Worlds of History

A Comparative Reader

Third Edition

Chapters taken from:

Volume One: To 1550
Volume Two: Since 1400

Kevin Reilly
Raritan Valley College

A Custom Edition for:

Making of the Modern World 4 (1200-1750)
Eleanor Roosevelt College
University of California, San Diego

Bedford/St. Martin's
Boston • New York

Manufactured in the United States of America.

4   3   2   1   0   9
f   e   d   c   b

For information, write: Bedford/St. Martin's, 75 Arlington Street, Boston, MA 02116   (617-399-4000)

ISBN-10: 0-312-60643-5
ISBN-13: 978-0-312-60643-5

Acknowledgments
Acknowledgments and copyrights are continued at the back of the book on pages 227–236, which constitutes a continuation of the copyright page.

Contents

From *Volume One: 400–1550* C.E.

8. Medieval Civilizations

European, Islamic, and Chinese Societies,
600–1400 C.E.   *268*

Three great civilizations spanned Eurasia between 500 and 1500. Of the three, China and Islam were the strongest, Europe the weakest. But their differences can be best understood by looking separately at the social structure, economy, politics, and culture of each.

HISTORICAL CONTEXT   *268*

THINKING HISTORICALLY
Distinguishing Social, Economic, Political,
and Cultural Aspects   *268*

Reflections   *299*

9. Love and Marriage

Medieval Europe, India, and Japan, 400–1200 C.E.   *301*

Love and marriage make the world go 'round today, but not a thousand years ago. Love meant different things to different people in Europe, India, and Japan, and we use cultural comparisons to find out how and why.

10. The First Crusade

Muslims, Christians, and Jews during the First Crusade,
1095–1099 C.E.

The First Crusade initiated a centuries-long struggle and dialogue between Christians and Muslims that would have a lasting impact on both. Wars are windows on cultures, but they also make moving narratives. Using the selections here, put together your own version of the story.

11. Raiders of Steppe and Sea: Vikings and Mongols

Eurasia and the Atlantic, 750–1350 C.E.   *375*

From the late ninth through the tenth century, waves of Viking ships attacked across Europe; a few centuries later beginning in 1200, the Mongols swept across Eurasia, conquering all in their path and creating the largest empire the world had ever seen. What was the impact of these raiding peoples on settled societies and vice versa? In considering this question and the violent and destructive nature of these "barbarian" raids, we will consider the relationship of morality to history.

HISTORICAL CONTEXT   *375*

THINKING HISTORICALLY
Distinguishing Historical Understanding from
Moral Judgments   *377*

Reflections   *419*

12. The Black Death

Afro-Eurasia, 1346–1350 C.E.   *422*

The pandemic plague ravaged the population of Afro-Eurasia, killing about one-third of the population of Europe and Egypt. In this chapter, looking at both written and visual evidence, we examine the impact of the plague in various locales while also contemplating its causes and the relation between cause and effect.

HISTORICAL CONTEXT   *422*

THINKING HISTORICALLY
Considering Cause and Effect   *422*

13. On Cities

European, Chinese, Islamic, and Mexican Cities,
1000–1550 C.E.   455

What did increasing urbanization from the medieval period on mean for those who lived in cities and those who did not? Wandering through some of the great cities of medieval Europe, China, and the Islamic world, we attempt to answer this question while also considering the validity and merits of one historian's famous comparative thesis about urbanization.

HISTORICAL CONTEXT   455

THINKING HISTORICALLY
Evaluating a Comparative Thesis   455

14. Ecology, Technology, and Science

Europe, Asia, Oceania, and Africa, 500–1550 C.E.   493

Since the Middle Ages, the most significant changes have occurred in the fields of ecology, technology, and science. In this chapter we read and assess three grand theories about the origins of our technological transformation and of our environmental problems, drawing on written and visual primary source evidence to develop our conclusions.

From *Volume Two: 1400*

1. Overseas Expansion in the Early Modern Period
China and Europe, 1400–1600   *1*

Both China and Europe set sail for global expansion in the fifteenth century, but China's explorations ended just as Europe's began. What were the factors that led to their similar efforts yet different outcomes? We examine primary and secondary sources in search of clues.

2. Atlantic World Encounters
Europeans, Americans, and Africans, 1500–1750   42

European encounters with Africans and Americans were similar in some ways, yet markedly different in others. The cultural clash created a new Atlantic world that both integrated and divided these indigenous peoples. We compare primary sources, including visual evidence, to understand these first contacts and conflicts.

HISTORICAL CONTEXT   42

THINKING HISTORICALLY
Comparing Primary Sources   43

3. State and Religion
Asian, Islamic, and Christian States, 1500–1800   88

In this chapter, we view the relationship between religion and political authority through the prism of Chinese, Japanese, South Asian, and Western experience in the early modern period. By examining the competing and sometimes cooperating dynamics between church and state in the past, we explore the history of an issue much debated in our own time and gain new insights into church-state relations today.

HISTORICAL CONTEXT   88

THINKING HISTORICALLY
Relating Past and Present   89

4. Gender and Family
China, Southeast Asia, Europe,
and "New Spain," 1600–1750   122

With the blinds drawn on the domestic lives of our ancestors, one might assume their private worlds were uneventful and everywhere the same. By comparing different cultures we see historical variety in family and economic life and the roles of both men and women.

HISTORICAL CONTEXT   122

THINKING HISTORICALLY
Making Comparisons   123

5. The Scientific Revolution
Europe, the Ottoman Empire, China, Japan,
and the Americas, 1600–1800   159

The scientific revolution of the seventeenth and eighteenth centuries occurred in Europe, but had important roots in Asia, and its consequences reverberated throughout the world. In this chapter we seek to understand what changed and how. How "revolutionary" was the scientific revolution and how do we distinguish between mere change and "revolutionary" change?

6. Enlightenment and Revolution
Europe and the Americas, 1650–1850   *193*

The eighteenth-century Enlightenment applied scientific reason to politics, but reason meant different things to different people and societies. What were the goals of the political revolutions produced by the Enlightenment? A close reading of the period texts reveals disagreement and shared dreams.

Volume One: To 1550

8

Medieval Civilizations

European, Islamic, and Chinese
Societies, 600–1400 C.E.

HISTORICAL CONTEXT

In the centuries after 200 C.E., an influx of nomadic peoples from the grasslands of Eurasia into the Roman and Han Chinese empires brought an end to the classical civilizations. In their wake, three distinct civilizations developed: European Christian, Islamic (after 622 C.E.), and Chinese. Of the three, the Chinese was most like its preceding classical civilization; in some ways the Sui dynasty (589–618) revived the institutions of the Han. The greatest change occurred in Western Europe, especially the former urban areas of the Roman Empire, some of which virtually disappeared. The area from Byzantium to the Indus River was radically transformed by the rise of Islam, but a foreign observer might have been struck more by the continuity of urban growth and material progress than by the change of faith in Western Asia from the classical to Muslim period.

In any case, these three worlds of Eurasia in the Middle Ages were vastly different from each other. The goal of this chapter is to explore some of those differences.

THINKING HISTORICALLY
Distinguishing Social, Economic, Political, and Cultural Aspects

Comparing civilizations is a daunting undertaking; there are so many variables one must keep in mind. Consequently, when historians compare civilizations, or any social system, they first break them down into parts. Most commonly, historians distinguish between the political, economic, social, and cultural features of a system. The political refers to how a society or civilization is governed, the economic to how it supports itself, the social to how it organizes population groups, including families, and the cultural to how it explains and represents itself, including its religion.

In this chapter, you are asked to be systematic in distinguishing among these features for each of the three main civilizations. We will break them down to compare each part — for example, European and Chinese politics, Muslim and Chinese culture — but also to see how the parts of each civilization make a whole: for example, how Chinese politics and Chinese culture fit together.

45

Feudalism: An Oath of Homage and Fealty

This primary source is from France, selected to illustrate one of the important institutions of Europe in the Middle Ages: feudalism. This document details the mutual obligation between a feudal lord and his vassal. In this case, the feudal lord is a religious institution, the monastery of St. Mary of Grasse. Acting for the monastery and its lands is the abbot, Leo. The vassal who holds the properties of the monastery as a fief, and in return pledges homage and fealty, is Bernard Atton, viscount of Carcassonne.* The year is 1110.

What exactly does the viscount of Carcassonne promise to do? What is Leo the abbot's responsibility on behalf of the monastery? How new or old does this agreement appear to be? What else does this document tell you about the relationship of lords and vassals in European feudalism?

Thinking Historically

Using the distinctions suggested in the chapter introduction, how would you characterize this agreement? In short, is it an economic, political, social, or cultural agreement? Because it obviously has more

---

*cahr cas OHN

"Charter of Homage and Fealty of the Viscount of Carcassone, 1110," in D. C. Munro, *Translations and Reprints from the Original Sources of European History*, vol. IV, bk. 3 (Philadelphia: University of Pennsylvania Press, 1897), 18–20.

than one of these elements, how might you argue for each of the four characterizations?

What would be the closest equivalent to this sort of agreement today? Would you characterize the modern equivalent as economic, political, social, or cultural?

In the name of the Lord, I, Bernard Atton, Viscount of Carcassonne, in the presence of my sons, Roger and Trencavel, and of Peter Roger of Barbazan, and William Hugo, and Raymond Mantellini, and Peter de Vietry, nobles, and of many other honorable men, who had come to the monastery of St. Mary of Grasse, to the honor of the festival of the august St. Mary; since lord Leo, abbot of the said monastery, has asked me, in the presence of all those above mentioned, to acknowledge to him the fealty and homage for the castles, manors, and places which the patrons, my ancestors, held from him and his predecessors and from the said monastery as a fief, and which I ought to hold as they held, I have made to the lord abbot Leo acknowledgment and homage as I ought to do.

Therefore, let all present and to come know that I the said Bernard Atton, lord and viscount of Carcassonne, acknowledge verily to thee my lord Leo, by the grace of God, abbot of St. Mary of Grasse, and to thy successors that I hold and ought to hold as a fief, in Carcassonne, the following: . . . Moreover, I acknowledge that I hold from thee and from the said monastery as a fief the castle of Termes in Narbonne; and in Minerve the castle of Ventaion, and the manors of Cassanolles, and of Ferral and Aiohars; and in Le Rogès, the little village of Longville; for each and all of which I make homage and fealty with hands and with mouth to thee my said lord abbot Leo and to thy successors, and I swear upon these four gospels of God that I will always be a faithful vassal to thee and to thy successors and to St. Mary of Grasse in all things in which a vassal is required to be faithful to his lord, and I will defend thee, my lord, and all thy successors, and the said monastery and the monks present and to come and the castles and manors and all your men and their possessions against all malefactors and invaders, at my request and that of my successors at my own cost; and I will give to thee power over all the castles and manors above described, in peace and in war, whenever they shall be claimed by thee or by thy successors.

Moreover I acknowledge that, as a recognition of the above fiefs, I and my successors ought to come to the said monastery, at our own expense, as often as a new abbot shall have been made, and there do homage and return to him the power over all the fiefs described above. And when the abbot shall mount his horse I and my heirs, viscounts of

Carcassonne, and our successors ought to hold the stirrup for the honor of the dominion of St. Mary of Grasse; and to him and all who come with him, to as many as two hundred beasts, we should make the abbot's purveyance in the borough of St. Michael of Carcassonne, the first time he enters Carcassonne, with the best fish and meat and with eggs and cheese, honorably according to his will, and pay the expense of the shoeing of the horses, and for straw and fodder as the season shall require.

And if I or my sons or their successors do not observe to thee or to thy successors each and all the things declared above, and should come against these things, we wish that all the aforesaid fiefs should by that very fact be handed over to thee and to the said monastery of St. Mary of Grasse and to thy successors.

I, therefore, the aforesaid lord Leo, by the grace of God, abbot of St. Mary of Grasse, receive thy homage and fealty for all the fiefs of castles and manors and places which are described above; in the way and with the agreements and understandings written above; and likewise I concede to thee and thy heirs and their successors, the viscounts of Carcassonne, all the castles and manors and places aforesaid, as a fief, along with this present charter, divided through the alphabet. And I promise to thee and thy heirs and successors, viscounts of Carcassonne, under the religion of my order, that I will be a good and faithful lord concerning all those things described above.

Moreover, I, the aforesaid viscount, acknowledge that the little villages of [twelve are listed] with the farmhouse of Mathus and the chateaux of Villalauro and Claromont, with the little villages of St. Stephen of Surlac, and of Upper and Lower Agrifolio, ought to belong to the said monastery, and whoever holds anything there holds from the same monastery, as we have seen and have heard read in the privileges and charters of the monastery, and as was there written.

Made in the year of the Incarnation of the Lord 1110, in the reign of Louis. Seal of [the witnesses named in paragraph one, Bernard Atton and abbot Leo] who has accepted this acknowledgment of the homage of the said viscount.

And I, the monk John, have written this charter at the command of the said lord Bernard Atton, viscount of Carcassonne and of his sons, on the day and year given above, in the presence and witness of all those named above.

Manorialism: Duties of a Villein

Manorialism is another term used to describe medieval European civilization. It concerns the life around the manor houses that were the centers of life in the countryside. Manors were owned by feudal lords whose income derived, at least in good part, from the work of free peasants and dependent serfs (*villeins*).*

This document, from England in 1307, delineates the duties required of a villein, John of Cayworth, to the lord of the manor, Battle Abbey. What duties does the abbey require of John of Cayworth? What does he get in return? In what ways is this document similar to the previous one? In what ways is it different?

Thinking Historically

How is the social status of John of Cayworth different from that of Bernard Atton in the previous selection? What would you imagine about the differences in their economic welfare?

What would be the modern equivalent of this document? Would you call that modern equivalent economic, political, social, or cultural? Which word best characterizes this document?

They say that John of Cayworth holds one house and thirty acres of land, and he owes 2 s.[1] a year at Easter and Michaelmas, and he owes one cock and two hens at Christmas worth 4 s.

And he ought to harrow for two days at the sowing at Lent with one man and his own horse and harrow, the value of the work is 4 d.;[2] and he receives from the lord on each day three meals worth 3 d.; and the lord will thus lose 1 d.; and so this harrowing is worth nothing to the service of the lord.

And he ought to carry the manure of the lord for two days with one cart using his own two oxen, the work to value 8 s., and he receives from the lord three meals of the above value each day; and so the work is worth 3 d. clear.

---

*vih LAYN

[1]Shilling, a British measure of money traditionally worth ¹⁄₂₀ of a pound. [Ed.]

[2]Pence, smallest measure of British currency traditionally worth ¹⁄₁₂ of a shilling. "d." comes from Roman *denarius*. [Ed.]

"Services Due from a Villein, 1307," in *Customals of Battle Abbey*, ed. S. R. Scargill-Bird (The Camden Society, 1887), 19–23.

And he should find one man for two days to mow the meadow of the lord, who can mow an estimated one acre and a half: the value of mowing one acre is 6 *d.*; and the total is 9 *d.*; and he receives for each day three meals of the above value, and thus the mowing is worth 4 *d.* clear.

And he ought to collect and carry that same hay which he has mowed, the value of the work is 3 *d.* And he has from the lord two meals to one man worth 1½ *d.*; thus the work is worth 1½ *d.* clear.

And he ought to carry the hay of the lord for one day with one cart and three animals of his own, the price of the work is 6 *d.*; and he has from the lord three meals worth 2½ *d.*; and thus the work has a value of 3½ *d.* clear.

And he ought to carry in the autumn beans or oats for two days with one cart and three of his own animals, the price of the work is 12 *d.*; and he has from the lord three meals of the above price for each day, and thus the work is worth 7 *d.* clear.

And he ought to carry wood from the woods of the lord to the manor house for two days in summer with one cart and three of his own animals, the price of the work is 9 *d.*; and he receives from the lord for each day three meals of the above price. And so the work is worth 4 *d.* clear.

And he ought to find one man for two days to cut heath, the price of the work is 4 [*d.*]; and he will have three meals for each day of the above price; and so the lord loses if he receives the work 1 *d.*; and thus that cutting is worth nothing to the work of the lord.

And he ought to carry the heath that he has cut, the price of the work is 5 *d.*; and he receives from the lord three meals of the price of 2½ *d.*; and thus the work is worth 2½ *d.* clear.

And he ought to carry to Battle [Abbey] two times in the summer half a load of grain each time, the price of the work is 4 *d.*; and he will receive in the manor each time one meal worth 2 *d.*; and thus the work is worth 2 *d.* clear.

The sum of the rents, with the price of the chickens is 2 *s.* 4 *d.*; the sum of the value of the work is 2 *s.* 3½ *d.*; owed from the said John per year. . . .

And it must be noted that all the aforesaid villeins may not marry their daughters nor have their sons tonsured, nor can they cut down timber growing on the lands they hold, without the personal approval of the bailiff or servant of the lord, and then for building and no other purpose.

And after the death of any one of the aforesaid villeins the lord will have as a heriot the best animal that he had; if, however, he had no living beast, the lord will have no heriot, as they say.

The sons or daughters of the aforesaid villeins will give to enter the tenement after the death of their ancestors as much as they gave in rent per year.

From the Magna Carta

The Magna Carta was a contract between King John of England and his nobles (or "liegemen") in which the king agreed to recognize certain rights and liberties of the nobility. In return the nobles accepted certain obligations to the king. What were some of these rights and obligations? Can you tell from these provisions what some of the nobles' complaints had been? Did the signing of this agreement in 1215 improve the position of the common people, women, or foreigners? What does the document tell you about English society in the early thirteenth century?

Thinking Historically

This is obviously a political document, as it details the mutual obligations of King John and his nobles, the barons. But in addition to political matters, it covers a number of issues that might be considered economic, social, and cultural. Which items would you characterize as falling into one of those categories?

What does the Magna Carta have in common with the other European documents on feudalism and manorialism? What does this commonality tell you about European society in the Middle Ages?

John, by the grace of God, King of England, Lord of Ireland, Duke of Normandy and Aquitaine, and Count of Anjou: To the Archbishops, Bishops, Abbots, Earls, Barons, Justiciaries, Foresters, Sheriffs, Reeves, Ministers, and all Bailiffs and others, his faithful subjects, Greeting. Know ye that in the presence of God, and for the health of Our soul, and the souls of Our ancestors and heirs, to the honor of God, and the exaltation of Holy Church, and amendment of Our Kingdom, by the advice of Our reverend Fathers, Stephen, Archbishop of Canterbury, Primate of all England, and Cardinal of the Holy Roman Church; Henry, Archbishop of Dublin; William of London, Peter of Winchester, Jocelin of Bath and Glastonbury, Hugh of Lincoln, Walter of Worcester, William of Coventry, and Benedict of Rochester, Bishops; Master Pandulph, the Pope's subdeacon and familiar; Brother Aymeric, Master

---

"Magna Carta," trans. E. P. Cheney, in *Translations and Reprints from the Original Sources of European History*, ed. D. C. Munro, vol. I, bk. 6 (Philadelphia: University of Pennsylvania Press, 1897), 6–15, passim.

of the Knights of the Temple in England; and the noble persons, William Marshal, Earl of Pembroke; William, Earl of Salisbury; William, Earl of Warren; William, Earl of Arundel; Alan de Galloway, Constable of Scotland; Warin Fitz-Gerald, Peter Fitz-Herbert, Hubert de Burgh, Seneschal of Poitou, Hugh de Neville, Matthew Fitz-Herbert, Thomas Basset, Alan Basset, Philip Daubeny, Robert de Roppelay, John Marshal, John Fitz-Hugh, and others, Our liegemen:

1. We have, in the first place, granted to God, and by this Our present Charter confirmed for Us and Our heirs forever — That the English Church shall be free and enjoy her rights in their integrity and her liberties untouched. And that We will this so to be observed appears from the fact that We of Our own free will, before the outbreak of the dissensions between Us and Our barons, granted, confirmed, and procured to be confirmed by Pope Innocent III the freedom of elections, which if considered most important and necessary to the English Church, which Charter We will both keep Ourself and will it to be kept with good faith by Our heirs forever. We have also granted to all the free men of Our kingdom, for Us and Our heirs forever, all the liberties underwritten, to have and to hold to them and their heirs of Us and Our heirs.

2. If any of Our earls, barons, or others who hold of Us in chief by knight's service shall die, and at the time of his death his heir shall be of full age and owe a relief[1] he shall have his inheritance by ancient relief; to wit, the heir or heirs of an earl of an entire earl's barony, £100; the heir or heirs of a baron of an entire barony, £100; the heir or heirs of a knight of an entire knight's fee, 100s. at the most; and he that owes less shall give less, according to the ancient custom of fees.

3. If, however, any such heir shall be under age and in ward, he shall, when he comes of age, have his inheritance without relief or fine.

4. The guardian of the land of any heir thus under age shall take therefrom only reasonable issues, customs, and services, without destruction or waste of men or property; and if We shall have committed the wardship of any such land to the sheriff or any other person answerable to Us for the issues thereof, and he commit destruction or waste, We will take an amends from him, and the land shall be committed to two lawful and discreet men of that fee, who shall be answerable for the issues to Us or to whomsoever We shall have assigned them. And if We shall give or sell the wardship of any such land to anyone, and he commit destruction or waste upon it, he shall lose the wardship, which shall be committed to two lawful and discreet men of that fee, who shall, in like manner, be answerable unto Us as has been aforesaid.

---

[1] A form of tax. [Ed.]

5. The guardian, so long as he shall have the custody of the land, shall keep up and maintain the houses, parks, fishponds, pools, mills, and other things pertaining thereto, out of the issues of the same, and shall restore the whole to the heir when he comes of age, stocked with ploughs and tillage, according as the season may require and the issues of the land can reasonably bear.

6. Heirs shall be married without loss of station, and the marriage shall be made known to the heir's nearest of kin before it be contracted.

7. A widow, after the death of her husband, shall immediately and without difficulty have her marriage portion and inheritance. She shall not give anything for her marriage portion, dower, or inheritance which she and her husband held on the day of his death, and she may remain in her husband's house for forty days after his death, within which time her dower shall be assigned to her.

8. No widow shall be compelled to marry so long as she has a mind to live without a husband, provided, however, that she give security that she will not marry without Our assent, if she holds of Us, or that of the lord of whom she holds, if she holds of another.

9. Neither We nor Our bailiffs shall seize any land or rent for any debt so long as the debtor's chattels are sufficient to discharge the same; nor shall the debtor's sureties be distrained so long as the debtor is able to pay the debt. If the debtor fails to pay, not having the means to pay, then the sureties shall answer the debt, and, if they desire, they shall hold the debtor's lands and rents until they have received satisfaction of the debt which they have paid for him, unless the debtor can show that he has discharged his obligation to them.

10. If anyone who has borrowed from the Jews any sum of money, great or small, dies before the debt has been paid, the heir shall pay no interest on the debt so long as he remains under age, of whomsoever he may hold. If the debt shall fall into Our hands, We will take only the principal sum named in the bond. . . .

13. The City of London shall have all her ancient liberties and free customs, both by land and water. Moreover, We will and grant that all other cities, boroughs, towns, and ports shall have their liberties and free customs.

14. For obtaining the common counsel of the kingdom concerning the assessment of aids (other than in the three cases aforesaid) or of scutage, We will cause to be summoned, severally by Our letters, the archbishops, bishops, abbots, earls, and great barons; We will also cause to be summoned, generally, by Our sheriffs and bailiffs, all those who hold lands directly of Us, to meet on a fixed day, but with at least forty days' notice, and at a fixed place. In all letters of such summons We will explain the cause thereof. The summons being thus made, the business shall proceed on the day appointed, according to the advice of

those who shall be present, even though not all the persons summoned have come. . . .

16. No man shall be compelled to perform more service for a knight's fee or other free tenement than is due therefrom.

17. Common Pleas shall not follow Our Court, but shall be held in some certain place. . . .

20. A free man shall be amerced[2] for a small fault only according to the measure thereof, and for a great crime according to its magnitude, saving his position; and in like manner a merchant saving his trade, and a villein saving his tillage, if they should fall under Our mercy. None of these amercements shall be imposed except by the oath of honest men of the neighborhood.

21. Earls and barons shall be amerced only by their peers, and only in proportion to the measure of the offense.

22. No amercement shall be imposed upon a clerk's[3] lay property, except after the manner of the other persons aforesaid, and without regard to the value of his ecclesiastical benefice.

23. No village or person shall be compelled to build bridges over rivers except those bound by ancient custom and law to do so. . . .

28. No constable or other of Our bailiffs shall take corn or other chattels of any man without immediate payment, unless the seller voluntarily consents to postponement of payment.

29. No constable shall compel any knight to give money in lieu of castle-guard when the knight is willing to perform it in person or (if reasonable cause prevents him from performing it himself) by some other fit man. Further, if We lead or send him into military service, he shall be quit of castle-guard for the time he shall remain in service by Our command.

30. No sheriff or other of Our bailiffs, or any other man, shall take the horses or carts of any free man for carriage without the owner's consent.

31. Neither We nor Our bailiffs will take another man's wood for Our castles or for any other purpose without the owner's consent. . . .

35. There shall be one measure of wine throughout Our kingdom, and one of ale, and one measure of corn, to wit, the London quarter, and one breadth of dyed cloth, russets, and haberjets[4] to wit, two cells within the selvages. As with measure so shall it also be with weights. . . .

38. In the future no bailiff shall upon his own unsupported accusation put any man to trial without producing credible witnesses to the truth of the accusation.

[2]Fined. [Ed.]
[3]Clergyman. [Ed.]
[4]Types of cloth. [Ed.]

39. No free man shall be taken, imprisoned, disseised,[5] outlawed, banished, or in any way destroyed, nor will We proceed against or prosecute him, except by the lawful judgment of his peers and by the law of the land.

40. To no one will We sell, to none will We deny or delay, right or justice.

41. All merchants shall have safe conduct to go and come out of and into England, and to stay in and travel through England by land and water for purposes of buying and selling, free of illegal tolls, in accordance with ancient and just customs, except, in time of war, such merchants as are of a country at war with Us. If any such be found in Our dominion at the outbreak of war, they shall be attached, without injury to their persons or goods, until it be known to Us or Our Chief Justiciary how Our merchants are being treated in the country at war with Us, and if Our merchants be safe there, then theirs shall be safe with Us.

42. In the future it shall be lawful (except for a short period in time of war, for the common benefit of the realm) for anyone to leave and return to Our kingdom safely and securely by land and water, saving his fealty to Us. Excepted are those who have been imprisoned or outlawed according to the law of the land, people of the country at war with Us, and merchants, who shall be dealt with as aforesaid. . . .

52. If anyone has been disseised or deprived by Us, without the legal judgment of his peers, of lands, castles, liberties, or rights, We will immediately restore the same, and if any dispute shall arise thereupon, the matter shall be decided by judgment of the twenty-five barons mentioned below in the clause for securing the peace. With regard to all those things, however, of which any man was disseised or deprived, without legal judgment of his peers, by King Henry Our Father or Our Brother King Richard, and which remain in Our warranty, We shall have respite during the term commonly allowed to the Crusaders, except as to those matters on which a plea had arisen, or an inquisition had been taken by Our command, prior to Our taking the Cross. Immediately after Our return from Our pilgrimage, or if by chance We should remain behind from it, We will at once do full justice.

---

[5]Dispossessed. [Ed.]

48

Islam: Sayings Ascribed to the Prophet

For Muslims the Koran was the word of God. Therefore no other writing was comparable. Nevertheless, when Muslims engaged in politics, considered laws, or studied social, economic, cultural, or other issues they could also refer to a body of writing called *hadiths*, or the sayings of the Prophet. These were writings attributed to Muhammad's contemporaries that described the decisions, acts, and the statements of the Prophet of Islam and the religion's first governor. What likely effect would the sayings included here have on the thinking of a devout Muslim? Under what circumstances would he or she be likely to be rebellious?

Thinking Historically

Most of these sayings deal with religion and government. What attitude toward politics do they express? If this selection was all you had to construct a Muslim idea of government, what would it be? How are these political ideas different from those in medieval Europe? What accounts for the differences?

I charge the Caliph[1] after me to fear God, and I commend the community of the Muslims to him, to respect the great among them and have pity on the small, to honor the learned among them, not to strike them and humiliate them, not to oppress them and drive them to unbelief, not to close his doors to them and allow the strong to devour the weak.

The Imams[2] are of Quraysh;[3] the godly among them rulers of the godly, and the wicked among them rulers of the wicked. If Quraysh gives a crop-nosed Ethiopian slave authority over you, hear him and obey him as long as he does not force any of you to choose between his Islam and his neck. And if he does force anyone to choose between his Islam and his neck, let him offer his neck.

[1]KAY lihf   Successor to the prophet; supreme authority. [Ed.]

[2]A leader, especially in prayer; clergyman. [Ed.]

[3]An aristocratic trading clan of Mecca; hostile to Muhammad, but after his death regained prominence. That religious leaders come from Quraysh was agreed after victory of the Meccan faction in 661. [Ed.]

Al-Muttaqi, *Kanz al'Ummal*, quoted in *Islam from the Prophet Muhammad to the Capture of Constantinople*, ed. and trans. Bernard Lewis, vol. I (New York: Harper, 1974), 150–51.

Hear and obey, even if a shaggy-headed black slave is appointed over you.

Whosoever shall try to divide my community, strike off his head.

If allegiance is sworn to two Caliphs, kill the other.

He who sees in his ruler something he disapproves should be patient, for if anyone separates himself from the community, even by a span, and dies, he dies the death of a pagan.

Obey your rulers, whatever happens. If their commands accord with the revelation I brought you, they will be rewarded for it, and you will be rewarded for obeying them; if their commands are not in accord with what I brought you, they are responsible and you are absolved. When you meet God, you will say, "Lord God! No evil." And He will say, "No evil!" And you will say, "Lord God! Thou didst send us Prophets, and we obeyed them by Thy leave; and Thou didst appoint over us Caliphs, and we obeyed them by Thy leave; and Thou didst place over us rulers, and we obeyed them for Thy sake." And He will say, "You speak truth. They are responsible, and you are absolved."

If you have rulers over you who ordain prayer and the alms tax and the Holy War for God, then God forbids you to revile them and allows you to pray behind them.

If anyone comes out against my community when they are united and seeks to divide them, kill him, whoever he may be.

He who dies without an Imam dies the death of a pagan, and he who throws off his obedience will have no defense on the Day of Judgment.

Do not revile the Sultan, for he is God's shadow on God's earth. Obedience is the duty of the Muslim man, whether he like it or not, as long as he is not ordered to commit a sin. If he is ordered to commit a sin, he does not have to obey.

The nearer a man is to government, the further he is from God; the more followers he has, the more devils; the greater his wealth, the more exacting his reckoning.

He who commends a Sultan in what God condemns has left the religion of God.

AL-TANUKHI

A Government Job

Al-Tanukhi* (d. 994) was a judge in Baghdad. In this selection, he relates the story of his great uncle Abu Qasim's[†] response when he asked him why he gave up a government job. What does Abu Qasim's story tell you about the job of government officials in Muslim Baghdad in the tenth century? How was government in Muslim Baghdad different from government in medieval Europe? How were ideas of government different?

Thinking Historically

This story concerns a political post, but in what ways is the story an economic one as well? Would you say the lesson of the story is political, economic, or religious?

How did you come to repent of being in Government service, Abu Qasim? I once asked, What was the cause?

This was the cause, said my great-uncle. Abu Ali Jubbai (the great Rationalist theologian) used to stay with me when he came to Ahwaz. I was Clerk to the Ahwaz municipality as well as deputy Finance Minister, so that all business used to pass through my hands. I really ran the whole place. Once a year, when the Land Tax collections began, Abu Ali Jubbai used to come to Ahwaz to arrange to have the taxes due from certain persons, who over the years had come to regard themselves as his dependents, added to the Land Tax on his own private estate at Jubba. Everybody treated him with the highest honor and respect whenever he came to town. As a rule he would only stay with me; and I used to settle his business with the Governor. The Governor, of course, was not always a friend of mine, nor was he always a man who realized Abu Ali's position, or else the amount at which his assessment was fixed would have been even lower than it was. But he would always remit at least half or a third of the tax due from him.

*ahl tah NOO kee
[†]ah BOO kah SEEM

Judge Muhassin Tanukhi, "Resurrections of Loquacity or Table-talk (10th century)," in Eric Schroeder, *Muhammad's People: A Tale by Anthology* (Portland, ME: Bond Wheelwright Company, 1955), 566–68.

Returning to Jubba, Abu Ali never kept for himself any of the money which in an ordinary case would have been taken in taxes from an estate like his. He used to deduct from the gross amount the sum he was to pay to Government, and then distribute the remainder among the members of his religious following, stipulating in return that each of them should entertain for a whole year one of the poor students who attended his lectures; the actual expense these students put them to was small, not a fifth of the amount due which Abu Ali's high standing had sufficed to get remitted. Then he would go to his own house, and there take out of the revenues of his estate a full tithe, which he used to give in alms among the poor people of his village, Pool, where he maintained his disciples. And he did all this every year.

On one occasion, he was staying with me at the usual season, I had done what he wanted in the matter of his Land Tax, and we were sitting talking in the evening.

Abu Ali, I said to him, are you afraid of the consequences to me in the Hereafter of the profession I am following?

How could I but be anxious, Abu Qasim? he replied. For be sure of this: if you should die employed as you now are, you will never breathe the fragrance of the Garden.

Why not? I asked. How am I guilty? I am only an accountant — I act merely as a copyist, an employee of the Treasury. It may be that somebody will come to me with a grievance, some man whose Land Tax has been unduly raised; and if I reduce it for him and set matters straight, he is only too glad to give me a present. At times perhaps I may appropriate something which really belongs to the Sovereign; but it only represents a share in the booty of the Muslims, to which I have a right.

Abu Qasim, he rejoined, GOD IS NOT DECEIVED. Tell me this: is it not you who appoints the land surveyors and sends them out to make their surveys, which are supposed to be accurate? And don't they go out into the country, and raise the acreage figures by ten or twenty per cent, with pen on paper, and then hand in these falsifications of theirs, and do you not make up your assessment registers on the basis of these same falsifications? And then hand over these registers to the Collector's officer, and tell him that unless he produces so much money at the Collector's Office within so many days his hands will be nailed to his feet?

Yes, I admitted.

And then the officer sets out with his escort of soldiers, horse and foot, his despatch riders and speed-up men, and flogs and cuffs and fetters? and all the time he is acting on your instructions. For if you bid him let a man off, or give him time, he does that; whereas if you give no such permission he is merciless until the man pays up.

Yes, said I.

And then the money is deposited at the Collector's Office, and the receipt forms are issued to him from your office, with your mark on them?

Yes, said I.

Then what part of the whole business, asked Abu Ali, is not of your undertaking? What part are you not answerable for? Beware of God, or you are lost. Give up your Government job. Provide for your future.

From such exhortations, from such grave warnings he would not desist until at last I burst into tears.

You are not more highly favored, he then said, nor more highly placed than Ja'far ibn Harb was: he held high office at court, his privileges and rank were almost those of a Vizier; and he was also an orthodox Believer, and a famous scholar, the author of more than one book which is still read. And yet Ja'far, when he was in office, and riding one day in a superb cavalcade, on the very crest of pomp and circumstance, suddenly heard a man reading the verse: *IS NOT THE HOUR YET COME WHEN ALL WHO TRULY BELIEVE MUST BE BROKEN AND CONTRITE OF HEART AT THE VERY MENTION OF GOD AND OF TRUTH REVEALED?* Ay, the hour is come! Ja'far exclaimed. Over and over again he said it, weeping. And he dismounted, and stripped off his dress, and waded into Tigris until the water came up to his neck. Nor did he come out again until he had given away everything he owned to atone for wrongs he had done, in reparations, pious foundations, and alms, doing everything that his system of Belief demanded, or that he thought his duty. Some passer-by, who saw him standing in the water and was told his story, gave him a shirt and a pair of breeches to cover his coming out; and he put them on. He gave himself to study and devotion from then until his death.

After a moment, Abu Ali said to me: Go, and do thou likewise, Abu Qasim. But if you cannot bring yourself to go the whole way, at least repent of being an official.

What Jubbai said made a great impression on me. I resolved that I would repent, that I would give up my job. For some time I conducted my affairs with this in view; and when I saw an opportunity of getting out of Government service, I repented, my mind made up that I would never take public office again.

Egyptian Invitation

This document is an invitation issued by the sultan of Egypt between 1280 and 1290. Egypt had been a part of the Muslim world since the Arab invasion under Omar in 639. Like other Arab dominions, Egypt was ruled by the Umayyad caliphate in Damascus before 747 and then nominally by the Abbasid caliphate in Baghdad after 750. (See Map 7.3.) But other powers created dynasties that effectively ruled Egypt after 868: first Turks, then Persians, then the North African Fatimids (910–1171), followed by the Kurdish Ayyubid dynasty founded in 1174 by Saladin that lasted until the Mongol invasion. The last Ayyubid ruler was murdered in 1250 and was replaced as sultan (political leader) by his Mamluk slave general. The use of purchased or captured non-Muslim slaves as soldiers gave Muslim rulers loyal forces that had no ties to other tribal leaders. Converted to Islam, well trained, and given considerable power and authority, these Mamluk troops and administrators owed everything to the Sultan. Between 1250 and 1517, two dynasties of Mamluks ruled Egypt. At first, Mamluk status was strictly nonhereditary, and their sons were prevented from sharing power. Eventually, however, Mamluk dynasties were grafted onto the tribal structure.

To whom is this invitation addressed? What did the Sultan hope to achieve by issuing it? What does the content of the document tell us about Mamluk Egyptian society? Every society needs soldiers and merchants. Using this document and those you have read from Europe, compare the Mamluk Egyptian method of supplying this need with the method of medieval Europe.

Thinking Historically

The purpose of this invitation is clearly economic. Yet this economic purpose has political, social, and cultural dimensions as well. What are these other dimensions? How is economics related to other aspects of medieval Islamic society?

A decree has been issued, may God exalt the Sultan's exalted command, and may his [the Sultan's] justice keep the subjects in assured protection. He requests the prayers of the people of both east and west

Islam from the Prophet Muhammad to the Conquest of Constantinople, ed. and trans. Bernard Lewis, vol. II, *Religion and Society* (New York: Harper & Row, 1974), 166–68.

for his thriving reign, and let all of them be sincere. He offers a genuine welcome to those who come to his realm, as to the garden of Eden, by whatever gate they may choose to enter, from Iraq, from Persia, from Asia Minor, from the Ḥijāz, from India, and from China. Whoever wishes to set forth — the distinguished merchants, the men of great affairs, and the small traders, from the countries enumerated and also those which have not been enumerated — and whoever wishes to enter our realms may sojourn or travel at will and to come to our country of broad lands and leafy shades, then let him, like those whom God has destined for this, make firm resolve on this worthy and beneficial act, and let him come to a country whose inhabitants have no need either of supplies or reserves of food, for it is an earthly paradise for those who dwell in it, and a consolation for those who are far from their own homes, a delight of which the eye does not weary, a place from which one is never driven by excessive cold, for one lives there in perpetual spring and permanent well-being. It is enough to say that one of its descriptions is that it is God's beauty spot on His earth. God's blessing accrues in the baggage of whoever does a good deed by lending or receives a good deed by borrowing. Another of its features is that anyone who comes there hoping for anything, gets what he wants, for it is a land of Islam, with armies whose swords are beyond reproach. For justice has made its lands prosper and has multiplied its inhabitants. The buildings have increased so that it is a land of great cities. The needy is at ease there, and does not fear the violence of the creditors, for demands there are not exacting and deferments easily obtained. The rest of the people and all the merchants have no fear there of any oppression, for justice protects.

Whoever becomes aware of this our decree, among the merchants who live in Yemen and India and China and Sind and elsewhere, let them prepare to travel and come to our country, where they will find the reality better than the word and will see a beneficence beyond the mere fulfillment of their promises and will sojourn in "a fair land under a forgiving Lord" [Qur'ān, xxxv, 15] and in comfort deserving of gratitude (for only the grateful is rewarded) and in security of person and property, and felicity which illuminates their circumstances and fulfills their hopes. They will receive from us all the justice that they expect. Our justice responds to those who call on it, has procedure which will be praised by their way of life, will leave their property to their descendants, and will protect and preserve them so that they will take shelter under its shadow and be protected. Whoever brings merchandise with him, such as spices and other articles imported by the Kārimī[1]

---

[1] An association of merchants in Egypt and Arabia, engaged in the eastern trade.

merchants, will suffer no unjust impost nor be subjected to any burdensome demand, for [our] justice will leave with them what is desirable and remove what is burdensome. If anyone brings [white] male slaves [mamlūk] or slave-girls, he will find their sale price beyond his expectations and [will be accorded] the tolerance in fixing a profitable price which is customarily accorded to those who import such slaves from near and all the more from distant lands; for our desire is directed toward the increase of our troops, and those who import mamlūks have gained a title to our generosity. Let whoever can do so increase his import of mamlūks, and let him know that the purpose in demanding them is to increase the armies of Islam. For thanks to them, Islam today is in glory with flag unfurled and the Sultan al-Manṣūr [Qalawun]. The mamlūk who is thus imported is removed from darkness to light. Yesterday he was blamed for unbelief; today he is praised for faith and fights for Islam against his own tribe and people.

This is our decree for all traveling merchants to whose knowledge it comes, "They seek the bounty of God, while others fight in the cause of God." [Qur'ān, lxxiii, 20] Let them read in it the orders which will ease their task; let them be guided by its star, nourished by its wisdom. Let them mount the neck of the hope which impels them to leave their homes and stretch out their hands in prayer for him who wishes people to come to his country, so that they may benefit from his generosity in all clarity and in all beneficence; and let them take advantage of the occasions for profit, for they are ripe for picking. These true promises are sent to them to confirm their high hopes and reaffirm to them that the noble rescript is valid, by the command of God, in accordance with what the pens have written, and [God is] the best Guarantor.

ICHISADA MIYAZAKI

The Chinese Civil Service Exam System

The Chinese civil service examination system originated fourteen hundred years ago, making it the first in the world. As a device for ensuring government by the brightest young men, regardless of class or social standing, it may also be viewed as one of the world's earliest democratic systems. It was not perfect. Like democratic systems in the West only two hundred years ago, it excluded women. The system also put enormous pressure on young boys of ambitious families.

This selection consists of two passages from a book by a noted modern Japanese historian of China. The first passage concerns the elaborate early preparations for the exams.

What did young boys have to learn? In what ways was their education different from your own? What effects did the examination system have on the goals and values of young people?

Thinking Historically

The Chinese examination system was primarily a political system, a way for the emperor to rule most effectively, employing the most talented administrators. In what sense did this system make China more "democratic" than the political systems of Western Europe or the Muslim world? In what sense was it less so? Did it become more or less democratic over the course of Chinese history? How did its purpose change from the Tang dynasty to the Sung dynasty?

Like any political system, the civil service system had a major impact on other aspects of life — social, economic, and cultural. How did it affect Chinese society, families, class differences, boys and girls? What were the economic effects of the system? How did it influence Chinese cultural values, ideas, and education?

Judging from this excerpt and your readings about Western Europe and the Islamic world, what was the single most important difference between Chinese and Western European civilizations? Between Chinese and Muslim civilization?

Ichisada Miyazaki, *China's Examination Hell*, trans. Conrad Schirokauer (New York: Weatherhill, 1976), 13–17, 111–16, passim.

Preparing for the Examinations

Competition for a chance to take the civil service examinations began, if we may be allowed to exaggerate only a little, even before birth. On the back of many a woman's copper mirror the five-character formula "Five Sons Pass the Examinations" expressed her heart's desire to bear five successful sons. Girls, since they could not take the examinations and become officials but merely ran up dowry expenses, were no asset to a family; a man who had no sons was considered to be childless. People said that thieves warned each other not to enter a household with five or more girls because there would be nothing to steal in it. The luckless parents of girls hoped to make up for such misfortune in the generation of their grandchildren by sending their daughters into marriage equipped with those auspicious mirrors.

Prenatal care began as soon as a woman was known to be pregnant. She had to be very careful then, because her conduct was thought to have an influence on the unborn child, and everything she did had to be right. She had to sit erect, with her seat and pillows arranged in exactly the proper way, to sleep without carelessly pillowing her head on an arm, to abstain from strange foods, and so on. She had to be careful to avoid unpleasant colors, and she spent her leisure listening to poetry and the classics being read aloud. These preparations were thought to lead to the birth of an unusually gifted boy.

If, indeed, a boy was born the whole family rejoiced, but if a girl arrived everyone was dejected. On the third day after her birth it was the custom to place a girl on the floor beneath her bed, and to make her grasp a tile and a pebble so that even then she would begin to form a lifelong habit of submission and an acquaintance with hardship. In contrast, in early times when a boy was born arrows were shot from an exorcising bow in the four directions of the compass and straight up and down. In later times, when literary accomplishments had become more important than the martial arts, this practice was replaced by the custom of scattering coins for servants and others to pick up as gifts. Frequently the words "First-place Graduate" were cast on those coins, to signify the highest dreams of the family and indeed of the entire clan.

It was thought best for a boy to start upon his studies as early as possible. From the very beginning he was instructed almost entirely in the classics, since mathematics could be left to merchants, while science and technology were relegated to the working class. A potential grand official must study the Four Books, the Five Classics, and other Confucian works, and, further, he must know how to compose poems and write essays. For the most part, questions in civil service examinations did not go beyond these areas of competence.

When he was just a little more than three years old, a boy's education began at home, under the supervision of his mother or some other suitable person. Even at this early stage the child's home environment exerted a great effect upon his development. In cultivated families, where books were stacked high against the walls, the baby sitter taught the boy his first characters while playing. As far as possible these were characters written with only a few strokes.

First a character was written in outline with red ink on a single sheet of paper. Then the boy was made to fill it in with black ink. Finally he himself had to write each character. At this stage there was no special need for him to know the meanings of the characters.

After he had learned in this way to hold the brush and to write a number of characters, he usually started on the *Primer of One Thousand Characters*. This is a poem that begins:

Heaven is dark, earth is yellow,
The universe vast and boundless . . .

It consists of a total of two hundred and fifty lines, and since no character is repeated, it provided the student with a foundation of a thousand basic ideograms.

Upon completing the *Primer*, a very bright boy, who could memorize one thing after another without difficulty, would go on to a history text called *Meng Ch'iu* (*The Beginner's Search*) and then proceed to the Four Books and the Five Classics normally studied in school. If rumors of such a prodigy reached the capital, a special "tough examination" was held, but often such a precocious boy merely served as a plaything for adults and did not accomplish much in later life. Youth examinations were popular during the Sung dynasty, but declined and finally were eliminated when people realized how much harm they did to the boys.

Formal education began at about seven years of age (or eight, counting in Chinese style). Boys from families that could afford the expense were sent to a temple, village, communal, or private school staffed by former officials who had lost their positions, or by old scholars who had repeatedly failed the examinations as the years slipped by. Sons of rich men and powerful officials often were taught at home by a family tutor in an elegant small room located in a detached building, which stood in a courtyard planted with trees and shrubs, in order to create an atmosphere conducive to study.

A class usually consisted of eight or nine students. Instruction centered on the Four Books, beginning with the *Analects*, and the process of learning was almost entirely a matter of sheer memorization. With their books open before them, the students would parrot the teacher, phrase by phrase, as he read out the text. Inattentive students, or those who amused themselves by playing with toys hidden in their sleeves, would be scolded by the teacher or hit on the palms and thighs with his fan-shaped "warning ruler." The high regard for discipline was reflected in the saying, "If education is not strict, it shows that the teacher is lazy."

Students who had learned how to read a passage would return to their seats and review what they had just been taught. After reciting it a hundred times, fifty times while looking at the book and fifty with the book face down, even the least gifted would have memorized it. At first the boys were given twenty to thirty characters a day, but as they became more experienced they memorized one, two, or several hundred each day. In order not to force a student beyond his capacity, a boy who could memorize four hundred characters would be assigned no more than two hundred. Otherwise he might become so distressed as to end by detesting his studies.

Along with the literary curriculum, the boys were taught proper conduct, such as when to use honorific terms, how to bow to superiors and to equals, and so forth — although from a modern point of view their training in deportment may seem somewhat defective, as is suggested by the incident concerning a high-ranking Chinese diplomat in the late Ch'ing dynasty who startled Westerners by blowing his nose with his fingers at a public ceremony.

It was usual for a boy to enter school at the age of eight and to complete the general classical education at fifteen. The heart of the curriculum was the classics. If we count the number of characters in the classics that the boys were required to learn by heart, we get the following figures:

Analects	11,705
Mencius	34,685
Book of Changes	24,107
Book of Documents	25,700
Book of Poetry	39,234
Book of Rites	99,010
Tso Chuan	196,845

The total number of characters a student had to learn, then, was 431,286.

The *Great Learning* and the *Doctrine of the Mean*, which together with the *Analects* and the *Mencius* constitute the Four Books, are not counted separately, since they are included in the *Book of Rites*. And, of course, those were not 431,286 *different* characters: Most of the ideographs would have been used many times in the several texts. Even so, the task of having to memorize textual material amounting to more than 400,000 characters is enough to make one reel. They required exactly six years of memorizing, at the rate of two hundred characters a day.

After the students had memorized a book, they read commentaries, which often were several times the length of the original text, and practiced answering questions involving passages selected as examination topics. On top of all this, other classical, historical, and literary works had to be scanned, and some literary works had to be examined carefully, since the students were required to write poems and essays modeled upon them. Anyone not very vigorous mentally might well become sick of it all halfway through the course.

Moreover, the boys were at an age when the urge to play is strongest, and they suffered bitterly when they were confined all day in a classroom as though under detention. Parents and teachers, therefore, supported a lad, urging him on to "become a great man!" From ancient times, many poems were composed on the theme, "If you study while young, you will get ahead." The Sung emperor Chen-tsung wrote such a one:

> To enrich your family, no need to buy good land:
> Books hold a thousand measures of grain.
> For an easy life, no need to build a mansion:
> In books are found houses of gold.
> Going out, be not vexed at absence of followers:
> In books, carriages and horses form a crowd.
> Marrying, be not vexed by lack of a good go-between:
> In books there are girls and faces of jade.
> A boy who wants to become a somebody
> Devotes himself to the classics, faces the window, and reads.

In later times this poem was criticized because it tempted students with the promise of beautiful women and riches, but that was the very reason it was effective.

Nonetheless, in all times and places students find shortcuts to learning. Despite repeated official and private injunctions to study the Four Books and Five Classics honestly, rapid-study methods were devised with the sole purpose of preparing candidates for the examinations. Because not very many places in the classics were suitable as subjects for examination questions, similar passages and problems were often repeated. Aware of this, publishers compiled collections of examination answers, and a candidate who, relying on these compilations, guessed successfully during the course of his own examinations could obtain a good rating without having worked very hard. But if he guessed wrong he faced unmitigated disaster because, unprepared, he would have submitted so bad a paper that the officials could only shake their heads and fail him. Reports from perturbed officials caused the government to issue frequent prohibitions of the publication of such collections of model answers, but since it was a profitable business with a steady demand, ways of issuing them surreptitiously were arranged, and time and again the prohibitions rapidly became mere empty formalities.

An Evaluation of the Examination System

Did the examination system serve a useful purpose? . . .

The purpose of instituting the examinations, some fourteen hundred years ago under the Sui rulers, was to strike a blow against government by the hereditary aristocracy, which had prevailed until then, and to establish in its place an imperial autocracy. The period of disunion lasting from the third to the sixth century was the golden age of the Chinese aristocracy: during that time it controlled political offices in central and local governments. . . .

The important point in China, as in Japan, was that the power of the aristocracy seriously constrained the emperor's power to appoint officials. He could not employ men simply on the basis of their ability, since any imperial initiative to depart from the traditional personnel policy evoked a sharp counterattack from the aristocratic officials. This was the situation when the Sui emperor, exploiting the fact that he had reestablished order and that his authority was at its height, ended the power of the aristocracy to become officials merely by virtue of family status. He achieved this revolution when he enacted the examination system (and provided that only its graduates were to be considered qualified to hold government office), kept at hand a reserve of such officials, and made it a rule to use only them to fill vacancies in central and local government as they occurred. This was the origin of the examination system.

The Sui dynasty was soon replaced by the T'ang, which for the most part continued the policies of its predecessor. Actually, as the T'ang was in the process of winning control over China, a new group of aristocrats appeared who hoped to transmit their privileges to their descendants. To deal with this problem the emperor used the examination system and favored its *chin-shih*[1] trying to place them in important posts so that he could run the government as he wished. The consequence was strife between the aristocrats and the *chin-shih*, with the contest gradually turning in favor of the latter. Since those who gained office simply through their parentage were not highly regarded, either by the imperial government or by society at large, career-minded aristocrats, too, seem to have found it necessary to enter officialdom through the examination system. Their acceptance of this hard fact meant a real defeat for the aristocracy.

The T'ang can be regarded as a period of transition from the aristocratic government inherited from the time of the Six Dynasties to the purely bureaucratic government of future regimes. The examination

---

[1] Highest degree winners. [Ed.]

system made a large contribution to what was certainly a great advance for China's society, and in this respect its immense significance in Chinese history cannot be denied. Furthermore, that change was begun fourteen hundred years ago, at about the time when in Europe the feudal system had scarcely been formed. In comparison, the examination system was immeasurably progressive, containing as it did a superb idea the equal of which could not be found anywhere else in the world at that time.

This is not to say that the T'ang examination system was without defects. First, the number of those who passed through it was extremely small. In part this was an inevitable result of the limited diffusion of China's literary culture at a time when printing had not yet become practical and hand-copied books were still both rare and expensive, thus restricting the number of men able to pursue scholarly studies. Furthermore, because the historical and economic roots of the new bureaucratic system were still shallow, matters did not always go smoothly and sometimes there were harsh factional conflicts among officials. The development of those conflicts indicates that they were caused by the examination system itself and constituted a second serious defect.

As has been indicated, a master-disciple relationship between the examiner and the men he passed was established, much like that between a political leader and his henchmen, while the men who passed the examination in the same year considered one another as classmates and helped one another forever after. When such combinations became too strong, factions were born.

These two defects of the examination system were eliminated during the Sung regime. For one thing, the number of men who were granted degrees suddenly rose, indicating a similar rise in the number of candidates. This was made possible by the increase in productive power and the consequent accumulation of wealth, which was the underlying reason that Chinese society changed so greatly from the T'ang period to the Sung. A new class appeared in China, comparable to the bourgeoisie in early modern Europe. In China this newly risen class concentrated hard on scholarship, and with the custom of this group, publishers prospered mightily. The classic books of Buddhism and Confucianism were printed; the collected writings of contemporaries and their discourses and essays on current topics were published; and the government issued an official gazette, so that in a sense China entered upon an age of mass communications. As a result learning was so widespread that candidates for the examinations came from virtually every part of the land, and the government could freely pick the best among them to form a reserve of officials.

In the Sung dynasty the system of conducting the examinations every three years was established. Since about three hundred men were selected each time, the government obtained an average of one hundred men a year who were qualified for the highest government positions. Thus the most important positions in government were occupied by *chin-shih*, and no longer were there conflicts between men who differed in their preparatory backgrounds, such as those between *chin-shih* and non–*chin-shih* that had arisen in the T'ang period.

Another improvement made during the Sung period was the establishment of the palace examination as the apex of the normal examination sequence. Under the T'ang emperors the conduct of the examinations was completely entrusted to officials, but this does not mean that emperors neglected them, because they were held by imperial order. It even happened that Empress Wu (r. 684–705) herself conducted the examinations in an attempt to win popularity. . . .

The position of the emperor in the political system changed greatly from T'ang times to Sung. No longer did the emperor consult on matters of high state policy with two or three great ministers deep in the interior of the palace, far removed from actual administrators. Now he was an autocrat, directly supervising all important departments of government and giving instructions about every aspect of government. Even minor matters of personnel needed imperial sanction. Now the emperor resembled the pivot of a fan, without which the various ribs of government would fall apart and be scattered. The creation of the palace examination as the final examination, given directly under the emperor's personal supervision, went hand in hand with this change in his function in the nation's political machinery and was a necessary step in the strengthening of imperial autocracy.

Thus, the examination system changed, along with Chinese society as a whole. Created to meet an essential need, it changed in response to that society's demand. It was most effective in those early stages when, first in the T'ang period, it was used by the emperor to suppress the power of the aristocracy, and then later, in the Sung period, when the cooperation of young officials with the *chin-shih* was essential for the establishment of imperial autocracy. Therefore, in the early Sung years *chin-shih* enjoyed very rapid promotion; this was especially true of the first-place *chin-shih*, not a few of whom rose to the position of chief councilor in fewer than ten years.

LIU TSUNG-YUAN

Camel Kuo the Gardener

Liu Tsung-yuan* (773–819) was one of the great writers of the T'ang dynasty (618–907). He was especially loved for his scenes of nature, a topic he uses here for an allegory about government. What is the message of the allegory?

Thinking Historically

Are the ideas of government expressed here more like those of Confucius or Lao Tzu? How do you think Liu Tsung-yuan felt about the civil service system? Can we assume that Chinese government was practiced as the author desired, or that it was not?

How does this view of government differ from that of Western European or Muslim societies? In what sense is it more typically Chinese?

Whatever name Camel Kuo may have had to begin with is not known. But he was a hunchback and walked in his bumpy way with his face to the ground, very like a camel, and so that was what the country folk called him. When Camel Kuo heard them he said, "Excellent. Just the right name for me." — And he forthwith discarded his real name and himself adopted "Camel" also.

He lived at Feng-lo, to the west of Ch'ang-an. Camel was a grower of trees by profession; and all the great and wealthy residents of Ch'ang-an who planted trees for their enjoyment or lived off the sale of their fruit would compete for the favour of his services. It was a matter of observation that when Camel Kuo had planted a tree, even though it was uprooted from elsewhere, there was never a one but lived, and grew strong and glossy, and fruited early and abundantly. Other growers, however they spied on him and tried to imitate his methods, never could achieve his success.

*lee OU   tsung WAHN

Liu Tsung-yuan, "Camel Kuo the Gardener," in *Anthology of Chinese Literature,* ed. and trans. Cyril Birch (New York: Grove Press, 1965), 258–59.

Once, when questioned on the point, Camel replied: "I cannot make a tree live for ever or flourish. What I *can* do is comply with the nature of the tree so that it takes the way of its kind. When a tree is planted its roots should have room to breathe, its base should be firmed, the soil it is in should be old, and the fence around it should be close. When you have it this way, then you must neither disturb it nor worry about it, but go away and not come back. If you care for it like this when you plant it, and neglect it like this *after* you have planted it, then its nature will be fulfilled and it will take the way of its kind. And so all *I* do is avoid harming its growth — I have no power to make it grow; I avoid hindering the fruiting — I have no power to bring it forward or make it more abundant.

"With other growers it is not the same. They coil up the roots and they use fresh soil. They firm the base either too much or not enough. Or if they manage to avoid these faults, then they dote too fondly and worry too anxiously. They inspect the tree every morning and cosset it every night; they cannot walk away from it without turning back for another look. The worst of them will even scrape off the bark to see if it is still living, or shake the roots to test whether they are holding fast. And with all this the tree gets further every day from what a tree should be. This is not mothering but smothering, not affection but affliction. This is why they cannot rival my results: what other skill can I claim?"

"Would it be possible to apply this philosophy of yours to the art of government?" asked the questioner.

"My only art is the growing of trees," said Camel Kuo in answer. "Government is not my business. But living here in the country I have seen officials who go to a lot of trouble issuing orders as though they were deeply concerned for the people; yet all they achieve is an increase of misfortune. Morning and evening runners come yelling, 'Orders from the government: plough at once! Sow right away! Harvest inspection! Spin your silk! Weave your cloth! Raise your children! Feed your livestock!' Drums roll for assembly, blocks are struck to summon us. And we the common people miss our meals to receive the officials and still cannot find the time: how then can we expect to prosper our livelihood and find peace in our lives? This is why we are sick and weary; and in this state of affairs I suppose there may be some resemblance to my profession?"

"Wonderful!" was the delighted cry of the man who had questioned him. "The art I sought was of cultivating trees; the art I found was of cultivating men. Let this be passed on as a lesson to all in office!"

FAN ZHONGYAN

Rules for the Fan Lineage's Charitable Estate

From the time of the Sung dynasty (960–1279), many wealthy Chinese families formed charitable trusts for their descendants. One of the first men to set up such a trust was Fan Zhongyan (989–1052), an important political official.

This selection presents the rules that Fan set down for the way in which his descendants would share the income from his estate. What activities did the lineage support? What other activities would have been left to individual families? Why would lineages be more common among wealthy than poor families?

Thinking Historically

Lineage was both a social and economic organization. What impact would these lineages have on Chinese social life? Would they strengthen or weaken Chinese families? How might they affect Chinese economic life?

How did lineages make Chinese society different from that of Western Europe? Were there similar social institutions in Islamic society? Is there a modern equivalent?

1. One pint of rice per day may be granted for each person whom a branch has certified to be one of its members. (These quantities refer to polished rice. If hulled rice is used, the amount should be increased proportionately.)

2. Children of both sexes over five years of age are counted in the total.

3. Female servants may receive rice if they have borne children by men in the lineage and the children are over fifteen or they themselves are over fifty.

4. One bolt of silk for winter clothing may be granted for each individual, except children between five and ten years of age who may receive half a bolt.

Fan Zhongyan, *Fan Wengzheng gong ji*, in *Chinese Civilization: A Sourcebook*, 2nd ed., ed. and trans. Patricia Buckley Ebrey (New York: The Free Press, 1993), 155–56.

5. Each branch may receive a rice ration for a single slave, but not any silk.

6. Every birth, marriage, death, or other change in the number of lineage members must immediately be recorded.

7. Each branch should make a list of those entitled to grain rations. At the end of the month the manager should examine these requests. He must not make any prior arrangements or exceed the stipulated monthly rations. The manager should also keep his own register in which he records the quantity due each branch based on the number of its members. If the manager spends money wastefully or makes advance payments to anyone, the branches have the authority to require him to pay an indemnity.

8. For the expenses of marrying a daughter, thirty strings of cash may be granted, unless the marriage is a second one, in which case twenty strings may be granted.

9. For the expenses of taking a first wife, twenty strings may be granted (but nothing for a second wife).

10. Lineage members who become officials may receive the regular rice and silk grants and the special grants for weddings and funerals if they are living at home awaiting a post, awaiting selection, or mourning their parents. They may also receive the grants if they leave their families at home while they serve in Sichuan, Gwangdong, or Fujien, or for any other good reason.

11. For the expenses of mourning and funerals in the various branches, if the deceased is a senior member, when mourning begins, a grant of ten strings of cash may be made, and a further fifteen at the time of the burial. For more junior members, the figures are five and ten strings respectively. In the case of low-ranking members or youths under nineteen, seven strings for both expenses; for those under fifteen, three strings; for those under ten, two strings. No grant should be made for children who die before seven, or slaves or servants.

12. If any relatives through marriage living in the district face dire need or unexpected difficulties, the branches should jointly determine the facts and discuss ways to provide assistance from the income of the charitable estate.

13. A stock of rice should be stored by the charitable estate from year to year. The monthly rations and the grants of silk for winter clothing should start with the tenth month of 1050. Thereafter, during each year with a good harvest, two years' worth of grain rations should be hulled and stored. If a year of dearth occurs, no grants should be made except for the rice rations. Any surplus over and above the two years' reserve should be used first for funeral and mourning expenses, then marriage expenses. If there is still a remainder, winter clothes may be issued. However, if the surplus is not very large, the priorities should be discussed, and the amount available divided up and granted in equi-

table proportions. If grants cannot be made to all entitled to them, they should be made first to those who have suffered bereavement, next to those with weddings. In cases where more than one death has occurred at the same time, senior members take precedence over junior ones. Where the relative seniority of those concerned is the same, the grant should be made on the basis of which death or burial took place first. If, after paying out the rations and the allowances for marriages and burials, a surplus still remains, it must not be sold off, but hulled and put into storage for use as rations for three or more years. If there is a danger that the stored grain might go bad, it may be sold off and replaced with fresh rice after the autumn harvest. All members of the branches of the lineage will carefully comply with the above rules.

Tenth month, 1050. Academician of the Zizheng Hall, Vice-president of the Board of Rites, and Prefect of Hangzhou, Fan. Sealed.

REFLECTIONS

Whatever particular period or region historians work on — in the case of this chapter, medieval Europe, Islam, and China — they also tend to specialize in particular kinds of documents and related aspects of life. They are social historians, or economic historians, or cultural historians. As a matter of fact, most of them would characterize their work even more precisely than that. A particular social historian might prefer to be called a historian of gender or a historian of the family. A political historian might be a diplomatic historian. A cultural historian might be a historian of religion, or even of medieval Christianity, or of Christian anti-Semitism. As in the sciences, historians are able to dig deeper and learn more by specializing. And, as in any field, the more you specialize, the more you discover you do not know, the more questions you have, and the more you can learn.

All of this begins, however, with some basic categories, like those we have used in this chapter. That is why you were asked to think in terms of political, economic, social, and cultural history.

To pull together and compare some of the characterizations you made from the selections in this chapter, make a chart: Write the names of the three civilizations — European, Islamic, and Chinese — across the top of the page, and the categories social, economic, political, and cultural down the left margin, allowing a quarter page for each. Try to fill in as many of the blocks as you can. You might use more than one characterization for each. For instance, in the box for social aspects of European civilization you would, no doubt, write "feudalism." You might also write "nobles," "monasteries," "fealty and homage," "vassals defend," and "sons inherit status." Or your style of observing and characterizing might lead you to such notes as "churches can be land-lords," "lots of witnesses," and "they were very formal." All of these descriptions are correct: Just make sure your comments are about society, social behavior, social relationships, social organization, or various social elements — class, family, men and women, population, and age. Repeat this exercise with the other three categories. These are by no means exclusive, but try not to use the same words in describing, say, a social and an economic aspect.

After you have filled in as many of the blanks as you can, you can make comparisons in a number of interesting ways. (You have already done some of this, but here you can be more systematic.) First, compare how one category, say society, is different in Europe and Islam, or Europe and China, or China and Islam. You might, for example, say that European society was less centralized than Chinese or Islamic society or that the extended family was more important in China.

After doing the same for economics, politics, and culture, notice how the four categories of any civilization fit together. How does the type of society in medieval Europe, for instance, "fit" medieval Europe's economy? This interaction is what constitutes a civilization. See if you used a word repetitively in characterizing each of the four aspects of a particular civilization. Then try to categorize the civilization as a whole.

Now you are ready to compare each of these civilizations to another one. These characterizations may be general, or they may be qualified and later modified, but at the very least you now have a general starting point for more in-depth analysis of these three great civilizations in future chapters.

9

Love and Marriage

Medieval Europe, India, and Japan, 400–1200 C.E.

HISTORICAL CONTEXT

Love and marriage, love and marriage,
Go together like a horse and carriage.
This I tell ya, brother,
You can't have one without the other.[1]

Despite the lyrics of the song, love and marriage had little to do with each other throughout most of human history. Parents arranged marriages with their own economic needs foremost. Few people had the time to cultivate the idea of romantic love. One group who did, the ancient Greeks, wrote of love as a sickness; its symptoms were sweaty palms, palpitating heart, blushing complexion, and stammering speech. Marriage cured the disease, ending all symptoms, returning the couple to the steady sanity of daily life. But the idea of love as affliction, accident, or attack (symbolized by the random shot of Cupid's arrow) was evidently too enticing to disappear with the end of the classical world. Cultivated in the religious poetry of the Islamic world, ideas of fevered emotional dedication revived in Europe in the Middle Ages.

A thousand years ago, romantic love was experienced by very few people—often members of a leisure class who seemed to have time on their hands. And the set of ideas, feelings, and actions they exhibited might strike modern readers as rather bizarre. We have to look closely to see the roots of one of our favorite modern emotions.

---

[1]Written by Sammy Cahn and Jimmy Van Heusen.

THINKING HISTORICALLY
Analyzing Cultural Differences

In the previous chapter, we distinguished among the economic, social, political, and cultural aspects of a society. In this chapter we will examine cultural aspects alone. Actually, culture is never alone, any more than are economics, politics, or social behavior. Culture is nothing less than all our thoughts and feelings and the way we express them by the way we walk, talk, dream, and read history books. Even love, a single ingredient of a culture, is related to aspects of behavior, economics, and even politics. Yet we will isolate this one cultural piece—love—to see how its meaning is different in different cultures. We will analyze these differences to understand better the different cultures and also to understand something about the history of love.

$$\boxed{54}$$

KEVIN REILLY
Love in Medieval Europe, India, and Japan

We hesitantly introduce this piece as a secondary source. It might be better called a tertiary source because it is based so much on the work of others and is part of a chapter in a college textbook. Nevertheless, it sets the stage for our discussion about love. The selection begins with the classic argument that romantic love was a product of medieval Europe, originating in the troubadour tradition of southern France around the twelfth century. The story of Ulrich von Liechtenstein, although probably not typical, details all the facets of the new idea of love, as well as the courts of chivalry that developed its code of behavior. What, according to this interpretation, are the elements of romantic love? How is it similar to, or different from, other kinds of love? How does it relate to sex and marriage? How is the medieval Indian tradition of *bhakti* different from European romantic love? How were medieval Hindu ideas of sex different from Christian ideas of sex? How was the Japanese idea of love during the Heian* period (794–1185) different from European romantic love? How was it similar?

*hay AHN

Kevin Reilly, *The West and the World*, 3rd ed. (Princeton, N.J.: Markus Wiener, 1997), 279–80, 282–83, 287–92.

Thinking Historically

Every culture encompasses a wide variety of ideas and behavior at any one time, making it difficult to argue that a certain idea or behavior defines the culture as a whole. Nevertheless, if there were no commonalities there could be no culture. One way to understand what makes one culture different from another is to discount the extreme behavior at the fringes and focus on what most people think or do. But another way is to compare the extremes of one culture with the extremes of another, on the assumption that the extremists of any culture will magnify the culture's main trait. You might think of Ulrich von Liechtenstein as an extreme example of medieval European ideas of romantic love. A question to ask after you read about other societies is: Could there have been an Ulrich elsewhere? Could medieval India or Japan have produced an Ulrich? If not, why not?

Notice also that this selection highlights particular social classes as well as particular cultures. How do cultures and classes interact to form the ideal of romantic love in Europe and something both similar and different in Japan?

In the Service of Woman

In the twelfth century the courtly love tradition of the troubadours traveled north into France and Germany, and it became a guide to behavior for many young knights.

We are lucky to have the autobiography of one of these romantic knights, a minor noble who was born in Austria about 1200. His name was Ulrich von Liechtenstein, and he called his autobiography, appropriately enough, *In the Service of Woman*.[1]

At an early age Ulrich learned that the greatest honor and happiness for a knight lay in the service of a beautiful and noble woman. He seems to have realized, at least subconsciously, that true love had to be full of obstacles and frustrations in order to be spiritually ennobling. So at the age of twelve Ulrich chose as the love of his life a princess. She was a perfect choice: Far above him socially, she was also older than Ulrich and already married. Ulrich managed to become a page in her court so that he could see her and touch the same things that she touched. Sometimes he was even able to steal away to his room with the very water that she had just washed her hands in, and he would secretly drink it.

By the age of seventeen Ulrich had become a knight and took to the countryside to joust the tournaments wearing the lady's colors. Finally

[1]Paraphrased from Martin Hunt, *The National History of Love* (New York: Alfred A. Knopf, 1959), 132–39. Quotations from Hunt.

after a number of victories, Ulrich gained the courage to ask his niece to call on the lady and tell her that he wanted to be a distant, respectful admirer. The princess would have none of it. She told Ulrich's niece that she was repulsed by Ulrich's mere presence, that he was low class and ugly—especially with that harelip of his. On hearing her reply Ulrich was overjoyed that she had noticed him. He went to have his harelip removed, recuperated for six weeks, and wrote a song to the princess. When the lady heard of this she finally consented to let Ulrich attend a riding party she was having, suggesting even that he might exchange a word with her if the opportunity arose. Ulrich had his chance. He was next to her horse as she was about to dismount, but he was so tongue-tied that he couldn't say a word. The princess thought him such a boor that she pulled out a lock of his hair as she got off her horse.

Ulrich returned to the field for the next three years. Finally the lady allowed him to joust in her name, but she wouldn't part with as much as a ribbon for him to carry. He sent her passionate letters and songs that he had composed. She answered with insults and derision. In one letter the princess derided Ulrich for implying that he had lost a finger while fighting for her when he had actually only wounded it slightly. Ulrich responded by having a friend hack off the finger and send it to the lady in a green velvet case. The princess was evidently so impressed with the power that she had over Ulrich that she sent back a message that she would look at it every day—a message that Ulrich received as he had the others—"on his knees, with bowed head and folded hands."

More determined than ever to win his lady's love, Ulrich devised a plan for a spectacular series of jousts, in which he challenged all comers on a five-week trip. He broke eight lances a day in the service of his princess. After such a showing, the princess sent word that Ulrich might at last visit her, but that he was to come disguised as a leper and sit with the other lepers who would be there begging. The princess passed him, said nothing, and let him sleep that night out in the rain. The following day she sent a message to Ulrich that he could climb a rope to her bedroom window. There she told him that she would grant no favors until he waded across the lake; then she dropped the rope so that he fell into the stinking moat.

Finally, after all of this, the princess said that she would grant Ulrich her love if he went on a Crusade in her name. When she learned that he was making preparations to go, she called it off and offered her love. After almost fifteen years Ulrich had proved himself to the princess.

What was the love that she offered? Ulrich doesn't say, but it probably consisted of kisses, an embrace, and possibly even a certain amount of fondling. Possibly more, but probably not. That was not the point. Ulrich had not spent fifteen years for sex. In fact, Ulrich had not spent fifteen years to win. The quest is what kept him going. His real reward was in the suffering and yearning. Within two years Ulrich was after another perfect lady.

Oh yes. We forgot one thing. Ulrich mentions that in the middle of his spectacular five-week joust, he stopped off for three days to visit the wife and kids. He was married? He was married. He speaks of his wife with a certain amount of affection. She was evidently quite good at managing the estate and bringing up the children. But what were these mundane talents next to the raptures of serving the ideal woman? Love was certainly not a part of the "details of crops, and cattle, fleas and fireplaces, serfs and swamp drainage." In fact, Ulrich might expect that his wife would be proud of him if she knew what he was up to. The love of the princess should make Ulrich so much more noble and esteemed in his wife's eyes.

Courtly Love

The behavior of Ulrich von Liechtenstein reflected in exaggerated form a new idea of love in the West. Historians have called it "courtly love" because it developed in the courts of Europe, where noble ladies and knights of "quality" came together. For the first time since the Greeks a man could idealize a woman, but only if he minimized her sexuality. The evidence is overwhelming that these spiritual affairs would ideally never be consummated.

It is difficult for us to understand how these mature lords and ladies could torture themselves with passionate oaths, feats of endurance, fainting spells when they heard their lover's name or voice, in short the whole repertoire of romance, and then refrain from actually consummating that love. Why did they insist on an ideal of "pure love" that allowed even naked embraces but drew the line at intercourse, which they called "false love"? No doubt the Christian antipathy for sex was part of the problem. Earlier Christian monks had practiced a similar type of *agape*, Christianity had always taught that there was a world of difference between love and lust. The tendency of these Christian men to think of their ladies as replicas of the Virgin Mother also made sex inappropriate, if not outright incestuous.

But these lords and ladies were also making a statement about their "class" or good breeding. They were saying (as did Sigmund Freud almost a thousand years later) that civilized people repress their animal lust. They were distinguishing themselves from the crude peasants and soldiers around them who knew only fornication and whoring and raping. They were cultivating their emotions and their sensitivity, and priding themselves on their self-control. They were privileged (as members of the upper class) to know that human beings were capable of loyalty and love and enjoying beauty without behaving like animals. They were telling each other that they were refined, that they had "class." . . .

Further, despite the new romanticized view of the woman (maybe because of it), wives were just as excluded as they had always been. Noble, uplifting love, genuine romantic love, could not be felt for someone who swept the floor any more than it could be felt *by* someone whose life was preoccupied with such trivia. The lords and one of their special ladies, Marie, the countess of Champagne, issued the following declaration in 1174:

> We declare and we hold as firmly established that love cannot exert its power between two people who are married to each other. For lovers give each other everything freely, under no compulsion of necessity, but married people are in duty bound to give in to each other's desires and deny themselves to each other in nothing.[2]

The Court of Love

The proclamation was one of many that were made by the "courts of love" that these lords and ladies established in order to settle lovers' quarrels—and to decide for themselves the specifics of the new morality. . . .

No one did more to formulate these rules than Andreas Capellanus. Andreas not only summarized the numerous cases that came before the court, but he used these decisions to write a manual of polite, courtly love. He called his influential book *A Treatise on Love and Its Remedy*, a title that indicated his debt to Sappho and the Greek romantic idea of love as a sickness. Andreas, however, did not think that he was advocating a "romantic" idea of love. The word was not even used in his day. He considered himself to be a modern twelfth-century Ovid—merely updating the Roman's *Art of Love*. He called himself Andreas the Lover and, like Ovid, considered himself an expert on all aspects of love.

But Andreas only used the same word as Ovid. The similarity ended there. The "aspects" of love that Andreas taught concerned the loyalty of the lovers, courteous behavior, the spiritual benefits of "pure love," the importance of gentleness, the subservience of the man to his lover, and the duties of courtship. There is none of Ovid's preoccupation with the techniques of seduction. Andreas is not talking about sex. In fact, he clearly advises against consummating the relationship.

Ovid made fun of infatuation and silly emotional behavior, but urged his readers to imitate such sickness in order to get the woman in bed. Andreas valued the passionate emotional attachment that Ovid mocked. Sincerity and honesty were too important to Andreas to dream

---

[2]Andreas, *Tractatus de Amore*, 1:6, 7th Dialogue. Quoted in Hunt, 143–44.

of trickery, deceit, or pretense. Love, for Andreas, was too noble an emotion, too worthy a pursuit, to be put on like a mask. In short, the Roman had been after sexual gratification; the Christian wanted to refine lives and cleanse souls. They both called it love, but Andreas never seemed to realize that they were not talking the same language.

A Medieval Indian Alternative: Mystical Eroticism

Sometimes the best way to understand our own traditions is to study those of a different culture. It is difficult, for instance, for us to see Christian sexual morality as unusual because it has shaped our culture to such a great extent.

There have been alternatives, however. One of the most remarkable was the Indian ecstatic religion of the Middle Ages. Here the erotic played a central role, not as temptation to be shunned but as a source of salvation. Most medieval temple sculpture was erotic. The temples at Khajuraho and Orissa are full of sexual imagery: sensuous nudes and embracing couples. The temple architecture itself suggests fertility and reproduction. The temple sculptures, like the popular story *Gita Govinda* of the twelfth century, tell of the loves of the god Krishna. He is shown scandalizing young women, dancing deliriously, and bathing with scores of admirers. Krishna's erotic appeal is a testament to his charisma. He is "divine in proportion to his superiority as a great lover."

> Worshippers were encouraged to commit excesses during festivals as the surest way to achieve . . . ecstasy, the purging climax of the orgiastic feast, the surmounting of duality.[3]

Among the most popular forms of medieval Hindu worship were the *bhakti* cults, which originated in devotion to Krishna in the *Bhagavad Gita*. Bhakti cults underline the difference between Indian and European devotion. While the Christian church discouraged spiritual love that might easily lead to "carnal love," the Indian *bhakti* sects encouraged rituals of ecstasy and sensual love precisely because they obliterated moral distinctions. The ecstatic union with the divine Krishna, Vishnu, or Shiva enabled the worshiper to transcend the limitations of self and confining definitions of good and evil.

Thus, Indian ecstatic religion sought sexual expression as a path to spiritual fulfillment. It is interesting that the word *bhakti* meant sex as well as worship, while we use the word "devotion" to mean worship and love. Hindu eroticism had nothing to do with the private expression of romantic love. In fact, it was the opposite. While romantic love depended

[3]Richard Lannoy, *The Speaking Tree: A Study of Indian Culture and Society* (Oxford: Oxford University Press, 1971), 64.

on the development of the individual personality and the cultivation of individual feelings, *bhakti* depended on the loss of self in the sexual act.

Bhakti cults differed from the European courtly love tradition in one other important respect. They were not expressions of upper-class control. They were popular expressions of religious feeling. In essence they were directed against the dominating *brahman* and *kshatriya* castes because they challenged the importance of caste distinctions altogether. The ecstatic communion with the deity that they preached was open to all, regardless of caste. They appealed even to women and untouchables, as well as to farmers and artisans.

As Christianity did in Europe, popular Hinduism of the Middle Ages replaced a classical formal tradition with a spiritual passion. Ovid's *Art of Love* and the *Kama Sutra* were mechanical, passionless exercises for tired ruling classes. Both India and Europe turned to more emotionally intense religious experiences in the Middle Ages. Perhaps the classical ideals seemed sterile after the spread of salvation religions like Christianity, Buddhism, and revived Hinduism. The similarity between Christian and Hindu emotionalism may be a product of uncertain times, barbarian threats, and diseases that stalked the Eurasian continent. But the differences between Christian courtly love and *bhakti* cults were also profound. In India, sexual passion was an avenue to spiritual salvation. In Christian Europe sexual passion was at best a dead end, and at worst a road to hell.

Polygamy, Sexuality, and Style: A Japanese Alternative

At the same time that feudal Europe was developing a code of chivalry that romanticized love and almost desexualized marriage, the aristocracy of feudal Japan was evolving a code of polygamous sexuality without chivalry and almost without passion. We know about the sexual lives of Japanese aristocrats between 950 and 1050—the apex of the Heian period—through a series of remarkable novels and diaries, almost all of which were written by women. These first classics of Japanese literature, like *The Tale of Genji* and *The Pillow Book*, were written by women because Japanese men were still writing the "more important" but less-informative laws and theological studies in Chinese (just as Europeans still wrote in a Latin that was very different from the everyday spoken language).

When well-born Japanese in the Heian court spoke of "the world" they were referring to a love affair, and the novels that aristocratic women like Murasaki Shikibu or Sei Shonagon had time to compose in the spoken language were full of stories of "the world."

In *The World of the Shining Prince* Ivan Morris distinguishes three types of sexual relationships between men and women of the Heian aristocracy. (Homosexuality among the court ladies was "probably quite common," he writes, "as in any society where women were obliged to live in continuous and close proximity," but male homosexuality among "warriors, priests, and actors" probably became prevalent in later centuries.) The first type of heterosexual relationship was between the male aristocrat and his "principal wife." She was often several years older than her boy-husband and frequently served more as a guardian than as a bride. She was always chosen for her social standing, usually to cement a political alliance between ruling families. Although the match must frequently have been loveless, her status was inviolate; it was strictly forbidden, for instance, for a prince to exalt a secondary wife to principal wife. Upon marriage the principal wife would normally continue to live with her family, visited by her husband at night, until he became the head of his own household on the death or retirement of his father. Then the principal wife would be installed with all of her servants and aides as the head of the north wing of her husband's residence. An aristocratic woman (but never a peasant woman) might also become a secondary wife or official concubine. If she were officially recognized as such (much to the pleasure of her family), she might be moved into another wing of the official residence (leading to inevitable conflicts with the principal wife and other past and future secondary wives), or she might be set up in her own house. The arrangements were virtually limitless. The third and most frequent type of sexual relationship between men and women was the simple (or complex) affair—with a lady at court, another man's wife or concubine, but usually with a woman of a far lower class than the man. Ivan Morris writes of this kind of relationship:

> Few cultured societies in history can have been as tolerant about sexual relations as was the world of *The Tale of Genji*. Whether or not a gentleman was married, it redounded to his prestige to have as many affairs as possible; and the palaces and great mansions were full of ladies who were only too ready to accommodate him if approached in the proper style. From reading the *Pillow Book* we can tell how extremely commonplace these casual affairs had become in court circles, the man usually visiting the girl at night behind her screen of state and leaving her at the crack of dawn.[4]

That emphasis on "the proper style" is what distinguishes the sexuality of medieval Japan from that of ancient Rome, and reminds us of the medieval European's display of form—the aristocracy's mark of "class." Perhaps because the sexuality of the Heian aristocracy was potentially more explosive than the repressed rituals of European chivalry, style was that much more important. Polygamous sexuality could be practiced

[4]Ivan Morris, *The World of the Shining Prince: Court Life in Ancient Japan* (Baltimore: Penguin Books, 1969), 237.

without tearing the society apart (and destroying aristocratic dominance in the process) only if every attention were given to style. Listen, for instance, to what the lady of *The Pillow Book* expected from a good lover:

> A good lover will behave as elegantly at dawn as at any other time. He drags himself out of bed with a look of dismay on his face. The lady urges him on: "Come, my friend, it's getting light. You don't want anyone to find you here." He gives a deep sigh, as if to say that the night has not been nearly long enough and that it is agony to leave. Once up, he does not instantly pull on his trousers. Instead he comes close to the lady and whispers whatever was left unsaid during the night. Even when he is dressed, he still lingers, vaguely pretending to be fastening his sash.
>
> Presently he raises the lattice, and the two lovers stand together by the side door while he tells her how he dreads the coming day, which will keep them apart; then he slips away. The lady watches him go, and this moment of parting will remain among her most charming memories.
>
> Indeed, one's attachment to a man depends largely on the elegance of his leave-taking. When he jumps out of bed, scurries about the room, tightly fastens his trouser-sash, rolls up the sleeves of his Court cloak, over-robe, or hunting costume, stuffs his belongings into the breast of his robe and then briskly secures the outer sash—one really begins to hate him.[5]

The stylistic elegance of the lover's departure was one of the principal themes of Heian literature. Perhaps no situation better expressed the mood of the Japanese word *aware* (a word that was used over a thousand times in *The Tale of Genji*), which meant the poignant or the stylishly, even artistically, sorrowful—a style of elegant resignation. The word also suggests the mood of "the lady in waiting" and even the underlying anguish and jealousy of a precariously polygamous existence for the women consorts and writers of the Japanese feudal age. The ladies of the court were trained in calligraphy, poetry, and music; they were dressed in elaborate, colorful silks, painted with white faces and black teeth, and rewarded by sexual attention that always had to be justified by its cultured style. . . .

Aristocracies have behaved in similar ways throughout the world, and throughout history. They demonstrate their "class" or "good breeding" with elaborate rituals that differentiate their world from the ordinary. But the example of aristocratic Heian Japan a thousand years ago points to some of the differences between Japanese and Christian culture. The Japanese developed rituals of courtship and seduction for the leisured few that were sexually satisfying and posed no threat to

---

[5]*The Pillow Book of Sei Shonagon*, trans. Ivan Morris (Baltimore: Penguin Books, 1971), 49–50.

marriage. They were rituals that showed artistic refinement rather than sexual "purity" or chastity. They could be sexual because Japanese culture did not disparage sexuality. Rather it disparaged lack of "taste." The affair did not threaten marriage because the culture did not insist on monogamy. The new sexual interest could be carried on outside or inside the polygamous estate of the Japanese aristocrat. Perhaps the main difference, then, is that the Japanese aristocrat invented stylized sex rather than romantic love.

$$\boxed{55}$$

ULRICH VON LIECHTENSTEIN

The Service of Ladies

This selection is drawn from Ulrich von Liechtenstein's own account of his adventures. After over ten years of service, as a page and then a distant admirer, in 1226, Ulrich undertook a spectacular series of jousts to impress and win his lady, the princess. In the course of a five-week itinerary in northern Italy and southern German-speaking areas in which he took on all comers, he claims to have broken three hundred and seven lances. In the first part of this selection he details his preparation for the traveling tournament. In the second part of the selection, he tells of a brief interruption in his jousting for a stop at home. What does this selection tell you about Ulrich's ideas of love and marriage?

Thinking Historically

Sometimes the best entry point for analyzing cultural differences is to begin with the surprising or incomprehensible. If we can refrain from merely dismissing what seems beyond the pale, this can be an opportunity to understand how cultures can be truly different from our own.

Even a moderately careful reading of the two selections from Ulrich's autobiography should evoke some surprise. In the first selection, Ulrich sketches a visual image of himself on horseback that is far from our expectations. Imagine what he must have looked like. Imagine how others must have seen him. Recognizing that this was not some Halloween prank, that others proceeded to joust with him rather than laugh him out of town, we are forced to rethink what his outfit and

Ulrich von Liechtenstein, *The Service of Ladies*, trans. J. W. Thomas (Suffolk, England and Rochester, N.Y.: The Boydell Press, 2004; published by arrangement with University of North Carolina Press, Chapel Hill, 1969), 46–49, 85–86.

presentation meant to him and those in his society. The recognition that the meaning of an act (like donning women's clothing) could be vastly different in Europe of the thirteenth century from what it is today offers the entry to comparative analysis.

We may also note that there are many things in Ulrich's description of love that are not at all surprising. This may be because they have become second nature to our own society. Certainly some of the elements of romantic love, which were fresh in Ulrich's day, have become clichés in modern film and television. What do you make of the elements of this story that are familiar? What do you make of those that surprise you?

"My service must be God's command.
Now let me tell you what I've planned.
I'll take on woman's dress and name
and thus disguised will strive for fame.
Sweet God protect me and sustain!
I'll travel with a knightly train
up to Bohemia from the sea.
A host of knights shall fight with me.

"This very winter I shall steal
out of the land and shall conceal
my goal from everyone but you.
I'll travel as a pilgrim who
to honor God is bound for Rome
(no one will question this at home).
I'll stop in Venice and shall stay
in hiding till the first of May.

"I'll carefully remain unseen
but deck myself out like a queen;
it should be easy to acquire
some lovely feminine attire
which I'll put on—now hear this last—
and when St. George's day is past,
the morning afterwards, I'll ride
(I pray that God is on my side)

"from the sea to Mestre, near
by Venice. He who breaks a spear
with me to serve, by tourneying,
his lady fair will get a ring

of gold and it will be quite nice.
I'll give it to him with this advice,
that he present it to his love,
the one he's in the service of.

"Messenger, I'll make the trip
so there will never be a slip
and no one possibly can guess
whose form is hid beneath the dress.
For I'll be clad from head to toe
in woman's garb where'er I go,
fully concealed from people's eyes.
They'll see me only in disguise.

"If you would please me, messenger,
then travel once again to her.
Just tell her what I have in mind
and ask if she will be so kind
as to permit that I should fight
throughout this journey as her knight.
It's something she will not repent
and I'll be glad of her assent."

He rode at once to tell her this
and swore upon his hope of bliss
my loyalty would never falter,
that I was true and would not alter.
He told my plan in full detail
and said, "My lady, should you fail
to let him serve and show your trust
in him, it wouldn't seem quite just."

"Messenger," she spoke, "just let
him have this message, don't forget.
This trip, if I have understood
you right, will surely do him good
and he will win a rich reward
in praise from many a lady and lord.
Whether it helps with me or not,
from others he will gain a lot."

The messenger was pleased and sure.
He found me by the river Mur
at Liechtenstein where I was then.
'T was nice to have him there again.

I spoke, "O courtly youth, now tell
me if the lady's feeling well.
For, if my darling's doing fine,
then shall rejoice this heart of mine."

He spoke, "She's fair and happy too;
she bade me bring this word to you
about your journey. If you should
go through with it 't will do you good
and, whether it helps with her or not,
from others you will gain a lot.
She certainly supports your aim
and says that you'll be rich in fame."

I listened to the news he had,
and heart and body both were glad.
It was a joy for me to know
my undertaking pleased her so.
I didn't linger but began
at once to carry out my plan
and was quite happy, I admit,
that he also approved of it.

I soon was ready, I assure
you, to begin my knightly tour.
I started out as pilgrim dressed
and left the land. I thought it best
to take a staff and pouch at least,
for looks (I got them from a priest);
one would have thought me bound for Rome.
I prayed God bring me safely home.

I got to Venice without delay
and found a house in which to stay,
right on the edge of town, a place
where none would ever see my face
who might have recognized me there.
I was as cautious everywhere
and all the winter long I hid.
But let me tell you what I did:

I had some woman's clothing made
to wear throughout the masquerade.
They cut and sewed for me twelve skirts
and thirty fancy lady's shirts.

I bought two braids for my disguise,
the prettiest they could devise,
and wound them with some pearls I got
which didn't cost an awful lot.

I bade the tailors then prepare
three velvet cloaks for me to wear,
all white. The saddles too on which
the master labored, stitch by stitch,
were silver white. As for a king
was made the saddle covering,
long and broad and gleaming white.
The bridles all were rich and bright.

The tailors sewed for every squire
(there were a dozen) white attire.
A hundred spears were made for me
and all as white as they could be.
But I need not continue so,
for all I wore was white as snow
and everything the squires had on
was just as white as any swan.

My shield was white, the helmet too.
I had them make ere they were through
a velvet cover for each steed
as armor. These were white, indeed,
as was the battle cape which I
should wear for jousting by and by,
the cloth of which was very fine.
I was quite pleased to call it mine.

At last I had my horses sent
to me (none knew just where they went)
and got some servants, as I'd planned,
each native to a foreign land.
They carefully did not let slip
a thing about my coming trip
and I took heed that those who came
to serve me never learned my name.

. . .

They rode toward me with armor on;
I had not waited long to don
a rich and splendid battle dress.

Von Ringenberg with full success
broke off a spear on me. The one
I jousted with when this was done
I knocked down backwards off his horse,
which made him feel ashamed, of course.

The spears I broke then numbered four.
On the field had come no more
with armor on and lance in hand
and so I stopped. At my command
the servants gave six rings away.
I sought the inn where I should stay
and found a pretty hostel there;
I got some other things to wear.

I changed my clothing under guard,
and then the hostel door was barred.
I took with me a servant who
would not say anything, I knew.
We stole away without a sound
and rode with joy to where I found
my dearest wife whom I adore;
I could not ever love her more.

She greeted me just as a good
and loving woman always should
receive a husband she holds dear.
That I had come to see her here
had made her really very pleased.
My visit stilled her grief and eased
her loneliness. We shared our bliss,
my sweet and I, with many a kiss.

She was so glad to see her knight,
and I had comfort and delight
till finally the third day came;
to give me joy was her sole aim.
When dawn appeared it was the third.
I dressed, an early mass was heard,
I prayed God keep me from transgressing,
and then received a friendly blessing.

Right after that I took my leave,
lovingly, you may believe,
and rode with joyful heart to where

I'd left my servants unaware.
I entered Gloggnitz hastily
and found them waiting there for me,
prepared to journey on again.
At once we left the city then.

We rode to Neunkirchen gaily decked
and were received as I'd expect
of those whose manners are refined.
Each knight was courteous and kind
who waited there with spear and shield.
When I came riding on the field
I found them all prepared, adorned
with trappings no one would have scorned.

Nine waited there, not more nor less,
to joust with me, in battle dress.
I saw them and it wasn't long
till I'd donned armor, bright and strong.
The first to come I'd heard much of;
his great desire was ladies' love.
It was Sir Ortold von Graz, a name
already widely known to fame.

All that he wore was of the best.
The good man cut me in the chest
so strong and skilful was his joust;
through shield and armor went the thrust.
When I beheld the wound indeed
and saw that it began to bleed
I hid it quickly with my coat
before the other knights took note.

I broke nine lances there in haste
and found my inn. I dared not waste
much time before I got in bed.
I sent nine rings of golden red
to each of them who with his spear
had earned from me a present here.
My injuries were deftly bound
by a doctor whom my servants found.

ANDREAS CAPELLANUS

From The Art of Courtly Love

Andreas Capellanus (Andreas the Chaplain) compiled this guide to
courtly love between 1184 and 1186. He probably intended his book
to update Ovid's *Art of Love,* as discussed in selection 54, but his approach reflects many of the new ideas of love circulating among the
upper classes of Europe in the twelfth century. Andreas says that
love is suffering, but also that it is wonderful. What does he mean?
Compare his ideas about sex and marriage to those of Ulrich von
Liechtenstein. The bishop of Paris condemned Andreas's ideas in
1277, but do they seem religious or Christian in any way? Notice the
author's attention to passion and proper behavior. How does he combine or balance the two?

Thinking Historically

How unusual are these ideas about love? Do you think that most
people in most societies would agree with these ideas or are they
unique? How might these ideas be considered European?

Introduction to the Treatise on Love

We must first consider what love is, whence it gets its name, what the
effect of love is, between what persons love may exist, how it may be
acquired, retained, increased, decreased, and ended, what are the signs
that one's love is returned, and what one of the lovers ought to do if the
other is unfaithful.

What Love Is

Love is a certain inborn suffering derived from the sight of and excessive meditation upon the beauty of the opposite sex, which causes
each one to wish above all things the embraces of the other and by
common desire to carry out all of love's precepts in the other's embrace.

That love is suffering is easy to see, for before the love becomes
equally balanced on both sides there is no torment greater, since the

---

Andreas Capellanus, *The Art of Courtly Love,* trans. John J. Parry (New York: Columbia
University Press, 1990), 28–32, 159–86.

lover is always in fear that his love may not gain its desire and that he is wasting his efforts. He fears, too, that rumors of it may get abroad, and he fears everything that might harm it in any way, for before things are perfected a slight disturbance often spoils them. If he is a poor man, he also fears that the woman may scorn his poverty; if he is ugly, he fears that she may despise his lack of beauty or may give her love to a more handsome man; if he is rich, he fears that his parsimony in the past may stand in his way. To tell the truth, no one can number the fears of one single lover. This kind of love, then, is a suffering which is felt by only one of the persons and may be called "single love." But even after both are in love the fears that arise are just as great, for each of the lovers fears that what he has acquired with so much effort may be lost through the effort of someone else, which is certainly much worse for a man than if, having no hope, he sees that his efforts are accomplishing nothing, for it is worse to lose the things you are seeking than to be deprived of a gain you merely hope for. The lover fears, too, that he may offend his loved one in some way; indeed he fears so many things that it would be difficult to tell them.

That this suffering is inborn I shall show you clearly, because if you will look at the truth and distinguish carefully you will see that it does not arise out of any action; only from the reflection of the mind upon what it sees does this suffering come. For when a man sees some woman fit for love and shaped according to his taste, he begins at once to lust after her in his heart; then the more he thinks about her the more he burns with love, until he comes to a fuller meditation. Presently he begins to think about the fashioning of the woman and to differentiate her limbs, to think about what she does, and to pry into the secrets of her body, and he desires to put each part of it to the fullest use. Then after he has come to this complete meditation, love cannot hold the reins, but he proceeds at once to action; straightway he strives to get a helper to find an intermediary. He begins to plan how he may find favor with her, and he begins to seek a place and a time opportune for talking; he looks upon a brief hour as a very long year, because he cannot do anything fast enough to suit his eager mind. It is well known that many things happen to him in this manner. This inborn suffering comes, therefore, from seeing and meditating. Not every kind of meditation can be the cause of love, an excessive one is required; for a restrained thought does not, as a rule, return to the mind, and so love cannot arise from it.

Between What Persons Love May Exist

Now, in love you should note first of all that love cannot exist except between persons of opposite sexes. Between two men or two women love can find no place, for we see that two persons of the same sex are not at all fitted for giving each other the exchanges of love or for practicing the acts natural to it. Whatever nature forbids, love is ashamed to accept.

What the Effect of Love Is

Now it is the effect of love that a true lover cannot be degraded with any avarice. Love causes a rough and uncouth man to be distinguished for his handsomeness; it can endow a man even of the humblest birth with nobility of character; it blesses the proud with humility; and the man in love becomes accustomed to performing many services gracefully for everyone. O what a wonderful thing is love, which makes a man shine with so many virtues and teaches everyone, no matter who he is, so many good traits of character! There is another thing about love that we should not praise in few words: it adorns a man, so to speak, with the virtue of chastity, because he who shines with the light of one love can hardly think of embracing another woman, even a beautiful one. For when he thinks deeply of his beloved the sight of any other woman seems to his mind rough and rude.

If One of the Lovers Is Unfaithful to the Other

If one of the lovers should be unfaithful to the other, and the offender is the man, and he has an eye to a new love affair, he renders himself wholly unworthy of his former love, and she ought to deprive him completely of her embraces.

But what if he should be unfaithful to his beloved—not with the idea of finding a new love, but because he has been driven to it by an irresistible passion for another woman? What, for instance, if chance should present to him an unknown woman in a convenient place or what if at a time when Venus is urging him on to that which I am talking about he should meet with a little strumpet or somebody's servant girl? Should he, just because he played with her in the grass, lose the love of his beloved? We can say without fear of contradiction that just for this a lover is not considered unworthy of the love of his beloved unless he indulges in so many excesses with a number of women that we may conclude that he is overpassionate. But if whenever he becomes acquainted with a woman he pesters her to gain his end, or if he attains his object as a result of his efforts, then rightly he does deserve to be deprived of his former love, because there is strong presumption that he has acted in this way with an eye toward a new one, especially where he has strayed with a woman of the nobility or otherwise of an honorable estate.

I know that once when I sought advice I got the answer that a true lover can never desire a new love unless he knows that for some definite and sufficient reason the old love is dead; we know from our own experience that this rule is very true. We have fallen in love with a woman of the most admirable character, although we have never had, or hope to have, any fruit of this love. For we are compelled to pine away for love of a woman of such lofty station that we dare not say one word about it, nor dare we throw ourself upon her mercy, and so at length we are forced to find our body shipwrecked. But although rashly and without foresight we have fallen into such great waves in this tempest, still we cannot think about a new love or look for any other way to free ourself.

But since you are making a special study of the subject of love, you may well ask whether a man can have a pure love for one woman and a mixed or common love with another. We will show you, by an unanswerable argument, that no one can feel affection for two women in this fashion. For although pure love and mixed love may seem to be very different things, if you will look at the matter properly you will see that pure love, so far as its substance goes, is the same as mixed love and comes from the same feeling of the heart. The substance of the love is the same in each case, and only the manner and form of loving are different, as this illustration will make clear to you. Sometimes we see a man with a desire to drink his wine unmixed, and at another time his appetite prompts him to drink only water or wine and water mixed; although his appetite manifests itself differently, the substance of it is the same and unchanged. So likewise when two people have long been united by pure love and afterwards desire to practice mixed love, the substance of the love remains the same in them, although the manner and form and the way of practicing it are different. . . .

The Rules of Love

Let us come now to the rules of love, and I shall try to present to you very briefly those rules which the King of Love[1] is said to have proclaimed with his own mouth and to have given in writing to all lovers. . . .

   I.   Marriage is no real excuse for not loving.
   II. He who is not jealous cannot love.
   III. No one can be bound by a double love.
   IV. It is well known that love is always increasing or decreasing.
   V.   That which a lover takes against the will of his beloved has no relish.
   VI. Boys do not love until they arrive at the age of maturity.
   VII. When one lover dies, a widowhood of two years is required of the survivor.
   VIII. No one should be deprived of love without the very best of reasons.

---

[1]King Arthur of Britain. [Ed.]

IX. No one can love unless he is impelled by the persuasion of love.

X. Love is always a stranger in the home of avarice.

XI. It is not proper to love any woman whom one should be ashamed to seek to marry.

XII. A true lover does not desire to embrace in love anyone except his beloved.

XIII. When made public love rarely endures.

XIV. The easy attainment of love makes it of little value; difficulty of attainment makes it prized.

XV. Every lover regularly turns pale in the presence of his beloved.

XVI. When a lover suddenly catches sight of his beloved his heart palpitates.

XVII. A new love puts to flight an old one.

XVIII. Good character alone makes any man worthy of love.

XIX. If love diminishes, it quickly fails and rarely revives.

XX. A man in love is always apprehensive.

XXI. Real jealousy always increases the feeling of love.

XXII. Jealousy, and therefore love, are increased when one suspects his beloved.

XXIII. He whom the thought of love vexes, eats and sleeps very little.

XXIV. Every act of a lover ends in the thought of his beloved.

XXV. A true lover considers nothing good except what he thinks will please his beloved.

XXVI. Love can deny nothing to love.

XXVII. A lover can never have enough of the solaces of his beloved.

XXVIII. A slight presumption causes a lover to suspect his beloved.

XXIX. A man who is vexed by too much passion usually does not love.

XXX. A true lover is constantly and without intermission possessed by the thought of his beloved.

XXXI. Nothing forbids one woman being loved by two men or one man by two women.

KALIDASA
From Shakuntala

Kalidasa (c. 400 C.E.) was one of the greatest Indian dramatists. His play *Shakuntala*, a classic of the Hindu literary tradition, tells the story of a love between a king and a hermit girl. The two fall passionately in love with each other although they have barely exchanged words. Despite their different stations in life, they are equally overcome by *kama*, one of the four great forces in the Hindu culture—the force of love and physical attraction. In this selection from Act 3 (of seven acts), Shakuntala is urged by her friends, Priyamvada and Anasuya, who say they "don't know what it is to be in love," to write a letter to the king, who overhears their conversation. In what ways is this similar to European ideas of romantic love? In what ways is it different?

Thinking Historically

The description of feelings in this selection might seem overly florid, but the emotions are not unfamiliar to a modern reader. Can you think of a play or film that is similar to this? What is the similarity? Is there any unfamiliar aspect? If you were to present this story to a modern American audience, how might you change it? Why?

PRIYAMVADĀ: Compose a love letter and I'll hide it in a flower. I'll deliver it to his hand on the pretext of bringing a gift from our offering to the deity.

ANASŪYĀ: This subtle plan pleases me. What does Shakuntalā say?

SHAKUNTALĀ: I'll try my friend's plan.

PRIYAMVADĀ: Then compose a poem to declare your love!

SHAKUNTALĀ: I'm thinking, but my heart trembles with fear that he'll reject me.

KING [IN HIDING]: (*delighted*):
The man whom you fear will reject you
waits longing to love you, timid girl—
a suitor may be lucky or cursed,
but his goodness of fortune always wins.

Kalidasa, *Shakuntala*, Act III, trans. Barbara Stoler Miller, in *Theater of Memory: The Plays of Kalidasa*, ed. Barbara Stoler Miller (New York: Columbia University Press, 1984), 114–18.

BOTH FRIENDS: Why do you devalue your own virtues? Who would keep autumn moonlight from cooling the body by covering it with a bit of cloth?

SHAKUNTALĀ (*smiling*): I'm following your advice. (*She sits thinking*)

KING: As I stare at her, my eyes forget to blink.
 She arches an eyebrow
 struggling to compose the verse —
 the down rises on her cheek,
 showing the passion she feels.

SHAKUNTALĀ: I have thought of a song, but there's nothing I can write it on.

PRIYAMVADĀ: Engrave the letters with your nails on this lotus leaf! It's as delicate as a parrot's breast.

SHAKUNTALĀ (*miming what Priyamvadā described*): Listen and tell me if this makes sense!

BOTH FRIENDS: We're both paying attention.

SHAKUNTALĀ (*sings*):
 I don't know your heart,
 but day and night Love
 violently burns my limbs
 with desire for you, cruel man.

KING (*Having been listening to them, entering suddenly*):
 Love torments you, slender girl,
 but he utterly consumes me —
 daylight makes the moon fade
 when it folds the white lotus.

BOTH FRIENDS (*Looking, rising with delight*): Welcome to the swift success of love's desire!
 (*Shakuntalā tries to rise.*)

KING: Don't strain yourself!
 Limbs on a couch of crushed flowers
 and fragrant tips of lotus stalks
 are too frail from suffering
 to perform ceremonial acts . . .

ANASŪYĀ: We've heard that kings have many loves. Will our beloved friend become a sorrow to her relatives after you've spent your time with her?

KING: Noble lady, enough of this! I may have many wives, but my royal line rests on two foundations: the sea-bound earth and this friend of yours!

BOTH FRIENDS: We are assured.

PRIYAMVADĀ (*casting a glance*): Anasūyā this fawn is looking for its mother. Let's take it to her!
 (*They both begin to leave.*)

SHAKUNTALĀ: Come back! Don't leave me unprotected!

BOTH FRIENDS: The protector of the earth is at your side.

SHAKUNTALĀ: Why have they gone?

KING: Don't be alarmed! A servant worships at your side.

Shall I set moist winds in motion
with lotus-leaf fans to cool your pain,
or put your pale red lotus feet on my lap
and stroke them, voluptuous girl?

SHAKUNTALĀ: I cannot sin against those I respect! (*standing as if she wants to leave*)

KING: Beautiful Shakuntalā, the day is still hot.

Why leave this couch of flowers
and its shield of lotus leaves
to venture into the heat
with your frail wan limbs?
(*Saying this, he forces her to turn around.*)

SHAKUNTALĀ: Puru king, control yourself! Though I'm burning with love I'm not free to give myself to you.

KING: Don't fear your elders! The father of your family knows the law. When he finds out, he will not fault you. Many kings' daughters first marry in secret and their fathers bless them.

SHAKUNTALĀ: Release me! I must ask my friends' advice!

KING: Yes, I shall release you.

SHAKUNTALĀ: When?

KING:

Only let my thirsting mouth
gently drink from your lips,
the way a bee sips nectar
from a fragile virgin blossom.

58

MIRABAI
Bhakti Poems

Mirabai (b. c. 1550) was one of the great poets of the medieval Indian
Bhakti or Hindu devotional tradition. Bhakti philosophers and poets
expressed a Hinduism suffused with love for the deity. Typically,
Mirabai's religious experience of personal love represented a form of
protest against the religious formalism of caste and the authority of
Brahmin sacrifice. According to legend, Mirabai refused to consum-
mate her marriage to a king because she had fallen in love with the
god Khrishna, who was often pictured as the deep blue "dark Lord"
and the lifter of mountains. How is Mirabai's imagery similar to that
of medieval European courtly love? How is it different?

Thinking Historically

India was not the only society that produced women who expressed
an almost sexual passion toward a god. The great Muslim mystic
Rabia al-Adawiyya (b. c. 717) and the Sufis used similar language,
and St. Teresa of Avila (1515–1582) is perhaps the best known
among Christian devotees who wrote with an almost erotic passion.
The Hindu celebration of *kama* and the development of Bhakti Hinduism were particularly Indian. Still, can you think of cases in your
own culture where love of a deity faded into, or felt like, love for another person? How about Ulrich's "worship" of the princess? How
unique is this Indian cultural form after all?

Colored by Devotion to Krishna

The motif of being dyed with the color of devotion to the Dark Lord is
common in bhakti poetry, as is dancing before him. The poison cup
refers to an incident when the Rānā tried to poison her, but the only effect was to make her glow with the beauty of Krishna. The "mountain
lifter" is a reference to one of Krishna's miracles.

[From Mīrābāī, in Parashurām Caturvedī, Mīrābāī kī Padāvalī, no.
37, trans. by J.S.H. and M.J.]

Poems of Mirabai, trans. John S. Hawley and Mark Juergensmeyer, in *Sources of Indian Tradition*, vol. I, *From the Beginning to 1800*, 2nd ed., ed. Ainslee Embree (New York: Columbia
University Press, 1988), 365–69.

326

I'm colored with the color of dusk, O Rānā
   colored with the color of my Lord.
Drumming out the rhythm on the drums, I danced,
   dancing in the presence of the saints,
      colored with the color of my Lord.
They thought me mad for the Wily One,
   raw for my dear dark love,
      colored with the color of my Lord.
The Rānā sent me a poison cup:
   I didn't look, I drank it up,
      colored with the color of my Lord.
The clever Mountain Lifter is the Lord of Mīrā.
   Life after life he's true—
      colored with the color of my Lord.

Marriage with Krishna

This poem echoes Mīrā's consciousness of having been married to Krishna in previous births. She is filled with longing for him and is begging him to unite with her now in this life.

[From Mīrābāī, *Mīrābāī Kī Padāvalī*, no. 51, trans. by J.S.H. and M. J.]

I have talked to you, talked,
   Dark Lifter of Mountains,
About this old love,
   from birth after birth.
Don't go, don't,
   Lifter of Mountains,
Let me offer a sacrifice—myself—
   beloved,
      to your beautiful face.
Come, here in the courtyard,
   Dark Lord,
The women are singing auspicious wedding songs;
My eyes have fashioned
   an altar of pearl tears,
And here is my sacrifice:
   the body and mind
of Mīrā,
   the servant who clings to your feet,
      through life after life,
         a virginal harvest for you to reap.

Life without Krishna

Mīrā's love for Krishna leads to the enmity of her family, but at the same time gives her a refuge to which she can escape.

[From Mīrābāī, *Mīrābāī kī Padāvalī*, no. 42, trans. by J. S. H. and M. J.]

Life without Hari is no life, friend,
And though my mother-in-law fights,
    my sister-in-law teases,
    the *rānā* is angered,
A guard is stationed on the stoop outside,
    and a lock is mounted on the door,
How can I abandon the love I have loved
    in life after life?
Mīrā's Lord is the clever Mountain-Lifter:
    Why would I want anyone else?

The Sound of Krishna's Flute

Muralī is the bamboo flute that is one of Krishna's chief symbols. It is the medium through which Krishna entrances the women of Braj, calling them to love. Sometimes the flute is pictured as a woman herself, with more immediate access to Krishna than has anyone else. So the sound of the flute fills Mīrā with the intense pain of longing for love, a longing that is one of the constant themes of love poetry in the Indian tradition.

[From Mīrābāī, no. 166, trans. by J.S.H. and M. J.]

Muralī sounds on the banks of the Jumna,
Muralī snatches away my mind;
My senses cut away from their moorings—
Dark waters, dark garments, Dark Lord.
I listen close to the sounds of Muralī
And my body withers away—
Lost thoughts, lost even the power to think.
    Mīrā's Lord, clever Mountain-Lifter,
    Come quick, snatch away my pain.

MURASAKI SHIKIBU

From The Tale of Genji

The Tale of Genji is, by some measures, the world's first novel. It was written by Murasaki Shikibu, a woman at the Japanese court, probably in the first decade after the year 1000. During the Heian period (794–1185) of Japanese history, women in the Japanese aristocracy differentiated their culture from the Chinese one that had dominated it since the seventh century.

While Japanese men were still using a dated form of Chinese for official documents, women like Lady Murasaki were fashioning the Japanese language into an effective and contemporary medium of communication. As ladies of the court, they also had the experience and leisure for writing intriguing, richly evocative stories.

The Tale of Genji is about Prince Genji—an attractive, talented, and sensitive son of the emperor—and his love interests. This chapter, occurring near the end of the novel, tells of one of Prince Genji's many flirtations. It also reveals much about the culture of the Japanese court. Notice the cultivation of music, dance, and poetry among the court nobility. What, if anything, does this display of sensitivity have to do with ideas of love and marriage? What signs do you see here of the persistence of Chinese culture in Heian Japan?

Also, notice the absence of monogamy in the court. The emperor is married but has taken in turn three consorts: Kokiden, Kiritsubo, and now Fujitsubo. What is the relationship between marriage and sex in this society? What does that tell you about the mores of the time?

Thinking Historically

Would you call this a story of romantic love? In what ways is the love Lady Murasaki describes similar to or different from the love Andreas Capellanus describes in selection 56? What aspects of Heian Japanese culture are different from the culture of medieval Europe? Is the dominant-upper class idea of love in Japan during this period different from that of Europe?

Murasaki Shikibu, *The Tale of Genji*, trans. Arthur Waley (1929; reprint, Garden City, N.Y.: Anchor Books, 1955), 201–10.

About the twentieth day of the second month the Emperor gave a Chinese banquet under the great cherry-tree of the Southern Court. Both Fujitsubo and the Heir Apparent were to be there. Kokiden, although she knew that the mere presence of the Empress was sufficient to spoil her pleasure, could not bring herself to forgo so delightful an entertainment. After some promise of rain the day turned out magnificent; and in full sunshine, with the birds singing in every tree, the guests (royal princes, noblemen, and professional poets alike) were handed the rhyme words which the Emperor had drawn by lot, and set to work to compose their poems. It was with a clear and ringing voice that Genji read out the word "Spring" which he had received as the rhyme-sound of his poem. Next came To no Chujo who, feeling that all eyes were upon him and determined to impress himself favourably on his audience, moved with the greatest possible elegance and grace; and when on receiving his rhyme he announced his name, rank, and titles, he took great pains to speak pleasantly as well as audibly. Many of the other gentlemen were rather nervous and looked quite pale as they came forward, yet they acquitted themselves well enough. But the professional poets, particularly owing to the high standard of accomplishment which the Emperor's and Heir Apparent's lively interest in Chinese poetry had at that time diffused through the Court, were very ill at ease; as they crossed the long space of the garden on their way to receive their rhymes they felt utterly helpless. A simple Chinese verse is surely not much to ask of a professional poet; but they all wore an expression of the deepest gloom. One expects elderly scholars to be somewhat odd in their movements and behaviour, and it was amusing to see the lively concern with which the Emperor watched their various but always uncouth and erratic methods of approaching the Throne. Needless to say a great deal of music had been arranged for. Towards dusk the delightful dance known as the Warbling of Spring Nightingales was performed, and when it was over the Heir Apparent, remembering the Festival of Red Leaves, placed a wreath on Genji's head and pressed him so urgently that it was impossible for him to refuse. Rising to his feet he danced very quietly a fragment of the sleeve-turning passage in the Wave Dance. In a few moments he was seated again, but even into this brief extract from a long dance he managed to import an unrivalled charm and grace. Even his father-in-law who was not in the best of humour with him was deeply moved and found himself wiping away a tear.

"And why have we not seen To no Chujo?" said the Heir Apparent. Whereupon Chujo danced the Park of Willow Flowers, giving a far more complete performance than Genji, for no doubt he knew that he would be called upon and had taken trouble to prepare his dance. It was a great success and the Emperor presented him with a cloak, which everyone said was a most unusual honour. After this the other young noblemen who were present danced in no particular order, but it was now so dark that it was impossible to discriminate between their performances.

Then the poems were opened and read aloud. The reading of Genji's verses was continually interrupted by loud murmurs of applause. Even the professional poets were deeply impressed, and it may well be imagined with what pride the Emperor, to whom at times Genji was a source of consolation and delight, watched him upon such an occasion as this. Fujitsubo, when she allowed herself to glance in his direction, marvelled that even Kokiden could find it in her heart to hate him. "It is because he is fond of me; there can be no other reason," she decided at last, and the verse, "Were I but a common mortal who now am gazing at the beauty of this flower, from its sweet petals not long should I withhold the dew of love," framed itself on her lips, though she dared not utter it aloud.

It was now very late and the banquet was over. The guests had scattered. The Empress and the Heir Apparent had both returned to the Palace—all was still. The moon had risen very bright and clear, and Genji, heated with wine, could not bear to quit so lovely a scene. The people at the Palace were probably all plunged in a heavy sleep. On such a night it was not impossible that some careless person might have left some door unfastened, some shutter unbarred. Cautiously and stealthily he crept towards Fujitsubo's apartments and inspected them. Every bolt was fast. He sighed; here there was evidently nothing to be done. He was passing the loggia of Kokiden's palace when he noted that the shutters of the third arch were not drawn. After the banquet Kokiden herself had gone straight to the Emperor's rooms. There did not seem to be anyone about. A door leading from the loggia into the house was standing open, but he could hear no sound within. "It is under just such circumstances as this that one is apt to drift into compromising situations," thought Genji. Nevertheless he climbed quietly on to the balustrade and peeped. Everyone must be asleep. But no; a very agreeable young voice with an intonation which was certainly not that of any waiting-woman or common person was softly humming the last two lines of the *Oborozuki-yo*.[1] Was not the voice coming towards him? It seemed so, and stretching out his hand he suddenly found that he was grasping a lady's sleeve. "Oh, how you frightened me!" she cried. "Who is it?" "Do not be alarmed," he whispered. "That both of us were not content to miss the beauty of this departing night is proof more clear than the half-clouded moon that we were meant to meet," and as he recited the words he took her gently by the hand and led her into the house, closing the door behind them. Her surprised and puzzled air fascinated him. "There is someone there," she whispered

---

[1] A famous poem by Oye no Chisato (ninth century): "What so lovely as a night when the moon though dimly clouded is never wholly lost to sight!"

tremulously, pointing to the inner room. "Child," he answered, "I am allowed to go wherever I please and if you send for your friends they will only tell you that I have every right to be here. But if you will stay quietly here...." It was Genji. She knew his voice and the discovery somewhat reassured her. She thought his conduct rather strange, but she was determined that he should not think her prudish or stiff. And so because he on his side was still somewhat excited after the doings of the evening, while she was far too young and pliant to offer any serious resistance, he soon got his own way with her.

Suddenly they saw to their discomfiture that dawn was creeping into the sky. She looked, thought Genji, as though many disquieting reflections were crowding into her mind. "Tell me your name," he said. "How can I write you unless you do? Surely this is not going to be our only meeting?" She answered with a poem in which she said that names are of this world only and he would not care to know hers if he were resolved that their love should last till worlds to come. It was a mere quip and Genji, amused at her quickness, answered, "You are quite right. It was a mistake on my part to ask." And he recited the poem: "While still I seek to find on which blade dwells the dew, a great wind shakes the grasses of the level land." "If you did not repent of this meeting," he continued, "you would surely tell me who you are. I do not believe that you want...." But here he was interrupted by the noise of people stirring in the next room. There was a great bustle and it was clear that they would soon be starting out to fetch Princess Kokiden back from the palace. There was just time to exchange fans in token of their new friendship before Genji was forced to fly precipitately from the room. In his own apartments he found many of his gentlemen waiting for him. Some were awake, and these nudged one another when he entered the room as though to say, "Will he never cease these disreputable excursions?" But discretion forbad them to show that they had seen him and they all pretended to be fast asleep. Genji too lay down, but he could not rest. He tried to recall the features of the lady with whom he had just spent so agreeable a time. Certainly she must be one of Kokiden's sisters. Perhaps the fifth or sixth daughter, both of whom were still unmarried. . . . But at present he could think of no way to make sure. She had not behaved at all as though she did not want to see him again. Why then had she refused to give him any chance of communicating with her? In fact he worried about the matter so much and turned it over in his mind with such endless persistency that it soon became evident he had fallen deeply in love with her. Nevertheless no sooner did the recollection of Fujitsubo's serious and reticent demeanour come back to his mind than he realized how incomparably more she meant to him than this light-hearted lady.

That day the after-banquet kept him occupied till late at night. At the Emperor's command he performed on the thirteen-stringed zithern and had an even greater success than with his dancing on the day before. At dawn Fujitsubo retired to the Emperor's rooms. Disappointed in his hope that the lady of last night would somewhere or somehow make her appearance on the scene, he sent for Yoshikiyo and Koremitsu with whom all his secrets were shared and bade them keep watch upon the lady's family. When he returned next day from duty at the Palace they reported that they had just witnessed the departure of several coaches which had been drawn up under shelter in the Courtyard of the Watch. "Among a group of persons who seemed to be the domestic attendants of those for whom the coaches were waiting two gentlemen came threading their way in a great hurry. These we recognized as Shii no Shosho and Uchuben, so there is little doubt that the carriages belonged to Princess Kokiden. For the rest we noted that the ladies were by no means ill-looking and that the whole party drove away in three carriages." Genji's heart beat fast. But he was no nearer than before to finding out which of the sisters it had been. Supposing her father, the Minister of the Right, should hear anything of this, what a to-do there would be! It would indeed mean his absolute ruin. It was a pity that while he was about it he did not stay with her till it was a little lighter. But there it was! He did not know her face, but yet he was determined to recognize her. How? . . . He still had her fan. It was a folding fan with ribs of hinoki-wood and tassels tied in a splice-knot. One side was covered with silverleaf on which was painted a dim moon, giving the impression of a moon reflected in water. It was a device which he had seen many times before, but it had agreeable associations for him, and continuing the metaphor of the "grass on the moor" which she had used in her poem, he wrote on the fan—"Has mortal man ever puzzled his head with such a question before as to ask where the moon goes to when she leaves the sky at dawn?" And he put the fan safely away. . . .

Fugitive as their meeting had been, it had sufficed to plunge the lady whose identity Prince Genji was now seeking to establish into the depths of despair; for in the fourth month she was to become the Heir Apparent's wife. Turmoil filled her brain. Why had not Genji visited her again? He must surely know whose daughter she was. But how should he know which daughter? Besides, her sister Kokiden's house was not a place where, save under very strange circumstances, he was likely to feel at all at his ease. And so she waited in great impatience and distress; but of Genji there was no news.

About the twentieth day of the third month her father, the Minister of the Right, held an archery meeting in which most of the young noblemen and princes were present. It was followed by a wistaria feast. The cherry blossom was for the most part over, but two trees, which the Minister seemed somehow to have persuaded to flower later than all the rest, were still an enchanting sight. He had had his house rebuilt

only a short time ago when celebrating the initiation of his grand-
daughters, the children of Kokiden. It was now a magnificent building
and not a thing in it but was of the very latest fashion. He had invited
Genji when he had met him at the Palace only a few days before and
was extremely annoyed when he did not appear. . . . It was very late indeed when at last he [Genji] made his appearance at the party. He was
dressed in a cloak of thin Chinese fabric, white outside but lined with
yellow. His robe was of a deep wine-red colour with a very long train.
The dignity and grace with which he carried this fancifully regal attire
in a company where all were dressed in plain official robes were indeed
remarkable, and in the end his presence perhaps contributed more to
the success of the party than did the fragrance of the Minister's boasted
flowers. His entry was followed by some very agreeable music. It was
already fairly late when Genji, on the plea that the wine had given him
a headache, left his seat and went for a walk. He knew that his two
stepsisters, the daughters of Kokiden, were in the inner apartments of
the palace. He went to the eastern portico and rested there. It was on
this side of the house that the wistaria grew. The wooden blinds were
raised and a number of ladies were leaning out of the window to enjoy
the blossoms. They had hung bright-coloured robes and shawls over
the windowsill just as is done at the time of the New Year dancing and
other gala days and were behaving with a freedom of allure which con-
trasted very oddly with the sober decorum of Fujitsubo's household. "I
am feeling rather overpowered by all the noise and bustle of the flower-
party," Genji explained. "I am very sorry to disturb my sisters, but I
can think of nowhere else to seek refuge . . ." and advancing towards
the main door of the women's apartments, he pushed back the curtain
with his shoulder. . . . A scent of costly perfumes pervaded the room;
silken skirts rustled in the darkness. There could be little doubt that
these were Kokiden's sisters and their friends. Deeply absorbed, as indeed was the whole of his family, in the fashionable gaieties of the moment, they had flouted decorum and posted themselves at the window
that they might see what little they could of the banquet which was
proceeding outside. Little thinking that his plan could succeed, yet led
on by delightful recollections of his previous encounter, he advanced
towards them chanting in a careless undertone the song:

> At Ishikawa, Ishikawa
> A man from Koma [Korea] took my belt away . . .

But for "belt" he substituted "fan" and by this means he sought to discover which of the ladies was his friend. "Why, you have got it wrong!
I never heard of *that* Korean," one of them cried. Certainly it was not
she. But there was another who though she remained silent seemed to
him to be sighing softly to herself. He stole towards the curtain-of-state

behind which she was sitting and taking her hand in his at a venture he whispered the poem: "If on this day of shooting my arrow went astray, 'twas that in dim morning twilight only the mark had glimmered in my view." And she, unable any longer to hide that she knew him, answered with the verse: "Had it been with the arrows of the heart that you had shot, though from the moon's slim bow no brightness came, would you have missed your mark?" Yes, it was her voice. He was delighted, and yet . . .

REFLECTIONS

Cultural comparisons, formerly a staple of historical studies, have come under harsh criticism in recent years, and for good reason. The ambitious general histories and philosophical anthropologies written at the beginning of the twentieth century were full of gross generalizations about the "essence" of various cultures and the advantages of one civilization over another. These grand overviews, predating serious empirical studies of African, Asian, and Latin American societies, invariably argued that such "pre-modern," or "traditional," societies lacked some critical cultural attribute honed in Europe that enabled Europeans to conquer the world after 1500. It goes without saying that these sweeping interpretations were written by Europeans and their North American descendants.

The comparative history of love got caught up in the whirlwind with historians and anthropologists, seeking to explain European expansion, industrialization, and modernization, arguing that conjugal love—the nonromantic familial variety—created family units in Europe and America that were different from those in other parts of the world. They saw the Western family as the stimulus of modern society. Still others found the Western practices of dating, mate choosing, and individual decision making unique.

Toward the end of the twentieth century, in a postcolonial age that had grown skeptical of Western claims of objectivity, cultural comparisons were seen for what they often were—thinly veiled exercises in self-aggrandizement and implicit rationales for Western domination. For example, Western scientific racism, in which the reigning Western anthropologists and scientists divided the world by cranial sizes, nose width, or culture-bound intelligence tests (always putting themselves on top), came crashing down, after its rationale was exposed as the foundation for the horrific genocides of World War II. `

There is a growing debate about the strategy of explaining Western growth and dominance by looking for Western traits that non-Western cultures lacked. But whether or not such a strategy is wise, we would

be foolish to stop trying to compare cultures. Cultures are rich reposi-
tories of human thought and behavior; they differ over time and across
the globe; and the process of comparison is essential to learning and
creating knowledge. In any case, historical comparisons should not be
about establishing which culture is better or worse. Culture, almost by
definition, is good for the particular society in which it arises. That
people in different parts of the world have found different ways of dealing with the same human problems should not surprise us. To call some
better than others is meaningless.

What we can learn from cultural comparison is something about
the malleability of human nature and the range of options available to
us. We also learn much about ourselves when we peer at another face
in the mirror. The differences leap out at us over time as well as space.
In some ways, Ulrich's mirror is as foreign as Genji's. In other ways it is
not. Both reflect elements of our own culture, call it European, Western, global, or something else. In response to an age of prejudice and
cultural stereotyping, many well-intentioned people choose to deny or
celebrate cultural differences. A far wiser course is to understand what
these differences reveal about our world and us.

10

The First Crusade

Muslims, Christians, and Jews during the First Crusade, 1095–1099 C.E.

HISTORICAL CONTEXT

In the eleventh century the Seljuk Turks, recently converted to Islam, emerged from the grasslands of central Asia to conquer much of the land held by the weakened Caliphate at Baghdad, the Egyptian Fatimid Caliphate, and the Byzantine Empire. By 1095 the Seljuks controlled the important cities of Baghdad and Jerusalem and threatened to take Constantinople.

Alexius, the Byzantine emperor, appealed to the Roman pope for help and found a receptive audience. Pope Urban II was continuing recent papal efforts to strengthen the Roman church's power over the scattered nobles and princes of European feudal society. He sought to reform the church of abuses such as the sale of church offices, and to bring peace to the fractious countryside, riddled with private armies of knights that fought each other or preyed on Christian peasants. Urban II's efforts to revitalize Christendom found a mission in the Seljuk occupation of Jerusalem, and in 1095 the First Crusade began with his urgent call for Christians to rout the new Muslim occupiers of the Holy Land. (See Map 10.1.)

The Crusades were an important chapter in the religious and military history—or more broadly, the cultural and political history—of both European and Islamic civilizations. They brought large numbers of European Christians and Muslims into contact with each other in a struggle and dialogue that would last for centuries.

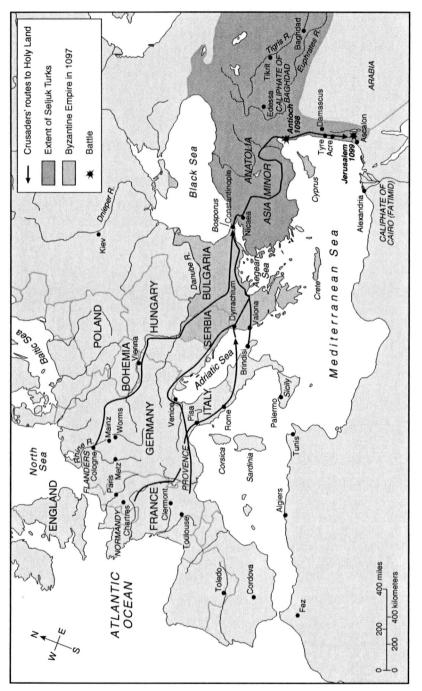

Map 10.1 The First Crusade, 1096–1099.

THINKING HISTORICALLY
Analyzing and Writing Narrative

When most people think of history, they think of narrative—the story itself. Narrative settles on specific details—one at a time—neither indiscriminately nor as examples of general laws, but usually chronologically, as they happen, woven in a chain of cause and effect. The "truth" of narrative is different from that of social science, which aspires to generality. The social scientist writes, "Holy wars among states are a dime a dozen." The narrative historian immerses us in the specific details of the battle: "The Duke's trumpets sounded, the shimmering line swayed forward, the long lances came down to point at the foe, their pennons shadowing the ground before them." A good narrative has the appeal of a good story: It places the reader on the scene, enables us to feel the drama of the moment, to experience what happened as it happened.

In this chapter you will read a number of brief narratives about the Crusades. You will analyze each narrative for what it tells you and to reflect on the way the story conveys that information, and then you will be encouraged to write your own narrative.

Keep in mind that narrative, or storytelling, is only one way of providing information. Storytelling is often considered a low-level skill, less sophisticated than analysis or synthesis. In college classes instructors will often say: "Don't just tell me the story" when they want you to analyze or make comparisons. Most professional historians write analytical books devoted to answering a particular historical question or challenging an interpretation. Generally historians only write narratives for a popular audience, not for each other. But the power of narrative is so strong some have even suggested that we might be hardwired for story telling—that we ought to be aware of how this form of knowing and presenting affects our understanding of historical events.

60

FULCHER OF CHARTRES

Pope Urban at Clermont

The Chronicle of Fulcher of Chartres is one of the few firsthand accounts of the First Crusade. Born in 1059, Fulcher was present at the Council of Clermont, where Pope Urban II issued his call for the First Crusade in 1095. In response to Urban's plea, Fulcher joined the army of Robert of Normandy, Stephen of Blois, and Robert of Flanders. He then joined Baldwin of Boulogne in Edessa (see Map 10.1, p. 338), the first Crusader state, and later visited Jerusalem after its capture by the Crusaders. In 1100 when Baldwin became King of Jerusalem, Fulcher returned to the Holy City to become his chaplain. There he wrote his history from 1101 until about 1128. The reliability of Fulcher's Chronicles, therefore, depends on his important contacts as well as his own observations.

Why, according to Fulcher, did Pope Urban II call the Council of Clermont? What did he hope to accomplish? How important among the pope's concerns was the capture of Jerusalem? How important was strengthening the Church?

Thinking Historically

What indications do you see in Urban's speech that the call to capture Jerusalem was only part of his agenda, perhaps even an afterthought? Fulcher's account of the speech and his section on "events after the council" mainly address the issue of Jerusalem. That emphasis is appropriate in a history of the crusade. A historical narrative must follow a particular thread. If Fulcher was writing a history of church reforms rather than of the First Crusade, what kind of "events after the council" might he have included?

A narrative, or story, is different from an explanation. What do you think were the causes of the First Crusade, based on what you have read so far? How is your answer an explanation rather than a narrative? How would you make your answer more of a narrative?

The First Crusade: The Chronicle of Fulcher of Chartres and Other Source Materials, 2nd ed., ed. Edward Peters (Philadelphia: University of Pennsylvania Press, 1998), 49–55.

I. The Council of Clermont

1. In the year 1095 from the Lord's Incarnation, with Henry reigning in Germany as so-called emperor,[1] and with Philip as king in France, manifold evils were growing in all parts of Europe because of wavering faith. In Rome ruled Pope Urban II, a man distinguished in life and character, who always strove wisely and actively to raise the status of the Holy Church above all things.

2. He saw that the faith of Christianity was being destroyed to excess by everybody, by the clergy as well as by the laity. He saw that peace was altogether discarded by the princes of the world, who were engaged in incessant warlike contention and quarreling among themselves. He saw the wealth of the land being pillaged continuously. He saw many of the vanquished, wrongfully taken prisoner and very cruelly thrown into foulest dungeons, either ransomed for a high price or, tortured by the triple torments of hunger, thirst, and cold, blotted out by a death hidden from the world. He saw holy places violated; monasteries and villas burned. He saw that no one was spared of any human suffering, and that things divine and human alike were held in derision.

3. He heard, too, that the interior regions of Romania, where the Turks ruled over the Christians, had been perniciously subjected in a savage attack.[2] Moved by long-suffering compassion and by love of God's will, he descended the mountains to Gaul, and in Auvergne he called for a council to congregate from all sides at a suitable time at a city called Clermont. Three hundred and ten bishops and abbots, who had been advised beforehand by messengers, were present.

4. Then, on the day set aside for it, he called them together to himself and, in an eloquent address, carefully made the cause of the meeting known to them. In the plaintive voice of an aggrieved Church, he expressed great lamentation, and held a long discourse with them about the raging tempests of the world, which have been mentioned, because faith was undermined.

5. One after another, he beseechingly exhorted them all, with renewed faith, to spur themselves in great earnestness to overcome the Devil's devices and to try to restore the Holy Church, most unmercifully weakened by the wicked, to its former honorable status.

---

[1]Henry IV (1056–1106). Fulcher uses the term "so-called emperor," since Henry was not recognized as rightful emperor by adherents of Gregory VII and Urban II.

[2]This refers to the Seljuk conquest of Anatolia, probably to Manzikert, 1071.

II. The Decree of Pope Urban in the Council

1. "Most beloved brethren," he said, "by God's permission placed over the whole world with the papal crown, I, Urban, as the messenger of divine admonition, have been compelled by an unavoidable occasion to come here to you servants of God. I desired those whom I judged to be stewards of God's ministries to be true stewards and faithful, with all hypocrisy rejected.[3]

2. "But with temperance in reason and justice being remote, I, with divine aid, shall strive carefully to root out any crookedness or distortion which might obstruct God's law. For the Lord appointed you temporarily as stewards over His family to serve it nourishment seasoned with a modest savor. Moreover, blessed will you be if at last the Overseer find you faithful.[4]

3. "You are also called shepherds; see that you are not occupied after the manner of mercenaries. Be true shepherds, always holding your crooks in your hands; and sleeping not, guard on every side the flock entrusted to you.

4. "For if through your carelessness or negligence, some wolf seizes a sheep, you doubtless will lose the reward prepared for you by our Lord.[5] Nay, first most cruelly beaten by the whips of the lictors, you afterwards will be angrily cast into the keeping of a deadly place.

5. "Likewise, according to the evangelical sermon, you are the 'salt of the earth.'[6] But if you fail, it will be disputed wherewith it was salted. O how much saltiness, indeed, is necessary for you to salt the people in correcting them with the salt of wisdom, people who are ignorant and panting with desire after the wantonness of the world; so that, unsalted, they might not be rotten with sins and stink whenever the Lord might wish to exhort them.

6. "For if because of the sloth of your management, He should find in them worms, that is, sin, straightway, He will order that they, despised, be cast into the dungheap. And because you could not make restoration for such a great loss, He will banish you, utterly condemned in judgment, from the familiarity of His love.

7. "It behooves saltiness of this kind to be wise, provident, temperate, learned, peace-making, truth-seeking, pious, just, equitable, pure. For how will the unlearned be able to make men learned, the intemper-

---

[3]Reference to I Corinthians 4:1, 2.
[4]Reference to Matthew 24:45, 46.
[5]Reference to John 10:12–16.
[6]Matthew 5:13.

ate make temperate, the impure make them pure? If one despises peace, how will he appease? Or if one has dirty hands, how will he be able to wipe the filth off another one defiled? For it is read, 'If the blind lead the blind, both shall fall into a ditch.'[7]

8. "Set yourselves right before you do others, so that you can blamelessly correct your subjects. If you wish to be friends of God, gladly practice those things which you feel will please Him.

9. "Especially establish ecclesiastical affairs firm in their own right, so that no simoniac heresy will take root among you. Take care lest the vendors and moneychangers, flayed by the scourges of the Lord, be miserably driven out into the narrow streets of destruction.[8]

10. "Uphold the Church in its own ranks altogether free from all secular power. See that the tithes of all those who cultivate the earth are given faithfully to God; let them not be sold or held back.

11. "Let him who has seized a bishop be considered an outlaw. Let him who has seized or robbed monks, clerics, nuns and their servants, pilgrims, or merchants, be excommunicated. Let the robbers and burners of homes and their accomplices, banished from the Church, be smitten with excommunication.

12. "It must be considered very carefully, as Gregory says, by what penalty he must be punished who seizes other men's property, if he who does not bestow his own liberally is condemned to Hell. For so it happened to the rich man in the well-known Gospel, who on that account was not punished because he had taken away the property of others, but because he had misused that which he had received.

13. "And so by these iniquities, most beloved, you have seen the world disturbed too long; so long, as it was told to us by those reporting, that perhaps because of the weakness of your justice in some parts of your provinces, no one dares to walk in the streets with safety, lest he be kidnapped by robbers by day or thieves by night, either by force or trickery, at home or outside.

14. "Wherefore the Truce,[9] as it is commonly called, now for a long time established by the Holy Fathers, must be renewed. In admonition, I entreat you to adhere to it most firmly in your own bishopric. But if anyone affected by avarice or pride breaks it of his own free will, let him be excommunicated by God's authority and by the sanction of the decrees of this Holy Council."

---

[7]Matthew 15:14.

[8]Reference to John 2:15.

[9]Truce of God—Cessation of all feuds from Wednesday evening to Monday morning in every week and during church festivals, ordered by the Church in 1041. This was proclaimed anew at the Council of Clermont.

III. The Pope's Exhortation Concerning the Expedition to Jerusalem

1. These and many other things having been suitably disposed of, all those present, both clergy and people, at the words of Lord Urban, the Pope, voluntarily gave thanks to God and confirmed by a faithful promise that his decrees would be well kept. But straightway he added that another thing not less than the tribulation already spoken of, but even greater and more oppressive, was injuring Christianity in another part of the world, saying:

2. "Now that you, O sons of God, have consecrated yourselves to God to maintain peace among yourselves more vigorously and to uphold the laws of the Church faithfully, there is work to do, for you must turn the strength of your sincerity, now that you are aroused by divine correction, to another affair that concerns you and God. Hastening to the way, you must help your brothers living in the Orient, who need your aid for which they have already cried out many times.

3. "For, as most of you have been told, the Turks, a race of Persians,[10] who have penetrated within the boundaries of Romania[11] even to the Mediterranean to that point which they call the Arm of Saint George, in occupying more and more of the lands of the Christians, have overcome them, already victims of seven battles, and have killed and captured them, have overthrown churches, and have laid waste God's kingdom. If you permit this supinely for very long, God's faithful ones will be still further subjected.

4. "Concerning this affair, I, with suppliant prayer—not I, but the Lord—exhort you, heralds of Christ, to persuade all of whatever class, both knights and footmen, both rich and poor, in numerous edicts, to strive to help expel that wicked race from our Christian lands before it is too late.

5. "I speak to those present, I send word to those not here; moreover, Christ commands it. Remission of sins will be granted for those going thither, if they end a shackled life either on land or in crossing the sea, or in struggling against the heathen. I, being vested with that gift from God, grant this to those who go.

6. "O what a shame, if a people, so despised, degenerate, and enslaved by demons would thus overcome a people endowed with the trust of almighty God, and shining in the name of Christ! O how many evils will be imputed to you by the Lord Himself, if you do not help those who, like you, profess Christianity!

---

[10]Really Seljuk Turks who conquered lands from east to west by way of Persia.

[11]Fulcher uses the term *Romania* to refer to the Anatolian as well as to the European provinces of the Byzantine Empire, but here, of course, he means the Anatolian. The Seljuks called the state which they founded here *Rum*.

7. "Let those," he said, "who are accustomed to wage private wars wastefully even against Believers, go forth against the Infidels in a battle worthy to be undertaken now and to be finished in victory. Now, let those, who until recently existed as plunderers, be soldiers of Christ; now, let those, who formerly contended against brothers and relations, rightly fight barbarians; now, let those, who recently were hired for a few pieces of silver, win their eternal reward. Let those, who wearied themselves to the detriment of body and soul, labor for a twofold honor. Nay, more, the sorrowful here will be glad there, the poor here will be rich there, and the enemies of the Lord here will be His friends there.

8. "Let no delay postpone the journey of those about to go, but when they have collected the money owed to them and the expenses for the journey, and when winter has ended and spring has come, let them enter the crossroads courageously with the Lord going on before."

IV. The Bishop of Puy and the Events after the Council

1. After these words were spoken, the hearers were fervently inspired. Thinking nothing more worthy than such an undertaking, many in the audience solemnly promised to go, and to urge diligently those who were absent. There was among them one Bishop of Puy, Ademar by name, who afterwards, acting as vicar-apostolic, ruled the whole army of God wisely and thoughtfully, and spurred them to complete their undertaking vigorously.

2. So, the things that we have told you were well established and confirmed by everybody in the Council. With the blessing of absolution given, they departed; and after returning to their homes, they disclosed to those not knowing, what had taken place. As it was decreed far and wide throughout the provinces, they established the peace, which they call the Truce, to be upheld mutually by oath.

3. Many, one after another, of any and every occupation, after confession of their sins and with purified spirits, consecrated themselves to go where they were bidden.

4. Oh, how worthy and delightful to all of us who saw those beautiful crosses, either silken or woven of gold, or of any material, which the pilgrims sewed on the shoulders of their woolen cloaks or cassocks by the command of the Pope, after taking the vow to go. To be sure, God's soldiers, who were making themselves ready to battle for His honor, ought to have been marked and fortified with a sign of victory. And so by embroidering the symbol [of the cross] on their clothing in recognition of their faith, in the end they won the True Cross itself. They imprinted the ideal so that they might attain the reality of the ideal.

5. It is plain that good meditation leads to doing good work and that good work wins salvation of the soul. But, if it is good to mean well, it is better, after reflection, to carry out the good intention. So, it is best to win salvation through action worthy of the soul to be saved. Let each and everyone, therefore, reflect upon the good, that he makes better in fulfillment, so that, deserving it, he might finally receive the best, which does not diminish in eternity.

6. In such a manner Urban, a wise man and reverenced,
Meditated a labor, whereby the world floresced.

For he renewed peace and restored the laws of the Church to their former standards; also he tried with vigorous instigation to expel the heathen from the lands of the Christians. And since he strove to exalt all things of God in every way, almost everyone gladly surrendered in obedience to his paternal care. . . .

┌─────┐
│ 61 │
└─────┘

Chronicle of Solomon bar Simson

Solomon bar Simson (who is known only from this chronicle) provides the most complete of the Hebrew chronicles of the First Crusade. He takes up the story after Pope Urban II's appeal. Franks and Germans have organized their armies of knights, suppliers, aides, and followers, and have set off for Jerusalem by way of Constantinople. Why did these Crusaders stop at Mainz* and other German cities to murder Jews?

Thinking Historically

This narrative, like the previous selection, includes quotations from speeches. How can you tell that some of these quotations do not contain the exact words that were spoken?

Solomon bar Simson's narrative contains another element that, while absent from modern histories, is found in other narratives of the Crusades and is especially pronounced here. This is not just a narra-

*myntz

"Chronicle of Solomon bar Simson," in *The Jews and the Crusaders: The Hebrew Chronicles of the First and Second Crusades*, ed. and trans. Shlomo Eidelberg (Madison: University of Wisconsin Press, 1977), 21–26.

tive of human action and intention, but it interprets divine action and intention as well. Why is this narrative strategy necessary for this author? If you were writing a narrative of the Crusades today, would you want to tell both of these stories, or only the human one? Why?

I will now recount the event of this persecution in other martyred communities as well—the extent to which they clung to the Lord, God of their fathers, bearing witness to His Oneness to their last breath.

In the year four thousand eight hundred and fifty-six, the year one thousand twenty-eight of our exile, in the eleventh year of the cycle Ranu, the year in which we anticipated salvation and solace, in accordance with the prophecy of Jeremiah: "Sing with gladness for Jacob, and shout at the head of the nations," etc.—this year turned instead to sorrow and groaning, weeping and outcry. Inflicted upon the Jewish People were the many evils related in all the admonitions; those enumerated in Scripture as well as those unwritten were visited upon us.

At this time arrogant people, a people of strange speech, a nation bitter and impetuous, Frenchmen and Germans, set out for the Holy City, which had been desecrated by barbaric nations, there to seek their house of idolatry and banish the Ishmaelites and other denizens of the land and conquer the land for themselves. They decorated themselves prominently with their signs, placing a profane symbol—a horizontal line over a vertical one—on the vestments of every man and woman whose heart yearned to go on the stray path to the grave of their Messiah. Their ranks swelled until the number of men, women, and children exceeded a locust horde covering the earth; of them it was said: "The locusts have no king [yet go they forth all of them by bands]." Now it came to pass that as they passed through the towns where Jews dwelled, they said to one another: "Look now, we are going a long way to seek out the profane shrine and to avenge ourselves on the Ishmaelites, when here, in our very midst, are the Jews—they whose forefathers murdered and crucified him for no reason. Let us first avenge ourselves on them and exterminate them from among the nations so that the name of Israel will no longer be remembered, or let them adopt our faith and acknowledge the offspring of promiscuity."

When the Jewish communities became aware of their intentions, they resorted to the custom of our ancestors, repentance, prayer, and charity. The hands of the Holy Nation turned faint at this time, their hearts melted, and their strength flagged. They hid in their innermost rooms to escape the swirling sword. They subjected themselves to great endurance, abstaining from food and drink for three consecutive days and nights, and then fasting many days from sunrise to sunset, until their skin was shriveled and dry as wood upon their bones. And they cried out loudly and bitterly to God.

But their Father did not answer them; He obstructed their prayers, concealing Himself in a cloud through which their prayers could not pass, and He abhorred their tent, and He removed them out of His sight—all of this having been decreed by Him to take place "in the day when I visit"; and this was the generation that had been chosen by Him to be His portion, for they had the strength and the fortitude to stand in His Sanctuary, and fulfill His word, and sanctify His Great Name in His world. It is of such as these that King David said: "Bless the Lord, ye angels of His, ye almighty in strength, that fulfil His word," etc.

That year, Passover fell on Thursday, and the New Moon of the following month, Iyar, fell on Friday and the Sabbath. On the eighth day of Iyar, on the Sabbath, the foe attacked the community of Speyer and murdered eleven holy souls who sanctified their Creator on the holy Sabbath and refused to defile themselves by adopting the faith of their foe. There was a distinguished, pious woman there who slaughtered herself in sanctification of God's Name. She was the first among all the communities of those who were slaughtered. The remainder were saved by the local bishop without defilement [i.e., baptism], as described above.

On the twenty-third of Iyar they attacked the community of Worms.[1] The community was then divided into two groups; some remained in their homes and others fled to the local bishop seeking refuge. Those who remained in their homes were set upon by the steppe-wolves who pillaged men, women, and infants, children, and old people. They pulled down the stairways and destroyed the houses, looting and plundering; and they took the Torah Scroll, trampled it in the mud, and tore and burned it. The enemy devoured the children of Israel with open maw.

Seven days later, on the New Moon of Sivan—the very day on which the Children of Israel arrived at Mount Sinai to receive the Torah—those Jews who were still in the court of the bishop were subjected to great anguish. The enemy dealt them the same cruelty as the first group and put them to the sword. The Jews, inspired by the valor of their brethren, similarly chose to be slain in order to sanctify the Name before the eyes of all, and exposed their throats for their heads to be severed for the glory of the Creator. There were also those who took their own lives, thus fulfilling the verse: "The mother was dashed in pieces with her children." Fathers fell upon their sons, being slaughtered upon one another, and they slew one another—each man his kin, his wife and children; bridegrooms slew their betrothed, and merciful

---

[1]Town in the Holy Roman Empire (now Germany). [Ed.]

women their only children. They all accepted the divine decree whole-heartedly and, as they yielded up their souls to the Creator, cried out: "Hear, O Israel, the Lord is our God, the Lord is One." The enemy stripped them naked, dragged them along, and then cast them off, sparing only a small number whom they forcibly baptized in their profane waters. The number of those slain during the two days was approximately eight hundred—and they were all buried naked. It is of these that the Prophet Jeremiah lamented: "They that were brought up in scarlet embrace dunghills." I have already cited their names above. May God remember them for good.

When the saints, the pious ones of the Most High, the holy community of Mainz, whose merit served as shield and protection for all the communities and whose fame had spread throughout the many provinces, heard that some of the community of Speyer had been slain and that the community of Worms had been attacked a second time, and that the sword would soon reach them, their hands became faint and their hearts melted and became as water. They cried out to the Lord with all their hearts, saying: "O Lord, God of Israel, will You completely annihilate the remnant of Israel? Where are all your wonders which our forefathers related to us, saying: 'Did You not bring us up from Egypt and from Babylonia and rescue us on numerous occasions?' How, then, have You now forsaken and abandoned us, O Lord, giving us over into the hands of evil Edom so that they may destroy us? Do not remove Yourself from us, for adversity is almost upon us and there is no one to aid us."

The leaders of the Jews gathered together and discussed various ways of saving themselves. They said: "Let us elect elders so that we may know how to act, for we are consumed by this great evil." The elders decided to ransom the community by generously giving of their money and bribing the various princes and deputies and bishops and governors. Then, the community leaders who were respected by the local bishop approached him and his officers and servants to negotiate this matter. They asked: "What shall we do about the news we have received regarding the slaughter of our brethren in Speyer and Worms?" They [the Gentiles] replied: "Heed our advice and bring all your money into our treasury. You, your wives, and your children, and all your belongings shall come into the courtyard of the bishop until the hordes have passed by. Thus will you be saved from the errant ones."

Actually, they gave this advice so as to herd us together and hold us like fish that are caught in an evil net, and then to turn us over to the enemy, while taking our money. This is what actually happened in the end, and "the outcome is proof of the intentions." The bishop assembled his ministers and courtiers—mighty ministers, the noblest in the land—for the purpose of helping us; for at first it had been his desire to save us with all his might, since we had given him and his ministers and servants a large bribe in return for their promise to help us. Ultimately, however, all the bribes and entreaties were of no avail to protect us on the day of wrath and misfortune.

It was at this time that Duke Godfrey [of Bouillon], may his bones be ground to dust, arose in the hardness of his spirit, driven by a spirit of wantonness to go with those journeying to the profane shrine, vowing to go on this journey only after avenging the blood of the crucified one by shedding Jewish blood and completely eradicating any trace of those bearing the name "Jew," thus assuaging his own burning wrath. To be sure, there arose someone to repair the breach—a God-fearing man who had been bound to the most holy of altars—called Rabbi Kalonymos, the *Parnass*[2] of the community of Mainz. He dispatched a messenger to King Henry in the kingdom of Pula, where the king had been dwelling during the past nine years, and related all that had happened.

The king was enraged and dispatched letters to all the ministers, bishops, and governors of all the provinces of his realm, as well as to Duke Godfrey, containing words of greeting and commanding them to do no bodily harm to the Jews and to provide them with help and refuge. The evil duke then swore that he had never intended to do them harm. The Jews of Cologne nevertheless bribed him with five hundred *zekukim* of silver, as did the Jews of Mainz. The duke assured them of his support and promised them peace.

However, God, the maker of peace, turned aside and averted His eyes from His people, and consigned them to the sword. No prophet, seer, or man of wise heart was able to comprehend how the sin of the people infinite in number was deemed so great as to cause the destruction of so many lives in the various Jewish communities. The martyrs endured the extreme penalty normally inflicted only upon one guilty of murder. Yet, it must be stated with certainty that God is a righteous judge, and we are to blame.

Then the evil waters prevailed. The enemy unjustly accused them of evil acts they did not do, declaring: "You are the children of those who killed our object of veneration, hanging him on a tree, and he himself had said: 'There will yet come a day when my children will come and avenge my blood.' We are his children and it is therefore obligatory for us to avenge him since you are the ones who rebel and disbelieve in him. Your God has never been at peace with you. Although He intended to deal kindly with you, you have conducted yourselves improperly before Him. God has forgotten you and is no longer desirous of you since you are a stubborn nation. Instead, He has departed from you and has taken us for His portion, casting His radiance upon us."

---

[2]Reference to the Greek mountain Parnassus, perhaps meaning "mainstay" of the community. [Ed.]

When we heard these words, our hearts trembled and moved out of their places. We were dumb with silence, abiding in darkness, like those long dead, waiting for the Lord to look forth and behold from heaven.

And Satan—the Pope of evil Rome—also came and proclaimed to all the nations believing in that stock of adultery—these are the stock of Seir[3]—that they should assemble and ascend to Jerusalem so as to conquer the city, and journey to the tomb of the superstition whom they call their god. Satan came and mingled with the nations, and they gathered as one man to fulfill the command, coming in great numbers like the grains of sand upon the seashore, the noise of them clamorous as a whirlwind and a storm. When the drops of the bucket had assembled, they took evil counsel against the people of the Lord and said: "Why should we concern ourselves with going to war against the Ishmaelites dwelling about Jerusalem, when in our midst is a people who disrespect our god—indeed, their ancestors are those who crucified him. Why should we let them live and tolerate their dwelling among us? Let us commence by using our swords against them and then proceed upon our stray path."

The heart of the people of our God grew faint and their spirit flagged, for many sore injuries had been inflicted upon them and they had been smitten repeatedly. They now came supplicating to God and fasting, and their hearts melted within them. But the Lord did as He declared, for we had sinned before Him, and He forsook the sanctuary of Shiloh—the Temple-in-Miniature—which He had placed among His people who dwelt in the midst of alien nations. His wrath was kindled and He drew the sword against them, until they remained but as the flagstaff upon the mountaintop and as the ensign on the hill, and He gave over His nation into captivity and trampled them underfoot. See, O Lord, and consider to whom Thou hast done thus: to Israel, a nation despised and pillaged, Your chosen portion! Why have You uplifted the shield of its enemies, and why have they gained in strength? Let all hear, for I cry out in anguish; the ears of all that hear me shall be seared: How has the staff of might been broken, the rod of glory—the sainted community comparable to fine gold, the community of Mainz! It was caused by the Lord to test those that fear Him, to have them endure the yoke of His pure fear. . . .

---

[3]An enemy of ancient Israel.

ANNA COMNENA
From The Alexiad

Anna Comnena was the daughter of Emperor Alexius (r. 1081–1118) of Byzantium. Threatened on three sides—by the Seljuk Turks to the east, the Norman Kingdom of southern Italy to the west, and rebellions to the north—Alexius appealed for aid to Pope Urban II of Rome in 1095. He expected a mercenary army, but because the pope saw a chance to send a massive force against Muslim occupiers of Jerusalem as well as against those threatening Constantinople, Alexius instead received an uncontrollable ragtag force of Christians and Crusaders that included his Norman enemies, led by Bohemond.

Princess Anna, the emperor's daughter, recalled the story of the First Crusade's appearance in Byzantium some forty years later in her history titled *The Alexiad* after her father. According to Anna, how did Alexius respond to the approach of the Crusader army? Did Alexius fear the Franks more than he feared the Turks?

Thinking Historically

This is a third perspective on the history of the First Crusade—the view of a Christian ally of Rome, more directly threatened than the Roman church by the Muslim armies. Yet, Byzantium and Rome were also at odds. Since 1054, they had accepted a parting of ways, theologically and institutionally. And with the advancing Frankish armies, Anna and Alexius were not sure whether they were facing friend or foe. How does Anna's critical perspective change our idea of the Crusaders? How might her idea of the Franks change our narrative of the early stage of the crusade?

Notice how this narrative combines a sequence of events with generalizations (often about the "race" or nature of the Franks) to explain specific events. Does a narrative history have to include generalizations as well as a sequence of specific events? Can the events alone provide sufficient explanation?

Anna Comnena, *The Alexiad of the Princess Anna Comnena*, trans. Elizabeth A. S. Dawes (London: Routledge & Kegan Paul Ltd., 1967), 247–52. Reprinted in William H. McNeill and Schuyler O. Houser, *Medieval Europe* (Oxford: Oxford University Press, 1971), 135–40.

Before he had enjoyed even a short rest, he heard a report of the approach of innumerable Frankish armies. Now he dreaded their arrival for he knew their irresistible manner of attack, their unstable and mobile character and all the peculiar natural and concomitant characteristics which the Frank retains throughout; and he also knew that they were always agape for money, and seemed to disregard their truces readily for any reason that cropped up. For he had always heard this reported of them, and found it very true. However, he did not lose heart, but prepared himself in every way so that, when the occasion called, he would be ready for battle. And indeed the actual facts were far greater and more terrible than rumour made them. For the whole of the West and all the barbarian tribes which dwell between the further side of the Adriatic and the pillars of Heracles, had all migrated in a body and were marching into Asia through the intervening Europe, and were making the journey with all their household. The reason of this upheaval was more or less the following. A certain Frank, Peter by name, nicknamed Cucupeter, had gone to worship at the Holy Sepulchre and after suffering many things at the hands of the Turks and Saracens who were ravaging Asia, he got back to his own country with difficulty. But he was angry at having failed in his object, and wanted to undertake the same journey again. However, he saw that he ought not to make the journey to the Holy Sepulchre alone again, lest worse things befall him, so he worked out a cunning plan. This was to preach in all the Latin countries that "the voice of God bids me announce to all the Counts in France" that they should all leave their homes and set out to worship at the Holy Sepulchre, and to endeavour wholeheartedly with hand and mind to deliver Jerusalem from the hand of Hagarenes.[1] And he really succeeded. For after inspiring the souls of all with this quasi-divine command he contrived to assemble the Franks from all sides, one after the other, with arms, horses and all the other paraphernalia of war. And they were all so zealous and eager that every highroad was full of them. And those Frankish soldiers were accompanied by an unarmed host more numerous than the sand or the stars, carrying palms and crosses on their shoulders, women and children, too, came away from their countries and the sight of them was like many rivers streaming from all sides, and they were advancing towards us through Dacia generally with all their hosts. Now the coming of these many peoples was preceded by a locust which did not touch the wheat, but made a terrible attack on the vines. This was really a presage as the diviners of the time interpreted it, and meant that this enormous Frankish army would, when it came, refrain from interference in Christian affairs, but fall very heavily upon the barbarian

---

[1] Saracens, who were considered "children of Hagar" (cf. Gen. 16). [Ed.]

Ishmaelites who were slaves to drunkenness, wine, and Dionysus.[2] For this race is under the sway of Dionysus and Eros,[3] rushes headlong into all kind of sexual intercourse, and is not circumcised either in the flesh or in their passions. It is nothing but a slave, nay triply enslaved, to the ills wrought by Aphrodite. For this reason they worship and adore Astarte and Ashtaroth[4] too and value above all the image of the moon, and the golden figure of Hobar[5] in their country. Now in these symbols Christianity was taken to be the corn because of its wineless and very nutritive qualities; in this manner the diviners interpreted the vines and the wheat. However let the matter of the prophecy rest.

The incidents of the barbarians' approach followed in the order I have described, and persons of intelligence could feel that they were witnessing a strange occurrence. The arrival of these multitudes did not take place at the same time nor by the same road (for how indeed could such masses starting from different places have crossed the straits of Lombardy all together?). Some first, some next, others after them and thus successively all accomplished the transit, and then marched through the Continent. Each army was preceded, as we said, by an unspeakable number of locusts; and all who saw this more than once recognized them as forerunners of the Frankish armies. When the first of them began crossing the straits of Lombardy sporadically the Emperor summoned certain leaders of the Roman forces, and sent them to the parts of Dyrrachium and Valona[6] with instructions to offer a courteous welcome to the Franks who had crossed, and to collect abundant supplies from all the countries along their route; then to follow and watch them covertly all the time, and if they saw them making any foraging-excursions, they were to come out from under cover and check them by light skirmishing. These captains were accompanied by some men who knew the Latin tongue, so that they might settle any disputes that arose between them.

Let me, however, give an account of this subject more clearly and in due order. According to universal rumour Godfrey,[7] who sold his country, was the first to start on the appointed road; this man was very rich and very proud of his bravery, courage and conspicuous lineage; for every Frank is anxious to outdo the others. And such an upheaval

---

[2] Anna's account of the beliefs of the Muslims was highly biased. Muhammad forbade his followers to drink intoxicating liquors.

[3] Dionysus was the Greek god associated with wine and revelry; Eros was the patron of lovers, and son of Aphrodite, goddess of love.

[4] Names of the Semitic goddess of fertility.

[5] I.e., Hathor, the Egyptian goddess of love, usually depicted with the head of a cow. (N.B. Idol worship was strictly forbidden by Islamic law.)

[6] Ports on the Adriatic, directly opposite the heel of Italy in modern Albania.

[7] Godfrey of Bouillon, the duke of Lower Lorraine (c. 1060–1100). To raise money for the Crusade, he sold two of his estates, and pledged his castle at Bouillon to the bishop of Liège.

of both men and women took place then as had never occurred within human memory, the simpler-minded were urged on by the real desire of worshipping at our Lord's Sepulchre, and visiting the sacred places; but the more astute, especially men like Bohemund and those of like mind, had another secret reason, namely, the hope that while on their travels they might by some means be able to seize the capital [Constantinople] itself, looking upon this as a kind of corollary. And Bohemund disturbed the minds of many nobler men by thus cherishing his old grudge against the Emperor. Meanwhile Peter, after he had delivered his message, crossed the straits of Lombardy before anybody else with eighty thousand men on foot, and one hundred thousand on horseback, and reached the capital by way of Hungary.[8] For the Frankish race, as one may conjecture, is always very hotheaded and eager, but when once it has espoused a cause, it is uncontrollable.

The Emperor, knowing what Peter had suffered before from the Turks, advised him to wait for the arrival of the other Counts, but Peter would not listen for he trusted the multitude of his followers, so he crossed and pitched his camp near a small town called Helenopolis.[9] After him followed the Normans numbering ten thousand, who separated themselves from the rest of the army and devastated the country round Nicaea, and behaved most cruelly to all. For they dismembered some of the children and fixed others on wooden spits and roasted them at the fire, and on persons advanced in age they inflicted every kind of torture. But when the inhabitants of Nicaea became aware of these doings, they threw open their gates and marched out upon them, and after a violent conflict had taken place they had to dash back inside their citadel as the Normans fought so bravely. And thus the latter recovered all the booty and returned to Helenopolis. Then a dispute arose between them and the others who had not gone out with them, as is usual in such cases, for the minds of those who stayed behind were aflame with envy, and thus caused a skirmish after which the headstrong Normans drew apart again, marched to Xerigordus[10] and took it by assault. When the Sultan[11] heard what had happened, he dispatched Elchanes[12] against them with a substantial force. He came, and recaptured Xerigordus and sacrificed some of the Normans to the sword, and took others captive, at the same time laid plans to catch those who had remained behind with Cucupeter. He placed ambushes in suitable spots so that any coming from the camp in the direction of Nicaea would fall into them unexpectedly and be killed. Besides this, as he knew the Franks' love of money, he sent for two active-minded men

---

[8]Peter's contingent probably numbered about twenty thousand including noncombatants.

[9]I.e., Peter moved his forces across the Bosphorus and into Asia Minor.

[10]A castle held by the Turks.

[11]Qilij Arslan I, ruled 1092–1106.

[12]An important Turkish military commander.

and ordered them to go to Cucupeter's camp and proclaim there that
the Normans had gained possession of Nicaea, and were now dividing
everything in it. When this report was circulated among Peter's followers, it upset them terribly. Directly [When] they heard the words "parti-
tion" and "money" they started in a disorderly crowd along the road to
Nicaea, all but unmindful of their military experience and the discipline
which is essential for those starting out to battle. For, as I remarked
above, the Latin race is always very fond of money, but more especially
when it is bent on raiding a country; it then loses its reason and gets beyond control. As they journeyed neither in ranks nor in squadrons, they
fell foul of the Turkish ambuscades near the river Dracon and perished
miserably. And such a large number of Franks and Normans were the
victims of the Ishmaelite sword, that when they piled up the corpses of
the slaughtered men which were lying on either side they formed, I say,
not a very large hill or mound or a peak, but a high mountain as it
were, of very considerable depth and breadth—so great was the pyramid of bones. And later men of the same tribe as the slaughtered barbarians built a wall and used the bones of the dead to fill the interstices
as if they were pebbles, and thus made the city their tomb in a way.
This fortified city is still standing today with its walls built of a mixture
of stones and bones. When they had all in this way fallen prey to the
sword, Peter alone with a few others escaped and reentered Helenopolis,[13] and the Turks who wanted to capture him, set fresh ambushes for
him. But when the Emperor received reliable information of all this,
and the terrible massacre, he was very worried lest Peter should have
been captured. He therefore summoned Constantine Catacalon Eu-
phorbenus (who has already been mentioned many times in this history), and gave him a large force which was embarked on ships of war
and sent him across the straits to Peter's succour. Directly the Turks
saw him land they fled. Constantine, without the slightest delay, picked
up Peter and his followers, who were but few, and brought them safe
and sound to the Emperor. On the Emperor's reminding him of his
original thoughtlessness and saying that it was due to his not having
obeyed his, the Emperor's, advice that he had incurred such disasters,
Peter, being a haughty Latin, would not admit that he himself was
the cause of the trouble, but said it was the others who did not listen
to him, but followed their own will, and he denounced them as
robbers and plunderers who, for that reason, were not allowed by the
Saviour to worship at His Holy Sepulchre. Others of the Latins, such as
Bohemund and men of like mind, who had long cherished a desire for
the Roman Empire, and wished to win it for themselves, found a pretext in Peter's preaching, as I have said, deceived the more single-

---

[13]According to other accounts of the battle, Peter was in Constantinople at the time.

minded, caused this great upheaval and were selling their own estates under the pretence that they were marching against the Turks to redeem the Holy Sepulchre.

63

FULCHER OF CHARTRES

The Siege of Antioch

We return here to Fulcher's Chronicles (Book I, Chapters 16 and 17). Antioch, in northern Syria, was the largest and most formidable Muslim-controlled city on the Crusaders' route to Jerusalem. After laying siege to the city for more than two years, the Crusader forces had suffered losses that seriously reduced their strength and morale. After their initial success, what events seem to have caused these reversals? What were the strengths and weaknesses of the Crusader armies?

Thinking Historically

Like the narrative of Solomon bar Simson, this narrative operates on two levels: the human and the divine. Notice how Fulcher attempts to interpret both of these narrative lines, separately and in their interaction. How much of Fulcher's narrative recounts God's work? How much recounts the work of the Crusaders? How does he combine these two threads? Of course, modern historians are normally limited to the human thread. Try to write a narrative that shows how the human Crusaders conquered Antioch.

XVI. The Wretched Poverty of the Christians and the Flight of the Count of Blois

1. In the year of the Lord 1098, after the region all around Antioch had been wholly devastated by the multitude of our people, the strong as well as the weak were more and more harassed by famine.

The First Crusade: The Chronicle of Fulcher of Chartres and Other Source Materials, 2nd ed., ed. Edward Peters (Philadelphia: University of Pennsylvania Press, 1998), 73–75.

2. At that time, the famished ate the shoots of beanseeds growing in the fields and many kinds of herbs unseasoned with salt; also thistles, which, being not well cooked because of the deficiency of firewood, pricked the tongues of those eating them; also horses, asses, and camels, and dogs and rats. The poorer ones ate even the skins of the beasts and seeds of grain found in manure.

3. They endured winter's cold, summer's heat, and heavy rains for God. Their tents became old and torn and rotten from the continuation of rains. Because of this, many of them were covered by only the sky.

4. So like gold thrice proved and purified sevenfold by fire, long predestined by God, I believe, and weighed by such a great calamity, they were cleansed of their sins. For even if the assassin's sword had not failed, many, long agonizing, would have voluntarily completed a martyr's course. Perhaps they borrowed the grace of such a great example from Saint Job, who, purifying his soul by the torments of his body, ever held God fast in mind. Those who fight with the heathen, labor because of God.

5. Granting that God—who creates everything, regulates everything created, sustains everything regulated, and rules by virtue—can destroy or renew whatsoever He wishes, I feel that He assented to the destruction of the heathen after the scourging of the Christians. He permitted it, and the people deserved it, because so many times they cheaply destroyed all things of God. He permitted the Christians to be killed by the Turks, so that the Christians would have the assurance of salvation; the Turks, the perdition of their souls. It pleased God that certain Turks, already predestined for salvation, were baptized by priests. "For those whom He predestined, He also called and glorified."

6. So what then? There were some of our men, as you heard before, who left the siege because it brought so much anguish; others, because of poverty; others, because of cowardice; others, because of fear of death; first the poor and then the rich.

7. Stephen, Count of Blois, withdrew from the siege and returned home to France by sea. Therefore all of us grieved, since he was a very noble man and valiant in arms. On the day following his departure, the city of Antioch was surrendered to the Franks. If he had persevered, he would have rejoiced much in the victory with the rest. This act disgraced him. For a good beginning is not beneficial to anyone unless it be well consummated. I shall cut short many things in the Lord's affairs lest I wander from the truth, because lying about them must be especially guarded against.

8. The siege lasted continuously from this same month of October, as it was mentioned, through the following winter and spring until June. The Turks and Franks alternately staged many attacks and counter-attacks; they overcame and were overcome. Our men, however, triumphed more often than theirs. Once it happened that many of the fleeing Turks fell into the Fernus River, and being submerged in it,

they drowned. On the near side of the river, and on the far side, both forces often waged war alternately.

9. Our leaders constructed castles before the city, from which they often rushed forth vigorously to keep the Turks from coming out [of the city]. By this means, the Franks took the pastures from their animals. Nor did they get any help from Armenians outside the city, although these Armenians often did injury to our men.

XVII. The Surrender of the City of Antioch

1. When it pleased God that the labor of His people should be consummated, perhaps pleased by the prayers of those who daily poured out supplications and entreaties to Him, out of His compassion He granted that through a fraud of the Turks the city be returned to the Christians in a secret surrender. Hear, therefore, of a fraud, and yet not a fraud.

2. Our Lord appeared to a certain Turk, chosen beforehand by His grace, and said to him: "Arise, thou who sleepest! I command thee to return the city to the Christians." The astonished man concealed that vision in silence.

3. However, a second time, the Lord appeared to him: "Return the city to the Christians," He said, "for I am Christ who command this of thee." Meditating what to do, he went away to his ruler, the prince of Antioch, and made that vision known to him. To him the ruler responded: "You do not wish to obey the phantom, do you, stupid?" Returning, he was afterwards silent.

4. The Lord again appeared to him, saying: "Why hast thou not fulfilled what I ordered thee? Thou must not hesitate, for I, who command this, am Lord of all." No longer doubting, he discreetly negotiated with our men, so that by his zealous plotting they might receive the city.

5. He finished speaking, and gave his son as hostage to Lord Bohemond, to whom he first directed that discourse, and whom he first persuaded. On a certain night, he sent twenty of our men over the wall by means of ladders made of ropes. Without delay, the gate was opened. The Franks, already prepared, entered the city. Forty of our soldiers, who had previously entered by ropes, killed sixty Turks found there, guards of the tower. In a loud voice, altogether the Franks shouted: "God wills it! God wills it!" For this was our signal cry, when we were about to press forward on any enterprise.

6. After hearing this, all the Turks were extremely terrified. Then, when the redness of dawn had paled, the Franks began to go forward to attack the city. When the Turks had first seen Bohemond's red banner on high, furling and unfurling, and the great tumult aroused on all sides, and the Franks running far and wide through the streets with their naked swords and wildly killing people, and had heard their horns sounding on the top of the wall, they began to flee here and there,

bewildered. From this scene, many who were able fled into the citadel situated on a cliff.

7. Our rabble wildly seized everything that they found in the streets and houses. But the proved soldiers kept to warfare, in following and killing the Turks.

$$\boxed{64}$$

IBN AL-QALANISI
From The Damascus Chronicle

Here we switch to a Muslim view of the events of 1098 and 1099: especially the battles of Antioch, Jerusalem, and Ascalon (modern Ashkelon, Israel). Ibn al-Qalanisi* (d. 1160) was a scholar in Damascus, Syria. How does his account of the battle for Antioch differ from the previous selection by Fulcher of Chartres? How do you resolve these differences?

Thinking Historically

We noticed how the medieval Christian historian provided two historical threads—the human and divine. How does this Muslim account integrate the threads of human action and divine will?

Modern historians restrict their accounts to human action but they seek to include the view of both sides in a conflict. How do you integrate both sides into your narrative? Also, what signs do you see here of a possible second conflict, this one between Muslims?

A.H. 491

(*9th December, 1097, to 27th November, 1098*)

At the end of First Jumādā (beginning of June, 1098) the report arrived that certain of the men of Antioch among the armourers in the train of the amīr Yāghī Siyān had entered into a conspiracy against Antioch and

---

*IH buhn   ahl kahl ah NEE see

H. A. R. Gibb, *The Damascus Chronicle of the Crusades*, extracted and translated from the *Chronicle of Ibn al-Qalanisi* (Mineola, N.Y.: Dover Publications, 2002), 44–49.

had come to an agreement with the Franks to deliver the city up to them, because of some ill-usage and confiscations which they had formerly suffered at his hands. They found an opportunity of seizing one of the city bastions adjoining the Jabal, which they sold to the Franks, and thence admitted them into the city during the night. At daybreak they raised the battle cry, whereupon Yāghī Siyān took to flight and went out with a large body, but not one person amongst them escaped to safety. When he reached the neighbourhood of Armanāz, an estate near Ma ʿarrat Masrīn, he fell from his horse to the ground. One of his companions raised him up and remounted him, but he could not maintain his balance on the back of the horse, and after falling repeatedly he died. As for Antioch, the number of men, women, and children, killed, taken prisoner, and enslaved from its population is beyond computation. About three thousand men fled to the citadel and fortified themselves in it, and some few escaped for whom God had decreed escape.

In Shaʿbān (July) news was received that al-Afdal, the commander-in-chief (amīr al-juyūsh), had come up from Egypt to Syria at the head of a strong ʿaskar.[1] He encamped before Jerusalem, where at that time were the two amīrs Sukmān and Il-Ghāzī, sons of Ortuq, together with a number of their kinsmen and followers and a large body of Turks, and sent letters to them, demanding that they should surrender Jerusalem to him without warfare or shedding of blood. When they refused his demand, he opened an attack on the town, and having set up mangonels[2] against it, which effected a breach in the wall, he captured it and received the surrender of the Sanctuary of David[3] from Sukmān. On his entry into it, he shewed kindness and generosity to the two amīrs, and set both them and their supporters free. They arrived in Damascus during the first ten days of Shawwāl (September), and al-Afdal returned with his ʿaskar to Egypt.

In this year also the Franks set out with all their forces to Maʿarrat al-Nuʿmān,[4] and having encamped over against it on 29th Dhu'l-Hijja (27th November), they opened an attack on the town and brought up a tower and scaling-ladders against it.

Now after the Franks had captured the city of Antioch through the devices of the armourer, who was an Armenian named Fīrūz,[5] on the eve

[1]Small military force of slaves and freed men, under Muslim amirs. [Ed.]

[2]A catapult that could hurl large stones as far as four hundred feet to break down a wall. [Ed.]

[3]The Citadel of Jerusalem.

[4]Maʿarrat al-Numān or Maʿarat al-Numān: Syrian city south of Antioch. Conquest of Antioch did not provide enough food so crusaders marched on to this next city on route to Jerusalem. There they massacred the population of 10,000–20,000 and by some accounts cannibalized some of them. [Ed.]

[5]In the text Nairūz.

of Friday, 1st Rajab (night of Thursday 3rd June), and a series of reports were received confirming this news, the armies of Syria assembled in uncountable force and proceeded to the province of Antioch, in order to inflict a crushing blow upon the armies of the Franks. They besieged the Franks until their supplies of food were exhausted and they were reduced to eating carrion; but thereafter the Franks, though they were in the extremity of weakness, advanced in battle order against the armies of Islām, which were at the height of strength and numbers, and they broke the ranks of the Muslims and scattered their multitudes. The lords of the pedigree steeds[6] were put to flight, and the sword was unsheathed upon the footsoldiers who had volunteered for the cause of God, who had girt themselves for the Holy War, and were vehement in their desire to strike a blow for the Faith and for the protection of the Muslims. This befel on Tuesday, the [twenty] sixth of Rajab, in this year (29th June, 1098).

A.H. 492

(28th November, 1098, to 16th November, 1099)

In Muharram of this year (December, 1098), the Franks made an assault on the wall of Ma'arrat al-Nu'mān from the east and north. They pushed up the tower until it rested against the wall, and as it was higher, they deprived the Muslims of the shelter of the wall. The fighting raged round this point until sunset on 14th Muharram (11th December), when the Franks scaled the wall, and the townsfolk were driven off it and took to flight. Prior to this, messengers had repeatedly come to them from the Franks with proposals for a settlement by negotiation and the surrender of the city, promising in return security for their lives and property, and the establishment of a [Frankish] governor amongst them, but dissension among the citizens and the fore-ordained decree of God prevented acceptance of these terms. So they captured the city after the hour of the sunset prayer, and a great number from both sides were killed in it. The townsfolk fled to the houses of al-Ma'arra, to defend themselves in them, and the Franks, after promising them safety, dealt treacherously with them. They erected crosses over the town, exacted indemnities from the townsfolk, and did not carry out any of the terms upon which they had agreed, but plundered everything that they found, and demanded of the people sums which they could not pay. On Thursday 17th Safar (13th January, 1099) they set out for Kafr Tāb.

Thereafter they proceeded towards Jerusalem, at the end of Rajab (middle of June) of this year, and the people fled in panic from their

---

[6]Literally "of the short-haired and swift-paced."

abodes before them. They descended first upon al-Ramla, and captured it after the ripening of the crops. Thence they marched to Jerusalem, the inhabitants of which they engaged and blockaded, and having set up the tower against the city they brought it forward to the wall. At length news reached them that al-Afdal was on his way from Egypt with a mighty army to engage in the Holy War against them, and to destroy them, and to succour and protect the city against them. They therefore attacked the city with increased vigour, and prolonged the battle that day until the daylight faded, then withdrew from it, after promising the inhabitants to renew the attack upon them on the morrow. The townsfolk descended from the wall at sunset, whereupon the Franks renewed their assault upon it, climbed up the tower, and gained a footing on the city wall. The defenders were driven down, and the Franks stormed the town and gained possession of it. A number of the townsfolk fled to the sanctuary [of David], and a great host were killed. The Jews assembled in the synagogue, and the Franks burned it over their heads. The sanctuary was surrendered to them on guarantee of safety on the 22nd of Sha'bān (14th July) of this year, and they destroyed the shrines and the tomb of Abraham. Al-Afdal arrived with the Egyptian armies, but found himself forestalled, and having been reinforced by the troops from the Sāhil,[7] encamped outside Ascalon on 14th Ramadān (4th August), to await the arrival of the fleet by sea and of the Arab levies. The army of the Franks advanced against him and attacked him in great force. The Egyptian army was thrown back towards Ascalon, al-Afdal himself taking refuge in the city. The swords of the Franks were given mastery over the Muslims, and death was meted out to the footmen, volunteers, and townsfolk, about ten thousand souls, and the camp was plundered. Al-Afdal set out for Egypt with his officers, and the Franks besieged Ascalon, until at length the townsmen agreed to pay them twenty thousand dinars as protection money, and to deliver this sum to them forthwith. They therefore set about collecting this amount from the inhabitants of the town, but it befel that a quarrel broke out between the [Frankish] leaders, and they retired without having received any of the money. It is said that the number of the people of Ascalon who were killed in this campaign—that is to say of the witnesses, men of substance, merchants, and youths, exclusive of the regular levies—amounted to two thousand seven hundred souls.

[7]The Sāhil was the general name given to the coastal plain and the maritime towns, from Ascalon to Bairūt.

RAYMOND OF ST. GILES, COUNT OF TOULOUSE

The Capture of Jerusalem by the Crusaders

The author of this letter or proclamation was the secular military leader chosen by Pope Urban II to lead the crusade. By the time of the capture of Jerusalem in 1099, he was certainly—with the Norman Bohemond and a couple other nobles—among the top military leaders. How does he account for their capture of Jerusalem? How would you explain it? Raymond tells how immediately after conquering Jerusalem, the Crusaders went to meet an Egyptian army (mistakenly identified as Babylonian) at Ascalon. How does Raymond explain their success? How did Ibn al-Qalanisi explain it? How might you explain it?

Thinking Historically

A letter can read much like a historical narrative, as does this one by Raymond of St. Giles. The author clearly wants to tell his readers what has happened. But this letter addressed to the pope, his bishops, and "the whole Christian people" is as much a testament to God's work as it is a history. Why does this make it difficult to construct the human narrative? Which events could you confidently include in your history of the crusade?

To lord Paschal, pope of the Roman church, to all the bishops, and to the whole Christian people, from the archbishop of Pisa, duke Godfrey, now, by the grace of God, defender of the church of the Holy Sepulchre, Raymond, count of St. Giles, and the whole army of God, which is in the land of Israel, greeting.

Multiply your supplications and prayers in the sight of God with joy and thanksgiving, since God has manifested His mercy in fulfilling by our hands what He had promised in ancient times. For after the capture of Nicaea, the whole army, made up of more than three hundred thousand soldiers, departed thence. And, although this army was so

---

Raymond of St. Giles, Count of Toulouse, "The Capture of Jerusalem by the Crusaders," in D. C. Munro, ed., *Translations and Reprints from the Original Sources of European History*, 4th ed., vol. I, bk. 4 (New York: AMC Press, Inc., 1971), 8–12.

great that it could have in a single day covered all Romania and drunk up all the rivers and eaten up all the growing things, yet the Lord conducted them amid so great abundance that a ram was sold for a penny and an ox for twelve pennies or less. Moreover, although the princes and kings of the Saracens rose up against us, yet, by God's will, they were easily conquered and overcome. Because, indeed, some were puffed up by these successes, God opposed to us Antioch, impregnable to human strength. And there He detained us for nine months and so humbled us in the siege that there were scarcely a hundred good horses in our whole army. God opened to us the abundance of His blessing and mercy and led us into the city, and delivered the Turks and all of their possessions into our power.

Inasmuch as we thought that these had been acquired by our own strength and did not worthily magnify God who had done this, we were beset by so great a multitude of Turks that no one dared to venture forth at any point from the city. Moreover, hunger so weakened us that some could scarcely refrain from eating human flesh. It would be tedious to narrate all the miseries which we suffered in that city. But God looked down upon His people whom He had so long chastised and mercifully consoled them. Therefore, He at first revealed to us, as a recompense for our tribulation and as a pledge of victory, His lance which had lain hidden since the days of the apostles. Next, He so fortified the hearts of the men, that they who from sickness or hunger had been unable to walk, now were endued with strength to seize their weapons and manfully to fight against the enemy.

After we had triumphed over the enemy, as our army was wasting away at Antioch from sickness and weariness and was especially hindered by the dissensions among the leaders, we proceeded into Syria, stormed Barra and Marra, cities of the Saracens, and captured the fortresses in that country. And while we were delaying there, there was so great a famine in the army that the Christian people now ate the putrid bodies of the Saracens.[1] Finally, by the divine admonition, we entered into the interior of Hispania,[2] and the most bountiful, merciful and victorious hand of the omnipotent Father was with us. For the cities and fortresses of the country through which we were proceeding sent ambassadors to us with many gifts and offered to aid us and to surrender their walled places. But because our army was not large and it was the unanimous wish to hasten to Jerusalem, we accepted their pledges and made them tributaries. One of the cities forsooth, which

---

[1]Radulph of Caen, another Crusader chronicler, wrote, "In Ma'arra our troops boiled pagan adults alive in cooking-pots; they impaled children on spits and devoured them grilled." [Ed.]

[2]Probably a metaphor for an extremely fertile Muslim land, as Muslim Spain was known to be. [Ed.]

was on the sea-coast, had more men than there were in our whole army. And when those at Antioch and Laodicea and Archas heard how the hand of the Lord was with us, many from the army who had remained in those cities followed us to Tyre. Therefore, with the Lord's companionship and aid, we proceeded thus as far as Jerusalem.

And after the army had suffered greatly in the siege, especially on account of the lack of water, a council was held and the bishops and princes ordered that all with bare feet should march around the walls of the city, in order that He who entered it humbly in our behalf might be moved by our humility to open it to us and to exercise judgment upon His enemies. God was appeased by this humility and on the eighth day after the humiliation He delivered the city and His enemies to us. It was the day indeed on which the primitive church was driven thence, and on which the festival of the dispersion of the apostles is celebrated. And if you desire to know what was done with the enemy who were found there, know that in Solomon's Porch and in his temple our men rode in the blood of the Saracens up to the knees of their horses.

Then, when we were considering who ought to hold the city, and some moved by love for their country and kinsmen wished to return home, it was announced to us that the king of Babylon had come to Ascalon with an innumerable multitude of soldiers. His purpose was, as he said, to lead the Franks, who were in Jerusalem, into captivity, and to take Antioch by storm. But God had determined otherwise in regard to us.

Therefore, when we learned that the army of the Babylonians was at Ascalon, we went down to meet them, leaving our baggage and the sick in Jerusalem with a garrison. When our army was in sight of the enemy, upon our knees we invoked the aid of the Lord, that He who in our other adversities had strengthened the Christian faith, might in the present battle break the strength of the Saracens and of the devil and extend the kingdom of the church of Christ from sea to sea, over the whole world. There was no delay; God was present when we cried for His aid, and furnished us with so great boldness, that one who saw us rush upon the enemy would have taken us for a herd of deer hastening to quench their thirst in running water. It was wonderful, indeed, since there were in our army not more than 5,000 horsemen and 15,000 foot-soldiers, and there were probably in the enemy's army 100,000 horsemen and 400,000 foot-soldiers. Then God appeared wonderful to His servants. For before we engaged in fighting, by our very onset alone, He turned this multitude in flight and scattered all their weapons, so that if they wished afterwards to attack us, they did not have the weapons in which they trusted. There can be no question how great the spoils were, since the treasures of the king of Babylon were captured. More than 100,000 Moors perished there by the sword. Moreover, their panic was so great that about 2,000 were suffocated at the gate of the city. Those who perished in the sea were innumerable. Many were entangled in the thickets. The whole world was certainly fighting for us, and if many of ours had not been detained in plundering the camp, few of the great multitude of the enemy would have been able to escape from the battle.

And although it may be tedious, the following must not be omitted: On the day preceding the battle the army captured many thousands of camels, oxen, and sheep. By the command of the princes these were divided among the people. When we advanced to battle, wonderful to relate, the camels formed in many squadrons and the sheep and oxen did the same. Moreover, these animals accompanied us, halting when we halted, advancing when we advanced, and charging when we charged. The clouds protected us from the heat of the sun and cooled us.

Accordingly, after celebrating the victory, the army returned to Jerusalem. Duke Godfrey remained there; the count of St. Giles, Robert, count of Normandy, and Robert, count of Flanders, returned to Laodicea. There they found the fleet belonging to the Pisans and to Bohemond. After the archbishop of Pisa had established peace between Bohemond and our leaders, Raymond prepared to return to Jerusalem for the sake of God and his brethren.

Therefore, we call upon you of the Catholic Church of Christ and of the whole Latin church to exult in the so admirable bravery and devotion of your brethren, in the so glorious and very desirable retribution of the omnipotent God, and in the so devoutedly hoped-for remission of all our sins through the grace of God. And we pray that He may make you—namely, all bishops, clerks, and monks who are leading devout lives, and all the laity—to sit down at the right hand of God, who liveth and reigneth God for ever and ever. And we ask and beseech you in the name of our Lord Jesus, who has ever been with us and aided us and freed us from all our tribulations, to be mindful of your brethren who return to you, by doing them kindnesses and by paying their debts, in order that God may recompense you and absolve you from all your sins and grant you a share in all the blessings which either we or they have deserved in the sight of the Lord. Amen.

66

IBN AL-ATHIR

The Conquest of Jerusalem

Ibn al-Athir* (1160–1233) was an influential Arab historian who wrote a history of the first three crusades, having witnessed the third himself. The following selection, taken from his work *The Perfect History*, is one of the most authoritative, roughly contemporaneous histories of the First Crusade from the Muslim perspective. What reason does al-Athir give for the Egyptian capture of Jerusalem from the Turks? Why were the Franks successful in wresting Jerusalem and other lands from Muslim control? What is the significance of the poem at the end of the selection?

Thinking Historically

There are always more than two sides to a story, but it is certainly useful to have battle descriptions from two sides of a conflict. In constructing your own narrative of the battle of Jerusalem, you might first look for points of agreement. On what points does Ibn al-Athir agree with other accounts you have read? How else would you decide which elements from each account to include in your narrative?

Taj ad-Daula Tutūsh was the Lord of Jerusalem but had given it as a feoff to the amīr Suqmān ibn Artūq the Turcoman. When the Franks defeated the Turks at Antioch the massacre demoralized them, and the Egyptians, who saw that the Turkish armies were being weakened by desertion, besieged Jerusalem under the command of al-Afdal ibn Badr al-Jamali. Inside the city were Artūq's sons, Suqmān and Ilghazi, their cousin Sunij and their nephew Yaquti. The Egyptians brought more than forty siege engines to attack Jerusalem and broke down the walls at several points. The inhabitants put up a defense, and the siege and fighting went on for more than six weeks. In the end the Egyptians forced the city to capitulate, in Sha'bān 489/August 1096. Suqmān, Ilghazi, and their friends were well treated by al-Afdal, who gave them

*IH buhn   ahl AH tuhr

Francesco Gabrieli, ed., *Arab Historians of the Crusades: Selected and Translated from the Arabic Sources*, ed. and trans. E. J. Costello. Islamic World Series (Berkeley: University of California Press, 1969), 10–12.

large gifts of money and let them go free. They made for Damascus and then crossed the Euphrates. Suqmān settled in Edessa and Ilghazi went on into Iraq. The Egyptian governor of Jerusalem was a certain Iftikhār ad-Daula, who was still there at the time of which we are speaking.

After their vain attempt to take Acre by siege, the Franks moved on to Jerusalem and besieged it for more than six weeks. They built two towers, one of which, near Sion, the Muslims burnt down, killing everyone inside it. It had scarcely ceased to burn before a messenger arrived to ask for help and to bring the news that the other side of the city had fallen. In fact Jerusalem was taken from the north on the morning of Friday 22 Sha'bān 492/July 15, 1099. The population was put to the sword by the Franks, who pillaged the area for a week. A band of Muslims barricaded themselves into the Oratory of David and fought on for several days. They were granted their lives in return for surrendering. The Franks honoured their word, and the group left by night for Ascalon. In the Masjid al-Aqsa the Franks slaughtered more than 70,000 people, among them a large number of Imams and Muslim scholars, devout and ascetic men who had left their homelands to live lives of pious seclusion in the Holy Place. The Franks stripped the Dome of the Rock of more than forty silver candelabra, each of them weighing 3,600 drams, and a great silver lamp weighing forty-four Syrian pounds, as well as a hundred and fifty smaller silver candelabra and more than twenty gold ones, and a great deal more booty. Refugees from Syria reached Baghdād in Ramadan, among them the qadi Abu Sa'd al-Hárawi. They told the Caliph's ministers a story that wrung their hearts and brought tears to their eyes. On Friday they went to the Cathedral Mosque and begged for help, weeping so that their hearers wept with them as they described the sufferings of the Muslims in that Holy City: the men killed, the women and children taken prisoner, the homes pillaged. Because of the terrible hardships they had suffered, they were allowed to break the fast. . . .

It was the discord between the Muslim princes, as we shall describe, that enabled the Franks to overrun the country. Abu l-Muzaffar al-Abiwardi composed several poems on this subject, in one of which he says:

> We have mingled blood with flowing tears, and there is no room left in us for pity[?]
> To shed tears is a man's worst weapon when the swords stir up the embers of war.
> Sons of Islām, behind you are battles in which heads rolled at your feet.
> Dare you slumber in the blessed shade of safety, where life is as soft as an orchard flower?

How can the eye sleep between the lids at a time of disasters that would waken any sleeper?

While your Syrian brothers can only sleep on the backs of their chargers, or in vultures' bellies!

Must the foreigners feed on our ignominy, while you trail behind you the train of a pleasant life, like men whose world is at peace?

When blood has been spilt, when sweet girls must for shame hide their lovely faces in their hands!

When the white swords' points are red with blood, and the iron of the brown lances is stained with gore!

At the sound of sword hammering on lance young children's hair turns white.

This is war, and the man who shuns the whirlpool to save his life shall grind his teeth in penitence.

This is war, and the infidel's sword is naked in his hand, ready to be sheathed again in men's necks and skulls.

This is war, and he who lies in the tomb at Medina seems to raise his voice and cry: "O sons of Hashim!

I see my people slow to raise the lance against the enemy: I see the Faith resting on feeble pillars.

For fear of death the Muslims are evading the fire of battle, refusing to believe that death will surely strike them."

Must the Arab champions then suffer with resignation, while the gallant Persians shut their eyes to their dishonour?

67

Letter from a Jewish Pilgrim in Egypt

The following letter was written in 1100 by an anonymous Jewish pilgrim from Alexandria, unable to make his pilgrimage to Jerusalem because of the ongoing war. How does the letter's author regard the Egyptian Sultan? How does he view the struggle between the Sultan and the Franks? What does this suggest about the lives of Jews under Muslim rule during this time period?

"Contemporary Letters on the Capture of Jerusalem by the Crusaders," trans. S. D. Goitein, *Journal of Jewish Studies*, vol. 3, no. 4 (London: Jewish Chronicle Publications, 1952), 162–77.

Thinking Historically

What does this letter add to your understanding of the Crusaders' capture of Jerusalem? How would you write a narrative of the First Crusade that took advantage of Christian, Muslim, and Jewish sources?

In Your name, You Merciful.

If I attempted to describe my longing for you, my Lord, my brother *and cousin,*—may God prolong your days and make permanent your honour, success, happiness, health, and welfare; and . . . subdue your enemies—all the paper in the world would not suffice. My longing will but increase and double, just as the days will grow and double. May *the Creator of the World* presently make us meet together in joy when I return under His guidance to my homeland *and to the inheritance of my Fathers* in complete happiness, *so that we rejoice and be happy through His great mercy and His vast bounty; and thus may be His will*!

You may remember, my Lord, that many years ago I left our country to seek God's mercy and help in my poverty, to behold Jerusalem and return thereupon. However, when I was in Alexandria God brought about circumstances which caused a slight delay. Afterwards, however, "the sea grew stormy," and many armed bands made their appearance in Palestine; "*and he who went forth and he who came had no peace,*" so that hardly one survivor out of a whole group came back to us from Palestine and told us that scarcely anyone could save himself from those armed bands, since they were so numerous and were gathered round . . . every town. There was further the journey through the desert, among [the bedouins] and whoever escaped from the one, fell into the hands of the other. Moreover, mutinies [spread throughout the country and reached] even Alexandria, so that we ourselves were besieged several times and the city was ruined; . . . the end however *was good*, for the Sultan—may God bestow glory upon his victories—conquered the city and caused justice to abound in it in a manner unprecedented in the history of any king in the world; not even a dirham was looted from anyone. Thus I had come to hope that because of his justice and strength God would give the land into his hands, and I should thereupon go to Jerusalem in safety and tranquility. For this reason I proceeded from Alexandria to Cairo, in order to start [my journey] from there.

When, however, God had given Jerusalem, the blessed, into his hands this state of affairs continued for too short a time to allow for making a journey there. The Franks arrived and killed everybody in the city, whether of *Ishmael or of Israel*; and the few who survived the slaughter were made prisoners. Some of these have been ransomed since, while others are still in captivity in all parts of the world.

Now, all of us had anticipated that our Sultan—may God bestow glory upon his victories—would set out against them [the Franks] with his troops and chase them away. But time after time our hope failed. Yet, to this very present moment we do hope that God will give his [the Sultan's] enemies into his hands. For it is inevitable that the armies will join in battle this year; and, if God grants us victory through him [the Sultan] and he conquers Jerusalem—and so it may be, with God's will—I for one shall not be amongst those who will linger, but shall go there to behold the city; and shall afterwards return straight to you—if God wills it. My salvation is in God, for this [is unlike] the other previous occasions [of making a pilgrimage to Jerusalem]. God, indeed, will exonerate me, since at my age I cannot afford to delay and wait any longer; I want to return home under any circumstances, if I still remain alive—whether I shall have seen Jerusalem or have given up the hope of doing it—both of which are possible.

You know, of course, my Lord, what has happened to us in the course of the last five years: the plague, the illnesses, and ailments have continued unabated for four successive years. As a result of this the wealthy became impoverished and a great number of people died *of the plague*, so that entire families perished in it. I, too, was affected with a grave illness, from which I recovered only about a year ago; then I was taken ill the following year so that (on the margin) for four years I have remained. . . . He who has said: *The evil diseases of Egypt* . . . he who hiccups does not live . . . ailments and will die . . . otherwise . . . will remain alive.

REFLECTIONS

The First Crusade (1095–1099) only marks the beginning of a protracted conflict between Christians and Muslims that continued until, perhaps, the eighteenth century. In the Holy Land there were crusades intermittently over the next forty years culminating in what was called the Second Crusade from 1147–1149. Meanwhile, the conquest of Muslims in Spain, which had been equated with the crusade by Pope Urban II, continued, as did frequent crusades into Eastern Europe.

The establishment of Latin kingdoms in Palestine could not be maintained without continual reinforcements, and they were vulnerable to Muslim attack. In 1187 Saladin reconquered most of Palestine, including Jerusalem, for the Muslims, a trauma for the Christians that led to the Third Crusade (1189–1192) and German Crusade

(1197–1198) by which Christians retook settlements on the coast. Popular enthusiasm continued in the Children's Crusade (1212) and the Crusade of the Shepherds (1251). The armies of the Fourth Crusade (1202–1204) were diverted to Constantinople, which they sacked in 1204. A Fifth Crusade (1217–1229) recovered Jerusalem, which was retaken by the Muslims in 1244, leading to crusades initiated by King Louis IX of France. Other crusading armies invaded Egypt, Tunisia, Muslim Spain, northwest Africa, southern France, Poland, Latvia, Germany, Russia, the Mongol Empire, Finland, Bosnia, and Italy, against papal enemies and Eastern Orthodox Christians as well as Muslims. Recent histories of the Crusades have ended their narratives in 1521, 1560, 1588, and 1798, according to Jonathan Riley-Smith who ends the recent *Oxford History of the Crusades* with images of the crusades in twentieth-century wars. Does the imagery of the Crusades still animate our wars?

While Americans, like President George W. Bush, learned the effects of using the term *crusade* in the context of American aspirations in the Middle East, the interference of Western forces in the region is a constant reminder to Muslims of a long history of Western intervention that began with the First Crusade. In Syria, Lebanon, Jordan, Palestine, and Israel one can still see crusader castles looming over the landscape and meet the descendants and coreligionists of the founders of Crusader states. From the perspective of many Muslims, unquestioned U.S. support of Israel, especially in Jerusalem, is a direct continuation of the Crusades. On more than one occasion, leaders of Middle Eastern countries have pictured themselves as a modern-day Saladin, the twelfth-century Kurdish Muslim warrior from Tikrit, Iraq, who retook Jerusalem in 1187, eighty-eight years after the events described by Raymond of St. Giles and Ibn al-Athir.

Writing a narrative of the First Crusade is difficult enough given the many sides to the conflict. Anna Comnena and the orthodox Christians of Byzantium had a very different perspective than the Franks or Roman Christian Crusaders of Western Europe. Nor were Muslims a single force of opposition. The Seljuk Turks had different interests than the Caliph of Baghdad, and, contrary to the opinion of Raymond St. Giles, the Fatimid Egyptian forces at Ascalon were neither Biblical Babylonians nor Abbasids from Baghdad. Then too there were Jews, and those in Germany may have had different interests from those in Egypt, despite an agreement about Christian crusading. Still, there are more sources than we have been able to explore here, and more interpretations than we have been able to include.

After trying your hand at writing a narrative of the First Crusade, you might think of how narratives are constructed. Each story leaves out some information to include other information, lest it read like a phone book. How do you decide whose "numbers" to include? To stimulate your thoughts about narrative choices, you might choose a subject a little closer to home where you have greater knowledge of the primary sources. Try a narrative of your own life up to now. If you dare, ask someone close to you to point out what you missed or over-emphasized.

11

Raiders of Steppe and Sea: Vikings and Mongols

Eurasia and the Atlantic, 750–1350 C.E.

HISTORICAL CONTEXT

Ever since the first urban settlements emerged five thousand years ago, they have been at risk of attack. The domestication of the horse and the development of sailing ships about four thousand years ago increased that risk. Much of ancient history is the story of the conflict between settled peoples and raiders on horseback or sailors on fleet ships. Eventually — between the third and fifth centuries C.E. — the great empires of Rome and Han dynasty China succumbed to raiding nomadic tribes from central Asia. As nomadic peoples settled themselves, new waves of raiders appeared.

In the previous chapter, we explored the impact of the Seljuk Turks who conquered cities in the Middle East that had been taken hundreds of years earlier by Arab armies on horseback. At about the same time as the Turks emerged from central Asia to threaten settlements south of the great Eurasian steppe grasslands, a new force from the north, Viking raiders on sailing ships, burst across the northern seas to attack the coastal enclaves and river cities of Europe and what came to be known in their wake as Russia. As generations oscillated between raiding and trading, new waves of Norsemen explored the edges of known waters to plant new settlements as far west as Iceland, Greenland, and North America. (See Map 11.1.) Who were these people? What did they hope to accomplish? How were they different from the land-raiders who preceded them?

At about the time that the Vikings were becoming farmers and grandfathers, around the year 1200, the Eurasian steppe exploded with its last and largest force of nomadic tribesmen on horseback: the

Map 11.1 Viking Invasions and Voyages of the Ninth and Tenth Centuries.

Mongols. Between the election of Chingis [or Genghis] Khan* (c. 1162–1227) as the Khan of Khans in 1206 and the Black Death of 1350 (or the end of the Mongol Yuan dynasty in China in 1368), the Mongols swept across Eurasia and created the largest empire the world had ever seen. (See Map 11.2.) Who were the Mongols? What made them so successful? How were they similar to, and different from, the Norsemen?

What was the impact of these raiding peoples on settled societies? How did they change each other? How did they change themselves? How did they create some of the conditions necessary for the modern world to come into being?

THINKING HISTORICALLY
Distinguishing Historical Understanding from Moral Judgments

The ancient Greeks called non-Greeks "barbarians" (because their languages contained "bar-bar"-like sounds that seemed foreign, untutored, and, thus, uncivilized). Since then the terms *barbarian* and *civilized* have been weighted with the same combination of descriptive and moral meaning. In the nineteenth century it was even fashionable among historians and anthropologists to distinguish between nomadic peoples and settled, urban peoples with the terms *barbarian* and *civilized*. As our first reading (and perhaps modern common sense) makes clear, rural or nomadic people are not necessarily less "moral" than city people; technological development is hardly the same thing as moral development (or the opposite).

What connection, if any, is there between history and morality? Stories of the past are frequently used to celebrate or condemn past individuals or groups. Sometimes we find past behavior shocking or reprehensible. Is it logical or proper to make moral judgments about the past? Can historians find answers to moral questions by studying the past?

Perhaps the place to begin is by recognizing that just as the "is" is different from the "ought," so too the "was" is different from the "should have been." Historians must begin by finding out what was. Our own moral values may lead us to ask certain questions about the past, but the historian's job is only to find out what happened. We will see in the following selections how difficult it has been for past observers to keep their own moral judgments from coloring their

*chihn GIHZ kahn

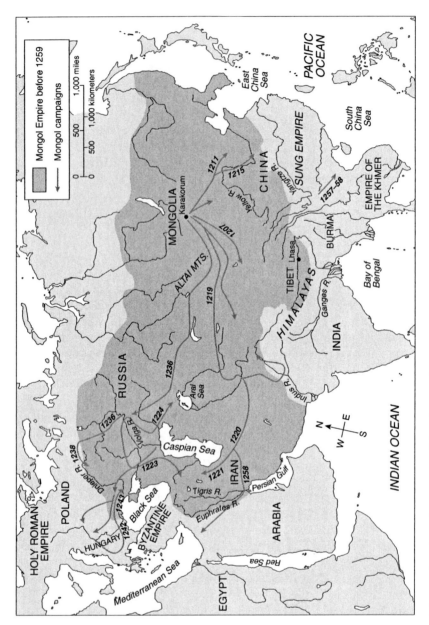

Map 11.2   Mongol Invasions of the Thirteenth Century.

descriptions of peoples and events they found disagreeable. This part of our study may help us realize how our own moral feelings affect our responses.

Then, assuming we have established the facts fairly, can our moral sentiments legitimately come into play? As "consumers" of history, readers, and thinking people, we cannot avoid making judgments about the past. Under what conditions are such judgments fair, helpful, or appropriate? We will explore this much larger and more complex question in this chapter.

68

GREGORY GUZMAN

Were the Barbarians
a Negative or Positive Factor
in Ancient and Medieval History?

Gregory Guzman is a modern world historian. In this essay he asks some questions about the peoples who have been called "barbarians." How were the lives of pastoral nomads different from those of settled people? How did the horse shape life on the steppe? How effective were these herders as rulers of settled societies? What were the achievements of the pastoral nomads?

Thinking Historically

Why, according to Guzman, have most histories of the barbarians made them look bad? How have city people or historians let their own prejudices block an appreciation of the achievements of pastoralists?

According to the general surveys of ancient and medieval history found in most textbooks, barbarian peoples and/or primitive savages repeatedly invaded the early Eurasian civilized centers in Europe, the Middle East, India, and China. All accounts of the early history of these four

Gregory Guzman, "Were the Barbarians a Negative or Positive Factor in Ancient and Medieval History?" *The Historian* L (August 1988): 558–72.

civilizations contain recurrent references to attacks by such familiar and famous barbarians as the Hittites, Hyksos, Kassites, Aryans, Scythians, Sarmatians, Hsiung-nu, Huns, Germans, Turks, and Mongols, and they also record the absorption and assimilation of these Inner Asian barbarian hordes into the respective cultures and lifestyles of the more advanced coastal civilizations. The early sources generally equate the barbarians with chaos and destruction. The barbarians are presented as evil and despicable intruders, associated only with burning, pillaging, and slaughtering, while the civilized peoples are portrayed as the good and righteous forces of stability, order, and progress.

But it must be remembered that most of these early sources are not objective; they are blatantly one-sided, biased accounts written by members of the civilized societies. Thus, throughout recorded history, barbarians have consistently received bad press — bad PR to use the modern terminology. By definition, barbarians were illiterate, and thus they could not write their own version of events. All written records covering barbarian-civilized interaction came from the civilized peoples at war with the barbarians — often the sedentary peoples recently defeated and overwhelmed by those same barbarians. Irritated and angered coastal historians tended to record and emphasize only the negative aspects of their recent interaction with the barbarians. These authors tended to condemn and denigrate the way their barbarian opponents looked and to associate them with the devil and evil, rather than to report with objectivity what actually happened. For example, the Roman historian Ammianus Marcellinus, whose description is distorted by hatred and fear, described the barbarians as "two-footed beasts, seemingly chained to their horses from which they take their meat and drink, never touching a plough and having no houses." While living in Jerusalem, St. Jerome also left a vivid description of the Huns who ". . . filled the whole earth with slaughter and panic alike as they flittered hither and thither on their swift horses. . . . They were at hand everywhere before they were expected; by their speed they outstripped rumor, and they took pity neither upon religion nor rank nor age nor wailing childhood. Those who had just begun to live were compelled to die. . . ."

Such reports obviously made the barbarians look bad, while their nomadic habits and practices, which differed from those of the sedentary coastal peoples, were clearly portrayed as inferior and less advanced: the incarnation of evil itself. These horror-filled and biased descriptions were not the accounts of weak and defenseless peoples. Rather, they were written by the citizens of the most advanced and powerful states and empires in Europe, the Middle East, India, and China. The individual barbarian tribes were, nevertheless, able to attack and invade these strong and well-organized civilized states with relative impunity — pillaging and killing almost at will.

Several important questions, not addressed by the ancient and medieval historians, need to be answered here. Who were these barbarians?

Why and how did they manage to repeatedly defeat and overwhelm so easily the wealthiest and most advanced civilizations of the day? And why were they so vehemently condemned and hated in recorded history, if these barbarian Davids were able to consistently defeat such mighty Goliath civilized centers? Since the rich and populous civilized states enjoyed tremendous advantages in the confrontations, why have the barbarians so often been denied the popular role of the underdog?

In the process of answering those questions, this study would like to suggest that maybe the barbarians were not really the "bad guys." While they may not deserve to be called the "good guys," they made a much more positive contribution to human civilization than presented in the grossly distorted written sources. The barbarians deserve much more credit than they have been given, for they created a complex pastoral lifestyle as an alternative to sedentary agriculture, and in that achievement they were not subhuman savages only out to loot, pillage, and destroy. As this study will show, the barbarians played a much more positive and constructive role in the development and diffusion of early human history than that with which they are usually credited.

Before proceeding further, it is necessary to identify these much-maligned barbarians and describe how their way of life and their basic practices differed from those of the sedentary coastal peoples in order to better evaluate the barbarian role and its impact on the history of humanity.

In terms of identity, the barbarians were the steppe nomads of Inner Asia or Central Eurasia. This area represents one of the toughest and most inhospitable places in the world in which to survive. The climate of the interior of the large Eurasian landmass is not moderated by the distant seas, resulting in extremes of climate, of hot and cold, wet and dry. It is an area of ice, forest, desert, and mountains — with bitter winds, dust, and poor soil. Unlike the coastal regions with their dependable moisture and warmth, the soil of Inner Asia was too cold, poor, and dry for agriculture; thus the sedentary urban lifestyle of the coastal civilized centers was not an option in the Eurasian heartland. The people living there had to be tough to endure such a hostile environment, where they constantly fought both nature and other people for survival.

Due to necessity, the people of Inner Asia were nomads, wandering in search of food and pasture, and they became herdsmen, shepherds, and warriors. These steppe nomads, the barbarians of recorded history, were frequently nothing more than migrants looking for new homes; these people needed little encouragement to seek safety, security, and better living conditions in the warm, rich, and fertile coastal civilization centers. Thus the steppe barbarians were not always savage marauders coming only to loot and pillage. Many of the so-called barbarian invaders constituted a surplus population which harsh Inner Asia could not support, or they represented whole tribes being pushed out of their ancestral homeland by stronger tribes behind them. At any rate, these repeated waves of nomadic peoples leaving the steppes soon encountered the coastal civilizations.

These Inner Asian barbarians were more or less harmless outsiders until the horse dramatically changed their lifestyle on the vast steppes. They adopted the pastoral system as the best way of providing for basic needs. The natural pasture provided by the steppe grassland proved ideal for grazing large herds and flocks of animals. Soon their whole life revolved around their animals; they became shepherds, herders, and keepers of beasts. . . .

The dominant feature of this emerging barbarian pastoralism was its mounted nature; it was essentially a horse culture by 1000 B.C. At first small horses were kept only for food and milk, but bigger horses eventually led to riding. Once an accomplished fact, mounted practices dramatically changed the lifestyle of the barbarian steppe peoples. Horseback riding made the tending of scattered herds faster and less tiring, and it enlarged the size of herds while increasing the range of pastoral movement. It also made possible, when necessary, the total migration of entire tribes and clans. Mastery of the horse reduced the vast expanses of steppe pasturage to more manageable proportions. Steppe nomads moved twice a year between traditional winter and summer pastures; the spring and fall were spent moving between the necessary grazing grounds. All peoples and possessions moved with regularity; the nomads became used to living in the saddle, so to speak.

The horse thus became the center of pastoral life on the steppes. The barbarian nomads could literally live off their animals which provided meat, milk, and hides for clothing, coverings, boots, etc. Tools and weapons were made from the bones and sinews, and dried dung was used as fuel. The barbarians ate, sold, negotiated, slept, and took care of body functions in the saddle as indicated in the following quotations: "From their horses, by day and night every one of that nation buys and sells, eats and drinks, and bowed over the narrow neck of the animal relaxes in a sleep so deep as to be accompanied by many dreams." "All the time they let themselves be carried by their horses. In that way they fight wars, participate in banquets, attend public and private business. On their back, they move, stand still, carry on trade, and converse." These mounted practices led to the emergence of the centaur motif in Middle Eastern art, as the civilized people tended to view the horse and rider as one inseparable unit.

Military action also became an integral part of nomadic steppe life. Warfare was simply cavalry action by the pastoral herdsmen who served as soldiers for the duration of the conflict. Steppe military service differed little from the normal, on-the-move pastoral life. Large-scale steppe alliances were hard to organize and even harder to hold together among the independent nomads. Such temporary alliances, called hordes, rose swiftly to great strength and power, but they usually declined and disintegrated just as quickly.

At any rate, these barbarian nomads were tough and hardy warriors. The horse gave them speed and mobility over both the light and heavily armed infantry of the civilized centers, but for this speed and mobility the barbarians gave up any type of defensive armor. They learned to guide their horses with their knees, since both arms needed to be free for the bow and arrow, their primary offensive weapon. By 1000 B.C. the compound bow was in common use by barbarians. This shorter bow could be handled with ease from horseback, and arrows could be shot up to three hundred yards with accuracy. As steppe hunters, all barbarians made excellent archers.

Early civilized armies had no cavalry. The famous Macedonian phalanx and the formidable Roman legions contained only light and heavily armed infantry. At first these brave foot soldiers had no tactical maneuvers to face and contain a barbarian cavalry charge. Even more devastating was the storm of arrows raining down upon them long before they could engage in the traditional hand-to-hand combat. The formidable steppe cavalry thus subjected civilized defenses to continuous pressure. Every nomad with a horse and bow was a potential frontline soldier who was tough, resourceful, and ferocious, whereas only a small percentage of the civilized population was equipped and trained for war. The nomadic lifestyle and the speed of the horse eliminated the need for expensive and heavy metal armor and its accompanying technological skills. Cavalry tactics gave an initial military advantage to the barbarians and the mounted horsemen won most of the early battles. The best defense against barbarian cavalry was an insurmountable obstacle, a wall. Ten- to twenty-foot-high walls of dirt, wood, or stone were built around cities and along some frontiers, i.e., the Great Wall of China. The old statement that Rome fell because China built a wall may not be such a simple overstatement after all.

Since they had the military advantage of cavalry tactics, the steppe nomads attacked and conquered various coastal civilizations with regularity. In a typical conquest, the victorious barbarians were the new military/political rulers. These new rulers possessed strengths obvious to all. The barbarians had vigorous and dynamic leadership; good, able, and charismatic leadership had been needed to organize the independent nomads into an effective horde in the first place. The new rulers had the complete loyalty of their followers; their group identity based on common blood and ancestors resulted in an intense personal and individual allegiance and commitment.

The first century after the initial conquest was usually an era of dynamic leadership, good government, and economic prosperity, as nomadic strengths mixed with the local advances and practices of that civilization. The new ruling family was often a fusion of the best of both sides as the barbarian victors married into the previous ruling dynasty. This brought forth an age of powerful and successful rulers, and produced an era of energetic leadership, good government, low taxes, agricultural revival, and peace. . . .

After this early period of revitalized and dynamic rule, slow decline usually set in. Royal vigor and ability sank as the rulers became soft, both mentally and physically. Without physical exercise and self-discipline, the rulers became overindulgent, instantly acquiring everything they wanted — excessive amounts of food or drink, harems, puppets, and yes-men as advisers. At the same time court rivalries and internal divisiveness began to emerge once the strong unity required for the conquest was no longer needed. A rivalry that often arose was between the ruler and various groups of his followers — his military, his bureaucracy, his harem (especially the queen mothers), his conquered subjects, and his old nomadic supporters. His steppe horsemen began to give first loyalty to their new family land rather than to their individual leader who was now weak, impaired, and soft. Such internal rivalries weakened the central government and led to chaos and civil wars. Thus, a civilized center was ripe for the next series of invasions and conquest by the next group of unified, tough, and well-led barbarians who would, in turn, be assimilated and absorbed in this process of ongoing revitalization of stagnant civilizations.

Despite the usual negative view and definition of barbarians provided by the sedentary civilized peoples, the steppe nomads had developed a complex pastoral and nomadic society. They were tough and hardy horsemen whose cavalry tactics gave them the military advantage for several centuries. The barbarians used this advantage, and their periodic attacks on civilization centers caused destruction, sometimes severe destruction. But the barbarian role in mankind's history was not always negative. The barbarians can and should be viewed as representing a dynamic and vital element in human history for they periodically revived many stagnating coastal civilizations. Many of these sedentary centers flourished, growing rich and powerful. In the process they also became conservative, settled into a fixed routine. Preferring the status quo, they tended to use old answers and ways to face new problems and issues, and as a consequence they lost the vitality and flexibility required for healthy and progressive growth.

The barbarians were active and dynamic. In their conquests of civilized centers, they frequently destroyed and eliminated the old and outdated and preserved and passed on only the good and useful elements. Sometimes, the mounted invaders also introduced new ideas and practices. Some of these new barbarian innovations (horseback riding, archery, trousers, and boots, etc.) fused with the good and useful practices of the sedentary peoples. Old and new practices and processes merged, and provided viable alternatives to the old, outdated civilized ways which had failed or outlived their usefulness. This fusion brought forth dynamic creativity and development. The ongoing encounters with barbarian strangers inevitably fostered innovation and progress in the civilized centers — due to their need to adjust in order to survive. . . .

It can be argued that barbarians also played a positive role in the spread and diffusion of civilization itself. The four major Eurasian civilization centers were separated from each other by deserts, mountains, and the vast expanses of the steppe heartland of Inner Asia. In its early stages each civilization was somewhat isolated from the others. Overland trade and contact was possible only through the barbarian steppe highway which stretched over five thousand miles across Eurasia, from Hungary to Manchuria. There was little early sea contact between the four sedentary centers, as naval travel was longer and more dangerous than the overland routes.

Thus the steppe barbarians were the chief agency through which the ideas and practices of one civilization were spread to another before 1500 A.D. According to [historian] William H. McNeill, there was much conceptual diffusion carried along the steppe highway by the barbarians. Writing originated in the ancient Middle East. The concept, not the form, of writing then spread eastward from the Middle East, as the Indian and Chinese forms and characters were significantly different than Middle Eastern cuneiform. The making and use of bronze and chariots also spread from the Middle East to Europe, India, and China. Chariots were introduced to China, on the eastern end of the steppe highway, a few centuries after their appearance in the Middle East. Needless to say, this type of early cultural diffusion is difficult to document with any degree of certainty, but enough evidence exists to make it highly probable, even if not scientifically provable.

The late medieval period provides even more examples of cultural diffusion via the movement of barbarians along the Inner Asian steppe highway. The great Eurasian *Pax Mongolica* opened the way for much cultural cross-fertilization in the late-thirteenth and early-fourteenth centuries. Chinese inventions like gunpowder and printing made their way to the Middle East and Europe in this period. Records show that Chinese artillerymen accompanied the Mongol armies into the Middle East. Papal envoys like John of Plano Carpini and William of Rubruck traveled to the Mongol capital of Karakorum in the 1240s and 1250s. In the 1280s, Marco Polo brought with him from Kublai Khan's court in China a Mongol princess to be the bride of the Mongol Khan of Persia. . . .

This cultural interaction and exchange between Eurasian coastal civilizations ended with the collapse of the Mongol Khanates in Persia and China in the mid-fourteenth century. The barbarian Mongols, therefore, provided the last period of great cultural cross-fertilization before the modern age.

Historical evidence that exists enables one to argue that the barbarian nomads played an active and positive role in the history of mankind. The barbarian invaders revitalized stagnant and decaying civilizations and were responsible for a certain amount of cultural diffusion between emerging ancient and medieval civilizations. The traditional portrayal of barbarians as mere marauders and destroyers is misleading and incorrect. Unfortunately this is the usual role they are given when historians center their study of the past narrowly on the civilized centers and the biased written sources produced by those peoples. All too often historians tend to adopt and reflect the biases and values of their subjects under study, and thus continue to denigrate and condemn all barbarians without objectively evaluating their real contributions to human development. The study of the steppe nomads, the barbarians, is just as valid a topic for historical analysis as the traditional study of coastal sedentary civilizations. Only by knowing and understanding the pastoral barbarian can historians accurately evaluate the constant interaction between the two lifestyles and come to understand the full picture of humanity's early growth and development in the ancient and medieval periods of Eurasian history.

69

IBN FADLAN

The Viking Rus

In 921 C.E. the Muslim caliph of Baghdad sent Ibn Fadlan* on a mission to the King of the Bulgars.[1] The Muslim king of the Bulgars may have been looking for an alliance with the caliph of Baghdad against the Khazars, sandwiched between them, just west of the Caspian Sea. North and west of the Bulgars was the area that became Ukraine and Russia. The Volga River, which had its source in the Ural Mountains,

---

*IH buhn   fahd LAHN

[1]These Bulgars, with a Muslim king, had recently been forced north of the Caspian Sea (while other Bulgars moved west to what is today Bulgaria where they were converted to Christianity by Byzantium).

Albert Stanburrough Cook, "Ibn Fadlan's Account of Scandinavian Merchants on the Volga in 922," in *Journal of English and Germanic Philology*, vol. 22, no. 1 (1923): 56–63.

flowed north through this land into the Baltic Sea. In the eighth and ninth centuries this area was inhabited by various tribes, many of which spoke early Slavic languages. At some point these tribes were united under the command of a people called the Rus. The origins of the Rus are disputed, but most experts believe that they were either Vikings or the descendants of Vikings and Slavs.

Ibn Fadlan provides our earliest description of these Rus (or Northmen, as he calls them here), whom he encountered on the Volga near the modern city of Kazan' during his trip to the Bulgar king. (See Map 11.1 on page 376 for his route.) They or their ancestors had sailed downriver from the Baltic Sea on raiding and trading expeditions. What does Ibn Fadlan tell us about these Scandinavian raiders who gave their name to Russia?

Thinking Historically

Notice Ibn Fadlan's moral judgments about the Viking Rus. Notice your own moral judgments. How are Ibn Fadlan's judgments different from your own? What do you think accounts for those differences?

I saw how the Northmen had arrived with their wares, and pitched their camp beside the Volga. Never did I see people so gigantic; they are tall as palm trees, and florid and ruddy of complexion. They wear neither camisoles nor *chaftans*, but the men among them wear a garment of rough cloth, which is thrown over one side, so that one hand remains free. Every one carries an axe, a dagger, and a sword, and without these weapons they are never seen. Their swords are broad, with wavy lines, and of Frankish make. From the tip of the finger-nails to the neck, each man of them is tattooed with pictures of trees, living beings, and other things. The women carry, fastened to their breast, a little case of iron, copper, silver, or gold, according to the wealth and resources, of their husbands. Fastened to the case they wear a ring, and upon that a dagger, all attached to their breast. About their necks they wear gold and silver chains. If the husband possesses ten thousand dirhems, he has one chain made for his wife; if twenty thousand, two; and for every ten thousand, one is added. Hence it often happens that a Scandinavian woman has a large number of chains about her neck. Their most highly prized ornaments consist of small green shells, of one of the varieties which are found in [the bottoms of] ships. They make great efforts to obtain these, paying as much as a dirhem for such a shell, and stringing them as a necklace for their wives.

They are the filthiest race that God ever created. They do not wipe themselves after going to stool, nor wash themselves after a nocturnal pollution, any more than if they were wild asses.

They come from their own country, anchor their ships in the Volga, which is a great river, and build large wooden houses on its banks. In every such house there live ten or twenty, more or fewer. Each man has a couch, where he sits with the beautiful girls he has for sale. Here he is as likely as not to enjoy one of them while a friend looks on. At times several of them will be thus engaged at the same moment, each in full view of the others. Now and again a merchant will resort to a house to purchase a girl, and find her master thus embracing her, and not giving over until he has fully had his will.

Every morning a girl comes and brings a tub of water, and places it before her master. In this he proceeds to wash his face and hands, and then his hair, combing it out over the vessel. Thereupon he blows his nose, and spits into the tub, and, leaving no dirt behind, conveys it all into this water. When he has finished, the girl carries the tub to the man next [to] him, who does the same. Thus she continues carrying the tub from one to another till each of those who are in the house has blown his nose and spit into the tub, and washed his face and hair.

As soon as their ships have reached the anchorage, every one goes ashore, having at hand bread, meat, onions, milk, and strong drink, and betakes himself to a high, upright piece of wood, bearing the likeness of a human face; this is surrounded by smaller statues, and behind these there are still other tall pieces of wood driven into the ground. He advances to the large wooden figure, prostrates himself before it, and thus addresses it: "O my Lord, I am come from a far country, bringing with me so and so many girls, and so and so many pelts of sable" [or, marten]; and when he has thus enumerated all his merchandise, he continues, "I have brought thee this present," laying before the wooden statue what he has brought, and saying: "I desire thee to bestow upon me a purchaser who has gold and silver coins, who will buy from me to my heart's content, and who will refuse none of my demands." Having so said, he departs. If his trade then goes ill, he returns and brings a second, or even a third present. If he still continues to have difficulty in obtaining what he desires, he brings a present to one of the small statues, and implores its intercession, saying: "These are the wives and daughters of our lord." Continuing thus, he goes to each statue in turn, invokes it, beseeches its intercession, and bows humbly before it. If it then chances that his trade goes swimmingly, and he disposes of all his merchandise, he reports: "My lord has fulfilled my desire; now it is my duty to repay him." Upon this, he takes a number of cattle and sheep, slaughters them, gives a portion of the meat to the poor, and carries the rest before the large statue and the smaller ones that surround it, hanging the heads of the sheep and cattle on the large piece of wood which is planted in the earth. When night falls, dogs come and devour it all. Then he who has so placed it exclaims: "I am well pleasing to my lord; he has consumed my present."

If one of their number falls sick, they set up a tent at a distance, in which they place him, leaving bread and water at hand. Thereafter they never approach nor speak to him, nor visit him the whole time, especially if he is a poor person or a slave. If he recovers and rises from his sick bed, he returns to his own. If he dies, they cremate him; but if he is a slave they leave him as he is till at length he becomes the food of dogs and birds of prey.

If they catch a thief or a robber, they lead him to a thick and lofty tree, fasten a strong rope round him, string him up, and let him hang until he drops to pieces by the action of wind and rain.

I was told that the least of what they do for their chiefs when they die, is to consume them with fire. When I was finally informed of the death of one of their magnates, I sought to witness what befell. First they laid him in his grave — over which a roof was erected — for the space of ten days, until they had completed the cutting and sewing of his clothes. In the case of a poor man, however, they merely build for him a boat, in which they place him, and consume it with fire. At the death of a rich man, they bring together his goods, and divide them into three parts. The first of these is for his family; the second is expended for the garments they make; and with the third they purchase strong drink, against the day when the girl resigns herself to death, and is burned with her master. To the use of wine they abandon themselves in mad fashion, drinking it day and night; and not seldom does one die with the cup in his hand.

When one of their chiefs dies, his family asks his girls and pages: "Which one of you will die with him?" Then one of them answers, "I." From the time that he [or she] utters this word, he is no longer free: should he wish to draw back, he is not permitted. For the most part, however, it is the girls that offer themselves. So, when the man of whom I spoke had died, they asked his girls, "Who will die with him?" One of them answered, "I." She was then committed to two girls, who were to keep watch over her, accompany her wherever she went, and even, on occasion, wash her feet. The people now began to occupy themselves with the dead man — to cut out the clothes for him, and to prepare whatever else was needful. During the whole of this period, the girl gave herself over to drinking and singing, and was cheerful and gay.

When the day was now come that the dead man and the girl were to be committed to the flames, I went to the river in which his ship lay, but found that it had already been drawn ashore. Four corner-blocks of birch and other woods had been placed in position for it, while around were stationed large wooden figures in the semblance of human beings. Thereupon the ship was brought up, and placed on the timbers above mentioned. In the mean time the people began to walk to and fro, uttering words which I did not understand. The dead man, meanwhile, lay at a distance in his grave, from which they had not yet removed him. Next they brought a couch, placed it in the ship, and covered it with Greek cloth of gold, wadded and quilted, with pillows of the same material. There came an old crone, whom they call the angel of death, and spread the articles mentioned on the couch. It was she who attended to the sewing of the garments, and to all the equipment; it was she, also, who was to slay the girl. I saw her; she was dark, . . . thickset, with a lowering countenance.

When they came to the grave, they removed the earth from the wooden roof, set the latter aside, and drew out the dead man in the loose wrapper in which he had died. Then I saw that he had turned quite black, by reason of the coldness of that country. Near him in the grave they had placed strong drink, fruits, and a lute; and these they now took out. Except for his color, the dead man had not changed. They now clothed him in drawers, leggings, boots, and a *kurtak* and *chaftan* of cloth of gold, with golden buttons, placing on his head a cap made of cloth of gold, trimmed with sable! Then they carried him into a tent placed in the ship, seated him on the wadded and quilted covering, supported him with the pillows, and, bringing strong drink, fruits, and basil, placed them all beside him. Then they brought a dog, which they cut in two, and threw into the ship; laid all his weapons beside him; and led up two horses which they chased until they were dripping with sweat, whereupon they cut them in pieces with their swords, and threw the flesh into the ship. Two oxen were then brought forward, cut in pieces, and flung into the ship. Finally they brought a cock and a hen, killed them, and threw them in also.

The girl who had devoted herself to death meanwhile walked to and fro, entering one after another of the tents which they had there. The occupant of each tent lay with her, saying, "Tell your master, 'I [the man] did this only for love of you.'"

When it was now Friday afternoon, they led the girl to an object which they had constructed, and which looked like the framework of a door. She then placed her feet on the extended hands of the men, was raised up above the framework, and uttered something in her language, whereupon they let her down. Then again they raised her, and she did as at first. Once more they let her down, and then lifted her a third time, while she did as at the previous times. They then handed her a hen, whose head she cut off and threw away; but the hen itself they cast into the ship. I inquired of the interpreter what it was that she had done. He replied: "The first time she said, 'Lo, I see here my father and mother'; the second time, 'Lo, now I see all my deceased relatives sitting'; the third time, 'Lo, there is my master, who is sitting in Paradise. Paradise is so beautiful, so green. With him are his men and boys. He calls me, so bring me to him.'" Then they led her away to the ship.

Here she took off her two bracelets, and gave them to the old woman who was called the angel of death, and who was to murder her. She also drew off her two anklets, and passed them to the two serving-maids, who were the daughters of the so-called angel of death. Then they lifted her into the ship, but did not yet admit her to the tent. Now men came up with shields and staves, and handed her a cup of strong drink. This she took, sang over it, and emptied it. "With this," so the interpreter told me, "she is taking leave of those who are dear to her." Then another cup was handed her, which she also took, and began a lengthy song. The crone admonished her to drain the cup without lingering, and to enter the tent where her master lay. By this time, as it seemed to me, the girl had become dazed [or, possibly, crazed]; she made as though she would enter the tent, and had brought her head forward between the tent and the ship, when the hag seized her by the head, and dragged her in. At this moment the men began to beat upon their shields with the staves, in order to drown the noise of her outcries, which might have terrified the other girls, and deterred then from seeking death with their masters in the future. Then six men followed into the tent, and each and every one had carnal companionship with her. Then they laid her down by her master's side, while two of the men seized her by the feet and two by the hands. The old woman known as the angel of death now knotted a rope around her neck, and handed the ends to two of the men to pull. Then with a broad-bladed dagger she smote her between the ribs, and drew the blade forth while the two men strangled her with the rope till she died.

The next of kin to the dead man now drew near, and, taking a piece of wood, lighted it, and walked backwards toward the ship holding the stick in one hand, with the other placed upon his buttocks (he being naked), until the wood which had been piled under the ship was ignited. Then the others came up with staves and firewood, each one carrying a stick already lighted at the upper end, and threw it all on the pyre. The pile was soon aflame, then the ship, finally the tent, the man, and the girl, and everything else in the ship. A terrible storm began to blow up, and thus intensified the flames, and gave wings to the blaze.

At my side stood one of the Northmen, and I heard him talking with the interpreter, who stood near him. I asked the interpreter what the Northman had said, and received this answer: "'You Arabs,' he said, must be a stupid set! You take him who is to you the most revered and beloved of men, and cast him into the ground, to be devoured by creeping things and worms. We, on the other hand, burn him in a twinkling, so that he instantly, without a moment's delay, enters into Paradise.' At this he burst out into uncontrollable laughter, and then continued: 'It is the love of the Master [God] that causes the wind to blow and snatch him away in an instant.'" And, in very truth, before an hour had passed, ship, wood, and girl had with the man, turned to ashes.

Thereupon they heaped over the place where the ship had stood something like a rounded hill, and erecting on the centre of it a large birchen post, wrote on it the name of the deceased, along with that of the king of the Northmen. Having done this, they left the spot.

70

BARRY CUNLIFFE

The Western Vikings

The Vikings who sailed down the rivers of Russia to raid, trade, and settle came mainly from eastern Scandinavia — what is today Sweden and Finland. Their cousins in western Scandinavia sailed to the south and west. In this selection from a wide-ranging history of the European Atlantic world, the author, a modern archaeologist, discusses the expansion of Western Vikings — mainly Danes and Norwegians — into the Atlantic. How would you compare the expansion of the Western Vikings with that of the Eastern Vikings into what became Russia?

Thinking Historically

The modern historian lets us hear enough from the medieval victims of the Vikings for us to feel their fear, and his list of destroyed cities and massacred peoples registers the horror they must have unleashed in their era. But Cunliffe also gives us information that enables us to put the Viking attacks in some perspective. What is that information? What perspective on the Vikings does the reading give you?

The Coming of the Northmen

About 790 Beaduheard, the king's reeve at Dorchester in southern Britain, got news that three foreign ships had landed at Portland and, assuming them to be traders, he went to welcome them. He was wrong.

Barry Cunliffe, *Facing the Ocean: The Atlantic and Its Peoples* (Oxford: Oxford University Press, 2001), 482–83, 488–95, 499, 514–16.

They were raiders from Scandinavia and he died for his mistake. The Dorset landing was a foretaste. A few years later, in 793, the raiding began in earnest with the attack on the monastery of St Cuthbert on Lindisfarne: "Never before has such terror appeared in Britain as we have now suffered from a pagan race, nor was it thought that such an in-road from the sea could be made. Behold, the church of St Cuthbert spattered with the blood of the priests of God, despoiled of all its ornaments; a place more venerable than all in Britain is given as prey to pagan people." So wrote the English cleric Alcuin at the court of Charlemagne. Many more raids followed around the coasts of Britain and Ireland. The Franks were soon to suffer, so too the Bretons. By the 840s Viking war bands were exploring further south along the Atlantic coasts. A vast fleet of 150 ships sailed up the Garonne and plundered almost to Toulouse. Then it moved onwards to attack Galicia and Lisbon before sailing into the Guadalquivir. Here, from their base on the Isla Menor, the Vikings pillaged Seville but were severely mauled by the Moors. Those captured were hanged from the city's palm trees, and two hundred Viking heads were sent by the Emir to his allies in Tangier as an effective witness to his military prowess. Undeterred, the Viking force continued through the Straits of Gibraltar harassing the coasts as they sailed to the mouth of the Rhône where, on an island in the Camargue, a base was established for raiding upriver into the heart of France and across the sea to the coasts of Italy. In 861 they returned to their base on the Loire. The expedition had been "at once profitable and honourable."

The Mediterranean venture, while a notable feat, was of little lasting consequence. But meanwhile, in the north, raids and settlement had reached significant proportions. Some indication of what was going on is given by the pained lamentation of Ermentarius, a monk at Noirmoutier, writing in the 860s:

> The number of ships increases, the endless flood of Vikings never ceases to grow bigger. Everywhere Christ's people are the victims of massacre, burning, and plunder. The Vikings overrun all that lies before them, and no one can withstand them. They seize Bordeaux, Périgueux, Limoges, Angoulême, Toulouse; Angers, Tours, and Orleans are made deserts. Ships past counting voyage up the Seine . . . Rouen is laid waste, looted, and burnt; Paris, Beauvais, Meaux are taken, Melun's stronghold is razed to the ground, Chartres occupied, Evreux and Bayeux looted, and every town invested. . . .

Why the Raids of the Northmen Began

The raids of the Danes and Norwegians began in the last decade of the eighth century, and over the next seventy years rose to a devastating crescendo. No single factor was responsible for unleashing the fury, but there can be little doubt that the overseas ventures became possible only after the longship had reached its peak of excellence by the middle of the eighth century. The Scandinavian landscape demanded good shipping. The long Atlantic coastline of Norway, with its deeply indented fjords, was accessible with ease only by sea, while the sounds and islands of Denmark had, for millennia, been bound together by boat. The Baltic, too, was a cradle for navigation — a great inland sea providing ease of access between the extensive littorals and their productive hinterlands, and to the river routes penetrating far south across the North European Plain. Throughout Scandinavia settlements favoured the sea coasts and the inland lakes and waterways. They faced the open water and kept their backs to the forest. Thus communities depended upon ships for their livelihood, their rulers able to maintain their power only by command of the sea. In such a world it is easy to see how the ship became a symbol of authority, honed to perfection to reflect the status of the elite. A ship, either real or symbolic, might also accompany its owner in his burial. . . . By the early years of the ninth century, all the features characteristic of the classic Viking ship had been brought together, creating fast and highly efficient seagoing vessels suitable for carrying men across the ocean in search of land and plunder.

. . . In the course of the eighth century, trade between continental Europe and England developed apace, with well-established links leading northwards to the Baltic. In this way the volume of mercantile traffic in the southern North Sea increased dramatically, while the rulers of Denmark became increasingly aware of the wealth to be had to the south. Through the various traders who visited the Scandinavian ports they would also have learnt the political geography of western Europe — most notably the whereabouts of its rich, isolated monasteries and the distracting factional disputes endemic among its ruling households. To the Scandinavian elite there was much prestige to be had in leading a successful raid: the spoils would enrich the begetters and would bind followers closer to their leader. In the competitive emulation which accompanied the early raiding expeditions the number, intensity, and duration of the raids inevitably escalated.

Another, quite different, factor at work was the desire for new land to settle. With a growing population the narrow coastal zone of Norway was too restricted a territory to provide the social space needed for enterprising sons to establish themselves. The only solution was to find new territories overseas in Britain and Ireland, and further afield on the more remote islands of the north Atlantic. For the most part what was sought was new farmland, like the home territories, where families could set up new farms with plenty of space around for expansion by successive generations. It was this that the north Atlantic could supply in plenty. What England had to offer was rather different but no less acceptable — well-run estates which new Scandinavian lords could leave largely undisturbed, simply taking the profits.

Another incentive to moving overseas was the possibility of setting up merchant colonies emulating those that were so successful in the Baltic and along the eastern coasts of the North Sea. York, already a developing English market, was taken over by the Northmen in 866 and rapidly expanded to become the principal entrepôt in northern Britain, while an entirely new port-of-trade was established at Dublin and soon became a centre for Irish Sea commerce. In all of these ventures the ship was vital.

It would be wrong to give the impression that overseas activities were narrowly focused: trading could soon turn into raiding, while raiding could dissipate itself into settlement. One was never exclusive of the other. This is evocatively summed up in an account of the lifestyle of Svein Asleifarson recorded in the twelfth-century *Orkneyinga Saga*, no doubt referring wistfully to a long-gone era when Vikings behaved like Vikings:

> In the spring he had more than enough to occupy him, with a great deal of seed to sow which he saw to carefully himself. Then when the job was done, he would go off plundering in the Hebrides and in Ireland on what he called his "spring-trip," then back home just after midsummer where he stayed till the cornfields had been reaped and the grain was safely in. After that he would go off raiding again, and never came back till the first month of winter was ended. This he used to call his "autumn trip."

The Vikings in the West: A Brief Progress

. . . *Viking* is the word frequently used by the English sources to describe raiders and settlers from Scandinavia, while the Carolingian sources prefer *Northmen*. Both words include, without differentiation, Danes and Norwegians. Until the mid-ninth century it is possible to make a broad distinction between Norwegians, who settled northern and western Scotland and the Northern and Western Isles and were active in the Irish Sea, and Danes, who raided the North Sea and Channel coasts, but thereafter the distinction becomes blurred.

The progress of the settlement of north-western Britain by the Norwegians is unrecorded, but contact began as early as the seventh century and it is quite likely that the colonization was largely completed during the course of the eighth century. The newly settled areas provided the springboard for attacks on Ireland and the Irish Sea coasts, becoming increasingly widespread and frequent in the period 795–840.

The rich and unprotected monasteries were the target. Iona was attacked three times, in 795, 802, and 806, in the first flush of activity. Thereafter raids thrust further and further south — 821 Wexford, 822 Cork, and 824 the isolated monastery of Skelling Michael in the Atlantic off the Kerry coast. Having picked off the vulnerable coastal communities the attacks then began to penetrate inland, but usually no more than 30 kilometres or so from the safety of navigable water. These early attacks were opportunistic hit-and-run affairs, meeting no significant organized opposition.

Meanwhile in the North Sea the Danes adopted similar tactics. In 820 a massive Danish fleet of two hundred vessels threatened Saxony, and in three successive years, beginning in 834, the great trading port of Dorestad was devastated. Frisia became the immediate focus of contention. In 838 the Danish king Harik demanded of the Frankish king Louis that "The Frisians be given over to him" — a request that was roundly refused. The vulnerability of the coast was vividly brought home when, in 835, the monastery of St-Philibert on the island of Noirmoutier south of the Loire estuary was attacked. England suffered only sporadic raids at first, but these intensified in the 830s. . . .

The events of 840–865 saw the Scandinavians working the full length of the Atlantic zone from the Rhine to Gibraltar and beyond, but they were at their most active and most persistent along the major rivers — the Seine, the Thames, the Loire, and the Garonne — feeding off the cities that owed their wealth and well-being to their command of the river routes. The rivers that brought them their commercial advantage through access to the sea now brought men who sought to take it for themselves.

The 860s saw a change of pace from raid to settlement, accompanied by intensified and co-ordinated opposition by those whose land the Northmen were intent on taking. The Franks were the first to come to terms with the new reality by building fortified bridges across the rivers Seine and Loire, by fortifying towns and monasteries, and by paying tribute to groups of Vikings in return for protection or military services. These tactics protected the heart of the kingdom while leaving the lower reaches of the two rivers to the roving bands of invaders who had now taken up residence in the areas. The strategy kept Frankia free from further incursions until a new wave of attacks began on Paris in 885. . . .

Towards the end of the tenth century, with the rise of a strong dynasty in Denmark under Harald Bluetooth and his son, Sven Forkbeard, a new phase of Viking raiding was initiated, and once more it was the Atlantic coastal regions as far south as Iberia that took the brunt of the attack. England was particularly vulnerable. In 991 Sven Forkbeard led his first raid against the English, his activities culminating in the conquest of the kingdom in 1013. Three years later, after his death, his son Knut was formally recognized as king of England. Dynastic squabbles and claims and counter-claims to the English throne rumbled on throughout the eleventh century, but the failure of the threatened Danish conquest of England to materialize in 1085 was the effective end of the Viking episode. Occasional Norwegian expeditions to the Northern and Western Isles were the last ripples, three centuries after the Viking wave first struck.

The Northmen and the Atlantic Communities

That the impact of the Scandinavians on the Atlantic communities was profound and lasting there can be no doubt, but sufficient will have been said to show that it varied significantly from region to region.

In lightly inhabited or empty lands like the Northern and Western Isles, the Faroes, Iceland, and Greenland, Scandinavian culture was directly transplanted in its entirety and flourished much in the style of the Norwegian homeland, but elsewhere the Scandinavian component fused with indigenous culture. In regions where the local systems were well established and comparatively stable, as in eastern England and the maritime region of France (soon to become Normandy), the new order emerged imperceptibly from the old with little disruption to the social or economic balance, but in other areas, like Ireland, where warfare between rival factions of the elite was endemic, the Scandinavian presence was a catalyst for widespread change. Here the ferocity of the Irish warlords matched their own. For this reason the small enclaves established at harbours around the coast remained small, developing as isolated trading colonies in an otherwise hostile landscape. Apart from certain areas of the north-east, large-scale land-taking and settlement was not possible. Much the same pattern can be seen in south-west Wales.

The Scandinavian settlements of the Irish Sea zone chose good docking facilities, initially to serve as protected anchorages for the vessels of the early raiders, but these quickly developed as trading centres, making the Irish Sea the major focus of exchange in the Scandinavian maritime system. From here ships might go south to Andalucía, north to Iceland and beyond, or around Britain eastwards to the Baltic. In this way the Irish Sea became the hub of a complex network of communications built upon the long-distance exchange systems which had already been established in the preceding centuries.

In Brittany a rather different pattern of interaction emerged. Here the long-term hostility between the Bretons and the Franks provided a situation in which raiding and mercenary activity could profitably be maintained, while the internecine warfare that broke out in both kingdoms in the painful periods when succession was being contested offered the raiders further opportunities for easy intervention.

Throughout this time the Loire formed the focus of Scandinavian activity and Nantes was often in their control, but there is, as yet, little evidence that a major trading enclave developed here. It may simply have been that the political turmoil in the region allowed warfare in its various modes to provide the necessary economic underpinning to sustain Viking society. From the Breton point of view the Scandinavian presence, disruptive though it was, was an important factor in helping to maintain their independence from the Franks.

South of the Loire, Viking military activity was sporadic and superficial, at least in so far as the historical record allows us to judge, but given their interest in trade it is difficult to believe that there were not regular visits by merchants to the Gironde and Garonne and along the Atlantic seaboard of Iberia. In this they would simply have been following the routes plied by their predecessors.

Some measure of the integration of the multifaceted maritime system that emerged is provided by a wreck excavated at Skuldelev in the Danish fjord of Roskilde. It was one of six that had been sunk to block the fjord from seaward attack some time in the late eleventh or early twelfth century. The vessel was a typical Viking longship suitable for carrying fifty to sixty warriors. Dendrochronology has shown that the ship had been built about 1060 at, or in the vicinity of, Dublin. What service it saw as a raiding vessel in the seas around Britain and France we will never know, but its final resting place 2,200 kilometres from the yard in which it had been built is a vivid reminder of the capacity of the sea in bringing the communities of Atlantic Europe ever closer together.

$$\boxed{71}$$

Eirik's Saga

Scandinavian seafarers spread out in all directions in the tenth century. While Swedes and Finns sailed down the rivers of Russia to the Black and Caspian seas, Danes conquered and colonized from England down the coast of France into the Mediterranean as far as Italy, North Africa, and Arabia. The Vikings of Norway sailed mainly

---

"Eirik's Saga," in *The Vinland Sagas: The Norse Discovery of America*, trans. and introduction by Magnus Magnusson and Hermann Palsson (Harmondsworth, Middlesex, England: Penguin Books, 1965), 75–78.

westward, colonizing Iceland, Greenland, and North America (certainly Newfoundland but likely further south). The Norsemen discovered Iceland in about 860 and began settlement some fourteen years later. By 930, Iceland contained the families and retainers of many lords who fled Western Norway to escape the conquering Harald Fairhair.

Eirik the Red (950–1003) came to Iceland with his family in 960 after his father had to flee Norway because of "some killings." In turn, Eirik was exiled from Iceland in 982 after he committed murder in the heat of two quarrels. Exile meant searching for a settlement even further west, leading Eirik to Greenland. While not the first to see or land in Greenland, Eirik established the first colony there.

This excerpt from "Eirik's Saga," written about 1260, insofar as it captures the oral tradition, gives us an idea of Viking thought in the tenth century. Does this account change your idea of Viking society? How? How does it contribute to your understanding of the Viking expansion?

Thinking Historically

How does this internal view of Viking society inevitably change our moral perspective from that of an outsider? How might the religious differences between Ibn Fadlan and this author lead to different moral perspectives?

There was a warrior king called Olaf the White, who was the son of King Ingjald. Olaf went on a Viking expedition to the British Isles, where he conquered Dublin and the adjoining territory and made himself king over them. He married Aud the Deep-Minded, the daughter of Ketil Flat-Nose; they had a son called Thorstein the Red.

Olaf was killed in battle in Ireland, and Aud and Thorstein the Red then went to the Hebrides. There Thorstein married Thurid, the daughter of Eyvind the Easterner; they had many children.

Thorstein the Red became a warrior king, and joined forces with Earl Sigurd the Powerful, together they conquered Caithness, Sutherland, Ross, and Moray, and more than half of Argyll. Thorstein ruled over these territories as king until he was betrayed by the Scots and killed in battle.

Aud the Deep-Minded was in Caithness when she learned of Thorstein's death; she had a ship built secretly in a forest, and when it was ready she sailed away to Orkney. There she gave away in marriage Groa, daughter of Thorstein the Red.

After that, Aud set out for Iceland; she had twenty freeborn men aboard her ship. She reached Iceland and spent the first winter with her brother Bjorn at Bjarnarhaven. Then she took possession of the entire Dales district between Dogurdar River and Skraumuhlaups River, and made her home at Hvamm. She used to say prayers at Kross Hills; she had crosses erected there, for she had been baptized and was a devout Christian.

Many well-born men, who had been taken captive in the British Isles by Vikings and were now slaves, came to Iceland with her. One of them was called Vifil; he was of noble descent. He had been taken prisoner in the British Isles and was a slave until Aud gave him his freedom.

When Aud gave land to members of her crew, Vifil asked her why she did not give him some land like the others. Aud replied that it was of no importance, and said that he would be considered a man of quality wherever he was. She gave him Vifilsdale, and he settled there. He married, and had two sons called Thorbjorn and Thorgeir; they were both promising men, and grew up with their father.

Eirik Explores Greenland

There was a man called Thorvald, who was the father of Eirik the Red. He and Eirik left their home in Jaederen because of some killings and went to Iceland. They took possession of land in Hornstrands, and made their home at Drangar. Thorvald died there, and Eirik the Red then married Thjodhild, and moved south to Haukadale; he cleared land there and made his home at Eirikstead, near Vatnshorn.

Eirik's slaves started a landslide that destroyed the farm of a man called Valthjof, at Valthjofstead; so Eyjolf Saur, one of Valthjof's kinsmen, killed the slaves at Skeidsbrekkur, above Vatnshorn. For this, Eirik killed Eyjolf Saur; he also killed Hrafn the Dueller, at Leikskalar. Geirstein and Odd of Jorvi, who were Eyjolf's kinsmen, took action over his killing, and Eirik was banished from Haukadale.

Eirik then took possession of Brok Island and Oxen Island, and spent the first winter at Tradir, in South Island. He lent his bench-boards to Thorgest of Breidabolstead. After that, Eirik moved to Oxen Island, and made his home at Eirikstead. He then asked for his bench-boards back, but they were not returned; so Eirik went to Breidabolstead and seized them. Thorgest pursued him, and they fought a battle near the farmstead at Drangar. Two of Thorgest's sons and several other men were killed there.

After this, both Eirik and Thorgest maintained a force of fighting-men at home. Eirik was supported by Styr Thorgrimsson, Eyjolf of Svin Island, Thorbjorn Vifilsson, and the sons of Thorbrand of Alptafjord;

Thorgest was supported by Thorgeir of Hitardale, Aslak of Langadale and his son Illugi, and the sons of Thord Gellir.

Eirik and his men were sentenced to outlawry at the Thorsness Assembly. He made his ship ready in Eiriksbay, and Eyjolf of Svin Island hid him in Dimunarbay while Thorgest and his men were scouring the islands for him.

Thorbjorn Vifilsson and Styr and Eyjolf accompanied Eirik out beyond the islands, and they parted in great friendship; Eirik said he would return their help as far as it lay within his power, if ever they had need of it. He told them he was going to search for the land that Gunnbjorn, the son of Ulf Crow, had sighted when he was driven westwards off course and discovered the Gunnbjarnar Skerries; he added that he would come back to visit his friends if he found this country.

Eirik put out to sea past Snæfells Glacier, and made land near the glacier that is known as Blaserk. From there he sailed south to find out if the country were habitable there. He spent the first winter on Eiriks Island, which lies near the middle of the Eastern Settlement. In the spring he went to Eiriksfjord, where he decided to make his home. That summer he explored the wilderness to the west and gave names to many landmarks there. He spent the second winter on Eiriks Holms, off Hvarfs Peak. The third summer he sailed all the way north to Snæfell and into Hrafnsfjord, where he reckoned he was farther inland than the head of Eiriksfjord. Then he turned back and spent the third winter on Eiriks Island, off the mouth of Eiriksfjord.

He sailed back to Iceland the following summer and put in at Breidafjord. He stayed the winter with Ingolf of Holmlatur. In the spring he fought a battle with Thorgest of Breidabolstead and was defeated. After that a reconciliation was arranged between them.

That summer Eirik set off to colonize the country he had discovered; he named it *Greenland*, for he said that people would be much more tempted to go there if it had an attractive name.

72

The Poetic Edda, Selections from the Havamol

The Poetic Edda constitutes a collection of poems, songs, stories, and proverbs from the rich body of Nordic mythology. In addition to the Edda, there are the Sagas — the historic stories like selection 71 and the epic tales of gods, giants, heroes, and the end of the world. Much of the Sagas have enriched the imaginations of generations from the operas of Richard Wagner to *The Lord of the Rings*. The Edda are shorter and less well known, but more immediately accessible than the grand stories. The Havamol is the part of *The Poetic Edda* that contains an abundance of practical guidance and moral lessons. These poems were part of an oral tradition in northern Europe for centuries before they were written down about the eleventh century. This version was translated from an Icelandic poetic Edda of the thirteenth century. What do these brief poems tell you about the culture and life of the people who told and wrote them?

Thinking Historically

Of all Norse, Viking, or Icelandic literature, the poems of the Havamol most directly express moral values. What do they tell you about the moral values of their authors? The Havamol has sometimes been compared to other books of wisdom literature, including the book of Proverbs in the Hebrew Bible. No single book can represent the ideas of an entire people throughout time and space. However, to the extent that these selections can stand for the ideas of the Vikings, how would you characterize their ideas of morality? What if any of these values do you see reflected in the behavior of the people described by Ibn Fadlan? How were the Vikings different from the barbarians who toppled the Roman and Han empires in the third to sixth centuries?

The Poetic Edda, trans. from the Icelandic with an introduction and notes by Henry Adams Bellows (Princeton, N.J.: Princeton University Press, 1936). Scanned at sacred-texts.com, April–July 2001, available online at http://www.sacred-texts.com/neu/poe/poe04.htm.

1. Within the gates | ere a man shall go,
(Full warily let him watch,)
Full long let him look about him;
For little he knows | where a foe may lurk,
And sit in the seats within.

3. Fire he needs | who with frozen knees
Has come from the cold without;
Food and clothes | must the farer have,
The man from the mountains come.

4. Water and towels | and welcoming speech
Should he find who comes, to the feast;
If renown he would get, | and again be greeted,
Wisely and well must he act.

5. Wits must he have | who wanders wide,
But all is easy at home;
At the witless man | the wise shall wink
When among such men he sits.

34. Crooked and far | is the road to a foe,
Though his house on the highway be;
But wide and straight | is the way to a friend,
Though far away he fare.

35. Forth shall one go, | nor stay as a guest
In a single spot forever;
Love becomes loathing | if long one sits
By the hearth in another's home.

36. Better a house, | though a hut it be,
A man is master at home;
A pair of goats | and a patched-up roof
Are better far than begging.

38. Away from his arms | in the open field
A man should fare not a foot;
For never he knows | when the need for a spear
Shall arise on the distant road.

39. If wealth a man | has won for himself,
Let him never suffer in need;
Oft he saves for a foe | what he plans for a friend,
For much goes worse than we wish.

78. Cattle die, | and kinsmen die,
And so one dies one's self;
One thing now | that never dies,
The fame of a dead man's deeds.

81. Give praise to the day at evening, | to a woman on her pyre,
To a weapon which is tried, | to a maid at wed lock,
To ice when it is crossed, | to ale that is drunk.

82. When the gale blows hew wood, | in fair winds seek the water;
Sport with maidens at dusk, | for day's eyes are many;
From the ship seek swiftness, | from the shield protection,
Cuts from the sword, | from the maiden kisses.

90. The love of women | fickle of will
Is like starting o'er ice | with a steed unshod,
A two-year-old restive | and little tamed,
Or steering a rudderless | ship in a storm,
Or, lame, hunting reindeer | on slippery rocks.

91. Clear now will I speak, | for I know them both,
Men false to women are found;
When fairest we speak, | then falsest we think,
Against wisdom we work with deceit.

92. Soft words shall he speak | and wealth shall he offer
Who longs for a maiden's love,
And the beauty praise | of the maiden bright;
He wins whose wooing is best.

139. I ween that I hung | on the windy tree,
Hung there for nights full nine;
With the spear I was wounded, | and offered I was
To Othin, myself to myself,
On the tree that none | may ever know
What root beneath it runs.

73

From The Secret History
of the Mongols

This Mongol account records the early years of Mongol expansion under Chingis Khan, the founder of the empire. Born Temujin in 1155 or 1167, the young son of a minor tribal chieftain attracted the support of Mongol princes in the years between 1187 and 1206 through a series of decisive military victories over other tribes and competing Mongol claimants to the title of Great Khan.

The Mongols were illiterate before the time of Chingis Khan, who adopted the script of the Uighurs, one of the more literate peoples of the steppe. Thus the *Secret History* was written in Mongolian with Uighur letters. The only surviving version is a fourteenth-century Chinese translation. The author is unknown, but the book provides detailed accounts of the early years of Temujin and ends with the reign of his son and successor, Ogodai, in 1228 — only a year after his father's death.

Because so much about the Mongols was written by their literate enemies, *The Secret History* is an invaluable resource: It is clearly an "insider's" account of the early years of Mongol expansion. While it includes mythic elements — it begins with the augury of the birth of a blue wolf to introduce Chingis Khan — *The Secret History* is, without doubt, an authentic representation of a Mongol point of view.

In this selection, you will read three passages. The first describes a meeting in about 1187 of several tribal leaders who agree that the twenty-year-old Temujin should become Great Khan (Chingis Khan). What do these tribal leaders expect to gain from this alliance under Temujin? What do they offer in return?

The second passage deals with an early Mongol victory in 1202 over the neighboring Tatars, a tribe that Europeans often confused with the Mongols. How merciful or harsh does Chingis Khan seem?

The third passage recounts the story of an important Mongol victory over the Naiman in 1204. What does this section tell you about the sources of Mongol military strength?

How does this "insider's" view of the Mongols provide unique information or a perspective that would be unattainable from non-Mongols?

Adapted by K. Reilly from R. P. Lister, *Genghis Khan* (New York: Barnes & Noble, 1993), 99–100, 136–39, 166–76, 191–93. While this volume is a retelling of the almost indecipherable *The Secret History of the Mongols* in Lister's own words, the selections that follow simplify without contextualizing or explaining the original work. More scholarly editions, trans. and ed. Francis Woodman Cleaves (Cambridge, Mass.: Harvard University Press, 1982) and Paul Kahn (San Francisco: North Point Press, 1984) are less accessible.

Thinking Historically

What moral values does this selection reveal? Do the Mongols think of themselves as "moral" people? Is the author-historian interested in describing what happened objectively, or in presenting an unblemished, sanitized view?

In what ways does this written Mongol history make you more sympathetic to the Mongols? Notice that the "Mongols Conquer the Naiman" passage begins with an account of the Naiman. How fair does the Mongol author seem to be toward the Naiman? Would this be a good source for understanding the Naiman? Do you think the Mongol authors described the Naiman more accurately than Chinese or Europeans described the Mongols?

The Choosing of the Khan

. . . A general council of all the chieftains was called, and the three most notable men among them, Prince Altan, Khuchar, and Sacha Beki, came forward. They addressed Temujin formally, in the following manner:

> We will make you Khan; you shall ride at our head, against our foes.
> We will throw ourselves like lightning on your enemies;
> We will bring you their finest women and girls, their rich tents like palaces.
> From all the peoples and nations we will bring you the fair girls and the high-stepping horses;
> When you hunt wild beasts, we will drive them towards you; we will encircle them, pressing hard at their heels.
>
> If on the day of battle we disobey you,
> Take our flocks from us, our women and children, and cast our worthless heads on the steppe.
> If in times of peace we disobey you,
> Part us from our men and our servants, our wives and our sons;
> Abandon us and cast us out, masterless, on the forsaken earth. . . .

Mongol Conquest of Tatars

. . . Temujin came up against the Tatars at Dalan Namurgas, on the Khalkha, east of Buir Nor, and defeated them in battle. They fell back; the Mongol armies pursued them, slaying and capturing them in large numbers.

The princes, Altan, Khuchar, and Daritai, were less assiduous in the pursuit. Finding a great number of animals roaming the steppes in the absence of their Tatar owners, they followed the usual custom of rounding them up, and collecting anything that took their fancy in the abandoned Tatar camps.

Temujin, having issued a clear order [against looting], could not tolerate their disobedience. He detached portions of his army, placed them under the command of Jebe and Khubilai, and sent them off after the disobedient princes, with orders to take away from them everything they had captured. The outcome was what might have been expected. Prince Altan and Khuchar, retiring in haste with as much of their booty as they could take with them, departed from their allegiance to him. They re-established themselves as independent chieftains, entering into such arrangements with Ong Khan, Jamukha, and other rulers as seemed desirable.

Daritai, however, seeing a little more clearly than the others, submitted to having his booty taken away from him.

Owing to his determined pursuit of the Tatars, Temujin found that he had a very considerable number of Tatar prisoners. They were kept under guard in the Mongol camp, and for the most part they were not greatly perturbed by their situation. Some of the chieftains might expect to be executed, but the lesser men had a reasonable hope of surviving. Some might have to serve as warriors under the Mongols, or even be enslaved, but a slave of talents could always hope to become a warrior again.

Temujin held a council to decide what to do with them. It was a great matter, and nobody was present at this council but his own family. The Khan's intention [was] to wipe out his enemies on a large scale. . . .

Belgutai had . . . made friends among the Tatar prisoners. One of these was Yeke Charan, the principal Tatar leader. . . . When Yeke Charan asked him what decision the family council had come to, Belgutai did not hesitate to tell him.

"We agreed to measure you against the linchpin,"[1] he said.

Yeke Charan told his fellow prisoners of the Khan's decision. Having nothing to lose, they rose up against their guards and fought their way out of the camp, taking with them what weapons they could seize. They gathered themselves together on a hilltop in a tight formation of fierce warriors. Men who are going to be killed whatever happens, and know it, fight well. The destruction of the Tatars, which was in due course accomplished, cost many Mongol lives.

Temujin was remarkably lenient towards Belgutai.

"Because Belgutai revealed the decision of the family council," he said, "Our army suffered great losses. From now on, Belgutai will take

---

[1]This was not an unknown procedure, though it had never been applied on quite such a vast scale. Prisoners were led past the wheel of a wagon. Those who were taller than the linchpin were beheaded; the children, who were smaller, survived to be taken into the Mongol armies when they grew up.

no part in the council. While it is being held, he will remain outside, keeping order in the camp, and he will sit in judgment during that time over the quarrelsome, the thieves, and the liars. When the council is finished and the wine is all drunk, then Belgutai can come in."

He ordered at the same time that Daritai should be banned from the family councils, for disobeying his *yasakh*.[2] . . .

Mongols Conquer the Naiman

When the news was brought to [the Naiman] Tayang Khan that someone claiming to be Ong Khan had been slain at the Neikun watercourse, his mother, Gurbesu, said: "Ong Khan was the great Khan of former days. Bring his head here! If it is really he, we will sacrifice to him."

She sent a message to Khorisu, commanding him to cut the head off and bring it in. When it was brought to her, she recognised it as that of Ong Khan. She placed it on a white cloth, and her daughter-in-law carried out the appropriate rites. . . . A wine-feast was held and stringed instruments were played. Gurbesu, taking up a drinking-bowl, made an offering to the head of Ong Khan.

When the sacrifice was made to it, the head grinned.

"He laughs!" Tayang Khan cried. Overcome by religious awe, he flung the head on the floor and trampled on it until it was mangled beyond recognition.

The great general Kokse'u Sabrakh was present at these ceremonies, and observed them without enthusiasm. It was he who had been the only Naiman general to offer resistance to Temujin and Ong Khan on their expedition against Tayang Khan's brother Buyiruk.

"First of all," he remarked, "you cut off the head of a dead ruler, and then you trample it into the dust. What kind of behaviour is this? Listen to the baying of those dogs: It has an evil sound. The Khan your father, Inancha Bilgei, once said: 'My wife is young, and I, her husband, am old. Only the power of prayer has enabled me to beget my son, this same Tayang. But will my son, born a weakling, be able to guard and hold fast my common and evil-minded people?'

"Now the baying of the dogs seems to announce that some disaster is at hand. The rule of our queen, Gurbesu, is firm; but you, my Khan, Torlukh Tayang, are weak. It is truly said of you that you have no thought for anything but the two activities of hawking and driving game, and no capacity for anything but these."

Tayang Khan was accustomed to the disrespect of his powerful general, but he was stung into making a rash decision.

---

[2]Order, law.

"There are a few Mongols in the east. From the earliest days this old and great Ong Khan feared them, with their quivers; now they have made war on him and driven him to death. No doubt they would like to be rulers themselves. There are indeed in Heaven two shining lights, the sun and the moon, and both can exist there; but how can there be two rulers here on earth? Let us go and gather those Mongols in."

His mother Gurbesu said: "Why should we start making trouble with them? The Mongols have a bad smell; they wear black clothes. They are far away, out there; let them stay there. Though it is true," she added, "that we could have the daughters of their chieftains brought here; when we had washed their hands and feet, they could milk our cows and sheep for us."

Tayang Khan said: "What is there so terrible about them? Let us go to these Mongols and take away their quivers."

"What big words you are speaking," Kokse'u Sabrakh said. "Is Tayang Khan the right man for it? Let us keep the peace."

Despite these warnings, Tayang Khan decided to attack the Mongols. It was a justifiable decision; his armies were stronger, but time was on Temujin's side. Tayang sought allies, sending a messenger to Alakhu Shidigichuri of the Onggut, in the south, the guardians of the ramparts between Qashin and the Khingan. "I am told that there are a few Mongols in the east," he said. "Be my right hand! I will ride against them from here, and we will take their quivers away from them."

[Alakhu Shidigichuri's] reply was brief: "I cannot be your right hand." He in his turn sent a message to Temujin. "Tayang Khan of the Naiman wants to come and take away your quivers. He sent to me and asked me to be his right hand. I refused. I make you aware of this, so that when he comes your quivers will not be taken away."[3]

When he received Alakhu's message Temujin, having wintered near Guralgu, was holding one of his . . . roundups of game on the camel-steppes of Tulkinche'ut, in the east. The beasts had been encircled by the clansmen and warriors; the chieftains were gathered together, about to begin the great hunt.

"What shall we do now?" some of them said to each other. "Our horses are lean at this season."

. . . The snow had only lately left the steppe; the horses had found nothing to graze on during these recent months. Their ribs stuck out and they lacked strength.

The Khan's youngest brother, Temuga, spoke up. . . .

---

[3]Temujin, grateful for this warning, sent him five hundred horses and a thousand sheep. His friendship with Alakhu was valuable to him at a later time.

"How can that serve as an excuse," he said, "that the horses are lean? My horses are quite fat enough. How can we stay sitting here, when we receive a message like that?"

Prince Belgutai spoke. . . .

"If a man allows his quivers to be taken away during his lifetime, what kind of an existence does he have? For a man who is born a man, it is a good enough end to be slain by another man, and lie on the steppe with his quiver and bow beside him. The Naiman make fine speeches, with their many men and their great kingdom. But suppose, having heard their fine speeches, we ride against them, would it be so difficult to take their quivers away from them? We must mount and ride; it is the only thing to do."

Temujin was wholly disposed to agree with these sentiments. He broke off the hunt, set the army in motion, and camped near Ornu'u on the Khalkha. Here he paused for a time while he carried out a swift reorganisation of the army. A count was held of the people; they were divided up into thousands, hundreds, and tens, and commanders of these units were appointed. Also at this time he chose his personal bodyguards, the seventy day-guards and eighty night-guards. . . .

Having reorganised the army, he marched away from the mountainside of Ornu'u on the Khalkha, and took the way of war against the Naiman.

The spring of the Year of the Rat [1204] was by now well advanced. During this westward march came the Day of the Red Disc, the sixteenth day of the first moon of summer. On this day, the moon being at the full, the Khan caused the great yak's-tail banner to be consecrated, letting it be sprinkled with fermented mare's milk, with the proper observances.

They continued the march up the Kerulen, with Jebe and Khubilai in the van. When they came on to the Saari steppes, they met with the first scouts of the Naiman. There were a few skirmishes between the Naiman and Mongol scouts; in one of these, a Mongol scout was captured, a man riding a grey horse with a worn saddle. The Naiman studied this horse with critical eyes, and thought little of it. "The Mongols' horses are inordinately lean," they said to each other.

The Mongol army rode out on to the Saari steppes, and began to deploy themselves for the forthcoming battle. . . . Dodai Cherbi, one of the newly appointed captains, put a proposal before the Khan.

"We are short in numbers compared to the enemy; besides this, we are exhausted after the long march, our horses in particular. It would be a good idea to settle in this camp, so that our horses can graze on the steppe, until they have had as much to eat as they need. Meanwhile, we can deceive the enemy by making puppets and lighting innumerable fires. For every man, we will make at least one puppet, and we will burn fires in five places. It is said that the Naiman people are very numerous, but it is rumoured also that their king is a weakling, who has never left his tents. If we keep them in a state of uncertainty about our numbers, with our puppets and our fires, our geldings can stuff themselves till they are fat."

The suggestion pleased Temujin, who had the order passed on to the soldiers to light fires immediately. Puppets were constructed and placed all over the steppe, some sitting or lying by the fires, some of them even mounted on horses.

At night, the watchers of the Naiman saw, from the flanks of the mountain, fires twinkling all over the steppe. They said to each other: "Did they not say that the Mongols were very few? Yet they have more fires than there are stars in Heaven."

Having previously sent to Tayang Khan news of the lean grey horse with the shabby saddle, they now sent him the message: "The warriors of the Mongols are camped out all over the Saari steppes. They seem to grow more numerous every day; their fires outnumber the stars."

When this news was brought to him from the scouts, Tayang Khan was at the watercourse of Khachir. He sent a message to his son Guchuluk.

"I am told that the geldings of the Mongols are lean, but the Mongols are, it seems, numerous. Once we start fighting them, it will be difficult to draw back. They are such hard warriors that when several men at once come up against one of them, he does not move an eyelid; even if he is wounded, so that the black blood flows out, he does not flinch. I do not know whether it is a good thing to come up against such men.

"I suggest that we should assemble our people and lead them back to the west, across the Altai; and all the time, during this retreat, we will fight off the Mongols as dogs do, by running in on them from either side as they advance. Our geldings are too fat; in this march we shall make them lean and fit. But the Mongols' lean geldings will be brought to such a state of exhaustion they will vomit in the Mongols' faces."

On receiving this message, Guchuluk Khan, who was more warlike than his father, said: "That woman Tayang has lost all his courage, to speak such words. Where does this great multitude of Mongols come from? Most of the Mongols are with Jamukha, who is here with us. Tayang speaks like this because fear has overcome him. He has never been farther from his tent than his pregnant wife goes to urinate. He has never dared to go so far as the inner pastures where the knee-high calves are kept." So he expressed himself on the subject of his father, in the most injurious and wounding terms.

When he heard these words, Tayang Khan said: "I hope the pride of this powerful Guchuluk will not weaken on the day when the clash of arms is heard and the slaughter begins. Because once we are committed to battle against the foe, it will be hard to disengage again."

Khorisu Beki, a general who commanded under Tayang Khan, said: "Your father, Inancha Bilgei, never showed the back of a man or the haunch of a horse to opponents who were just as worthy as these. How can you lose your courage so early in the day? We would have done better to summon your mother Gurbesu to command over us. It is a pity that Kokse'u Sabrakh has grown too old to lead us. Our army's discipline has become lax. For the Mongols, their hour has come. It is finished! Tayang, you have failed us." He belted on his quiver and galloped off.

Tayang Khan grew angry. "All men must die," he said. "Their bodies must suffer. It is the same for all men. Let us fight, then."

So, having created doubt and dismay, and lost the support of some of his best leaders, he decided to give battle. He broke away from the watercourse of Khachir, marched down the Tamir, crossed the Orkhon and skirted the eastern flanks of the mountain Nakhu. When they came to Chakirma'ut, Temujin's scouts caught sight of them and brought back the message: "The Naiman are coming!"

The Battle of Chakirma'ut

When the news was brought to Temujin he said: "Sometimes too many men are just as big a handicap as too few."

Then he issued his general battle orders. "We will march in the order 'thick grass,' take up positions in the 'lake' battle order, and fight in the manner called 'gimlet.'"[4] He gave Kasar the command of the main army, and appointed Prince Otchigin to the command of the reserve horses, a special formation of great importance in Mongol warfare.

The Naiman, having advanced as far as Chakirma'ut, drew themselves up in a defensive position on the foothills of Nakhu, with the mountain behind them. . . . The Mongols forced their scouts back on to the forward lines, and then their forward lines back on to the main army, and drove tightly knit formations of horsemen again and again into the Naiman ranks. The Naiman, pressed back on themselves, could do nothing but retreat gradually up the mountain. Many of their men . . . hardly had the chance to fight at all, but were cut down in an immobile mass of men as soon as the Mongols reached them.

Tayang Khan, with his advisers, also retreated up the mountain as the day advanced. From the successive spurs to which they climbed, each one higher than the last, they could see the whole of this dreadful disaster as it took place below them.

Jamukha was with Tayang Khan. . . .

"Who are those people over there," Tayang Khan asked him, "who throw my warriors back as if they were sheep frightened by a wolf, who come huddling back to the sheepfold?"

---

[4]These were the names of various tactical disciplines in which he had drilled his army.

Jamukha said: "My *anda*[5] Temujin has four hounds whom he brought up on human flesh, and kept in chains. They have brows of copper, snouts like chisels, tongues like bradawls, hearts of iron, and tails that cut like swords. They can live on dew, and ride like the wind. On the day of battle they eat the flesh of men. You see how, being set loose, they come forward slavering for joy. Those two are Jebe and Khubilai; those two are Jelmei and Subetai. That is who those four hounds are."

He pointed out to him also the Uru'ut and the Mangqut, who, as Tayang Khan remarked, seemed to bound like foals set loose in the morning, when, after their dams have suckled them, they frisk around her on the steppe. "They hunt down men who carry lances and swords," he said. "Having struck them down, they slay them, and rob them of all they possess. How joyful and boisterous they look, as they ride forward!"

"Who is it coming up there in the rear," Tayang Khan asked him, "who swoops down on our troops like a ravening falcon?"

"That is my *anda* Temujin. His entire body is made of sounding copper; there is no gap through which even a bodkin could penetrate. There he is, you see him? He advances like an eagle about to seize his prey. You said formerly that if you once set eyes on the Mongols you would not leave so much of them as the skin of a lamb's foot. What do you think of them now?"

By this time the chieftains were standing on a high spur. Below them, the great army of the Naiman, Jamukha's men with them, were retreating in confusion, fighting desperately as the Mongols hemmed them in.

"Who is that other chieftain," Tayang asked Jamukha, "who draws ever nearer us, in a dense crowd of men?"

"Mother Hoelun brought up one of her own sons on human flesh. He is nine feet tall; he eats a three-year-old cow every day. If he swallows an armed man whole, it makes no difference to his appetite. When he is roused to anger, and lets fly with one of his *angqu'a* [forked] arrows, it will go through ten or twenty men. His normal range is a thousand yards; when he draws his bow to its fullest extent, he shoots over eighteen hundred yards. He is mortal, but he is not like other mortals; he is more than a match for the serpents of Guralgu. He is called Kasar."

They were climbing high up the mountain now, to regroup below its summit. Tayang Khan saw a new figure among the Mongols.

"Who is that coming up from the rear?" he asked Jamukha.

"That is the youngest son of Mother Hoelun. He is called Otchigin [Odeigin] the Phlegmatic. He is one of those people who go to bed

---

[5]Sworn brother, blood brother, declared ally.

early and get up late. But when he is behind the army, with the reserves, he does not linger; he never comes too late to the battle lines."

"We will climb to the peak of the mountain," Tayang Khan said.

Jamukha, seeing that the battle was lost, slipped away to the rear and descended the mountain, with a small body of men. One of these he sent to Temujin with a message. "Say this to my *anda*. Tayang Khan, terrified by what I have told him, has completely lost his senses. He has retreated up the mountain as far as he can. He could be killed by one harsh word. Let my *anda* take note of this: They have climbed to the top of the mountain, and are in no state to defend themselves any more. I myself have left the Naiman."

Since the evening was drawing on, Temujin commanded his troops in the forefront of the attack to draw back. Bodies of men were sent forward on the wings, east and west, to encircle the summit of Mount Nakhu. There they stood to arms during the night. During the night, the Naiman army tried to break out of the encircling ring. Bodies of horsemen plunged down the mountainside in desperate charges; many fell and were trampled to death, the others were slain. In the first light they were seen lying about the mountain in droves, like fallen trees. Few were left defending the peak; they put up little resistance to the force sent up against them.

74

JOHN OF PLANO CARPINI

History of the Mongols

Chingis Khan united the tribes of the steppe and conquered northern China, capturing Peking by 1215. He then turned his armies against the West, conquering the tribes of Turkestan and the Khorezmian Empire, the great Muslim power of central Asia, by 1222 and sending an army around the Caspian Sea into Russia. In 1226, he turned again to the East, subduing and destroying the kingdom of Tibet before he

---

John of Plano Carpini, "History of the Mongols," in *Mission to Asia: Narratives and Letters of the Franciscan Missionaries in Mongolia and China in the Thirteenth and Fourteenth Centuries*, trans. a nun of Stanbrook Abbey, ed. Christopher Dawson (1955; reprint, New York: Harper & Row, 1966), 60–69.

died in 1227. One historian, Christopher Dawson, summarizes the career of Chingis Khan this way:

> In spite of the primitive means at his disposal, it is possible that [Chingis Khan] succeeded in destroying a larger portion of the human race than any modern expert in total warfare. Within a dozen years from the opening of his campaign against China, the Mongol armies had reached the Pacific, the Indus, and the Black Sea, and had destroyed many of the great cities in India. For Europe especially, the shock was overwhelming.

European fears intensified in 1237 as the principal Mongol armies under Batu Khan systematically destroyed one Russian city after another. In April 1241, one Mongol army destroyed a combined force of Polish and German armies, while another defeated the Hungarian army and threatened Austria. In 1245, desperate to learn as much as possible about Mongol intentions, Pope Innocent IV sent a mission to the Mongols. For this important task, he sent two Franciscan monks — one of whom was John of Plano Carpini — with two letters addressed to the Emperor of the Tartars (a compounded error that changed the Tatars, the Mongols' enemy, into the denizens of Tartarus, or Hell).

In May, the barefoot sixty-five-year-old Friar John reached Batu's camp on the Volga River, from which he was relayed to Mongolia by five fresh horses a day in order to reach the capital at Karakorum in time for the installation of the third Great Khan, Guyuk (r. 1246–1248) in July and August.

In this selection from his *History of the Mongols*, John writes of his arrival in Mongolia for the installation of Guyuk (here written as Cuyuc). In what ways does John's account change or expand your understanding of the Mongols? Was John a good observer? How does he compensate for his ignorance (as an outside observer) of Mongol society and culture? In what ways does he remain a victim of his outsider status?

Thinking Historically

How would you characterize John's moral stance towards the Mongols? Consider your own moral judgment, if any, of the Mongols. How is it related to your historical understanding?

. . . On our arrival Cuyuc had us given a tent and provisions, such as it is the custom for the Tartars to give, but they treated us better than other envoys. Nevertheless we were not invited to visit him for he had not yet been elected, nor did he yet concern himself with the government. The translation of the Lord Pope's letter, however, and the things I had said had been sent to him by Bati. After we had stayed there for five or six days he sent us to his mother where the solemn court was assembling. By the time we got there a large pavilion had already been put up made of white velvet, and in my opinion it was so big that more than two thousand men could have got into it. Around it had been erected a wooden palisade, on which various designs were painted. On the second or third day we went with the Tartars who had been appointed to look after us and there all the chiefs were assembled and each one was riding with his followers among the hills and over the plains round about.

On the first day they were all clothed in white velvet, on the second in red — that day Cuyuc came to the tent — on the third day they were all in blue velvet, and on the fourth in the finest brocade. In the palisade round the pavilion were two large gates, through one of which the Emperor alone had the right to enter and there were no guards placed at it although it was open, for no one dare enter or leave by it; through the other gate all those who were granted admittance entered and there were guards there with swords and bows and arrows. . . . The chiefs went about everywhere armed and accompanied by a number of their men, but none, unless their group of ten was complete, could go as far as the horses; indeed those who attempted to do so were severely beaten. There were many of them who had, as far as I could judge, about twenty marks' worth of gold on their bits, breastplates, saddles, and cruppers. The chiefs held their conference inside the tent and, so I believe, conducted the election. All the other people however were a long way away outside the aforementioned palisade. There they remained until almost midday and then they began to drink mare's milk and they drank until the evening, so much that it was amazing to see. We were invited inside and they gave us mead as we would not take mare's milk. They did this to show us great honour, but they kept on plying us with drinks to such an extent that we could not possibly stand it, not being used to it, so we gave them to understand that it was disagreeable to us and they left off pressing us.

Outside were Duke Jerozlaus of Susdal in Russia and several chiefs of the Kitayans and Solangi, also two sons of the King of Georgia, the ambassador of the Caliph of Baghdad, who was a Sultan, and more than ten other Sultans of the Saracens, so I believe and so we were told by the stewards. There were more than four thousand envoys there, counting those who were carrying tribute, those who were bringing gifts, the Sultans and other chiefs who were coming to submit to them, those summoned by the Tartars and the governors of territories. All these were put together outside the palisade and they were given drinks at the same time, but when we were outside with them we and Duke Jerozlaus were always given the best places. I think, if I remember rightly, that we had been there a good four weeks when, as I believe, the election took place; the result however was not made public at that time; the chief ground for my supposition was that whenever Cuyuc left the tent they sang before him and as long as he remained outside they dipped to him beautiful rods on the top of which was scarlet wool, which they did not do for any of the other chiefs. They call this court the Sira Orda.

Leaving there we rode all together for three or four leagues to another place, where on a pleasant plain near a river among the mountains another tent had been set up, which is called by them the Golden Orda, it was here that Cuyuc was to be enthroned on the feast of the Assumption of Our Lady. . . .

At that place we were summoned into the presence of the Emperor, and Chingay the protonotary wrote down our names and the names of those who had sent us, also the names of the chief of the Solangi and of others, and then calling out in a loud voice he recited them before the Emperor and all the chiefs. When this was finished each one of us genuflected four times on the left knee and they warned us not to touch the lower part of the threshold. After we had been most thoroughly searched for knives and they had found nothing at all, we entered by a door on the east side, for no one dare enter from the west with the sole exception of the Emperor or, if it is a chief's tent, the chief; those of lower rank do not pay much attention to such things. This was the first time since Cuyuc had been made Emperor that we had entered his tent in his presence. He also received all the envoys in that place, but very few entered his tent.

So many gifts were bestowed by the envoys there that it was marvellous to behold — gifts of silk, samite, velvet, brocade, girdles of silk threaded with gold, choice furs, and other presents. The Emperor was also given a sunshade or little awning such as is carried over his head, and it was all decorated with precious stones. . . .

Leaving there we went to another place where a wonderful tent had been set up all of red velvet, and this had been given by the Kitayans; there also we were taken inside. Whenever we went in we were given mead and wine to drink, and cooked meat was offered us if we wished to have it. A lofty platform of boards had been erected, on which the Emperor's throne was placed. The throne, which was of ivory, was wonderfully carved and there was also gold on it, and precious stones, if I remember rightly, and pearls. Steps led up to it and it was rounded behind. Benches were also placed round the throne, and here the ladies sat in their seats on the left; nobody, however, sat on the right, but the chiefs were on benches in the middle and the rest of the people sat beyond them. Every day a great crowd of ladies came.

Finally, after some time, John was to be brought again before the Emperor. When he heard from them that we had come to him he ordered us to go back to his mother, the reason being that he wished on the following day to raise his banner against the whole of the Western world — we were told this definitely by men who knew . . . — and he wanted us to be kept in ignorance of this. On our return we stayed for a few days, then we went back to him again and remained with him for a good month, enduring such hunger and thirst that we could scarcely keep alive, for the food provided for four was barely sufficient for one, moreover, we were unable to find anything to buy, for the market was a very long way off. If the Lord had not sent us a certain Russian, by name Cosmas, a goldsmith and a great favourite of the Emperor, who supported us to some extent, we would, I believe, have died, unless the Lord had helped us in some other way. . . .

After this the Emperor sent for us, and through Chingay his protonotary told us to write down what we had to say and our business, and give it to him. We did this and wrote out for him all that we said earlier to Bati. . . . A few days passed by; then he had us summoned again and told us through Kadac, the procurator of the whole empire, in the presence of Bala and Chingay his protonotaries and many other scribes, to say all we had to say: We did this willingly and gladly. Our interpreter on this as on the previous occasion was Temer, a knight of Jerozlaus': and there were also present a cleric who was with him and another cleric who was with the Emperor. On this occasion we were asked if there were any people with the Lord Pope who understood the writing of the Russians or Saracens or even of the Tartars. We gave answer that we used neither the Ruthenian nor Saracen writing; there were however Saracens in the country but they were a long way from the Lord Pope; but we said that it seemed to us that the most expedient course would be for them to write in Tartar and translate it for us, and we would write it down carefully in our own script and we would take both the letter and the translation to the Lord Pope. Thereupon they left us to go to the Emperor.

On St. Martin's day we were again summoned, and Kadac, Chingay, and Bala, the aforementioned secretaries, came to us and translated the letter for us word by word. When we had written it in Latin, they had it translated so that they might hear a phrase at a time, for they wanted to know if we had made a mistake in any word. When both letters were written, they made us read it once and a second time in case we had left out anything. . . .

It is the custom for the Emperor of the Tartars never to speak to a foreigner, however important he may be, except through an intermediary, and he listens and gives his answer, also through the intermediary. Whenever his subjects have any business to bring before Kadac, or while they are listening to the Emperor's reply, they stay on their knees until the end of the conversation, however important they may be. It is not possible nor indeed is it the custom for anyone to say anything about any matter after the Emperor has declared his decision. This Emperor not only has a procurator and protonotaries and secretaries, but all officials for dealing with both public and private matters, except that he has no advocates, for everything is settled according to the decision of the Emperor without the turmoil of legal trials. The other princes of the Tartars do the same in those matters concerning them.

The present Emperor may be forty or forty-five years old or more; he is of medium height, very intelligent, and extremely shrewd, and most serious and grave in his manner. He is never seen to laugh for a slight cause nor to indulge in any frivolity, so we were told by the Christians who are constantly with him. The Christians of his household also told us that they firmly believed he was about to become a Christian, and they have clear evidence of this, for he maintains Christian clerics and provides them with supplies of Christian things; in addition he always has a chapel before his chief tent and they sing openly and in public and beat the board for services after the Greek fashion like other Christians, however big a crowd of Tartars or other men be there. The other chiefs do not behave like this.

. . . on the feast of St. Brice [November 13th], they gave us a permit to depart and a letter sealed with the Emperor's seal, and sent us to the Emperor's mother. She gave each of us a fox-skin cloak, which had the fur outside and was lined inside, and a length of velvet; our Tartars stole a good yard from each of the pieces of velvet and from the piece given to our servant they stole more than half. This did not escape our notice, but we preferred not to make a fuss about it.

We then set out on the return journey. . . .

REFLECTIONS

The great Chinese artist Cheng Ssu-hsaio (1241–1318) continued to paint his delicate Chinese orchids in the years after the Mongol defeat of the Sung dynasty, under the alien rule of Khubilai Khan (r. 1260–1294), the fifth Great Khan and the founder of the Mongol Yuan dynasty of China. But when Cheng was asked why he always painted the orchids without earth around their roots, he replied that the earth had been stolen by the barbarians.

Just as it would be a mistake to see a fifth-generation Mongol ruler like Khubilai as a barbarian, it would also be a mistake to assume that Cheng's hardened resistance remained the norm. In fact, a younger generation of artists found opportunity and even freedom in Khubilai's China. Khubilai appointed some of the most famous Chinese painters of his era to positions of government — Ministries of War, Public

Works, Justice, Personnel, Imperial Sacrifices — actively recruiting the bright young men, artists and intellectuals, for his government. While some painters catered to the Mongol elite's inclination for paintings of horses, others relished the wider range of subjects allowed by a regime free of highly cultivated prejudices.

If conquest invariably brings charges of barbarism, it also eventually turns to issues of government and administration. Administrators need officials. Though Khubilai abolished the Chinese civil service examination system because it would have forced him to rely on Chinese officials, the Chinese language, and an educational system based on the Chinese classics, he actively sought ways of governing that were neither too Chinese nor too Mongolian. Typically, he promulgated a Chinese alphabet that was based on Tibetan, hoping that its phonetic symbols would make communication easier and less classical. Many of his achievements were unintended. While his officials continued to use Chinese characters and the Uighur script, the Yüan dynasty witnessed a flowering of literary culture, including theater and novels. For some, no doubt, the wind from the steppe blew away the dust and cobwebs that had accumulated for too long.

Our judgment of the Mongols depends to a great extent on the period of Mongol history we consider. But while it is easy to condemn Chingis Khan and the initial conquests and praise the later enlightened governance, two considerations come to mind. First, in the great sweep of history, many "barbarians" became benign, even indulgent, administrators. Second, the Mongols were not unique in making that transition.

Before the Mongols, the Vikings had already made the transition from raiding to trading and from conquering to colonizing. In fact, as Cunliffe points out, the Vikings had always been farmer-sailors who were as hungry for land as for plunder. Unlike the Mongols who were born on horses, continually picking up and remaking camp in new pastureland, the Vikings became nomadic in emergencies when a search for new settlements was necessary.

The memory of Viking assaults also faded faster than that of the Mongols. The Viking Rus had the Mongols to thank. The Rus of Viking cities like Novgorod became the national heroes of anti-Mongol Russian legend. The Viking Rus became the Russians. In Europe, too, the descendants of Vikings helped establish new national identities. The last great Viking king, Harald the Hard Ruler, "Thunderbolt of the North," won back his father's crown as King of Norway after preparing himself in Russian trading cities and Byzantine courts. He married a Russian princess and fought for the Byzantines in Asia Minor, Jerusalem, and the Caucasus Mountains. In 1066, this King of Norway lost his control of England when he was killed by an English earl. A few days later the new English king was killed by William Duke of

Normandy, a Viking son who had previously conquered much of France. Norman rule was to last over a hundred years, from 1066 to 1215, and create a new English identity.

In the North Atlantic and North America the Vikings traded with indigenous peoples whom they called "wretches" and later generations were to call Eskimos, Inuit, and Indians. But the land did not allow much contact and they learned very little from each other.

At the end of the day, history is neither moral nor immoral. History is what happened, for better or worse, and moralistic history is generally bad history. The Vikings and Mongols of our period were no more morally frozen in time than were the Christian and Muslim crusaders of the same era who visited such violence upon each other.

Just as the role of nomads and settlers changes over time, so does the degree to which a people are particularly aggressive or peaceful. It is hard to imagine a more fearful people than the Mongols of the thirteenth century or the Vikings of the tenth century. Yet modern Scandinavia, Iceland, and Mongolia are among the most peaceful places on the planet.

We can study societies or periods marked by unusually high levels of violence in order to understand the causes and avoid the repetition. History never offers simple lessons, but without its rich sources for explanation and reflection, we sail adrift bereft of markers or direction. Indeed, as history teaches us the consequences of our acts, we might say that without history there can hardly be morality.

The Black Death

Afro-Eurasia, 1346–1350 C.E.

HISTORICAL CONTEXT

The Mongol peace that made the Persian Ilkhanid dynasty (1256–1353) and the Chinese Yuan dynasty (1279–1368) sister empires nurtured a level of economic exchange and artistic communication greater than in the most cosmopolitan days of the early Roman/Han Silk Road. But the new caravan routes that spanned Central Asia could carry microbes as well as people. The plague that had long been endemic in country rats spread by fleas to city rats and other animals, including humans. As early as 1346, travelers reported millions killed in China, Central Asia, and the Middle East. In Europe and Egypt, approximately a third of the population perished. In some cities, the death toll was greater than half. This pandemic plague of 1348–1350 is sometimes called the Black Death, after the discolored wounds it caused.

THINKING HISTORICALLY
Considering Cause and Effect

The study of history, like the practice of medicine, is a process of understanding the causes of certain effects. In medicine the effects are diseases; in history they are more varied events. Nevertheless, understanding the causes of things is central to both disciplines. For medical specialists the goal of understanding causes is implicitly a part of the process of finding a cure. Historians rarely envision "cures" for social ills, but many believe that an understanding of cause and effect can improve society's chances of progress.

Still, the most hopeful medical researcher or historian would agree that the process of relating cause and effect, of finding causes and explaining effects, is fraught with difficulties. We will explore some of those difficulties in this chapter.

$$\boxed{75}$$

MARK WHEELIS

Biological Warfare at the 1346 Siege of Caffa

We are used to thinking of biological warfare as a recently developed threat. This article, published in a journal for public health professionals, suggests a longer history. According to the author, how and where did the Black Death originate? What was the significance of the Mongol siege of Caffa in 1346? The author draws on the contemporary account of the Black Death by Gabriele de Mussis. On what points does he agree and disagree with de Mussis?

Thinking Historically

The author of this selection, a professor of microbiology at the University of California, was trained as a bacterial physiologist and geneticist, but for more than the last ten years his research has concentrated on the history and control of biological weapons. Notice how he explains the causes of such events as the spread of plague and the infection at Caffa. Would you call his way of finding causes the method of a medical researcher or a historian, or does he employ the methods of both? If you see a distinction, try to note the places where he is thinking more like a medical scientist and those where he is thinking more like a historian.

The Black Death, which swept through Europe, the Near East, and North Africa in the mid-fourteenth-century, was probably the greatest public health disaster in recorded history and one of the most dramatic examples ever of emerging or reemerging disease. Europe lost an

Mark Wheelis, "Biological Warfare at the 1346 Siege of Caffa," *Emerging Infectious Diseases*, 8, no. 9 (September, 2002): 971–75. The journal is published by the U.S. Centers for Disease Control and Prevention (C.D.C.), Atlanta, and is also available online at http://www.cdc.gov/ncidod/EID/vol8no9/01-0536.htm.

estimated one quarter to one third of its population, and the mortality in North Africa and the Near East was comparable. China, India, and the rest of the Far East are commonly believed to have also been severely affected, but little evidence supports that belief.

A principal source on the origin of the Black Death is a memoir by the Italian Gabriele de' Mussis. This memoir has been published several times in its original Latin and has recently been translated into English (although brief passages have been previously published in translation). This narrative contains some startling assertions: that the Mongol army hurled plague-infected cadavers into the besieged Crimean city of Caffa, thereby transmitting the disease to the inhabitants; and that fleeing survivors of the siege spread plague from Caffa to the Mediterranean Basin. If this account is correct, Caffa should be recognized as the site of the most spectacular incident of biological warfare ever, with the Black Death as its disastrous consequence. After analyzing these claims, I have concluded that it is plausible that the biological attack took place as described and was responsible for infecting the inhabitants of Caffa; however, the event was unimportant in the spread of the plague pandemic.

Origin of the Fourteenth-Century Pandemic

The disease that caused this catastrophic pandemic has, since Hecker, generally been considered to have been a plague, a zoonotic disease caused by the gram-negative bacterium *Yersinia pestis,* the principal reservoir for which is wild rodents. The ultimate origin of the Black Death is uncertain — China, Mongolia, India, central Asia, and southern Russia have all been suggested. Known fourteenth-century sources are of little help; they refer repeatedly to an eastern origin, but none of the reports is firsthand. Historians generally agree that the outbreak moved west out of the steppes north of the Black and Caspian Seas, and its spread through Europe and the Middle East is fairly well documented (see Map 12.1). However, despite more than a century of speculation about an ultimate origin further east, the requisite scholarship using Chinese and central Asian sources has yet to be done. In any event, the Crimea clearly played a pivotal role as the proximal source from which the Mediterranean Basin was infected.

Historical Background to the Siege of Caffa

Caffa (now Feodosija, Ukraine) was established by Genoa in 1266 by agreement with the Kahn of the Golden Horde. It was the main port for the great Genoese merchant ships, which connected there to a coastal shipping industry to Tana (now Azov, Russia) on the Don

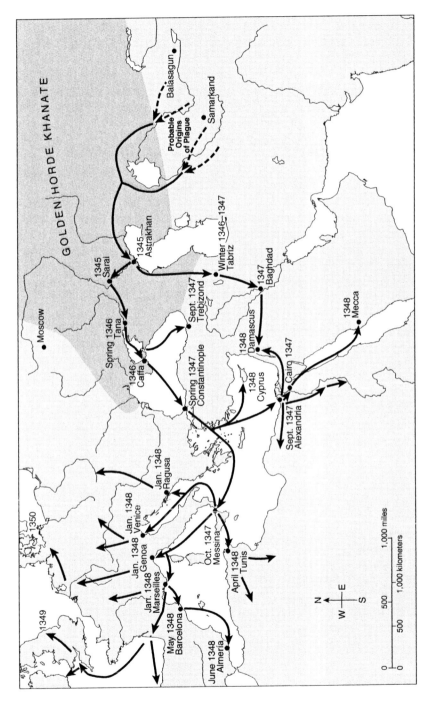

Map 12.1 Tentative Chronology of the Initial Spread of Plague in the Mid-Fourteenth Century.

River. Trade along the Don connected Tana to Central Russia, and overland caravan routes linked it to Sarai and thence to the Far East.

Relations between Italian traders and their Mongol hosts were uneasy, and in 1307 Toqtai, Kahn of the Golden Horde, arrested the Italian residents of Sarai, and besieged Caffa. The cause was apparently Toqtai's displeasure at the Italian trade in Turkic slaves (sold for soldiers to the Mameluke Sultanate). The Genoese resisted for a year, but in 1308 set fire to their city and abandoned it. Relations between the Italians and the Golden Horde remained tense until Toqtai's death in 1312.

Toqtai's successor, Özbeg, welcomed the Genoese back, and also ceded land at Tana to the Italians for the expansion of their trading enterprise. By the 1340s, Caffa was again a thriving city, heavily fortified within two concentric walls. The inner wall enclosed 6,000 houses, the outer 11,000. The city's population was highly cosmopolitan, including Genoese, Venetian, Greeks, Armenians, Jews, Mongols, and Turkic peoples.

In 1343 the Mongols under Janibeg (who succeeded Özbeg in 1340) besieged Caffa and the Italian enclave at Tana following a brawl between Italians and Muslims in Tana. The Italian merchants in Tana fled to Caffa (which, by virtue of its location directly on the coast, maintained maritime access despite the siege). The siege of Caffa lasted until February 1344, when it was lifted after an Italian relief force killed 15,000 Mongol troops and destroyed their siege machines. Janibeg renewed the siege in 1345 but was again forced to lift it after a year, this time by an epidemic of plague that devastated his forces. The Italians blockaded Mongol ports, forcing Janibeg to negotiate, and in 1347 the Italians were allowed to reestablish their colony in Tana.

Gabriele de' Mussis

Gabriele de' Mussis, born circa 1280, practiced as a notary in the town of Piacenza, over the mountains just north of Genoa. Tononi summarizes the little we know of him. His practice was active in the years 1300–1349. He is thought to have died in approximately 1356.

Although Henschel thought de' Mussis was present at the siege of Caffa, Tononi asserts that the Piacenza archives contain deeds signed by de' Mussis spanning the period 1344 through the first half of 1346. While this does not rule out travel to Caffa in late 1346, textual evidence suggests that he did not. He does not claim to have witnessed any of the Asian events he describes and often uses a passive voice for descriptions. After describing the siege of Caffa, de' Mussis goes on to say, "Now it is time that we passed from east to west to discuss all the things which we ourselves have seen. . . ."

The Narrative of Gabriele de' Mussis

The de' Mussis account is presumed to have been written in 1348 or early 1349 because of its immediacy and the narrow time period described. The original is lost, but a copy is included in a compilation of historical and geographic accounts by various authors, dating from approximately 1367. The account begins with an introductory comment by the scribe who copied the documents: "In the name of God, Amen. Here begins an account of the disease or mortality which occurred in 1348, put together by Gabrielem de Mussis of Piacenza."

The narrative begins with an apocalyptic speech by God, lamenting the depravity into which humanity has fallen and describing the retribution intended. It goes on:

". . . In 1346, in the countries of the East, countless numbers of Tartars and Saracens were struck down by a mysterious illness which brought sudden death. Within these countries broad regions, far-spreading provinces, magnificent kingdoms, cities, towns and settlements, ground down by illness and devoured by dreadful death, were soon stripped of their inhabitants. An eastern settlement under the rule of the Tartars called Tana, which lay to the north of Constantinople and was much frequented by Italian merchants, was totally abandoned after an incident there which led to its being besieged and attacked by hordes of Tartars who gathered in a short space of time. The Christian merchants, who had been driven out by force, were so terrified of the power of the Tartars that, to save themselves and their belongings, they fled in an armed ship to Caffa, a settlement in the same part of the world which had been founded long ago by the Genoese.

"Oh God! See how the heathen Tartar races, pouring together from all sides, suddenly invested the city of Caffa and besieged the trapped Christians there for almost three years. There, hemmed in by an immense army, they could hardly draw breath, although food could be shipped in, which offered them some hope. But behold, the whole army was affected by a disease which overran the Tartars and killed thousands upon thousands every day. It was as though arrows were raining down from heaven to strike and crush the Tartars' arrogance. All medical advice and attention was useless; the Tartars died as soon as the signs of disease appeared on their bodies: swellings in the armpit or groin caused by coagulating humours, followed by a putrid fever.

"The dying Tartars, stunned and stupefied by the immensity of the disaster brought about by the disease, and realizing that they had no hope of escape, lost interest in the siege. But they ordered corpses to be placed in catapults[1] and lobbed into the city in the hope that the intolerable stench would kill everyone inside.[2] What seemed like mountains of dead were thrown into the city, and the Christians could not hide or flee or escape from them, although they dumped as many of the bodies as they could in the sea. And soon the rotting corpses tainted the air and poisoned the water supply, and the stench was so overwhelming that hardly one in several thousand was in a position to flee the remains of the Tartar army. Moreover one infected man could carry the poison to others, and infect people and places with the disease by look alone. No one knew, or could discover, a means of defense.

"Thus almost everyone who had been in the East, or in the regions to the south and north, fell victim to sudden death after contracting this pestilential disease, as if struck by a lethal arrow which raised a tumor on their bodies. The scale of the mortality and the form which it took persuaded those who lived, weeping and lamenting, through the bitter events of 1346 to 1348 — the Chinese, Indians, Persians, Medes, Kurds, Armenians, Cilicians, Georgians, Mesopotamians, Nubians, Ethiopians, Turks, Egyptians, Arabs, Saracens, and Greeks (for almost all the East has been affected) — that the last judgement had come.

". . . As it happened, among those who escaped from Caffa by boat were a few sailors who had been infected with the poisonous disease. Some boats were bound for Genoa, others went to Venice and to other Christian areas. When the sailors reached these places and mixed with the people there, it was as if they had brought evil spirits with them: every city, every settlement, every place was poisoned by the contagious pestilence, and their inhabitants, both men and women, died suddenly. And when one person had contracted the illness, he poisoned his whole family even as he fell and died, so that those preparing to bury his body were seized by death in the same way. Thus death entered through the windows, and as cities and towns were depopulated their inhabitants mourned their dead neighbours."

The account closes with an extended description of the plague in Piacenza, and a reprise of the apocalyptic vision with which it begins.

---

[1]Technically trebuchets, not catapults. Catapults hurl objects by the release of tension on twisted cordage; they are not capable of hurling loads over a few dozen kilograms. Trebuchets are counter-weight-driven hurling machines, very effective for throwing ammunition weighing a hundred kilos or more.

[2]Medieval society lacked a coherent theory of disease causation. Three notions coexisted in a somewhat contradictory mixture: 1) disease was a divine punishment for individual or collective transgression: 2) disease was the result of "miasma," or the stench of decay: and 3) disease was the result of person-to-person contagion.

Commentary

In this narrative, de' Mussis makes two important claims about the siege of Caffa and the Black Death: that plague was transmitted to Europeans by the hurling of diseased cadavers into the besieged city of Caffa and that Italians fleeing from Caffa brought it to the Mediterranean ports.

Biological Warfare at Caffa

De' Mussis's account is probably secondhand and is uncorroborated; however, he seems, in general, to be a reliable source, and as a Piacenzian he would have had access to eyewitnesses of the siege. Several considerations incline me to trust his account: this was probably not the only, nor the first, instance of apparent attempts to transmit disease by hurling biological material into besieged cities; it was within the technical capabilities of besieging armies of the time; and it is consistent with medieval notions of disease causality.

Tentatively accepting that the attack took place as described, we can consider two principal hypotheses for the entry of plague into the city: it might, as de' Mussis asserts, have been transmitted by the hurling of plague cadavers; or it might have entered by rodent-to-rodent transmission from the Mongol encampments into the city.

Diseased cadavers hurled into the city could easily have transmitted plague, as defenders handled the cadavers during disposal. Contact with infected material is a known mechanism of transmission; for instance, among 284 cases of plague in the United States in 1970–1995 for which a mechanism of transmission could be reasonably inferred, 20 percent were thought to be by direct contact. Such transmission would have been especially likely at Caffa, where cadavers would have been badly mangled by being hurled, and many of the defenders probably had cut or abraded hands from coping with the bombardment. Very large numbers of cadavers were possibly involved, greatly increasing the opportunity for disease transmission. Since disposal of the bodies of victims in a major outbreak of lethal disease is always a problem, the Mongol forces may have used their hurling machines as a solution to their mortuary problem, in which case many thousands of cadavers could have been involved. de' Mussis's description of "mountains of dead" might have been quite literally true.

Thus it seems plausible that the events recounted by de' Mussis could have been an effective means of transmission of plague into the city. The alternative, rodent-to-rodent transmission from the Mongol encampments into the city, is less likely. Besieging forces must have camped at least a kilometer away from the city walls. This distance is necessary to have a healthy margin of safety from arrows and artillery and to provide space for logistical support and other military activities between the encampments and the front lines. Front-line location must have been approximately 250–300 m from the walls; trebuchets are known from modern reconstruction to be capable of hurling 100 kg more than 200 m, and historical sources claim 300 m as the working range of large machines. Thus, the bulk of rodent nests associated with the besieging armies would have been located a kilometer or more away from the cities, and none would have likely been closer than 250 m. Rats are quite sedentary and rarely venture more than a few tens of meters from their nest. It is thus unlikely that there was any contact between the rat populations within and outside the walls.

Given the many uncertainties, any conclusion must remain tentative. However, the considerations above suggest that the hurling of plague cadavers might well have occurred as de' Mussis claimed, and if so, that this biological attack was probably responsible for the transmission of the disease from the besiegers to the besieged. Thus, this early act of biological warfare, if such it were, appears to have been spectacularly successful in producing casualties, although of no strategic importance (the city remained in Italian hands, and the Mongols abandoned the siege).

Crimea as the Source of European and Near Eastern Plague

There has never been any doubt that plague entered the Mediterranean from the Crimea, following established maritime trade routes. Rat infestations in the holds of cargo ships would have been highly susceptible to the rapid spread of plague, and even if most rats died during the voyage, they would have left abundant hungry fleas that would infect humans unpacking the holds. Shore rats foraging on board recently arrived ships would also become infected, transmitting plague to city rat populations.

Plague appears to have been spread in a stepwise fashion, on many ships rather than on a few [see Map 12.1], taking over a year to reach Europe from the Crimea. This conclusion seems fairly firm, as the dates for the arrival of plague in Constantinople and more westerly cities are reasonably certain. Thus de' Mussis was probably mistaken in attributing the Black Death to fleeing survivors of Caffa, who should not have needed more than a few months to return to Italy.

Furthermore, a number of other Crimean ports were under Mongol control, making it unlikely that Caffa was the only source of infected ships heading west. And the overland caravan routes to the Middle East from Serai and Astrakhan insured that plague was also spreading south (Map 12.1), whence it would have entered Europe in any case. The siege of Caffa and its gruesome finale thus are unlikely to have been seriously implicated in the transmission of plague from the Black Sea to Europe.

Conclusion

Gabriele de' Mussis's account of the origin and spread of plague appears to be consistent with most known facts, although mistaken in its claim that plague arrived in Italy directly from the Crimea. His account of biological attack is plausible, consistent with the technology of the time, and it provides the best explanation of disease transmission into besieged Caffa. This thus appears to be one of the first biological attacks recorded and among the most successful of all time.

However, it is unlikely that the attack had a decisive role in the spread of plague to Europe. Much maritime commerce probably continued throughout this period from other Crimean ports. Overland caravan routes to the Middle East were also unaffected. Thus, refugees from Caffa would most likely have constituted only one of several streams of infected ships and caravans leaving the region. The siege of Caffa, for all of its dramatic appeal, probably had no more than anecdotal importance in the spread of plague, a macabre incident in terrifying times.

Despite its historical unimportance, the siege of Caffa is a powerful reminder of the horrific consequences when disease is successfully used as a weapon. The Japanese use of plague as a weapon in World War II and the huge Soviet stockpiles of *Y. pestis* prepared for use in an all-out war further remind us that plague remains a very real problem for modern arms control, six and a half centuries later.

$$\boxed{76}$$

GABRIELE DE' MUSSIS

Origins of the Black Death

Gabriele de' Mussis (d. 1356) was a lawyer who lived in the northern Italian city of Piacenza. The previous reading introduced you to de' Mussis and the importance of his history of the Black Death. Since Wheelis quoted abundantly from the story of the siege of Caffa, we pick up the story in de' Mussis's words of the spread of the plague to Europe where, as he wrote, he had direct evidence. How would you

---

The Black Death, trans. and ed. Rosemary Horrox (Manchester, England: Manchester University Press, 1994), 18–26.

rate de' Mussis as an eyewitness observer? According to his evidence, how did the Black Death spread in Italy? How deadly was it?

Thinking Historically

As in the previous selection, there are two causal chains in this account, but in this case they are not medical and historical. Rather, reminiscent of the readings on the First Crusade, they are divine and human chains of causation. What according to the author were the divine or religious causes of the Black Death? What were the human, physical, or scientific causes? What remedies does each type of cause call for?

Now it is time that we passed from east to west, to discuss all the things which we ourselves have seen, or known, or consider likely on the basis of the evidence, and, by so doing, to show forth the terrifying judgements of God. Listen everybody, and it will set tears pouring from your eyes. For the Almighty has said: "I shall wipe man, whom I created, off the face of the earth. Because he is flesh and blood, let him be turned to dust and ashes. My spirit shall not remain among man."

— "What are you thinking of, merciful God, thus to destroy your creation and the human race; to order and command its sudden annihilation in this way? What has become of your mercy; the faith of our fathers; the blessed virgin, who holds sinners in her lap; the precious blood of the martyrs; the worthy army of confessors and virgins; the whole host of paradise, who pray ceaselessly for sinners; the most precious death of Christ on the cross and our wonderful redemption? Kind God, I beg that your anger may cease, that you do not destroy sinners in this way, and, because you desire mercy rather than sacrifice, that you turn away all evil from the penitent, and do not allow the just to be condemned with the unjust."

— "I hear you, sinner, dropping words into my ears. I bid you weep. The time for mercy has passed. I, God, am called to vengeance. It is my pleasure to take revenge on sin and wickedness. I shall give my signs to the dying, let them take steps to provide for the health of their souls."

As it happened, among those who escaped from Caffa by boat were a few sailors who had been infected with the poisonous disease. Some boats were bound for Genoa, others went to Venice and to other Christian areas. . . .

— "We Genoese and Venetians bear the responsibility for revealing the judgements of God. Alas, once our ships had brought us to port we went to our homes. And because we had been delayed by tragic events, and because among us there were scarcely ten survivors from a thousand sailors, relations, kinsmen and neighbours flocked to us from all sides. But, to our anguish, we were carrying the darts of death. While they hugged and kissed us we were spreading poison from our lips even as we spoke."

When they returned to their own folk, these people speedily poisoned the whole family, and within three days the afflicted family would succumb to the dart of death. Mass funerals had to be held and there was not enough room to bury the growing numbers of dead. Priests and doctors, upon whom most of the care of the sick devolved, had their hands full in visiting the sick and, alas, by the time they left they too had been infected and followed the dead immediately to the grave. Oh fathers! Oh mothers! Oh children and wives! For a long time prosperity preserved you from harm, but one grave now covers you and the unfortunate alike. You who enjoyed the world and upon whom pleasure and prosperity smiled, who mingled joys with follies, the same tomb receives you and you are handed over as food for worms. Oh hard death, impious death, bitter death, cruel death, who divides parents, divorces spouses, parts children, separates brothers and sisters. We bewail our wretched plight. The past has devoured us, the present is gnawing our entrails, the future threatens yet greater dangers. What we laboured to amass with feverish activity, we have lost in one hour.

Where are the fine clothes of gilded youth? Where is nobility and the courage of fighters, where the mature wisdom of elders and the regal throng of great ladies, where the piles of treasure and precious stones? Alas! All have been destroyed; thrust aside by death. To whom shall we turn, who can help us? To flee is impossible, to hide futile. Cities, fortresses, fields, woods, highways and rivers are ringed by thieves — which is to say by evil spirits, the executioners of the supreme Judge, preparing endless punishments for us all.

We can unfold a terrifying event which happened when an army was camped near Genoa. Four of the soldiers left the force in search of plunder and made their way to Rivarolo on the coast, where the disease had killed all the inhabitants. Finding the houses shut up, and no one about, they broke into one of the houses and stole a fleece which they found on a bed. They then rejoined the army and on the following night the four of them bedded down under the fleece. When morning comes it finds them dead. As a result everyone panicked, and thereafter nobody would use the goods and clothes of the dead, or even handle them, but rejected them outright.

Scarcely one in seven of the Genoese survived. In Venice, where an inquiry was held into the mortality, it was found that more than 70 percent of the people had died, and that within a short period 20 out of 24 excellent physicians had died. The rest of Italy, Sicily, and Apulia and the neighbouring regions maintain that they have been virtually emptied of inhabitants. The people of Florence, Pisa, and Lucca, finding themselves bereft of their fellow residents, emphasise their losses. The Roman Curia at Avignon, the provinces on both sides of the Rhône, Spain,

France, and the Empire cry up their griefs and disasters — all of which makes it extraordinarily difficult for me to give an accurate picture.

By contrast, what befell the Saracens can be established from trustworthy accounts. In the city of Babylon alone (the heart of the Sultan's power), 480,000 of his subjects are said to have been carried off by disease in less than three months in 1348 — and this is known from the Sultan's register which records the names of the dead, because he receives a gold bezant for each person buried. I am silent about Damascus and his other cities, where the number of dead was infinite. In the other countries of the East, which are so vast that it takes three years to ride across them and which have a population of 10,000 for every one inhabitant of the west, it is credibly reported that countless people have died.

Everyone has a responsibility to keep some record of the disease and the deaths, and because I am myself from Piacenza I have been urged to write more about what happened there in 1348. . . .

I don't know where to begin. Cries and laments arise on all sides. Day after day one sees the Cross and the Host[1] being carried about the city, and countless dead being buried. The ensuing mortality was so great that people could scarcely snatch breath. The living made preparations for their burial, and because there was not enough room for individual graves, pits had to be dug in colonnades and piazzas, where nobody had ever been buried before. It often happened that man and wife, father and son, mother and daughter, and soon the whole household and many neighbours, were buried together in one place. The same thing happened in Castell' Arquato and Viguzzolo and in the other towns, villages, cities, and settlements, and last of all in the Val Tidone, where they had hitherto escaped the plague.

Very many people died. One Oberto de Sasso, who had come from the infected neighbourhood around the church of the Franciscans, wished to make his will and accordingly summoned a notary and his neighbours as witnesses, all of whom, more than sixty of them, died soon after. At this time the Dominican friar Syfredo de Bardis, a man of prudence and great learning who had visited the Holy Sepulchre, also died, along with 23 brothers of the same house. There also died within a short time the Franciscan friar Bertolino Coxadocha of Piacenza, renowned for his learning and many virtues, along with 24 brothers of the same house, nine of them on one day; seven of the Augustinians; the Carmelite friar Francesco Todischi with six of his brethren; four of the order of Mary; more than sixty prelates and parish priests from the city and district of Piacenza; many nobles; countless young people; numberless women, particularly those who were pregnant. It is too distressing to recite any more, or to lay bare the wounds inflicted by so great a disaster.

---

[1]The consecrated Eucharistic wafer. The reference is to priests taking the last sacrament to the dying.

Let all creation tremble with fear before the judgement of God. Let human frailty submit to its creator. May a greater grief be kindled in all hearts, and tears well up in all eyes as future ages hear what happened in this disaster. When one person lay sick in a house no one would come near. Even dear friends would hide themselves away, weeping. The physician would not visit. The priest, panic-stricken, administered the sacraments with fear and trembling.

Listen to the tearful voices of the sick: "Have pity, have pity, my friends. At least say something, now that the hand of God has touched me."

"Oh father, why have you abandoned me? Do you forget that I am your child?"

"Mother, where have you gone? Why are you now so cruel to me when only yesterday you were so kind? You fed me at your breast and carried me within your womb for nine months."

"My children, whom I brought up with toil and sweat, why have you run away?"

Man and wife reached out to each other, "Alas, once we slept happily together but now are separated and wretched."

And when the sick were in the throes of death, they still called out piteously to their family and neighbours, "Come here. I'm thirsty, bring me a drink of water. I'm still alive. Don't be frightened. Perhaps I won't die. Please hold me tight, hug my wasted body. You ought to be holding me in your arms."

At this, as everyone else kept their distance, somebody might take pity and leave a candle burning by the bed head as he fled. And when the victim had breathed his last, it was often the mother who shrouded her son and placed him in the coffin, or the husband who did the same for his wife, for everybody else refused to touch the dead body. . . .

I am overwhelmed, I can't go on. Everywhere one turns there is death and bitterness to be described. The hand of the Almighty strikes repeatedly, to greater and greater effect. The terrible judgement gains in power as time goes by.

— What shall we do? Kind Jesus, receive the souls of the dead, avert your gaze from our sins and blot out all our iniquities.

We know that whatever we suffer is the just reward of our sins. Now, therefore, when the Lord is enraged, embrace acts of penance, so that you do not stray from the right path and perish. Let the proud be humbled. Let misers, who withheld alms from the poor, blush for shame. Let the envious become zealous in almsgiving. Let lechers put aside their filthy habits and distinguish themselves in honest living. Let the raging and wrathful restrain themselves from violence. Let gluttons temper their appetites by fasting. Let the slaves of sloth arise and dress themselves in good works. Let adolescents and youths abandon their present delight in following fashion. Let there be good faith and equity among judges, and respect for the law among merchants. Let pettifogging

lawyers study and grow wise before they put pen to paper. Let members
of religious orders abandon hypocrisy. Let the dignity of prelates be put
to better use. Let all of you hurry to set your feet on the way of salvation. And let the overweening vanity of great ladies, which so easily
turns into voluptuousness, be bridled. It was against their arrogance that
Isaiah inveighed: "Because the daughters of Sion are haughty, and have
walked with stretched out necks and wanton glances of their eyes, and
made a noise as they walked with their feet, and moved in a set pace. . . .
Thy fairest men also shall fall by the sword: and thy valiant ones in battle. And her gates shall lament and mourn: and she shall sit desolate on
the ground" [Isaiah 3.16–26]. This was directed against the pride of
ladies and young people.

For the rest, so that the conditions, causes, and symptoms of this
pestilential disease should be made plain to all, I have decided to set
them out in writing. Those of both sexes who were in health, and in no
fear of death, were struck by four savage blows to the flesh. First, out
of the blue, a kind of chilly stiffness troubled their bodies. They felt a
tingling sensation, as if they were being pricked by the points of arrows. The next stage was a fearsome attack which took the form of an
extremely hard, solid boil. In some people this developed under the
armpit and in others in the groin between the scrotum and the body. As
it grew more solid, its burning heat caused the patients to fall into an
acute and putrid fever, with severe headaches. As it intensified its
extreme bitterness could have various effects. In some cases it gave rise
to an intolerable stench. In others it brought vomiting of blood, or
swellings near the place from which the corrupt humour arose: on the
back, across the chest, near the thigh. Some people lay as if in a
drunken stupor and could not be roused. Behold the swellings, the
warning signs sent by the Lord.[2] All these people were in danger of
dying. Some died on the very day the illness took possession of them,
others on the next day, others — the majority — between the third and
fifth day. There was no known remedy for the vomiting of blood.
Those who fell into a coma, or suffered a swelling or the stink of corruption very rarely escaped. But from the fever it was sometimes possible to make a recovery. . . .

Truly, then was a time of bitterness and grief, which served to turn
men to the Lord. I shall recount what happened. A warning was given
by a certain holy person, who received it in a vision, that in cities,
towns and other settlements, everyone, male and female alike, should
gather in their parish church on three consecutive days and, each with a
lighted candle in their hand, hear with great devotion the mass of the

---

[2]A pun: *bulla* is a swelling, but it is also the word for the papal seal, and hence for a
papal document (or bull). De' Mussis is playing on the idea of the swelling characteristic of
the plague being God's seal, notifying the victim of his imminent fate.

Blessed Anastasia, which is normally performed at dawn on Christmas day, and they should humbly beg for mercy, so that they might be delivered from the disease through the merits of the holy mass. Other people sought deliverance through the mediation of a blessed martyr; and others humbly turned to other saints, so that they might escape the abomination of disease. For among the aforesaid martyrs, some, as stories relate, are said to have died from repeated blows, and it was therefore the general opinion that they would be able to protect people against the arrows of death. Finally, in 1350, the most holy Pope Clement ordained a general indulgence, to be valid for a year, which remitted penance and guilt to all who were truly penitent and confessed. And as a result a numberless multitude of people made the pilgrimage to Rome, to visit with great reverence and devotion the basilicas of the blessed apostles Peter and Paul and St John.

Oh, most dearly beloved, let us therefore not be like vipers, growing ever more wicked, but let us rather hold up our hands to heaven to beg for mercy on us all, for who but God shall have mercy on us? With this, I make an end. May the heavenly physician heal our wounds — our spiritual rather than our bodily wounds. To whom be the blessing and the praise and the glory for ever and ever, Amen.

$$\boxed{77}$$

GIOVANNI BOCCACCIO

The Plague in Florence: *From* the Decameron

Giovanni Boccaccio* (1313–1375) was a poet in Florence, Italy, when the plague struck in 1348. His *Decameron*[†] is a collection of a hundred dred tales based on his experiences during the plague years. This selection is drawn from the Introduction. What does Boccaccio add to your understanding of the Black Death?

*boh KAH chee oh
†deh KAM uh rahn

Giovanni Boccaccio, *Decameron*, trans. G. H. McWilliam (Harmondsworth, England: Penguin, 1972), 50–58.

Thinking Historically

Compare Boccaccio's treatment of divine and human causes of the
plague. Boccaccio not only muses on the causes of the plague; he also
sees the plague as the cause of new forms of behavior. What were the
behavioral effects of the plague according to Boccaccio?

I say, then, that the sum of thirteen hundred and forty-eight years had
elapsed since the fruitful Incarnation of the Son of God, when the noble
city of Florence, which for its great beauty excels all others in Italy, was
visited by the deadly pestilence. Some say that it descended upon the
human race through the influence of the heavenly bodies, others that it
was a punishment signifying God's righteous anger at our iniquitous
way of life. But whatever its cause, it had originated some years earlier
in the East, where it had claimed countless lives before it unhappily
spread westward, growing in strength as it swept relentlessly on from
one place to the next.

In the face of its onrush, all the wisdom and ingenuity of man were
unavailing. Large quantities of refuse were cleared out of the city by officials specially appointed for the purpose, all sick persons were forbidden
entry, and numerous instructions were issued for safeguarding the people's
health, but all to no avail. Nor were the countless petitions humbly directed to God by the pious, whether by means of formal processions or
in any other guise, any less ineffectual. For in the early spring of the year
we have mentioned, the plague began, in a terrifying and extraordinary
manner, to make its disastrous effects apparent. It did not take the form
it had assumed in the East, where if anyone bled from the nose it was an
obvious portent of certain death. On the contrary, its earliest symptom,
in men and women alike, was the appearance of certain swellings in the
groin or the armpit, some of which were egg-shaped whilst others were
roughly the size of the common apple. Sometimes the swellings were
large, sometimes not so large, and they were referred to by the populace
as *gavòccioli*. From the two areas already mentioned, this deadly *gavòcciolo* would begin to spread, and within a short time it would appear at
random all over the body. Later on, the symptoms of the disease
changed, and many people began to find dark blotches and bruises on
their arms, thighs, and other parts of the body, sometimes large and few
in number, at other times tiny and closely spaced. These, to anyone unfortunate enough to contract them, were just as infallible a sign that he
would die as the *gavòcciolo* had been earlier, and as indeed it still was.

Against these maladies, it seemed that all the advice of physicians
and all the power of medicine were profitless and unavailing. Perhaps
the nature of the illness was such that it allowed no remedy; or perhaps
those people who were treating the illness (whose numbers had increased enormously because the ranks of the qualified were invaded by

people, both men and women, who had never received any training in medicine), being ignorant of its causes, were not prescribing the appropriate cure. At all events, few of those who caught it ever recovered, and in most cases death occurred within three days from the appearance of the symptoms we have described, some people dying more rapidly than others, the majority without any fever or other complications.

But what made this pestilence even more severe was that whenever those suffering from it mixed with people who were still unaffected, it would rush upon these with the speed of a fire racing through dry or oily substances that happened to be placed within its reach. Nor was this the full extent of its evil, for not only did it infect healthy persons who conversed or had any dealings with the sick, making them ill or visiting an equally horrible death upon them, but it also seemed to transfer the sickness to anyone touching the clothes or other objects which had been handled or used by its victims. . . .

Some people were of the opinion that a sober and abstemious mode of living considerably reduced the risk of infection. They therefore formed themselves into groups and lived in isolation from everyone else. Having withdrawn to a comfortable abode where there were no sick persons, they locked themselves in and settled down to a peaceable existence, consuming modest quantities of delicate foods and precious wines and avoiding all excesses. They refrained from speaking to outsiders, refused to receive news of the dead or sick, and entertained themselves with music and whatever other amusements they were able to devise.

Others took the opposite view, and maintained that an infallible way of warding off this appalling evil was to drink heavily, enjoy life to the full, go round singing and merrymaking, gratify all of one's cravings whenever the opportunity offered, and shrug the whole thing off as one enormous joke. Moreover, they practised what they preached to the best of their ability, for they would visit one tavern after another, drinking all day and night to immoderate excess; or alternatively (and this was their more frequent custom), they would do their drinking in various private houses, but only in the ones where the conversation was restricted to subjects that were pleasant or entertaining. Such places were easy to find, for people behaved as though their days were numbered, and treated their belongings and their own persons with equal abandon. Hence most houses had become common property, and any passing stranger could make himself at home as naturally as though he were the rightful owner. But for all their riotous manner of living, these people always took good care to avoid any contact with the sick.

In the face of so much affliction and misery, all respect for the laws of God and man had virtually broken down and been extinguished in our city. For like everybody else, those ministers and executors of the laws who were not either dead or ill were left with so few subordinates that they were unable to discharge any of their duties. Hence everyone was free to behave as he pleased.

There were many other people who steered a middle course between the two already mentioned, neither restricting their diet to the same degree as the first group, nor indulging so freely as the second in drinking and other forms of wantonness, but simply doing no more than satisfy their appetite. Instead of incarcerating themselves, these people moved about freely, holding in their hands a posy of flowers, or fragrant herbs, or one of a wide range of spices, which they applied at frequent intervals to their nostrils, thinking it an excellent idea to fortify the brain with smells of that particular sort; for the stench of dead bodies, sickness, and medicines seemed to fill and pollute the whole of the atmosphere.

Some people, pursuing what was possibly the safer alternative, callously maintained that there was no better or more efficacious remedy against a plague than to run away from it. Swayed by this argument, and sparing no thought for anyone but themselves, large numbers of men and women abandoned their city, their homes, their relatives, their estates, and their belongings, and headed for the countryside, either in Florentine territory or, better still, abroad. It was as though they imagined that the wrath of God would not unleash this plague against men for their iniquities irrespective of where they happened to be, but would only be aroused against those who found themselves within the city walls; or possibly they assumed that the whole of the population would be exterminated and that the city's last hour had come.

Of the people who held these various opinions, not all of them died. Nor, however, did they all survive. On the contrary, many of each different persuasion fell ill here, there, and everywhere, and having themselves, when they were fit and well, set an example to those who were as yet unaffected, they languished away with virtually no one to nurse them. It was not merely a question of one citizen avoiding another, and of people almost invariably neglecting their neighbours and rarely or never visiting their relatives, addressing them only from a distance; this scourge had implanted so great a terror in the hearts of men and women that brothers abandoned brothers, uncles their nephews, sisters their brothers, and in many cases wives deserted their husbands. But even worse, and almost incredible, was the fact that fathers and mothers refused to nurse and assist their own children, as though they did not belong to them.

Hence the countless numbers of people who fell ill, both male and female, were entirely dependent upon either the charity of friends (who were few and far between) or the greed of servants, who remained in short supply despite the attraction of high wages out of all proportion to the services they performed. Furthermore, these latter were men and women of coarse intellect and the majority were unused to such duties, and they did little more than hand things to the invalid when asked to do so and watch over him when he was dying. And in performing this kind of service, they frequently lost their lives as well as their earnings.

As a result of this wholesale desertion of the sick by neighbours, relatives, and friends, and in view of the scarcity of servants, there grew up a practice almost never previously heard of, whereby when a woman fell ill, no matter how gracious or beautiful or gently bred she might be, she raised no objection to being attended by a male servant, whether he was young or not. Nor did she have any scruples about showing him every part of her body as freely as she would have displayed it to a woman, provided that the nature of her infirmity required her to do so; and this explains why those women who recovered were possibly less chaste in the period that followed.

Moreover a great many people died who would perhaps have survived had they received some assistance. And hence, what with the lack of appropriate means for tending the sick, and the virulence of the plague, the number of deaths reported in the city whether by day or night was so enormous that it astonished all who heard tell of it, to say nothing of the people who actually witnessed the carnage. . . .

As for the common people and a large proportion of the bourgeoisie, they presented a much more pathetic spectacle, for the majority of them were constrained, either by their poverty or the hope of survival, to remain in their houses. Being confined to their own parts of the city, they fell ill daily in their thousands, and since they had no one to assist them or attend to their needs, they inevitably perished almost without exception. Many dropped dead in the open streets, both by day and by night, whilst a great many others, though dying in their own houses, drew their neighbours' attention to the fact more by the smell of their rotting corpses than by any other means. And what with these, and the others who were dying all over the city, bodies were here, there, and everywhere. . . .

[T]here were no tears or candles or mourners to honour the dead; in fact, no more respect was accorded to dead people than would nowadays be shown towards dead goats. For it was quite apparent that the one thing which, in normal times, no wise man had ever learned to accept with patient resignation (even though it struck so seldom and unobtrusively), had now been brought home to the feeble-minded as well, but the scale of the calamity caused them to regard it with indifference.

Such was the multitude of corpses (of which further consignments were arriving every day and almost by the hour at each of the churches), that there was not sufficient consecrated ground for them to be buried in, especially if each was to have its own plot in accordance with long-established custom. So when all the graves were full, huge trenches were excavated in the churchyards, into which new arrivals were placed in their hundreds, stowed tier upon tier like ships' cargo, each layer of corpses being covered over with a thin layer of soil till the trench was filled to the top.

But rather than describe in elaborate detail the calamities we experienced in the city at that time, I must mention that, whilst an ill wind was blowing through Florence itself, the surrounding region was no less badly affected. In the fortified towns, conditions were similar to those in the city itself on a minor scale; but in the scattered hamlets and the countryside proper, the poor unfortunate peasants and their families had no physicians or servants whatever to assist them, and collapsed by the wayside, in their fields, and in their cottages at all hours of the day and night, dying more like animals than human beings. Like the townspeople, they too grew apathetic in their ways, disregarded their affairs, and neglected their possessions. Moreover, they all behaved as though each day was to be their last, and far from making provision for the future by tilling their lands, tending their flocks, and adding to their previous labours, they tried in every way they could think of to squander the assets already in their possession. Thus it came about that oxen, asses, sheep, goats, pigs, chickens, and even dogs (for all their deep fidelity to man) were driven away and allowed to roam freely through the fields, where the crops lay abandoned and had not even been reaped, let alone gathered in. And after a whole day's feasting, many of these animals, as though possessing the power of reason, would return glutted in the evening to their own quarters without any shepherd to guide them.

But let us leave the countryside and return to the city. What more remains to be said, except that the cruelty of heaven (and possibly, in some measure, also that of man) was so immense and so devastating that between March and July of the year in question, what with the fury of the pestilence and the fact that so many of the sick were inadequately cared for or abandoned in their hour of need because the healthy were too terrified to approach them, it is reliably thought that over a hundred thousand human lives were extinguished within the walls of the city of Florence? Yet before this lethal catastrophe fell upon the city, it is doubtful whether anyone would have guessed it contained so many inhabitants.

$$\boxed{78}$$

Images of the Black Death

Contemporary accounts testify to the plague's terrifying physical, social, and psychological impact. Images from the period document the ravages of the epidemic as well, sometimes in gruesome detail. The engraving in Figure 12.1, for example, shows a plague victim covered in the dark blotches characteristic of the disease. The town in the back-

Figure 12.1   Plague Victim with Maiden, 1348.
Source: The Bridgeman Art Library International.

ground appears to be going up in flames while lightning flares in the
sky above. What else do you think is going on in this image? Who is
the woman depicted and what is she doing? If this is a group fleeing
with their belongings from the burning town, do you think the plague
victim is part of their entourage? What might be the significance of
the flag they carry?

Figures 12.2 and 12.3 show two well-documented phenomena of
the plague years: The first depicts a group of flagellants, members of a
movement who wandered from town to town beating themselves with
whips studded with iron nails in an effort to do penance for the sins
they believed had brought on the plague. Written accounts confirm
many elements in this picture: Flagellants usually carried crosses or
banners with crosses on them, wore long pleated skirts, and went
around bare-chested, the better to make their scourging as painful as
possible. Figure 12.3 illustrates a similar impulse toward punishment
as a means of coping with the plague, but this time the violence is

Figure 12.2 Flagellants, from a Fifteenth-Century Chronicle from Constance, Switzerland.

Source: © Bettmann/CORBIS.

Figure 12.3 The Burning of Jews in an Early Printed Woodcut.

Source: © Christel Gerstenberg/CORBIS.

directed outward, against Jews, so often the scapegoats in troubled times. Baseless accusations that Jews poisoned wells to spread the plague resulted in many such attacks against them during the period.

The final image, Figure 12.4, is one of a transi tomb from 1390. Transi tombs, which emerged during and after the plague era, were a major departure from standard funerary monuments that typically offered an idealized depiction of the deceased. Instead these tombs showed decaying or skeletal corpses covered with worms and other emblems of bodily corruption. Scholars differ over their meaning. How might you explain them?

Thinking Historically

What can these images tell us about fourteenth-century people's beliefs about the possible causes — medical or religious — of the plague? Think about the social and religious changes wrought by the plague recounted in the de' Mussis and Boccaccio readings. What evidence, if any, do you see in these images of these changes?

Figure 12.4 François de la Sarra, Tomb at La Sarraz, Switzerland, c. 1390.
Source: Reproduced courtesy of Harry N. Abrams, Inc.

79

AHMAD AL-MAQRIZI
The Plague in Cairo

Ahmad al-Maqrizi* (1364–1442) became a historian after pursuing a career as an administrator in post-plague Cairo. While he wrote his history of the plague period more than fifty years after the event, he probably had access to contemporary sources that are now lost to us. Compare al-Maqrizi's account of the plague in Cairo with the prior accounts of the plague in Italy. How was the experience of the Black Death in Cairo similar to, and different from, the experience in Florence?

Thinking Historically

Like Boccaccio, al-Maqrizi devotes more attention to the effects than to the causes of the Black Death. What effects were similar in Florence and Cairo? Al-Maqrizi discusses certain effects that were not mentioned in the Italian accounts. Which, if any, of these effects do you think also probably occurred in Italy?

In January 1349, there appeared new symptoms that consisted of spitting up of blood. The disease caused one to experience an internal fever, followed by an uncontrollable desire to vomit; then one spat up blood and died. The inhabitants of a house were stricken one after the other, and in one night or two, the dwelling became deserted. Each individual lived with this fixed idea that he was going to die in this way. He prepared for himself a good death by distributing alms; he arranged for scenes of reconciliation and his acts of devotion multiplied. . . .

By January 21, Cairo had become an abandoned desert, and one did not see anyone walking along the streets. A man could go from the Port Zuwayla to Bāb al-Nasr[1] without encountering a living soul. The dead were very numerous, and all the world could think of nothing else. Debris piled up in the streets. People went around with worried faces. Everywhere one heard lamentations, and one could not pass by any house without being overwhelmed by the howling. Cadavers

*ahk MAHD   ahl mah KREE zee
[1]This was apparently the busiest boulevard in medieval Cairo.

John Aberth, *The Black Death: The Great Mortality of 1348–1350, A Brief History with Documents* (Boston: Bedford/St. Martin's, 2005), 84–87.

formed a heap on the public highway, funeral processions were so many that they could not file past without bumping into each other, and the dead were transported in some confusion. . . .

One began to have to search for readers of the Koran for funeral ceremonies, and a number of individuals quit their usual occupations in order to recite prayers at the head of funeral processions. In the same way, some people devoted themselves to smearing crypts with plaster; others presented themselves as volunteers to wash the dead or carry them. These latter folk earned substantial salaries. For example, a reader of the Koran took ten *dirhams*.[2] Also, hardly had he reached the oratory when he slipped away very quickly in order to go officiate at a new [funeral]. Porters demanded 6 *dirhams* at the time they were engaged, and then it was necessary to match it [at the grave]. The gravedigger demanded fifty *dirhams* per grave. Most of the rest of these people died without having taken any profit from their gains. . . . Also families kept their dead on the bare ground, due to the impossibility of having them interred. The inhabitants of a house died by the tens and, since there wasn't a litter ready to hand, one had to carry them away in stages. Moreover, some people appropriated for themselves without scruple the immovable and movable goods and cash of their former owners after their demise. But very few lived long enough to profit thereby, and those who remained alive would have been able to do without. . . .

Family festivities and weddings had no more place [in life]. No one issued an invitation to a feast during the whole time of the epidemic, and one did not hear any concert. The *vizier*[3] lifted a third of what he was owed from the woman responsible [for collecting] the tax on singers. The call to prayer was canceled in various places, and in the exact same way, those places [where prayer] was most frequent subsisted on a *muezzin*[4] alone. . . .

The men of the [military] troop and the cultivators took a world of trouble to finish their sowing [of fields]. The plague emerged at the end of the season when the fields were becoming green. How many times did one see a laborer, at Gaza, at Ramleh, and along other points of the Syrian littoral,[5] guide his plow being pulled by oxen suddenly fall down dead, still holding in his hands his plow, while the oxen stood at their place without a conductor.

It was the same in Egypt: When the harvest time came, there remained only a very small number of *fellahs*.[6] The soldiers and their

---

[2] A silver coin used in the Muslim world.

[3] The chief minister of the caliph, or leader of the Muslim community.

[4] An official of the mosque who called the faithful to prayer from the minaret.

[5] The coastal plain of southern Palestine, where the most fertile land was located.

[6] Arabic word for ploughman or tiller, which also denoted the peasantry of Egypt and is the origin of the modern term, *fellahin*.

valets left for the harvest and attempted to hire workers, promising
them half of the crop, but they could not find anyone to help them reap
it. They loaded the grain on their horses, did the mowing themselves,
but, being powerless to carry out the greatest portion of the work, they
abandoned this enterprise.

The endowments[7] passed rapidly from hand to hand as a consequence of the multiplicity of deaths in the army. Such a concession
passed from one to the other until the seventh or eighth holder, to fall
finally [into the hands] of artisans, such as tailors, shoemakers, or public criers, and these mounted the horse, donned the [military] headdress, and dressed in military tunics.

Actually, no one collected the whole revenue of his endowment,
and a number of holders harvested absolutely nothing. During the
flooding of the Nile[8] and the time of the sprouting of vegetation, one
could procure a laborer only with difficulty: On half the lands only did
the harvest reach maturity. Moreover, there was no one to buy the
green clover [as feed] and no one sent their horses to graze over the
field. This was the ruin of royal properties in the suburbs of Cairo, like
Matarieh, Hums, Siryaqus, and Bahtit. In the canton [administrative
district] of Nay and Tanan, 1,500 *feddans*[9] of clover were abandoned
where it stood: No one came to buy it, either to pasture their beasts on
the place or to gather it into barns and use it as fodder.

The province of Upper Egypt was deserted, in spite of the vast
abundance of cultivable terrain. It used to be that, after the land surface
was cultivated in the territory of Asyūt,[10] 6,000 individuals were subject to payment of the property tax; now, in the year of the epidemic
[1348–49], one could not count on more than 106 contributors. Nevertheless, during this period, the price of wheat did not rise past fifteen
dirhams per *ardeb*.[11]

Most of the trades disappeared, for a number of artisans devoted
themselves to handling the dead, while the others, no less numerous,
occupied themselves in selling off to bidders [the dead's] movable goods
and clothing, so well that the price of linen and similar objects fell by a
fifth of their real value, at the very least, and still further until one
found customers. . . .

Thus the trades disappeared: One could no longer find either a
water carrier, or a laundress, or a domestic. The monthly salary of a

---

[7]Mamluk commanders and elite soldiers, like their Ayyubid predecessors, were paid out
of the revenues of land grants, known as *iqtas* (similar to fiefs in Europe). With the dearth of
labor caused by the Black Death, it became far more difficult to extract income from these
estates.

[8]This usually took place between September and November of every year.

[9]A *feddan* is equivalent to 1.038 acres.

[10]Located along the Nile in Upper Egypt, about midway between Cairo and Aswan.

[11]An *ardeb* is equivalent to 5.62 bushels.

groom rose from thirty *dirhams* to eighty. A proclamation made in Cairo invited the artisans to take up their old trades, and some of the recalcitrants reformed themselves. Because of the shortage of men and camels, a goatskin of water reached the price of eight *dirhams,* and in order to grind an *ardeb* of wheat, one paid fifteen *dirhams.*

80

WILLIAM H. McNEILL

Consequences of the Black Death in Europe

In this selection, William H. McNeill, a leading world historian (see selection 10), explores the psychological, cultural, and economic consequences of the Black Death in Europe. What, according to McNeill, were these consequences? Which do you think were most important?

Thinking Historically

McNeill uses the term *consequences* rather than *effects.* Do the words mean the same thing, or are his "consequences" too general to be attached to specific causes? In fact, he lists some of the major changes that occurred in European culture and economy in the centuries after the Black Death. Which of these consequences was likely caused by the Black Death? In the last sentence of this selection, McNeill makes a distinction between effects that depend on a single cause "alone" and on causes that "contributed" to a broader effect. What does he mean by this distinction?

Before pursuing this theme, however, it seems worth venturing a few remarks about the psychological, economic, and cultural consequences of Europe's encounter with the plague in the fourteenth and succeeding centuries; and then we must survey as best we can the disease consequences for Asia and Africa of the Mongol opening of the steppelands to regular transit.

William H. McNeill, *Plagues and Peoples* (Garden City, N.Y.: Anchor Books, 1976), 161–65.

At the psychological and cultural level European reactions were obvious and varied. In face of intense and immediate crisis, when an outbreak of plague implanted fear of imminent death in an entire community, ordinary routines and customary restraints regularly broke down. In time, rituals arose to discharge anxiety in socially acceptable ways; but in the fourteenth century itself, local panic often provoked bizarre behavior. The first important effort at ritualizing responses to the plague took extreme and ugly forms. In Germany and some adjacent parts of Europe companies of Flagellants aimed at propitiating God's wrath by beating each other bloody and attacking Jews, who were commonly accused of spreading the pestilence. The Flagellants disdained all established authorities of church and state and, if accounts are to be believed, their rituals were well-nigh suicidal for the participants.

Attacks on German-Jewish communities inspired by Flagellants and others probably accelerated an eastward shift of centers of Jewish population in Europe. Poland escaped the first round of plague almost entirely, and though popular rioting against Jews occurred there too, royal authorities welcomed German Jews for the urban skills they brought into the country. The subsequent development of east European Jewry was therefore significantly affected (and the rise in the Vistula and Nieman valleys of a market-oriented agriculture, largely under Jewish management, was probably accelerated) by the fourteenth-century pattern of popular reaction to plague.

These and other violent episodes attest the initial impact of the plague on European consciousness. In time, the fear and horror of the first onset relaxed. Writers as diverse as Boccaccio, Chaucer, and William Langland all treated the plague as a routine crisis of human life — an act of God, like the weather. Perhaps the plague had other, more lasting, consequences for literature: scholars have suggested, for instance, that the rise of vernacular tongues as a medium for serious writing and the decay of Latin as a *lingua franca* among the educated men of western Europe was hastened by the die-off of clerics and teachers who knew enough Latin to keep that ancient tongue alive. Painting also responded to the plague-darkened vision of the human condition provoked by repeated exposure to sudden, inexplicable death. Tuscan painters, for instance, reacted against Giotto's serenity, preferring sterner, hieratic portrayals of religious scenes and figures. The "Dance of Death" became a common theme for art; and several other macabre motifs entered the European repertory. The buoyancy and self-confidence, so characteristic of the thirteenth century, when Europe's great cathedrals were abuilding, gave way to a more troubled age. Acute social tensions between economic classes and intimate acquaintance with sudden death assumed far greater importance for almost everyone than had been true previously.

The economic impact of the Black Death was enormous, though local differences were greater than an earlier generation of scholars assumed. In highly developed regions like northern Italy and Flanders, harsh collisions between social classes manifested themselves as the boom times of the thirteenth century faded into the past. The plague, by disrupting wage and price patterns sharply, exacerbated these conflicts, at least in the short run. Some ninety years ago Thorold Rogers argued that the Black Death had improved the lot of the lower classes and advanced freedom by destroying serfdom. His idea was that labor shortage caused by plague deaths allowed wage earners to bargain among rival would-be employers and thus improve their real wages. This view is no longer widely believed. Local circumstances differed widely. Employers died as well as laborers; and manpower shortages proved evanescent in those towns where a vigorous market economy did effect a short-term rise in real wages.

In time, of course, the initial perturbations created by the plague tended to diminish. All the same, two general displacements of European culture and society can be discerned in the latter fourteenth and fifteenth centuries that seem plausibly related to the terrifying, constantly renewed experience of plague.

When the plague was raging, a person might be in full health one day and die miserably within twenty-four hours. This utterly discredited any merely human effort to explain the mysteries of the world. The confidence in rational theology, which characterized the age of Aquinas (d. 1274), could not survive such experiences. A world view allowing ample scope to arbitrary, inexplicable catastrophe alone was compatible with the grim reality of plague. Hedonism and revival of one or another form of fatalistic pagan philosophy were possible reactions, though confined always to a few. Far more popular and respectable was an upsurge of mysticism, aimed at achieving encounter with God in inexplicable, unpredictable, intense, and purely personal ways. Hesychasm[1] among the Orthodox, and more variegated movements among Latin Christians — e.g., the practices of the so-called Rhineland mystics, of the Brethren of the Common Life, and of heretical groups like the Lollards of England — all gave expression to the need for a more personal, antinomian access to God than had been offered by Thomist theology and the previously recognized forms of piety. Recurrence of plague refreshed this psychological need until the mid-seventeenth century; hence it is no accident that all branches of organized Christianity — Orthodox, Catholic, and Protestant — made more room for personal mysticism and other forms of communion with God, even though ecclesiastical

---

[1]Mystical religious practice by Orthodox monks which involved certain repetitive movements and recitation of prayer. [Ed.]

authorities always remained uncomfortable when confronting too much private zeal.

Secondly, the inadequacy of established ecclesiastical rituals and administrative measures to cope with the unexampled emergency of plague had pervasively unsettling effects. In the fourteenth century, many priests and monks died; often their successors were less well trained and faced more quizzical if not openly antagonistic flocks. God's justice seemed far to seek in the way plague spared some, killed others; and the regular administration of God's grace through the sacraments (even when consecrated priests remained available) was an entirely inadequate psychological counterpoise to the statistical vagaries of lethal infection and sudden death. Anticlericalism was of course not new in Christian Europe; after 1346, however, it became more open and widespread, and provided one of the elements contributing to Luther's later success.

Because sacred rituals remained vigorously conservative, it took centuries for the Roman Church to adjust to the recurrent crises created by outbreaks of plague. Hence it was mainly in the period of the Counter-Reformation that psychologically adequate ceremonies and symbols for coping with recurrent lethal epidemics defined themselves. Invocation of St. Sebastian, who in early Christian centuries had already attracted to himself many of the attributes once assigned to Apollo, became central in Catholic rituals of prophylaxis against the plague. The suffering saint, whose death by arrows was symbolic of deaths dealt by the unseen arrows of pestilential infection, began to figure largely in religious art as well. A second important figure was St. Roch. He had a different character, being an exemplar and patron of the acts of public charity and nursing that softened the impact of plague in those cities of Mediterranean Europe that were most exposed to the infection.

Protestant Europe never developed much in the way of special rituals for meeting epidemic emergencies. The Bible had little to say about how to cope with massive outbreaks of infectious disease, and since plague seldom affected the North (though when it came it was sometimes exceptionally severe), Protestants lacked sufficient stimulus to such a development.

In contrast to the rigidities that beset the church, city governments, especially in Italy, responded rather quickly to the challenges presented by devastating disease. Magistrates learned how to cope at the practical level, organizing burials, safeguarding food deliveries, setting up quarantines, hiring doctors, and establishing other regulations for public and private behavior in time of plague. The ability of city authorities to react in these more or less effective ways was symptomatic of their general vigor — a vigor that made the centuries between 1350 and 1550 a sort of golden age for European city-states, especially Germany and Italy, where competition with any superior secular government was minimal.

Italian and German city governments and businessmen not only managed their own local affairs with general success, but also pioneered the development of a far more closely integrated inter-regional market economy that ran throughout all of Europe. Ere long these same cities also defined a more secularized style of life and thought that by 1500 attracted the liveliest attention throughout the continent. The shift from medieval to renaissance cultural values, needless to say, did not depend on the plague alone; yet the plague, and the generally successful way city authorities managed to react to its ravages, surely contributed something to the general transformation of European sensibility.

When we turn attention from Europe and ask what the new plague pattern may have meant elsewhere in the Old World, a troublesome void presents itself. Scholarly discussion of the Black Death in Europe, its course and consequences, is more than a century old; nothing remotely comparable exists for other regions of the earth. Yet it is impossible to believe that the plague did not affect China, India, and the Middle East; and it is even more implausible to think that human life on the steppe was not also brought under new and unexampled stress by the establishment of a persistent reservoir of bubonic infection among the rodents of the Eurasian grasslands all the way from Manchuria to the Ukraine.

To be sure, there is ample evidence that plague became and remained, as in Europe, a dreaded recurrent affliction throughout the Islamic world. Egypt and Syria shared the plague experience of other parts of the Mediterranean coastlands with which they remained always in close contact. About a third of Egypt's population seems to have died in the first attack, 1347–1349, and the plague returned to the Nile Valley at frequent intervals thereafter, appearing there most recently in the 1940s.

REFLECTIONS

History is always written backwards. We study the rearview mirror to see where we are going. What can the Black Death tell us about the possibility of pandemic disease in the future? Historians who are sometimes embarrassed by their present-mindedness can take refuge in the conventions of the discipline: Histories begin in the past and work chronologically toward the present; narratives seem to only tell the story, just as it happened. But both chronological and narrative presentations imply a chain of cause and effect where analysis might reveal chance or no relationship at all.

We can all easily fall prey to the logical fallacy called in Latin "*post hoc, ergo propter hoc*" (meaning literally "after this, therefore because of this"). Just because "B" came after "A" doesn't mean that "B" was caused by "A." Still it is only natural to cast around for this sort of simple, uncomplicated causation when your world is falling apart. Consider how de' Mussis, Boccaccio, or the Flagellants and Europeans shown in Figures 12.2 and 12.3 and discussed in the McNeill reading explained what was happening to them. Nevertheless, in our lives, as in our understanding of history, we can only see the past from the standpoint of the immediate present, and all roads seem to lead inexorably to Now. Though most of us like to think we can shape our future, we gain some comfort from believing that we couldn't have changed our past.

At least for the purposes of historical accuracy, how do we break this mindset? We have already suggested (in our introduction to the reading by McNeill) the importance of recognizing multiple causation. Rarely if ever is any event the result of a single cause. Even a single premeditated act of an individual can be usefully understood in terms of a myriad of factors. Anything as complex as a social movement, economic trend, political revolution, or cultural style results from a profound web of causes. When we ask about the causes of the Protestant Reformation or the Communist Revolution in China, we are clearly dealing with multiple factors, all of which were imporant to some degree in these developments.

Finally, it is important to keep in mind that historical causation always underplays the role of chance or accident. We know our personal lives are full of chance events. Do these unpredictable events become more predictable in larger social groups or over longer time periods? Sometimes we realize later that an event we thought was chance actually had causes. Might this be true more generally? Are chance events merely those we have not yet been able to explain?

We end, perhaps, with more questions than answers. This is because the study of history involves nothing less than the study of everything that has happened to all of the very complex creatures we call human beings. We can formulate certain scientific methods for studying the past. We can even use these methods to improve our understanding of the past. But we never have a single or final explanation of any of it.

13

On Cities

European, Chinese, Islamic, and Mexican Cities, 1000–1550 C.E.

HISTORICAL CONTEXT

During the last five thousand years, cities have grown and multiplied, the world becoming increasingly urbanized. There have been interruptions in this process, however: the period of the Mongol invasions in the first half of the thirteenth century and the era of the Black Death, the plague that wiped out urban populations in the middle of the fourteenth century, for instance. But, by and large, the general course of world history has promoted the rise and expansion of cities and of urban over rural populations.

In this chapter, we ask what this increasing urbanization meant for those who lived in the cities and for those who did not. We compare cities in various parts of the world between 1000 and 1550. We will study primary and secondary sources, and you will be asked to note the ways in which these cities are similar and different.

THINKING HISTORICALLY
Evaluating a Comparative Thesis

Many of the chapters, even individual readings, in this volume have been comparative. Making comparisons is a critical skill in any disciplined thinking process. In the study of world history, comparisons are particularly important and potentially fruitful, since until recently the historical profession tended to study different nations' histories somewhat in isolation from each other or without reference to a broader comparative context.

455

Comparisons are not useful in and of themselves. They are merely a first step toward a thesis that attempts to explain the differences or similarities noticed. To say that something is bigger or smaller, hotter or colder, than something else, that one country is more densely populated or more religious than another, may or may not be obvious or interesting, but the observation is not meaningful in and of itself. The comparative observation becomes meaningful when it is explained by some general rule that covers both cases. Human behavior is too complex to attain what some call "covering laws" in science, but the effort to reach an explanation that covered both cases might be called a comparative thesis.

In history, there are many comparative theses. An example of one might run something like this: Canada has a more universal health care system than the United States because it has a longer tradition of mutual aid and trust in government. Now, one might agree or disagree with either the comparison or the explanation. If one disagrees with the comparison there is no need to go further. But if one agrees with the comparison, then one has to evaluate the comparative thesis.

In this chapter you will be asked to consider a comparative thesis about cities that is offered in the first reading. The other readings in the chapter will enable you to consider what evidence they offer for or against the initial comparison and its explanatory thesis.

81

FERNAND BRAUDEL

Towns and Cities

Fernand Braudel* (1902–1985) was one of the great historians of the twentieth century, and the following selection, which provides a broad overview of medieval towns and cities throughout the world, is from one of his interpretative works of world history. According to Braudel, what were some of the distinctive characteristics of Western, or European, towns? Why did Western towns acquire these character-

*broh DELL

Fernand Braudel, *The Structures of Everyday Life: The Limits of the Possible* (London: Collins, 1983), 509–15, 518–25.

istics? How does Braudel describe Chinese and Islamic cities? Why
and how did these towns develop differently?

Thinking Historically

Braudel begins with a comparative judgment—that European towns
"were marked by an unparalleled freedom." How does he explain this
supposed difference between European towns and those of other societies? He offers a kind of covering law in the form of a "Western
model" that relates urban freedom to a number of other features. He
says these towns were autonomous, self-governing, bodies of largely
middle-class citizens who thought of themselves as a community. They
were not governed by a king, emperor, or territorial state, but, rather,
governed themselves through a number of organizations. In addition to
governing councils and militaries, these organizations included guilds,
church groups, and various other voluntary societies in which citizens
exercised real power over their lives. On an even broader level, Braudel
attributes these differences to the long history of European feudalism
and weak states, and to the rise of capitalism and a middle class.

As you read Braudel, try to weigh his evidence for both the comparison and the larger model. Does it appear from the reading that inhabitants of European towns had greater freedom than the people of
other towns? If you agree with his comparison, try to evaluate his
model. Do the elements of the model fit together? Was there a
complex of features in Western society that did not occur elsewhere?
What is his evidence for that comparative thesis? What else would you
want to learn to challenge or confirm his thesis?

The Originality of Western Towns

. . . What were Europe's differences and original features? Its towns
were marked by an unparalleled freedom. They had developed as autonomous worlds and according to their own propensities. They had
outwitted the territorial state, which was established slowly and then
only grew with their interested co-operation—and was moreover only
an enlarged and often insipid copy of their development. They ruled
their countrysides autocratically, regarding them exactly as later powers regarded their colonies, and treating them as such. They pursued an
economic policy of their own via their satellites and the nervous system
of urban relay points; they were capable of breaking down obstacles
and creating or recreating protective privileges. Imagine what would
happen if modern states were suppressed so that the Chambers of Commerce of the large towns were free to act as they pleased!

Even without resort to doubtful comparisons these long-standing
realities leap to the eye. And they lead us to a key problem which can
be formulated in two or three different ways: What stopped the other

cities of the world from enjoying the same relative freedom? Or to take another aspect of the same problem, why was change a striking feature of the destiny of Western towns (even their physical existence was transformed) while the other cities have no history by comparison and seem to have been shut in long periods of immobility? Why were some cities like steam-engines while the others were like clocks, to parody Lévi-Strauss? Comparative history compels us to look for the reason for these differences and to attempt to establish a dynamic "model" of the turbulent urban evolution of the West, whereas a model representing city life in the rest of the world would run in a straight and scarcely broken line across time.

Free Worlds

Urban freedom in Europe is a classic and fairly well documented subject; let us start with it.

In a simplified form we can say:

1. The West well and truly lost its urban framework with the end of the Roman Empire. Moreover the towns in the Empire had been gradually declining since before the arrival of the barbarians. The very relative animation of the Merovingian period was followed, slightly earlier in some places, slightly later in others, by a complete halt.

2. The urban renaissance from the eleventh century was precipitated by and superimposed on a rise in rural vigour, a growth of fields, vineyards, and orchards. Towns grew in harmony with villages and clearly outlined urban law often emerged from the communal privileges of village groups. The town was often simply the country revived and remodeled. The names of a number of streets in Frankfurt (which remained very rural until the sixteenth century) recall the woods, clumps of trees, and marshland amid which the town grew up.

This rural rearrangement naturally brought to the nascent city the representatives of political and social authority: nobles, lay princes, and ecclesiastics.

3. None of this would have been possible without a general return to health and a growing monetary economy. Money, a traveler from perhaps distant lands (from Islam, according to Maurice Lombard), was the active and decisive force. Two centuries before Saint Thomas Aquinas, Alain de Lille said: "Money, not Caesar, is everything now." And money meant towns.

Thousands of towns were founded at this time, but few of them went on to brilliant futures. Only certain regions, therefore, were urbanized in depth, thus distinguishing themselves from the rest and playing a vitalizing role: such was the region between the Loire and the Rhine, for instance, or northern and central Italy, and certain key points on Mediterranean coasts. Merchants, craft guilds, industries, long-distance trade, and banks were quick to appear there, as well as a certain kind of bourgeoisie and even some sort of capitalism. The destinies of these very special cities were linked not only to the progress of the surrounding countryside but to international trade. Indeed, they often broke free of rural society and former political ties. The break might be achieved violently or amicably, but it was always a sign of strength, plentiful money, and real power.

Soon there were no states around these privileged towns. This was the case in Italy and Germany, with the political collapses of the thirteenth century. The hare beat the tortoise for once. Elsewhere—in France, England, Castile, even in Aragon—the earlier rebirth of the territorial state restricted the development of the towns, which in addition were not situated in particularly lively economic areas. They grew less rapidly than elsewhere.

But the main, the unpredictable thing was that certain towns made themselves into autonomous worlds, city-states, buttressed with privileges (acquired or extorted) like so many juridical ramparts. Perhaps in the past historians have insisted too much on the legal factors involved, for if such considerations were indeed sometimes more important than, or of equal importance to, geographical, sociological, and economic factors, the latter did count to a large extent. What is privilege without material substance?

In fact the miracle in the West was not so much that everything sprang up again from the eleventh century, after having been almost annihilated with the disaster of the fifth. History is full of examples of secular revivals, of urban expansion, of births and rebirths: Greece from the fifth to the second century B.C.E.; Rome perhaps; Islam from the ninth century; China under the Sungs. But these revivals always featured two runners, the state and the city. The state usually won and the city then remained subject and under a heavy yoke. The miracle of the first great urban centuries in Europe was that the city won hands down, at least in Italy, Flanders, and Germany. It was able to try the experiment of leading a completely separate life for quite a long time. This was a colossal event. Its genesis cannot be pinpointed with certainty, but its enormous consequences are visible.

Towns as Outposts of Modernity

It was on the basis of this liberty that the great Western cities, and other towns they influenced and to which they served as examples, built up a distinctive civilization and spread techniques which were new, or had been revived or rediscovered after centuries—it matters little which. The important thing is that these cities had the rare privilege of following through an unusual political, social, and economic experience.

In the financial sphere, the towns organized taxation, finances, public credit, customs, and excise. They invented public loans: the first issues of the Monte Vecchio in Venice could be said to go back to 1167, the first formulation of the Casa di San Giorgio to 1407. One after another, they reinvented gold money, following Genoa which may have minted the *genovino* as early as the late twelfth century. They organized industry and the guilds; they invented long-distance trade, bills of exchange, the first forms of trading companies and accountancy. They also quickly became the scene of class struggles. For if the towns were "communities" as has been said, they were also "societies" in the modern sense of the word, with their tensions and civil struggles: nobles against bourgeois; poor against rich ("thin people" *popolo magro* against "fat people" *popolo grosso*). The struggles in Florence were already more deeply akin to those of the industrial early nineteenth century than to the faction-fights of ancient Rome, as the drama of the Ciompi (1378) demonstrates.

This society divided from within also faced enemies from without— the worlds of the noble, prince, or peasant, of everybody who was not a citizen. The cities were the West's first focus for patriotism—and the patriotism they inspired was long to be more coherent and much more conscious than the territorial kind, which emerged only slowly in the first states. . . .

A new state of mind was established, broadly that of an early, still faltering, Western capitalism—a collection of rules, possibilities, calculations, the art both of getting rich and of living. It also included gambling and risk: the key words of commercial language, *fortuna, ventura, ragione, prudenza, sicurta*, define the risks to be guarded against. No question now of living from day to day as noblemen did, always putting up their revenues to try to meet the level of their expenditure, which invariably came first—and letting the future take care of itself. The merchant was economical with his money, calculated his expenditure according to his returns, his investments according to their yield. The hour-glass had turned back the right way. He would also be economical with his time: A merchant could already say that *chi tempo ha e tempo aspetta tempo perde*, which means much the same thing as "time is money."

Capitalism and towns were basically the same thing in the West. Lewis Mumford humorously claimed that capitalism was the cuckoo's egg laid in the confined nests of the medieval towns. By this he meant to convey that the bird was destined to grow inordinately and burst its tight framework (which was true), and then link up with the state, the conqueror of towns but heir to their institutions and way of thinking and completely incapable of dispensing with them. The important thing was that even when it had declined as a city the town continued to rule the roost all the time it was passing into the actual or apparent service of the prince. The wealth of the state would still be the wealth of the town: Portugal converged on Lisbon, the Netherlands on Amsterdam, and English primacy was London's primacy (the capital modelled England in its own image after the peaceful revolution of 1688). The latent defect in the Spanish imperial economy was that it was based on Seville—a controlled town rotten with dishonest officials and long dominated by foreign capitalists—and not on a powerful free town capable of producing and carrying through a really individual economic policy. Likewise, if Louis XIV did not succeed in founding a "royal bank," despite various projects (1703, 1706, 1709), it was because faced with the power of the monarch, Paris did not offer the protection of a town free to do what it wanted and accountable to no one.

Urban Patterns

Let us imagine we are looking at a comprehensive history of the towns of Europe covering the complete series of their forms from the Greek city-state to an eighteenth-century town—everything Europe was able to build at home and overseas, from Muscovy in the East to America in the West. . . .

Simplifying, one could say that the West has had three basic types of town in the course of its evolution: open towns, that is to say not differentiated from their hinterland, even blending into it (A); towns closed in on themselves in every sense, their walls marking the boundaries of an individual way of life more than a territory (B); finally towns held in subjection, by which is meant the whole range of known controls by prince or state (C).

Roughly, A preceded B, and B preceded C. But there is no suggestion of strict succession about this order. It is rather a question of directions and dimensions shaping the complicated careers of the Western towns. They did not all develop at the same time or in the same way. Later we will see if this "grid" is valid for classifying all the towns of the world.

Type A: the ancient Greek or Roman city was open to the surrounding countryside and on terms of equality with it. Athens accepted inside its walls as rightful citizens the Eupatrid horse-breeders as well as the vine-growing peasants so dear to Aristophanes. As soon as the smoke rose above the Pnyx, the peasant responded to the signal and attended the Assembly of the People, where he sat among his equals. At the beginning of the Peloponnesian war, the entire population of the Attic countryside evacuated itself to Athens where it took refuge while the Spartans ravaged the fields, olive groves, and houses. When the Spartans fell back at the approach of winter, the country people returned to their homes. The Greek city was in fact the sum of the town and its surrounding countryside. . . . Likewise, if one explores the ruins of Roman

cities, one is in open country immediately outside the gates: There are
no suburbs, which is as good as saying no industry or active and organized trades in their duly allotted place.

Type B: the closed city: the medieval town was the classic example of a
closed city, a self-sufficient unit, an exclusive, Lilliputian empire. Entering its gates was like crossing one of the serious frontiers of the world
today. You were free to thumb your nose at your neighbour from the
other side of the barrier. He could not touch you. The peasant who uprooted himself from his land and arrived in the town was immediately
another man. He was free—or rather he had abandoned a known and
hated servitude for another, not always guessing the extent of it beforehand. But this mattered little. If the town had adopted him, he could
snap his fingers when his lord called for him. And though obsolete elsewhere, such calls were still frequently to be heard in Silesia in the eighteenth century and in Muscovy up to the nineteenth.

   Though the towns opened their gates easily it was not enough to
walk through them to be immediately and really part of them. Full citizens were a jealous minority, a small town inside the town itself. A
citadel of the rich was built up in Venice in 1297 thanks to the *serrata*,
the closing of the Great Council to new members. The *nobili* of Venice
became a closed class for centuries. Very rarely did anyone force its
gates. The category of ordinary *cittadini*—at a lower level—was probably more hospitable. But the Signoria very soon created two types of
citizen, one *de intus*, the other *de intus et extra*, the latter full, the former partial. Fifteen years' residence were still required to be allowed to
apply for the first, twenty-five years for the second. A decree by the
Senate in 1386 even forbade new citizens (including those who were
full citizens) from trading directly in Venice with German merchants at
the Fondego dei Todeschi or outside it. The ordinary townspeople were
no less mistrustful or hostile to newcomers. According to Marin
Sanudo, in June 1520, the street people attacked the peasants who had
arrived from the mainland as recruits for the galleys or the army, crying
"*Poltroni ande arar!*" "Back to the plough, shirkers!"

   Of course Venice was an extreme example. Moreover, it owed the
preservation of its own constitution until 1797 to an aristocratic and
extremely reactionary regime, as well as to the conquest at the beginning of the fifteenth century of the Terra Firma, which extended its authority as far as the Alps and Brescia. It was the last *polis* in the West.
But citizenship was also parsimoniously granted in Marseilles in the
sixteenth century; it was necessary to have "ten years of domicile, to
possess property, to have married a local girl." Otherwise the man remained amongst the masses of non-citizens of the town. This limited
conception of citizenship was the general rule everywhere.

The main source of contention can be glimpsed throughout this vast process: to whom did industry and craft, their privileges and profits, belong? In fact they belonged to the town, to its authorities and to its merchant entrepreneurs. They decided if it were necessary to deprive, or to try to deprive, the rural area of the city of the right to spin, weave, and dye, or if on the contrary it would be advantageous to grant it these rights. Everything was possible in these interchanges, as the history of each individual town shows.

As far as work inside the walls was concerned (we can hardly call it industry without qualification), everything was arranged for the benefit of the craft guilds. They enjoyed exclusive contiguous monopolies, fiercely defended along the imprecise frontiers that so easily led to absurd conflicts. The urban authorities did not always have the situation under control. Sooner or later, with the help of money, they were to allow obvious, acknowledged, honorary superiorities, consecrated by money or power, to become apparent. The "Six Corps" (drapers, grocers, haberdashers, furriers, hosiers, goldsmiths) were the commercial aristocracy of Paris from 1625. In Florence it was the *arte dela lana* and the *Arte di Calimala* (engaged in dyeing fabric imported from the north, unbleached). But town museums in Germany supply the best evidence of these old situations. In Ulm, for example, each guild owned a picture hinged in triptych form. The side panels represented characteristic scenes of the craft. The centre, like a treasured family album, showed innumerable small portraits recalling the successive generations of masters of the guild over the centuries.

An even more telling example was the City of London and its annexes (running along its walls) in the eighteenth century, still the domain of fussy, obsolete, and powerful guilds. If Westminster and the suburbs were growing continually, noted a well-informed economist (1754), it was for obvious reasons: "These suburbs are free and present a clear field for every industrious citizen, while in its bosom London nourishes ninety-two of all sorts of those exclusive companies [guilds], whose numerous members can be seen adorning the Lord Mayor's Show every year with immoderate pomp." . . .

Type C: subjugated towns, of early modern times. Everywhere in Europe, as soon as the state was firmly established it disciplined the towns with instinctive relentlessness, whether or not it used violence. The Habsburgs did so just as much as the Popes, the German princes as much as the Medicis or the kings of France. Except in the Netherlands and England, obedience was imposed.

Take Florence as an example: The Medicis had slowly subjugated it, almost elegantly in Lorenzo's time. But after 1532 and the return of the Medicis to power the process accelerated. Florence in the seventeenth

century was no more than the Grand Duke's court. He had seized everything—money, the right to govern, and to distribute honours. From the
Pitti Palace, on the left bank of the Arno, a gallery—a secret passage in
fact—allowed the prince to cross the river and reach the Uffizi. This elegant gallery, still in existence today on the Ponte Vecchio, was the
thread from which the spider at the extremity of his web supervised the
imprisoned town. . . .

Different Types of Development

But we know, of course, that urban development does not happen of its
own accord: It is not an endogenous phenomenon produced under a
bell-jar. It is always the expression of a society which controls it from
within, but also from without, and in this respect, our classification is, I
repeat, too simple. That said, how does it work when applied outside
the narrow confines of Western Europe?

1. *Towns in colonial America.* We should say "in Latin America," because the English towns remained a separate case. They had to live by
their own resources and emerge from their wilderness to find a place in
the vast world; the real parallel for them is the medieval city. The
towns in Iberian America had a much simpler and more limited career.
Built like Roman camps inside four earth walls, they were garrisons lost
in the midst of vast hostile expanses, linked together by communications which were slow because they stretched across enormous empty
spaces. Curiously, at a period when the privileged medieval town had
spread over practically the whole of Europe, the ancient rule prevailed
in all Hispano-Portuguese America, apart from the large towns of
the viceroys: Mexico City, Lima, Santiago de Chile, San Salvador
(Bahia)—that is to say the official, already parasitical organisms.

There were scarcely any purely commercial towns in this part of
America, or if there were they were of minor importance. For example,
Recife—the merchants' town—stood next to aristocratic Olinda, town
of great plantation owners, *senhores de engenbos*,[1] and slave owners. It
was rather like Piraeus or Phalera in relation to Pericles' Athens.
Buenos Aires after its second foundation (the successful one in 1580)
was still a small market village—like Megara or Aegina. It had the misfortune to have nothing but Indian *bravos* round about, and its inhabitants complained of being forced to earn "their bread by the sweat of
their brow" in this America where the whites were *rentiers*.[2] But caravans of mules or large wooden carts arrived there from the Andes, from

[1] Men of talent. [Ed.]
[2] Property owners. [Ed.]

Lima, which was a way of acquiring Potosi silver. Sugar, and soon gold, came by sailing ship from Brazil. And contact with Portugal and Africa was maintained through the smuggling carried on by sailing ships bringing black slaves. But Buenos Aires remained an exception amidst the "barbarism" of nascent Argentina.

The American town was generally tiny, without these gifts from abroad. It governed itself. No one was really concerned with its fate. Its masters were the landowners who had their houses in the town, with rings for tethering their horses fixed on the front walls overlooking the street. These were the "men of property," *os homes bons* of the municipalities of Brazil, or the *hacendados* of the Spanish *cabildos*.[3] These towns were so many miniature versions of Sparta or of Thebes in the time of Epaminondas. It could safely be said that the history of the Western towns in America began again from zero. Naturally there was no separation between the towns and the hinterland and there was no industry to be shared out. Wherever industry appeared—in Mexico city, for example—it was carried on by slaves or semi-slaves. The medieval European town would not have been conceivable if its artisans had been serfs.

2. How should Russian towns be classified? One can tell at a glance that the towns that survived or grew up again in Muscovy after the terrible catastrophes of the Mongol invasion no longer lived according to the Western pattern. Although there were great cities among them, like Moscow or Novgorod, they were kept in hand sometimes brutally. In the sixteenth century a proverb still asked: "Who can set his face against God and the mighty Novgorod?" But the proverb was wrong. The town was harshly brought to heel in 1427 and again in 1477 (it had to deliver 300 cartloads of gold). Executions, deportations, confiscations followed in quick succession. Above all, these towns were caught up in the slow circulation of traffic over an immense, already Asiatic, still wild expanse. In 1650, as in the past, transport on the rivers or overland by sledge or by convoys of carts moved with an enormous loss of time. It was often dangerous even to go near villages, and a halt had to be called every evening in open country—as on the Balkan roads—deploying the carriages in a circle, with everyone on the alert to defend himself.

For all these reasons the Muscovy towns did not impose themselves on the vast surrounding countryside; quite the reverse. They were unable to dictate their wishes to a peasant world which was biologically extraordinarily strong, although poverty-stricken, restless, and perpetually on the move. The important fact was that "harvests per hectare in

[3]Town councils. [Ed.]

the European countries of the East remained constant on average, from the sixteenth to the nineteenth century"—at a low level. There was no healthy rural surplus and therefore no really prosperous town. Nor did the Russian towns have serving them those secondary towns that were a characteristic of the West and its lively trade.

Consequently, there were innumerable peasant serfs practically without land, insolvent in the eyes of their lords and even the state. It was of no importance whether they went to towns or to work in the houses of rich peasants. In the town they became beggars, porters, craftsmen, poor tradesmen, or very rarely merchants who got rich quickly. They might also stay put and become craftsmen in their own villages, or seek the necessary supplement to their earnings by becoming carriers or travelling pedlars. This irresistible tide of mendicancy could not be stemmed, and indeed it often served the interests of the landlord who gave it his blessing: All such artisans and traders remained his serfs whatever they did and however great their social success; they still owed him their dues.

These examples and others indicate a fate resembling what may after all have happened at the beginning of Western urbanization. Though a clearer case, it is comparable to the caesura[4] between the eleventh and thirteenth centuries, that interlude when almost everything was born of the villages and peasant vitality. We might call it an intermediate position between A and C, without the B type (the independent city) ever having arisen. The prince appeared too quickly, like the ogre in a fairy tale.

3. *Imperial towns in the East and Far East.* The same problems and ambiguities—only deeper—arise when we leave Europe and move east.

Towns similar to those in medieval Europe—masters of their fate for a brief moment—only arose in Islam when the empires collapsed. They marked some outstanding moments in Islamic civilization. But they only lasted for a time and the main beneficiaries were certain marginal towns like Cordoba, or the cities which were urban republics by the fifteenth century, like Ceuta before the Portuguese occupation in 1415, or Oran before the Spanish occupation in 1509. The usual pattern was the huge city under the rule of a prince or a Caliph: a Baghdad or a Cairo.

Towns in distant Asia were of the same type: imperial or royal cities, enormous, parasitical, soft, and luxurious—Delhi and Vijnayanagar, Peking and to some extent Nanking, though this was rather different. The great prestige enjoyed by the prince comes as no surprise to us.

---

[4]Pause. [Ed.]

And if one ruler was swallowed up by the city or more likely by his palace, another immediately took his place and the subjection continued. Neither will it surprise us to learn that these towns were incapable of taking over the artisanal trades from the countryside: They were both open towns and subject towns simultaneously. Besides, in India as in China, social structures already existing hampered the free movement of the towns. If the town did not win its independence, it was not only because of the bastinadoes[5] ordered by the mandarins or the cruelty of the prince to merchants and ordinary citizens. It was because society was prematurely fixed, crystallized in a certain mould.

In India, the caste system automatically divided and broke up every urban community. In China, the cult of the *gentes*[6] on the one hand was confronted on the other by a mixture comparable to that which created the Western town: Like the latter it acted as a melting-pot, breaking old bonds and placing individuals on the same level. The arrival of immigrants created an "American" environment, where those already settled set the tone and the way of life. In addition, there was no independent authority representing the Chinese town as a unit, in its dealings with the State or with the very powerful countryside. The rural areas were the real heart of living, active, and thinking China.

The town, residence of officials and nobles, was not the property of either guilds or merchants. There was no gradual "rise of the bourgeoisie" here. No sooner did a bourgeoisie appear than it was tempted by class betrayal, fascinated by the luxurious life of the mandarins. The towns might have lived their own lives, filled in the contours of their own destiny, if individual initiative and capitalism had had a clear field. But the tutelary State hardly lent itself to this. It did occasionally nod, intentionally or not: At the end of the sixteenth century a bourgeoisie seems to have emerged with a taste for business enterprise, and we can guess what part it played in the large iron-works near Peking, in the private porcelain workshops that developed in King-te-chen, and even more in the rise of the silk trade in Su-Chu, the capital of Kiang-tsu. But this was no more than a flash in the pan. With the Manchu conquest, the Chinese crisis was resolved in the seventeenth century in a direction completely opposed to urban freedoms.

Only the West swung completely over in favour of its towns. The towns caused the West to advance. It was, let us repeat, an enormous event, but the deep-seated reasons behind it are still inadequately explained. What would the Chinese towns have become if the junks had discovered the Cape of Good Hope at the beginning of the fifteenth century, and had made full use of such a chance of world conquest?

[5]Beatings (often on soles of the feet). [Ed.]
[6]People. [Ed.]

82

Charter of Henry I
for London, 1130–1133

In the last century types of cities have been distinguished by historians and sociologists who have recognized that European cities in the late Middle Ages were relatively independent of rulers and other cities due to charters of freedom. Town and city charters were frequently drawn up between European lords, princes, and kings, on the one hand, and the inhabitants, owners, or burghers, on the other. These charters, which were granted to the town for a fee, brought needed income to the lord or ruler while ensuring the ruler access to an active class of artisans, merchants, specialists, and luxury providers.

In this charter, for London, England, what does the king give to the townspeople? What powers does the king retain? What seems to have been the main concerns of the townspeople and king that are settled here?

Thinking Historically

Does this charter reflect King Henry's strength or his weakness? Would this sort of arrangement be more likely to develop in a feudal society like Europe than it would in a Mongol or Chinese empire? Why or why not? Does the charter support Braudel's comparative thesis?

Henry, by the grace of God, king of the English, to the archbishop of Canterbury, and to the bishops and abbots, and earls and barons and justices and sheriffs, and to all his liegemen, both French and English, of the whole of England, greeting. Know that I have granted to my citizens of London that they shall hold middlesex at "farm" for three hundred pounds "by tale" for themselves and their heirs from me and my heirs, so that the citizens shall appoint as sheriff from themselves whomsoever they may choose, and shall appoint from among themselves as justice whomsoever they choose to look after the pleas of my crown and the pleadings which arise in connexion with them. No other shall be justice over the same men of London. And the citizens shall not plead outside the walls of the city in respect of any plea; and they shall

Charter of Henry I for London (1130–1133), from *English Historical Documents*, vol. II, ed. David C. Douglas and George W. Greenaway (London: Eyre and Spottiswoode, Ltd., 1955), 945–46.

be quit of scot and of Danegeld[1] and the murder-fine. Nor shall any of them be compelled to offer trial by battle. And if any one of the citizens shall be impleaded in respect of the pleas of the crown, let him prove himself to be a man of London by an oath which shall be judged in the city. Let no one be billeted within the walls of the city, either of my household, or by the force of anyone else. And let all the men of London and their property be quit and free from toll and passage and lestage[2] and from all other customs throughout all England and at the seaports. And let the churches and barons and citizens hold and have well and in peace their sokes,[3] with all their customs, so that those who dwell in these sokes shall pay no customs except to him who possesses the soke, or to the steward whom he has placed there. And a man of London shall not be fined at mercy except according to his "were," that is to say, up to one hundred shillings: This applies to an offence which can be punished by a fine. And there shall no longer be "miskenning"[4] in the hustings court,[5] nor in the folk-moot,[6] nor in other pleas within the city. And the hustings court shall sit once a week, to wit, on Monday. I will cause my citizens to have their lands and pledges and debts within the city and outside it. And in respect of the lands about which they make claim to me, I will do them right according to the law of the city. And if anyone has taken toll or custom from the citizens of London, then the citizens of London may take from the borough or village where toll or custom has been levied as much as the man of London gave for toll, and more also may be taken for a penalty. And let all debtors to the citizens of London discharge their debts, or prove in London that they do not owe them; and if they refuse either to pay, or to come and make such proof, then the citizens to whom the debts are due may take pledges within the city either from the borough or from the village or from the county in which the debtor lives. And the citizens shall have their hunting chases, as well and fully as had their predecessors, to wit, in Chiltern and Middlesex and Surrey.

---

[1]A medieval land tax, originally levied to buy off raiding Danes (literally, "Dane's money"). First levied in England in 868, but generally discontinued in the twelfth century. [Ed.]

[2]Sometimes "lastage": a toll payable by traders attending fairs and markets. [Ed.]

[3]A right of local jurisdiction. [Ed.]

[4]A verbal error in making a formal oath. [Ed.]

[5]King's court or court of king's representatives. [Ed.]

[6]A general assembly of the people. [Ed.]

83

GREGORIO DATI

Corporations and Community in Florence

This is an account of the Italian city of Florence and its inhabitants from 1380 to 1405. While family identity was primary, residents of Florence were also members of many corporate organizations that served to channel their loyalty to the larger urban community. Among these were guilds and parish churches, as well as political, welfare, and religious organizations. On public holidays like the feast day of St. John the Baptist, the patron saint of Florence, these various groups would come together in a display of communal solidarity that was often more fraternal than the deliberations in the political arena. What seems to motivate people to participate in public acts and parades in Florence?

Thinking Historically

Would a chartered city be more or less likely than a city run by a king to hold these sorts of festivities? In what ways would you expect the politics of Florence to be similar to and different from those of London? What aspects of this account support Braudel's thesis?

When springtime comes and the whole world rejoices, every Florentine begins to think about organizing a magnificent celebration on the feast day of St. John the Baptist [June 24]. . . . For two months in advance, everyone is planning marriage feasts or other celebrations in honor of the day. There are preparations for the horse races, the costumes of the retinues, the flags, and the trumpets; there are the pennants and the wax candles and other things which the subject territories offer to the Commune. Messengers are sent to obtain provisions for the banquets, and horses come from everywhere to run in the races. The whole city is engaged in preparing for the feast, and the spirits of the young people and the women [are animated] by these preparations. . . . Everyone is filled with gaiety; there are dances and concerts and songfests and tournaments and other joyous activities. Up to the eve of the holiday, no one thinks about anything else.

Gregorio Dati, "*Istoria di Firenze dall'anno MCCCLXXX all'anno MCCCCV*" (History of Florence from 1380 to 1405) (Florence, 1735), in *The Society of Renaissance Florence*, ed. and trans. Gene Brucker (New York: Harper & Row, 1971), 75–78.

Early on the morning of the day before the holiday, each guild has a display outside of its shops of its fine wares, its ornaments, and jewels. There are cloths of gold and silk sufficient to adorn ten kingdoms. . . . Then at the third hour, there is a solemn procession of clerics, priests, monks, and friars, and there are so many [religious] orders, and so many relics of saints, that the procession seems endless. [It is a manifestation] of great devotion, on account of the marvelous richness of the adornments . . . and clothing of gold and silk with embroidered figures. There are many confraternities of men who assemble at the place where their meetings are held, dressed as angels, and with musical instruments of every kind and marvelous singing. They stage the most beautiful representations of the saints, and of those relics in whose honor they perform. They leave from S. Maria del Fiore [the cathedral] and march through the city and then return.

Then, after midday, when the heat has abated before sunset, all of the citizens assemble under [the banner of] their district, of which there are sixteen. Each goes in the procession in turn, the first, then the second, and so on with one district following the other, and in each group the citizens march two by two, with the oldest and most distinguished at the head, and proceeding down to the young men in rich garments. They march to the church of St. John [the Baptistery] to offer, one by one, a wax candle weighing one pound. . . . The walls along the streets through which they pass are all decorated, and there are . . . benches on which are seated young ladies and girls dressed in silk and adorned with jewels, pearls, and precious stones. This procession continues until sunset, and after each citizen has made his offering, he returns home with his wife to prepare for the next morning.

Whoever goes to the Piazza della Signoria on the morning of St. John's Day witnesses a magnificent, marvelous, and triumphant sight, which the mind can scarcely grasp. Around the great piazza are a hundred towers which appear to be made of gold. Some were brought on carts and others by porters. . . . [These towers] are made of wood, paper, and wax [and decorated] with gold, colored paints, and with figures. . . . Next to the rostrum of the palace [of the Signoria] are standards . . . which belong to the most important towns which are subject to the Commune: Pisa, Arezzo, Pistoia, Volterra, Cortona, Lucignano. . . .

First to present their offering, in the morning, are the captains of the Parte Guelfa, together with all of the knights, lords, ambassadors, and foreign knights. They are accompanied by a large number of the most honorable citizens, and before them, riding on a charger covered with a cloth . . . is one of their pages carrying a banner with the insignia of the Parte Guelfa. Then there follow the above-mentioned standards, each one carried by men on horseback . . . and they all go to make their offerings at the Baptistery. And these standards are given a tribute by the districts which have been acquired by the Commune of Florence. . . . The wax candles, which have the appearance of golden towers, are the tribute of the regions which in most ancient times were subject to the Florentines. In order of dignity, they are brought, one by one, to be offered to St. John, and on the following day, they are hung inside the church and there they remain for the entire year until the next feast day. . . . Then come . . . an infinite number of large wax candles, some weighing one hundred pounds and others fifty, some more and some less . . . carried by the residents of the villages [in the *contado*[1]] which offer them. . . .

Then the lord priors and their colleges come to make their offerings, accompanied by their rectors, that is, the podestà, the captain [of the *popolo*[2]], and the executor. . . . And after the lord [priors] come those who are participating in the horse race, and they are followed by the Flemings and the residents of Brabant who are weavers of woolen cloth in Florence. Then there are offerings by twelve prisoners who, as an act of mercy, have been released from prison . . . in honor of St. John, and these are poor people. . . . After all of these offerings have been made, men and women return home to dine. . . .

[1]Countryside. [Ed.]
[2]People. [Ed.]

84

MARCO POLO

From The Travels of Marco Polo

In *The Travels of Marco Polo,* the Venetian merchant recounted his travels across the Silk Road to Mongolia and China. According to his account he stayed in China from 1275 to 1292 before returning to Venice. In 1275, the Chinese Southern Song capital of Hangchou had just been conquered by Kubilai Khan, the grandson of Ghengis Khan. The Mongols were able to conquer China, but they could not radically change it. The structure and organization of towns and cities remained very much the way it had been under the Song. In addition to Hangchou, which Marco Polo calls Kinsay, he had been to the Mon-

Marco Polo, *The Travels of Marco Polo,* the Complete Yule-Currier ed., vol. 2 (New York: Dover, 1993), 185–206.

gol capital at Karakorum and to the Chinese cities of Peking and Changan. Why does he consider the city of Hangchou "the finest and the noblest in the world"? How does his description support that characterization? What do you see in this account of Hangchou that supports or challenges Braudel's comparison and thesis?

Thinking Historically

In what ways does the Hangchou that emerges from this document resemble London or Florence? In what ways was Hangchou significantly different? Does Marco Polo's description show signs that Chinese cities were autonomous or that they were not?

When you have left the city of Changan and have travelled for three days through a splendid country, passing a number of towns and villages, you arrive at the most noble city of Kinsay,[1] a name which is as much as to say in our tongue "The City of Heaven," as I told you before.

And since we have got thither I will enter into particulars about its magnificence; and these are well worth the telling, for the city is beyond dispute the finest and the noblest in the world. In this we shall speak according to the written statement which the Queen of this Realm sent to Bayan the conqueror of the country for transmission to the Great Kaan, in order that he might be aware of the surpassing grandeur of the city and might be moved to save it from destruction or injury. I will tell you all the truth as it was set down in that document. For truth it was, as the said Messer Marco Polo at a later date was able to witness with his own eyes. And now we shall rehearse those particulars.

First and foremost, then, the document stated the city of Kinsay to be so great that it hath an hundred miles of compass. And there are in it twelve thousand bridges of stone,[2] for the most part so lofty that a great fleet could pass beneath them. And let no man marvel that there are so many bridges, for you see the whole city stands as it were in the water and surrounded by water, so that a great many bridges are required to give free passage about it. [And though the bridges be so high, the approaches are so well contrived that carts and horses do cross them.]

The document aforesaid also went on to state that there were in this city twelve guilds of the different crafts, and that each guild had twelve thousand houses in the occupation of its workmen. Each of these houses contains at least twelve men, whilst some contain twenty and some forty,—not that these are all masters, but inclusive of the

---

[1]Kinsay simply means "capital." The current name is Hangchou. [Ed.]

[2]Generally assumed to be an exaggeration; one thousand would have been a lot. [Ed.]

journeymen who work under the masters. And yet all these craftsmen had full occupation, for many other cities of the kingdom are supplied from this city with what they require.

The document aforesaid also stated that the number and wealth of the merchants, and the amount of goods that passed through their hands, was so enormous that no man could form a just estimate thereof. And I should have told you with regard to those masters of the different crafts who are at the head of such houses as I have mentioned, that neither they nor their wives ever touch a piece of work with their own hands, but live as nicely and delicately as if they were kings and queens. The wives indeed are most dainty and angelical creatures! Moreover it was an ordinance laid down by the King that every man should follow his father's business and no other, no matter if he possessed 100,000 bezants.[3]

Inside the city there is a Lake which has a compass of some thirty miles:[4] and all round it are erected beautiful palaces and mansions, of the richest and most exquisite structure that you can imagine, belonging to the nobles of the city. There are also on its shores many abbeys and churches of the Idolaters. In the middle of the Lake are two Islands, on each of which stands a rich, beautiful, and spacious edifice, furnished in such style as to seem fit for the palace of an Emperor. And when any one of the citizens desired to hold a marriage feast, or to give any other entertainment, it used to be done at one of these palaces. And everything would be found there ready to order, such as silver plate, trenchers, and dishes [napkins and tablecloths], and whatever else was needful. The King made this provision for the gratification of his people, and the place was open to every one who desired to give an entertainment. . . .

The people are Idolaters; and since they were conquered by the Great Kaan they use paper money. [Both men and women are fair and comely, and for the most part clothe themselves in silk, so vast is the supply of that material, both from the whole district of Kinsay, and from the imports by traders from other provinces.] And you must know they eat every kind of flesh, even that of dogs and other unclean beasts, which nothing would induce a Christian to eat.

Since the Great Kaan occupied the city he has ordained that each of the twelve thousand bridges should be provided with a guard of ten men, in case of any disturbance, or of any being so rash as to plot treason or insurrection against him. [Each guard is provided with a hollow

---

[3]A gold coin struck at Byzantium (or Constantinople) and used throughout Europe from the ninth century. [Ed.]

[4]The circumference of the lake was more probably 30 li. A li was about a third of a mile, but it was sometimes used to mean a hundredth of a day's march. The entire circumference of the city could not have been more than 100 li. [Ed.]

instrument of wood and with a metal basin, and with a timekeeper to enable them to know the hour of the day or night. . . .

Part of the watch patrols the quarter, to see if any light or fire is burning after the lawful hours; if they find any they mark the door, and in the morning the owner is summoned before the magistrates, and unless he can plead a good excuse he is punished. Also if they find any one going about the streets at unlawful hours they arrest him, and in the morning they bring him before the magistrates. Likewise if in the daytime they find any poor cripple unable to work for his livelihood, they take him to one of the hospitals, of which there are many, founded by the ancient kings, and endowed with great revenues. Or if he be capable of work they oblige him to take up some trade. . . .

The Kaan watches this city with especial diligence because it forms the head of all Manzi;[5] and because he has an immense revenue from the duties levied on the transactions of trade therein, the amount of which is such that no one would credit it on mere hearsay.

All the streets of the city are paved with stone or brick, as indeed are all the highways throughout Manzi, so that you ride and travel in every direction without inconvenience. . . .

You must know also that the city of Kinsay has some three thousand baths, the water of which is supplied by springs. They are hot baths, and the people take great delight in them, frequenting them several times a month, for they are very cleanly in their persons. They are the finest and largest baths in the world; large enough for one hundred persons to bathe together.

And the Ocean Sea comes within twenty-five miles of the city at a place called Ganfu, where there is a town and an excellent haven, with a vast amount of shipping which is engaged in the traffic to and from India and other foreign parts, exporting and importing many kinds of wares, by which the city benefits. And a great river flows from the city of Kinsay to that sea-haven, by which vessels can come up to the city itself. This river extends also to other places further inland.

Know also that the Great Kaan hath distributed the territory of Manzi into nine parts, which he hath constituted into nine kingdoms. To each of these kingdoms a king is appointed who is subordinate to the Great Kaan, and every year renders the accounts of his kingdom to the fiscal office at the capital. This city of Kinsay is the seat of one of these kings, who rules over one hundred forty great and wealthy cities. For in the whole of this vast country of Manzi there are more than twelve hundred great and wealthy cities, without counting the towns and villages, which are in great numbers. And you may receive it for certain that in each of those twelve hundred cities the Great Kaan has a

[5]China. [Ed.]

garrison, and that the smallest of such garrisons musters one thousand men; whilst there are some of ten thousand, twenty thousand, and thirty thousand; so that the total number of troops is something scarcely calculable. . . . And all of them belong to the army of the Great Kaan.

I repeat that everything appertaining to this city is on so vast a scale, and the Great Kaan's yearly revenues therefrom are so immense, that it is not easy even to put it in writing, and it seems past belief to one who merely hears it told. But I *will* write it down for you. . . .

I must tell you that in this city there are 160 *tomans*[6] of fires, or in other words 160 *tomans* of houses. Now I should tell you that the *toman* is 10,000, so that you can reckon the total as altogether 1,600,000 houses, among which are a great number of rich palaces. There is one church only, belonging to the Nestorian Christians.

There is another thing I must tell you. It is the custom for every burgess of this city, and in fact for every description of person in it, to write over his door his own name, the name of his wife, and those of his children, his slaves, and all the inmates of his house, and also the number of animals that he keeps. And if any one dies in the house then the name of that person is erased, and if any child is born its name is added. So in this way the sovereign is able to know exactly the population of the city. And this is the practice also throughout all Manzi and Cathay.

And I must tell you that every hosteler who keeps an hostel for travellers is bound to register their names and surnames, as well as the day and month of their arrival and departure. And thus the sovereign hath the means of knowing, whenever it pleases him, who come and go throughout his dominions. And certes this is a wise order and a provident [one].

The position of the city is such that it has on one side a lake of fresh and exquisitely clear water (already spoken of), and on the other a very large river. The waters of the latter fill a number of canals of all sizes which run through the different quarters of the city, carry away all impurities, and then enter the Lake; whence they issue again and flow to the Ocean, thus producing a most excellent atmosphere. By means of these channels, as well as by the streets, you can go all about the city. Both streets and canals are so wide and spacious that carts on the one and boats on the other can readily pass to and fro, conveying necessary supplies to the inhabitants.

At the opposite side the city is shut in by a channel, perhaps forty miles in length, very wide, and full of water derived from the river aforesaid, which was made by the ancient kings of the country in order to relieve the river when flooding its banks. This serves also as a de-

---

[6]A *toman* is a Mongol measurement of ten thousand. [Ed.]

fence to the city, and the earth dug from it has been thrown inward, forming a kind of mound enclosing the city.

In this part are the ten principal markets, though besides these there are a vast number of others in the different parts of the town. The former are all squares of half a mile to the side, and along their front passes the main street, which is forty paces in width, and runs straight from end to end of the city, crossing many bridges of easy and commodious approach. At every four miles of its length comes one of those great squares of two miles (as we have mentioned) in compass. So also parallel to this great street, but at the back of the marketplaces, there runs a very large canal, on the bank of which toward the squares are built great houses of stone, in which the merchants from India and other foreign parts store their wares, to be handy for the markets. In each of the squares is held a market three days in the week, frequented by forty thousand or fifty thousand persons, who bring thither for sale every possible necessary of life, so that there is always an ample supply of every kind of meat and game, as of roebuck, red-deer, fallow-deer, hares, rabbits, partridges, pheasants, francolins, quails, fowls, capons, and of ducks and geese an infinite quantity; for so many are bred on the Lake that for a Venice groat of silver you can have a couple of geese and two couple of ducks. Then there are the shambles where the larger animals are slaughtered, such as calves, beeves, kids, and lambs, the flesh of which is eaten by the rich and the great dignitaries.

Those markets make a daily display of every kind of vegetables and fruits; and among the latter there are in particular certain pears of enormous size, weighing as much as ten pounds apiece, and the pulp of which is white and fragrant like a confection; besides peaches in their season both yellow and white, of every delicate flavour. . . .

All the ten marketplaces are encompassed by lofty houses, and below these are shops where all sorts of crafts are carried on, and all sorts of wares are on sale, including spices and jewels and pearls. Some of these shops are entirely devoted to the sale of wine made from rice and spices, which is constantly made fresh, and is sold very cheap.

Certain of the streets are occupied by the women of the town, who are in such a number that I dare not say what it is. They are found not only in the vicinity of the marketplaces, where usually a quarter is assigned to them, but all over the city. They exhibit themselves splendidly attired and abundantly perfumed, in finely garnished houses, with trains of waiting-women. These women are extremely accomplished in all the arts of allurement, and readily adapt their conversation to all sorts of persons, insomuch that strangers who have once tasted their attractions seem to get bewitched, and are so taken with their blandishments and their fascinating ways that they never can get these out of their heads. Hence it comes to pass that when they return home they say they have been to Kinsay or the City of Heaven, and their only desire is to get back thither as soon as possible.

Other streets are occupied by the Physicians, and by the Astrologers, who are also teachers of reading and writing; and an infinity of other professions have their places round about those squares. In each of the squares there are two great palaces facing one another, in which are established the officers appointed by the King to decide differences arising between merchants, or other inhabitants of the quarter. It is the daily duty of these officers to see that the guards are at their posts on the neighbouring bridges, and to punish them at their discretion if they are absent. . . .

The natives of the city are men of peaceful character, both from education and from the example of their kings, whose disposition was the same. They know nothing of handling arms, and keep none in their houses. You hear of no feuds or noisy quarrels or dissensions of any kind among them. Both in their commercial dealings and in their manufactures they are thoroughly honest and truthful, and there is such a degree of good will and neighbourly attachment among both men and women that you would take the people who live in the same street to be all one family.

And this familiar intimacy is free from all jealousy or suspicion of the conduct of their women. These they treat with the greatest respect, and a man who should presume to make loose proposals to a married woman would be regarded as an infamous rascal. They also treat the foreigners who visit them for the sake of trade with great cordiality, and entertain them in the most winning manner, affording them every help and advice on their business. But on the other hand they hate to see soldiers, and not least those of the Great Kaan's garrisons, regarding them as the cause of their having lost their native kings and lords.

85

S. D. GOITEIN

Cairo: An Islamic City
in Light of the Geniza

The author of this selection provides an especially detailed picture of medieval Cairo due to an unusual discovery of documents. "The Geniza" refers to a treasure trove of documents maintained by a Jewish synagogue in Cairo from the tenth to thirteenth centuries. It contains correspondence, legal documents, receipts, inventories, prescriptions, and notes—written in Hebrew characters in the Arabic language—and offers a rare opportunity to review virtually everything a community wrote over a long period of time. It is an extremely valuable resource that can answer most questions about medieval society in Cairo.

In this selection, S. D. Goitein studies the documents for the insight they provide into city life in Cairo. What do the Geniza documents tell us about city life in Cairo? What would it have been like to live in medieval Cairo?

Thinking Historically

In what ways would life in medieval Cairo have been similar to or different from life in a city of medieval Europe or medieval China? What is the significance of the lack of public buildings and guilds in Cairo? In what ways was the Muslim identity larger or more cosmopolitan than European urban identities? How does this support or challenge Braudel's thesis?

. . . It is astounding how rarely government buildings are mentioned in the Geniza documents. There were the local police stations and prisons, as well as the offices where one received the licenses occasionally needed, but even these are seldom referred to. The Mint and the Exchange are frequently referred to, but at least the latter was only semi-public in character, since the persons working there were not on the government payroll. Taxes were normally collected by tax farmers. Thus there was little direct contact between the government and the

---

S. D. Goitein, "Cairo: An Islamic City in Light of the Geniza," in *Middle Eastern Cities*, ed. Ira M. Lapidus (Berkeley and Los Angeles: University of California Press, 1969), 90–95.

populace and consequently not much need for public buildings. The imperial palace and its barracks formed a city by itself, occasionally mentioned in Ayyūbid times, but almost never in the Fāṭimid period.

Government, although not conspicuous by many public buildings, was present in the city in many other ways. A city was governed by a military commander called *amīr*, who was assisted by the *wālī* or superintendent of the police. Smaller towns had only a *wālī* and no *amīr*. Very powerful, sometimes more powerful than the *amīr*, was the *qāḍī*, or judge, who had administrative duties in addition to his substantial judicial functions. The chief *qāḍī* often held other functions such as the control of the taxes or of a port, as we read with regard to Alexandria or Tyre. The city was divided into small administrative units called *rabʿ* (which is not the classical *rub*, meaning quarter, but instead designates an area, or rather a compound). Each *rabʿ* had a superintendent called *ṣāḥib rabʿ* (pronounced rub), very often referred to in the Geniza papers. In addition to regular and mounted police there were plain clothesmen, or secret service men, called *aṣḥāb al-khabar*, "informants" who formed a government agency independent even of the *qāḍī*, a state of affairs for which there seem to exist parallels in more modern times.

An ancient source tells us that the vizier[1] al-Ma'mūn, mentioned above, instructed the two superintendents of the police of Fusṭāṭ[2] and Cairo, respectively, to draw up exact lists of the inhabitants showing their occupations and other circumstances and to permit no one to move from one house to another without notification of the police. This is described as an extraordinary measure aimed at locating any would-be assassins who might have been sent to the Egyptian capital by the Bāṭiniyya, an Ismāʿīlī group using murder as a political weapon. Such lists, probably with fewer details, no doubt were in regular use for the needs of taxation. In a letter from Sicily, either from its capital Palermo or from Mazara on its southwestern tip, the writer, an immigrant from Tunisia around 1063, informs his business friend in Egypt that he is going to buy a house and that he has already registered for the purpose in the *qānūn* (Greek *canon*) which must have designated an official list of inhabitants. With regard to non-Muslims, a differentiation was made between permanent residents and newcomers. Whether the same practice existed with respect to Muslims is not evident from the Geniza papers.

What were the dues that a town dweller had to pay to the government in his capacity as the inhabitant of a city, and what were the benefits that he derived from such payments? By right of conquest, the

---

[1]Prime minister. [Ed.]
[2]Old Cairo. [Ed.]

ground on which Fusṭāṭ stood belonged to the Muslims, that is, to the government (the same was the case in many other Islamic cities), and a ground rent, called *ḥikr*, had to be paid for each building. A great many deeds of sale, gift, and rent refer to this imposition. . . .

Besides the ground rent, every month a *ḥarāsa*, or "due for protection," had to be paid to the government. The protection was partly in the hands of a police force, partly in those of the superintendents of the compounds, and partly was entrusted to nightwatchmen, usually referred to as *ṭawwāfūn*, literally, "those that make the round," but known also by other designations. As we learn expressly from a Geniza source, the nightwatchmen, like the regular police, were appointed by the government (and not by a municipality or local body which did not exist). The amounts of the *ḥarāsa* in the communal accounts cannot be related to the value of the properties for which they were paid, but it is evident that they were moderate.

In a responsum[3] written around 1165, Rabbi Maimon, the father of Moses Maimonides,[4] states that the markets of Fusṭāṭ used to remain open during the nights, in contrast of course to what the writer was accustomed from having lived in other Islamic cities. In Fusṭāṭ, too, this had not been always the case. In a description of the festival of Epiphany from the year 941 in which all parts of the population took part, it is mentioned as exceptional that the streets were not closed during that particular night.

Sanitation must have been another great concern of the government, for the items "removal of rubbish" (called "throwing out of dust") and "cleaning of pipes" appear with great regularity in the monthly accounts preserved in the Geniza. One gets the impression that these hygienic measures were not left to the discretion of each individual proprietor of a house. The clay tubes bringing water (for washing purposes) to a house and those connecting it with a cesspool constantly needed clearing, and there are also many references to their construction. The amounts paid for both operations were considerable. The Geniza has preserved an autograph note by Maimonides permitting a beadle[5] to spend a certain sum on "throwing out of dust" (presumably from a synagogue). This may serve as an illustration for the fact that landlords may have found the payment of these dues not always easy.

In this context we may also draw attention to the new insights gained through the study of the documents from the Geniza about the

---

[3]A legal document. [Ed.]
[4](1135–1204), a Jewish rabbi, physician, and philosopher in Spain and Egypt. [Ed.]
[5]A minor official. [Ed.]

social life of Cairo. Massignon[6] had asserted, and he was followed by many, that the life-unit in the Islamic city was the professional corporation, the guilds of the merchants, artisans, and scholars which had professional, as well as social and religious functions. No one would deny that this was true to a large extent for the sixteenth through the nineteenth centuries. However, there is not a shred of evidence that this was true for the ninth through the thirteenth centuries. . . .

The term "guild" designates a medieval union of craftsmen or traders which supervised the work of its members in order to uphold standards, and made arrangements for the education of apprentices and their initiation into the union. The guild protected its members against competition, and in Christian countries was closely connected with religion.

Scrutinizing the records of the Cairo Geniza or the Muslim handbooks of market supervision contemporary with them, one looks in vain for an Arabic equivalent of the term "guild." There was no such word because there was no such institution. The supervision of the quality of the artisans' work was in the hands of the state police, which availed itself of the services of trustworthy and expert assistants.

Regarding apprenticeship and admission to a profession, no formalities and no rigid rules are to be discovered in our sources. Parents were expected to have their sons learn a craft and to pay for their instruction, and the Geniza has preserved several contracts to this effect.

The protection of the local industries from the competition of newcomers and outsiders is richly documented by the Geniza records, but nowhere do we hear about a professional corporation fulfilling this task. It was the Jewish local community, the central Jewish authorities, the state police, or influential notables, Muslim and Jewish, who were active in these matters.

As to the religious aspect of professional corporation, the associations of artisans and traders in imperial Rome, or at least a part of them, bore a religious character and were often connected with the local cult of the town from which the founders of an association had originated. Similarly, the Christian guilds of the late Middle Ages had their patron saints and special rites. The fourteenth century was the heyday of Muslim corporations, especially in Anatolia (the present day Turkey), which adopted the doctrines and ceremonies of Muslim mystic brotherhoods. One looks in vain for similar combinations of artisanship and religious cult in the period and the countries under discussion. On the other hand, we find partnerships of Muslims and Jews both in workshops and in mercantile undertakings, for free partnerships were the normal form of industrial cooperation, and were common as well in commercial ventures. The classical Islamic city was a

---

[6]Louis Massignon (1883–1962), a French scholar of Islam. [Ed.]

free enterprise society, the very opposite of a community organized in rigid guilds and tight professional corporations.

Further, we have stated before that no formal citizenship existed. The question is, however, how far did people feel a personal attachment to their native towns. "Homesickness," says Professor Gibb in his translation of the famous traveler Ibn Baṭṭūṭa, "was hardly to be expected in a society so cosmopolitan as that of medieval Islam." Indeed the extent of travel and migration reflected in the Geniza is astounding. No less remarkable, however, is the frequency of expressions of longing for one's native city and the wish to return to it, as well as the fervor with which compatriots stuck together when they were abroad. On the other hand, I cannot find much of neighborhood factionalism or professional *esprit de corps*, both of which were so prominent in the later Middle Ages. Under an ever more oppressive military feudalism and government-regimented economy, life became miserable and insecure, and people looked for protection and assistance in their immediate neighborhood. In an earlier period, in a free-enterprise, competitive society, there was no place for such factionalism. A man felt himself to be the son of a city which provided him with the security, the economic possibilities, and the spiritual amenities which he needed.

$$\boxed{86}$$

BERNAL DÍAZ
Cities of Mexico

Bernal Díaz (1492–1580) accompanied Hernando Cortés* and the band of Spanish conquistadors who were the first Europeans to see the cities of the central Mexican plateau, dominated by the Aztec capital of Tenochtitlan,† or Mexico, in 1519. Later in life, he recalled what he saw in this account of *The Conquest of New Spain*. What impressed Díaz about the cities of Mexico? How, according to Díaz, were they different from the cities of Europe?

*kohr TEHZ
†teh NOHCH teet LAHN

Bernal Díaz, *The Conquest of New Spain*, trans. J. M. Cohen (London: Penguin Books, 1963), 214–20, 230–35.

Thinking Historically

The cities of Mexico provide the best example of how much cities could differ. Unlike the cities of Eurasia, or even Islamic Africa, the development of Mexican cities was entirely separate from and uninfluenced by the other cultures we have studied. Therefore, this description of Mexico, and the other cities of the Mexican plateau, like Iztapalapa and Coyoacan, is enormously useful to us.

In what respects were these cities different from others you have read about? What other cities do they most resemble? How does this selection support or challenge Braudel's comparison and thesis?

Next morning, we came to a broad causeway[1] and continued our march towards Iztapalapa. And when we saw all those cities and villages built in the water, and other great towns on dry land, and that straight and level causeway leading to Mexico, we were astounded. These great towns and *cues*[2] and buildings rising from the water, all made of stone, seemed like an enchanted vision from the tale of Amadis. Indeed, some of our soldiers asked whether it was not all a dream. It is not surprising therefore that I should write in this vein. It was all so wonderful that I do not know how to describe this first glimpse of things never heard of, seen, or dreamed of before.

When we arrived near Iztapalapa we beheld the splendour of the other *Caciques*[3] who came out to meet us, the lord of that city whose name was Cuitlahuac, and the lord of Culuacan, both of them close relations of Montezuma. And when we entered the city of Iztapalapa, the sight of the palaces in which they lodged us! They were very spacious and well built, of magnificent stone, cedar wood, and the wood of other sweet-smelling trees, with great rooms and courts, which were a wonderful sight, and all covered with awnings of woven cotton.

When we had taken a good look at all this, we went to the orchard and garden, which was a marvellous place both to see and walk in. I was never tired of noticing the diversity of trees and the various scents given off by each, and the paths choked with roses and other flowers, and the many local fruit-trees and rose-bushes, and the pond of fresh water. Another remarkable thing was that large canoes could come into the garden from the lake, through a channel they had cut, and their crews did not have to disembark. Everything was shining with lime and decorated with different kinds of stonework and paintings which were a marvel to gaze

---

[1]The causeway of Cuitlahuac, which separated the lakes of Chalco and Xochimilco.
[2]Spanish for temple; probably refers to pyramids. [Ed.]
[3]Taino for rulers. [Ed.]

on. Then there were birds of many breeds and varieties which came to the pond. I say again that I stood looking at it, and thought that no land like it would ever be discovered in the whole world, because at that time Peru was neither known nor thought of. But today all that I then saw is overthrown and destroyed; nothing is left standing.

The Entrance into Mexico

Early next day we left Iztapalapa with a large escort of these great *Caciques*, and followed the causeway, which is eight yards wide and goes so straight to the city of Mexico that I do not think it curves at all. Wide though it was, it was so crowded with people that there was hardly room for them all. Some were going to Mexico and others coming away, besides those who had come out to see us, and we could hardly get through the crowds that were there. For the towers and the *cues* were full, and they came in canoes from all parts of the lake. No wonder, since they had never seen horses or men like us before!

With such wonderful sights to gaze on we did not know what to say, or if this was real that we saw before our eyes. On the land side there were great cities, and on the lake many more. The lake was crowded with canoes. At intervals along the causeway there were many bridges, and before us was the great city of Mexico [Tenochtitlan]. As for us, we were scarcely four hundred strong, and we well remembered the words and warnings of the people of Huexotzinco and Tlaxcala and Tlamanalco, and the many other warnings we had received to beware of entering the city of Mexico, since they would kill us as soon as they had us inside. Let the interested reader consider whether there is not much to ponder in this narrative of mine. What men in all the world have shown such daring? But let us go on.

We marched along our causeway to a point where another small causeway branches off to another city called Coyoacan, and there, beside some towerlike buildings, which were their shrines, we were met by many more *Caciques* and dignitaries in very rich cloaks. The different chieftains wore different brilliant liveries, and the causeways were full of them. Montezuma had sent these great *Caciques* in advance to receive us, and as soon as they came before Cortes they told him in their language that we were welcome, and as a sign of peace they touched the ground with their hands and kissed it. . . .

Who could now count the multitude of men, women, and boys in the streets, on the roof-tops and in canoes on the waterways, who had come out to see us? It was a wonderful sight and, as I write, it all comes before my eyes as if it had happened only yesterday.

They led us to our quarters, which were in some large houses capable of accommodating us all and had formerly belonged to the great

Montezuma's father, who was called Axayacatl. Here Montezuma now kept the great shrines of his gods, and a secret chamber containing gold bars and jewels. This was the treasure he had inherited from his father, which he never touched. Perhaps their reason for lodging us here was that, since they called us *Teules*[4] and considered us as such, they wished to have us near their idols. In any case they took us to this place, where there were many great halls, and a dais hung with the cloth of their country for our Captain, and matting beds with canopies over them for each of us.

On our arrival we entered the large court, where the great Montezuma was awaiting our Captain. Taking him by the hand, the prince led him to his apartment in the hall where he was to lodge, which was very richly furnished in their manner. Montezuma had ready for him a very rich necklace, made of golden crabs, a marvellous piece of work, which he hung round Cortes' neck. His captains were greatly astonished at this sign of honour.

After this ceremony, for which Cortes thanked him through our interpreters, Montezuma said: "Malinche,[5] you and your brothers are in your own house. Rest awhile." He then returned to his palace, which was not far off.

We divided our lodgings by companies, and placed our artillery in a convenient spot. Then the order we were to keep was clearly explained to us, and we were warned to be very much on the alert, both the horsemen and the rest of us soldiers. We then ate a sumptuous dinner which they had prepared for us in their native style.

So, with luck on our side, we boldly entered the city of Tenochtitlan or Mexico on 8 November in the year of our Lord 1519. . . .

I must now speak of the skilled workmen whom Montezuma employed in all the crafts they practised, beginning with the jewellers and workers in silver and gold and various kinds of hollowed objects, which excited the admiration of our great silversmiths at home. Many of the best of them lived in a town called Atzcapotzalco, three miles from Mexico. There were other skilled craftsmen who worked with precious stones and *chalchihuites*, and specialists in feather-work, and very fine painters and carvers. We can form some judgement of what they did then from what we can see of their work today. There are three Indians now living in the city of Mexico, named Marcos de

---

[4]Gods. [Ed.]

[5]mah LEEN cheh   Also known as Malintzin and Doña Marina. According to Díaz, she was a daughter of a cacique who was given away as a slave after her mother remarried. She had learned Nahuatl as a youth and Yucatec Mayan as a slave. Thus, with the help of a Spanish sailor who had learned Mayan, Cortés could initially translate between Nahuatl and Spanish. Malinche also learned Spanish and became Cortés's translator and mistress, eventually giving birth to Cortés's son, Martin. [Ed.]

Aquino, Juan de la Cruz, and El Crespillo, who are such magnificent painters and carvers that, had they lived in the age of the Apelles of old,[6] or of Michael Angelo,[7] or Berruguete[8] in our own day, they would be counted in the same rank.

Let us go on to the women, the weavers and sempstresses, who made such a huge quantity of fine robes with very elaborate feather designs. These things were generally brought from some towns in the province of Cotaxtla, which is on the north coast, quite near San Juan de Ulua. In Montezuma's own palaces very fine cloths were woven by those chieftains' daughters whom he kept as mistresses; and the daughters of other dignitaries, who lived in a kind of retirement like nuns in some houses close to the great *cue* of Huichilobos,[9] wore robes entirely of featherwork. Out of devotion for that god and a female deity who was said to preside over marriage, their fathers would place them in religious retirement until they found husbands. They would then take them out to be married.

Now to speak of the great number of performers whom Montezuma kept to entertain him. There were dancers and stilt-walkers, and some who seemed to fly as they leapt through the air, and men rather like clowns to make him laugh. There was a whole quarter full of these people who had no other occupation. He had as many workmen as he needed, too, stonecutters, masons, and carpenters, to keep his houses in repair. . . .

When we had already been in Mexico for four days, . . . Cortés said it would be a good thing to visit the large square of Tlatelolco and see the great *cue* of Huichilobos. So he sent Aguilar, Doña Marina,[10] and his own young page Orteguilla, who by now knew something of the language, to ask for Montezuma's approval of this plan. On receiving his request, the prince replied that we were welcome to go, but for fear that we might offer some offence to his idols he would himself accompany us with many of his chieftains. Leaving the palace in his fine litter, when he had gone about half way, he dismounted beside some shrines, since he considered it an insult to his gods to visit their dwelling in a litter. Some of the great chieftains then supported him by the arms, and his principal vassals walked before him, carrying two staves, like sceptres raised on high as a sign that the great Montezuma was approaching. When riding in his litter he had carried a rod, partly of gold and partly of wood, held up like a wand of justice. The prince now climbed

[6]Famous Ancient Greek painter. [Ed.]

[7]Michelangelo (1476–1564), Renaissance master painter and sculptor. [Ed.]

[8]Berruguete is either Pedro (1450–1504) or his son, Alonso (1488–1561), both famous Spanish painters. [Ed.]

[9]Huitzilopochtli. Aztec god of sun and war; required human sacrifice. [Ed.]

[10]Same as Malinche (footnote 5). [Ed.]

the steps of the great *cue*, escorted by many *papas*,[11] and began to burn incense and perform other ceremonies for Huichilobos. . . .

On reaching the market-place, escorted by the many *Caciques* whom Montezuma had assigned to us, we were astounded at the great number of people and the quantities of merchandise, and at the orderliness and good arrangements that prevailed, for we had never seen such a thing before. The chieftains who accompanied us pointed everything out. Every kind of merchandise was kept separate and had its fixed place marked for it.

Let us begin with the dealers in gold, silver, and precious stones, feathers, cloaks, and embroidered goods, and male and female slaves who are also sold there. They bring as many slaves to be sold in that market as the Portuguese bring Negroes from Guinea. Some are brought there attached to long poles by means of collars round their necks to prevent them from escaping, but others are left loose. Next there were those who sold coarser cloth, and cotton goods and fabrics made of twisted thread, and there were chocolate merchants with their chocolate. In this way you could see every kind of merchandise to be found anywhere in New Spain, laid out in the same way as goods are laid out in my own district of Medina del Campo, a centre for fairs, where each line of stalls has its own particular sort. So it was in this great market. There were those who sold sisal cloth and ropes and the sandals they wear on their feet, which are made from the same plant. All these were kept in one part of the market, in the place assigned to them, and in another part were skins of tigers and lions, otters, jackals, and deer, badgers, mountain cats, and other wild animals, some tanned and some untanned, and other classes of merchandise.

There were sellers of kidney-beans and sage and other vegetables and herbs in another place, and in yet another they were selling fowls, and birds with great dewlaps,[12] also rabbits, hares, deer, young ducks, little dogs, and other such creatures. Then there were the fruiterers; and the women who sold cooked food, flour and honey cake, and tripe, had their part of the market. Then came pottery of all kinds, from big water-jars to little jugs, displayed in its own place, also honey, honey-paste, and other sweets like nougat. Elsewhere they sold timber too, boards, cradles, beams, blocks, and benches, all in a quarter of their own.

Then there were the sellers of pitch-pine for torches, and other things of that kind, and I must also mention, with all apologies, that they sold many canoe-loads of human excrement, which they kept in the creeks near the market. This was for the manufacture of salt and

[11]Aztec priests. [Ed.]
[12]Turkeys.

the curing of skins, which they say cannot be done without it. I know that many gentlemen will laugh at this, but I assure them it is true. I may add that on all the roads they have shelters made of reeds or straw or grass so that they can retire when they wish to do so, and purge their bowels unseen by passers-by, and also in order that their excrement shall not be lost. . . .

We went on to the great *cue,* and as we approached its wide courts, before leaving the market-place itself, we saw many more merchants who, so I was told, brought gold to sell in grains, just as they extract it from the mines. This gold is placed in the thin quills of the large geese of that country, which are so white as to be transparent. They used to reckon their accounts with one another by the length and thickness of these little quills, how much so many cloaks or so many gourds of chocolate or so many slaves were worth, or anything else they were bartering.

Now let us leave the market, having given it a final glance, and come to the courts and enclosures in which their great *cue* stood. Before reaching it you passed through a series of large courts, bigger I think than the Plaza at Salamanca. These courts were surrounded by a double masonry wall and paved, like the whole place, with very large smooth white flagstones. Where these stones were absent everything was whitened and polished, indeed the whole place was so clean that there was not a straw or a grain of dust to be found there.

When we arrived near the great temple and before we had climbed a single step, the great Montezuma sent six *papas* and two chieftains down from the top, where he was making his sacrifices, to escort our Captain; and as he climbed the steps, of which there were one hundred and fourteen, they tried to take him by the arms to help him up in the same way as they helped Montezuma, thinking he might be tired, but he would not let them near him.

The top of the *cue* formed an open square on which stood something like a platform, and it was here that the great stones stood on which they placed the poor Indians for sacrifice. Here also was a massive image like a dragon, and other hideous figures, and a great deal of blood that had been spilled that day. Emerging in the company of two *papas* from the shrine which houses his accursed images, Montezuma made a deep bow to us all and said: "My lord Malinche, you must be tired after climbing this great *cue* of ours." And Cortes replied that none of us was ever exhausted by anything. Then Montezuma took him by the hand, and told him to look at his great city and all the other cities standing in the water, and the many others on the land round the lake; and he said that if Cortes had not had a good view of the great market-place he could see it better from where he now was. So we stood there looking, because that huge accursed *cue* stood so high that it dominated everything. We saw the three causeways that led into

Mexico: the causeway of Iztapalapa by which we had entered four days
before. . . . We saw the fresh water which came from Chapultepec to
supply the city, and the bridges that were constructed at intervals on
the causeways so that the water could flow in and out from one part of
the lake to another. We saw a great number of canoes, some coming
with provisions and others returning with cargo and merchandise; and
we saw too that one could not pass from one house to another of that
great city and the other cities that were built on the water except over
wooden drawbridges or by canoe. We saw *cues* and shrines in these
cities that looked like gleaming white towers and castles: a marvellous
sight. All the houses had flat roofs, and on the causeways were other
small towers and shrines built like fortresses.

Having examined and considered all that we had seen, we turned
back to the great market and the swarm of people buying and selling.
The mere murmur of their voices talking was loud enough to be heard
more than three miles away. Some of our soldiers who had been in
many parts of the world, in Constantinople, in Rome, and all over
Italy, said that they had never seen a market so well laid out, so large,
so orderly, and so full of people.

REFLECTIONS

Our selections certainly offer support for Braudel's thesis on the European city. London was hardly unique among European cities. The char-
tering of cities as independent corporations with their own laws,
courts, and independent citizenry was a phenomenon repeated throughout Europe, especially in the West and the Mediterranean from the
eleventh to the fifteenth century. The Florentine festival demonstrates
how citizens came together in so many groups to celebrate their collective identity as citizens. Europe was a world without emperors, in
which kings and lords were forced to bargain freedoms for favors.

Marco Polo unwittingly points to the power of the emperor, Song
or Mongol, in imperial China. The capital city especially is designed
and maintained according to his specifications. City life may be vibrant.
There may even be enormous markets and wealthy merchants, but it is
the emperor's city, not the merchants'. Rich merchants might train their
sons to govern, but only as officials of the emperor.

Neither Chinese nor Muslim urban dwellers find their primary
identities as citizens or even as residents of a particular city. They may
be Cairenes, but they are Muslims first. Muslims had no need for self-
governing cities when they could travel and work anywhere in the vast
world of Islam.

Braudel struggled with American cities. North American towns, he thought, were re-creations of European towns. In Latin America, he classified Mexico City as similar to the imperial capitals of other parts of the world. Like Hangchou, Mexico City could be astonishingly rich, but it was not an autonomous entity under Aztecs or Spaniards. The readings were selected not to stack the deck, but to show what Braudel meant. Consequently, some qualifications of Braudel's thesis might be in order.

First, we should not assume that autonomous or communal cities were limited to Europe. Rather, they were a product of a feudal, or politically weak and decentralized, society, where urban populations could bargain for special privileges. We could find similar examples of urban autonomy among, for example, Japanese port cities during the Japanese feudal era of the fourteenth to sixteenth centuries. One of these, Sakai, was called the Venice of Japan. Not until after 1600 and the re-centralization of Japan under the Tokugawa administration were these independent cities brought to heel. In many ways, Tokugawa developments paralleled those of Europe, where centralized states also subordinated the independence of commercial cities after 1700.

Second, the absence of a movement for urban autonomy in Islamic and Chinese cities—important as it was in the time and places discussed in this chapter—was not universal. Chinese cities before the Mongol Yüan dynasty, especially in the earlier Sung dynasty, had developed an extremely prosperous commercial class. And while it is true that they did not gain (or seek) urban independence, they were content to exercise sufficient influence on the local representatives of the emperor. No appointed official could think lightly of ignoring the advice of Chinese merchants, the uniquely Chinese class of civil-service exam graduates, and the many Chinese guilds (one of the more important forces for self-government in Europe).

Third, while medieval Muslim cities encouraged little urban autonomy or identity, a prosperous class of merchants—always at the core of Islam—were nourished by more enlightened sultans and emirs. The Turkish historian Halil Inalcik writes that it was "the deliberate policy" of the Ottoman government, as it founded its successive capitals at Bursa in 1326, Edirne in 1402, and Istanbul in 1453, to create commercial and industrial centers, and that it consequently used every means—from tax exemptions to force—to attract and settle merchants and artisans in the new capitals. With the same end in view, Mehmed II encouraged the Jews of Europe to migrate to his new capital at Istanbul as they were being expelled from Spain and Portugal.

Braudel's thesis emphasizes the differences among cities, but as he well knew, one could emphasize the similarities as well. All cities distinguished themselves from the countryside which they controlled and exploited. All cities built and concentrated the wealth, achievements, and opportunities of the culture within their walls. All cities were greater engines of change than were villages, farm, and pasture. And some have argued that all cities promote patriarchy and class stratification.

Today about half the world's people live in cities. In 1800 only 3 percent of the world's population lived in cities. It is expected that by 2030, 60 percent of the world's population will be urban. Does that mean the lives of so many people will change in a similar way? Does it mean increasing patriarchy? Increasing exploitation of the countryside? Increasing inequality? Do significant choices need to be made about the types of cities we inhabit? Can we find ways to make our cities of the future our own?

14

Ecology, Technology, and Science

Europe, Asia, Oceania, and Africa,
500–1550 C.E.

HISTORICAL CONTEXT

Everyone knows that the world has changed drastically since the Middle Ages. And most people would agree that the most important and far-reaching changes have occurred in the fields of ecology, technology, and science. Global population has grown tenfold. The world has become a single ecological unit where microbes, migrants, and money travel everywhere at jet speed. In most parts of the world, average life expectancy has doubled; cities have mushroomed, supplanting farm and pasture. Machines have replaced the labor of humans and animals. Powers that were only imagined in the Middle Ages — elixirs to cure disease, energy to harness rivers, machines that could fly — are now commonplace. Other aspects of life — among them religion, political behavior, music, and art — have also evolved, but even these were affected significantly by advances in modern science and technology.

Have the changes been for good or ill? The signs of environmental stress are visible everywhere. The hole in the earth's protective ozone layer over Antarctica continues to expand. The North Pole floats in the summer. Ten-thousand-year-old glaciers are disappearing. The oceans are rising two to four inches every ten years. Our atmosphere contains more carbon gasses than it has for at least 650,000 years. The stored energy of millions of years burns to service the richest members of a couple of generations. Ancient aquifers are drained to water the lawns of desert cities.

Precisely what change or changes occurred? When did the cycle of change begin and what caused it? We will examine these questions here. You will read three substantial answers. Lynn White Jr. defines the transformation to modernity in largely technological and ecological terms, but emphasizes the role of cultural causes. Lynda Shaffer discusses technological and scientific changes as spreading through contact and trade. Jared Diamond writes of cultural failures to meet new natural and technological crises.

These explanations of long-term change differ most markedly in how they explain the roots of the transformation. White, a historian of medieval European technology, focuses on the role of medieval European religion: Christianity. Shaffer, a world historian, underscores the role of India and South Asia. Diamond, a professor of geography with numerous specializations in fields like physiology, evolutionary biology, and biogeography, finds a failure of will in many societies.

THINKING HISTORICALLY
Evaluating Grand Theories

Big questions deserve big answers — or at least grand theories. Here we consider three grand theories about the origins of our technological transformation and ecological difficulties, the links between environmental decline and the growth of technology and science, and the role of Western (European and American) economic growth in undermining the environment. Grand theories are especially speculative. They give us much to question and challenge. But their scope and freshness can often suggest new insights. Grand theories almost inevitably have elements that seem partly wrong and partly right. You will be encouraged to weigh some of the many elements in these theories. Then you can evaluate the theories, decide where you agree and disagree, and, perhaps, begin to develop your own grand theory as well.

87

LYNN WHITE JR.

The Historical Roots of Our Ecological Crisis

This classic essay first appeared in the magazine *Science* in 1967 and has since been reprinted and commented on many times. What do you think of White's linkage of ecological crisis and Christianity? Which of White's arguments and evidence do you find most persuasive? Which do you find least convincing? Imagine a continuum that includes all of the world's people, from the most ecologically minded "tree-huggers" on the left to the most damaging polluters and destroyers of the environment on the right. Where on that continuum would you place the historical majority of Christians? Buddhists? Why?

Thinking Historically

A grand theory like this — that Christianity is responsible for our environmental problems — argues far more than can be proven in such a brief essay. White concentrates on making certain kinds of connections and marshaling certain kinds of evidence. In addition to weighing the arguments he makes, consider the gaps in his argument. What sorts of evidence would you seek to make White's theory more convincing?

A conversation with Aldous Huxley[1] not infrequently put one at the receiving end of an unforgettable monologue. About a year before his lamented death he was discoursing on a favorite topic: man's unnatural treatment of nature and its sad results. To illustrate his point he told how, during the previous summer, he had returned to a little valley in England where he had spent many happy months as a child. Once it had been composed of delightful grassy glades; now it was becoming overgrown with unsightly brush because the rabbits that formerly kept such growth under control had largely succumbed to a disease, myxomatosis, that was deliberately introduced by the local farmers to reduce

---

[1]Aldous Huxley (1894–1963), British author of novels, short stories, travel books, biography, and essays. Best known for *Brave New World* (1932). [Ed.]

Lynn White Jr., "The Historical Roots of Our Ecological Crisis," *Science* 155 (March 1967): 1203–7.

the rabbits' destruction of crops. Being something of a Philistine,[2] I could be silent no longer, even in the interests of great rhetoric. I interrupted to point out that the rabbit itself had been brought as a domestic animal to England in 1176, presumably to improve the protein diet of the peasantry.

All forms of life modify their contexts. The most spectacular and benign instance is doubtless the coral polyp. By serving its own ends, it has created a vast undersea world favorable to thousands of other kinds of animals and plants. Ever since man became a numerous species he has affected his environment notably. The hypothesis that his fire-drive[3] method of hunting created the world's great grasslands and helped to exterminate the monster mammals of the Pleistocene from much of the globe is plausible, if not proved. For six millennia at least, the banks of the lower Nile have been a human artifact rather than the swampy African jungle which nature, apart from man, would have made it. The Aswan Dam, flooding five thousand square miles, is only the latest stage in a long process. In many regions terracing or irrigation, overgrazing, and the cutting of forests by Romans to build ships to fight Carthaginians or by Crusaders to solve the logistics problems of their expeditions have profoundly changed some ecologies. Observation that the French landscape falls into two basic types, the open fields of the north and the *bocage*[4] of the south and west, inspired Marc Bloch to undertake his classic study of medieval agricultural methods. Quite unintentionally, changes in human ways often affect nonhuman nature. It has been noted, for example, that the advent of the automobile eliminated huge flocks of sparrows that once fed on the horse manure littering every street.

The history of ecologic change is still so rudimentary that we know little about what really happened, or what the results were. The extinction of the European aurochs[5] as late as 1627 would seem to have been a simple case of overenthusiastic hunting. On more intricate matters it often is impossible to find solid information. For a thousand years or more the Frisians and Hollanders have been pushing back the North Sea, and the process is culminating in our own time in the reclamation

---

[2]An anti-intellectual (though obviously White is not; he was only impatient with Huxley's pedantry). [Ed.]

[3]Paleolithic hunters used fires to drive animals to their deaths. [Ed.]

[4]Full of groves or woodlands. Marc Bloch reasoned that the open fields north of the Loire River in France must have been plowed by teams of oxen and heavy plows because of the hard soil. In the south farmers could use scratch plows on the softer soil and therefore did not clear large fields, preserving more woodlands. [Ed.]

[5]A now extinct European wild ox believed to be the ancestor of European domestic cattle. [Ed.]

of the Zuider Zee.[6] What, if any, species of animals, birds, fish, shore life, or plants have died out in the process? In their epic combat with Neptune have the Netherlanders overlooked ecological values in such a way that the quality of human life in the Netherlands has suffered? I cannot discover that the questions have ever been asked, much less answered.

People, then, have often been a dynamic element in their own environment, but in the present state of historical scholarship we usually do not know exactly when, where, or with what effects man-induced changes came. As we enter the last third of the twentieth century, however, concern for the problem of ecologic backlash is mounting feverishly. Natural science, conceived as the effort to understand the nature of things, had flourished in several eras and among several peoples. Similarly there had been an age-old accumulation of technological skills, sometimes growing rapidly, sometimes slowly. But it was not until about four generations ago that Western Europe and North America arranged a marriage between science and technology, a union of the theoretical and the empirical approaches to our natural environment. The emergence in widespread practice of the Baconian creed that scientific knowledge means technological power over nature can scarcely be dated before about 1850, save in the chemical industries, where it is anticipated in the eighteenth century. Its acceptance as a normal pattern of action may mark the greatest event in human history since the invention of agriculture, and perhaps in nonhuman terrestrial history as well.

Almost at once the new situation forced the crystallization of the novel concept of ecology; indeed, the word *ecology* first appeared in the English language in 1873. Today, less than a century later, the impact of our race upon the environment has so increased in force that it has changed in essence. When the first cannons were fired, in the early fourteenth century, they affected ecology by sending workers scrambling to the forests and mountains for more potash, sulfur, iron ore, and charcoal, with some resulting erosion and deforestation. Hydrogen bombs are of a different order: A war fought with them might alter the genetics of all life on this planet. By 1285 London had a smog problem arising from the burning of soft coal, but our present combustion of fossil fuels threatens to change the chemistry of the globe's atmosphere as a whole, with consequences which we are only beginning to guess. With the population explosion, the carcinoma of planless urbanism, the now geological deposits of sewage and garbage, surely no creature other than man has ever managed to foul its nest in such short order.

---

[6]Once a Dutch lake, it was joined to the North Sea by a flood in the thirteenth century but has since been reclaimed by the building of a dam. [Ed.]

There are many calls to action, but specific proposals, however worthy as individual items, seem too partial, palliative, negative: Ban the bomb, tear down the billboards, give the Hindus contraceptives and tell them to eat their sacred cows. The simplest solution to any suspect change is, of course, to stop it, or, better yet, to revert to a romanticized past: Make those ugly gasoline stations look like Anne Hathaway's cottage or (in the Far West) like ghost-town saloons. The "wilderness area" mentality invariably advocates deep-freezing an ecology, whether San Gimignano or the High Sierra, as it was before the first Kleenex was dropped. But neither atavism nor prettification will cope with the ecologic crisis of our time.

What shall we do? No one yet knows. Unless we think about fundamentals, our specific measures may produce new backlashes more serious than those they are designed to remedy.

As a beginning we should try to clarify our thinking by looking, in some historical depth, at the presuppositions that underlie modern technology and science. Science was traditionally aristocratic, speculative, intellectual in intent; technology was lower-class, empirical, action-oriented. The quite sudden fusion of these two, toward the middle of the nineteenth century, is surely related to the slightly prior and contemporary democratic revolutions which, by reducing social barriers, tended to assert a functional unity of brain and hand. Our ecologic crisis is the product of an emerging, entirely novel, democratic culture. The issue is whether a democratized world can survive its own implications. Presumably we cannot unless we rethink our axioms.

The Western Traditions of Technology and Science

One thing is so certain that it seems stupid to verbalize it: Both modern technology and modern science are distinctively *Occidental*. Our technology has absorbed elements from all over the world, notably from China; yet everywhere today, whether in Japan or in Nigeria, successful technology is Western. Our science is the heir to all the sciences of the past, especially perhaps to the work of the great Islamic scientists of the Middle Ages, who so often outdid the ancient Greeks in skill and perspicacity: al-Rāzī in medicine, for example; or ibn-al-Haytham in optics; or Omar Khayyám in mathematics. Indeed, not a few works of such geniuses seem to have vanished in the original Arabic and to survive only in medieval Latin translations that helped to lay the foundations for later Western developments. Today, around the globe, all significant science is Western in style and method, whatever the pigmentation or language of the scientists.

A second pair of facts is less well recognized because they result from quite recent historical scholarship. The leadership of the West, both in technology and in science, is far older than the so-called Scientific Revolution of the seventeenth century or the so-called Industrial Revolution of the eighteenth century. These terms are in fact outmoded and obscure the true nature of what they try to describe — significant stages in two long and separate developments. By A.D. 1000 at the latest — and perhaps, feebly, as much as two hundred years earlier — the West began to apply water power to industrial processes other than milling grain. This was followed in the late twelfth century by the harnessing of wind power. From simple beginnings, but with remarkable consistency of style, the West rapidly expanded its skills in the development of power machinery, labor-saving devices, and automation. Those who doubt should contemplate that most monumental achievement in the history of automation: the weight-driven mechanical clock, which appeared in two forms in the early fourteenth century. Not in craftsmanship but in basic technological capacity, the Latin West of the later Middle Ages far outstripped its elaborate, sophisticated, and esthetically magnificent sister cultures, Byzantium and Islam. In 1444 a great Greek ecclesiastic, Bessarion, who had gone to Italy, wrote a letter to a prince in Greece. He is amazed by the superiority of Western ships, arms, textiles, glass. But above all he is astonished by the spectacle of waterwheels sawing timbers and pumping the bellows of blast furnaces. Clearly, he had seen nothing of the sort in the Near East.

By the end of the fifteenth century the technological superiority of Europe was such that its small, mutually hostile nations could spill out over all the rest of the world, conquering, looting, and colonizing. The symbol of this technological superiority is the fact that Portugal, one of the weakest states of the Occident, was able to become, and to remain for a century, mistress of the East Indies. And we must remember that the technology of Vasco da Gama and Albuquerque was built by pure empiricism, drawing remarkably little support or inspiration from science.

In the present-day vernacular understanding, modern science is supposed to have begun in 1543, when both Copernicus and Vesalius published their great works. It is no derogation of their accomplishments, however, to point out that such structures as the *Fabrica*[7] and the *De revolutionibus*[8] do not appear overnight. The distinctive Western tradition of science, in fact, began in the late eleventh century with a massive movement of translation of Arabic and Greek scientific works into Latin. A

---

[7]*De Humani Corporis Fabrica* (1543), an illustrated work on human anatomy based on dissections, was produced by Andreas Vesalius (1514–1564), a Flemish anatomist, at the University of Padua in Italy. [Ed.]

[8]*De revolutionibus orbium coelestium* (1543; On the Revolutions of Heavenly Bodies) was published by Nicolas Copernicus (1473–1543); it showed the sun as the center of a system around which the Earth revolved. [Ed.]

few notable books — Theophrastus, for example — escaped the West's avid new appetite for science, but within less than two hundred years effectively the entire corpus of Greek and Muslim science was available in Latin, and was being eagerly read and criticized in the new European universities. Out of criticism arose new observation, speculation, and increasing distrust of ancient authorities. By the late thirteenth century Europe had seized global scientific leadership from the faltering hands of Islam. It would be as absurd to deny the profound originality of Newton, Galileo, or Copernicus as to deny that of the fourteenth-century scholastic scientists like Buridan or Oresme on whose work they built. Before the eleventh century, science scarcely existed in the Latin West, even in Roman times. From the eleventh century onward, the scientific sector of Occidental culture has increased in a steady crescendo.

Since both our technological and our scientific movements got their start, acquired their character, and achieved world dominance in the Middle Ages, it would seem that we cannot understand their nature or their present impact upon ecology without examining fundamental medieval assumptions and developments.

Medieval View of Man and Nature

Until recently, agriculture has been the chief occupation even in "advanced" societies; hence, any change in methods of tillage has much importance. Early plows, drawn by two oxen, did not normally turn the sod but merely scratched it. Thus, cross-plowing was needed and fields tended to be squarish. In the fairly light soils and semiarid climates of the Near East and Mediterranean, this worked well. But such a plow was inappropriate to the wet climate and often sticky soils of northern Europe. By the latter part of the seventh century after Christ, however, following obscure beginnings, certain northern peasants were using an entirely new kind of plow, equipped with a vertical knife to cut the line of the furrow, a horizontal share to slice under the sod, and a moldboard to turn it over. The friction of this plow with the soil was so great that it normally required not two but eight oxen. It attacked the land with such violence that cross-plowing was not needed, and fields tended to be shaped in long strips.

In the days of the scratch-plow, fields were distributed generally in units capable of supporting a single family. Subsistence farming was the presupposition. But no peasant owned eight oxen: to use the new and more efficient plow, peasants pooled their oxen to form large plow-teams, originally receiving (it would appear) plowed strips in proportion to their contribution. Thus, distribution of land was based no longer on the needs of a family but, rather, on the capacity of a power machine to till the earth. Man's relation to the soil was profoundly changed. Formerly man had been part of nature; now he was the exploiter of nature. Nowhere else in the world did farmers develop any analogous agricultural implement. Is it coincidence that modern technology, with its ruthlessness toward nature, has so largely been produced by descendants of these peasants of northern Europe?

This same exploitive attitude appears slightly before A.D. 830 in Western illustrated calendars. In older calendars the months were shown as passive personifications. The new Frankish calendars, which set the style for the Middle Ages, are very different: They show men coercing the world around them — plowing, harvesting, chopping trees, butchering pigs. Man and nature are two things, and man is master.

These novelties seem to be in harmony with larger intellectual patterns. What people do about their ecology depends on what they think about themselves in relation to things around them. Human ecology is deeply conditioned by beliefs about our nature and destiny — that is, by religion. To Western eyes this is very evident in, say, India or Ceylon. It is equally true of ourselves and of our medieval ancestors.

The victory of Christianity over paganism was the greatest psychic revolution in the history of our culture. It has become fashionable today to say that, for better or worse, we live in "the post-Christian age." Certainly the forms of our thinking and language have largely ceased to be Christian, but to my eye the substance often remains amazingly akin to that of the past. Our daily habits of action, for example, are dominated by an implicit faith in perpetual progress which was unknown either to Greco-Roman antiquity or to the Orient. It is rooted in, and is indefensible apart from, Judeo-Christian teleology.[9] The fact that Communists share it merely helps to show what can be demonstrated on many other grounds: that Marxism, like Islam, is a Judeo-Christian heresy. We continue today to live, as we have lived for about seventeen hundred years, very largely in a context of Christian axioms.

What did Christianity tell people about their relations with the environment?

While many of the world's mythologies provide stories of creation, Greco-Roman mythology was singularly incoherent in this respect. Like Aristotle, the intellectuals of the ancient West denied that the visible world had had a beginning. Indeed, the idea of a beginning was impossible in the framework of their cyclical notion of time. In sharp contrast, Christianity inherited from Judaism not only a concept of time as nonrepetitive and linear but also a striking story of creation. By gradual stages a loving and all-powerful God had created light and darkness, the heavenly bodies, the earth and all its plants, animals, birds, and fishes. Finally, God had created Adam and, as an afterthought,

[9]The Biblical idea that God's purpose is revealed in his creation, that human history can be seen as the result of God's intentions. [Ed.]

Eve to keep man from being lonely. Man named all the animals, thus establishing his dominance over them. God planned all of this explicitly for man's benefit and rule: No item in the physical creation had any purpose save to serve man's purposes. And, although man's body is made of clay, he is not simply part of nature: He is made in God's image.

Especially in its Western form, Christianity is the most anthropocentric religion the world has seen. As early as the second century both Tertullian and Saint Irenaeus of Lyons were insisting that when God shaped Adam he was foreshadowing the image of the incarnate Christ, the Second Adam. Man shares, in great measure, God's transcendence of nature. Christianity, in absolute contrast to ancient paganism and Asia's religions (except, perhaps, Zoroastrianism), not only established a dualism of man and nature but also insisted that it is God's will that man exploit nature for his proper ends.

At the level of the common people this worked out in an interesting way. In Antiquity every tree, every spring, every stream, every hill had its own *genius loci*, its guardian spirit. These spirits were accessible to men, but were very unlike men; centaurs, fauns, and mermaids show their ambivalence. Before one cut a tree, mined a mountain, or dammed a brook, it was important to placate the spirit in charge of that particular situation, and to keep it placated. By destroying pagan animism, Christianity made it possible to exploit nature in a mood of indifference to the feelings of natural objects.

It is often said that for animism the Church substituted the cult of saints. True; but the cult of saints is functionally quite different from animism. The saint is not *in* natural objects; he may have special shrines, but his citizenship is in heaven. Moreover, a saint is entirely a man; he can be approached in human terms. In addition to saints, Christianity of course also had angels and demons inherited from Judaism and perhaps, at one remove, from Zoroastrianism. But these were all as mobile as the saints themselves. The spirits *in* natural objects, which formerly had protected nature from man, evaporated. Man's effective monopoly on spirit in this world was confirmed, and the old inhibitions to the exploitation of nature crumbled.

When one speaks in such sweeping terms, a note of caution is in order. Christianity is a complex faith, and its consequences differ in differing contexts. What I have said may well apply to the medieval West, where in fact technology made spectacular advances. But the Greek East, a highly civilized realm of equal Christian devotion, seems to have produced no marked technological innovation after the late seventh century, when Greek fire was invented. The key to the contrast may perhaps be found in a difference in the tonality of piety and thought which students of comparative theology find between the Greek and the Latin Churches. The Greeks believed that sin was intellectual blindness, and that salvation was found in illumination, orthodoxy — that is, clear thinking. The Latins, on the other hand, felt that sin was moral evil, and that salvation was to be found in right conduct. Eastern theology has been intellectualist. Western theology has been voluntarist. The Greek saint contemplates; the Western saint acts. The implications of Christianity for the conquest of nature would emerge more easily in the Western atmosphere.

The Christian dogma of creation, which is found in the first clause of all the Creeds, has another meaning for our comprehension of today's ecologic crisis. By revelation, God had given man the Bible, the Book of Scripture. But since God had made nature, nature also must reveal the divine mentality. The religious study of nature for the better understanding of God was known as natural theology. In the early Church, and always in the Greek East, nature was conceived primarily as a symbolic system through which God speaks to men: The ant is a sermon to sluggards; rising flames are the symbol of the soul's aspiration. This view of nature was essentially artistic rather than scientific. While Byzantium preserved and copied great numbers of ancient Greek scientific texts, science as we conceive it could scarcely flourish in such an ambience.

However, in the Latin West by the early thirteenth century natural theology was following a very different bent. It was ceasing to be the decoding of the physical symbols of God's communication with man and was becoming the effort to understand God's mind by discovering how his creation operates. The rainbow was no longer simply a symbol of hope first sent to Noah after the Deluge: Robert Grosseteste, Friar Roger Bacon, and Theodoric of Freiberg produced startlingly sophisticated work on the optics of the rainbow, but they did it as a venture in religious understanding. From the thirteenth century onward, up to and including Leibnitz and Newton, every major scientist, in effect, explained his motivations in religious terms. Indeed, if Galileo had not been so expert an amateur theologian he would have got into far less trouble: The professionals resented his intrusion. And Newton seems to have regarded himself more as a theologian than as a scientist. It was not until the late eighteenth century that the hypothesis of God became unnecessary to many scientists.

It is often hard for the historian to judge, when men explain why they are doing what they want to do, whether they are offering real reasons or merely culturally acceptable reasons. The consistency with which scientists during the long formative centuries of Western science said that the task and the reward of the scientist was "to think God's thoughts after him" leads one to believe that this was their real motivation. If so, then modern Western science was cast in a matrix of Christian theology. The dynamism of religious devotion, shaped by the Judeo-Christian dogma of creation, gave it impetus.

An Alternative Christian View

We would seem to be headed toward conclusions unpalatable to many Christians. Since both *science* and *technology* are blessed words in our contemporary vocabulary, some may be happy at the notions, first, that, viewed historically, modern science is an extrapolation of natural theology and, second, that modern technology is at least partly to be explained as an Occidental, voluntarist realization of the Christian dogma of man's transcendence of, and rightful mastery over, nature. But, as we now recognize, somewhat over a century ago science and technology — hitherto quite separate activities — joined to give mankind powers which, to judge by many of the ecologic effects, are out of control. If so, Christianity bears a huge burden of guilt.

I personally doubt that disastrous ecologic backlash can be avoided simply by applying to our problems more science and more technology. Our science and technology have grown out of Christian attitudes toward man's relation to nature which are almost universally held not only by Christians and neo-Christians but also by those who fondly regard themselves as post-Christians. Despite Copernicus, all the cosmos rotates around our little globe. Despite Darwin, we are *not*, in our hearts, part of the natural process. We are superior to nature, contemptuous of it, willing to use it for our slightest whim. The newly elected Governor of California,[10] like myself a churchman but less troubled than I, spoke for the Christian tradition when he said (as is alleged), "when you've seen one redwood tree, you've seen them all." To a Christian a tree can be no more than a physical fact. The whole concept of the sacred grove is alien to Christianity and to the ethos of the West. For nearly two millennia Christian missionaries have been chopping down sacred groves, which are idolatrous because they assume spirit in nature.

What we do about ecology depends on our ideas of the man-nature relationship. More science and more technology are not going to get us out of the present ecologic crisis until we find a new religion, or rethink our old one. The beatniks, who are the basic revolutionaries of our time, show a sound instinct in their affinity for Zen Buddhism, which conceives of the man-nature relationship as very nearly the mirror image of the Christian view. Zen, however, is as deeply conditioned by Asian history as Christianity is by the experience of the West, and I am dubious of its viability among us.

Possibly we should ponder the greatest radical in Christian history since Christ: Saint Francis of Assisi. The prime miracle of Saint Francis is the fact that he did not end at the stake, as many of his left-wing fol-

---

[10]Ronald Reagan, governor from 1967 to 1975.

lowers did. He was so clearly heretical that a General of the Franciscan Order, Saint Bonaventura, a great and perceptive Christian, tried to suppress the early accounts of Franciscanism. The key to an understanding of Francis is his belief in the virtue of humility — not merely for the individual but for man as a species. Francis tried to depose man from his monarchy over creation and set up a democracy of all God's creatures. With him the ant is no longer simply a homily for the lazy, flames a sign of the thrust of the soul toward union with God; now they are Brother Ant and Sister Fire, praising the Creator in their own ways as Brother Man does in his.

Later commentators have said that Francis preached to the birds as a rebuke to men who would not listen. The records do not read so: He urged the little birds to praise God, and in spiritual ecstasy they flapped their wings and chirped rejoicing. Legends of saints, especially the Irish saints, had long told of their dealings with animals but always, I believe, to show their human dominance over creatures. With Francis it is different. The land around Gubbio in the Apennines was being ravaged by a fierce wolf. Saint Francis, says the legend, talked to the wolf and persuaded him of the error of his ways. The wolf repented, died in the odor of sanctity, and was buried in consecrated ground.

What Sir Steven Ruciman calls "the Franciscan doctrine of the animal soul" was quickly stamped out. Quite possibly it was in part inspired, consciously or unconsciously, by the belief in reincarnation held by the Cathar heretics who at that time teemed in Italy and southern France, and who presumably had got it originally from India. It is significant that at just the same moment, about 1200, traces of metempsychosis are found also in Western Judaism, in the Provençal *Cabbala*. But Francis held neither to transmigration of souls nor to pantheism. His view of nature and of man rested on a unique sort of pan-psychism of all things animate and inanimate, designed for the glorification of their transcendent Creator, who, in the ultimate gesture of cosmic humility, assumed flesh, lay helpless in a manger, and hung dying on a scaffold.

I am not suggesting that many contemporary Americans who are concerned about our ecologic crisis will be either able or willing to counsel with wolves or exhort birds. However, the present increasing disruption of the global environment is the product of a dynamic technology and science which were originating in the Western medieval world against which Saint Francis was rebelling in so original a way. Their growth cannot be understood historically apart from distinctive attitudes toward nature which are deeply grounded in Christian dogma. The fact that most people do not think of these attitudes as Christian is irrelevant. No new set of basic values has been accepted in our society to displace those of Christianity. Hence we shall continue to have a worsening ecologic crisis until we reject the Christian axiom that nature has no reason for existence save to serve man.

The greatest spiritual revolutionary in Western history, Saint Francis, proposed what he thought was an alternative Christian view of nature and man's relation to it: He tried to substitute the idea of the equality of all creatures, including man, for the idea of man's limitless rule of creation. He failed. Both our present science and our present technology are so tinctured with orthodox Christian arrogance toward nature that no solution for our ecologic crisis can be expected from them alone. Since the roots of our trouble are so largely religious, the remedy must also be essentially religious, whether we call it that or not. We must rethink and refeel our nature and destiny. The profoundly religious, but heretical, sense of the primitive Franciscans for the spiritual autonomy of all parts of nature may point a direction. I propose Francis as a patron saint for ecologists.

88

Life of Boniface:
Converting the Hessians

This story about the Christian missionary Boniface was told in the *Life of Boniface*, written between 754 and 768, by Willibald, one of his students. The Hessians, previously converted to Christianity, had reverted to paganism, and Boniface traveled from England to Germany to reconvert them. Hessians were widely regarded by the early Christian missionaries to Germany as a difficult people to convert. Boniface's success became a guide for future missions. What does this account tell us about the nature of Hessian paganism? What does Boniface do to reconvert them to Christianity? What, if anything, does the story tell us about Christianity?

Thinking Historically

How does this primary source relate to Lynn White Jr.'s article? Does it support his argument? Can a single piece like this ever prove an argument like White's, or can it only illustrate it?

The Anglo-Saxon Missionaries in Germany, trans. C. H. Talbot (London: Sheed and Ward, 1954), 45–46.

Now many of the Hessians who at that time had acknowledged the Catholic faith were confirmed by the grace of the Holy Spirit and received the laying-on of hands. But others, not yet strong in the spirit, refused to accept the pure teachings of the Church in their entirety. Moreover, some continued secretly, others openly, to offer sacrifices to trees and springs, to inspect the entrails of victims; some practised divination, legerdemain,[1] and incantations; some turned their attention to auguries, auspices, and other sacrificial rites; whilst others, of a more reasonable character, forsook all the profane practices of heathenism and committed none of these crimes. With the counsel and advice of the latter persons, Boniface in their presence attempted to cut down, at a place called Gaesmere, . . . a certain oak of extraordinary size called by the pagans of olden times the Oak of Jupiter. Taking his courage in his hands (for a great crowd of pagans stood by watching and bitterly cursing in their hearts the enemy of the gods), he cut the first notch. But when he had made a superficial cut, suddenly the oak's vast bulk, shaken by a mighty blast of wind from above, crashed to the ground shivering its topmost branches into fragments in its fall. As if by the express will of God (for the brethren present had done nothing to cause it) the oak burst asunder into four parts, each part having a trunk of equal length. At the sight of this extraordinary spectacle the heathens who had been cursing ceased to revile and began, on the contrary, to believe and bless the Lord. Thereupon the holy bishop took counsel with the brethren, built an oratory from the timber of the oak and dedicated it to St. Peter the Apostle. He then set out on a journey to Thuringia, having accomplished by the help of God all the things we have already mentioned. Arrived there, he addressed the elders and the chiefs of the people, calling on them to put aside their blind ignorance and to return to the Christian religion which they had formerly embraced. . . .

[1]Sleight of hand.

89

Image from a Cistercian Manuscript, Twelfth Century

This image of a monk chopping down a tree while his lay servant prunes the branches is from a manuscript of the Cistercian order of monks, from the twelfth century. The Cistercians, more than other orders, spoke out in favor of conserving forest resources, but they also celebrated manual labor. Does this image indicate that the monks were in favor of forest clearance?

Thinking Historically

Does this image lend support to White's argument? Why or why not? If there were many such images, would visual evidence like this convince you of White's argument? Would it be more convincing if almost all European images of trees showed someone chopping them down and virtually no Chinese tree images showed that? In other words, how much visual evidence would convince you of White's interpretation?

Image from a Cistercian manuscript, 12th c., monk chopping tree (Dijon, Bibliothèque municipale, MS 173), duplicated in *Cambridge Illustrated History of the Middle Ages*, Robert Fossier, ed. (Cambridge: Cambridge University Press, 1997), 72.

Figure 14.1 Twelfth-Century Manuscript.

Source: Courtesy of Tresorier Principal
Municipal, Dijon.

90

Image from a French Calendar, Fifteenth Century

This French calendar scene for March is from the early fifteenth century. What sorts of activities does it show? How does it relate specifically to White's argument about the changing images of European calendars? (See p. 501.) The top half of the calendar shows a zodiac. In what ways are these images of nature different from those in the bottom half?

Thinking Historically

What technologies are shown here? Were any of these technologies particularly recent or European? Does this image merely illustrate White's argument, or does it support it to some extent? What other visual evidence would you want to see in order to be persuaded by White's argument?

From *Les trés riches heures du duc de Berry*, Giraudon, Musée de Condé.

Figure 14.2 French Calendar Scene.
Source: Bridgeman-Giraudon/Art Resource, N.Y.

91

Image of a Chinese *Feng-Shui* Master

Although the Chinese celebrated the natural landscape in their paintings, they also created drawings that showcased their advanced technologies. The Chinese made and used the compass (as well as paper, printing, and gunpowder) long before Europeans. Instead of using it to subdue the natural world, however, they used it to find harmony with nature, specifically through the practice of *feng-shui*.* *Feng-shui*, which literally means wind over water, is the Chinese art of determining the best position and placement of structures such as houses within the natural environment. In the following image we see a type of compass used in the work of a Chinese *feng-shui* master. Before building, the *feng-shui* master would use instruments like this to ascertain the flow of energy (*chi*) on the site, resulting in new buildings that would be in harmony with, rather than obstruct, this flow. How might a compass detect energy? How was the Chinese use of a compass-like device different from the modern scientific use of the compass?

Thinking Historically

An image has many elements to read. What information is revealed about Chinese society in this image, in addition to the scientific devices? What significance do you attach to the artist's depiction of humans and the natural setting? In what ways does this image support Lynn White Jr.'s argument? In what ways does it challenge his interpretation? On balance, do you find it more supportive or critical of White's position?

*fung SHWEE

Joseph Needham, *Science and Civilization in China*, vol. 2 (Cambridge: Cambridge University Press, 1956), 362.

太保相宅圖

太保

Figure 14.3 Chinese *Feng-Shui* Master.

92

LYNDA NORENE SHAFFER

Southernization

The author of this selection began her career as a historian of China, but she is currently a world historian, having published books on Native American, Southeast Asian, and Chinese history. Shaffer coins the term *Southernization* to suggest that *Westernization* was preceded by an earlier "southern" process of technological expansion that eventually made it possible. Which of her examples of Southernization do you find most important in changing the world? Which least significant? Did India and Indian Ocean societies of the early Middle Ages play a role like that of the West today?

Thinking Historically

Shaffer did not write this essay to criticize Lynn White Jr., nor does her essay address precisely the same issues. Our exercise here is not the relatively simple task of weighing two debaters on a single issue. Rather, Shaffer's essay challenges some of the assumptions and arguments made by White and many other historians when they discuss the history of technology. What are some of the assumptions and arguments of White that Shaffer challenges? How might you use Shaffer to challenge White's grand theory? Which essay provides a more satisfying explanation of the origins of modern science and technology?

The term *Southernization* is a new one. It is used here to refer to a multifaceted process that began in Southern Asia and spread from there to various other places around the globe. The process included so many interrelated strands of development that it is impossible to do more here than sketch out the general outlines of a few of them. Among the most important that will be omitted from this discussion are the metallurgical, the medical, and the literary. Those included are the development of mathematics; the production and marketing of subtropical or tropical spices; the pioneering of new trade routes; the cultivation, processing, and marketing of southern crops such as sugar and cotton; and the development of various related technologies.

The term *Southernization* is meant to be analogous to *Westernization*. Westernization refers to certain developments that first occurred

---

Lynda Norene Shaffer, "Southernization," *Journal of World History* 5 (Spring 1994): 1–21.

in western Europe. Those developments changed Europe and eventually spread to other places and changed them as well. In the same way, southernization changed Southern Asia and later spread to other areas, which then underwent a process of change.

Southernization was well under way in Southern Asia by the fifth century c.e., during the reign of India's Gupta kings (320–535 c.e.). It was by that time already spreading to China. In the eighth century various elements characteristic of Southernization began spreading through the lands of the Muslim caliphates. Both in China and in the lands of the caliphate, the process led to dramatic changes, and by the year 1200 it was beginning to have an impact on the Christian Mediterranean. One could argue that within the Northern Hemisphere, by this time the process of Southernization had created an Eastern Hemisphere characterized by a rich south and a north that was poor in comparison. And one might even go so far as to suggest that in Europe and its colonies, the process of Southernization laid the foundation for Westernization.

The Indian Beginning

Southernization was the result of developments that took place in many parts of southern Asia, both on the Indian subcontinent and in Southeast Asia. By the time of the Gupta kings, several of its constituent parts already had a long history in India. Perhaps the oldest strand in the process was the cultivation of cotton and the production of cotton textiles for export. Cotton was first domesticated in the Indus River valley some time between 2300 and 1760 b.c.e., and by the second millennium b.c.e., the Indians had begun to develop sophisticated dyeing techniques. During these early millennia Indus River valley merchants are known to have lived in Mesopotamia, where they sold cotton textiles.

In the first century c.e. Egypt became an important overseas market for Indian cottons. By the next century there was a strong demand for these textiles both in the Mediterranean and in East Africa, and by the fifth century they were being traded in Southeast Asia. The Indian textile trade continued to grow throughout the next millennium. Even after the arrival of European ships in Asian ports at the turn of the sixteenth century, it continued unscathed. According to one textile expert, "India virtually clothed the world" by the mid-eighteenth century. The subcontinent's position was not undermined until Britain's Industrial Revolution, when steam engines began to power the production of cotton textiles.

Another strand in the process of Southernization, the search for new sources of bullion, can be traced back in India to the end of the

Mauryan Empire (321–185 B.C.E.). During Mauryan rule Siberia had been India's main source of gold, but nomadic disturbances in Central Asia disrupted the traffic between Siberia and India at about the time that the Mauryans fell. Indian sailors then began to travel to the Malay peninsula and the islands of Indonesia in search of an alternative source, which they most likely "discovered" with the help of local peoples who knew the sites. (This is generally the case with bullion discoveries, including those made by Arabs and Europeans.) What the Indians (and others later on) did do was introduce this gold to international trade routes.

The Indians' search for gold may also have led them to the shores of Africa. Although its interpretation is controversial, some archaeological evidence suggests the existence of Indian influence on parts of East Africa as early as 300 C.E. There is also one report that gold was being sought in East Africa by Ethiopian merchants, who were among India's most important trading partners.

The sixth-century Byzantine geographer Cosmas Indicopleustes described Ethiopian merchants who went to some location inland from the East African coast to obtain gold. "Every other year they would sail far to the south, then march inland, and in return for various made-up articles they would come back laden with ingots of gold." The fact that the expeditions left every other year suggests that it took two years to get to their destination and return. If so, their destination, even at this early date, may have been Zimbabwe. The wind patterns are such that sailors who ride the monsoon south as far as Kilwa can catch the return monsoon to the Red Sea area within the same year. But if they go beyond Kilwa to the Zambezi River, from which they might go inland to Zimbabwe, they cannot return until the following year.

Indian voyages on the Indian Ocean were part of a more general development, more or less contemporary with the Mauryan Empire, in which sailors of various nationalities began to knit together the shores of the "Southern Ocean," a Chinese term referring to all the waters from the South China Sea to the eastern coast of Africa. During this period there is no doubt that the most intrepid sailors were the Malays, peoples who lived in what is now Malaysia, Indonesia, the southeastern coast of Vietnam, and the Philippines.

Sometime before 300 B.C.E. Malay sailors began to ride the monsoons, the seasonal winds that blow off the continent of Asia in the colder months and onto its shores in the warmer months. Chinese records indicate that by the third century B.C.E. "Kunlun" sailors, the Chinese term for the Malay seamen, were sailing north to the southern coasts of China. They may also have been sailing west to India, through the straits now called Malacca and Sunda. If so they may have been the first to establish contact between India and Southeast Asia.

Malay sailors had reached the eastern coast of Africa at least by the first century B.C.E., if not earlier. Their presence in East African waters is testified to by the peoples of Madagascar, who still speak a Malayo-Polynesian language. Some evidence also suggests that Malay sailors had settled in the Red Sea area. Indeed, it appears that they were the first to develop a long-distance trade in a southern spice. In the last centuries B.C.E., if not earlier, Malay sailors were delivering cinnamon from South China Sea ports to East Africa and the Red Sea.

By about 400 C.E. Malay sailors could be found two-thirds of the way around the world, from Easter Island to East Africa. They rode the monsoons without a compass, out of sight of land, and often at latitudes below the equator where the northern pole star cannot be seen. They navigated by the wind and the stars, by cloud formations, the color of the water, and swell and wave patterns on the ocean's surface. They could discern the presence of an island some thirty miles from its shores by noting the behavior of birds, the animal and plant life in the water, and the swell and wave patterns. Given their manner of sailing, their most likely route to Africa and the Red Sea would have been by way of the island clusters, the Maldives, the Chagos, the Seychelles, and the Comoros.

Malay ships used balance lug sails, which were square in shape and mounted so that they could pivot. This made it possible for sailors to tack against the wind, that is, to sail into the wind by going diagonally against it, first one way and then the other. Due to the way the sails were mounted, they appeared somewhat triangular in shape, and thus the Malays' balance lug sail may well be the prototype of the triangular lateen, which can also be used to tack against the wind. The latter was invented by both the Polynesians to the Malays' east and by the Arabs to their west, both of whom had ample opportunity to see the Malays' ships in action.

It appears that the pepper trade developed after the cinnamon trade. In the first century C.E. southern India began supplying the Mediterranean with large quantities of pepper. Thereafter, Indian merchants could be found living on the island of Socotra, near the mouth of the Red Sea, and Greek-speaking sailors, including the anonymous author of the *Periplus of the Erythraean Sea*, could be found sailing in the Red Sea and riding the monsoons from there to India.

Indian traders and shippers and Malay sailors were also responsible for opening up an all-sea route to China. The traders' desire for silk drew them out into dangerous waters in search of a more direct way to its source. By the second century C.E. Indian merchants could make the trip by sea, but the route was slow, and it took at least two years to make a round trip. Merchants leaving from India's eastern coast rounded the shores of the Bay of Bengal. When they came to the Isthmus of Kra, the narrowest part of the Malay peninsula, the ships were un-loaded, and the goods were portaged across to the Gulf of Thailand. The cargo was then reloaded on ships that rounded the gulf until they reached Funan, a kingdom on what is now the Kampuchea-Vietnam border. There they had to wait for the winds to shift, before embarking upon a ship that rode the monsoon to China.

Some time before 400 C.E. travelers began to use a new all-sea route to China, a route that went around the Malay peninsula and thus avoided the Isthmus of Kra portage. The ships left from Sri Lanka and sailed before the monsoon, far from any coasts, through either the Strait of Malacca or the Strait of Sunda into the Java Sea. After waiting in the Java Sea port for the winds to shift, they rode the monsoon to southern China. The most likely developers of this route were Malay sailors, since the new stopover ports were located within their territories.

Not until the latter part of the fourth century, at about the same time as the new all-sea route began to direct commercial traffic through the Java Sea, did the fine spices — cloves, nutmeg, and mace — begin to assume importance on international markets. These rare and expensive spices came from the Moluccas, several island groups about a thousand miles east of Java. Cloves were produced on about five minuscule is-lands off the western coast of Halmahera; nutmeg and mace came from only a few of the Banda Islands, some ten islands with a total area of seventeen square miles, located in the middle of the Banda Sea. Until 1621 these Moluccan islands were the only places in the world able to produce cloves, nutmeg, and mace in commercial quantities. The Moluccan producers themselves brought their spices to the international markets of the Java Sea ports and created the market for them.

It was also during the time of the Gupta kings, around 350 C.E., that the Indians discovered how to crystallize sugar. There is consid-erable disagreement about where sugar was first domesticated. Some believe that the plant was native to New Guinea and domesticated there, and others argue that it was domesticated by Southeast Asian peoples living in what is now southern China. In any case, sugar culti-vation spread to the Indian subcontinent. Sugar, however, did not be-come an important item of trade until the Indians discovered how to turn sugarcane juice into granulated crystals that could be easily stored and transported. This was a momentous development, and it may have been encouraged by Indian sailing, for sugar and clarified butter (ghee) were among the dietary mainstays of Indian sailors.

The Indians also laid the foundation for modern mathematics dur-ing the time of the Guptas. Western numerals, which the Europeans called Arabic since they acquired them from the Arabs, actually come from India. (The Arabs call them Hindi numbers.) The most significant feature of the Indian system was the invention of the zero as a number concept. The oldest extant treatise that uses the zero in the modern way is a mathematical appendix attached to Aryabhata's text on astronomy, which is dated 499 C.E.

The Indian zero made the place-value system of writing numbers superior to all others. Without it, the use of this system, base ten or otherwise, was fraught with difficulties and did not seem any better than alternative systems. With the zero the Indians were able to perform calculations rapidly and accurately, to perform much more complicated calculations, and to discern mathematical relationships more aptly. These numerals and the mathematics that the Indians developed with them are now universal — just one indication of the global significance of Southernization.

As a result of these developments India acquired a reputation as a place of marvels, a reputation that was maintained for many centuries after the Gupta dynasty fell. As late as the ninth century Amr ibn Bahr al Jahiz (c. 776–868), one of the most influential writers of Arabic, had the following to say about India:

> As regards the Indians, they are among the leaders in astronomy, mathematics — in particular, they have Indian numerals — and medicine; they alone possess the secrets of the latter, and use them to practice some remarkable forms of treatment. They have the art of carving statues and painted figures. They possess the game of chess, which is the noblest of games and requires more judgment and intelligence than any other. They make Kedah swords, and excel in their use. They have splendid music. . . . They possess a script capable of expressing the sounds of all languages, as well as many numerals. They have a great deal of poetry, many long treatises, and a deep understanding of philosophy and letters; the book *Kalila wa-Dimna* originated with them. They are intelligent and courageous. . . . Their sound judgment and sensible habits led them to invent pins, cork, toothpicks, the drape of clothes, and the dyeing of hair. They are handsome, attractive, and forbearing; their women are proverbial; and their country produces the matchless Indian aloes which are supplied to kings. They were the originators of the science of *fikr*, by which a poison can be counteracted after it has been used, and of astronomical reckoning, subsequently adopted by the rest of the world. When Adam descended from Paradise, it was to their land that he made his way.

The Southernization of China

These Southern Asian developments began to have a significant impact on China after 350 C.E. The Han dynasty had fallen in 221 C.E., and for more than 350 years thereafter China was ruled by an ever-changing collection of regional kingdoms. During these centuries Buddhism became

increasingly important in China, Buddhist monasteries spread throughout the disunited realm, and cultural exchange between India and China
grew accordingly. By 581, when the Sui dynasty reunited the empire,
processes associated with Southernization had already had a major impact on China. The influence of Southernization continued during the
T'ang (618–906) and Sung (960–1279) dynasties. One might even go so
far as to suggest that the process of Southernization underlay the revolutionary social, political, economic, and technological developments of the
T'ang and Sung.

The Chinese reformed their mathematics, incorporating the advantages of the Indian system, even though they did not adopt the Indian
numerals at that time. They then went on to develop an advanced
mathematics, which was flourishing by the time of the Sung dynasty.
Cotton and indigo became well established, giving rise to the blue-
black peasant garb that is still omnipresent in China. Also in the Sung
period the Chinese first developed cotton canvas, which they used to
make a more efficient sail for ocean-going ships.

Although sugar had long been grown in some parts of southern
China it did not become an important crop in this region until the
process of Southernization was well under way. The process also introduced new varieties of rice. The most important of these was what the
Chinese called Champa rice, since it came to China from Champa, a
Malay kingdom located on what is now the southeastern coast of Vietnam. Champa rice was a drought-resistant, early ripening variety that
made it possible to extend cultivation up well-watered hillsides, thereby
doubling the area of rice cultivation in China. . . .

In southern China the further development of rice production
brought significant changes in the landscape. Before the introduction of
Champa rice, rice cultivation had been confined to lowlands, deltas,
basins, and river valleys. Once Champa rice was introduced and rice
cultivation spread up the hillsides, the Chinese began systematic terracing and made use of sophisticated techniques of water control on
mountain slopes. Between the mid-eighth and the early twelfth century
the population of southern China tripled, and the total Chinese population doubled. According to Sung dynasty household registration figures
for 1102 and 1110 — figures that Sung dynasty specialists have shown
to be reliable — there were 100 million people in China by the first
decade of the twelfth century.

Before the process of Southernization, northern China had always
been predominant, intellectually, socially, and politically. The imperial
center of gravity was clearly in the north, and the southern part of
China was perceived as a frontier area. But Southernization changed
this situation dramatically. By 600, southern China was well on its way
to becoming the most prosperous and most commercial part of the empire. The most telling evidence for this is the construction of the Grand
Canal, which was completed around 610, during the Sui dynasty. Even

though the rulers of the Sui had managed to put the pieces of the empire back together in 581 and rule the whole of China again from a single northern capital, they were dependent on the new southern crops. Thus it is no coincidence that this dynasty felt the need to build a canal that could deliver southern rice to northern cities.

The T'ang dynasty, when Buddhist influence in China was especially strong, saw two exceedingly important technological innovations — the invention of printing and gunpowder. These developments may also be linked to Southernization. Printing seems to have developed within the walls of Buddhist monasteries between 700 and 750, and subtropical Sichuan was one of the earliest centers of the art. The invention of gunpowder in China by Taoist alchemists in the ninth century may also be related to the linkages between India and China created by Buddhism. In 644 an Indian monk identified soils in China that contained saltpeter and demonstrated the purple flame that results from its ignition. As early as 919 C.E. gunpowder was used as an igniter in a flamethrower, and the tenth century also saw the use of flaming arrows, rockets, and bombs thrown by catapults. The earliest evidence of a cannon or bombard (1127) has been found in Sichuan, quite near the Tibetan border, across the Himalayas from India.

By the time of the Sung the Chinese also had perfected the "south-pointing needle," otherwise known as the compass. Various prototypes of the compass had existed in China from the third century B.C.E., but the new version developed during the Sung was particularly well suited for navigation. Soon Chinese mariners were using the south-pointing needle on the oceans, publishing "needle charts" for the benefit of sea captains, and following "needle routes" on the Southern Ocean.

Once the Chinese had the compass they, like Columbus, set out to find a direct route to the spice markets of Java and ultimately to the Spice Islands in the Moluccas. Unlike Columbus, they found them. They did not bump into an obstacle, now known as the Western Hemisphere, on their way, since it was not located between China and the Spice Islands. If it had been so situated, the Chinese would have found it some 500 years before Columbus.

Cities on China's southern coasts became centers of overseas commerce. Silk remained an important export, and by the T'ang dynasty it had been joined by a true porcelain, which was developed in China sometime before 400 C.E. China and its East Asian neighbors had a monopoly on the manufacture of true porcelain until the early eighteenth century. Many attempts were made to imitate it, and some of the resulting imitations were economically and stylistically important. China's southern ports were also exporting to Southeast Asia large quantities of ordinary consumer goods, including iron hardware, such as needles, scissors, and cooking pots. Although iron manufacturing was concentrated in the north, the large quantity of goods produced was a direct result of the size of the market in southern China and overseas. Until the

British Industrial Revolution of the eighteenth century, no other place ever equaled the iron production of Sung China.

The Muslim Caliphates

In the seventh century C.E., Arab cavalries, recently converted to the new religion of Islam, conquered eastern and southern Mediterranean shores that had been Byzantine (and Christian), as well as the Sassanian empire (Zoroastrian) in what is now Iraq and Iran. In the eighth century they went on to conquer Spain and Turko-Iranian areas of Central Asia, as well as northwestern India. Once established on the Indian frontier, they became acquainted with many of the elements of Southernization.

The Arabs were responsible for the spread of many important crops, developed or improved in India, to the Middle East, North Africa, and Islamic Spain. Among the most important were sugar, cotton, and citrus fruits. Although sugarcane and cotton cultivation may have spread to Iraq and Ethiopia before the Arab conquests, only after the establishment of the caliphates did these southern crops have a major impact throughout the Middle East and North Africa.

The Arabs were the first to import large numbers of enslaved Africans in order to produce sugar. Fields in the vicinity of Basra, at the northern end of the Persian Gulf, were the most important sugar-producing areas within the caliphates, but before this land could be used, it had to be desalinated. To accomplish this task, the Arabs imported East African (Zanj) slaves. This African community remained in the area, where they worked as agricultural laborers. The famous writer al Jahiz, whose essay on India was quoted earlier, was a descendant of Zanj slaves. In 869, one year after his death, the Zanj slaves in Iraq rebelled. It took the caliphate fifteen years of hard fighting to defeat them, and thereafter Muslim owners rarely used slaves for purposes that would require their concentration in large numbers.

The Arabs were responsible for moving sugarcane cultivation and sugar manufacturing westward from southern Iraq into other relatively arid lands. Growers had to adapt the plant to new conditions, and they had to develop more efficient irrigation technologies. By 1000 or so sugarcane had become an important crop in the Yemen; in Arabian oases; in irrigated areas of Syria, Lebanon, Palestine, Egypt, and the Mahgrib; in Spain; and on Mediterranean islands controlled by Muslims. By the tenth century cotton also had become a major crop in the lands of the caliphate, from Iran and Central Asia to Spain and the Mediterranean islands. Cotton industries sprang up wherever the plant was cultivated, producing for both local and distant markets. . . .

Under Arab auspices, Indian mathematics followed the same routes as the crops. Al-Kharazmi (c. 780–847) introduced Indian mathematics to the Arabic-reading world in his *Treatise on Calculation with the Hindu Numerals*, written around 825. Mathematicians within the caliphates then could draw upon the Indian tradition, as well as the Greek and Persian. On this foundation Muslim scientists of many nationalities, including al-Battani (d. 929), who came from the northern reaches of the Mesopotamian plain, and the Persian Omar Khayyám (d. 1123), made remarkable advances in both algebra and trigonometry.

The Arab conquests also led to an increase in long-distance commerce and the "discovery" of new sources of bullion. Soon after the Abbasid caliphate established its capital at Baghdad, the caliph al-Mansur (r. 745–75) reportedly remarked, "This is the Tigris; there is no obstacle between us and China; everything on the sea can come to us." By this time Arab ships were plying the maritime routes from the Persian Gulf to China, and they soon outnumbered all others using these routes. By the ninth century they had acquired the compass (in China, most likely), and they may well have been the first to use it for marine navigation, since the Chinese do not seem to have used it for this purpose until after the tenth century.

. . . Thus it was that the Arabs "pioneered" or improved an existing long-distance route across the Sahara, an ocean of sand rather than water. Routes across this desert had always existed, and trade and other contacts between West Africa and the Mediterranean date back at least to the Phoenician period. Still, the numbers of people and animals crossing this great ocean of sand were limited until the eighth century when Arabs, desiring to go directly to the source of the gold, prompted an expansion of trade across the Sahara. Also during the eighth century Abdul al-Rahman, an Arab ruler of Morocco, sponsored the construction of wells on the trans-Saharan route from Sijilmasa to Wadidara to facilitate this traffic. This Arab "discovery" of West African gold eventually doubled the amount of gold in international circulation. East Africa, too, became a source of gold for the Arabs. By the tenth century Kilwa had become an important source of Zimbabwean gold.

Developments after 1200:
The Mongolian Conquest and the Southernization of the European Mediterranean

By 1200 the process of Southernization had created a prosperous south from China to the Muslim Mediterranean. Although mathematics, the pioneering of new ocean routes, and "discoveries" of bullion are not inextricably connected to locations within forty degrees of the equator, several crucial elements in the process of Southernization were closely linked to latitude. Cotton generally does not grow above the fortieth parallel. Sugar, cinnamon, and pepper are tropical or subtropical crops, and the fine spices will grow only on particular tropical islands. Thus for many centuries the more southern parts of Asia and the Muslim Mediterranean enjoyed the profits that these developments brought, while locations that were too far north to grow these southern crops were unable to participate in such lucrative agricultural enterprises.

The process of Southernization reached its zenith after 1200, in large part because of the tumultuous events of the thirteenth century. During that century in both hemispheres there were major transformations in the distribution of power, wealth, and prestige. In the Western Hemisphere several great powers went down. Cahokia (near East St. Louis, Illinois), which for three centuries had been the largest and most influential of the Mississippian mound-building centers, declined after 1200, and in Mexico Toltec power collapsed. In the Mediterranean the prestige of the Byzantine empire was destroyed when Venetians seized its capital in 1204. From 1212 to 1270 the Christians conquered southern Spain, except for Granada. In West Africa, Ghana fell to Sosso, and so did Mali, one of Ghana's allies. But by about 1230 Mali, in the process of seeking its own revenge, had created an empire even larger than Ghana's. At the same time Zimbabwe was also becoming a major power in southern Africa.

The grandest conquerors of the thirteenth century were the Central Asians. Turkish invaders established the Delhi sultanate in India. Mongolian cavalries devastated Baghdad, the seat of the Abbasid caliphate since the eighth century, and they captured Kiev, further weakening Byzantium. By the end of the century they had captured China, Korea, and parts of mainland Southeast Asia as well.

Because the Mongols were pagans at the time of their conquests, the western Europeans cheered them on as they laid waste to one after another Muslim center of power in the Middle East. The Mongols were stopped only when they encountered the Mamluks of Egypt at Damascus. In East Asia and Southeast Asia only the Japanese and the Javanese were able to defeat them. The victors in Java went on to found Majapahit, whose power and prestige then spread through maritime Southeast Asia.

Both hemispheres were reorganized profoundly during this turmoil. Many places that had flourished were toppled, and power gravitated to new locales. In the Eastern Hemisphere the Central Asian conquerors had done great damage to traditional southern centers just about everywhere, except in Africa, southern China, southern India, and maritime Southeast Asia. At the same time the Mongols' control of overland routes between Europe and Asia in the thirteenth and early fourteenth centuries fostered unprecedented contacts between Europeans and peoples from those areas that had long been southernized. Marco Polo's long sojourn in Yüan Dynasty China is just one example of such interaction.

Under the Mongols overland trade routes in Asia shifted north and converged on the Black Sea. After the Genoese helped the Byzantines to retake Constantinople from the Venetians in 1261, the Genoese were granted special privileges of trade in the Black Sea. Italy then became directly linked to the Mongolian routes. Genoese traders were among the first and were certainly the most numerous to open up trade with the Mongolian states in southern Russia and Iran. In the words of one Western historian, in their Black Sea colonies they "admitted to citizenship" people of many nationalities, including those of "strange background and questionable belief," and they "wound up christening children of the best ancestry with such uncanny names as Saladin, Hethum, or Hulugu."

Such contacts contributed to the Southernization of the Christian Mediterranean during this period of Mongolian hegemony. Although European conquerors sometimes had taken over sugar and cotton lands in the Middle East during the Crusades, not until some time after 1200 did the European-held Mediterranean islands become important exporters. Also after 1200 Indian mathematics began to have a significant impact in Europe. Before that time a few western European scholars had become acquainted with Indian numerals in Spain, where the works of al-Kharazmi, al-Battani, and other mathematicians had been translated into Latin. Nevertheless, Indian numerals and mathematics did not become important in western Europe until the thirteenth century after the book *Liber abaci* (1202), written by Leonardo Fibonacci of Pisa (c. 1170–1250), introduced them to the commercial centers of Italy. Leonardo had grown up in North Africa (in what is now Bejala, Algeria), where his father, consul over the Pisan merchants in that port, had sent him to study calculation with an Arab master.

In the seventeenth century, when Francis Bacon observed the "force and virtue and consequences of discoveries," he singled out three technologies in particular that "have changed the whole face and state of things throughout the world." These were all Chinese inventions — the compass, printing, and gunpowder. All three were first acquired by Europeans during this time of hemispheric reorganization.

It was most likely the Arabs who introduced the compass to Mediterranean waters, either at the end of the twelfth or in the thirteenth century. Block printing, gunpowder, and cannon appeared first in Italy in the fourteenth century, apparently after making a single great leap from Mongolian-held regions of East Asia to Italy. How this great leap was accomplished is not known, but the most likely scenario is one suggested by Lynn White Jr., in an article concerning how various other Southern (rather than Eastern) Asian technologies reached western

Europe at about this time. He thought it most likely that they were introduced by "Tatar" slaves, Lama Buddhists from the frontiers of China whom the Genoese purchased in Black Sea marts and delivered to Italy. By 1450 when this trade reached its peak, there were thousands of these Asian slaves in every major Italian city.

Yet another consequence of the increased traffic and communication on the more northern trade routes traversing the Eurasian steppe was the transmission of the bubonic plague from China to the Black Sea. The plague had broken out first in China in 1331, and apparently rats and lice infected with the disease rode westward in the saddlebags of Mongolian post messengers, horsemen who were capable of traveling one hundred miles per day. By 1346 it had reached a Black Sea port, whence it made its way to the Middle East and Europe.

During the latter part of the fourteenth century the unity of the Mongolian empire began to disintegrate, and new regional powers began to emerge in its wake. Throughout much of Asia the chief beneficiaries of imperial disintegration were Turkic or Turko-Mongolian powers of the Muslim faith. The importance of Islam in Africa was also growing at this time, and the peoples of Southeast Asia, from the Malay peninsula to the southern Philippines, were converting to the faith.

Indeed, the world's most obvious dynamic in the centuries before Columbus was the expansion of the Islamic faith. Under Turkish auspices Islam was even spreading into eastern Europe, a development marked by the Ottoman conquest of Constantinople in 1453. This traumatic event lent a special urgency to Iberian expansion. The Iberians came to see themselves as the chosen defenders of Christendom. Ever since the twelfth century, while Christian Byzantium had been losing Anatolia and parts of southeastern Europe to Islam, they had been retaking the Iberian peninsula for Christendom.

One way to weaken the Ottomans and Islam was to go around the North African Muslims and find a new oceanic route to the source of West African gold. Before the Portuguese efforts, sailing routes had never developed off the western shore of Africa, since the winds there blow in the same direction all year long, from north to south. (Earlier European sailors could have gone to West Africa, but they would not have been able to return home.)

The Portuguese success would have been impossible without the Chinese compass, Arabic tables indicating the declination of the noonday sun at various latitudes, and the lateen sail, which was also an Arab innovation. The Portuguese caravels were of mixed, or multiple, ancestry, with a traditional Atlantic hull and a rigging that combined the traditional Atlantic square sail with the lateen sail of Southern Ocean provenance. With the lateen sail the Portuguese could tack against the wind for the trip homeward.

The new route to West Africa led to Portugal's rounding of Africa and direct participation in Southern Ocean trade. While making the voyages to West Africa, European sailors learned the wind patterns and ocean currents west of Africa, knowledge that made the Columbian voyages possible. The Portuguese moved the sugarcane plant from Sicily to Madeira, in the Atlantic, and they found new sources of gold, first in West Africa and then in East Africa. Given that there was little demand in Southern Ocean ports for European trade goods, they would not have been able to sustain their Asian trade without this African gold.

The Rise of Europe's North

The rise of the north, or more precisely, the rise of Europe's northwest, began with the appropriation of those elements of Southernization that were not confined by geography. In the wake of their southern European neighbors, they became partially southernized, but they could not engage in all aspects of the process due to their distance from the equator. Full Southernization and the wealth that we now associate with northwestern Europe came about only after their outright seizure of tropical and subtropical territories and their rounding of Africa and participation in Southern Ocean trade. . . .

Even though the significance of indigenous developments in the rise of northwestern Europe should not be minimized, it should be emphasized that many of the most important causes of the rise of the West are not to be found within the bounds of Europe. Rather, they are the result of the transformation of western Europe's relationships with other regions of the Eastern Hemisphere. Europe began its rise only after the thirteenth-century reorganization of the Eastern Hemisphere facilitated its Southernization, and Europe's northwest did not rise until it too was reaping the profits of Southernization. Thus the rise of the North Atlantic powers should not be oversimplified so that it appears to be an isolated and solely European phenomenon, with roots that spread no farther afield than Greece. Rather, it should be portrayed as one part of a hemisphere-wide process, in which a northwestern Europe ran to catch up with a more developed south — a race not completed until the eighteenth century.

JARED DIAMOND

Easter Island's End

In comparison with the grand theories of White and Shaffer, an essay on a small island in the Pacific might seem to be an exercise in the recent vogue of small-bore "micro-history." It is not. Jared Diamond, author of *Guns, Germs, and Steel,* uses small examples to big effect. In this selection and in his larger book-length treatment, *Collapse: How Societies Choose to Fail or Succeed,* Diamond teases a global lesson from the history of tiny Easter Island. What is that lesson? What does Diamond's essay suggest about the causes of environmental decline? Are we in danger of duplicating the fate of Easter Island? How can we avoid the fate of Easter Island?

Thinking Historically

How does Diamond's essay challenge the thesis of Lynn White Jr.? Do you see in this essay an alternative grand theory for understanding our environmental problems? If so, what is that theory? Do you agree or disagree with it? Why or why not?

In just a few centuries, the people of Easter Island wiped out their forest, drove their plants and animals to extinction, and saw their complex society spiral into chaos and cannibalism. Are we about to follow their lead?

Among the most riveting mysteries of human history are those posed by vanished civilizations. Everyone who has seen the abandoned buildings of the Khmer, the Maya, or the Anasazi is immediately moved to ask the same question: Why did the societies that erected those structures disappear?

Their vanishing touches us as the disappearance of other animals, even the dinosaurs, never can. No matter how exotic those lost civilizations seem, their framers were humans like us. Who is to say we won't succumb to the same fate? Perhaps someday New York's skyscrapers will stand derelict and overgrown with vegetation, like the temples at Angkor Wat and Tikal.

Among all such vanished civilizations, that of the former Polynesian society on Easter Island remains unsurpassed in mystery and isola-

Jared Diamond, "Easter Island's End," *Discover* 16, no. 8 (August 1995).

tion. The mystery stems especially from the island's gigantic stone statues and its impoverished landscape, but it is enhanced by our associations with the specific people involved: Polynesians represent for us the ultimate in exotic romance, the background for many a child's, and an adult's, vision of paradise. My own interest in Easter was kindled over 30 years ago when I read Thor Heyerdahl's fabulous accounts of his Kon-Tiki voyage.

But my interest has been revived recently by a much more exciting account, one not of heroic voyages but of painstaking research and analysis. My friend David Steadman, a paleontologist, has been working with a number of other researchers who are carrying out the first systematic excavations on Easter intended to identify the animals and plants that once lived there. Their work is contributing to a new interpretation of the island's history that makes it a tale not only of wonder but of warning as well.

Easter Island, with an area of only 64 square miles, is the world's most isolated scrap of habitable land. It lies in the Pacific Ocean more than 2,000 miles west of the nearest continent (South America), 1,400 miles from even the nearest habitable island (Pitcairn). Its subtropical location and latitude — at 27 degrees south, it is approximately as far below the equator as Houston is north of it — help give it a rather mild climate, while its volcanic origins make its soil fertile. In theory, this combination of blessings should have made Easter a miniature paradise, remote from problems that beset the rest of the world.

The island derives its name from its "discovery" by the Dutch explorer Jacob Roggeveen, on Easter (April 5) in 1722. Roggeveen's first impression was not of a paradise but of a wasteland: "We originally, from a further distance, have considered the said Easter Island as sandy; the reason for that is this, that we counted as sand the withered grass, hay, or other scorched and burnt vegetation, because its wasted appearance could give no other impression than of a singular poverty and barrenness."

The island Roggeveen saw was a grassland without a single tree or bush over ten feet high. Modern botanists have identified only 47 species of higher plants native to Easter, most of them grasses, sedges, and ferns. The list includes just two species of small trees and two of woody shrubs. With such flora, the islanders Roggeveen encountered had no source of real firewood to warm themselves during Easter's cool, wet, windy winters. Their native animals included nothing larger than insects, not even a single species of native bat, land bird, land snail, or lizard. For domestic animals, they had only chickens. European visitors throughout the eighteenth and early nineteenth centuries estimated Easter's human population at about 2,000, a modest number considering the island's fertility. As Captain James Cook recognized during his brief visit in 1774, the islanders were Polynesians (a Tahitian man accompanying Cook was able to converse with them). Yet despite the Polynesians' well-deserved fame as a great seafaring people, the Easter Islanders who came out to Roggeveen's and Cook's ships did so by swimming or paddling canoes that Roggeveen described as "bad and frail." Their craft, he wrote, were "put together with manifold small planks and light inner timbers, which they cleverly stitched together with very fine twisted threads. . . . But as they lack the knowledge and particularly the materials for caulking and making tight the great number of seams of the canoes, these are accordingly very leaky, for which reason they are compelled to spend half the time in bailing." The canoes, only ten feet long, held at most two people, and only three or four canoes were observed on the entire island.

With such flimsy craft, Polynesians could never have colonized Easter from even the nearest island, nor could they have traveled far offshore to fish. The islanders Roggeveen met were totally isolated, unaware that other people existed. Investigators in all the years since his visit have discovered no trace of the islanders' having any outside contacts: not a single Easter Island rock or product has turned up elsewhere, nor has anything been found on the island that could have been brought by anyone other than the original settlers or the Europeans. Yet the people living on Easter claimed memories of visiting the uninhabited Sala y Gomez reef 260 miles away, far beyond the range of the leaky canoes seen by Roggeveen. How did the islanders' ancestors reach that reef from Easter, or reach Easter from anywhere else?

Easter Island's most famous feature is its huge stone statues, more than 200 of which once stood on massive stone platforms lining the coast. [See Figure 14.4.] At least 700 more, in all stages of completion, were abandoned in quarries or on ancient roads between the quarries and the coast, as if the carvers and moving crews had thrown down their tools and walked off the job. Most of the erected statues were carved in a single quarry and then somehow transported as far as six miles — despite heights as great as 33 feet and weights up to 82 tons. The abandoned statues, meanwhile, were as much as 65 feet tall and weighed up to 270 tons. The stone platforms were equally gigantic: up to 500 feet long and 10 feet high, with facing slabs weighing up to 10 tons.

Roggeveen himself quickly recognized the problem the statues posed: "The stone images at first caused us to be struck with astonishment," he wrote, "because we could not comprehend how it was possible that these people, who are devoid of heavy thick timber for making any machines, as well as strong ropes, nevertheless had been able to erect such images." Roggeveen might have added that the islanders had no wheels, no draft animals, and no source of power except their own muscles. How did they transport the giant statues for miles, even before erecting them? To deepen the mystery, the statues were still standing in

Figure 14.4   Easter Island Statues.
Source: © Westend61/Alamy.

1770, but by 1864 all of them had been pulled down, by the islanders themselves. Why then did they carve them in the first place? And why did they stop?

The statues imply a society very different from the one Roggeveen saw in 1722. Their sheer number and size suggest a population much larger than 2,000 people. What became of everyone? Furthermore, that society must have been highly organized. Easter's resources were scattered across the island: the best stone for the statues was quarried at Rano Raraku near Easter's northeast end; red stone, used for large crowns adorning some of the statues, was quarried at Puna Pau, inland in the southwest; stone carving tools came mostly from Aroi in the northwest. Meanwhile, the best farmland lay in the south and east, and the best fishing grounds on the north and west coasts. Extracting and redistributing all those goods required complex political organization. What happened to that organization, and how could it ever have arisen in such a barren landscape?

Easter Island's mysteries have spawned volumes of speculation for more than two and a half centuries. Many Europeans were incredulous that Polynesians — commonly characterized as "mere savages" — could have created the statues or the beautifully constructed stone platforms. In the 1950s, Heyerdahl argued that Polynesia must have been settled by advanced societies of American Indians, who in turn must have received civilization across the Atlantic from more advanced societies of the Old World. Heyerdahl's raft voyages aimed to prove the feasibility of such prehistoric transoceanic contacts. In the 1960s the Swiss writer Erich von Däniken, an ardent believer in Earth visits by extraterrestrial astronauts, went further, claiming that Easter's statues were the work of intelligent beings who owned ultramodern tools, became stranded on Easter, and were finally rescued.

Heyerdahl and von Däeniken both brushed aside overwhelming evidence that the Easter Islanders were typical Polynesians derived from Asia rather than from the Americas and that their culture (including their statues) grew out of Polynesian culture. Their language was Polynesian, as Cook had already concluded. Specifically, they spoke an eastern Polynesian dialect related to Hawaiian and Marquesan, a dialect isolated since about A.D. 400, as estimated from slight differences in vocabulary. Their fishhooks and stone adzes resembled early Marquesan models. Last year DNA extracted from 12 Easter Island skeletons was also shown to be Polynesian. The islanders grew bananas, taro, sweet potatoes, sugarcane, and paper mulberry — typical Polynesian crops, mostly of Southeast Asian origin. Their sole domestic animal, the chicken, was also typically Polynesian and ultimately Asian, as were the rats that arrived as stowaways in the canoes of the first settlers.

What happened to those settlers? The fanciful theories of the past must give way to evidence gathered by hardworking practitioners in three fields: archeology, pollen analysis, and paleontology. Modern archeological excavations on Easter have continued since Heyerdahl's 1955 expedition. The earliest radiocarbon dates associated with human activities are around A.D. 400 to 700, in reasonable agreement with the approximate settlement date of 400 estimated by linguists. The period of statue construction peaked around 1200 to 1500, with few if any statues erected thereafter. Densities of archeological sites suggest a large population; an estimate of 7,000 people is widely quoted by archeologists, but other estimates range up to 20,000, which does not seem implausible for an island of Easter's area and fertility.

Archeologists have also enlisted surviving islanders in experiments aimed at figuring out how the statues might have been carved and erected. Twenty people, using only stone chisels, could have carved even the largest completed statue within a year. Given enough timber and fiber for making ropes, teams of at most a few hundred people could have loaded the statues onto wooden sleds, dragged them over lubricated wooden tracks or rollers, and used logs as levers to maneuver them into a standing position. Rope could have been made from the fiber of a small native tree, related to the linden, called the hauhau. However, that tree is now extremely scarce on Easter, and hauling one statue would have required hundreds of yards of rope. Did Easter's now barren landscape once support the necessary trees? That question can be answered by the technique of pollen analysis, which involves boring out a column of sediment from a swamp or pond, with the most recent deposits at the top and relatively more ancient deposits at the bottom. The absolute age of each layer can be dated by radiocarbon methods. Then begins the hard work: examining tens of thousands of pollen grains under a microscope, counting them, and identifying the plant species that produced each one by comparing the grains with modern pollen from known plant species. For Easter Island, the bleary-eyed scientists who performed that task were John Flenley, now at Massey University in New Zealand, and Sarah King of the University of Hull in England.

Flenley and King's heroic efforts were rewarded by the striking new picture that emerged of Easter's prehistoric landscape. For at least 30,000 years before human arrival and during the early years of Polynesian settlement, Easter was not a wasteland at all. Instead, a subtropical forest of trees and woody bushes towered over a ground layer of shrubs, herbs, ferns, and grasses. In the forest grew tree daisies, the rope-yielding hauhau tree, and the toromiro tree, which furnishes a dense, mesquite-like firewood. The most common tree in the forest was a species of palm now absent on Easter but formerly so abundant that the bottom strata of the sediment column were packed with its pollen. The Easter Island palm was closely related to the still-surviving Chilean wine palm, which grows up to 82 feet tall and 6 feet in diameter. The tall, unbranched trunks of the Easter Island palm would have been ideal for transporting and erecting statues and constructing large canoes. The palm would also have been a valuable food source, since its Chilean relative yields edible nuts as well as sap from which Chileans make sugar, syrup, honey, and wine.

What did the first settlers of Easter Island eat when they were not glutting themselves on the local equivalent of maple syrup? Recent excavations by David Steadman, of the New York State Museum at Albany, have yielded a picture of Easter's original animal world as surprising as Flenley and King's picture of its plant world. Steadman's expectations for Easter were conditioned by his experiences elsewhere in Polynesia, where fish are overwhelmingly the main food at archeological sites, typically accounting for more than 90 percent of the bones in ancient Polynesian garbage heaps. Easter, though, is too cool for the coral reefs beloved by fish, and its cliff-girded coastline permits shallow-water fishing in only a few places. Less than a quarter of the bones in its early garbage heaps (from the period 900 to 1300) belonged to fish; instead, nearly one-third of all bones came from porpoises.

Nowhere else in Polynesia do porpoises account for even 1 percent of discarded food bones. But most other Polynesian islands offered animal food in the form of birds and mammals, such as New Zealand's now extinct giant moas and Hawaii's now extinct flightless geese. Most other islanders also had domestic pigs and dogs. On Easter, porpoises would have been the largest animal available — other than humans. The porpoise species identified at Easter, the common dolphin, weighs up to 165 pounds. It generally lives out at sea, so it could not have been hunted by line fishing or spearfishing from shore. Instead, it must have been harpooned far offshore, in big seaworthy canoes built from the extinct palm tree.

In addition to porpoise meat, Steadman found, the early Polynesian settlers were feasting on seabirds. For those birds, Easter's remoteness and lack of predators made it an ideal haven as a breeding site, at least until humans arrived. Among the prodigious numbers of seabirds that bred on Easter were albatross, boobies, frigate birds, fulmars, petrels, prions, shearwaters, storm petrels, terns, and tropic birds. With at least 25 nesting species, Easter was the richest seabird breeding site in Polynesia and probably in the whole Pacific. Land birds as well went into early Easter Island cooking pots.

Steadman identified bones of at least six species, including barn owls, herons, parrots, and rail. Bird stew would have been seasoned with meat from large numbers of rats, which the Polynesian colonists inadvertently brought with them; Easter Island is the sole known Polynesian island where rat bones outnumber fish bones at archeological sites. (In case you're squeamish and consider rats inedible, I still recall recipes for creamed laboratory rat that my British biologist friends used to supplement their diet during their years of wartime food rationing.)

Porpoises, seabirds, land birds, and rats did not complete the list of meat sources formerly available on Easter. A few bones hint at the possibility of breeding seal colonies as well. All these delicacies were cooked in ovens fired by wood from the island's forests.

Such evidence lets us imagine the island onto which Easter's first Polynesian colonists stepped ashore some 1,600 years ago, after a long canoe voyage from eastern Polynesia. They found themselves in a pristine paradise. What then happened to it? The pollen grains and the bones yield a grim answer.

Pollen records show that destruction of Easter's forests was well under way by the year 800, just a few centuries after the start of human settlement. Then charcoal from wood fires came to fill the sediment cores, while pollen of palms and other trees and woody shrubs decreased or disappeared, and pollen of the grasses that replaced the forest became more abundant. Not long after 1400 the palm finally became extinct, not only as a result of being chopped down but also because the now ubiquitous rats prevented its regeneration: of the dozens of preserved palm nuts discovered in caves on Easter, all had been chewed by rats and could no longer germinate. While the hauhau tree did not become extinct in Polynesian times, its numbers declined drastically until there weren't enough left to make ropes from. By the time Heyerdahl visited Easter, only a single, nearly dead toromiro tree remained on the island, and even that lone survivor has now disappeared. (Fortunately, the toromiro still grows in botanical gardens elsewhere.)

The fifteenth century marked the end not only for Easter's palm but for the forest itself. Its doom had been approaching as people cleared land to plant gardens; as they felled trees to build canoes, to transport and erect statues, and to burn; as rats devoured seeds; and probably as the native birds died out that had pollinated the trees' flowers and dispersed their fruit. The overall picture is among the most extreme examples of forest destruction anywhere in the world: the whole forest gone, and most of its tree species extinct.

The destruction of the island's animals was as extreme as that of the forest: without exception, every species of native land bird became extinct. Even shellfish were overexploited, until people had to settle for small sea snails instead of larger cowries. Porpoise bones disappeared abruptly from garbage heaps around 1500; no one could harpoon porpoises anymore, since the trees used for constructing the big seagoing canoes no longer existed. The colonies of more than half of the seabird species breeding on Easter or on its offshore islets were wiped out.

In place of these meat supplies, the Easter Islanders intensified their production of chickens, which had been only an occasional food item. They also turned to the largest remaining meat source available: humans, whose bones became common in late Easter Island garbage heaps. Oral traditions of the islanders are rife with cannibalism; the most inflammatory taunt that could be snarled at an enemy was "The flesh of your mother sticks between my teeth." With no wood available to cook these new goodies, the islanders resorted to sugarcane scraps, grass, and sedges to fuel their fires.

All these strands of evidence can be wound into a coherent narrative of a society's decline and fall. The first Polynesian colonists found themselves on an island with fertile soil, abundant food, bountiful building materials, ample lebensraum, and all the prerequisites for comfortable living. They prospered and multiplied.

After a few centuries, they began erecting stone statues on platforms, like the ones their Polynesian forebears had carved. With passing years, the statues and platforms became larger and larger, and the statues began sporting ten-ton red crowns — probably in an escalating spiral of one-upmanship, as rival clans tried to surpass each other with shows of wealth and power. (In the same way, successive Egyptian pharaohs built ever-larger pyramids. Today Hollywood movie moguls near my home in Los Angeles are displaying their wealth and power by building ever more ostentatious mansions. Tycoon Marvin Davis topped previous moguls with plans for a 50,000-square-foot house, so now Aaron Spelling has topped Davis with a 56,000-square-foot house.

All that those buildings lack to make the message explicit are ten-ton red crowns.) On Easter, as in modern America, society was held together by a complex political system to redistribute locally available resources and to integrate the economies of different areas.

Eventually Easter's growing population was cutting the forest more rapidly than the forest was regenerating. The people used the land for gardens and the wood for fuel, canoes, and houses — and, of course, for lugging statues. As forest disappeared, the islanders ran out of timber and rope to transport and erect their statues. Life became more uncomfortable — springs and streams dried up, and wood was no longer available for fires.

People also found it harder to fill their stomachs, as land birds, large sea snails, and many seabirds disappeared. Because timber for building seagoing canoes vanished, fish catches declined and porpoises disappeared from the table. Crop yields also declined, since deforestation allowed the soil to be eroded by rain and wind, dried by the sun, and its nutrients to be leeched from it. Intensified chicken production and cannibalism replaced only part of all those lost foods. Preserved statuettes with sunken cheeks and visible ribs suggest that people were starving.

With the disappearance of food surpluses, Easter Island could no longer feed the chiefs, bureaucrats, and priests who had kept a complex society running. Surviving islanders described to early European visitors how local chaos replaced centralized government and a warrior class took over from the hereditary chiefs. The stone points of spears and daggers, made by the warriors during their heyday in the 1600s and 1700s, still litter the ground of Easter today. By around 1700, the population began to crash toward between one-quarter and one-tenth of its former number. People took to living in caves for protection against their enemies. Around 1770 rival clans started to topple each other's statues, breaking the heads off. By 1864 the last statue had been thrown down and desecrated.

As we try to imagine the decline of Easter's civilization, we ask ourselves, "Why didn't they look around, realize what they were doing, and stop before it was too late? What were they thinking when they cut down the last palm tree?"

I suspect, though, that the disaster happened not with a bang but with a whimper. After all, there are those hundreds of abandoned statues to consider. The forest the islanders depended on for rollers and rope didn't simply disappear one day — it vanished slowly, over decades. Perhaps war interrupted the moving teams; perhaps by the time the carvers had finished their work, the last rope snapped. In the meantime, any islander who tried to warn about the dangers of progressive deforestation would have been overridden by vested interests of carvers, bureaucrats, and chiefs, whose jobs depended on continued deforestation. Our Pacific Northwest loggers are only the latest in a long line of loggers to cry, "Jobs over trees!" The changes in forest cover from year to year would have been hard to detect: yes, this year we cleared those woods over there, but trees are starting to grow back again on this abandoned garden site here. Only older people, recollecting their childhoods decades earlier, could have recognized a difference. Their children could no more have comprehended their parents' tales than my eight-year-old sons today can comprehend my wife's and my tales of what Los Angeles was like 30 years ago.

Gradually trees became fewer, smaller, and less important. By the time the last fruit-bearing adult palm tree was cut, palms had long since ceased to be of economic significance. That left only smaller and smaller palm saplings to clear each year, along with other bushes and treelets. No one would have noticed the felling of the last small palm.

By now the meaning of Easter Island for us should be chillingly obvious. Easter Island is Earth writ small. Today, again, a rising population confronts shrinking resources. We too have no emigration valve, because all human societies are linked by international transport, and we can no more escape into space than the Easter Islanders could flee into the ocean. If we continue to follow our present course, we shall have exhausted the world's major fisheries, tropical rain forests, fossil fuels, and much of our soil by the time my sons reach my current age.

Every day newspapers report details of famished countries — Afghanistan, Liberia, Rwanda, Sierra Leone, Somalia, the former Yugoslavia, Zaire — where soldiers have appropriated the wealth or where central government is yielding to local gangs of thugs. With the risk of nuclear war receding, the threat of our ending with a bang no longer has a chance of galvanizing us to halt our course. Our risk now is of winding down, slowly, in a whimper. Corrective action is blocked by vested interests, by well-intentioned political and business leaders, and by their electorates, all of whom are perfectly correct in not noticing big changes from year to year. Instead, each year there are just somewhat more people, and somewhat fewer resources, on Earth. It would be easy to close our eyes or to give up in despair. If mere thousands of Easter Islanders with only stone tools and their own muscle power sufficed to destroy their society, how can billions of people with metal tools and machine power fail to do worse? But there is one crucial difference. The Easter Islanders had no books and no histories of other doomed societies. Unlike the Easter Islanders, we have histories of the past — information that can save us. My main hope for my sons' generation is that we may now choose to learn from the fates of societies like Easter's.

REFLECTIONS

Grand theories are difficult to evaluate, as are these. In part the difficulty is that they cover so much. How many images or primary sources could ever establish that a particular set of Christian ideas affected the way Christians actually behaved? And yet we know, or believe, that ideas matter. How many South Asian crops, tools, skills, and ideas constitute a global technological, let alone a scientific, revolution? And yet we know past historians have overemphasized the impact of European independence and Westernization. How many histories of societal collapse do we need to understand the threats to our own? And yet, we know that the more knowledge of how others have struggled and failed or succeeded we possess, the better our own chances for survival.

At least two issues lie beneath the surface of the debate in this chapter. One is the issue of culture, specifically the importance of cultural or religious ideas in shaping human behavior. White argues that religious ideas have a profound impact on how societies behave. Shaffer's study of material things rather than ideas, and even of ideas as things, offers a different view. By her account economic growth and technological development proceed with little regard to religions, ideologies, or belief systems. For Diamond too, not only are Christian or monotheistic ideas irrelevant, but historical processes leave precious little room for thoughtful intervention.

Historians are always working between ideas and things. Historians of ideas may have a tendency to see ideas shaping history, and historians of things (economic historians, for instance) may see ideas as mere rationalizations. But good historians are not predictable. Lynn White Jr. is perhaps best known for his book *Medieval Technology and Social Change* in which he argued, among other things, that the introduction of the stirrup into medieval Europe was the cause of the society and culture we call feudalism. While this idea is much debated today, one would have a hard time finding an example of a stronger argument of how a thing created a culture. Nor does Diamond, a professor of geography and physiology, ignore the role of ideas. In addition to the case of Easter Island, he surveys the example of Viking collapse in Greenland in his recent book, *Collapse: How Societies Choose to Fail or Succeed* (a title that suggests the power of will and ideas). The Vikings, he suggests, failed in Greenland because they were unable to change their culture in ways necessary to adapt to the new environment. For Diamond, ideas and political will offer the only hope against the blind destructiveness of entrenched interests and seemingly unstoppable historical processes.

Another issue below the surface of this debate is the relationship between ecology and economic development. We tend to think that one comes at the expense of the other. White criticizes Western (Christian) environmental behavior with the same lens that has allowed others to celebrate Western (Christian) economic development. This is a reason, by the way, why many contemporary world historians find both views too centered on the West or Europe. Lynda Shaffer's article on "Southernization" is in good part an effort to counter Europe-centered history with a more global version. But if Europe was not the source of modern technology, it was also not a source of our modern ecological predicament. Diamond is also critical of approaches that start and end in Europe. (His area of specialty is New Guinea.) Since he eliminated religious or cultural motives, his story of Easter Island can be read as an indictment of economic growth as the cause of ecological collapse. But the villain in Diamond's essay is not any kind of economic growth; it is the competitive economic exploitation of different tribes without any common plan or restraint. His message for our own predicament is to correct the anarchy of competing greedy corporations and interest groups with a common agenda and control.

Are not genuine economic growth and ecological balance mutually supportive? It is difficult to imagine long-term, healthy economic growth continuing while wrecking the environment. Similarly with environmental movements: White has us imagine that the true environmentalists are Buddhist mendicants and Hindu tree-huggers. But Buddhist monks might be content to cultivate their own gardens and ignore the rest of the world. After all, modern ecological political movements are largely products of rich societies with threatened environments. Might the most precarious ecologies display — by necessity — the greatest ecological concern? If that is the case, is the renewed popularity of environmental movements in our own age at least a sign of hope?

Volume Two: Since 1400

1

Overseas Expansion
in the Early Modern Period

China and Europe, 1400–1600

HISTORICAL CONTEXT

Between 1400 and 1500, the balance between Chinese and European sea power changed drastically. Before 1434, Chinese shipbuilding was the envy of the world. Chinese ships were larger, more numerous, safer, and better outfitted than European ships. The Chinese navy made frequent trips through the South China Sea to the Spice Islands, through the Indian Ocean, and as far as East Africa and the Persian Gulf (see Map 1.1). Every island, port, and kingdom along the route was integrated into the Chinese system of tributaries. Goods were exchanged, marriages arranged, and princes taken to visit the Chinese emperor.

In the second half of the fifteenth century, the Chinese navy virtually disappeared. At the same time, the Portuguese began a series of explorations down the coast of Africa and into the Atlantic Ocean. In 1434, Portuguese ships rounded the treacherous Cape Bojador, just south of Morocco. In 1488, Bartolomeu Dias rounded the Cape of Good Hope. Vasco da Gama sailed into the Indian Ocean, arriving in Calicut the following year. And in 1500 a fortuitous landfall in Brazil by Pedro Cabral gave the Portuguese a claim from the western Atlantic to the Indian Ocean. By 1512, Portuguese ships had reached the Bandas and Moluccas — the Spice Islands of what is today eastern Indonesia.

Beginning in 1492, after the defeat of the Moors (Muslims) and the voyages of Columbus, the Spanish claimed most of the Western Hemisphere until challenged by the Dutch, English, and French. European control in the Americas penetrated far deeper than in Asia, where it was limited to enclaves on the coast, and where European nations were in an almost perpetual state of war with each other. Taken together, the nations of Western Europe dominated the seas of the world after 1500 (see Map 1.2).

1

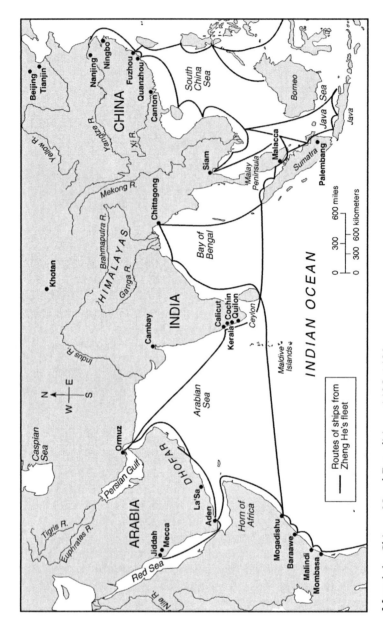

Map 1.1 Chinese Naval Expeditions, 1405–1433.

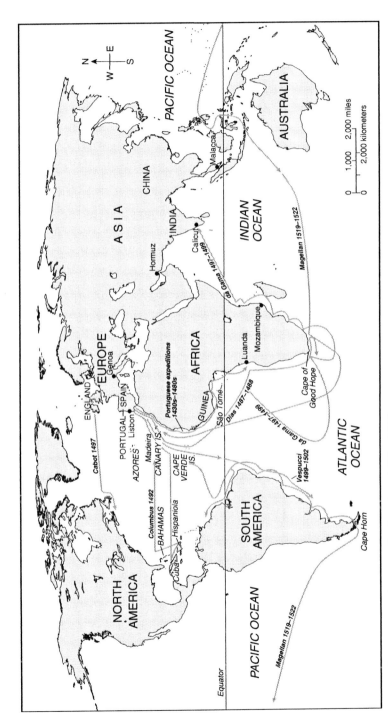

Map 1.2   European Overseas Exploration, 1430s–1530s.

What accounts for the different fortunes of China and Europe in the fifteenth century? Were the decline of China and the rise of Europe inevitable? Probably no objective observer of the time would have thought so. In what ways were the expansions of China and Europe similar? In what ways were they different? Think about these questions as you reflect on the readings in this chapter.

THINKING HISTORICALLY
Reading Primary and Secondary Sources

This chapter contains both primary and secondary sources. *Primary sources* are actual pieces of the past and include anything — art, letters, essays, and so on — from the historical period being studied. If a future historian were to study and research students in American colleges at the beginning of the twenty-first century, some primary sources might include diaries, letters, cartoons, music videos, posters, paintings, e-mail messages, blogs and Web sites, class notes, school newspapers, tests, and official and unofficial records. *Secondary sources* are usually books and articles *about* the past — interpretations of the past. These sources are "secondary" because they must be based on primary sources; therefore, a history written after an event occurs is a secondary source.

In your studies, you will be expected to distinguish primary from secondary sources. A quick glance at the introductions to this chapter's selections tells you that the first article is written by a modern journalist and the third and fifth are written by an amateur historian and an environmentalist, taken from books published in 2003 and 1991, respectively. In contrast, the second selection, an inscription ordered by Admiral Zheng He* that dates from the fifteenth century, and the fourth selection, a letter penned by Christopher Columbus more than five hundred years ago, are firsthand accounts of worlds long past.

Having determined whether selections are primary or secondary sources, we also explore some of the subtle complexities that are overlooked by such designations.

Note: Pronunciations of difficult-to-pronounce terms will be given throughout the chapter. The emphasis goes on the syllable appearing in all capital letters. [Ed.]
  *jung HUH

JOSEPH KAHN

"China Has an Ancient Mariner to Tell You About"

In this 2005 *New York Times* article journalist Joseph Kahn, currently Beijing bureau chief for the *Times*, combines a brief history of the life of Zheng He with a critical view of recent Chinese government efforts at reviving the reputation of the fifteenth-century admiral. Who was Zheng He? Why, according to Kahn, is China focusing attention on him?

Thinking Historically

Newspaper stories are not primary sources — unless the subject is the newspaper itself, the reporter of the story, or the way in which newspapers presented the particular story. Some historians would say that a newspaper story as brief as this one is hardly even a secondary source because it tells us very little of what modern historians know about Zheng He. For an understanding of the great Chinese admiral, this might better be called a third level, or tertiary, source. Still, even a news story must rely on sources. What primary and secondary sources does this article refer to?

The captivating tale of Zheng He, a Chinese eunuch who explored the Pacific and Indian Oceans with a mighty armada almost a century before Columbus discovered America, has long languished as a tantalizing footnote in China's imperial history.

Zheng He (pronounced jung huh) fell into disfavor before he completed the last of his early 15th-century voyages, and most historical records were destroyed. Authorities protected his old family home in Nanjing, but it was often shuttered, its rooms used to store unrelated relics.

Joseph Kahn, "Letter from Asia: China Has an Ancient Mariner to Tell You About," *New York Times*, July 20, 2005, Section A, p. 4.

Now, on the 600th anniversary of Zheng He's first mission in 1405, all that is changing. Zheng He's legacy is being burnished — some critics say glossed over — to give rising China a new image on the world stage.

Books and television shows, replicas of Zheng He's ships and a new $50 million museum in Nanjing promote Zheng He as a maritime cultural ambassador for a powerful but ardently peaceful nation.

Officials have even endorsed the theory, so far unproven, that one of Zheng He's ships foundered on the rocks near Lamu island, off the coast of today's Kenya, with survivors swimming ashore, marrying locals and creating a family of Chinese-Africans that is now being reunited with the Chinese motherland.

The message is that Zheng He foreshadowed China's 21st-century emergence as a world power, though one that differs in crucial respects from Spain, Britain, France, Germany, Japan, and, most pointedly, the United States.

"In the heyday of the Ming Dynasty, China did not seek hegemony," says Wan Ming, a leading scholar of the era. "Today, we are once again growing stronger all the time, and China's style of peaceful development has been welcomed all over the world."

The Communist Party hopes to signal to its own people that it has recaptured past glory, while reassuring foreign countries that China can be strong and non-threatening at the same time.

Even within China, though, the use of poorly documented history as a modern propaganda prop has generated a backlash.

Several scholars have publicly criticized the campaign as a distortion, saying Zheng He treated foreigners as barbarians and most foreign countries as vassal states. His voyages amounted to a wasteful tribute to a maniacal emperor, some argue.

Zheng He resonates, favorably or not, in Asia. Arguably for the first time since his final voyage in 1433, China is vying to become a major maritime power.

Beijing has upgraded its navy with Russian-built Sovremenny-class guided missile destroyers, Kilo-class diesel submarines, and a new nuclear submarine equipped to carry intercontinental ballistic missiles. It has flirted with the idea of building an aircraft carrier, according to conflicting reports in state media.

Sustained double-digit increases in defense spending have helped make China one of the largest military powers in the world, though still well behind the United States. China says it aims only to defend itself. But others are skeptical.

"Since no nation threatens China, one wonders: why this growing investment?" Defense Secretary Donald H. Rumsfeld asked recently in a speech on China's buildup during a visit to Singapore last month.

Beijing clearly hopes history will help answer the question.

Zheng He was a Chinese Muslim who, following the custom of the day, was castrated so he could serve in the household of a prince, Zhu Di.*

Zhu Di later toppled the emperor, his brother, and took the throne for himself. He rewarded Zheng He, his co-conspirator, with command of the greatest naval expedition that the world had ever seen. Beginning in July 1405, Zheng He made port calls all around Southeast Asia, rounded India, explored the Middle East and reached the eastern coast of Africa.

The three ships Columbus guided across the Atlantic 87 years later, the Niña, Pinta, and Santa María, could fit inside a single large vessel in Zheng He's armada, which at its peak had up to 300 ships and 30,000 sailors. Some of China's maritime innovations at the time, including watertight compartments, did not show up on European vessels for hundreds of years.

Zheng He was China's first big ocean trader, presenting gifts from the emperor to leaders in foreign ports and hauling back crabapples, myrrh, mastic gum, and even a giraffe.

In time, though, the emperor turned against seafaring, partly because of the exorbitant cost, partly because of China's religious certitude that it had nothing to learn from the outside world. By the latter part of the 15th century the country had entered a prolonged period of self-imposed isolation that lasted into the 20th century, leaving European powers to rule the seas.

For Chinese officials today, the sudden end of China's maritime ambitions 600 years ago conveniently signals something else: that China is a gentle giant with enduring good will.

Zheng He represents China's commitment to "good neighborliness, peaceful coexistence, and scientific navigation," government-run China Central Television said during an hour-long documentary on the explorer last week.

Earlier this month, authorities opened a $50 million memorial to Zheng He. Tributes to him fill courtyard-style exhibition halls, painted in stately vermillion and imperial yellow. A hulking statue of Zheng He, his chest flung forward as in many Communist-era likenesses of Mao, decorates the main hall.

As the Zheng He anniversary approached, delegations of Chinese diplomats and scholars also traveled to Kenya to investigate the claims that islanders there could trace their roots to sailors on Zheng He's fleet.

On one remote island, called Siyu, the Chinese found a 19-year-old high school student, Mwamaka Sharifu, who claimed Chinese ancestry.

---

*zhoo DEE

Beijing's embassy in Nairobi arranged for her to visit China to attend Zheng He celebrations. Beijing has invited her back to study in China, tuition-free, this fall.

"My family members have round faces, small eyes, and black hair, so we long believed we are Chinese," Ms. Sharifu said in a telephone interview. "Now we have a direct link to China itself."

The outreach effort has generated positive publicity for China in Kenya and some other African countries, as well as around Southeast Asia, where Zheng He is widely admired.

But Zheng He has been more coolly received by some scholars in China and abroad.

Geoff Wade, a China specialist at the National University of Singapore, argued in an academic essay that Zheng He helped the Ming state colonize neighboring countries. His far-flung expeditions aimed at enforcing a "pax Ming" through Southeast Asia, allowing China to wrest control of trade routes dominated at that time by Arabs, he wrote.

Several Chinese experts also questioned whether Zheng He's legacy is as salutary as government officials hope.

Ye Jun, a Beijing historian, said the official contention that Zheng He was a good-will ambassador is a "one-sided interpretation that blindly ignores the objective fact that Zheng He engaged in military suppression" to achieve the emperor's goals.

"These matters should be left to scholars," Mr. Ye said.

$$2$$

ZHENG HE

Inscription to the Goddess

This inscription was carved on a stone erected to the Chinese Daoist goddess called the Celestial Spouse at Changle in Fujian Province of China in 1431. Zheng He left other inscriptions to other deities on his travels so it would be a mistake to read much of a religious motive in this act by the admiral who had been raised a Muslim. In fact, in

Zheng He, "Inscription to the Goddess," in *China and Africa in the Middle Ages*, ed. Teobaldo Filesi, trans. David L. Morrison (London: Frank Cass, 1972), 57–61. Americanized and slightly simplified.

1411, Zheng He erected a monument in Sri Lanka dedicated to three deities in three languages. The Chinese portion praised Buddha, a section in Tamil was dedicated to the god Tenavarai-Nayanar, and a third section in Persian was inscribed to Allah.

This selection conveys some idea of how Zheng He must have perceived his mission or wanted it to be understood. Judging from this inscription, would you call Zheng He, to use Joseph Kahn's terms, a good-will ambassador or a military oppressor?

Thinking Historically

Primary sources like this one can be difficult for a modern reader to interpret because they were not written for us, but for another audience in a different time. A modern journalist like Joseph Kahn speaks directly to us; the fifteenth-century mariner does not. This lack of "fit" between ancient source and modern ear can actually be a benefit, however, because it better enables us to distinguish fact from propaganda, truth from spin. As you read this selection, ask yourself what the author wants the reader to believe and what in his writing he could not have crafted for the purpose of persuading or fooling the audience. Your answer to the latter part of this question provides us with historical knowledge of a high degree of certainty.

For an example of how this works, look at the first sentence, the title that declares the nature of the inscription: "Record of the miraculous answer (to prayer) of the goddess the Celestial Spouse." We *do not* learn from this that the author received a miraculous answer to his prayer. We cannot even be sure that he thought he did (since he may not be telling the truth). But we do learn some things beyond doubt. We learn from this sentence that some Chinese believed in a goddess called "the Celestial Spouse." We learn that some Chinese prayed to the goddess and that some believed she could provide "miraculous answers." We learn all of these things because the inscription would make no sense otherwise. These are the assumptions rather than the arguments of the inscription. We learn from primary sources by asking about the things they *assume.* Try this exercise with the rest of the selection.

Record of the miraculous answer (to prayer) of the goddess the Celestial Spouse.

The Imperial Ming Dynasty unifying seas and continents, surpassing the three dynasties even goes beyond the Han and Tang dynasties. The countries beyond the horizon and from the ends of the earth have all become subjects and to the most western of the western or the most northern of the northern countries, however far they may be, the distance and the routes may be calculated. Thus the barbarians from beyond the seas, though their countries are truly distant, have come to audience bearing precious objects and presents.

The Emperor, approving of their loyalty and sincerity, has ordered Zheng He and others at the head of several tens of thousands of officers and flag-troops to ascend more than one hundred large ships to go and confer presents on them in order to make manifest the transforming power of the imperial virtue and to treat distant people with kindness. From the third year of Yongle (1405) till now we have seven times received the commission of ambassadors to countries of the western ocean. The barbarian countries which we have visited are: by way of Zhancheng (Champa), Zhaowa (Java), Sanfoqi (Palembang) and Xianle (Siam) crossing straight over to Xilanshan (Ceylon) in South India, Guli (Calicut), and Kezhi (Cochin), we have gone to the western regions Hulumosi (Hormuz), Adan (Aden), Mugudushu (Mogadishu), altogether more than thirty countries large and small. We have traversed more than one hundred thousand li[1] of immense water spaces and have beheld in the ocean huge waves like mountains rising sky-high, and we have set eyes on barbarian regions far away hidden in a blue transparency of light vapors, while our sails loftily unfurled like clouds day and night continued their course rapid like a star, traversing those savage waves as if we were treading a public thoroughfare. Truly this was due to the majesty and the good fortune of the Court and moreover we owe it to the protecting virtue of the divine Celestial Spouse.

The power of the goddess having indeed been manifested in previous times has been abundantly revealed in the present generation. In the midst of the rushing waters it happened that, when there was a hurricane, suddenly there was a divine lantern shining in the mast, and as soon as this miraculous light appeared the danger was appeased, so that even in the danger of capsizing one felt reassured that there was no cause for fear. When we arrived in the distant countries we captured alive those of the native kings who were not respectful and exterminated those barbarian robbers who were engaged in piracy, so that consequently the sea route was cleansed and pacified and the natives put their trust in it. All this is due to the favors of the goddess.

It is not easy to enumerate completely all the cases where the goddess has answered prayers. Previously in a memorial to the Court we have requested that her virtue be registered in the Court of Sacrificial Worship and a temple be built at Nanking on the bank of the dragon river where regular sacrifices should be transmitted forever. We have respectfully received an Imperial commemorative composition exalting the miraculous favors, which is the highest recompense and praise in-

---

[1]A li = ⅓ mile. [Ed.]

deed. However, the miraculous power of the goddess resides wherever one goes. As for the temporary palace on the southern mountain at Changle, I have, at the head of the fleet, frequently resided there awaiting the favorable wind to set sail for the ocean.

We, Zheng He and others, on the one hand have received the high favor of a gracious commission of our Sacred Lord, and on the other hand carry to the distant barbarians the benefits of respect and good faith. Commanding the multitudes on the fleet and being responsible for a quantity of money and valuables, in the face of the violence of the winds and the nights, our one fear is not to be able to succeed; how should we then dare not to serve our dynasty with exertion of all our loyalty and the gods with the utmost sincerity? How would it be possible not to realize what is the source of the tranquility of the fleet and the troops and the salvation on the voyage both going and returning? Therefore we have made manifest the virtue of the goddess on stone and have moreover recorded the years and months of the voyages to the barbarian countries and the return in order to leave the memory for ever.

I. In the third year of Yongle (1405) commanding the fleet we went to Guli (Calicut) and other countries. At that time the pirate Chen Zuyi had gathered his followers in the country of Sanfoqi (Palembang), where he plundered the native merchants. When he also advanced to resist our fleet, supernatural soldiers secretly came to the rescue so that after one beating of the drum he was annihilated. In the fifth year (1407) we returned.

II. In the fifth year of Yongle (1407) commanding the fleet we went to Zhaowa (Java), Guli (Calicut), Kezhi (Cochin), and Xianle (Siam). The kings of these countries all sent as tribute precious objects, precious birds, and rare animals. In the seventh year (1409) we returned.

III. In the seventh year of Yongle (1409) commanding the fleet we went to the countries visited before and took our route by the country of Xilanshan (Ceylon). Its king Yaliekunaier (Alagakkonara) was guilty of a gross lack of respect and plotted against the fleet. Owing to the manifest answer to prayer of the goddess the plot was discovered and thereupon that king was captured alive. In the ninth year (1411) on our return the king was presented to the throne as a prisoner; subsequently he received the Imperial favor of returning to his own country.

IV. In the eleventh year of Yongle (1413) commanding the fleet we went to Hulumosi (Ormuz) and other countries. In the country of Sumendala (Samudra)[2] there was a false king Suganla (Sekandar) who was marauding and invading his country. Its king Cainu-liabiding

---

[2]Kerala, India. [Ed.]

(Zaynu-'l-Abidin) had sent an envoy to the Palace Gates in order to lodge a complaint. We went thither with the official troops under our command and exterminated some and arrested other rebels, and owing to the silent aid of the goddess we captured the false king alive. In the thirteenth year (1415) on our return he was presented to the Emperor as a prisoner. In that year the king of the country of Manlajia (Malacca) came in person with his wife and son to present tribute.

V. In the fifteenth year of Yongle (1417) commanding the fleet we visited the western regions. The country of Hulumosi (Ormuz) presented lions, leopards with gold spots, and large western horses. The country of Adan (Aden) presented qilin of which the native name is culafa (giraffe), as well as the long-horned animal maha (oryx). The country of Mugudushu (Mogadishu) presented huafu lu ("striped" zebras) as well as lions. The country of Bulawa (Brava)[3] presented camels which run one thousand li as well as camel-birds (ostriches). The countries of Zhaowa (Java) and Guli (Calicut) presented the animal miligao. They all vied in presenting the marvelous objects preserved in the mountains or hidden in the seas and the beautiful treasures buried in the sand or deposited on the shores. Some sent a maternal uncle of the king, others a paternal uncle or a younger brother of the king in order to present a letter of homage written on gold leaf as well as tribute.

VI. In the nineteenth year of Yongle (1421) commanding the fleet we conducted the ambassadors from Hulumosi (Ormuz) and the other countries that had been in attendance at the capital for a long time back to their countries. The kings of all these countries prepared even more tribute than previously.

VII. In the sixth year of Xuande (1431) once more commanding the fleet we have left for the barbarian countries in order to read to them (an Imperial edict) and to confer presents.

We have anchored in this port awaiting a north wind to take the sea, and recalling how previously we have on several occasions received the benefits of the protection of the divine intelligence we have thus recorded an inscription in stone.

---

[3]Baraawe, Somalia. [Ed.]

GAVIN MENZIES

From 1421: The Year China Discovered America

Writer Gavin Menzies has recently caused a stir among historians by arguing in his book *1421: The Year China Discovered America* that Zheng He's ships actually reached America. This selection from that same work contains the author's more reliable discussion of the preparations for the great Chinese naval expedition of 1421, Zheng He's sixth, setting events in the broader context of Chinese imperial history and its tribute system.

As Zheng He indicated in the "Inscription to the Goddess" (selection 2), the 1421 voyage was intended to return a number of foreign ambassadors to their home countries after they had participated in the inauguration of the emperor Zhu Di's new capital city at Beijing. How was such a voyage part of the Chinese system of trade and diplomacy? What did the Chinese stand to gain by such a system? What did those tribute-paying countries gain? Does Menzies's description support the Chinese government claim that the tribute system was peaceful, or does it seem to be the "military suppression" charged by at least one historian (see selection 1)?

Thinking Historically

This is clearly a secondary source. It depends on many primary and other secondary sources. As indicated in the first selection of this chapter, the gathering of primary sources about the Chinese treasure ships suffers from severe limitations. Most of the imperial archives as well as the ships were destroyed by the successor Ming emperors after 1435. Persuaded by the traditional Confucian bureaucracy to abandon the naval ventures favored by palace eunuchs, later emperors even banned Chinese habitation along the coastal corridor of the China Sea.

For this selection, however, on the preparations for the voyage of 1421, Gavin Menzies is able to use available primary and secondary sources on various aspects of Ming Chinese society and culture. Notice also how he uses information from other cultures and other periods to

Gavin Menzies, *1421: The Year China Discovered America* (New York: HarperCollins, 2003), 60–71.

help the reader understand the scale of these Ming treasure ships. The ordinary reader cannot distinguish Menzies's assumptions from his arguments as easily as with a primary source. One tends to read a secondary source less critically than a primary source. Nevertheless, what are the advantages of a secondary source like this? Without checking the footnotes (and Menzies provides very few), which of the details or interpretations in this selection are you most inclined to question? Why?

Chinese foreign policy was quite different from that of the Europeans who followed them to the Indian Ocean many years later. The Chinese preferred to pursue their aims by trade, influence, and bribery rather than by open conflict and direct colonization. Zhu Di's policy was to despatch huge armadas every few years throughout the known world, bearing gifts and trade goods; the massive treasure ships carrying a huge array of guns and a travelling army of soldiers were also a potent reminder of his imperial might: China alone had the necessary firepower to protect friendly countries from invasion and quash insurrections against their rulers. The treasure ships returned to China with all manner of exotic items: "dragon saliva [ambergris], incense and golden amber" and "lions, gold spotted leopards and camel-birds [ostriches] which are six or seven feet tall" from Africa; gold cloth from Calicut in south-west India, studded with pearls and precious stones; elephants, parrots, sandalwood, peacocks, hardwood, incense, tin, and cardamom from Siam (modern Thailand).

Those rulers who accepted the emperor's overlordship were rewarded with titles, protection, and trade missions. In south-east Asia, Malacca was rewarded for its loyalty by being promoted as a trading port at the expense of Java and Sumatra; the emperor even personally composed a poem for the Malaccan sultan, and can be said to have been the founder of Malaysia. The subservient Siamese were also extended trading privileges to the detriment of the truculent Cambodians. Korea was especially important to China: Zhu Di lost no time in despatching an envoy to the King of Korea, Yi Pang-Won, granting him an honorary Chinese title. The Koreans needed Chinese medicine, books, and astronomical instruments, and in return they agreed to set up an observatory to co-operate with Zhu Di in charting the world. They traded leopards, seals, gold, silver and horses — one thousand of them in 1403, ten thousand the next year. Despite some reluctance, they also found it expedient to comply with Chinese requests to fill Zhu Di's harem with virgins. Many Korean ships were to join the Chinese fleets when they left to sail the world.

As soon as he had expelled the last Mongols from China in 1382, Zhu Di had despatched his eunuch Isiha to the perennially troublesome region of Manchuria in the far north-east, and in 1413 the Jurchen people of Manchuria responded by sending a prestigious mission to Beijing, where its members were showered with titles, gifts, and trading rights. Japan was also assiduously courted. The third Ashikaga Shogun Yoshimitsu was a Sinophile[1]; he lost no time in kow-towing as "your subject, the King of Japan." His reward was a string of special ports opened to promote trade with Japan, at Ningbo, Quanzhou, and Guangdong (Canton). Like Korea, Japan also set up an observatory to aid Zhu Di's astronomical research, and Japanese ships also joined the globetrotting Chinese convoys.

Having pacified Manchuria and brought Korea and Japan into the Chinese tribute system, Zhu Di next turned his attention to Tibet. Another court eunuch, Hau-Xian, led a mission to court the famous holy man the Karmapa, leader of one of the four sects of Tibetan Buddhism, and bring him to China. When he arrived, a procession of Buddhist monks met him outside the city and Zhu Di bestowed upon him the title "Divine Son of India Below the Sky and Upon the Earth, Inventor of the Alphabet, Incarnated Buddha, Maintainer of the Kingdom's Prosperity, Source of Rhetoric." The emperor then presented the Karmapa with a square black hat bearing a diamond-studded emblem. It has been worn by successive incarnations of the Karmapa ever since.

Joining China's tribute system also gave rulers and their envoys the opportunity to visit the capital of the oldest and finest civilization in the world. The traditional imperial capital of Nanjing had received dignitaries from around the world, and now the new capital of Beijing began to welcome the latest arrivals. Although the emperor's main concern was to awe all countries into becoming tribute-bearing states, great efforts were also made to learn about their history, geography, manners, and customs. Beijing was to be not only the world's greatest city but its intellectual capital, with encyclopedias and libraries covering every subject known to man. In December 1404, Zhu Di had appointed two long-time advisers, Yao Guang Xiao and Lui Chi'ih, assisted by 2,180 scholars, to take charge of a project, the Yong-le-Dadian, to preserve all known literature and knowledge. It was the largest scholarly enterprise ever undertaken. The result, a massive encyclopedia of four thousand volumes containing some fifty million characters, was completed just before the Forbidden City was inaugurated.

In parallel with this great endeavour, Zhu Di ordered the opinions of 120 philosophers and sages of the Song dynasty to be collated and stored in the Forbidden City together with the complete commentaries of thinkers from the eleventh to the thirteenth centuries. In addition to this wealth of academic knowledge, hundreds of printed novels could be bought from Beijing market stalls. There was nothing remotely

---

[1]A lover of China and things Chinese. [Ed.]

comparable anywhere in the world. Printing was unknown in Europe — Gutenberg did not complete his printed Bible for another thirty years — and though Europe was on the eve of the Renaissance that was to transform its culture and scientific knowledge, it lagged far behind China. The library of Henry V (1387–1422) comprised six handwritten books, three of which were on loan to him from a nunnery, and the Florentine Francesco Datini, the wealthiest European merchant of the same era, possessed twelve books, eight of which were on religious subjects.

The voyage to the intellectual paradise of Beijing also offered foreign potentates and envoys many earthly delights. Carried in sumptuous comfort aboard the leviathan ships, they consumed the finest foods and wines, and pleasured themselves with the concubines whose only role was to please these foreign dignitaries. The formal inauguration of the Forbidden City was followed by a sumptuous banquet. Its scale and opulence emphasized China's position at the summit of the civilized world. In comparison, Europe was backward, crude, and barbaric. Henry V's marriage to Catherine of Valois took place in London just three weeks after the inauguration of the Forbidden City. Twenty-six thousand guests were entertained in Beijing, where they ate a ten-course banquet served on dishes of the finest porcelain; a mere six hundred guests attended Henry's nuptials and they were served stockfish (salted cod) on rounds of stale bread that acted as plates. Catherine de Valois wore neither knickers nor stockings at her wedding; Zhu Di's favourite concubine was clad in the finest silks and her jewellery included cornelians from Persia, rubies from Sri Lanka, Indian diamonds and jade from Kotan (in Chinese Turkestan). Her perfume contained ambergris from the Pacific, myrrh from Arabia, and sandalwood from the Spice Islands. China's army numbered one million men, armed with guns; Henry V could put five thousand men in the field, armed only with longbows, swords, and pikes. The fleet that would carry Zhu Di's guests home numbered over a hundred ships with a complement of thirty thousand men; when Henry went to war against France in June of that year, he ferried his army across the Channel in four fishing boats, carrying a hundred men on each crossing and sailing only in daylight hours.

For a further month after the inauguration of the Forbidden City, the rulers and envoys in Beijing were provided with lavish imperial hospitality — the finest foods and wines, the most splendid entertainments and the most beautiful concubines, skilled in the arts of love. Finally, on 3 March 1421, a great ceremony was mounted to commemorate the departure of the envoys for their native lands. A vast honour guard was assembled: "First came commanders of ten thousands, next commanders of thousands, all numbering about one hundred thousand men. . . . Behind them stood troops in serried ranks, two hundred thousand strong. . . . The whole body . . . stood so silent it seemed there was not a breathing soul there." At noon precisely, cymbals clashed, elephants lowered their trunks, and clouds of smoke wafted from incense-holders in the shape of tortoises and cranes. The emperor appeared, striding through the smoke to present the departing ambassadors with their farewell gifts — crates of blue and white porcelain, rolls of silk, bundles of cotton cloth, and bamboo cases of jade. His great fleets stood ready to carry them back to Hormuz, Aden, La'Sa, and Dhofar in Arabia; to Mogadishu, Brava, Malindi, and Mombasa in Africa; to Sri Lanka, Calicut, Cochin, and Cambay in India; to Japan, Vietnam, Java, Sumatra, Malacca, and Borneo in south-east Asia, and elsewhere.

Admiral Zheng He, dressed in his formal uniform — a long red robe and a tall black hat — presented the emperor with his compliments and reported that an armada comprising four of the emperor's great fleets was ready to set sail; the fifth, commanded by Grand Eunuch Yang Qing, had put to sea the previous month. The return of the envoys to their homelands was only the first part of this armada's overall mission. It was then to "proceed all the way to the end of the earth to collect tribute from the barbarians beyond the seas . . . to attract all under heaven to be civilised in Confucian harmony." Zheng He's reward for his lifelong, devoted service to his emperor had been the command of five previous treasure fleets tasked with promoting Chinese trade and influence in Asia, India, Africa, and the Middle East. Now he was to lead one of the largest armadas the world had ever seen. Zhu Di had also rewarded other eunuchs for their part in helping him to liberate China. Many of the army commanders in the war against the Mongols were now admirals and captains of his treasure fleets. Zheng He had become a master of delegation. By the fourth voyage fleets were sailing separately. On this great sixth voyage loyal eunuchs would command separate fleets. Zheng He would lead them to the Indian Ocean then return home confident that they would handle their fleets as he had taught them.

The envoys' parting gifts were packed into their carriages, the emperor made a short speech, and then, after kow-towing one last time, the envoys embarked and the procession moved off. Servants ran behind the carriages as they rumbled down to the Grand Canal a mile to the east of the city. There, a fleet of barges decked with silk awnings awaited them. Teams of horses, ten to twelve for each barge, stood on the banks, bamboo poles tied to their harnesses. When the envoys were aboard, whips cracked and the sturdy animals began to drag the barges on their slow journey down to the coast.

Two days and thirty-six locks later, they arrived at Tanggu (near the modern city of Tianjin) on the Yellow Sea. The sight that greeted the envoys at Tanggu was one that must have lingered long in their minds. More than one hundred huge junks rode at anchor, towering above the watchers on the quayside — the ships were taller by far than the thatched houses lining the bay. Surrounding them was a fleet of smaller merchant ships. Each capital ship was about 480 feet in length (444 *chi*, the standard Chinese unit of measurement, equivalent to about 12.5 inches or 32 centimetres) and 180 feet across — big enough to swallow fifty fishing boats. On the prow, glaring serpents' eyes served to frighten away evil spirits. Pennants streamed from the tips of a forest of a thousand masts; below them great sails of red silk, light but immensely strong, were furled on each ship's nine masts. "When their sails are spread, they are like great clouds in the sky."

The armada was composed very much like a Second World War convoy. At the centre were the great leviathan flagships, surrounded by a host of merchant junks, most 90 feet long and 30 feet wide. Around the perimeters were squadrons of fast, manoeuvrable warships. As the voyage progressed, trading ships of several other nations, especially Japan, Korea, Burma, Vietnam, and India, joined the convoy, taking advantage of the protection afforded by the warships and the opportunities offered as the magnificent armada, almost a trading country in its own right, swept over the oceans. By the time it reached Calicut, it comprised more than eight hundred vessels whose combined population exceeded that of any city between China and India. Each treasure ship had sixteen internal watertight compartments, any two of which could be flooded without sinking the ship. Some internal compartments could also be partially flooded to act as tanks for the trained sea-otters used in fishing, or for use by divers entering and leaving the sea. The otters, held on long cords, were employed to herd shoals of fish into nets, a method still practised in parts of China, Malaysia, and Bengal today. The admiral's sea cabin was above the stern of his flagship. Below were sixty staterooms for foreign ambassadors, envoys and their entourages. Their concubines were housed in adjacent cabins and most had balconies overlooking the sea. Chinese ambassadors, one for each country to be visited, were housed in less grand but nonetheless spacious apartments. Each ambassador had ten assistants as *chefs de protocol* and a further fifty-two eunuchs served as secretaries. The crewmen's quarters were on the lower decks.

In 1407, Zheng He had established a language school in Nanjing, the Ssu-i-Quan (Si Yi Guan), to train interpreters, and sixteen of its finest graduates travelled with the fleets, enabling the admirals to communicate with rulers from India to Africa in Arabic, Persian, Swahili, Hindi, Tamil, and many other languages. Zhu Di and Zheng He also actively sought out foreign navigators and cartographers; the diaries of one of them, an Indonesian by the name of Master Bentun, have survived. Religious tolerance was one of Zhu Di's great virtues, and the junks also habitually carried Islamic, Hindu, and Buddhist savants to provide advice and guidance. Buddhism, with its teachings of universal compassion and tolerance, had been the religion of the majority of the Chinese people for centuries. Buddhism in no way conflicted with Confucianism, which could be said to be a code of civic values rather than a religion. On this sixth and final voyage of the treasure fleets which would last until 1423, the Buddhist monk Sheng Hui and the religious leaders Ha San and Pu He Ri were aboard. After the inauguration of the Forbidden City and the dedication of the awesome encyclopedia the Yong-le-Dadian, thousands of scholars found themselves without an obvious role. It would have been natural for Zhu Di to send them overseas on the great voyages of exploration. Through interpreters, Chinese mathematicians, astronomers, navigators, engineers, and architects would have been able to converse with and learn from their counterparts throughout the Indian Ocean. Once the ambassadors and their entourages had disembarked, the vast ships with their labyrinths of cabins would have been well suited to use as laboratories for scientific experiments. Metallurgists could prospect for minerals in the countries the Chinese visited, physicians could search out new healing plants, medicines, and treatments that might help to combat plagues and epidemics, and botanists could propagate valuable food plants. Chinese agricultural scientists and farmers had millennia of experience of developing and propagating hybrids.

The native Chinese flora is perhaps the richest in the world: "In wealth of its endemic species and in the extent of the genus and species potential of its cultivated plants, China is conspicuous among other centres of origin of plant forms. Moreover the species are usually represented by enormous numbers of botanical varieties and hereditary forms." In Europe, a long period of economic and agricultural decline followed the fall of the Roman Empire. The plant forms known to the Western world from Theophrastus to the German fathers of botany show that European knowledge had slumped, but there was no corresponding "dark age" in Chinese scientific history. Botanical knowledge, and the number of plant species recorded by the Chinese, grew steadily as the centuries passed. The contrast between the voyages of discovery of the Chinese and those of the Europeans cannot be overestimated. The only interest of the Spanish and Portuguese was in gathering sustenance, gold, and spices, while warding off attacks from the natives. The great Chinese fleets undertook scientific expeditions the Europeans could not even begin to equal in scale or scope until Captain Cook set sail three and a half centuries later.

As the admirals and envoys embarked, and the armada was readied for sea, the water around the great ships was still black with smaller craft shuttling from ship to shore. For days the port had been in turmoil as cartloads of vegetables and dried fish and hundreds of tons of water were hauled aboard to provision this armada of thirty thousand men for their voyage. Even at this late hour, barges were still bringing final supplies of fresh water and rice. The great armada's ships could remain at sea for over three months and cover at least 4,500 miles without making landfall to replenish food or water, for separate grain ships and water tankers sailed with them. The grain ships also carried an array of flora the Chinese intended to plant in foreign lands, some as further benefits of the tribute system and others to provide food for the Chinese colonies that would be created in new lands. Dogs were also taken aboard as pets, others to be bred for food and to hunt rats, and there were coops of Asiatic chickens as valuable presents for foreign dignitaries. The larger ships even kept sties of Chinese pigs. Separate horse-ships carried the mounts for the cavalry.

The staggering size of the individual ships, not to mention the armada itself, can best be understood by comparison with other navies of the same era. In 1421, the next most powerful fleet afloat was that of Venice. The Venetians possessed around three hundred galleys — fast, light, thin-skinned ships built with soft-wood planking, rowed by oarsmen and only suitable for island-hopping in the calm of a Mediterranean summer. The biggest Venetian galleys were some 150 feet long and 20 feet wide and carried at best 50 tons of cargo. In comparison, Zhu Di's treasure ships were ocean-going monsters built of teak. The rudder of one of these great ships stood 36 feet high — almost as long as the whole of the flagship the *Niña* in which Columbus was later to set sail for the New World. Each treasure ship could carry more than two thousand tons of cargo and reach Malacca in five weeks, Hormuz in the Persian Gulf in twelve. They were capable of sailing the wildest oceans of the world, in voyages lasting years at a time. That so many ships were lost on the Chinese voyages of discovery testifies not to any lack of strength in their construction but rather to the perilous, uncharted waters they explored and the hurricanes and tsunami they encountered along rocky coasts and razor-sharp coral reefs to the ice-strewn oceans of the far north and far south. Venetian galleys were protected by archers; Chinese ships were armed with gunpowder weapons, brass and iron cannon, mortars, flaming arrows, and exploding shells that sprayed excrement over their adversaries. In every single respect — construction, cargo capacity, damage control, armament, range, communications, the ability to navigate in the trackless ocean and to repair and maintain their ships at sea for months on end — the Chinese were centuries ahead of Europe. Admiral Zheng He would have had no difficulty in destroying any fleet that crossed his path. A battle between this Chinese armada and the other navies of the world combined would have resembled one between a pack of sharks and a shoal of sprats.

By the end of the middle watch — four in the morning — the last provisions had been lashed down and the armada weighed anchor. A prayer was said to Ma Tsu, Taoist goddess of the sea, and then, as their red silk sails slowly filled, the ships, resembling great houses, gathered way before the winds of the north-east monsoon. As they sailed out across the Yellow Sea, the last flickering lights of Tanggu faded into the darkness while the sailors clustered at the rails, straining for a last sight of their homeland. In the long months they would spend travelling the oceans, their only remaining links to the land would be memories, keepsakes, and the scented roses many brought with them, growing them in pots and even sharing their water rations with them. The majority of those seamen at the rails would never see China again. Many would die, many others would be shipwrecked or left behind to set up colonies on foreign shores. Those who eventually returned after two and a half years at sea would find their country convulsed and transformed beyond all recognition.

4

CHRISTOPHER COLUMBUS
Letter to King Ferdinand and Queen Isabella

Christopher Columbus sent this letter to his royal backers, King Ferdinand and Queen Isabella of Spain, on his return in March 1493 from his first voyage across the Atlantic. (See Map 1.3.)

An Italian sailor from Genoa, Columbus, in 1483–1484, tried to convince King John II of Portugal to underwrite his plan to sail across the western ocean to the spice-rich East Indies. Relying on a Florentine map that used Marco Polo's overstated distance from Venice to Japan across Asia and an understated estimate of the circumference of the globe, Columbus believed that Japan lay only 2,500 miles west of the Portuguese Azores. King John II rejected the proposal because more accurate estimates indicated that sailing around Africa was the shorter route, a feat achieved in 1488 by Portuguese navigator Bartolomeu Dias.

Less knowledgeable about navigation, the new Spanish monarchs, Ferdinand and Isabella, supported Columbus and financed his plan to sail west to Asia. In four voyages, Columbus touched a number of Caribbean islands and the coast of Central America, settled Spaniards on Hispaniola (Española), and began to create one of the largest

---

"First Voyage of Columbus," in *The Four Voyages of Columbus*, ed. Cecil Jane (New York: Dover, 1988), 1–18.

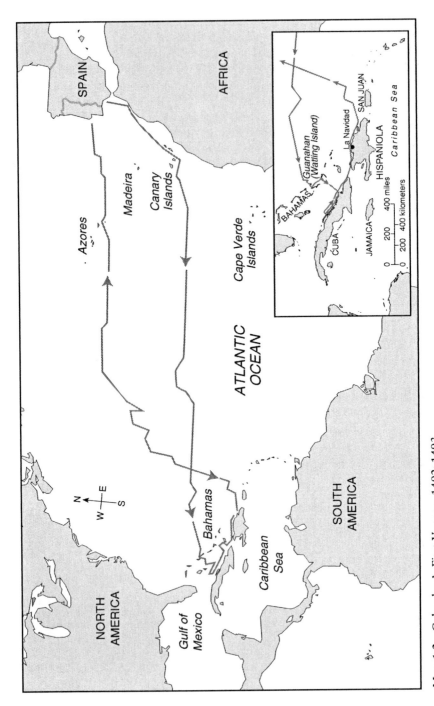

Map 1.3 Columbus's First Voyage, 1492–1493.
Source: Lawrence V. Mott.

empires in world history for Spain — all the while thinking he was near China and Japan, in the realm of the Great Khan whom Marco Polo had met and who had died hundreds of years earlier.

In what ways was the voyage of Columbus similar to that of Zheng He? In what ways was it different? How were the relationships of the explorers with their kings similar and different? Were the motives driving Chinese and European expansion more alike or different?

Thinking Historically

Because this document comes from the period we are studying and is written by Columbus himself, it is a primary source. Primary sources, like this letter and Zheng He's inscription, have a great sense of immediacy and can often "transport" us to the past intellectually. However, involvement when reading does not always lead to understanding, so it is important to think critically about the source and the writer's intended audience as you read. First we must determine the source of the document. Where does it come from? Is it original? If not, is it a copy or a translation? Next, we must determine who wrote it, when it was written, and for what purpose. After answering these questions, we are able to read the document with a critical eye, which leads to greater understanding.

The original letter by Columbus has been lost. This selection is an English translation based on three different printed Spanish versions of the letter. So this text is a reconstruction, not an original, though it is believed to be quite close to the original.

The original letter was probably composed during a relaxed time on the return voyage before its date of February 15, 1493 — possibly as early as the middle of January — and sent to the Spanish monarchs from Lisbon in order to reach them by the time Columbus arrived in Barcelona.

What does Columbus want to impart to Ferdinand and Isabella? First and foremost, he wants them to know that he reached the Indies, that the voyage was a success. And so, the letter's opening sentence tells us something that Columbus certainly did not intend or know. We learn that on his return in 1493, Columbus thought he had been to the Indies when in fact he had not. (It is due to Columbus's confusion that we call the islands he visited the West Indies and Native Americans "Indians.")

Knowing what the author wants a reader to believe is useful information because it serves as a point of reference for other statements the author makes. The success of Columbus's voyage is a case in point. Columbus does not admit to the loss of one of his ships in his letter, nor does he explain fully why he had to build a fort at Navidad and leave some of his crew there, returning home without them. Clearly, Columbus had reason to worry that his voyage would be viewed as a failure. He had not found the gold mines he sought or the Asian cities described by Marco Polo. He thought he had discovered many spices, though only the chili peppers were new. Notice, as you read this letter, how Columbus presents his voyage in the best light.

Aside from what Columbus intends, what facts do you learn from the letter about Columbus, his first voyage, and his encounter with the New World? What seems to drive Columbus to do what he does? What is Columbus's attitude toward the "Indians"? What does Columbus's letter tell us about the society and culture of the Taino* — the people he met in the Caribbean?

Sir, As I know that you will be pleased at the great victory with which Our Lord has crowned my voyage, I write this to you, from which you will learn how in thirty-three days, I passed from the Canary Islands to the Indies with the fleet which the most illustrious king and queen, our sovereigns, gave to me. And there I found very many islands filled with people innumerable, and of them all I have taken possession for their highnesses, by proclamation made and with the royal standard unfurled, and no opposition was offered to me. To the first island which I found, I gave the name *San Salvador*, in remembrance of the Divine Majesty, Who has marvellously bestowed all this; the Indians call it "Guanahani."† To the second, I gave the name *Isla de Santa María de Concepción*; to the third, *Fernandina*; to the fourth, *Isabella*; to the fifth, *Isla Juana*, and so to each one I gave a new name.

When I reached Juana, I followed its coast to the westward, and I found it to be so extensive that I thought that it must be the mainland, the province of Catayo. And since there were neither towns nor villages on the seashore, but only small hamlets, with the people which I could not have speech, because they all fled immediately, I went forward on the same course, thinking that I should not fail to find great cities and towns. And, at the end of many leagues, seeing that there was no change and that the coast was bearing me northwards, which I wished to avoid, since winter was already beginning and I proposed to make from it to the south, and as moreover the wind was carrying me forward, I determined not to wait for a change in the weather and retraced my path as far as a certain harbour known to me. And from that point, I sent two men inland to learn if there were a king or great cities. They travelled three days' journey and found an infinity of small hamlets and people without number, but nothing of importance. For this reason, they returned.

I understood sufficiently from other Indians, whom I had already taken, that this land was nothing but an island. And therefore I fol-

*TY noh
†gwah nah HAH nee

lowed its coast eastwards for one hundred and seven leagues to the point where it ended. And from that cape, I saw another island, distant eighteen leagues from the former, to the east, to which I at once gave the name "Española." And I went there and followed its northern coast, as I had in the case of Juana, to the eastward for one hundred and eighty-eight great leagues in a straight line. This island and all the others are very fertile to a limitless degree, and this island is extremely so. In it there are many harbours on the coast of the sea, beyond comparison with others which I know in Christendom, and many rivers, good and large, which is marvellous. Its lands are high, and there are in it very many sierras and very lofty mountains, beyond comparison with the island of Teneriffe. All are most beautiful, of a thousand shapes, and all are accessible and filled with trees of a thousand kinds and tall, and they seem to touch the sky. And I am told that they never lose their foliage, as I can understand, for I saw them as green and as lovely as they are in Spain in May, and some of them were flowering, some bearing fruit, and some in another stage, according to their nature. And the nightingale was singing and other birds of a thousand kinds in the month of November there where I went. There are six or eight kinds of palm, which are a wonder to behold on account of their beautiful variety, but so are the other trees and fruits and plants. In it are marvellous pine groves, and there are very large tracts of cultivatable lands, and there is honey, and there are birds of many kinds and fruits in great diversity. In the interior are mines of metals, and the population is without number. Española is a marvel.

The sierras and mountains, the plains and arable lands and pastures, are so lovely and rich for planting and sowing, for breeding cattle of every kind, for building towns and villages. The harbours of the sea here are such as cannot be believed to exist unless they have been seen, and so with the rivers, many and great, and good waters, the majority of which contain gold. In the trees and fruits and plants, there is a great difference from those of Juana. In this island, there are many spices and great mines of gold and of other metals.

The people of this island, and of all the other islands which I have found and of which I have information, all go naked, men and women, as their mothers bore them, although some women cover a single place with the leaf of a plant or with a net of cotton which they make for the purpose. They have no iron or steel or weapons, nor are they fitted to use them, not because they are not well built men and of handsome stature, but because they are very marvellously timorous. They have no other arms than weapons made of canes, cut in seeding time, to the ends of which they fix a small sharpened stick. And they do not dare to make use of these, for many times it has happened that I have sent ashore two or three men to some town to have speech, and countless people have come out to them, and as soon as they have seen my men approaching they have fled, even a father not waiting for his son. And this, not because ill has been done to anyone; on the contrary, at every point where I have been and have been able to have speech, I have given to them of all that I had, such as cloth and many other things, without receiving anything for it; but so they are, incurably timid. It is true that, after they have been reassured and have lost their fear, they are so guileless and so generous with all they possess, that no one would believe it who has not seen it. They never refuse anything which they possess, if it be asked of them; on the contrary, they invite anyone to share it, and display as much love as if they would give their hearts, and whether the thing be of value or whether it be of small price, at once with whatever trifle of whatever kind it may be that is given to them, with that they are content. I forbade that they should be given things so worthless as fragments of broken crockery and scraps of broken glass, and ends of straps, although when they were able to get them, they fancied that they possessed the best jewel in the world. So it was found that a sailor for a strap received gold to the weight of two and a half *castellanos*, and others much more for other things which were worth much less. As for new *blancas*, for them they would give everything which they had, although it might be two or three *castellanos'* weight of gold or an *arroba* or two of spun cotton. . . . They took even the pieces of the broken hoops of the wine barrels and, like savages, gave what they had, so that it seemed to me to be wrong and I forbade it. And I gave a thousand handsome good things, which I had brought, in order that they might conceive affection, and more than that, might become Christians and be inclined to the love and service of their highnesses and of the whole Castilian nation, and strive to aid us and to give us of the things which they have in abundance and which are necessary to us. And they do not know any creed and are not idolaters; only they all believe that power and good are in the heavens, and they are very firmly convinced that I, with these ships and men, came from the heavens, and in this belief they everywhere received me, after they had overcome their fear. And this does not come because they are ignorant; on the contrary, they are of a very acute intelligence and are men who navigate all those seas, so that it is amazing how good an account they give of everything, but it is because they have never seen people clothed or ships of such a kind.

And as soon as I arrived in the Indies, in the first island which I found, I took by force some of them, in order that they might learn and give me information of that which there is in those parts, and so it was that they soon understood us, and we them, either by speech or signs, and they have been very serviceable. I still take them with me, and they are always assured that I come from Heaven, for all the intercourse which they have had with me; and they were the first to announce this wherever I went, and the others went running from house to house and to the neighbouring towns, with loud cries of, "Come! Come to see the people from Heaven!" So all, men and women alike, when their minds were set at rest concerning us, came, so that not one, great or small, remained behind, and all brought something to eat and drink, which they gave with extraordinary affection. In all the island, they have very many canoes, like rowing *fustas*, some larger, some smaller, and some are larger than a *fusta* of eighteen benches. They are not so broad, because they are made of a single log of wood, but a *fusta* would not keep up with them in rowing, since their speed is a thing incredible. And in these they navigate among all those islands, which are innumerable, and carry their goods. One of these canoes I have seen with seventy and eighty men in her, and each one with his oar.

In all these islands, I saw no great diversity in the appearance of the people or in their manners and language. On the contrary, they all understand one another, which is a very curious thing, on account of which I hope that their highnesses will determine upon their conversion to our holy faith, towards which they are very inclined.

I have already said how I have gone one hundred and seven leagues in a straight line from west to east along the seashore of the island Juana, and as a result of that voyage, I can say that this island is larger than England and Scotland together, for, beyond these one hundred and seven leagues, there remain to the westward two provinces to which I have not gone. One of these provinces they call "Avan," and there the people are born with tails; and these provinces cannot have a length of less than fifty or sixty leagues, as I could understand from those Indians whom I have and who know all the islands.

The other, Española, has a circumference greater than all Spain, from Colibre, by the sea-coast, to Fuenterabia in Vizcaya, since I voyaged along one side one hundred and eighty-eight great leagues in a straight line from west to east. It is a land to be desired and, seen, it is never to be left. And in it, although of all I have taken possession for their highnesses and all are more richly endowed than I know how, or am able, to say, and I hold them all for their highnesses, so that they may dispose of them as, and as absolutely as, of the kingdoms of Castile, in this Española, in the situation most convenient and in the best position for the mines of gold and for all intercourse as well with the mainland here as with that there, belonging to the Grand Khan, where will be great trade and gain, I have taken possession of a large town, to which I gave the name *Villa de Navidad*, and in it I have made fortifications and a fort, which now will by this time be entirely finished, and I have left in it sufficient men for such a purpose with arms and artillery and provisions for more than a year, and a *fusta*, and one, a master of all seacraft, to build others, and great friendship with the king of that land, so much so, that he was proud to call me, and to treat me as, a brother. And even if he were to change his attitude to one of hostility towards these men, he and his do not know what arms are and they go naked, as I have already said, and are the most timorous people that there are in the world, so that the men whom I have left there alone would suffice to destroy all that land, and the island is without danger for their persons, if they know how to govern themselves.

In all these islands, it seems to me that all men are content with one woman, and to their chief or king they give as many as twenty. It appears to me that the women work more than the men. And I have not been able to learn if they hold private property; what seemed to me to appear was that, in that which one had, all took a share, especially of eatable things.

In these islands I have so far found no human monstrosities, as many expected, but on the contrary the whole population is very well-formed, nor are they negros as in Guinea, but their hair is flowing, and they are not born where there is intense force in the rays of the sun; it is true that the sun has there great power, although it is distant from the equinoctial line twenty-six degrees. In these islands, where there are high mountains, the cold was severe this winter, but they endure it, being used to it and with the help of meats which they eat with many and extremely hot spices. As I have found no monsters, so I have had no report of any, except in an island "Quaris," the second at the coming into the Indies, which is inhabited by a people who are regarded in all the islands as very fierce and who eat human flesh. They have many canoes with which they range through all the islands of India and pillage and take as many as they can. They are no more malformed than the others, except that they have the custom of wearing their hair long like women, and they use bows and arrows of the same cane stems, with a small piece of wood at the end, owing to lack of iron which they do not possess. They are ferocious among these other people who are cowardly to an excessive degree, but I make no more account of them than of the rest. These are those who have intercourse with the women of "Matinino," which is the first island met on the way from Spain to the Indies, in which there is not a man. These women engage in no feminine occupation, but use bows and arrows of cane, like those already mentioned, and they arm and protect themselves with plates of copper, of which they have much.

In another island, which they assure me is larger than Española, the people have no hair. In it, there is gold incalculable, and from it and from the other islands, I bring with me Indians as evidence.

In conclusion, to speak only of that which has been accomplished on this voyage, which was so hasty, their highnesses can see that I will give them as much gold as they may need, if their highnesses will render me very slight assistance; moreover, spice and cotton, as much as their highnesses shall command; and mastic, as much as they shall order to be shipped and which, up to now, has been found only in Greece, in the island of Chios, and the Seignory sells it for what it pleases; and aloe wood, as much as they shall order to be shipped, and slaves, as many as they shall order to be shipped and who will be from the idolaters. And I believe that I have found rhubarb and cinnamon, and I shall find a thousand other things of value, which the people whom I have left there will have discovered, for I have not delayed at any point, so far as the wind allowed me to sail, except in the town of Navidad, in order to leave it secured and well established, and in truth, I should have done much more, if the ships had served me, as reason demanded.

This is enough . . . and the eternal God, our Lord, Who gives to all those who walk in His way triumph over things which appear to be impossible, and this was notably one; for, although men have talked or have written of these lands, all was conjectural, without suggestion of ocular evidence, but amounted only to this, that those who heard for the most part listened and judged it to be rather a fable than as having any vestige of truth. So that, since Our Redeemer has given this victory to our most illustrious king and queen, and to their renowned kingdoms, in so great a matter, for this all Christendom ought to feel delight and make great feasts and give solemn thanks to the Holy Trinity with many solemn prayers for the great exaltation which they shall have, in the turning of so many peoples to our holy faith, and afterwards for temporal benefits, for not only Spain but all Christians will have hence refreshment and gain.

This, in accordance with that which has been accomplished, thus briefly.

Done in the caravel,[1] off the Canary Islands, on the fifteenth of February, in the year one thousand four hundred and ninety-three.

At your orders.   El Almirante.

After having written this, and being in the sea of Castile, there came on me so great a south-south-west wind, that I was obliged to lighten ship. But I ran here to-day into this port of Lisbon, which was the greatest marvel in the world, whence I decided to write to their highnesses. In all the Indies, I have always found weather like May; where I went in thirty-three days and I had returned in twenty-eight, save for these storms which have detained me for fourteen days, beating about in this sea. Here all the sailors say that never has there been so bad a winter nor so many ships lost.

Done on the fourth day of March.

---

[1]Sailing ship, in this case the *Santa María*. [Ed.]

5

KIRKPATRICK SALE

From The Conquest of Paradise

In this selection from his popular study of Columbus, Sale is concerned with Columbus's attitude toward nature in the New World. Do you think Sale's comments are accurate? Are they insightful? Do they help us understand Columbus?

Sale regards Columbus as a symbol of European expansion. Let us for the moment grant him that. If Columbus is distinctly European, what is Sale saying about European expansion? How and what does Sale add to your understanding of the similarities and differences between Chinese and European expansion?

Was Columbus much different from Zheng He? Or were the areas and peoples they visited causes for different responses?

Thinking Historically

Clearly, this selection is a secondary source; Sale is a modern writer, not a fifteenth-century contemporary of Columbus. Still, you will not have to read very far into the selection to realize that Sale has a distinct point of view. Secondary sources, like primary ones, should be analyzed for bias and perspective and should identify the author's interpretation.

Sale is an environmentalist and a cultural critic. Do his beliefs and values hinder his understanding of Columbus, or do they inform and illuminate aspects of Columbus that might otherwise be missed? Does Sale help you recognize things you would not have seen on your own, or does he persuade you to see things that might not truly be there?

Notice how Sale uses primary sources in his text. He quotes from Columbus's journal and his letter to King Ferdinand and Queen Isabella. Do these quotes help you understand Columbus, or do they simply support Sale's argument? What do you think about Sale's use of the Spanish "Colón"* for "Columbus"? Does Sale "take possession" of Columbus by, in effect, "renaming" him for modern readers? Is the effect humanizing or debunking?

*koh LOHN

Kirkpatrick Sale, *The Conquest of Paradise* (New York: Penguin, 1991), 92–104.

Notice how Sale sometimes calls attention to what the primary source did *not* say rather than what it did say. Is this a legitimate way to understand someone, or is Sale projecting a twentieth-century perspective on Columbus to make a point?

Toward the end of the selection, Sale extends his criticism beyond Columbus to include others. Who are the others? What is the effect of this larger criticism?

Admiral Colón spent a total of ninety-six days exploring the lands he encountered on the far side of the Ocean Sea — four rather small coralline islands in the Bahamian chain and two substantial coastlines of what he finally acknowledged were larger islands — every one of which he "took possession of" in the name of his Sovereigns.

The first he named San Salvador, no doubt as much in thanksgiving for its welcome presence after more than a month at sea as for the Son of God whom it honored; the second he called Santa María de la Concepcíon, after the Virgin whose name his flagship bore; and the third and fourth he called Fernandina and Isabela, for his patrons, honoring Aragon before Castile for reasons never explained (possibly protocol, possibly in recognition of the chief sources of backing for the voyage). The first of the two large and very fertile islands he called Juana, which Fernando [Columbus's son] says was done in honor of Prince Juan, heir to the Castilian throne, but just as plausibly might have been done in recognition of Princess Juana, the unstable child who eventually carried on the line; the second he named la Ysla Española, the "Spanish Island," because it resembled (though he felt it surpassed in beauty) the lands of Castile.

It was not that the islands were in need of names, mind you, nor indeed that Colón was ignorant of the names that native peoples had already given them, for he frequently used those original names before endowing them with his own. Rather, the process of bestowing new names went along with "taking possession of" those parts of the world he deemed suitable for Spanish ownership, showing the royal banners, erecting various crosses, and pronouncing certain oaths and pledges. If this was presumption, it had an honored heritage: It was Adam who was charged by his Creator with the task of naming "every living creature," including the product of his own rib, in the course of establishing "dominion over" them.

Colón went on to assign no fewer than sixty-two other names on the geography of the islands — capes, points, mountains, ports — with a blithe assurance suggesting that in his (and Europe's) perception the act of name-giving was in some sense a talisman of conquest, a rite that changed raw neutral stretches of far-off earth into extensions of

Europe. The process began slowly, even haltingly — he forgot to record, for example, until four days afterward that he named the landfall island San Salvador — but by the time he came to Española at the end he went on a naming spree, using more than two-thirds of all the titles he concocted on that one coastline. On certain days it became almost a frenzy: on December 6 he named six places, on the nineteenth six more, and on January 11 no fewer than ten — eight capes, a point, and a mountain. It is almost as if, as he sailed along the last of the islands, he was determined to leave his mark on it the only way he knew how, and thus to establish his authority — and by extension Spain's — even, as with baptism, to make it thus sanctified, and real, and official. . . .

This business of naming and "possessing" foreign islands was by no means casual. The Admiral took it very seriously, pointing out that "it was my wish to bypass no island without taking possession" (October 15) and that "in all regions [I] always left a cross standing" (November 16) as a mark of Christian dominance. There even seem to have been certain prescriptions for it (the instructions from the Sovereigns speak of "the administering of the oath and the performing of the rites prescribed in such cases"), and Rodrigo de Escobedo was sent along as secretary of the fleet explicitly to witness and record these events in detail.

But consider the implications of this act and the questions it raises again about what was in the Sovereigns' minds, what in Colón's. Why would the Admiral assume that these territories were in some way *un*possessed — even by those clearly inhabiting them — and thus available for Spain to claim? Why would he not think twice about the possibility that some considerable potentate — the Grand Khan of China, for example, whom he later acknowledged (November 6) "must be" the ruler of Española — might descend upon him at any moment with a greater military force than his three vessels commanded and punish him for his territorial presumption? Why would he make the ceremony of possession his very first act on shore, even before meeting the inhabitants or exploring the environs, or finding out if anybody there objected to being thus possessed — particularly if they actually owned the great treasures he hoped would be there? No European would have imagined that anyone — three small boatloads of Indians, say — could come up to a European shore or island and "take possession" of it, nor would a European imagine marching up to some part of North Africa or the Middle East and claiming sovereignty there with impunity. Why were these lands thought to be different?

Could there be any reason for the Admiral to assume he had reached "unclaimed" shores, new lands that lay far from the domains of any of the potentates of the East? Can that really have been in his mind — or can it all be explained as simple Eurocentrism, or Eurosuperiority, mixed with cupidity and naiveté? . . .

Once safely "possessed,"[1] San Salvador was open for inspection. Now the Admiral turned his attention for the first time to the "naked people" staring at him on the beach — he did not automatically give them a name, interestingly enough, and it would be another six days before he decided what he might call them — and tried to win their favor with his trinkets.

> They all go around as naked as their mothers bore them; and also the women, although I didn't see more than one really young girl. All that I saw were young people [*mancebos*], none of them more than 30 years old. They are very well built, with very handsome bodies and very good faces; their hair [is] coarse, almost like the silk of a horse's tail, and short. They wear their hair over their eyebrows, except for a little in the back that they wear long and never cut. Some of them paint themselves black (and they are the color of the Canary Islanders, neither black nor white), and some paint themselves white, and some red, and some with what they find. And some paint their faces, and some of them the whole body, and some the eyes only, and some of them only the nose.

It may fairly be called the birth of American anthropology.

A crude anthropology, of course, as superficial as Colón's descriptions always were when his interest was limited, but simple and straightforward enough, with none of the fable and fantasy that characterized many earlier (and even some later) accounts of new-found peoples. There was no pretense to objectivity, or any sense that these people might be representatives of a culture equal to, or in any way a model for, Europe's. Colón immediately presumed the inferiority of the natives, not merely because (a sure enough sign) they were naked, but because (his society could have no surer measure) they seemed so technologically backward. "It appeared to me that these people were very poor in everything," he wrote on that first day, and, worse still, "they have no iron." And they went on to prove their inferiority to the Admiral by being ignorant of even such a basic artifact of European life as a sword: "They bear no arms, nor are they acquainted with them," he wrote, "for I showed them swords and they grasped them by the blade and cut themselves through ignorance." Thus did European arms spill the first drops of native blood on the sands of the New World, accompanied not with a gasp of compassion but with a smirk of superiority.

Then, just six sentences further on, Colón clarified what this inferiority meant in his eyes:

[1]Given Spanish names. [Ed.]

They ought to be good servants and of good intelligence [*ingenio*]. . . .
I believe that they would easily be made Christians, because it seemed
to me that they had no religion. Our Lord pleasing, I will carry off six
of them at my departure to Your Highnesses, in order that they may
learn to speak.

No clothes, no arms, no possessions, no iron, and now no religion —
not even speech: hence they were fit to be servants, and captives. It may
fairly be called the birth of American slavery.

Whether or not the idea of slavery was in Colón's mind all along is
uncertain, although he did suggest he had had experience as a slave
trader in Africa (November 12) and he certainly knew of Portuguese
plantation slavery in the Madeiras and Spanish slavery of Guanches in
the Canaries. But it seems to have taken shape early and grown ever
firmer as the weeks went on and as he captured more and more of the
helpless natives. At one point he even sent his crew ashore to kidnap
"seven head of women, young ones and adults, and three small children"; the expression of such callousness led the Spanish historian Salvador de Madariaga to remark, "It would be difficult to find a starker
utterance of utilitarian subjection of man by man than this passage
[whose] form is no less devoid of human feeling than its substance."

To be sure, Colón knew nothing about these people he encountered
and considered enslaving, and he was hardly trained to find out very
much, even if he was moved to care. But they were in fact members of
an extensive, populous, and successful people whom Europe, using its
own peculiar taxonomy, subsequently called "Taino" (or "Taíno"),
their own word for "good" or "noble," and their response when asked
who they were. They were related distantly by both language and culture to the Arawak people of the South American mainland, but it is
misleading (and needlessly imprecise) to call them Arawaks, as historians are wont to do, when the term "Taino" better establishes their ethnic and historical distinctiveness. They had migrated to the islands from
the mainland at about the time of the birth of Christ, occupying the
three large islands we now call the Greater Antilles and arriving at
Guanahani (Colón's San Salvador) and the end of the Bahamian chain
probably sometime around A.D. 900. There they displaced an earlier
people, the Guanahacabibes (sometimes called Guanahatabeys), who
by the time of the European discovery occupied only the western third
of Cuba and possibly remote corners of Española; and there, probably
in the early fifteenth century, they eventually confronted another people
moving up the islands from the mainland, the Caribs, whose culture
eventually occupied a dozen small islands of what are called the Lesser
Antilles.

The Tainos were not nearly so backward as Colón assumed from
their lack of dress. (It might be said that it was the Europeans, who

generally kept clothed head to foot during the day despite temperatures regularly in the eighties, who were the more unsophisticated in garmenture — especially since the Tainos, as Colón later noted, also used their body paint to prevent sunburn.) Indeed, they had achieved a means of living in a balanced and fruitful harmony with their natural surroundings that any society might well have envied. They had, to begin with, a not unsophisticated technology that made exact use of their available resources, two parts of which were so impressive that they were picked up and adopted by the European invaders: *canoa* (canoes) that were carved and fire-burned from large silk-cotton trees, "all in one piece, and wonderfully made" (October 13), some of which were capable of carrying up to 150 passengers; and *hamaca* (hammocks) that were "like nets of cotton" (October 17) and may have been a staple item of trade with Indian tribes as far away as the Florida mainland. Their houses were not only spacious and clean — as the Europeans noted with surprise and appreciation, used as they were to the generally crowded and slovenly hovels and huts of south European peasantry — but more apropos, remarkably resistant to hurricanes; the circular walls were made of strong cane poles set deep and close together ("as close as the fingers of a hand," Colón noted), the conical roofs of branches and vines tightly interwoven on a frame of smaller poles and covered with heavy palm leaves. Their artifacts and jewelry, with the exception of a few gold trinkets and ornaments, were based largely on renewable materials, including bracelets and necklaces of coral, shells, bone, and stone, embroidered cotton belts, woven baskets, carved statues and chairs, wooden and shell utensils, and pottery of variously intricate decoration depending on period and place.

Perhaps the most sophisticated, and most carefully integrated, part of their technology was their agricultural system, extraordinarily productive and perfectly adapted to the conditions of the island environment. It was based primarily on fields of knee-high mounds, called *conucos*, planted with *yuca* (sometimes called manioc), *batata* (sweet potato), and various squashes and beans grown all together in multicrop harmony: The root crops were excellent in resisting erosion and producing minerals and potash, the leaf crops effective in providing shade and moisture, and the mound configurations largely resistant to erosion and flooding and adaptable to almost all topographic conditions including steep hillsides. Not only was the *conuco* system environmentally appropriate — "conuco agriculture seems to have provided an exceptionally ecologically well-balanced and protective form of land use," according to David Watts's recent and authoritative *West Indies* — but it was also highly productive, surpassing in yields anything known in Europe at the time, with labor that amounted to hardly more than two or three hours a week, and in continuous yearlong harvest. The pioneering American geographical scholar Carl Sauer calls

Taino agriculture "productive as few parts of the world," giving the "highest returns of food in continuous supply by the simplest methods and modest labor," and adds, with a touch of regret, "The white man never fully appreciated the excellent combination of plants that were grown in conucos."

In their arts of government the Tainos seem to have achieved a parallel sort of harmony. Most villages were small (ten to fifteen families) and autonomous, although many apparently recognized loose allegiances with neighboring villages, and they were governed by a hereditary official called a *kaseke* (*cacique,** in the Spanish form), something of a cross between an arbiter and a prolocutor, supported by advisers and elders. So little a part did violence play in their system that they seem, remarkably, to have been a society without war (at least we know of no war music or signals or artifacts, and no evidence of intertribal combats) and even without overt conflict (Las Casas reports that no Spaniard ever saw two Tainos fighting). And here we come to what was obviously the Tainos' outstanding cultural achievement, a proficiency in the social arts that led those who first met them to comment unfailingly on their friendliness, their warmth, their openness, and above all — so striking to those of an acquisitive culture — their generosity.

"They are the best people in the world and above all the gentlest," Colón recorded in his *Journal* (December 16), and from first to last he was astonished at their kindness:

> They became so much our friends that it was a marvel. . . . They traded and gave everything they had, with good will [October 12].
>
> I sent the ship's boat ashore for water, and they very willingly showed my people where the water was, and they themselves carried the full barrels to the boat, and took great delight in pleasing us [October 16].
>
> They are very gentle and without knowledge of what is evil; nor do they murder or steal [November 12].
>
> Your Highnesses may believe that in all the world there can be no better or gentler people . . . for neither better people nor land can there be. . . . All the people show the most singular loving behavior and they speak pleasantly [December 24].
>
> I assure Your Highnesses that I believe that in all the world there is no better people nor better country. They love their neighbors as themselves, and they have the sweetest talk in the world, and are gentle and always laughing [December 25].

Even if one allows for some exaggeration — Colón was clearly trying to convince Ferdinand and Isabella that his Indians could be easily

*kah SEEK

conquered and converted, should that be the Sovereigns' wish — it is obvious that the Tainos exhibited a manner of social discourse that quite impressed the rough Europeans. But that was not high among the traits of "civilized" nations, as Colón and Europe understood it, and it counted for little in the Admiral's assessment of these people. However struck he was with such behavior, he would not have thought that it was the mark of a benign and harmonious society, or that from it another culture might learn. For him it was something like the wondrous behavior of children, the naive guilelessness of prelapsarian[2] creatures who knew no better how to bargain and chaffer and cheat than they did to dress themselves: "For a lacepoint they gave good pieces of gold the size of two fingers" (January 6), and "They even took pieces of the broken hoops of the wine casks and, like beasts [*como besti*], gave what they had" (Santangel Letter)[3]. Like beasts; such innocence was not human.

It is to be regretted that the Admiral, unable to see past their nakedness, as it were, knew not the real virtues of the people he confronted. For the Tainos' lives were in many ways as idyllic as their surroundings, into which they fit with such skill and comfort. They were well fed and well housed, without poverty or serious disease. They enjoyed considerable leisure, given over to dancing, singing, ballgames, and sex, and expressed themselves artistically in basketry, woodworking, pottery, and jewelry. They lived in general harmony and peace, without greed or covetousness or theft. . . .

It is perhaps only natural that Colón should devote his initial attention to the handsome, naked, naive islanders, but it does seem peculiar that he pays almost no attention, especially in the early days, to the spectacular scenery around them. Here he was, in the middle of an old-growth tropical forest the likes of which he could not have imagined before, its trees reaching sixty or seventy feet into the sky, more varieties than he knew how to count much less name, exhibiting a lushness that stood in sharp contrast to the sparse and denuded lands he had known in the Mediterranean, hearing a melodious multiplicity of bird songs and parrot calls — why was it not an occasion of wonder, excitement, and the sheer joy at nature in its full, arrogant abundance? But there is not a word of that: He actually said nothing about the physical surroundings on the first day, aside from a single phrase about "very green trees" and "many streams," and on the second managed only that short sentence about a big island with a big lake and green trees. Indeed, for the whole two weeks of the first leg of his voyage through the Bahamas to Cuba, he devoted only a third of the lines of descrip-

---

[2]Before the Fall. In other words, before the time, according to the Old Testament, when Adam and Eve sinned and were banished by God from the Garden of Eden. [Ed.]

[3]Santangel was the minister of Ferdinand and Isabella who received the letter (see selection 4).

tion to the phenomena around him. And there are some natural sights he seems not to have noticed at all: He did not mention (except in terms of navigation) the nighttime heavens, the sharp, glorious configurations of stars that he must have seen virtually every night of his journey, many for the first time.

Eventually Colón succumbed to the islands' natural charms as he sailed on — how could he not? — and began to wax warmly about how "these islands are very green and fertile and the air very sweet" (October 15), with "trees which were more beautiful to see than any other thing that has ever been seen" (October 17), and "so good and sweet a smell of flowers or trees from the land" (October 19). But his descriptions are curiously vapid and vague, the language opaque and lifeless:

> The other island, which is very big [October 15] . . . this island is very large [October 16] . . . these islands are very green and fertile [October 15] . . . this land is the best and most fertile [October 17] . . . in it many plants and trees . . . if the others are very beautiful, this is more so [October 19] . . . here are some great lagoons . . . big and little birds of all sorts . . . if the others already seen are very beautiful and green and fertile, this one is much more so [October 21] . . . full of very good harbors and deep rivers [October 28].

You begin to see the Admiral's problem: He cares little about the features of nature, at least the ones he doesn't use for sailing, and even when he admires them he has little experience in assessing them and less acquaintance with a vocabulary to describe them. To convey the lush density and stately grandeur of those tropical forests, for example, he had little more than the modifiers "green" and "very": "very green trees" (October 12), "trees very green" (October 13), "trees . . . so green and with leaves like those of Castile" (October 14), "very green and very big trees" (October 19), "large groves are very green" (October 21), "trees . . . beautiful and green" (October 28). And when he began to be aware of the diversity among those trees, he was still unable to make meaningful distinctions: "All the trees are as different from ours as day from night" (October 17), "trees of a thousand kinds" (October 21), "a thousand sorts of trees" (October 23), "trees . . . different from ours" (October 28), "trees of a thousand sorts" (November 14), "trees of a thousand kinds" (December 6).

Such was his ignorance — a failing he repeatedly bemoaned ("I don't recognize them, which gives me great grief," October 19) — that when he did stop to examine a species he often had no idea what he was looking at. "I saw many trees very different from ours," he wrote on October 16, "and many of them have branches of many kinds, and all on one trunk, and one twig is of one kind and another of another, and so different that it is the greatest wonder in the world how much diversity there is of one kind from the other. That is to say, one branch has leaves like a cane, and another like mastic, and thus on one tree five or six kinds, and all so different." There is no such tree in existence, much less "many of them," and never was: Why would anyone imagine, or so contrive, such a thing to be?

Colón's attempts to identify species were likewise frequently wrongheaded, usually imputing to them commercial worth that they did not have, as with the worthless "aloes" he loaded such quantities of. The "amaranth" he identified on October 28 and the "oaks" and "arbutus" of November 25 are species that do not grow in the Caribbean; the "mastic" he found on November 5 and loaded on board to sell in Spain was gumbo-limbo, commercially worthless. (On the other hand, one of the species of flora he deemed of no marketable interest — "weeds [*tizon*] in their hands to drink in the fragrant smoke" [November 6] — was tobacco.) Similarly, the "whales" he spotted on October 16 must have been simply large fish, the "geese" he saw on November 6 and again on December 22 were ducks, the "nightingales" that kept delighting him (November 6; December 7, 13) do not exist in the Americas, and the skulls of "cows" he identified on October 29 were probably not those of land animals but of manatees.

This all seems a little sad, revealing a man rather lost in a world that he cannot come to know, a man with a "geographic and naturalistic knowledge that doesn't turn out to be very deep or nearly complete," and "a limited imagination and a capacity for comparisons conditioned by a not very broad geographic culture," in the words of Gaetano Ferro, a Columbus scholar and professor of geography at the University of Genoa. One could not of course have expected that an adventurer and sailor of this era would also be a naturalist, or necessarily even have some genuine interest in or curiosity about the natural world, but it is a disappointment nonetheless that the Discoverer of the New World turns out to be quite so simple, quite so inexperienced, in the ways of discovering his environment.

Colón's limitations, I hasten to say, were not his alone; they were of his culture, and they would be found in the descriptions of many others — Vespucci, Cortés, Hawkins, Juet, Cartier, Champlain, Ralegh — in the century of discovery to follow. They are the source of what the distinguished English historian J. H. Elliott has called "the problem of description" faced by Europeans confronting the uniqueness of the New World: "So often the physical appearance of the New World is either totally ignored or else described in the flattest and most conventional phraseology. This off-hand treatment of nature contrasts strikingly with the many precise and acute descriptions of the native inhabitants. It is as if the American landscape is seen as no more than a backcloth against which the strange and perennially fascinating peoples of the New World are dutifully grouped." The reason, Elliott thinks, and this is telling, may be "a lack of interest among sixteenth-century

Europeans, and especially those of the Mediterranean world, in landscape and in nature." This lack of interest was reflected in the lack of vocabulary, the lack of that facility common to nature-based peoples whose cultures are steeped in natural imagery. Oviedo, for example, setting out to write descriptions for his *Historia general* in the next century, continually threw his hands up in the air: "Of all the things I have seen," he said at one point, "this is the one which has most left me without hope of being able to describe it in words"; or at another, "It needs to be painted by the hand of a Berruguete or some other excellent painter like him, or by Leonardo da Vinci or Andrea Mantegna, famous painters whom I knew in Italy." Like Colón, visitor after visitor to the New World seemed mind-boggled and tongue-tied trying to convey the wonders before them, and about the only color they seem to have eyes for is green — and not very many shades of that, either. . . .

REFLECTIONS

It is difficult to ignore moral issues when considering explorations and explorers. The prefix *great* is used liberally, and words like *discovery* and *courage* readily fit when describing "firsts" and "unknowns." However, celebratory images, national myths, and heroic biographies inevitably engender the reverse. Ye Jun and a new breed of Beijing historians condemn Zheng He for military suppression. Kirkpatrick Sale charges Columbus with arrogance, ignorance, and insufficient curiosity.

On the matter of preparation, the difference between the Chinese and Columbian voyages is especially striking. The floating Chinese scientific laboratories, traveling experts, sages, and interpreters contrast starkly with the lack of a single artist or naturalist on board Columbus's ships. But the inability to distinguish shades of green is not a moral failure. We might say that Columbus's voyage was premature, Zheng He's meticulously planned and prepared. Like the designers of a modern aircraft, the Chinese built in redundancies: separate compartments that could fill with water without sinking the ship, more rice and fresh water than they would need, experts to find plants that might cure diseases yet unknown. By contrast, Columbus seems like a loose cannon, unaware of where he was going or where he had been, capable of lighting a match inside a dark powder shed.

These were, and in many ways still are, the differences between Chinese and European (now Western) scientific innovation. No European could (or can) organize an enterprise on the scale of Zhu Di. No Chinese emperor had reason to sanction an experimental voyage into the unknown. In the same book from which we excerpted a noncontroversial section, Gavin Menzies argues that Zheng He's voyage of 1421 led eventually around Africa and across the Atlantic to the Americas. But in addition to the weakness of the evidence that Zheng He reached the Americas, this would have been out of character for Chinese imperial tribute missions. There were, no doubt, Chinese sailors who came upon unknown lands, possibly even across the great Pacific Ocean; but the domain of the emperor was the known world, of which he was the center. In the Europe of closely competing princes, a Columbus could hatch a personal scheme with minimal supervision and barely sufficient funding and the consequences could still be — indeed, were — momentous. (See Chapter 2.) Was such a system irresponsible? Today, as we begin to probe the heavens around us, even as we tamper with technologies that change the balance of natural forces on earth, we might consider whether the Confucian scholars of six hundred years ago were on to something when they burned the ships and destroyed all of the records of their age of great discovery.

Primary sources are not limited to written records, however. When the Chinese recently revived the memory of Zheng He, Joseph Kahn tells us, they drew on an unlikely record of Chinese settlement in east Africa: the young woman from Kenya, Mwamaka Sharifu, who claimed Chinese ancestry. Chinese-African faces on the coast of East Africa are evidence of contact, but not of contact in 1421. Combined, however, with family stories, DNA tests, local histories, archaeological finds, a single living primary source may become the basis for a new interpretation of a broader history. In the case of Mwamaka Sharifu, members of her family, and other residents of coastal Somalia and Kenya, the evidence has proved convincing.

Lawyers are fond of saying that the absence of evidence is not the same as the evidence of absence. Still, the absence of primary evidence, despite Gavin Menzies's Herculean but ultimately fruitless efforts at finding evidence of Chinese settlement in the Americas, seriously challenges his secondary interpretation. The absence of any fifteenth-century Chinese remains in the Western Hemisphere contrasts starkly with the archaeological and genetic record of the Indian Ocean. Primary sources, then, reveal by their silences as well as their inclusions. As Menzies himself notes, Zheng He's account of his voyages dots the Indian Ocean ports from Ceylon to India to Arabia to East Africa, as far as the Somali ports of Mogadishu and Brava — but no further (see Map 1.1). Sometimes primary sources are more reliable than secondary ones, if the Zheng He and Menzies selections are any indication. But both kinds of sources are necessary to develop the historical sensibility required to engage the difficult moral issues that the past and, of course, the future confront us with.

2

Atlantic World Encounters

Europeans, Americans,
and Africans, 1500–1750

HISTORICAL CONTEXT

European expansion in the Atlantic that began with Portuguese voyages along the African coast in the 1440s and Columbus's discovery of the Americas in 1492 had by 1750 created a new Atlantic zone of human contact and communication that embraced four continents and one ocean. Until this point, nothing — neither the Chinese contacts with Africa in the early fifteenth century, nor the expansion of Islam throughout Eurasia in the almost thousand years since the Prophet Muhammad's death in 632 — had so thoroughly and so permanently changed the human and ecological balance of the world.

Sub-Saharan Africa had already been integrated into the world of Eurasia by 1450. African populations became more mixed, as peoples from the Niger River area migrated east and south throughout the continent during the fifteen hundred years before the arrival of the Portuguese. Muslims from North Africa and the Middle East had aided or established Muslim states and trading ports south of the Sahara in East and West Africa after 1000. Cultural and technical innovations of the Middle East, like the literacy that came with Islam, penetrated slowly, and the spread of the many plants and animals of the northern hemisphere was slowed by the Sahara and equator. However, microbes traveled swiftly and easily from Eurasia to Africa, creating a single set of diseases and immunities for the peoples of the Afro-Eurasian Old World.

The peoples of the Americas, having been isolated ecologically for more than a thousand years, were not so fortunate. The arrival of Europeans and Africans in the Americas after 1492 had devastating consequences for Native American populations. Old World diseases like smallpox were responsible for millions of Native American deaths — a tragedy far worse in scope than the casualties caused by wars. To work the mines and plantations of the New World, Europeans used Indian labor, but increasingly, especially for lowland plantations, they used African slaves (see Map 2.1). By 1750, the combination of Indian "die off" and African and European migration resulted in vastly different populations in the Americas. On some Caribbean islands and in plantation areas like northeastern Brazil, Indian populations were entirely replaced by Africans. At the same time, European animals (for example, goats, cattle, horses) multiplied in the absence of natural predators.

The new Atlantic ecological system was not a uniform zone, however. Coastal regions in Western Europe and towns on the eastern seaboard of the Americas prospered, while American interiors and African populations in Africa stagnated or declined. The Atlantic Ocean became a vast lake that united port cities and plantations with sailing ships that carried African slaves to the Caribbean, Caribbean sugar and rum to North American and European industrial ports, and guns, pots, and liquor to the African "Slave Coast."

Thus, the Atlantic world was integrated with the Old World. Trade routes that began in Boston or Bahia, Brazil, stretched across Eurasia and around southern Africa into the Indian Ocean and the China Sea. Crops that had previously been known only to Native Americans — corn, potatoes, and tomatoes — fueled population explosions from Ireland to China and graced the tables of peasants and princes in between. What began as an effort by European merchants to import Asian spices directly became after 1650 (as European tastes for pepper and Asian spices moderated) a new global pantry of possibilities.

In this chapter, we will read selections that describe some of the first contacts that led to this new global dynamic. We will read of Europeans in Mexico, North America, and West Africa and examine European depictions of natives from both North and South America. We will also explore some of the African and American responses to this European expansion. When studying these accounts and images, notice how these individuals at the frontier of a new age understand and treat each other. Consider how these initial exchanges, so apparently fortuitous and transitory at the time, changed the face of the world.

THINKING HISTORICALLY
Comparing Primary Sources

By comparing and contrasting one thing with another, we learn more about each, and by examining related works in their proper context, we learn more about the whole of which they are part. In the first chapter we compared China and Europe or Chinese and European (mainly

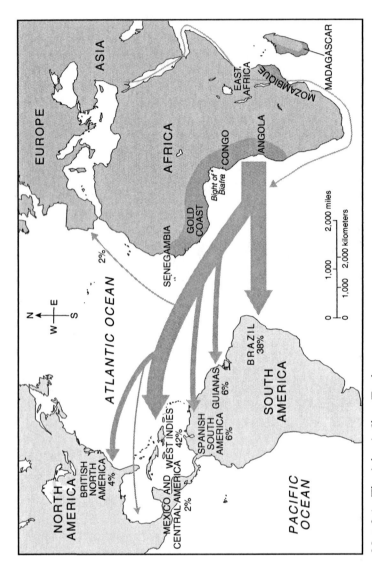

Map 2.1 The Atlantic Slave Trade.

Spanish) expansion in the fifteenth century. In this chapter we look at the Atlantic world, specifically at Europeans in Africa and the Americas. We begin with three views of the Spanish conquest of Mexico — separate accounts by the Spanish conquistadors, by the Mexicans, and by a Dominican friar. The fourth selection juxtaposes two European depictions of Native Americans. The fifth selection recounts the Dutch conquest of the Algonquin nation in North America (in what is today New York City), and allows us to compare Dutch and Spanish colonial policies.

The final three readings examine encounters between Europeans and Africans and the development of the Atlantic slave trade. Did Europeans treat Native Americans and Africans differently? If so, why?

6

BERNAL DÍAZ

From The Conquest of New Spain

Bernal Díaz del Castillo was born in Spain in 1492, the year Columbus sailed to America. After participating in two explorations of the Mexican coast, Díaz joined the expedition of Hernán Cortés to Mexico City in 1519. He wrote this history of the conquest much later, when he was in his seventies; he died circa 1580, a municipal official with a small estate in Guatemala.

The conquest of Mexico did not automatically follow from the first Spanish settlements in Santo Domingo, Hispaniola, and then Cuba in the West Indies. The Spanish crown had given permission for trade and exploration, not colonization. But many Spaniards, from fortune-seeking peasant-soldiers to minor nobility, were eager to conquer their own lands and exploit the populations of dependent Indians.

Cortés, of minor noble descent, sailed to the Indies at the age of nineteen, where he established a sizeable estate on the island of Hispaniola. When he heard stories of Montezuma's gold, he was determined to find the fabled capital of the Aztec empire, Tenochtitlán*

*teh nohch teet LAHN

Bernal Díaz, *The Conquest of New Spain*, trans. J. M. Cohen (Baltimore: Penguin Books, 1963), 217–19, 221–25, 228–38, 241–43.

(modern Mexico City). He gathered more than five hundred amateur soldiers, eleven ships, sixteen horses, and several pieces of artillery, then sailed across the Caribbean and Gulf of Mexico and there began the long march from the coast up to the high central plateau of Mexico.

The Aztecs were new to central Mexico, arriving from the North American desert only about two hundred years before the Spanish, around 1325. By 1500 they had established dominion over almost all other city-states of Mexico, ruling an empire that stretched as far south as Guatemala and as far east as the Mayan lands of the Yucatan Peninsula.

Aztec power relied on a combination of old and new religious ideas and a military system that conquered through terror. The older religious tradition that the Aztecs adopted from Toltec culture centered on Quetzalcoatl* — the feathered serpent, god of creation and brotherhood, whose nurturing forces continued in Aztec society in a system of universal education and in festivals dedicated to life, creativity, and procreation. But the Aztecs also worshipped Huitzilopochtli,[†] a warrior god primed for death and sacrifice, who was given dominant status in the Aztec pantheon. Huitzilopochtli (rendered "Huichilobos"[‡] in this selection) was a force for building a powerful Aztec empire. Drawing on the god's need for human sacrifice — a need not unknown among religions of central Mexico (or Christians) — Montezuma's predecessors built altars to Huitzilopochtli at Tenochtitlán, Cholula, and other sites. The war god required a neverending supply of human hearts, a need that prompted armies to evermore remote sections of Central America in search of sacrificial victims and creating an endless supply of enemies of the Aztecs, among these, the Tlaxcalans.

With the help of his Indian captive and companion Doña Marina — called La Malinche[§] by some of the Indians (thus, Montezuma sometimes calls Cortés "Lord Malinche" in the selection) — Cortés was able to communicate with the Tlaxcalans and other Indians who were tired of Aztec domination. On his march toward Tenochtitlán, Cortés stopped to join forces with the Tlaxcalans, perhaps cementing the relationship and demonstrating his resolve through a brutal massacre of the people of Cholula, an Aztec ally and arch enemy of the Tlaxcalans. By the time Cortés arrived at Tenochtitlán, Montezuma knew of the defeat of his allies at Cholula.

This selection from Bernal Díaz begins with the Spanish entry into Tenochtitlán. What impresses Díaz, and presumably other Spanish

*keht zahl koh AH tuhl
[†]wheat zee loh poácht lee
[‡]wee chee LOH bohs
[§]La Malinche (lah   mah LEEN cheh). A variation on "Marina." In contemporary Mexico a traitor is often called a "Malinchisto."

conquistadors, about the Mexican capital city? What parts of the city attract his attention the most? What conclusions does he draw about Mexican (or Aztec) civilization? Does he think Spanish civilization is equal, inferior, or superior to that of Mexico?

Thinking Historically

Díaz gives us a dramatic account of the meeting of Cortés and Montezuma. What do you think each is thinking and feeling? Do you see any signs of tension in their elaborate greetings? Why are both behaving so politely? What do they want from each other?

Notice how the initial hospitality turns tense. What causes this? Is either side more to blame for what happens next? Was conflict inevitable? Could the encounter have ended in some sort of peaceful resolution?

Remember, we are going to compare Díaz's view with a Mexican view of these events. From your reading of Díaz, does he seem able to understand the Mexican point of view? Would you call him a sympathetic observer?

When Cortes saw, heard, and was told that the great Montezuma was approaching, he dismounted from his horse, and when he came near to Montezuma each bowed deeply to the other. Montezuma welcomed our Captain, and Cortes, speaking through Doña Marina, answered by wishing him very good health. Cortes, I think, offered Montezuma his right hand, but Montezuma refused it and extended his own. Then Cortes brought out a necklace which he had been holding. It was made of those elaborately worked and coloured glass beads called *margaritas*, . . . and was strung on a gold cord and dipped in musk to give it a good odour. This he hung round the great Montezuma's neck, and as he did so attempted to embrace him. But the great princes who stood round Montezuma grasped Cortes' arm to prevent him, for they considered this an indignity.

Then Cortes told Montezuma that it rejoiced his heart to have seen such a great prince, and that he took his coming in person to receive him and the repeated favours he had done him as a high honour. After this Montezuma made him another complimentary speech, and ordered two of his nephews who were supporting him, the lords of Texcoco and Coyoacan, to go with us and show us our quarters. Montezuma returned to the city with the other two kinsmen of his escort, the lords of Cuitlahuac and Tacuba; and all those grand companies of *Caciques*[1] and dignitaries who had come with him returned also in his train. . . .

---

[1]Chiefs. Kah SEEK [Ed.]

On our arrival we entered the large court, where the great Montezuma was awaiting our Captain. Taking him by the hand, the prince led him to his apartment in the hall where he was to lodge, which was very richly furnished in their manner. Montezuma had ready for him a very rich necklace, made of golden crabs, a marvellous piece of work, which he hung round Cortes' neck. His captains were greatly astonished at this sign of honour.

After this ceremony, for which Cortes thanked him through our interpreters, Montezuma said: "Malinche, you and your brothers are in your own house. Rest awhile." He then returned to his palace, which was not far off.

We divided our lodgings by companies, and placed our artillery in a convenient spot. Then the order we were to keep was clearly explained to us, and we were warned to be very much on the alert, both the horsemen and the rest of us soldiers. We then ate a sumptuous dinner which they had prepared for us in their native style.

So, with luck on our side, we boldly entered the city of Tenochtitlán or Mexico on 8 November in the year of our Lord 1519.

The Stay in Mexico

. . . Montezuma had ordered his stewards to provide us with everything we needed for our way of living: maize, grindstones, women to make our bread, fowls, fruit, and plenty of fodder for the horses. He then took leave of us all with the greatest courtesy, and we accompanied him to the street. However, Cortes ordered us not to go far from our quarters for the present until we knew better what conduct to observe.

Next day Cortes decided to go to Montezuma's palace. But first he sent to know whether the prince was busy and to inform him of our coming. He took four captains with him: Pedro de Alvarado, Juan Velazquez de Leon, Diego de Ordaz, and Gonzalo de Sandoval, and five of us soldiers.

When Montezuma was informed of our coming, he advanced into the middle of the hall to receive us, closely surrounded by his nephews, for no other chiefs were allowed to enter his palace or communicate with him except upon important business. Cortes and Montezuma exchanged bows, and clasped hands. Then Montezuma led Cortes to his own dais, and setting him down on his right, called for more seats, on which he ordered us all to sit also.

Cortes began to make a speech through our interpreters, saying that we were all now rested, and that in coming to see and speak with such a great prince we had fulfilled the purpose of our voyage and the orders of our lord the King. The principal things he had come to say on behalf of our Lord God had already been communicated to Montezuma through his three ambassadors, on that occasion in the sand-hills when he did us the favour of sending us the golden moon and sun. We had then told him that we were Christians and worshipped one God alone, named Jesus Christ, who had suffered His passion and death to save us; and that what they worshipped as gods were not gods but devils, which were evil things, and if they were ugly to look at, their deeds were uglier. But he had proved to them how evil and ineffectual their gods were, as both the prince and his people would observe in the course of time, since, where we had put up crosses such as their ambassadors had seen, they had been too frightened to appear before them.

The favour he now begged of the great Montezuma was that he should listen to the words he now wished to speak. Then he very carefully expounded the creation of the world, how we are all brothers, the children of one mother and father called Adam and Eve; and how such a brother as our great Emperor, grieving for the perdition of so many souls as their idols were leading to hell, where they burnt in living flame, had sent us to tell him this, so that he might put a stop to it, and so that they might give up the worship of idols and make no more human sacrifices — for all men are brothers — and commit no more robbery or sodomy. He also promised that in the course of time the King would send some men who lead holy lives among us, much better than our own, to explain this more fully, for we had only come to give them warning. Therefore he begged Montezuma to do as he was asked.

As Montezuma seemed about to reply, Cortes broke off his speech, saying to those of us who were with him: "Since this is only the first attempt, we have now done our duty."

"My lord Malinche," Montezuma replied, "these arguments of yours have been familiar to me for some time. I understand what you said to my ambassadors on the sandhills about the three gods and the cross, also what you preached in the various towns through which you passed. We have given you no answer, since we have worshipped our own gods here from the beginning and know them to be good. No doubt yours are good also, but do not trouble to tell us any more about them at present. Regarding the creation of the world, we have held the same belief for many ages, and for this reason are certain that you are those who our ancestors predicted would come from the direction of the sunrise. As for your great King, I am in his debt and will give him of what I possess. For, as I have already said, two years ago I had news of the Captains who came in ships, by the road that you came, and said they were servants of this great king of yours. I should like to know if you are all the same people."

Cortes answered that we were all brothers and servants of the Emperor, and that they had come to discover a route and explore the seas and ports, so that when they knew them well we could follow, as we had done. Montezuma was referring to the expeditions of Francisco

Hernandez de Cordoba and of Grijalva, the first voyages of discovery. He said that ever since that time he had wanted to invite some of these men to visit the cities of his kingdom, where he would receive them and do them honour, and that now his gods had fulfilled his desire, for we were in his house, which we might call our own. Here we might rest and enjoy ourselves, for we should receive good treatment. If on other occasions he had sent to forbid our entrance into his city, it was not of his own free will, but because his vassals were afraid. For they told him we shot out flashes of lightning, and killed many Indians with our horses, and that we were angry *Teules*, and other such childish stories. But now that he had seen us, he knew that we were of flesh and blood and very intelligent, also very brave. Therefore he had a far greater esteem for us than these reports had given him, and would share with us what he had.

We all thanked him heartily for his . . . good will, and Montezuma replied with a laugh, because in his princely manner he spoke very gaily: "Malinche, I know that these people of Tlascala with whom you are so friendly have told you that I am a sort of god or *Teule*, and keep nothing in any of my houses that is not made of silver and gold and precious stones. But I know very well that you are too intelligent to believe this and will take it as a joke. See now, Malinche, my body is made of flesh and blood like yours, and my houses and palaces are of stone, wood, and plaster. It is true that I am a great king, and have inherited the riches of my ancestors, but the lies and nonsense you have heard of us are not true. You must take them as a joke, as I take the story of your thunders and lightnings."

Cortes answered also with a laugh that enemies always speak evil and tell lies about the people they hate, but he knew he could not hope to find a more magnificent prince in that land, and there was good reason why his fame should have reached our Emperor.

While this conversation was going on, Montezuma quietly sent one of his nephews, a great *Cacique*, to order his stewards to bring certain pieces of gold, which had apparently been set aside as a gift for Cortes, and ten loads of fine cloaks which he divided: the gold and cloaks between Cortes and the four captains, and for each of us soldiers two gold necklaces, each worth ten pesos, and two loads of cloaks. The gold that he then gave us was worth in all more than a thousand pesos, and he gave it all cheerfully, like a great and valiant prince.

As it was now past midday and he did not wish to be importunate, Cortes said to Montezuma: "My lord, the favours you do us increase, load by load, every day, and it is now the hour of your dinner." Montezuma answered that he thanked us for visiting him. We then took our leave with the greatest courtesy, and returned to our quarters, talking as we went of the prince's fine breeding and manners and deciding to show him the greatest respect in every way, and to remove our quilted caps in his presence, which we always did.

The great Montezuma was about forty years old, of good height, well proportioned, spare and slight, and not very dark, though of the usual Indian complexion. He did not wear his hair long but just over his ears, and he had a short black beard, well-shaped and thin. His face was rather long and cheerful, he had fine eyes, and in his appearance and manner could express geniality or, when necessary, a serious composure. He was very neat and clean, and took a bath every afternoon. He had many women as his mistresses, the daughters of chieftains, but two legitimate wives who were *Caciques* in their own right, and when he had intercourse with any of them it was so secret that only some of his servants knew of it. He was quite free from sodomy. The clothes he wore one day he did not wear again till three or four days later. He had a guard of two hundred chieftains lodged in rooms beside his own, only some of whom were permitted to speak to him. When they entered his presence they were compelled to take off their rich cloaks and put on others of little value. They had to be clean and walk barefoot, with their eyes downcast, for they were not allowed to look him in the face, and as they approached they had to make three obeisances, saying as they did so, "Lord, my lord, my great lord!" Then, when they had said what they had come to say, he would dismiss them with a few words. They did not turn their backs on him as they went out, but kept their faces towards him and their eyes downcast, only turning round when they had left the room. Another thing I noticed was that when other great chiefs came from distant lands about disputes or on business, they too had to take off their shoes and put on poor cloaks before entering Montezuma's apartments; and they were not allowed to enter the palace immediately but had to linger for a while near the door, since to enter hurriedly was considered disrespectful. . . .

Montezuma had two houses stocked with every sort of weapon; many of them were richly adorned with gold and precious stones. There were shields large and small, and a sort of broadsword, and two-handed swords set with flint blades that cut much better than our swords, and lances longer than ours, with five-foot blades consisting of many knives. Even when these are driven at a buckler or a shield they are not deflected. In fact they cut like razors, and the Indians can shave their heads with them. They had very good bows and arrows, and double and single-pointed javelins as well as their throwing-sticks and many slings and round stones shaped by hand, and another sort of shield that can be rolled up when they are not fighting, so that it does not get in the way, but which can be opened when they need it in battle and covers their bodies from head to foot. There was also a great deal of cotton armour richly worked on the outside with different coloured feathers, which they used as devices and distinguishing marks, and they had casques and helmets made of wood and bone which were also highly decorated with feathers on the outside. They had other arms of different kinds which I will not mention through fear of prolixity, and workmen skilled in the manufacture of such things, and stewards who were in charge of these arms. . . .

I have already described the manner of their sacrifices. They strike open the wretched Indian's chest with flint knives and hastily tear out the palpitating heart which, with the blood, they present to the idols in whose name they have performed the sacrifice. Then they cut off the arms, thighs, and head, eating the arms and thighs at their ceremonial banquets. The head they hang up on a beam, and the body of the sacrificed man is not eaten but given to the beasts of prey. They also had many vipers in this accursed house, and poisonous snakes which have something that sounds like a bell in their tails. These, which are the deadliest snakes of all, they kept in jars and great pottery vessels full of feathers, in which they laid their eggs and reared their young. They were fed on the bodies of sacrificed Indians and the flesh of the dogs that they bred. We know for certain, too, that when they drove us out of Mexico and killed over eight hundred and fifty of our soldiers, they fed those beasts and snakes on their bodies for many days, as I shall relate in due course. These snakes and wild beasts were dedicated to their fierce idols, and kept them company. As for the horrible noise when the lions and tigers roared, and the jackals and foxes howled, and the serpents hissed, it was so appalling that one seemed to be in hell. . . .

When our Captain and the Mercedarian friar realized that Montezuma would not allow us to set up a cross at Huichilobos' *cue*[2] or build a church there, it was decided that we should ask his stewards for masons so that we could put up a church in our own quarters. For every time we had said mass since entering the city of Mexico we had had to erect an altar on tables and dismantle it again.

The stewards promised to tell Montezuma of our wishes, and Cortes also sent our interpreters to ask him in person. Montezuma granted our request and ordered that we should be supplied with all the necessary material. We had our church finished in two days, and a cross erected in front of our lodgings, and mass was said there each day until the wine gave out. For as Cortes and some other captains and a friar had been ill during the Tlascalan campaign, there had been a run on the wine that we kept for mass. Still, though it was finished, we still went to church every day and prayed on our knees before the altar and images, firstly because it was our obligation as Christians and a good habit, and secondly so that Montezuma and all his captains should observe us and, seeing us worshipping on our knees before the cross — especially when we intoned the Ave Maria — might be inclined to imitate us.

---

[2]The temple of the sun god who demanded human sacrifice. [Ed.]

It being our habit to examine and inquire into everything, when we were all assembled in our lodging and considering which was the best place for an altar, two of our men, one of whom was the carpenter Alonso Yañez, called attention to some marks on one of the walls which showed that there had once been a door, though it had been well plastered up and painted. Now as we had heard that Montezuma kept his father's treasure in this building, we immediately suspected that it must be in this room, which had been closed up only a few days before. Yañez made the suggestion to Juan Velazquez de Leon and Francisco de Lugo, both relatives of mine, to whom he had attached himself as a servant; and they mentioned the matter to Cortes. So the door was secretly opened, and Cortes went in first with certain captains. When they saw the quantity of golden objects — jewels and plates and ingots — which lay in that chamber they were quite transported. They did not know what to think of such riches. The news soon spread to the other captains and soldiers, and very secretly we all went in to see. The sight of all that wealth dumbfounded me. Being only a youth at the time and never having seen such riches before, I felt certain that there could not be a store like it in the whole world. We unanimously decided that we could not think of touching a particle of it, and that the stones should immediately be replaced in the doorway, which should be blocked again and cemented just as we had found it. We resolved also that not a word should be said about this until times changed, for fear Montezuma might hear of our discovery.

Let us leave this subject of the treasure and tell how four of our most valiant captains took Cortes aside in the church, with a dozen soldiers who were in his trust and confidence, myself among them, and asked him to consider the net or trap in which we were caught, to look at the great strength of the city and observe the causeways and bridges, and remember the warnings we had received in every town we had passed through that Huichilobos had counselled Montezuma to let us into the city and kill us there. We reminded him that the hearts of men are very fickle, especially among the Indians, and begged him not to trust the good will and affection that Montezuma was showing us, because from one hour to another it might change. If he should take it into his head to attack us, we said, the stoppage of our supplies of food and water, or the raising of any of the bridges, would render us helpless. Then, considering the vast army of warriors he possessed, we should be incapable of attacking or defending ourselves. And since all the houses stood in the water, how could our Tlascalan allies come in to help us? We asked him to think over all that we had said, for if we wanted to preserve our lives we must seize Montezuma immediately, without even a day's delay. We pointed out that all the gold Montezuma had given us, and all that we had seen in the treasury of his father Axayacatl, and all the food we ate was turning to poison in our bodies, for we could not sleep by night or day or take any rest while these thoughts were in our minds. If any of our soldiers gave him less drastic advice, we concluded, they would be senseless beasts charmed by the gold and incapable of looking death in the eye.

When he had heard our opinion, Cortes answered: "Do not imagine, gentlemen, that I am asleep or that I do not share your anxiety. You must have seen that I do. But what strength have we got for so bold a course as to take this great lord in his own palace, surrounded as he is by warriors and guards? What scheme or trick can we devise to prevent him from summoning his soldiers to attack us at once?"

Our captains (Juan Velazquez de Leon, Diego de Ordaz, Gonzalo de Sandoval, and Pedro de Alvarado) replied that Montezuma must be got out of his palace by smooth words and brought to our quarters. Once there, he must be told that he must remain as a prisoner, and that if he called out or made any disturbance he would pay for it with his life. If Cortes was unwilling to take this course at once, they begged him for permission to do it themselves. With two very dangerous alternatives before us, the better and more profitable thing, they said, would be to seize Montezuma rather than wait for him to attack us. Once he did so, what chance would we have? Some of us soldiers also remarked that Montezuma's stewards who brought us our food seemed to be growing insolent, and did not serve us as politely as they had at first. Two of our Tlascalan allies had, moreover, secretly observed to Jeronimo de Aguilar that for the last two days the Mexicans had appeared less well disposed to us. We spent a good hour discussing whether or not to take Montezuma prisoner, and how it should be done. But our final advice, that at all costs we should take him prisoner, was approved by our Captain, and we then left the matter till next day. All night we prayed God to direct events in the interests of His holy service. . . .

7

From The Broken Spears:
The Aztec Account of
the Conquest of Mexico

This Aztec account of the encounter between the Spanish and the Indians of Mexico was written some years after the events described. Spanish Christian monks helped a postconquest generation of Aztec Nahuatl* speakers translate the illustrated manuscripts of the conquest period. According to this account, how did Montezuma respond to Cortés? Was Montezuma's attitude toward the Spanish shared by other Aztecs? How reliable is this account, do you think, in describing Montezuma's thoughts, motives, and behavior?

Thinking Historically

How does the Aztec account of the conquest differ from that of the Spanish, written by Díaz? Is this difference merely a matter of perspective, or do the authors disagree about what happened? To the extent to which there are differences, how do you decide which account to believe and accept?

Speeches of Motecuhzoma and Cortes

When Motecuhzoma[1] had given necklaces to each one, Cortes asked him: "Are you Motecuhzoma? Are you the king? Is it true that you are the king Motecuhzoma?"

And the king said: "Yes, I am Motecuhzoma." Then he stood up to welcome Cortes; he came forward, bowed his head low and addressed him in these words: "Our lord, you are weary. The journey has tired you, but now you have arrived on the earth. You have come to your city, Mexico. You have come here to sit on your throne, to sit under its canopy.

"The kings who have gone before, your representatives, guarded it and preserved it for your coming. The kings Itzcoatl, Motecuhzoma the Elder, Axayacatl, Tizoc, and Ahuitzol ruled for you in the City of

*nah WAH tuhl
[1]Original Indian spelling of Montezuma. [Ed.]

The Broken Spears: The Aztec Account of the Conquest of Mexico, ed. Miguel Leon-Portilla (Boston: Beacon Press, 1990), 64–76.

Mexico. The people were protected by their swords and sheltered by their shields.

"Do the kings know the destiny of those they left behind, their posterity? If only they are watching! If only they can see what I see!

"No, it is not a dream. I am not walking in my sleep. I am not seeing you in my dreams. . . . I have seen you at last! I have met you face to face! I was in agony for five days, for ten days, with my eyes fixed on the Region of the Mystery. And now you have come out of the clouds and mists to sit on your throne again.

"This was foretold by the kings who governed your city, and now it has taken place. You have come back to us; you have come down from the sky. Rest now, and take possession of your royal houses. Welcome to your land, my lords!"

When Motecuhzoma had finished, La Malinche translated his address into Spanish so that the Captain could understand it. Cortes replied in his strange and savage tongue, speaking first to La Malinche: "Tell Motecuhzoma that we are his friends. There is nothing to fear. We have wanted to see him for a long time, and now we have seen his face and heard his words. Tell him that we love him well and that our hearts are contented."

Then he said to Motecuhzoma: "We have come to your house in Mexico as friends. There is nothing to fear."

La Malinche translated this speech and the Spaniards grasped Motecuhzoma's hands and patted his back to show their affection for him.

Attitudes of the Spaniards and the Native Lords

The Spaniards examined everything they saw. They dismounted from their horses, and mounted them again, and dismounted again, so as not to miss anything of interest.

The chiefs who accompanied Motecuhzoma were: Cacama, king of Tezcoco; Tetlepanquetzaltzin, king of Tlacopan; Itzcuauhtzin the Tlacochcalcatl, lord of Tlatelolco; and Topantemoc, Motecuhzoma's treasurer in Tlatelolco. These four chiefs were standing in a file.

The other princes were: Atlixcatzin [chief who has taken captives];[2] Tepeoatzin, the Tlacochcalcatl; Quetzalaztatzin, the keeper of the chalk; Totomotzin; Hecateupatiltzin; and Cuappiatzin.

When Motecuhzoma was imprisoned, they all went into hiding. They ran away to hide and treacherously abandoned him!

---

[2]Military title given to a warrior who had captured four enemies.

The Spaniards Take Possession of the City

When the Spaniards entered the Royal House, they placed Motecuhzoma under guard and kept him under their vigilance. They also placed a guard over Itzcuauhtzin, but the other lords were permitted to depart.

Then the Spaniards fired one of their cannons, and this caused great confusion in the city. The people scattered in every direction; they fled without rhyme or reason; they ran off as if they were being pursued. It was as if they had eaten the mushrooms that confuse the mind, or had seen some dreadful apparition. They were all overcome by terror, as if their hearts had fainted. And when night fell, the panic spread through the city and their fears would not let them sleep.

In the morning the Spaniards told Motecuhzoma what they needed in the way of supplies: tortillas, fried chickens, hens' eggs, pure water, firewood, and charcoal. Also: large, clean cooking pots, water jars, pitchers, dishes, and other pottery. Motecuhzoma ordered that it be sent to them. The chiefs who received this order were angry with the king and no longer revered or respected him. But they furnished the Spaniards with all the provisions they needed — food, beverages, and water, and fodder for the horses.

The Spaniards Reveal Their Greed

When the Spaniards were installed in the palace, they asked Motecuhzoma about the city's resources and reserves and about the warriors' ensigns and shields. They questioned him closely and then demanded gold.

Motecuhzoma guided them to it. They surrounded him and crowded close with their weapons. He walked in the center, while they formed a circle around him.

When they arrived at the treasure house called Teucalco, the riches of gold and feathers were brought out to them: ornaments made of quetzal feathers, richly worked shields, disks of gold, the necklaces of the idols, gold nose plugs, gold greaves, and bracelets and crowns.

The Spaniards immediately stripped the feathers from the gold shields and ensigns. They gathered all the gold into a great mound and set fire to everything else, regardless of its value. Then they melted down the gold into ingots. As for the precious green stones, they took only the best of them; the rest were snatched up by the Tlaxcaltecas. The Spaniards searched through the whole treasure house, questioning and quarreling, and seized every object they thought was beautiful.

The Seizure of
Motecuhzoma's Treasures

Next they went to Motecuhzoma's storehouse, in the place called Toto-calco [Place of the Palace of the Birds],[3] where his personal treasures were kept. The Spaniards grinned like little beasts and patted each other with delight.

When they entered the hall of treasures, it was as if they had arrived in Paradise. They searched everywhere and coveted everything; they were slaves to their own greed. All of Motecuhzoma's possessions were brought out: fine bracelets, necklaces with large stones, ankle rings with little gold bells, the royal crowns, and all the royal finery — everything that belonged to the king and was reserved to him only. They seized these treasures as if they were their own, as if this plunder were merely a stroke of good luck. And when they had taken all the gold, they heaped up everything else in the middle of the patio.

La Malinche called the nobles together. She climbed up to the palace roof and cried: "Mexicanos, come forward! The Spaniards need your help! Bring them food and pure water. They are tired and hungry; they are almost fainting from exhaustion! Why do you not come forward? Are you angry with them?"

The Mexicans were too frightened to approach. They were crushed by terror and would not risk coming forward. They shied away as if the Spaniards were wild beasts, as if the hour were midnight on the blackest night of the year. Yet they did not abandon the Spaniards to hunger and thirst. They brought them whatever they needed, but shook with fear as they did so. They delivered the supplies to the Spaniards with trembling hands, then turned and hurried away.

The Preparations for the Fiesta

The Aztecs begged permission of their king to hold the fiesta of Huitzilopochtli.[3] The Spaniards wanted to see this fiesta to learn how it was celebrated. A delegation of the celebrants came to the palace where Motecuhzoma was a prisoner, and when their spokesman asked his permission, he granted it to them.

As soon as the delegation returned, the women began to grind seeds of the *chicalote*.[4] These women had fasted for a whole year. They ground the seeds in the patio of the temple.

The Spaniards came out of the palace together, dressed in armor and carrying their weapons with them. They stalked among the women

---

[3]The zoological garden attached to the royal palaces.
[4]Edible plants also used in medicines.

and looked at them one by one; they stared into the faces of the women who were grinding seeds. After this cold inspection, they went back into the palace. It is said that they planned to kill the celebrants if the men entered the patio.

The Statue of Huitzilopochtli

On the evening before the fiesta of Toxcatl, the celebrants began to model a statue of Huitzilopochtli. They gave it such a human appearance that it seemed the body of a living man. Yet they made the statue with nothing but a paste made of the ground seeds of the chicalote, which they shaped over an armature of sticks.

When the statue was finished, they dressed it in rich feathers, and they painted crossbars over and under its eyes. They also clipped on its earrings of turquoise mosaic; these were in the shape of serpents, with gold rings hanging from them. Its nose plug, in the shape of an arrow, was made of gold and was inlaid with fine stones.

They placed the magic headdress of hummingbird feathers on its head. They also adorned it with an *anecuyotl*, which was a belt made of feathers, with a cone at the back. Then they hung around its neck an ornament of yellow parrot feathers, fringed like the locks of a young boy. Over this they put its nettle-leaf cape, which was painted black and decorated with five clusters of eagle feathers.

Next they wrapped it in its cloak, which was painted with skull and bones, and over this they fastened its vest. The vest was painted with dismembered human parts: skulls, ears, hearts, intestines, torsos, breasts, hands, and feet. They also put on its *maxtlatl*, or loincloth, which was decorated with images of disseevered limbs and fringed with amate paper. This *maxtlatl* was painted with vertical stripes of bright blue.

They fastened a red paper flag at its shoulder and placed on its head what looked like a sacrificial flint knife. This too was made of red paper; it seemed to have been steeped in blood.

The statue carried a *tehuehuelli*, a bamboo shield decorated with four clusters of fine eagle feathers. The pendant of this shield was blood-red, like the knife and the shoulder flag. The statue also carried four arrows.

Finally, they put the wristbands on its arms. These bands, made of coyote skin, were fringed with paper cut into little strips.

The Beginning of the Fiesta

Early the next morning, the statue's face was uncovered by those who had been chosen for that ceremony. They gathered in front of the idol in single file and offered it gifts of food, such as round seedcakes or perhaps human flesh. But they did not carry it up to its temple on top of the pyramid.

All the young warriors were eager for the fiesta to begin. They had sworn to dance and sing with all their hearts, so that the Spaniards would marvel at the beauty of the rituals.

The procession began, and the celebrants filed into the temple patio to dance the Dance of the Serpent. When they were all together in the patio, the songs and the dance began. Those who had fasted for twenty days and those who had fasted for a year were in command of the others; they kept the dancers in file with their pine wands. (If anyone wished to urinate, he did not stop dancing, but simply opened his clothing at the hips and separated his clusters of heron feathers.)

If anyone disobeyed the leaders or was not in his proper place they struck him on the hips and shoulders. Then they drove him out of the patio, beating him and shoving him from behind. They pushed him so hard that he sprawled to the ground, and they dragged him outside by the ears. No one dared to say a word about this punishment, for those who had fasted during the year were feared and venerated; they had earned the exclusive title "Brothers of Huitzilopochtli."

The great captains, the bravest warriors, danced at the head of the files to guide the others. The youths followed at a slight distance. Some of the youths wore their hair gathered into large locks, a sign that they had never taken any captives. Others carried their headdresses on their shoulders; they had taken captives, but only with help.

Then came the recruits, who were called "the young warriors." They had each captured an enemy or two. The others called to them: "Come, comrades, show us how brave you are! Dance with all your hearts!"

The Spaniards Attack the Celebrants

At this moment in the fiesta, when the dance was loveliest and when song was linked to song, the Spaniards were seized with an urge to kill the celebrants. They all ran forward, armed as if for battle. They closed the entrances and passageways, all the gates of the patio: the Eagle Gate in the lesser palace, the Gate of the Canestalk and the Gate of the Serpent of Mirrors. They posted guards so that no one could escape, and then rushed into the Sacred Patio to slaughter the celebrants. They came on foot, carrying their swords and their wooden or metal shields.

They ran in among the dancers, forcing their way to the place where the drums were played. They attacked the man who was drumming and cut off his arms. Then they cut off his head, and it rolled across the floor.

They attacked all the celebrants, stabbing them, spearing them, striking them with their swords. They attacked some of them from behind, and these fell instantly to the ground with their entrails hanging out. Others they beheaded: they cut off their heads, or split their heads to pieces.

They struck others in the shoulders, and their arms were torn from their bodies. They wounded some in the thigh and some in the calf. They slashed others in the abdomen, and their entrails all spilled to the ground. Some attempted to run away, but their intestines dragged as they ran; they seemed to tangle their feet in their own entrails. No matter how they tried to save themselves, they could find no escape.

Some attempted to force their way out, but the Spaniards murdered them at the gates. Others climbed the walls, but they could not save themselves. Those who ran into the communal houses were safe there for a while; so were those who lay down among the victims and pretended to be dead. But if they stood up again, the Spaniards saw them and killed them.

The blood of the warriors flowed like water and gathered into pools. The pools widened, and the stench of blood and entrails filled the air. The Spaniards ran into the communal houses to kill those who were hiding. They ran everywhere and searched everywhere; they invaded every room, hunting and killing.

8

BARTOLOMEO DE LAS CASAS

From The Devastation of the Indies

Las Casas (1484–1566) emigrated with his father from Spain to the island of Hispaniola in 1502. Eight years later he became a priest, served as a missionary to the Taino of Cuba (1512), attempted to create a utopian society for the Indians of Venezuela, and became a Dominican friar in 1522. Repelled by his early experience among the conquistadors, Las Casas the priest and friar devoted his adult life to aiding the Indians in the Americas and defending their rights in the Spanish court. This selection is drawn from his brief history, *The Devastation of the Indies*, published in 1555. The work for this book and

Bartolomeo de Las Casas, *The Devastation of the Indies: A Brief Account*, trans. Herma Briffault (Baltimore: Johns Hopkins University Press, 1992), 32–35, 40–41.

a larger volume, *In Defense of the Indians*, presented his case against Indian slavery in the great debate at the Spanish court at Valladolid in 1550. Along with his monumental *History of the Indies*, published after his death, the writings of Las Casas constituted such an indictment of Spanish colonialism that Protestant enemies were able to argue that Catholic slavery and exploitation of the "New World" was worse than their own, a dubious proposition that became known as "the Black Legend." What do you make of this account by Las Casas? Does he exaggerate, or is it likely that these events happened?

Thinking Historically

Compare this account with the two previous selections. Do you think the Spanish treated the people of Hispaniola and Mexico differently? Do these three readings offer different interpretations of the role of Christianity in the Americas?

This [Hispaniola][1] was the first land in the New World to be destroyed and depopulated by the Christians, and here they began their subjection of the women and children, taking them away from the Indians to use them and ill use them, eating the food they provided with their sweat and toil. The Spaniards did not content themselves with what the Indians gave them of their own free will, according to their ability, which was always too little to satisfy enormous appetites, for a Christian eats and consumes in one day an amount of food that would suffice to feed three houses inhabited by ten Indians for one month. And they committed other acts of force and violence and oppression which made the Indians realize that these men had not come from Heaven. And some of the Indians concealed their foods while others concealed their wives and children and still others fled to the mountains to avoid the terrible transactions of the Christians.

And the Christians attacked them with buffets and beatings, until finally they laid hands on the nobles of the villages. Then they behaved with such temerity and shamelessness that the most powerful ruler of the islands had to see his own wife raped by a Christian officer.

From that time onward the Indians began to seek ways to throw the Christians out of their lands. They took up arms, but their weapons were very weak and of little service in offense and still less in defense. (Because of this, the wars of the Indians against each other are little more than games played by children.) And the Christians, with their horses and swords and pikes began to carry out massacres and strange

[1]The island that today includes the Dominican Republic and Haiti. [Ed.]

cruelties against them. They attacked the towns and spared neither the children nor the aged nor pregnant women nor women in childbed, not only stabbing them and dismembering them but cutting them to pieces as if dealing with sheep in the slaughter house. They laid bets as to who, with one stroke of the sword, could split a man in two or could cut off his head or spill out his entrails with a single stroke of the pike. They took infants from their mothers' breasts, snatching them by the legs and pitching them headfirst against the crags or snatched them by the arms and threw them into the rivers, roaring with laughter and saying as the babies fell into the water, "Boil there, you offspring of the devil!" Other infants they put to the sword along with their mothers and anyone else who happened to be nearby. They made some low wide gallows on which the hanged victim's feet almost touched the ground, stringing up their victims in lots of thirteen, in memory of Our Redeemer and His twelve Apostles, then set burning wood at their feet and thus burned them alive. To others they attached straw or wrapped their whole bodies in straw and set them afire. With still others, all those they wanted to capture alive, they cut off their hands and hung them round the victim's neck, saying, "Go now, carry the message," meaning, Take the news to the Indians who have fled to the mountains. They usually dealt with the chieftains and nobles in the following way: they made a grid of rods which they placed on forked sticks, then lashed the victims to the grid and lighted a smoldering fire underneath, so that little by little, as those captives screamed in despair and torment, their souls would leave them.

I once saw this, when there were four or five nobles lashed on grids and burning; I seem even to recall that there were two or three pairs of grids where others were burning, and because they uttered such loud screams that they disturbed the captain's sleep, he ordered them to be strangled. And the constable, who was worse than an executioner, did not want to obey that order (and I know the name of that constable and know his relatives in Seville), but instead put a stick over the victims' tongues, so they could not make a sound, and he stirred up the fire, but not too much, so that they roasted slowly, as he liked. I saw all these things I have described, and countless others.

And because all the people who could do so fled to the mountains to escape these inhuman, ruthless, and ferocious acts, the Spanish captains, enemies of the human race, pursued them with the fierce dogs they kept which attacked the Indians, tearing them to pieces and devouring them. And because on few and far between occasions, the Indians justifiably killed some Christians, the Spaniards made a rule among themselves that for every Christian slain by the Indians, they would slay a hundred Indians. . . .

Because the particulars that enter into these outrages are so numerous they could not be contained in the scope of much writing, for in

truth I believe that in the great deal I have set down here I have not revealed the thousandth part of the sufferings endured by the Indians, I
now want only to add that, in the matter of these unprovoked and destructive wars, and God is my witness, all these acts of wickedness I
have described, as well as those I have omitted, were perpetrated
against the Indians without cause, without any more cause than could
give a community of good monks living together in a monastery. And
still more strongly I affirm that until the multitude of people on this island of Hispaniola were killed and their lands devastated, they committed no sin against the Christians that would be punishable by man's
laws, and as to those sins punishable by God's law, such as vengeful
feelings against such powerful enemies as the Christians have been,
those sins would be committed by the very few Indians who are hard-
hearted and impetuous. And I can say this from my great experience
with them: their hardness and impetuosity would be that of children, of
boys ten or twelve years old. I know by certain infallible signs that the
wars waged by the Indians against the Christians have been justifiable
wars and that all the wars waged by the Christians against the Indians
have been unjust wars, more diabolical than any wars ever waged anywhere in the world. This I declare to be so of all the many wars they
have waged against the peoples throughout the Indies.

After the wars and the killings had ended, when usually there survived only some boys, some women, and children, these survivors were
distributed among the Christians to be slaves. The *repartimiento* or distribution was made according to the rank and importance of the Christian to whom the Indians were allocated, one of them being given
thirty, another forty, still another, one or two hundred, and besides the
rank of the Christian there was also to be considered in what favor he
stood with the tyrant they called Governor. The pretext was that these
allocated Indians were to be instructed in the articles of the Christian
Faith. As if those Christians who were as a rule foolish and cruel and
greedy and vicious could be caretakers of souls! And the care they took
was to send the men to the mines to dig for gold, which is intolerable
labor, and to send the women into the fields of the big ranches to hoe
and till the land, work suitable for strong men. Nor to either the men
or the women did they give any food except herbs and legumes, things
of little substance. The milk in the breasts of the women with infants
dried up and thus in a short while the infants perished.

Two European Views of Native Americans

Las Casas's sympathetic view of the Indians was hardly one shared by the average Frenchman, Italian, or Scot. Indeed, many Europeans harbored fantastical and negative notions about the inhabitants of the "New World," envisioning them as wild and cannibalistic, savage and ruthless toward their enemies. Reinforcing this impression were images that circulated throughout Europe during the sixteenth and seventeenth centuries, such as this engraving from the 1590s, part of a series by Flemish engraver Theodore de Bry, based on paintings by an artist who had accompanied a French expedition to Florida a few decades earlier. Figure 2.1 shows the cannibalistic practices by natives supposedly witnessed by the explorers. What is going on in this picture? It is likely that de Bry made adjustments to his engravings from the originals to please potential buyers. If so, what does this tell us about the expectations of European audiences about the Americas and their inhabitants?

Almost seventy-five years later, a very different set of no less remarkable images emerged from a Dutch colony in northeastern Brazil. Count Johan Maurits, the humanist governor general of the colony from 1636 to 1644, brought several artists and scientists with him to observe and record the region's flora and fauna as well as its inhabitants. Johan Maurits, who was fascinated by the local peoples and their cultures, commissioned from artist Albert Eckhout a number of still-lifes and group and individual portraits, including one showing a female Tapuya Indian (see Figure 2.2). According to Dutch accounts, the Tapuya were more warlike and less "civilized" than some of the other local peoples — for example, they sometimes consumed their dead instead of burying them. Aside from the body parts this woman carries in her hand and in her bag, what other signs of this warlike tendency do you see in Figure 2.2? Look closely at the many interesting details in this painting. What does the artist seem to be interested in showing?

Thinking Historically

What are the differences in style and content between Figures 2.1 and 2.2, and how do you account for them? Which of the following factors do you think is most important in explaining their differences: chronology, agenda of the artist, the potential audience for the image, the setting in which they were produced? What might be the pitfalls for students of history in comparing these two images? How do you reconcile Las Casas's account in the previous source with the scene

Figure 2.1 Cannibalism, Engraving by Theodore de Bry.

Source: Service Historique de la Marine, Vincennes, France, Giraudon/The Bridgeman Art Library International.

portrayed in Figure 2.1? Which source would you consider more reliable and why? Which source would a sixteenth-century Spaniard have considered more reliable and why? Consider how women (or woman) are depicted in these works. What differences and similarities do you see? What might that tell us about European notions of women and gender in the New World?

Figure 2.2   Tapuya Indian, by Albert Eckhout.
Source: National Museum of Denmark.

DAVID PIETERZEN DeVRIES

A Dutch Massacre of the Algonquins

David Pieterzen DeVries was a ship's captain who became a landlord or "patroonship" holder in the Dutch colony of New Amsterdam (now New York). After a disastrous venture to establish a farming and whaling colony, Swanendael on the Delaware River (near modern Philadelphia), he was granted the first patroonship on Staten Island. There he had frequent contact with the Algonquin and Raritan Indians. He was a member of the Board of Directors (the Twelve Men), responsible to the Dutch West India Company for the governance of New Amsterdam. When in 1642, a new governor, Dutch merchant Willem Kieft, urged increased settlement and Indian removal, DeVries urged caution. He described what happened in February 1643 in his book, *Voyages from Holland to America*.

Why did DeVries oppose the governor's plan to attack the Algonquins? What does his story suggest about Dutch-Indian relations before 1643? What were the consequences of the massacre?

Thinking Historically

How is the Dutch treatment of the Algonquins different from the Spanish treatment of the Native Americans? What accounts for these differences? Consider this source in light of the images in the previous document. How might seventeenth-century Europeans reconcile the scene in Figure 2.1 with what DeVries describes in his account?

Do you think an Algonquin account of this encounter would be significantly different from that of DeVries? How might it differ?

The 24th of February, sitting at a table with the Governor, he began to state his intentions, that he had a mind to *wipe the mouths* of the savages; that he had been dining at the house of Jan Claesen Damen, where Maryn Adriaensen and Jan Claesen Damen, together with Jacob Planck, had presented a petition to him to begin this work. I answered him that they were not wise to request this; that such work could not

David Pieterzen DeVries, *Voyages from Holland to America*, A.D. *1632–1644*, trans. H. C. Murphy (New York: Billing Brothers, 1853), 114–17.

be done without the approbation of the Twelve Men; that it could not take place without my assent, who was one of the Twelve Men; that moreover I was the first patroon, and no one else hitherto had risked there so many thousands, and also his person, as I was the first to come from Holland or Zeeland to plant a colony; and that he should consider what profit he could derive from this business, as he well knew that on account of trifling with the Indians we had lost our colony in the South River at Swanendael, in the Hoere-kil, with thirty-two men, who were murdered in the year 1630; and that in the year 1640, the cause of my people being murdered on Staten Island was a difficulty which he had brought on with the Raritan Indians, where his soldiers had for some trifling thing killed some savages. . . . But it appeared that my speaking was of no avail. He had, with his comurderers, determined to commit the murder, deeming it a Roman deed, and to do it without warning the inhabitants in the open lands that each one might take care of himself against the retaliation of the savages, for he could not kill all the Indians. When I had expressed all these things in full, sitting at the table, and the meal was over, he told me he wished me to go to the large hall, which he had been lately adding to his house. Coming to it, there stood all his soldiers ready to cross the river to Pavonia to commit the murder. Then spoke I again to Governor Willem Kieft: "Let this work alone; you wish to break the mouths of the Indians, but you will also murder our own nation, for there are none of the settlers in the open country who are aware of it. My own dwelling, my people, cattle, corn, and tobacco will be lost." He answered me, assuring me that there would be no danger; that some soldiers should go to my house to protect it. But that was not done. So was this business begun between the 25th and 26th of February in the year 1643. I remained that night at the Governor's, sitting up. I went and sat by the kitchen fire, when about midnight I heard a great shrieking, and I ran to the ramparts of the fort, and looked over to Pavonia. Saw nothing but firing, and heard the shrieks of the savages murdered in their sleep. I returned again to the house by the fire. Having sat there awhile, there came an Indian with his squaw, whom I knew well, and who lived about an hour's walk from my house, and told me that they two had fled in a small skiff, which they had taken from the shore at Pavonia; that the Indians from Fort Orange had surprised them; and that they had come to conceal themselves in the fort. I told them that they must go away immediately; that this was no time for them to come to the fort to conceal themselves; that they who had killed their people at Pavonia were not Indians, but the Swannekens, as they call the Dutch, had done it. They then asked me how they should get out of the fort. I took them to the door, and there was no sentry there, and so they betook themselves to the woods. When it was day the soldiers returned to the fort, having

massacred or murdered eighty Indians, and considering they had done
a deed of Roman valor, in murdering so many in their sleep; where infants were torn from their mothers' breasts, and hacked to pieces in the
presence of the parents, and the pieces thrown into the fire and in the
water, and other sucklings, being bound to small boards, were cut,
stuck, and pierced, and miserably massacred in a manner to move a
heart of stone. Some were thrown into the river, and when the fathers
and mothers endeavored to save them, the soldiers would not let them
come on land but made both parents and children drown — children
from five to six years of age, and also some old and decrepit persons.
Those who fled from this onslaught, and concealed themselves in the
neighboring sedge, and when it was morning, came out to beg a piece
of bread, and to be permitted to warm themselves, were murdered in
cold blood and tossed into the fire or the water. Some came to our people in the country with their hands, some with their legs cut off, and
some holding their entrails in their arms, and others had such horrible
cuts and gashes, that worse than they were could never happen. And
these poor simple creatures, as also many of our own people, did not
know any better than that they had been attacked by a party of other
Indians — the Maquas. After this exploit, the soldiers were rewarded
for their services, and Director Kieft thanked them by taking them by
the hand and congratulating them. At another place, on the same night,
on Corler's Hook near Corler's plantation, forty Indians were in the
same manner attacked in their sleep, and massacred there in the same
manner. Did the Duke of Alva[1] in the Netherlands ever do anything
more cruel? This is indeed a disgrace to our nation, who have so generous a governor in our Fatherland as the Prince of Orange, who has always endeavored in his wars to spill as little blood as possible. As soon
as the savages understood that the Swannekens had so treated them, all
the men whom they could surprise on the farmlands, they killed; but
we have never heard that they have ever permitted women or children
to be killed. They burned all the houses, farms, barns, grain, haystacks,
and destroyed everything they could get hold of. So there was an open
destructive war begun. They also burnt my farm, cattle, corn, barn, to-
bacco-house, and all the tobacco. My people saved themselves in the
house where I alone lived, which was made with embrasures, through
which they defended themselves. Whilst my people were in alarm the
savage whom I had aided to escape from the fort in the night came
there, and told the other Indians that I was a good chief, that I had
helped him out of the fort, and that the killing of the Indians took place

---

[1]Spanish tyrant who ruled over the Netherlands before the Dutch gained their independence in 1581. [Ed.]

contrary to my wish. Then they all cried out together to my people that they would not shoot them; that if they had not destroyed my cattle they would not do it, nor burn my house; that they would let my little brewery stand, though they wished to get the copper kettle, in order to make darts for their arrows; but hearing now that it had been done contrary to my wish, they all went away, and left my house unbesieged. When now the Indians had destroyed so many farms and men in revenge for their people, I went to Governor Willem Kieft, and asked him if it was not as I had said it would be, that he would only effect the spilling of Christian blood. Who would now compensate us for our losses? But he gave me no answer. He said he wondered that no Indians came to the fort. I told him that I did not wonder at it; "why should the Indians come here where you have so treated them?"

$$11$$

NZINGA MBEMBA
Appeal to the King of Portugal

Europeans were unable to conquer Africa as they did the Americas until the end of the nineteenth century. Rivers that fell steeply to the sea, military defenses, and diseases like malaria proved insurmountable to Europeans before the age of the steamship, the machine gun, and quinine pills. Before the last half of the nineteenth century, Europeans had to be content with alliances with African kings and rulers. The Portuguese had been the first to meet Africans in the towns and villages along the Atlantic coast, and they became the first European missionaries and trading partners.

Nzinga Mbemba, whose Christian name was Affonso, was king of the west African state of Congo (comprising what is today parts of Angola as well as the two Congo states) from about 1506 to 1543. He succeeded his father, King Nzinga a Kuwu who, shortly after their first Portuguese contact in 1483, sent officials to Lisbon to learn European ways. In 1491 father and son were baptized, and Portuguese

Basil Davidson, *The African Past* (Boston: Little, Brown, and Company, 1964), 191–94.

priests, merchants, artisans, and soldiers were provided with a coastal settlement.

What exactly is the complaint of the King of Congo? What seems to be the impact of Portuguese traders (factors) in the Congo? What does King Affonso want the King of Portugal to do?

Thinking Historically

This selection offers an opportunity to compare European expansion in the Americas and Africa. Portuguese contact with Nzinga Mbemba of the Congo was roughly contemporaneous with Spanish colonialism in the Americas. What differences do you see between these two cases of early European expansion? Can you think of any reasons that Congo kings converted to Christianity while Mexican kings did not?

Compare the European treatment of Africans with their treatment of Native Americans. Why did Europeans enslave Africans and not, for the most part, American Indians?

Sir, Your Highness [of Portugal] should know how our Kingdom is being lost in so many ways that it is convenient to provide for the necessary remedy, since this is caused by the excessive freedom given by your factors and officials to the men and merchants who are allowed to come to this Kingdom to set up shops with goods and many things which have been prohibited by us, and which they spread throughout our Kingdoms and Domains in such an abundance that many of our vassals, whom we had in obedience, do not comply because they have the things in greater abundance than we ourselves; and it was with these things that we had them content and subjected under our vassalage and jurisdiction, so it is doing a great harm not only to the service of God, but to the security and peace of our Kingdoms and State as well.

And we cannot reckon how great the damage is, since the mentioned merchants are taking every day our natives, sons of the land and the sons of our noblemen and vassals and our relatives, because the thieves and men of bad conscience grab them wishing to have the things and wares of this Kingdom which they are ambitious of; they grab them and get them to be sold; and so great, Sir, is the corruption and licentiousness that our country is being completely depopulated, and Your Highness should not agree with this nor accept it as in your service. And to avoid it we need from those [your] Kingdoms no more than some priests and a few people to teach in schools, and no other goods except wine and flour for the holy sacrament. That is why we beg of Your Highness to help and assist us in this matter, commanding your factors that they should not send here either merchants or wares, because it is *our will that in these Kingdoms there should not be any trade of slaves nor outlet for them.*[1] Concerning what is referred above, again we beg of Your Highness to agree with it, since otherwise we cannot remedy such an obvious damage. Pray Our Lord in His mercy to have Your Highness under His guard and let you do for ever the things of His service. I kiss your hands many times.

At our town of Congo, written on the sixth day of July.
João Teixeira did it in 1526.
The King. Dom Affonso.
[On the back of this letter the following can be read:
To the most powerful and excellent prince Dom João, King our Brother.]

Moreover, Sir, in our Kingdoms there is another great inconvenience which is of little service to God, and this is that many of our people [*naturaes*], keenly desirous as they are of the wares and things of your Kingdoms, which are brought here by your people, and in order to satisfy their voracious appetite, seize many of our people, freed and exempt men; and very often it happens that they kidnap even noblemen and the sons of noblemen, and our relatives, and take them to be sold to the white men who are in our Kingdoms; and for this purpose they have concealed them; and others are brought during the night so that they might not be recognized.

And as soon as they are taken by the white men they are immediately ironed and branded with fire, and when they are carried to be embarked, if they are caught by our guards' men the whites allege that they have bought them but they cannot say from whom, so that it is our duty to do justice and to restore to the freemen their freedom, but it cannot be done if your subjects feel offended, as they claim to be.

And to avoid such a great evil we passed a law so that any white man living in our Kingdoms and wanting to purchase goods in any way should first inform three of our noblemen and officials of our court whom we rely upon in this matter, and these are Dom Pedro Manipanza and Dom Manuel Manissaba, our chief usher, and Gonçalo Pires our chief freighter, who should investigate if the mentioned goods are captives or free men, and if cleared by them there will be no further doubt nor embargo for them to be taken and embarked. But if the white men do not comply with it they will lose the aforementioned goods. And if we do them this favor and concession it is for the part Your Highness has in it, since we know that it is in your service too that these goods are taken from our Kingdom, otherwise we should not consent to this. . . .

---

[1]Emphasis in the original.

Sir, Your Highness has been kind enough to write to us saying that we should ask in our letters for anything we need, and that we shall be provided with everything, and as the peace and the health of our Kingdom depend on us, and as there are among us old folks and people who have lived for many days, it happens that we have continuously many and different diseases which put us very often in such a weakness that we reach almost the last extreme; and the same happens to our children, relatives, and natives owing to the lack in this country of physicians and surgeons who might know how to cure properly such diseases. And as we have got neither dispensaries nor drugs which might help us in this forlornness, many of those who had been already confirmed and instructed in the holy faith of Our Lord Jesus Christ perish and die; and the rest of the people in their majority cure themselves with herbs and breads and other ancient methods, so that they put all their faith in the mentioned herbs and ceremonies if they live, and believe that they are saved if they die; and this is not much in the service of God.

And to avoid such a great error and inconvenience, since it is from God in the first place and then from your Kingdoms and from Your Highness that all the goods and drugs and medicines have come to save us, we beg of you to be agreeable and kind enough to send us two physicians and two apothecaries and one surgeon, so that they may come with their drug-stores and all the necessary things to stay in our kingdoms, because we are in extreme need of them all and each of them. We shall do them all good and shall benefit them by all means, since they are sent by Your Highness, whom we thank for your work in their coming. We beg of Your Highness as a great favor to do this for us, because besides being good in itself it is in the service of God as we have said above.

12

WILLIAM BOSMAN

Slave Trader

William Bosman was the chief agent of the Dutch West India Company on the African coast where he lived from 1686 to 1702. Here he explains how slaves were brought to Whydah, an English fort on the coast of Dahomey (between the Gold Coast of Ghana and the slave coast of Nigeria). Bosman discusses various ways in which he received slaves. What were these ways? Which does he seem to prefer?

Thinking Historically

Compare Bosman's description of the slave trade with that of Nzinga Mbemba in the preceding selection. How do you account for the differences? Are they due to Dutch and Portuguese practice, to policies of the Congo and Dahomey, or to the passage of time between 1526 and 1700?

The author, a Dutchman, makes certain comparisons between Dutch slave ships and those of other Europeans. Do you see any evidence for his claims?

The first business of one of our factors [agents] when he comes to Fida [Whydah], is to satisfy the customs of the king and the great men, which amounts to about a hundred pounds in Guinea value, as the goods must yield there. After which we have free license to trade, which is published throughout the whole land by the crier.

But yet before we can deal with any person, we are obliged to buy the king's whole stock of slaves at a set price, which is commonly one third or one fourth higher than ordinary; after which, we obtain free leave to deal with all his subjects, of what rank soever. But if there happen to be no stock of slaves, the factor must then resolve to run the risk of trusting the inhabitants with goods to the value of one or two hundred slaves; which commodities they send into the inland country, in

William Bosman, *A New and Accurate Description of the Coast of Guinea, Divided into the Gold, the Slave, and the Ivory Coasts*, 2nd ed., trans. from Dutch (London: 1721), Barnes & Noble, 1967, pp. 363a–365a.

order to buy with them slaves at all markets, and that sometimes two hundred miles deep in the country. For you ought to be informed, that markets of men are here kept in the same manner as those of beasts with us.

Not a few in our country fondly imagine that parents here sell their children, men their wives, and one brother the other. But those who think so, do deceive themselves; for this never happens on any other account but that of necessity, or some great crime; but most of the slaves that are offered to us, are prisoners of war, which are sold by the victors as their booty.

When these slaves come to Fida, they are put in prison all together; and when we treat concerning buying them, they are all brought out together in a large plain; where, by our surgeons, whose province it is, they are thoroughly examined, even to the smallest member, and that naked, both men and women, without the least distinction or modesty. Those that are approved as good, are set on one side; and the lame or faulty are set by as invalids, which are here called *mackrons*: these are such as are above five and thirty years old, or are maimed in the arms, legs, or feet; have lost a tooth, are grey-haired, or have films over their eyes; as well as all those which are affected with any venereal distemper, or several other diseases.

The invalids and the maimed being thrown out, as I have told you, the remainder are numbered, and it is entered who delivered them. In the meanwhile, a burning iron, with the arms or name of the companies, lies in the fire, with which ours are marked on the breast. This is done that we may distinguish them from the slaves of the English, French, or others (which are also marked with their mark), and to prevent the Negroes exchanging them for worse, at which they have a good hand. I doubt not but this trade seems very barbarous to you, but since it is followed by mere necessity, it must go on; but we yet take all possible care that they are not burned too hard, especially the women, who are more tender than the men.

We are seldom long detained in the buying of these slaves, because their price is established, the women being one fourth or fifth part cheaper than the men. The disputes which we generally have with the owners of these slaves are, that we will not give them such goods as they ask for them, especially the *boesies* [cowry shells] (as I have told you, the money of this country) of which they are very fond, though we generally make a division on this head, in order to make one part of the goods help off another; because those slaves which are paid for in *boesies*, cost the company one half more than those bought with other goods. . . .

When we have agreed with the owners of the slaves, they are returned to their prison; where, from that time forwards, they are kept at our charge, cost us two pence a day a slave; which serves to subsist them, like our criminals, on bread and water: so that to save charges, we send them on board our ships with the very first opportunity, before which their masters strip them of all they have on their backs; so that they come to us stark-naked, as well women as men: in which condition they are obliged to continue, if the master of the ship is not so charitable (which he commonly is) as to bestow something on them to cover their nakedness.

You would really wonder to see how these slaves live on board; for though their number sometimes amounts to six or seven hundred, yet by the careful management of our masters of ships, they are so [well] regulated, that it seems incredible. And in this particular our nation exceeds all other Europeans; for as the French, Portuguese, and English slave-ships are always foul and stinking; on the contrary, ours are for the most part clean and neat.

The slaves are fed three times a day with indifferent good victuals, and much better than they eat in their own country. Their lodging place is divided into two parts; one of which is appointed for the men, the other for the women, each sex being kept apart. Here they lie as close together as it is possible for them to be crowded.

We are sometimes sufficiently plagued with a parcel of slaves which come from a far inland country, who very innocently persuade one another, that we buy them only to fatten, and afterwards eat them as a delicacy. When we are so unhappy as to be pestered with many of this sort, they resolve and agree together (and bring over the rest of their party) to run away from the ship, kill the Europeans, and set the vessel ashore; by which means they design to free themselves from being our food.

I have twice met with this misfortune; and the first time proved very unlucky to me, I not in the least suspecting it; but the uproar was timely quashed by the master of the ship and myself, by causing the abettor to be shot through the head, after which all was quiet.

But the second time it fell heavier on another ship, and that chiefly by the carelessness of the master, who having fished up the anchor of a departed English ship, had laid it in the hold where the male slaves were lodged, who, unknown to any of the ship's crew, possessed themselves of a hammer, with which, in a short time they broke all their fetters in pieces upon the anchor: After this, they came above deck, and fell upon our men, some of whom they grievously wounded, and would certainly have mastered the ship, if a French and English ship had not very fortunately happened to lie by us; who perceiving by our firing a distressed-gun, that something was in disorder on board, immediately came to our assistance with shallops and men, and drove the slaves under deck: notwithstanding which, before all was appeased, about twenty of them were killed.

The Portuguese have been more unlucky in this particular than we; for in four years time they lost four ships in this manner.

13

OLAUDAH EQUIANO

Enslaved Captive

The Interesting Narrative of the Life of Olaudah Equiano,* or Gustavus Vassa the African, written by himself was published in 1789. It tells the story of a young boy sold into slavery in Africa and transported to the Americas, who after winning his freedom became a spokesman for the abolition of slavery in England and America. Recent research suggests that the author, Equiano, may have actually been born a slave in South Carolina and that his tale of earlier African slavery may be a composite of the stories of others. If *The Interesting Narrative* is less autobiographical than once believed, it is no less interesting, and still conveys a wealth of useful information about African experiences of slavery. How was slavery in Africa different from slavery in America? What were the worst aspects of the Atlantic slave trades according to the author? Why does Equiano address his audience as "nominal Christians"?

Thinking Historically

Compare Equiano's attitude toward slavery with that of another author in this chapter. Is Equiano opposed to all forms of slavery or only to certain kinds of slavery? How does Equiano's attitude towards Europeans compare with that of other authors in this chapter?

I hope the reader will not think I have trespassed on his patience in introducing myself to him with some account of the manners and customs of my country. They had been implanted in me with great care, and made an impression on my mind, which time could not erase, and which all the adversity and variety of fortune I have since experienced, served only to rivet and record: for, whether the love of one's country be real or imaginary, or a lesson of reason, or an instinct of nature, I still look back with pleasure on the first scenes of my life, though that pleasure has been for the most part mingled with sorrow.

*oh law OO dah   eh kwee AH noh

"Olaudah Equiano of the Niger Ibo," ed. G. I. Jones, in *Africa Remembered*, ed. Philip D. Curtin (Madison: University of Wisconsin Press, 1967), 60–98.

I have already acquainted the reader with the time and place of my birth. My father, besides many slaves, had a numerous family, of which seven lived to grow up, including myself and sister, who was the only daughter. As I was the youngest of the sons, I became, of course, the greatest favorite with my mother, and was always with her; and she used to take particular pains to form my mind. I was trained up from my earliest years in the art of war: my daily exercise was shooting and throwing javelins, and my mother adorned me with emblems, after the manner of our greatest warriors. In this way I grew up till I had turned the age of eleven, when an end was put to my happiness in the following manner: Generally, when the grown people in the neighborhood were gone far in the fields to labor, the children assembled together in some of the neighboring premises to play; and commonly some of us used to get up a tree to look out for any assailant, or kidnapper, that might come upon us — for they sometimes took those opportunities of our parents' absence, to attack and carry off as many as they could seize. . . . Alas! ere long it was my fate to be thus attacked, and to be carried off, when none of the grown people were nigh.

One day, when all our people were gone out to their works as usual, and only I and my dear sister were left to mind the house, two men and a woman got over our walls, and in a moment seized us both, and, without giving us time to cry out, or make resistance, they stopped our mouths, and ran off with us into the nearest wood. Here they tied our hands, and continued to carry us as far as they could, till night came on, when we reached a small house, where the robbers halted for refreshment, and spent the night. We were then unbound, but were unable to take any food; and, being quite overpowered by fatigue and grief, our only relief was some sleep, which allayed our misfortune for a short time. The next morning we left the house, and continued travelling all the day. For a long time we had kept the woods, but at last we came into a road which I believed I knew. I had now some hopes of being delivered; for we had advanced but a little way before I discovered some people at a distance, on which I began to cry out for their assistance; but my cries had no other effect than to make them tie me faster and stop my mouth, and then they put me into a large sack. They also stopped my sister's mouth, and tied her hands; and in this manner we proceeded till we were out of sight of these people. When we went to rest the following night, they offered us some victuals, but we refused it; and the only comfort we had was in being in one another's arms all that night, and bathing each other with our tears. But alas! we were soon deprived of even the small comfort of weeping together.

The next day proved a day of greater sorrow than I had yet experienced; for my sister and I were then separated, while we lay clasped in each other's arms. It was in vain that we besought them not to part us; she was torn from me, and immediately carried away, while I was left in a state of distraction not to be described. I cried and grieved continually; and for several days did not eat anything but what they forced into my mouth. At length, after many days' travelling, during which I had often changed masters, I got into the hands of a chieftain, in a very pleasant country. This man had two wives and some children, and they all used me extremely well, and did all they could do to comfort me; particularly the first wife, who was something like my mother. Although I was a great many days' journey from my father's house, yet these people spoke exactly the same language with us. This first master of mine, as I may call him, was a smith, and my principal employment was working his bellows, which were the same kind as I had seen in my vicinity. They were in some respects not unlike the stoves here in gentlemen's kitchens, and were covered over with leather; and in the middle of that leather a stick was fixed, and a person stood up, and worked it in the same manner as is done to pump water out of a cask with a hand pump. I believe it was gold he worked, for it was of a lovely bright yellow color, and was worn by the women on their wrists and ankles. . . .

Soon after this, my master's only daughter, and child by his first wife, sickened and died, which affected him so much that for some time he was almost frantic, and really would have killed himself, had he not been watched and prevented. However, in a short time afterwards he recovered, and I was again sold. I was now carried to the left of the sun's rising, through many dreary wastes and dismal woods, amidst the hideous roarings of wild beasts. The people I was sold to used to carry me very often, when I was tired, either on their shoulders or on their backs. I saw many convenient well-built sheds along the road, at proper distances, to accommodate the merchants and travellers, who lay in those buildings along with their wives, who often accompany them; and they always go well armed. . . .

After travelling a considerable time. I came to a town called Tinmah, in the most beautiful country I had yet seen in Africa. It was extremely rich, and there were many rivulets which flowed through it, and supplied a large pond in the centre of the town, where the people washed. Here I saw for the first time cocoanuts, which I thought superior to any nuts I had ever tasted before; and the trees, which were loaded, were also interspersed among the houses, which had commodious shades adjoining, and were in the same manner as ours, the insides being neatly plastered and whitewashed. Here I also saw and tasted for the first time, sugar-cane. Their money consisted of little white shells, the size of the fingernail. I was sold here for one hundred and seventy-two of them, by a merchant who lived and brought me there.

I had been about two or three days at his house, when a wealthy widow, a neighbor of his, came there one evening, and brought with her an only son, a young gentleman about my own age and size. Here they saw me; and, having taken a fancy to me, I was bought of the merchant, and went home with them. Her house and premises were situated close to one of those rivulets I have mentioned, and were the finest I ever saw in Africa: they were very extensive, and she had a number of slaves to attend her. The next day I was washed and perfumed, and when meal time came, I was led into the presence of my mistress, and ate and drank before her with her son. This filled me with astonishment; and I could scarce help expressing my surprise that the young gentleman should suffer me, who was bound, to eat with him who was free; and not only so, but that he would not at any time either eat or drink till I had taken first, because I was the eldest, which was agreeable to our custom. Indeed, every thing here, and all their treatment of me, made me forget that I was a slave. The language of these people resembled ours so nearly, that we understood each other perfectly. They had also the very same customs as we. There were likewise slaves daily to attend us, while my young master and I, with other boys, sported with our darts and bows and arrows, as I had been used to do at home. In this resemblance to my former happy state, I passed about two months; and I now began to think I was to be adopted into the family, and was beginning to be reconciled to my situation, and to forget by degrees my misfortunes, when all at once the delusion vanished; for, without the least previous knowledge, one morning early, while my dear master and companion was still asleep, I was awakened out of my reverie to fresh sorrow, and hurried away. . . .

Thus, at the very moment I dreamed of the greatest happiness, I found myself most miserable; and it seemed as if fortune wished to give me this taste of joy only to render the reverse more poignant. The change I now experienced was as painful as it was sudden and unexpected. It was a change indeed, from a state of bliss to a scene which is inexpressible by me, as it discovered to me an element I had never before beheld, and till then had no idea of, and wherein such instances of hardship and cruelty continually occurred, as I can never reflect on but with horror. . . .

Thus I continued to travel, sometimes by land, sometimes by water, through different countries and various nations, till, at the end of six or seven months after I had been kidnapped, I arrived at the sea coast. . . .

The first object which saluted my eyes when I arrived on the coast was the sea, and a slave ship, which was then riding at anchor, and waiting for its cargo. These filled me with astonishment, which was soon converted into terror, when I was carried on board. I was immediately handled, and tossed up to see if I were sound, by some of the crew; and I was now persuaded that I had gotten into a world of bad spirits, and that they were going to kill me. Their complexions, too, differing so much from ours, their long hair, and the language they spoke (which was very different from any I had ever heard), united to confirm me in this belief. . . . When I looked round the ship too, and saw a large furnace of copper boiling, and a multitude of black people of every description chained together, every one of their countenances expressing dejection and sorrow, I no longer doubted of my fate; and, quite overpowered with horror and anguish, I fell motionless on the deck and fainted. . . .

I now saw myself deprived of all chance of returning to my native country, or even the least glimpse of hope of gaining the shore, which I now considered as friendly; and I even wished for my former slavery in preference to my present situation, which was filled with horrors of every kind, still heightened by my ignorance of what I was to undergo. I was not long suffered to indulge my grief; I was soon put down under the decks, and there I received such a salutation in my nostrils as I had never experienced in my life: so that, with the loathsomeness of the stench, and crying together, I became so sick and low that I was not able to eat, nor had I the least desire to taste anything. I now wished for the last friend, death, to relieve me; but soon, to my grief, two of the white men offered me eatables; and, on my refusing to eat, one of them held me fast by the hands, and laid me across, I think, the windlass, and tied my feet, while the other flogged me severely. I had never experienced anything of this kind before, and, although not being used to the water, I naturally feared that element the first time I saw it, yet, nevertheless, could I have got over the nettings, I would have jumped over the side, but I could not; and besides, the crew used to watch us very closely who were not chained down to the decks, lest we should leap into the water; and I have seen some of these poor African prisoners most severely cut for attempting to do so, and hourly whipped for not eating. This indeed was often the case with myself.

In a little time after, amongst the poor chained men, I found some of my own nation, which in a small degree gave ease to my mind. I inquired of them what was to be done with us? They gave me to understand we were to be carried to these white people's country to work for them. I then was a little revived, and thought, if it were no worse than working, my situation was not so desperate: but still I feared I should be put to death, the white people looked and acted, as I thought, in so savage a manner; for I had never seen among any people such instances of brutal cruelty; and this not only shown towards us blacks, but also to some of the whites themselves. One white man in particular I saw, when we were permitted to be on deck, flogged so unmercifully with a large rope near the foremast, that he died in consequence of it; and they tossed him over the side as they would have done a brute. This made me fear these people the more; and I expected nothing less than to be treated in the same manner. I could not help expressing my fears and apprehensions to some of my countrymen: I asked them if these people had no country, but lived in this hollow place the ship? They told me they did not, but came from a distant one. "Then," said I, "how comes it in all our country we never heard of them?" They told me, because they lived so very far off. I then asked, where were their women? Had they any like themselves? I was told they had. "And why," said I, "do we not see them?" They answered, because they were left behind. I asked how the vessel could go? They told me they could not tell; but that there were cloth put upon the masts by the help of the ropes I saw, and then the vessel went on; and the white men had some spell or magic they put in the water when they liked in order to stop the vessel. I was exceedingly amazed at this account, and really thought they were spirits. I therefore wished much to be from amongst them, for I expected they would sacrifice me: but my wishes were vain — for we were so quartered that it was impossible for any of us to make our escape. . . .

At last, when the ship we were in had got in all her cargo, they made ready with many fearful noises, and we were all put under deck, so that we could not see how they managed the vessel. But this disappointment was the least of my sorrow. The stench of the hold while we were on the coast was so intolerably loathsome, that it was dangerous to remain there for any time, and some of us had been permitted to stay on the deck for the fresh air; but now that the whole ship's cargo were confined together, it became absolutely pestilential. The closeness of the place, and the heat of the climate, added to the number in the ship, which was so crowded that each had scarcely room to turn himself, almost suffocated us. This produced copious perspirations, so that the air soon became unfit for respiration, from a variety of loathsome smells, and brought on a sickness amongst the slaves, of which many died — thus falling victims to the improvident avarice, as I may call it, of their purchasers. This wretched situation was again aggravated by the galling of the chains, now become insupportable; and the filth of the necessary tubs, into which the children often fell, and were almost suffocated. The shrieks of the women, and the groans of the dying, rendered the whole a scene of horror almost inconceivable. Happily perhaps for myself I was soon reduced so low here that it was thought necessary to keep me almost always on deck; and from my extreme youth I was not put in fetters. In this situation I expected every hour to share the fate of my companions, some of whom were almost daily brought upon deck at the point of death, which I began to hope would soon put an end to my miseries. Often did I think many of the inhabitants of the deep much more happy than myself; I envied them the freedom they enjoyed, and as often wished I could change my condition for theirs. Every circumstance I met with served only to render my state more painful, and heighten my apprehensions and my opinion of the cruelty of the whites.

One day they had taken a number of fishes; and when they had killed and satisfied themselves with as many as they thought fit, to our astonishment who were on the deck, rather than give any of them to us to eat, as we expected, they tossed the remaining fish into the sea again, although we begged and prayed for some as well as we could, but in vain; and some of my countrymen, being pressed by hunger, took an opportunity, when they thought no one saw them, of trying to get a little privately; but they were discovered, and the attempt procured them some very severe floggings.

One day, when we had a smooth sea, and moderate wind, two of my wearied countrymen, who were chained together (I was near them at the time), preferring death to such a life of misery, somehow made through the nettings, and jumped into the sea; immediately another quite dejected fellow, who, on account of his illness, was suffered to be out of irons, also followed their example; and I believe many more would very soon have done the same, if they had not been prevented by the ship's crew, who were instantly alarmed. Those of us that were the most active were in a moment put down under the deck; and there was such a noise and confusion amongst the people of the ship as I never heard before, to stop her, and get the boat out to go after the slaves. However, two of the wretches were drowned, but they got the other, and afterwards flogged him unmercifully, for thus attempting to prefer death to slavery. In this manner we continued to undergo more hardships than I can now relate; hardships which are inseparable from this accursed trade. Many a time we were near suffocation, from the want of fresh air, which we were often without for whole days together. This, and the stench of the necessary tubs, carried off many.

During our passage I first saw flying fishes, which surprised me very much: They used frequently to fly across the ship, and many of them fell on the deck. I also now first saw the use of the quadrant. I had often with astonishment seen the mariners make observations with it, and I could not think what it meant. They at last took notice of my surprise; and one of them, willing to increase it, as well as to gratify my curiosity, made me one day look through it. The clouds appeared to me to be land, which disappeared as they passed along. This heightened my wonder, and I was now more persuaded than ever that I was in another world, and that every thing about me was magic.

At last, we came in sight of the island of Barbadoes, at which the whites on board gave a great shout, and made many signs of joy to us. We did not know what to think of this; but, as the vessel drew nearer, we plainly saw the harbour, and other ships of different kinds and sizes; and we soon anchored amongst them off Bridge Town. Many merchants and planters now come on board, though it was in the evening. They put us in separate parcels, and examined us attentively.

They also made us jump, and pointed to the land, signifying we were to go there. We thought by this we should be eaten by these ugly men, as they appeared to us; and when, soon after we were all put down under the deck again, there was much dread and trembling among us, and nothing but bitter cries to be heard all the night from these apprehensions, insomuch that at last the white people got some old slaves from the land to pacify us. They told us we were not to be eaten, but to work, and were soon to go on land where we should see many of our country people. This report eased us much; and sure enough, soon after we landed, there came to us Africans of all languages.

We were conducted immediately to the merchant's yard, where we were all pent up together like so many sheep in a fold, without regard to sex or age. As every object was new to me, everything I saw filled me with surprise. What struck me first was, that the houses were built with bricks, in stories, and in every other respect different from those I have seen in Africa; but I was still more astonished on seeing people on horseback. I did not know what this could mean; and indeed I thought these people were full of nothing but magical arts. . . .

We were not many days in the merchant's custody, before we were sold after their usual manner, which is this: On a signal given (as the beat of a drum), the buyers rush at once into the yard where the slaves are confined, and make choice of that parcel they like best. The noise and clamor with which this is attended, and the eagerness visible in the countenances of the buyers, serve not a little to increase the apprehension of the terrified Africans, who may well be supposed to consider them as the ministers of that destruction to which they think themselves devoted. In this manner, without scruple, are relations and friends separated, most of them never to see each other again.

I remember in the vessel in which I was brought over, in the men's apartment, there were several brothers who, in the sale, were sold in different lots; and it was very moving on this occasion to see and hear their cries at parting. O, ye nominal Christians! Might not an African ask you — learned you this from your God, who says unto you, Do unto all men as you would men should do unto you. Is it not enough that we are torn from our country and friends to toil for your luxury and lust of gain? Must every tender feeling be likewise sacrificed to your avarice? Are the dearest friends and relations, now rendered more dear by their separation from their kindred, still to be parted from each other, and thus preventing from cheering the gloom of slavery with the small comfort of being together, and mingling their sufferings and sorrows? Why are parents to love their children, brothers their sisters, or husbands their wives? Surely this is a new refinement in cruelty, which, while it has no advantage to atone for it, thus aggravates distress, and adds fresh horrors even to the wretchedness of slavery.

REFLECTIONS

This chapter asks you to compare European encounters with Native Americans and Africans. Why did Europeans enslave Africans and not, for the most part, American Indians? Because so many Africans were brought to the Americas to work on plantations, this topic is especially compelling.

Initially, of course, Indians *were* enslaved. Recall the letter of Columbus (selection 4). Part of the reason this enslavement did not continue was the high mortality of Native Americans exposed to small-pox and other Old World diseases. In addition, Native Americans who survived the bacterial onslaught had the "local knowledge" and support needed to escape from slavery.

Above and beyond this were the humanitarian objections of Spanish priests like Bartolomeo de Las Casas and the concerns of the Spanish monarchy that slavery would increase the power of the conquistadors at the expense of the crown. In 1542, the enslavement of Indians was outlawed in Spanish dominions of the New World. Clearly, these "New Laws" were not always obeyed by Spaniards in the Americas or by the Portuguese subjects of the unified Spanish-Portuguese crown between 1580 and 1640. Still, the different legal positions of Africans and Indians in the minds of Europeans require further explanation.

Some scholars have suggested that the difference in treatment lies in the differing needs of the main European powers involved in the encounter. The anthropologist Marvin Harris makes the argument this way:

> The most plausible explanation of the New Laws [of 1542] is that they represented the intersection of the interests of three power groups: the Church, the Crown, and the colonists. All three of these interests sought to maximize their respective control over the aboriginal populations. Outright enslavement of the Indians was the method preferred by the colonists. But neither the Crown nor the Church could permit this to happen without surrendering their own vested and potential interests in the greatest resource of the New World — its manpower.

Why then did they permit and even encourage the enslavement of Africans? In this matter all three power groups stood to gain. Africans who remained in Africa were of no use to anybody, since effective military and political domination of that continent by Europeans was not achieved until the middle of the nineteenth century. To make use of African manpower, Africans had to be removed from their homelands. The only way to accomplish this was to buy them as slaves from dealers on the coast. For both the Crown and the Church, it was better to have Africans under the control of the New World colonists than to leave Africans under the control of Africans.[1]

But of course the Atlantic world slave trade was just one of the lasting outcomes of Atlantic world encounters. Towards the end of his dramatic account of the Spanish conquest of Mexico (selection 6), Bernal Díaz describes a grizzly discovery made by the victorious conquistadors:

> I solemnly swear that all the houses and stockades in the lake were full of heads and corpses. I do not know how to describe it but it was the same in the streets and courts of Tlatelolco. We could not walk without treading on the bodies and heads of dead Indians. (Díaz, 1963, 405)

After two years of continual and heavy warfare, the fortunes of the Spanish turned in their favor and they seized a ravaged city where, according to Bernal Díaz, "the stench was so bad, no one could endure it." Díaz assumed that the Mexicans had been starved and denied fresh water, but we now know that at least part of the cause was the spread of smallpox, a disease which the Spanish carried from the Old World and for which the Native Americans had no immunities. Because of thousands of years of contact, Africans shared many of the same immunities as Europeans, but Native Americans, having inhabited a separate biological realm for over ten thousand years, were completely vulnerable to the new diseases and perished in droves.

Ultimately, slavery came to an end, even if in some cases — the work of Italians on Brazilian sugar plantations, Chinese rail workers, or free African day laborers — it was hard to tell the difference. In any case, the long-term impact of the "Columbian exchange" was more ecological than economic. The potatoes of South America and the corn of Mexico fed more families in Afro-Eurasia than had ever existed in the Americas. The flora and fauna of the New World became new again, through the introduction of the grasses, trees, fruits, grains, horses, cattle, pigs, and chickens that the Old World had known for centuries.

---

[1]Marvin Harris, *Patterns of Race in the Americas* (New York: W. W. Norton, 1964), 17.

3

State and Religion

Asian, Islamic, and Christian States, 1500–1800

HISTORICAL CONTEXT

The relationship between state and religion is a matter of concern and debate almost everywhere in the modern world. In the United States, the issue of the separation of church and state engenders conflicts about the legality of abortion, prayer in the schools, government vouchers for religious schools, and the public display of religious symbols like the Ten Commandments, Nativity scenes, and Chanukah menorahs. Governments in countries as diverse as France and Turkey have recently debated the wearing of headscarves and the display of religious symbols in public schools and other public spaces.

Few states in the world today are dedicated to a single religion as are Saudi Arabia, Israel, and the Vatican. Yet even such places where religious devotion is extreme allow citizenship, residence, and rights in some measure for people of other religions. A few other states have official religions: Brazil is officially Roman Catholic, as was Italy until 1984; Iran is officially Muslim. But, with some notable exceptions, these designations often have little effect on what people believe or how they behave.

While the role of religion in public life and the relationship between church and state are important current issues, from the long-term historical view, the state has only become more important in peoples' lives while religion has become less influential. In the period before 1500, with the notable exception of China, many religious organizations were more important in people's lives than political entities. But, in much of the world, the story of the last five hundred years has been the replacement of religious authority by that of the state.

From the shortened perspective of the last fifty years, such changes may seem negligible. In some places in the world — the United States and the Middle East — religious commitment and fundamentalism have been on the rise in recent decades, becoming more pervasive than fifty years ago, if not more than five hundred years ago. In this chapter, we look at religion and the state in three parts of the world two to five hundred years ago to see how different things were but also to locate the roots of present church-state conflicts. We look first at China where state formation began over two thousand years ago and official Confucianism supported the authority of the emperor. Japan, by contrast, emerged from feudalism to begin state formation only after 1600. Both East Asian societies struggled with the claims of Buddhists, Christians, Muslims, and popular religious sects. Next we look at India, conquered by the Muslim Mughals after 1500, many of whom were remarkably tolerant of Hindus and Hinduism. We conclude with the West, Europe, and colonial America to understand how Christian states struggled with some of the challenges posed by religion. Ultimately, we will be looking for the roots of religious toleration.

Kings and political leaders are almost all more comfortable with some kind of orthodoxy (conventional belief and practice) than with heterodoxy (dissident or heretical belief and practice). But one person's orthodox belief is another's heterodoxy. Most Muslim states, for instance, see Iran's Shi'ism as heterodox, but for most Iranian governments Shi'ism has been the orthodox norm and Sunni Islam more heretical. Orthodoxy frequently undermines religious toleration, but toleration is not the same as heterodoxy. In modern society, we see toleration as a product of secularism. In fact, its history suggests something very different.

THINKING HISTORICALLY
Relating Past and Present

"The past," novelist L. P. Hartley famously wrote, "is a foreign country. They do things differently there." Understanding the past can be like learning a foreign language or exercising muscles gone slack from the daily grind of the commonplace and predictable. These are the muscles that help us imagine and tolerate differences, accept the strange as a possible norm, and allow us to hold conflicting ideas together without forcing agreement or rushing to judgment.

The issue of "state and religion" or "church and state" is a very modern one. We are invoking that modern concern in framing our study of the period between 1500 and 1800. But we should be wary of how past ideas of state and religion may differ from our own. Even the words we use reflect our modern vocabulary and understanding. For the most part, before the sixteenth century, the world's people did not make a distinction between state and religion. Not only were states few and far between, but religious life was not separated from politics or other aspects of life.

In this chapter we ask questions about the history of religious toleration. This too is a modern question. Toleration is a modern idea, but, as we shall see, that does not mean that emperors or governments did not practice it. Various empires throughout history have allowed a variety of beliefs and practices among their subjects, not because they believed it was morally the right thing to do, but because it made good practical political sense.

As you read the following selections, you will be asked to flex your imaginative muscles and reflect on how our modern conceptions of an apparently familiar topic are often different from those of our "foreign" predecessors. Then we can ask how those differences affect our ability to use the past to understand the present.

14

JONATHAN SPENCE

The Ming Chinese State and Religion

In this brief introduction to China of the Ming dynasty (1368–1644), a leading modern historian of China paints a picture of an advanced civilization where a confident government need not "tolerate other centers of authority." What were the elements of Chinese state authority? What religious authorities might have challenged these? Why was the Chinese state able to control these challenges?

Thinking Historically

Spence uses architectural imagery to describe China in 1600. Architecture can tell us much about a society's priorities and values, if only because building represents such a large investment in resources and labor. What does Ming architecture tell us about state and religion in China? What priorities and values might you deduce from our own society's architecture?

Jonathan D. Spence, *The Search for Modern China* (New York: W. W. Norton, 1990), 7–9.

Architectural monuments and buildings offer a constant reminder of the past. But because construction continues from one generation to the next and some buildings last longer than others, we rarely see a single period of the past on a city street or even a single building. We must "read" the architectural styles and details to separate the various layers of the past found in any city or complex settlement.

Oddly, our interest in imagining the past is evoked more by ruins. We cannot help imagining how people might have lived in an ancient city ruin, its building blocks askew, like the Roman Forum or the Mayan remains at Tulum on the Yucatán Peninsula. We are less likely to imagine what a place that has been rebuilt over the generations, such as a modern city, was like in past ages. In such "living museums" the past is drowned out by current distractions. The study of history is based on evidence and facts, but it is nourished by imagination. Look around. Imagine what your surroundings looked like fifty years ago and five hundred years ago.

In the year A.D. 1600, the empire of China was the largest and most sophisticated of all the unified realms on earth. The extent of its territorial domains was unparalleled at a time when Russia was only just beginning to coalesce as a country, India was fragmented between Mughal and Hindu rulers, and a grim combination of infectious disease and Spanish conquerors had laid low the once great empires of Mexico and Peru. And China's population of some 120 million was far larger than that of all the European countries combined.

There was certainly pomp and stately ritual in capitals from Kyoto to Prague, from Delhi to Paris, but none of these cities could boast of a palace complex like that in Peking, where, nestled behind immense walls, the gleaming yellow roofs and spacious marble courts of the Forbidden City symbolized the majesty of the Chinese emperor. Laid out in a meticulous geometrical order, the grand stairways and mighty doors of each successive palace building and throne hall were precisely aligned with the arches leading out of Peking to the south, speaking to all comers of the connectedness of things personified in this man the Chinese termed the Son of Heaven.

Rulers in Europe, India, Japan, Russia, and the Ottoman Empire were all struggling to develop systematic bureaucracies that would expand their tax base and manage their swelling territories effectively, as well as draw to new royal power centers the resources of agriculture and trade. But China's massive bureaucracy was already firmly in place, harmonized by a millennium of tradition and bonded by an immense body of statutory laws and provisions that, in theory at least, could offer pertinent advice on any problem that might arise in the daily life of China's people.

One segment of this bureaucracy lived in Peking, serving the emperor in an elaborate hierarchy that divided the country's business among six ministries dealing respectively with finance and personnel, rituals and laws, military affairs and public works. Also in Peking were the senior scholars and academicians who advised the emperor on ritual matters, wrote the official histories, and supervised the education of the imperial children. This concourse of official functionaries worked in uneasy proximity with the enormous palace staff who attended to the emperor's more personal needs: the court women and their eunuch watchmen, the imperial children and their nurses, the elite bodyguards, the banquet-hall and kitchen staffs, the grooms, the sweepers, and the water carriers.

The other segment of the Chinese bureaucracy consisted of those assigned to posts in the fifteen major provinces into which China was divided during the Ming dynasty. These posts also were arranged in elaborate hierarchies, running from the provincial governor at the top, down through the prefects in major cities to the magistrates in the countries. Below the magistrates were the police, couriers, militiamen, and tax gatherers who extracted a regular flow of revenue from China's farmers. A group of officials known as censors kept watch over the integrity of the bureaucracy both in Peking and in the provinces.

The towns and cities of China did not, in most cases, display the imposing solidity in stone and brick of the larger urban centers in post-Renaissance Europe. Nor, with the exception of a few famous pagodas, were Chinese skylines pierced by towers as soaring as those of the greatest Christian cathedrals or the minarets of Muslim cities. But this low architectural profile did not signify an absence of wealth or religion. There were many prosperous Buddhist temples in China, just as there were Daoist temples dedicated to the natural forces of the cosmos, ancestral meeting halls, and shrines to Confucius, the founding father of China's ethical system who had lived in the fifth century B.C. A scattering of mosques dotted some eastern cities and the far western areas, where most of China's Muslims lived. There were also some synagogues, where descendants of early Jewish travelers still congregated, and dispersed small groups with hazy memories of the teachings of Nestorian Christianity, which had reached China a millennium earlier. The lesser grandeur of China's city architecture and religious centers represented not any absence of civic pride or disesteem of religion, but rather a political fact: The Chinese state was more effectively centralized than those elsewhere in the world; its religions were more effectively controlled; and the growth of powerful, independent cities was prevented by a watchful government that would not tolerate rival centers of authority.

15

MATTEO RICCI

Jesuit Missionaries in Ming China

Matteo Ricci (1555–1610) was born in Italy, studied law and mathematics, entered the Jesuit monastic order (founded by the Spaniard Ignatius Loyola in 1540), and sailed to Portuguese Goa in India where he was ordained into the priesthood, learned Chinese, and directed a Jesuit expedition to China. After living in the southern capital of Nanking, Ricci was expelled and set up a mission in the secondary city of Nanchang (referred to in the following document as "Nancian"), where the events described in this selection took place in 1606 and 1607. Ricci went on to live in the northern capital of Peking for the rest of his life. There he gained the attention of the emperor with his fluent Chinese, his incomparable memory, and his work in astronomy and mathematics. He published a remarkably accurate map of the world, translated the books of Euclid, the Greek mathematician, into Chinese, and published a number of other books in Chinese.

The following selection is excerpted from Ricci's journals, published posthumously by one of his fellow Jesuits in 1615. What does this selection tell you about Jesuit missionary life in China at this time? How would you describe Chinese attitudes toward Christianity? What does this selection tell you about Chinese ideas regarding religion and the state?

Thinking Historically

Parts of this story evoke the feeling that "some things never change." Consider for instance, the envy generated by the Jesuit purchase of a larger house, or the conflict between two intellectual elites: the new Bachelors (Confucian literati who have passed their exams) and the foreign Jesuit community. What other elements in the story strike you as fairly universal or constant throughout history? Are there elements of the story that strike you as foreign or strange, suggesting a very different way of doing things in the Chinese Ming dynasty?

When we get to the point where we can feel somewhat "at home" in a particular past, we may also find elements in a primary source that surprise us because they run counter to our expectations. In this story do any elements that you would have expected to be very different turn

China in the Sixteenth Century: The Journals of Matthew Ricci: 1583–1610, trans. Louis J. Gallagher, S.J. (New York: Random House, 1953), 522–30.

out to be very similar to modern ways of doing things? How do you account for that "strange familiarity"?

During 1606 and the year following, the progress of Christianity in Nancian was in no wise retarded, . . .

Through the efforts of Father Emanuele Dias another and a larger house was purchased, in August of 1607, at a price of a thousand gold pieces. This change was necessary, because the house he had was too small for his needs and was situated in a flood area. Just as the community was about to change from one house to the other, a sudden uprising broke out against them. It happened that some of the pedants among the lettered Bachelors[1] had become dissatisfied with the growing popularity of the Christian faith. So they wrote out a complaint against the Fathers and took it to the governing Pimpithau, the Mayor, who had charge of all city affairs. They were neither well received nor patiently listened to, and he answered them saying, "If this Christian law, against which you are complaining, does not seem good to you, then do not accept it. I have not as yet heard that anyone has been forced into it. If the house which they have bought happens to be large, you are not the ones who are paying for it, and they will never interfere with your property." This answer only aroused their anger, and they went to the Governor of the metropolitan district. It happened that this man, whose name was Lu, was a friend of Father Ricci, with whom he had become acquainted, some years before, in Pekin. He accepted their complaint and then disregarded it, and the lawyers who presented it could not persuade him to give them an answer. This second rebuff also had its effect on their impatience.

At the beginning of each month, the Magistrates hold a public assembly, together with the Bachelors in Philosophy, in the temple of their great Philosopher.[2] When the rites of the new-moon were completed in the temple, and these are civil rather than religious rites, one of those present took advantage of the occasion to speak on behalf of the others, and to address the highest Magistrate present, the Pucinsu. "We wish to warn you," he said, "that there are certain foreign priests in this royal city, who are preaching a law, hitherto unheard of in this kingdom, and who are holding large gatherings of people in their house." Having said this, he referred them to their local Magistrate, called Ticho, who was also head of the school to which the speaker was attached, and he in turn ordered the plaintiffs to present their case in

---

[1] The Confucian literati. [Ed.]
[2] Confucius. [Ed.]

writing, assuring them that he would support it with all his authority, in an effort to have the foreign priests expelled. The complaint was written out that same day and signed with twenty-seven signatures. They gave one copy to the Director of the school and one to the Supreme Magistrate. The content of the document was somewhat as follows.

"Matthew Ricci, Giovanni Soeiro, Emanuele Dias, and certain other foreigners from western kingdoms, men who are guilty of high treason against the throne, are scattered amongst us, in five different provinces. They are continually communicating with each other and are here and there practicing brigandage on the rivers, collecting money, and then distributing it to the people, in order to curry favor with the multitudes. They are frequently visited by the Magistrates, by the high nobility and by the Military Prefects, with whom they have entered into a secret pact, binding unto death.

"These men teach that we should pay no respect to the images of our ancestors, a doctrine which is destined to extinguish the love of future generations for their forebears. Some of them break up the idols, leaving the temples empty and the gods to be pitied, without any patronage. In the beginning they lived in small houses, but by this time they have bought up large and magnificent residences. The doctrine they teach is something infernal. It attracts the ignorant into its fraudulent meshes, and great crowds of this class are continually assembled at their houses. Their doctrine gets beyond the city walls and spreads itself through the neighboring towns and villages and into the open country, and the people become so wrapt up in its falsity, that students are not following their courses, laborers are neglecting their work, farmers are not cultivating their acres, and even the women have no interest in their housework. The whole city has become disturbed, and, whereas in the beginning there were only a hundred or so professing their faith, now there are more than twenty thousand. These priests distribute pictures of some Tartar or Saracen, who they say is God, who came down from heaven to redeem and to instruct all of humanity, and who alone according to their doctrine, can give wealth and happiness; a doctrine by which the simple people are very easily deceived. These men are an abomination on the face of the earth, and there is just ground for fear that once they have erected their own temples, they will start a rebellion, as they did in recent years, according to report, in the provinces of Fuchian and Nankin. Wherefore, moved by their interest in the maintenance of the public good, in the conservation of the realm, and in the preservation, whole and entire, of their ancient laws, the petitioners are presenting this complaint and demanding, in the name of the entire province, that a rescript of it be forwarded to the King, asking that these foreigners be sentenced to death, or banished from the realm, to some deserted island in the sea."

Such, in brief, was the content of the complaint, eloquently worded, with alleged proofs and testimony, and couched in a persuasive style, at which the quasi-literati are very adept. Each of the Magistrates to whom the indictment was presented asserted that the spread of Christianity should be prohibited, and that the foreign priests should be expelled from the city, if the Mayor saw fit, after hearing the case, and notifying the foreigners. All those who knew nothing about the method of conducting affairs in the Chinese kingdom, were fairly well persuaded that the Fathers would at least be chased out of the metropolitan city, and as a result their many friends hesitated to come to their assistance, in what looked like a hopeless case. But the Fathers, themselves, were not too greatly disturbed, placing their confidence in Divine Providence, which had always been present to assist them on other such dangerous occasions. Their first problem was to decide upon the initial step to be taken in a matter of so grave importance.

Many of their friends thought they should seek out an intercessor, who might be induced for a consideration to have the sentence of the Magistrates revoked, as a favor to him. Instead, Father Emanuele, in his own defense, wrote out a request for justice, which he began with an instant petition to the Magistrates to make an exact inquiry into the crimes of which they had been accused, and if they were found guilty, to punish them to the full extent of the law. The Mayor and the same Magistrate, Director of the Schools, received copies of this document, and after the Chief Justice had heard the Fathers and kept them a long time on their knees, clad as criminals, he broke forth with the following questions: "Why is it that you have not left the city, after arousing the hatred of the Baccalaureates? What is this law that you are promulgating? What is this crime you have committed? Why do you forbid the people to honor their ancestors? What infernal image is this that you honor? Where did you get the money to buy these houses?" These and more questions were hurled at them, with little show of civility. Father Emanuele undertook to answer these questions with one of his Lay Brothers acting as an interpreter. First he gave a brief outline of the Christian doctrine. Then he showed that according to the divine law, the first to be honored, after God, were a man's parents. But the judge had no mind to hear or to accept any of this and he made it known that he thought it was all false. After that repulse, with things going from bad to worse, it looked as if they were on the verge of desperation, so much so, indeed, that they increased their prayers, their sacrifices and their bodily penances, in petition for a favorable solution of their difficulty. Their adversaries appeared to be triumphantly victorious. They were already wrangling about the division of the furniture of the Mission residences, and to make results doubly certain, they stirred up the flames anew with added accusations and indictments. They persuaded the civil leaders to urge on the Magistrates. One of the minor Magistrates to whom a copy of the new indictment was given, in order to flatter their zeal, said there was no need to inquire, as to whether or not the Christian law was true. The fact that it was being preached by foreigners was sufficient reason for suppressing it, adding that he himself would exterminate such men, if the complaint had not been handed on to the higher court.

The Mayor, who was somewhat friendly with the Fathers, realizing that there was much in the accusation that was patently false, asked the Magistrate Director of the Schools, if he knew whether or not this man Emanuele was a companion of Matthew Ricci, who was so highly respected at the royal court, and who was granted a subsidy from the royal treasury, because of the gifts he had presented to the King. Did he realize that the Fathers had lived in Nankin for twelve years, and that no true complaint had ever been entered against them for having violated the laws. Then he asked him if he had really given full consideration as to what was to be proven in the present indictment. To this the Director of the Schools replied that he wished the Mayor to make a detailed investigation of the case and then to confer with him. The Chief Justice then ordered the same thing to be done. Fortunately, it was this same Justice who was in charge of city affairs when Father Ricci first arrived in Nancian. It was he who first gave the Fathers permission, with the authority of the Viceroy, to open a house there. After that, through a series of promotions he returned to Nancian, to occupy the highest position in this metropolis. He exercised great prudence in handling the public rebuff the Fathers had received, being careful not to favor either side in the case. He was set on making the truth appear, and yet he did not wish to throw out the case of the quasi-literati because he himself was at one time the Director of their schools.

At that time, some of the accusing element, feeling certain that they had gained a victory, went into the houses of the neophytes looking for pictures of the Saviour, two or three of which they tore to pieces. Father Emanuele then advised the new Christians to hide the pictures from these bandits and, for the time being, not to hang them in their living rooms. He told them that in so doing they were not denying their faith but just preventing further sacrilege. He told them also that they could carry their rosaries in public if they wished to, but that there was no obligation to do so.

After the Mayor had examined the charges of the plaintiffs and the reply of the defendants, he subjected the quasi-literati to an examination in open court, and taking the Fathers under his patronage, he took it upon himself to refute the calumnies of their accusers. He said he was fully convinced that these strangers were honest men, and that he knew that there were only two of them in their local residence and not twenty, as had been asserted. To this they replied that the Chinese were becoming their disciples. To which the Justice in turn replied: "What of it? Why should we be afraid of our own people? Perhaps you are unaware of the fact that Matthew Ricci's company is cultivated by everyone in Pekin, and that he is being subsidized by the royal treasury. How dare the Magistrates who are living outside of the royal city, expel men who have permission to live at the royal court? These men here have lived peacefully in Nankin for twelve years. I command," he added, "that they buy no more large houses, and that the people are not to follow their law." Then in the presence of the court he addressed the Fathers, very kindly, saying that there were some in the city who were angry because they had bought the larger house, when the smaller one would have served their needs.

Relative to the Christian law, he told Father Emanuele that he had no objection whatsoever to its observance by him and by his own people, but that he should not teach it to the people of this country, because in this respect they are not trustworthy. He warned him, that even if the people did accept his religion, in the beginning, they would afterwards turn against it. All this he told them, calmly, and more of a similar nature, and what he said was accepted by all as being quite favorable. Afterwards, while speaking with one of his associates, in open court, he told them that the law which this man professed was quite in keeping with right reason, and that Father Emanuele was a good example of a man who lived according to what he preached. He explained that the Baccalaureates were bold enough to enter charges against Father Emanuele because he was a foreigner and, as they thought, unprotected by any patronage. The Chief Justice then told the Director of the Schools not to make any trouble for the Father, because it was evident that the general charges made by the Baccalaureates were fictitious and trumped up for the purpose of securing bribe money. He said the people of Nancian were a hard lot to please, and that he would give Father Emanuele permission to buy the house because, formerly, when he was Mayor, he gave Father Ricci permission to buy whatever house he wished.

16

Japanese Edicts Regulating Religion

The history of the state in Japan was very different from that of China. Between 1200 and 1600 Japan went through a period in which the state was eclipsed by aristocratic, warrior, and religious groups. When the Tokugawa Shogunate reasserted the authority of a central state in 1600, the memory of monk-soldiers and numerous independent armies called for a series of measures directed at controlling religious institutions and other independent powers. In one measure, all farmers were forbidden to have swords. Another regulated all religious temples. Between 1633 and 1639 the Tokugawa government took the further step of closing the country to all foreign religions, a move directed mainly at the influence previously enjoyed by Portuguese Catholic missionaries.

The first of the two documents in this selection is a vow by which Japanese Christians renounced their faith in 1645. The second document is a government edict regulating temples, mainly Buddhist temples, in 1665. What do these documents tell you about the relationship between the state and religion in Tokugawa Japan?

Thinking Historically

We tend to think of religions as fixed phenomena: eternal and unchanging. In fact, religious ideas and behavior change over time. Religious change is particularly striking in cases where missionaries convert people from a foreign culture. Inevitably, the religion that the convert accepts is different from the religion the missionary preaches. Can you identify some of the changes Christianity underwent in Japan?

Similarly, the regulation of Buddhist temples by the new centralizing Tokugawa government brought changes in Buddhism. How would you expect the edict of 1665 to have changed Japanese Buddhism?

Much in these documents will strike the modern reader as very foreign, even to the extent of requiring an imaginative leap to understand how people might have thought. Choose one of these passages and explain how and why it is so strange to you. Try also to explain how you might understand it.

Yosaburo Takekoshi, *The Economic Aspects of the History of the Civilization of Japan*, vol. 2 (New York: Macmillan, 1930), 88–89. Reprinted in *Japan: A Documentary History*, vol. I, ed. David J. Lu (Armonk, N.Y.: M. E. Sharpe, 2005), 224–25.
Japan: A Documentary History, vol. I, ed. David J. Lu (Armonk, N.Y.: M. E. Sharpe, 2005), 219–20.

Renouncing the Kirishitan Faith, 1645

Vow of Namban (Southern Barbarians): We have been Kirishitans for many years. But the more we learn of the Kirishitan doctrines the greater becomes our conviction that they are evil. In the first place, we who received instructions from the padre regarding the future life were threatened with excommunication which would keep us away from association with the rest of humanity in all things in the present world, and would cast us into hell in the next world. We were also taught that, unless a person committing a sin confesses it to the padre and secures his pardon, he shall not be saved in the world beyond. In that way the people were led into believing in the padres. All that was for the purpose of taking the lands of others.

When we learned of it, we "shifted" from Kirishitan and became adherents of Hokkekyō while our wives became adherents of Ikkōshō. We hereby present a statement in writing to you, worshipful Magistrate, as a testimony.

Hereafter we shall not harbor any thought of the Kirishitan in our heart. Should we entertain any thought of it at all, we shall be punished by Deus Paternus (God the Father), Jesus (His Son), Spirito Santo (the Holy Ghost), as well as by Santa Maria (St. Mary), various angels, and saints.

The grace of God will be lost altogether. Like Judas Iscariot, we shall be without hope, and shall be mere objects of ridicule to the people. We shall never rise. The foregoing is our Kirishitan vow.

Japanese Pledge: We have no thought of the Kirishitan in our hearts. We have certainly "shifted" our faith. If any falsehood be noted in our declaration now or in the future, we shall be subject to divine punishment by Bonten, Taishaku, the four deva kings, the great or little gods in all the sixty or more provinces of Japan, especially the Mishima Daimyōjin, the representatives of the god of Izu and Hakone, Hachiman Daibosatsu, Temman Daijizai Tenjin, especially our own family gods, Suwa Daimyōjin, the village people, and our relatives. This is to certify to the foregoing.

The second year of Shōhō [1645]
Endorsement.

Regulations for Buddhist Temples, 1665

1. The doctrines and rituals established for different sects must not be mixed and disarranged. If there is anyone who does not behave in accordance with this injunction, an appropriate measure must be taken expeditiously.

2. No one who does not understand the basic doctrines or rituals of a given sect is permitted to become the chief priest of a temple. Addendum: If a new rite is established, it must not preach strange doctrines.

3. The regulations which govern relationships between the main temple and branch temples must not be violated. However, even the main temple cannot take measures against branch temples in an unreasonable manner.

4. Parishioners of the temples can choose to which temple they wish to belong and make contributions. Therefore priests must not compete against one another for parishioners.

5. Priests are enjoined from engaging in activities unbecoming of priests, such as forming groups or planning to fight one another.

6. If there is anyone who has violated the law of the land, and that fact is communicated to a temple, it must turn him away without question.

7. When making repairs to a temple or a monastery, do not make them ostentatiously. Addendum: Temples must be kept clean without fail.

8. The estate belonging to a temple is not subject to sale, nor can it be mortgaged.

9. Do not allow anyone who has expressed a desire to become a disciple but is not of good lineage to enter the priesthood freely. If there is a particular candidate who has an improper and questionable background, the judgment of the domanial lord or magistrate of his domicile must be sought and then act accordingly.

The above articles must be strictly observed by all the sects. . . .

Fifth year of Kanbun [1665], seventh month, 11th day.

17

BADA'UNI

Akbar and Religion

At the same time the Chinese and Japanese confronted Christian missionaries, the descendents of Muslim Turkic and Mongol peoples of central Asia were conquering the Hindu kingdoms of northern India. Babur (1483–1530), the first of these Mughal rulers, swept into India from Afghanistan in 1525. Successive Mughal emperors enlarged the empire so that by the time of Akbar (r. 1556–1605) it included all of northern India. Like his contemporaries Philip II of Spain (r. 1556–1598) and Elizabeth of England (r. 1558–1603), Akbar created an elaborate and enduring administrative bureaucracy. But unlike Philip and Elizabeth, who waged religious wars against each other and forcibly converted their domestic subjects and newly conquered peoples, Akbar reached out to his Hindu subjects in ways that would have astonished his European contemporaries. In fact, he angered many of his own Muslim advisors, including Bada'uni, the author of the following memoir. What bothered Bada'uni about Akbar? What does this selection tell you about Akbar's rule? What factors might have motivated his toleration of heterodoxy?

Thinking Historically

What strikes the modern reader here is Akbar's evident curiosity about religious ideas and his lack of doctrinal rigidity. These are not qualities most people expect from a Muslim ruler, perhaps especially a premodern one. Why are we modern readers surprised by this? How might our ideas about Islam and Hinduism in the modern world influence our understanding of these religious traditions in the past?

We know from other sources that Akbar made special efforts to include Hindus in his administration. About a third of his governing bureaucracy were Hindus and he gave Hindu-governed territories a large degree of self-rule — allowing them to retain their own law and courts. Various taxes normally paid by non-Muslims were abolished. Among Akbar's five thousand wives his favorite was the mother of his

Bada'uni, 'Abdul Qadir. *Muntakhab ut-Tawarikh*, vol. 2, trans. G. S. A. Ranking and W. H. Lowe (Calcutta: Asiatic Society of Bengal 1895–1925), 200–201, 255–61 *passim*, 324. Edited and reprinted in *Sources of Indian Tradition*, ed. Ainslie T. Embree (New York: Columbia University Press, 1988), 465–68.

successor, Jahangir (r. 1605–1628). Akbar's policy of toleration continued under his son and grandson, Jahangir and Shah Jahan (r. 1628–1658), but was largely reversed by his great grandson, Aurangzeb (r. 1658–1707). How does this understanding of a particular past affect our ideas about the present? Does it make conflict seem less inevitable?

In the year nine hundred and eighty-three [1605] the buildings of the 'Ibādatkhāna[1] were completed. The cause was this. For many years previously the emperor had gained in succession remarkable and decisive victories. The empire had grown in extent from day to day; everything turned out well, and no opponent was left in the whole world. His Majesty had thus leisure to come into nearer contact with ascetics and the disciples of his reverence [the late] Muʿīn, and passed much of his time in discussing the word of God and the word of the Prophet. Questions of Sufism,[2] scientific discussions, inquiries into philosophy and law, were the order of the day.

And later that day the emperor came to Fatehpur. There he used to spend much time in the Hall of Worship in the company of learned men and shaikhs and especially on Friday nights, when he would sit up there the whole night continually occupied in discussing questions of religion, whether fundamental or collateral. The learned men used to draw the sword of the tongue on the battlefield of mutual contradiction and opposition, and the antagonism of the sects reached such a pitch that they would call one another fools and heretics. The controversies used to pass beyond the differences of Sunni, and Shīʿa, of Hanafī and Shāfiʿī, of lawyer and divine, and they would attack the very bases of belief. And Makhdūm-ul-Mulk wrote a treatise to the effect that Shaikh ʿAbd-al-Nabī had unjustly killed Khizr Khān Sarwānī, who had been suspected of blaspheming the Prophet [peace be upon him!], and Mīr Habsh, who had been suspected of being a Shīʿa, and saying that it was not right to repeat the prayers after him, because he was undutiful toward his father, and was himself afflicted with hemorrhoids. Shaikh ʿAbd-al-Nabī replied to him that he was a fool and a heretic. Then the mullās [Muslim theologians] became divided into two parties, and one party took one side and one the other, and became very Jews and Egyptians for hatred of each other. And persons of

[1]Hall of Religious Discussions. [Ed.]
[2]Mystical, poetic Islamic tradition. [Ed.]

novel and whimsical opinions, in accordance with their pernicious ideas and vain doubts, coming out of ambush, decked the false in the garb of the true, and wrong in the dress of right, and cast the emperor, who was possessed of an excellent disposition, and was an earnest searcher after truth, but very ignorant and a mere tyro, and used to the company of infidels and base persons, into perplexity, till doubt was heaped upon doubt, and he lost all definite aim, and the straight wall of the clear law and of firm religion was broken down, so that after five or six years not a trace of Islam was left in him: and everything was turned topsy-turvy. . . .

And samanas [Hindu or Buddhist ascetics] and brāhmans (who as far as the matter of private interviews is concerned gained the advantage over everyone in attaining the honor of interviews with His Majesty, and in associating with him, and were in every way superior in reputation to all learned and trained men for their treatises on morals, and on physical and religious sciences, and in religious ecstasies, and stages of spiritual progress and human perfections) brought forward proofs, based on reason and traditional testimony, for the truth of their own, and the fallacy of our religion, and inculcated their doctrine with such firmness and assurance, that they affirmed mere imaginations as though they were self-evident facts, the truth of which the doubts of the sceptic could no more shake "Than the mountains crumble, and the heavens be cleft!" And the Resurrection, and Judgment, and other details and traditions, of which the Prophet was the repository, he laid all aside. And he made his courtiers continually listen to those revilings and attacks against our pure and easy, bright and holy faith. . . .

Some time before this a brāhman, named Puruk'hotam, who had written a commentary on the Book, *Increase of Wisdom* (Khirad-afzā), had had private interviews with him, and he had asked him to invent particular Sanskrit names for all things in existence. And at one time a brāhman, named Debi, who was one of the interpreters of the *Mahābhārata*, was pulled up the wall of the castle sitting on a bedstead till he arrived near a balcony, which the emperor had made his bedchamber. Whilst thus suspended he instructed His Majesty in the secrets and legends of Hinduism, in the manner of worshiping idols, the fire, the sun and stars, and of revering the chief gods of these unbelievers, such as Brahma, Mahadev [Shiva], Bishn [Vishnu], Kishn [Krishna], Ram, and Mahama (whose existence as sons of the human race is a supposition, but whose nonexistence is a certainty, though in their idle belief they look on some of them as gods, and some as angels). His Majesty, on hearing further how much the people of the country prized their institutions, began to look upon them with affection. . . .

Sometimes again it was Shaikh Tāj ud-dīn whom he sent for. This shaikh was son of Shaikh Zakarīya of Ajodhan. . . . He had been a pupil of Rashīd Shaikh Zamān of Panipat, author of a commentary on the *Paths* (*Lawā'ih*), and of other excellent works, was most excellent in Sufism, and in the knowledge of theology second only to Shaikh Ibn 'Arabī and had written a comprehensive commentary on the *Joy of the Souls* (*Nuzhat ul-Arwāh*). Like the preceding he was drawn up the wall of the castle in a blanket, and His Majesty listened the whole night to his Sufic obscenities and follies. The shaikh, since he did not in any great degree feel himself bound by the injunctions of the law, introduced arguments concerning the unity of existence, such as idle Sufis discuss, and which eventually lead to license and open heresy. . . .

Learned monks also from Europe, who are called *Padre*, and have an infallible head, called *Papa*,[3] who is able to change religious ordinances as he may deem advisable for the moment, and to whose authority kings must submit, brought the Gospel, and advanced proofs for the Trinity. His Majesty firmly believed in the truth of the Christian religion, and wishing to spread the doctrines of Jesus, ordered Prince Murād to take a few lessons in Christianity under good auspices, and charged Abū'l Fazl to translate the Gospel. . . .

Fire worshipers also came from Nousarī in Gujarat, proclaimed the religion of Zardusht [Zarathustra] as the true one, and declared reverence to fire to be superior to every other kind of worship. They also attracted the emperor's regard, and taught him the peculiar terms, the ordinances, the rites and ceremonies of the Kaianians [a pre-Muslim Persian dynasty]. At last he ordered that the sacred fire should be made over to the charge of Abū'l Fazl, and that after the manner of the kings of Persia, in whose temples blazed perpetual fires, he should take care it was never extinguished night or day, for that it is one of the signs of God, and one light from His lights. . . .

His Majesty also called some of the yogis, and gave them at night private interviews, inquiring into abstract truths; their articles of faith; their occupation; the influence of pensiveness; their several practices and usages; the power of being absent from the body; or into alchemy, physiognomy, and the power of omnipresence of the soul.

---

[3]The Roman Catholic Pope. [Ed.]

18

DONALD QUATAERT

Ottoman Inter-communal Relations

Between 1500 and 1922 the Ottoman Empire, centered in Turkey, embraced a greater variety of religious and ethnic groups than any other state in world history. Many of these peoples, like the Jews expelled from Spain in 1492, came as exiles. According to this history of the empire by modern historian Donald Quataert, Ottoman administration of this incredibly diverse empire was remarkably tolerant. The degree of intercommunal peace and cooperation declined in later centuries, however. What evidence does the author offer of a generally cooperative interchange in the early centuries? Why, according to the author, did this situation change after 1800?

Thinking Historically

As the author points out in the beginning of this selection, the number of recent conflicts occurring in the territory of the old Ottoman Empire has engendered much interest in this topic. It is common to imagine that intractable contemporary conflicts have an ancient history. Often the participants in a conflict have a stake in overemphasizing the longevity of the conflict. But in this selection, the author argues that the roots of these conflicts are not nearly so deep. The causes are more recent than ancient. If he is right, how does that change our present understanding of these conflicts? How might it change our ability to deal with these conflicts?

The subject of historical intergroup relations in the Ottoman empire looms large because of the many conflicts that currently plague the lands it once occupied. Recall, for example, the Palestinian-Israeli struggle, the Kurdish issue, the Armenian question, as well as the horrific events that have befallen Bosnia and Kossovo. All rage in lands once Ottoman. What then, is the connection between these struggles of today and the inter-communal experiences of the Ottoman past?

Donald Quataert, *The Ottoman Empire, 1700–1922* (Cambridge: Cambridge University Press, 2000), 172–77.

There was nothing inevitable about these conflicts — all were historically conditioned. Other outcomes historically were possible but did not happen because of a particular unfolding of events. Nor are any of these struggles ancient ones reflecting millennia-old hatreds. Rather, each of them can be explained with reference to the nineteenth and twentieth centuries, through the unfolding of specific events rather than racial animosities. But because these contemporary struggles loom so large and because we assume that present-day hostilities have ancient and general rather than recent and specific causes, our understanding of the Ottoman inter-communal record has been profoundly obscured.

Despite all stereotypes and preconceptions to the contrary, inter-group relations during most of Ottoman history were rather good relative to the standards of the age. For many centuries, persons who were of minority status enjoyed fuller rights and more legal protection in the Ottoman lands than, for example, did minorities in the realm of the French king or of the Habsburg emperor. It is also true that Ottoman inter-communal relations worsened in the eighteenth and nineteenth centuries. In large part, this chapter argues, the deterioration derives directly from the explosive mixture of Western capital, Great Power interference in internal Ottoman affairs, and the transitional nature of an Ottoman polity struggling to establish broader political rights. Such an assessment does *not* aim to idealize the Ottoman record of inter-communal relations, which was hardly unblemished, or explain away the major injustices and atrocities inflicted on Ottoman subjects.

Nonetheless, the goal is to replace the stereotypes that too long have prevailed regarding relations among the religious and ethnic Ottoman communities. One's religion — as Muslim, Christian, or Jew — was an important means of differentiation in the Ottoman world. Indeed, ethnic terms confusingly often described what actually were religious differences. In the Balkan and Anatolian lands, Ottoman Christians informally spoke of "Turks" when in fact they meant Muslims. "Turk" was a kind of shorthand for referring to Muslims of every sort, whether Kurds, Turks, or Albanians (but not Arabs). Today's Bosnian Muslims are called Turks by the Serbian Christians even though they actually have a common Slavic ethnicity. In the Arab world, Muslim Arabs used "Turk" when sometimes they meant Albanian or Circassian Muslim, one who had come from outside the region.

Stereotypes present distorted pictures of Ottoman subjects living apart, in sharply divided, mutually impenetrable religious communities called *millets* that date back to the fifteenth century. In this incorrect view, each community lived in isolation from one another, adjacent but separate. And supposedly implacable hatreds prevailed: Muslims hated Christians who hated Jews who hated Christians who hated Muslims. Recent scholarship shows this view to be fundamentally wrong on almost every score. To begin with, the term *millet* as a designator for

Ottoman non-Muslims is not ancient but dates from the reign of Sultan Mahmut II, in the early nineteenth century. Before then, *millet* in fact meant Muslims within the empire and Christians *outside* it.

Let us continue this exploration of inter-communal relations with two different versions of the past in Ottoman Bulgaria during the 1700–1922 era. In the first version, we hear the voices of Father Paissiy (1722–1773) and S. Vrachanski (1739–1813) calling their Ottoman overlords "ferocious and savage infidels," "Ishmaelites," "sons of infidels," "wild beasts," and "loathsome barbarians." Somewhat later, another Bulgarian Christian writer Khristo Botev (1848–1876) wrote of the Ottoman administration:

> And the tyrant rages
> and ravages our native home:
> impales, hangs, flogs, curses
> and fines the people thus enslaved.

In the first quotation are the words of Bulgarian emigré intelligentsia who were seeking to promote a Bulgarian nation state and break from Ottoman rule.[1] To justify this separation, they invented a new past in which the Ottomans had brought an abrupt end to the Bulgarian cultural renaissance of the medieval era, destroying its ties to the West and preventing Bulgaria from participating in and contributing to western civilization.

And yet, hear two other Bulgarian Christian voices speaking about Bulgarian Muslims, the first during the period just before formal independence in 1908 and the other a few years later:

> Turks and Bulgarians lived together and were good neighbors. On holidays they exchanged pleasantries. We sent the Turks *kozunak* and red eggs at Easter, and they sent us baklava at Bayram. And on these occasions we visited each other.[2]
>
> In Khaskovo, our neighbors were Turks. They were good neighbors. They got on well together. They even had a little gate between their gardens. Both my parents knew Turkish well. My father was away fighting [during the Balkan Wars]. My mother was alone with four children. And the neighbors said: "You're not going anywhere. You'll stay with us. . . ." So Mama stayed with the Turks. . . . What I'm trying to tell you is that we lived well with these people."[3]

---

[1]The quotations provided from the oral interviews conducted in Bulgaria by Barbara Reeves-Ellington, Binghamton University.

[2]Interview with Simeon Radev, 1879–1967, describing his childhood before 1900, provided by Barbara Reeves-Ellington.

[3]Interview with Iveta Gospodarova, personal narrative, Sofia, January 19, 1995, provided by Barbara Reeves-Ellington.

Concepts of the "other" abound in history. The ancient Greeks divided the world into that of the civilized Greek and of the barbarian others. Barbarians could be brave and courageous but they did not possess civilization. For Jews, there are the *goyim* — the non-Jew, the other — whose lack of certain characteristics keeps them outside the chosen, Jewish, community. For Muslims, the notion of the *dhimmi* is another way of talking about difference. In this case, Muslims regard Christians and Jews as "the People of the Book" (*dhimmi*), who received God's revelation before Muhammad and therefore only incompletely. Thus, *dhimmi* have religion, civilization, and God's message. But since they received only part of that message, they are inherently different from and inferior to Muslims.

In the Ottoman world, people were acutely aware of differences between Muslims and non-Muslims. Muslims, as such, shared their religious beliefs with the dynasty and most members of the Ottoman state apparatus. The state itself, among its many attributes, called itself an Islamic one and many sultans included the term "*gazi*," warrior for the Islamic faith, among their titles. Later on, as seen, they revived the title of caliph, one with deep roots in the early Islamic past. Further, for many centuries military service primarily was carried out as a Muslim duty, although there were always some non-Muslims in the military service such as Christian Greeks serving as sailors in the navy during the 1840s. Yet, in a real sense, the military obligation had become a Muslim one. Even when an 1856 law required Ottoman Christian military service, the purchase of exemption quickly became institutionalized as a special tax. A 1909 law ended this loophole but then hundreds of thousands of Ottoman Christians fled the empire rather than serve. Thus, subjects understood that Muslims needed to fight but non-Muslims did not.

A variety of mechanisms maintained difference and distinction. Clothing laws . . . distinguished among the various religious communities, delineating the religious allegiance of passersby. They reassured maintenance of the differences not simply as instruments of discipline but useful markers of community boundaries, immediately identifying outsiders and insiders. Apparel gave a sense of group identity to members of the specific community.

Until the nineteenth century, the legal system was predicated on religious distinctions. Each religious community maintained its own courts, judges, and legal principles for the use of coreligionists. Since Muslims theologically were superior, so too, in principle, was their court system. Muslim courts thus held sway in cases between Muslims and non-Muslims. The latter, moreover, simply did not possess the necessary authority (*velayet*) and so, with a few exceptions, could not testify against Muslims. The state used the religious authorities and courts to announce decrees and taxes and, more generally, as instruments of

imperial control. The ranking government official of an area, for example, the governor, received an imperial order and summoned the various religious authorities. They in turn informed their communities
which negotiated within themselves over enforcement of the order or
distribution of the taxes being imposed.

Muslim courts often provided rights to Christians and Jews that
were unavailable in their own courts. And so non-Muslims routinely
sought out Muslim courts when they were under no obligation to do
so. Once they appeared before the Islamic court, its decisions took
precedence. They often appealed to Muslim courts to gain access to the
provisions of Islamic inheritance laws which absolutely guaranteed certain shares of estates to relatives — daughters, fathers, uncles, sisters.
Thus, persons who feared disinheritance or a smaller share in the will
of a Christian or Jew placed themselves under Islamic law. Christian
widows frequently registered in the Islamic courts because these provided a greater share to the wife of the deceased than did ecclesiastical
law. Or, take the case of *dhimmi* girls being forced into arranged marriages by fellow Christians or Jews. Since Islamic law required the female's consent to the marriage contract, the young woman in question
could go to the Muslim court that took her side, thus preventing the
unwanted arranged marriage.

With the Tanzimat reforms,[4] the old system of differentiation and
distinction and of Muslim legal superiority formally disappeared. Equality of status meant equality of obligation and military service for all. The
clothing laws disappeared and, while the religious courts remained,
many of their functions vanished. New courts appeared: so-called mixed
courts at first heard commercial, criminal, and then civil cases involving
persons of different religious communities. Then, beginning in 1869,
secular courts (*nizamiye*) presided over civil and criminal cases involving
Muslim and non-Muslim. Whether or not these changes automatically
and always improved the rights and status of individuals — Christian,
Jew, or Muslim — currently is being debated by scholars. Some, for example, argue that women's legal rights overall declined with the replacement of Islamic by secular law, but others disagree.

So, how equal were Ottoman subjects and how well were non-
Muslims treated? Quite arbitrarily, I offer the testimony of the Jewish
community of Ottoman Salonica, as recorded in the "Annual Report of
the Jews of Turkey" of the *Bulletin de l'Alliance Israélite Universelle* in
1893. French Jews had founded the Alliance Israélite Universelle in
1860 to work for Jewish emancipation and combat discrimination all
over the world. The organization placed great stress on schools and education as a liberating device, establishing its first Ottoman school in
1867 and within a few decades, some fifty more. It published a journal,

[4]1839–1876. [Ed.]

the *Bulletin*, in Paris, to which Jewish communities from all over the world sent letters reporting on local conditions. Here then is the statement which the Jewish community of Salonica sent to the *Bulletin* in 1893:

> There are but few countries, even among those which are considered the most enlightened and the most civilized, where Jews enjoy a more complete equality than in Turkey [the Ottoman Empire]. H. M. the sultan and the government of the Porte display towards Jews a spirit of largest toleration and liberalism.

To place these words in context, we need to consider several points. First of all, the statement likely can be read at face value since it was not prepared for circulation within the empire. Second, Ottoman Jewish-Muslim relations were better than Muslim-Christian (or Jewish-Christian) relations. Nonetheless, this statement likely represents the sentiments of large numbers of Ottoman non-Muslim subjects, Christian and Jewish alike during the eighteenth and nineteenth centuries.

19

MARTIN LUTHER

Law and the Gospel: Princes and Turks

Martin Luther (1483–1546) launched the Protestant Reformation when he published his "95 Theses" in 1517, challenging the domination of Christianity by Rome and the Papacy. Luther's immediate complaint centered on the authority of the Pope and his agents to sell indulgences, which promised lessened time in purgatory for deceased loved ones on receipt of a contribution to a building fund for St. Peter's Cathedral. As Luther's criticism of papal practices reached the point of a breach, Luther turned to the German princes to support churches independent of Rome.

The issue of religious and political authority has long been debated and negotiated in Christian Europe. Unlike Islam, which was founded

The Table-Talk of Martin Luther, trans. William Hazlitt, Esq. (Philadelphia: The Lutheran Publication Society, 1997).

by a prophet who also governed, Christianity was founded and grew in an anti-Roman and even antipolitical environment. Typically, Christianity settled on an ambiguous or dualistic relationship between government and God. "Render to Caesar the things that are Caesar's, and to God the things that are God's," Jesus declared according to Mark (12:17) and Matthew (22:21). St. Augustine distinguished between the two cities: the city of God and the city of Man. In the Middle Ages, the doctrine of the two swords, temporal and spiritual, suggested a similar duality. Periodically one force asserted superiority over the other. In 800 Charlemagne took the coronation crown from the hands of the Pope. In 1054, the Holy Roman Emperor was said to crawl through the snow on his hands and knees to beg forgiveness from the Pope. The popes of the Italian Renaissance lived like kings, but in the sixteenth century, secular princes increased the power of the state.

Martin Luther's initial break with Rome encouraged other protests against both secular and religious authorities. His stress on individual interpretation of scripture and the power of following one's own conscience inspired more radical groups like the German Anabaptists to defy all worldly authority. In the wake of a peasant's revolt throughout Germany in 1523–1525, Luther joined forces with the German princes and voiced approval of the authority of the state.

This selection is drawn from a collection of conversational statements by Luther that were recorded by his followers and published under the title *Table-Talk* in 1566, after Luther's death.

What was Luther's attitude toward law and the state? What role did he think princes or governments ought to have in enforcing religious doctrine or behavior? What did he think of the Ottoman Turks?

Thinking Historically

Luther's ideas live on today in the minds of modern Protestants, especially Lutherans. Even the words Luther used — *law, conscience, government* — are as familiar now as they were in the sixteenth century. But Luther's ideas are also the product of a sixteenth-century thinker in sixteenth-century circumstances. Consequently, we can never assume that when we use these words or express these ideas we mean what Luther meant.

Notice, for instance, how Martin Luther dealt with the laws of the state and the call of conscience or the Gospel in the selections on "Law and the Gospel." What did "law" mean for the first Protestant? How did "conscience" or "the Gospel" provide better footing for Luther's challenge of the church? How do people compare or contrast law and conscience today? Would Luther have understood a modern appeal to conscience that led to civil disobedience?

In the selections on "Princes and Potentates" Luther turns his attention to the laws that would be enforced by his allies, the German princes. What vision of religion and politics is implied in these selections? What role did Luther leave for conscience or nonconformity? Would we want to allow a greater freedom of conscience today? Do we?

In what ways are Luther's ideas of the Ottoman Turks similar to European ideas of Muslim countries today? Was Luther poorly informed or prejudiced? Are we?

Of the Law and the Gospel

CCLXXI

We must reject those who so highly boast of Moses' laws, as to temporal affairs, for we have our written imperial and country laws, under which we live, and unto which we are sworn. Neither Naaman the Assyrian, nor Job, nor Joseph, nor Daniel, nor many other good and godly Jews, observed Moses' laws out of their country, but those of the Gentiles among whom they lived. Moses' law bound and obliged only the Jews in that place which God made choice of. Now they are free. If we should keep and observe the laws and rites of Moses, we must also be circumcised, and keep the mosaical ceremonies; for there is no difference; he that holds one to be necessary, must hold the rest so too. Therefore let us leave Moses to his laws, excepting only the *Moralia*,[1] which God has planted in nature, as the ten commandments, which concern God's true worshipping and service, and a civil life. . . .

CCLXXXVIII

In what darkness, unbelief, traditions, and ordinances of men have we lived, and in how many conflicts of the conscience we have been ensnared, confounded, and captivated under popedom, is testified by the books of the papists, and by many people now living. From all which snares and horrors we are now delivered and freed by Jesus Christ and his Gospel, and are called to the true righteousness of faith; insomuch that with good and peaceable consciences we now believe in God the Father, we trust in him, and have just cause to boast that we have sure and certain remission of our sins through the death of Christ Jesus, dearly bought and purchased. Who can sufficiently extol these treasures of the conscience, which everywhere are spread abroad, offered, and presented merely by grace? We are now conquerors of sin, of the

[1]Moral code. [Ed.]

law, of death, and of the devil; freed and delivered from all human traditions. If we would but consider the tyranny of auricular confession,[2]
one of the least things we have escaped from, we could not show ourselves sufficiently thankful to God for loosing us out of that one snare.
When popedom stood and flourished among us, then every king would
willingly have given ten hundred thousand guilders, a prince one hundred thousand, a nobleman one thousand, a gentleman one hundred, a
citizen or countryman twenty or ten, to have been freed from that
tyranny. But now seeing that such freedom is obtained for nothing, by
grace, it is not much regarded, neither give we thanks to God for it.

CCLXXXIX

. . . We must make a clear distinction; we must place the Gospel in
heaven, and leave the law on earth; we must receive of the Gospel a heavenly and a divine righteousness; while we value the law as an earthly and
human righteousness, and thus directly and diligently separate the righteousness of the gospel from the righteousness of the law, even as God has
separated and distinguished heaven from earth, light from darkness, day
from night, etc., so that the righteousness of the Gospel be the light and
the day, but the righteousness of the law, darkness and night. Therefore
all Christians should learn rightly to discern the law and grace in their
hearts, and know how to keep one from the other, in deed and in truth,
not merely in words, as the pope and other heretics do, who mingle them
together, and, as it were, make thereout a cake not fit to eat. . . .

Of Princes and Potentates

DCCXI

Government is a sign of the divine grace, of the mercy of God, who has
no pleasure in murdering, killing, and strangling. If God left all things
to go where they would, as among the Turks and other nations, without good government, we should quickly dispatch one another out of
this world.

DCCXII

Parents keep their children with greater diligence and care than rulers
and governors keep their subjects. Fathers and mothers are masters naturally and willingly; it is a self-grown dominion; but rulers and magis-

---

[2]Catholic confession to a priest. [Ed.]

trates have a compulsory mastery; they act by force, with a prepared dominion; when father and mother can rule no more, the public police must take the matter in hand. Rulers and magistrates must watch over the sixth commandment.

DCCXIII

The temporal magistrate is even like a fish net, set before the fish in a pond or a lake, but God is the plunger, who drives the fish into it. For when a thief, robber, adulterer, murderer, is ripe, he hunts him into the net, that is, causes him to be taken by the magistrate, and punished; for it is written: "God is judge upon earth." Therefore repent, or thou must be punished.

DCCXIV

Princes and rulers should maintain the laws and statues, or they will be condemned. They should, above all, hold the Gospel in honor, and bear it ever in their hands, for it aids and preserves them, and ennobles the state and office of magistracy, so that they know where their vocation and calling is, and that with good and safe conscience they may execute the works of their office. At Rome, the executioner always craved pardon of the condemned malefactor, when he was to execute his office, as though he were doing wrong, or sinning in executing the criminal; whereas 'tis his proper office, which God has set.

St. Paul says: "He beareth not the sword in vain"; he is God's minister, a revenger, to execute wrath upon him that does evil. When the magistrate punishes, God himself punishes.

On the Turks

DCCCXXVII

The power of the Turk is very great; he keeps in his pay, all the year through, hundreds of thousands of soldiers. He must have more than two millions of florins annual revenue. We are far less strong in our bodies, and are divided out among different masters, all opposed the one to the other, yet we might conquer these infidels with only the Lord's prayer, if our own people did not spill so much blood in religious quarrels, and in persecuting the truths contained in that prayer. God will punish us as he punished Sodom and Gomorrah, but I would fain 'twere by the hand of some pious potentate, and not by that of the accursed Turk. . . .

DCCCXXX

News came from Torgau that the Turks had led out into the great square at Constantinople twenty-three Christian prisoners, who, on their refusing to apostatize, were beheaded. Dr. Luther said: Their blood will cry up to heaven against the Turks, as that of John Huss[3] did against the papists. 'Tis certain, tyranny and persecution will not avail to stifle the Word of Jesus Christ. It flourishes and grows in blood. Where one Christian is slaughtered, a host of others arise. 'Tis not on our walls or our arquebusses[4] I rely for resisting the Turk, but upon the *Pater Noster.* 'Tis that will triumph. The Decalogue is not, of itself, sufficient. I said to the engineers at Wittenberg: Why strengthen your walls — they are trash; the walls with which a Christian should fortify himself are made, not of stone and mortar, but of prayer and faith. . . .

DCCCXXXV

. . . The Turks pretend, despite the Holy Scriptures, that they are the chosen people of God, as descendants of Ishmael. They say that Ishmael was the true son of the promise, for that when Issac was about to be sacrificed, he fled from his father, and from the slaughter knife, and, meanwhile, Ishmael came and truly offered himself to be sacrificed, whence he became the child of the promise; as gross a lie as that of the papists concerning one kind in the sacrament. The Turks make a boast of being very religious, and treat all other nations as idolaters. They slanderously accuse the Christians of worshipping three gods. They swear by one only God, creator of heaven and earth, by his angels, by the four evangelists, and by the eighty heaven-descended prophets, of whom Mohammed is the greatest. They reject all images and pictures, and render homage to God alone. They pay the most honorable testimony to Jesus Christ, saying that he was a prophet of preeminent sanctity, born of the Virgin Mary, and an envoy from God, but that Mohammed succeeded him, and that while Mohammed sits, in heaven, on the right hand of the Father, Jesus Christ is seated on his left. The Turks have retained many features of the law of Moses, but, inflated with the insolence of victory, they have adopted a new worship; for the glory of warlike triumphs is, in the opinion of the world, the greatest of all.

Luther complained of the emperor Charles's[5] negligence, who, taken up with other wars, suffered the Turk to capture one place after

---

[3]In Czech, known as Jan Hus. Hus (1369–1415) was a Czech forerunner of the Protestant Reformation. [Ed.]

[4]Primitive firearms used from the fifteenth to the seventeenth centuries. [Ed.]

[5]Charles V (1500–1558), the Habsburg Emperor, fought the French as well as the Ottomans. [Ed.]

another. 'Tis with the Turks as heretofore with the Romans, every subject is a soldier, as long as he is able to bear arms, so they have always a disciplined army ready for the field; whereas we gather together ephemeral bodies of vagabonds, untried wretches, upon whom is no dependence. My fear is, that the papists will unite with the Turks to exterminate us. Please God, my anticipation come not true, but certain it is, that the desperate creatures will do their best to deliver us over to the Turks.

20

ROGER WILLIAMS

The Bloody Tenent of Persecution for Cause of Conscience

Roger Williams (1603–1683), a minister of the Church of England sympathetic to its puritan reformist wing, sailed from England in 1630 to join the newly founded Massachusetts Bay Colony. But for Williams the colony remained too close to the Church of England, especially in its continuing legacies of Catholicism: bishops, infant baptism, ritual kneeling, and making the sign of the cross. Williams moved on to the more separatist Pilgrim colony in Plymouth and to a church in Salem in 1633. There he became engaged in a series of conflicts with the General Court of Massachusetts for defaming the churches and the civil authority of the colony. For his "dangerous opinions" he was given six weeks to leave. In the howling winter of 1635, he brought his small band of followers south to Narragansett Bay where he bought a tract of land from the Indians which he called Providence and which would later become Rhode Island.

The Bloody Tenent, written sometime between 1636 and 1644 when it was finally published (and then burned) in London, summarized the disagreements that Williams had with the Massachusetts authorities, the Church of England, and, one might add, the long history of Catholicism. What did Williams mean by the "bloody tenent"

Roger Williams, *The Bloody Tenent of Persecution for Cause of Conscience, Discussed in a Conference between Truth and Peace*, ed. Richard Groves (Macon, Ga.: Mercer University Press, 2001) (tenet or doctrine) of persecution for conscience? Why does he call this doctrine bloody? According to Williams, what should be the relationship between church and state? Why? How is Williams's idea of this relationship different from Luther's? How do you account for that difference?

Thinking Historically

In Protestant America of the 1630s the more fervent advocates of religious purity rallied around symbols and signs that more mainstream Protestants dismissed as unimportant. But the religious purists and the mainstreamers of the American seventeenth century argued the exact opposite of what we might expect to hear today. Roger Williams and his Separatist followers objected to the display of the most sacred Christian symbol, the cross, on the English flag. For them the cross on the flag was a sacrilegious confusion of nation and church, politics and faith. Some of the Separatists of Salem got into trouble with the Massachusetts government for desecrating the flag by cutting out the cross. Williams and the Separatists also objected to political officials taking an oath of office saying "so help me God." The judges and officials of the state should not presume to act for God, Williams argued, and nonbelievers should not be forced to take the name of "the Lord thy God" in vain. Nothing good could come from governments policing faith or from communities of the faithful mucking about in worldly affairs. What do you think Roger Williams would have thought of prayer in the public schools, the idea that America was a "Christian nation," or politicians saying "God Bless America"?

In this selection, Williams makes reference to a number of different historical periods. First he refers to the religious wars between Catholics and Protestants that had ravaged Europe. Like Luther, he also refers to two of the most important historical markers for Christians: Ancient Israel of the Old Testament and the coming of Christ. Why does he say what he says about ancient Israel? What is his attitude toward Jews and non-Christians alike after the coming of Christ? Christian theology was (and is) highly historical. It envisions a timeline that stretches into the future as well. What future developments does Williams envision?

First, that the blood of so many hundred thousand souls of Protestants and papists, spilled in the wars of present and former ages for their respective consciences, is not required nor accepted by Jesus Christ the Prince of Peace.

Secondly, pregnant scriptures and arguments are throughout the work proposed against the doctrine of persecution for cause of conscience.

Thirdly, satisfactory answers are given to scriptures and objections produced by Mr. Calvin, Beza,[1] Mr. Cotton, and the ministers of the New English churches, and others former and later, tending to prove the doctrine of persecution for cause of conscience.

Fourthly, the doctrine of persecution for cause of conscience is proved guilty of all the blood of the souls crying for vengeance under the altar.

Fifthly, all civil states, with their officers of justice, in their respective constitutions and administrations, are proved essentially civil, and therefore not judges, governors, or defenders of the spiritual, or Christian, state and worship.

Sixthly, it is the will and command of God that, since the coming of his Son the Lord Jesus, a permission of the most paganish, Jewish, Turkish, or anti-Christian consciences and worships be granted to all men in all nations and countries, and they are only to be fought against with that sword which is only, in soul matters, able to conquer, to wit, the sword of God's Spirit, the word of God.

Seventhly, the state of the land of Israel, the kings and people thereof, in peace and war, is proved figurative and ceremonial, and no pattern nor precedent for any kingdom or civil state in the world to follow.

Eighthly, God requires not a uniformity of religion to be enacted and enforced in any civil state; which enforced uniformity, sooner or later, is the greatest occasion of civil war, ravishing of conscience, persecution of Christ Jesus in his servants, and of the hypocrisy and destruction of millions of souls.

Ninthly, in holding an enforced uniformity of religion in a civil state, we must necessarily disclaim our desires and hopes of the Jews' conversion to Christ.

Tenthly, an enforced uniformity of religion throughout a nation or civil state confounds the civil and religious, denies the principles of Christianity and civility, and that Jesus Christ is come in the flesh.

Eleventhly, the permission of other consciences and worships that a state professes only can, according to God, procure a firm and lasting peace; good assurance being taken, according to the wisdom of the civil state, for uniformity of civil obedience from all sorts.

Twelfthly, lastly, true civility and Christianity may both flourish in a state or kingdom, notwithstanding the permission of divers and contrary consciences, either of Jew or Gentile.

---

[1] Theodore Beza (1519–1605), John Calvin's successor. [Ed.]

REFLECTIONS

School prayer, abortion, the public display of religious symbols — what is the proper relationship of government and religion? Roger Williams reminds us that the principle of the separation of church and state, a pillar of modern civic society, originated not as a secular humanist denigration of religion but as an effort by the most fervent Protestant Separatists to preserve their religion's purity and independence.

Luther's discussion of government and religion strikes a more expected tone. The great reformer was able to dismiss thousands of years of law from ancient Israel and the Roman papacy, but he gave German princes far greater authority over religious matters than most Christians would allow today. How do we account for the differences between Martin Luther and Roger Williams on this issue? Is it simply a matter of each preaching the politics of their position — the privileged versus the persecuted?

The Christian debate was unique. Muslims also quarreled about who had the truth, but they lacked a tradition of separating religious and secular authority. In the Ottoman Empire the sultan issued edicts on matters that were not covered in the Koran, but this body of secular law merely supplemented Koranic law, and both were administered by the same judges and officials. There was neither the theoretical possibility that the two systems would disagree nor that separate judicial institutions might come into conflict. Nevertheless, the Ottomans developed a tolerance for differences that would have struck many Catholics and Protestants, in their less accommodating moods, as sheer folly. In the Ottoman Empire, non-Muslims were subject to the religious law of their own communities, and when they violated the secular law of the states, Muslims often suffered more severe punishment on the principle that Muslims should set a better example.

Like Christians, however, Muslims held religious truths that they believed applied to all people. As a consequence both Christian and Muslim society gave rise to religious zealots who wanted the state to enshrine God's Truth. In that way, Christians and Muslims were very different from the rulers, subjects, and thinkers of China and Japan.

Neither the Chinese nor Japanese traditions held religious orthodoxies. But both required proper observance of certain social and political proprieties. Strong governments, as in most of Chinese history, turned principles like Confucian filial piety into virtual religions but they had the force of law and made little appeal to conscience or individual choice. Daoism and Buddhism appealed to the inner lives of Chinese and Japanese devotees, but posed no conflict to state power. Only in periods of unrest, feudalism, or the breakdown of the state did Buddhist or Daoist priests and monks exercise political power. Even then, however, they did not challenge the state as much as they filled the vacuum left by its disappearance. In both Japan and Europe, the post-feudal age was one in which the state's rise depended, in part, on the reclamation and monopolization of powers previously exercised by religious institutions.

Three pasts, but increasingly one present. As cultural differences meld with the force of rockets and the speed of the Internet, one might well ask what separate histories matter to a common present. Increasingly principles of toleration are enshrined by international organizations in declarations of human rights and the proceedings of international tribunals. Whether we see the roots of modern principles of tolerance in Confucian secularism, Christian separation of church and state, or Muslim cosmopolitanism, we live in a world where intolerance is widely condemned and legitimately prosecuted.

And yet, fanaticism and intolerance have not disappeared. Religious fundamentalists of various stripes declare their missions to take over governments, convert populations, and bring about the rule of God. History has shown that tolerance need not be secular. Indeed even the aggressively secular regimes of the twentieth and twenty-first centuries have demonstrated and continue to demonstrate a capacity for brutal persecution of dissidents, religious and otherwise.

The study of the past may be more proficient at telling us what we want than how we can achieve it. But the knowledge of how to get there from here begins with the knowledge of where we are and where we have been. At the very least, the knowledge of how things have changed from the past to the present holds the key to unlocking the future.

4

Gender and Family

China, Southeast Asia, Europe, and "New Spain," 1600–1750

HISTORICAL CONTEXT

Women are half of humanity. The family is the oldest and most important social institution. Marriage is one of the most important passages in one's life. Yet up until the last few decades these subjects rarely registered as important topics in world history. There were at least two reasons for this: One was the tendency to think of history as the story of public events only — the actions of political officials, governments, and their representatives — instead of the private and domestic sphere. The second was the assumption that the private or domestic sphere had no history, and that it had always been the same. As the documents in this chapter will show, nothing could be further from the truth.

Since the urban revolution five thousand years ago most societies have been patriarchal. The laws, social codes, and dominant ideas have enshrined the power and prestige of men over women, husbands over wives, fathers over children, gods over goddesses, even brothers over sisters. Double standards for adultery, inheritance laws that favor sons, and laws that deny women property or political rights all attest to the power of patriarchal culture and norms. Almost everywhere patriarchies have limited women to the domestic sphere while granting men public and political power. Nevertheless, we will see in this chapter that not all patriarchies were alike. Some were less stringent than others, and in many societies during this period, women, individually, in families, and even in larger groups, discovered ways both large and small to assert their social, cultural, and economic independence. As you read about women in China, Southeast Asia, Europe, and the Americas, consider how women's lives varied from one patriarchal society to another and how women found openings to express themselves and create their own worlds.

THINKING HISTORICALLY
Making Comparisons

We learn by making comparisons. Every new piece of knowledge we acquire leads to a comparison with what we already know. For example, we arrive in a new town and we are struck by something that we have not seen before. The town has odd street lamps, flowerpots on the sidewalks, or lots of trucks on the street. We start to formulate a theory about the differences between what we observe in the new town and what we already know about our old town. We think we're on to something, but our theory falls apart when we make more observations by staying in the new town another day, or traveling on to the next town, or going halfway across the world. As we gain more experience and make more observations, our original theory explaining an observed difference is supplanted by a much more complex theory about *types* of towns.

History is very much like travel. We learn by comparison, one step at a time, and the journey is never ending. On this trip we begin in China and then move on to other regions of the world. We begin with primary sources, but make comparisons based on secondary sources as well. In fact, we conclude with a secondary source that will allow us to draw upon our previous readings to make increasingly informed and complex comparisons. Welcome aboard. Next stop, China.

$$\boxed{21}$$

Family Instructions for the Miu Lineage

Chinese families in Ming times (1368–1644) often organized themselves into groups by male lineage. These groups often shared common land, built ancestral halls, published genealogies, honored their common ancestors, and ensured the success and well-being of future generations. To accomplish the last of these, lineage groups frequently compiled lists of family rules or instructions. This particular example, from the various lines of the Miu family of the Guangdong province

"Family Instructions for the Miu Lineage, Late Sixteenth Century," trans. Clara Yu, in *Chinese Civilization: A Sourcebook*, 2nd ed., ed. Patricia Ebrey (New York: Free Press, 1993), 238–40, 241–43.

in the south, shows how extensive these instructions could be. What values did these family instructions encourage? What activities did the Miu lineage regulate? What kind of families, and what kind of individuals, were these rules intended to produce? How would these rules have had a different impact on women and men?

Thinking Historically

It is difficult to read this selection without thinking of one's own family and of families in one's own society. How many of the Miu lineage's concerns are concerns of families you know? Family instructions and lineage organizations are not common features of modern American society, even among Chinese Americans who may have a sense of their lineage and family identity. What institutions in modern American society regulate the activities addressed by these family instructions? Or are these activities allowed to regulate themselves or to go unregulated? From reading this document, what do you think are some of the differences between Ming-era Chinese families and modern American families?

Work Hard at *One of the Principal Occupations*

1. To be filial to one's parents, to be loving to one's brothers, to be diligent and frugal — these are the first tenets of a person of good character. They must be thoroughly understood and faithfully carried out.

One's conscience should be followed like a strict teacher and insight should be sought through introspection. One should study the words and deeds of the ancients to find out their ultimate meanings. One should always remember the principles followed by the ancients, and should not become overwhelmed by current customs. For if one gives in to cruelty, pride, or extravagance, all virtues will be undermined, and nothing will be achieved.

Parents have special responsibilities. *The Book of Changes*[1] says: "The members of a family have strict sovereigns." The "sovereigns" are the parents. Their position in a family is one of unique authority, and they should utilize their authority to dictate matters to maintain order, and to inspire respect, so that the members of the family will all be obedient. If the parents are lenient and indulgent, there will be many troubles which in turn will give rise to even more troubles. Who is to blame for all this? The elders in a family must demand discipline of themselves, following all rules and regulations to the letter, so that the younger members emulate their good behavior and exhort each other

---

[1]The *I Ching*, a Chinese classic. [Ed.]

to abide by the teachings of the ancient sages. Only in this way can the family hope to last for generations. If, however, the elders of a family should find it difficult to abide by these regulations, the virtuous youngsters of the family should help them along. Because the purpose of my work is to make such work easier, I am not afraid of giving many small details. . . .

2. Those youngsters who have taken Confucian scholarship as their hereditary occupation should be sincere and hard-working, and try to achieve learning naturally while studying under a teacher. Confucianism is the only thing to follow if they wish to bring glory to their family. Those who know how to keep what they have but do not study are as useless as puppets made of clay or wood. Those who study, even if they do not succeed in the examinations, can hope to become teachers or to gain personal benefit. However, there are people who study not for learning's sake, but as a vulgar means of gaining profit. These people are better off doing nothing.

Youngsters who are incapable of concentrating on studying should devote themselves to farming; they should personally grasp the ploughs and eat the fruit of their own labor. In this way they will be able to support their families. If they fold their hands and do nothing, they will soon have to worry about hunger and cold. If, however, they realize that their forefathers also worked hard and that farming is a difficult way of life, they will not be inferior to anyone. In earlier dynasties, officials were all selected because they were filial sons, loving brothers, and diligent farmers. This was to set an example for all people to devote themselves to their professions, and to ensure that the officials were familiar with the hardships of the common people, thereby preventing them from exploiting the commoners for their own profit.

3. Farmers should personally attend to the inspection, measurement, and management of the fields, noting the soil as well as the terrain. The early harvest as well as the grain taxes and the labor service obligations should be carefully calculated. Anyone who indulges in indolence and entrusts these matters to others will not be able to distinguish one kind of crop from another and will certainly be cheated by others. I do not believe such a person could escape bankruptcy.

4. The usual occupations of the people are farming and commerce. If one tries by every possible means to make a great profit from these occupations, it usually leads to loss of capital. Therefore it is more profitable to put one's energy into farming the land; only when the fields are too far away to be tilled by oneself should they be leased to others. One should solicit advice from old farmers as to one's own capacity in farming.

Those who do not follow the usual occupations of farming or business should be taught a skill. Being an artisan is a good way of life and will also shelter a person from hunger and cold. All in all, it is important to remember that one should work hard when young, for when youth expires one can no longer achieve anything. Many people learn this lesson only after it is too late. We should guard against this mistake.

5. Fish can be raised in ponds by supplying them with grass and manure. Vegetables need water. In empty plots one can plant fruit trees such as the pear, persimmon, peach, prune, and plum, and also beans, wheat, hemp, peas, potatoes, and melons. When harvested, these vegetables and fruits can sustain life. During their growth, one should give them constant care, nourishing them and weeding them. In this way, no labor is wasted and no fertile land is left uncultivated. On the contrary, to purchase everything needed for the morning and evening meals means the members of the family will merely sit and eat. Is this the way things should be?

6. Housewives should take full charge of the kitchen. They should make sure that the store of firewood is sufficient, so that even if it rains several days in succession, they will not be forced to use silver or rice to pay for firewood, thereby impoverishing the family. Housewives should also closely calculate the daily grocery expenses, and make sure there is no undue extravagance. Those who simply sit and wait to be fed only are treating themselves like pigs and dogs, but also are leading their whole households to ruin. . . .

Exercise Restraint

1. Our young people should know their place and observe correct manners. They are not permitted to gamble, to fight, to engage in lawsuits, or to deal in salt[2] privately. Such unlawful acts will only lead to their own downfall.

2. If land or property is not obtained by righteous means, descendants will not be able to enjoy it. When the ancients invented characters, they put gold next to two spears to mean "money," indicating that the danger of plunder or robbery is associated with it. If money is not accumulated by good means, it will disperse like overflowing water; how could it be put to any good? The result is misfortune for oneself as well as for one's posterity. This is the meaning of the saying: "The way of Heaven detests fullness, and only the humble gain." Therefore, accumulation of great wealth inevitably leads to great loss. How true are the words of Laozi![3]

---

[2]Get involved in the salt trade, a state monopoly. Salt was used as a preservative for fish, meat, and other foods. [Ed.]

[3]Lao Tzu, legendary Chinese philosopher and author of the *Dao de Jing*, the Daoist classic. [Ed.]

A person's fortune and rank are predestined. One can only do one's best according to propriety and one's own ability; the rest is up to Heaven. If one is easily contented, then a diet of vegetables and soups provides a lifetime of joy. If one does not know one's limitations and tries to accumulate wealth by immoral and dishonest means, how can one avoid disaster? To be able to support oneself through life and not leave one's sons and grandsons in hunger and cold is enough; why should one toil so much?

3. Pride is a dangerous trait. Those who pride themselves on wealth, rank, or learning are inviting evil consequences. Even if one's accomplishments are indeed unique, there is no need to press them on anyone else. "The way of Heaven detests fullness, and only the humble gain." I have seen the truth of this saying many times.

4. Taking concubines in order to beget heirs should be a last resort, for the sons of the legal wife and the sons of the concubine are never of one mind, causing innumerable conflicts between half brothers. If the parents are in the least partial, problems will multiply, creating misfortune in later generations. Since families have been ruined because of this, it should not be taken lightly.

5. Just as diseases are caused by what goes into one's mouth, misfortunes are caused by what comes out of one's mouth. Those who are immoderate in eating and unrestrained in speaking have no one else to blame for their own ruin.

6. Most men lack resolve and listen to what their women say. As a result, blood relatives become estranged and competitiveness, suspicion, and distance arise between them. Therefore, when a wife first comes into a family, it should be made clear to her that such things are prohibited. "Start teaching one's son when he is a baby; start teaching one's daughter-in-law when she first arrives." That is to say, preventive measures should be taken early.

7. "A family's fortune can be foretold from whether its members are early risers" is a maxim of our ancient sages. Everyone, male and female, should rise before dawn and should not go to bed until after the first drum. Never should they indulge themselves in a false sense of security and leisure, for such behavior will eventually lead them to poverty.

8. Young family members who deliberately violate family regulations should be taken to the family temple, have their offenses reported to the ancestors, and be severely punished. They should then be taught to improve themselves. Those who do not accept punishment or persist in their wrongdoings will bring harm to themselves.

9. As a preventive measure against the unpredictable, the gates should be closed at dusk, and no one should be allowed to go out. Even when there are visitors, dinner parties should end early, so that there will be no need for lighting lamps and candles. On very hot or very cold days, one should be especially considerate of the kitchen servants.

10. For generations this family had dwelt in the country, and everyone has had a set profession; therefore, our descendants should not be allowed to change their place of residence. After living in the city for three years, a person forgets everything about farming; after ten years, he does not even know his lineage. Extravagance and leisure transform people, and it is hard for anyone to remain unaffected. I once remarked that the only legitimate excuse to live in a city temporarily is to flee from bandits.

11. The inner and outer rooms, halls, doorways, and furniture should be swept and dusted every morning at dawn. Dirty doorways and courtyards and haphazardly placed furniture are sure signs of a declining family. Therefore, a schedule should be followed for cleaning them, with no excuses allowed.

12. Those in charge of cooking and kitchen work should make sure that breakfast is served before nine o'clock in the morning and dinner before five o'clock in the afternoon. Every evening the iron wok and other utensils should be washed and put away, so that the next morning, after rising at dawn, one can expect tea and breakfast to be prepared immediately and served on time. In the kitchen no lamps are allowed in the morning or at night. This is not only to save the expense, but also to avoid harmful contamination of food. Although this is a small matter, it has a great effect on health. Furthermore, since all members of the family have their regular work to do, letting them toil all day without giving them meals at regular hours is no way to provide comfort and relief for them. If these rules are deliberately violated, the person in charge will be punished as an example to the rest.

13. On the tenth and twenty-fifth days of every month, all the members of this branch, from the honored aged members to the youngsters, should gather at dusk for a meeting. Each will give an account of what he has learned, by either calling attention to examples of good and evil, or encouraging diligence, or expounding his obligations, or pointing out tasks to be completed. Each member will take turns presenting his own opinions and listening attentively to others. He should examine himself in the matters being discussed and make efforts to improve himself. The purpose of these meetings is to encourage one another in virtue and to correct each other's mistakes.

The members of the family will take turns being the chairman of these meetings, according to schedule. If someone is unable to chair a meeting on a certain day, he should ask the next person in line to take his place. The chairman should provide tea, but never wine. The meetings may be canceled on days of ancestor worship, parties, or other such occasions, or if the weather is severe. Those who are absent from these meetings for no reason are only doing themselves harm.

There are no set rules for where the meeting should be held, but the place should be convenient for group discussions. The time of the meeting should always be early evening, for this is when people have free time. As a general precaution the meeting should never last until late at night.

14. Women from lower-class families who stop at our houses tend to gossip, create conflicts, peek into the kitchens, or induce our women to believe in prayer and fortune-telling, thereby cheating them out of their money and possessions. Consequently, one should question these women often and punish those who come for no reason, so as to put a stop to the traffic.

15. Blood relatives are as close as the branches of a tree, yet their relationships can still be differentiated according to importance and priority: Parents should be considered before brothers, and brothers should be considered before wives and children. Each person should fulfill his own duties and share with others profit and loss, joy and sorrow, life and death. In this way, the family will get along well and be blessed by Heaven. Should family members fight over property or end up treating each other like enemies, then when death or misfortune strikes they will be of even less use than strangers. If our ancestors have consciousness, they will not tolerate these unprincipled descendants who are but animals in man's clothing. Heaven responds to human vices with punishments as surely as an echo follows a sound. I hope my sons and grandsons take my words seriously.

16. To get along with patrilineal relatives, fellow villages, and relatives through marriage, one should be gentle in speech and mild in manners. When one is opposed by others, one may remonstrate with them; but when others fall short because of their limitations, one should be tolerant. If one's youngsters or servants get into fights with others, one should look into oneself to find the blame. It is better to be wronged than to wrong others. Those who take affront and become enraged, who conceal their own shortcomings and seek to defeat others, are courting immediate misfortune. Even if the other party is unbearably unreasonable, one should contemplate the fact that the ancient sages had to endure much more. If one remains tolerant and forgiving, one will be able to curb the other party's violence.

22

MAO XIANG

How Dong Xiaowan Became My Concubine

Mao Xiang* (1611–1693) was one of the great poets, artists, and cal-ligraphers of the late Ming dynasty and, after its demise in 1644, a persistent critic of the succeeding Manchu or Ching dynasty. He was also known for his love of beautiful women, especially three fa-mous courtesans who were also talented artists: Dong Xiaowan† (1625–1651), Cai Han (1647–1686), and Qin Yue (c. 1660–1690). (Note what these dates reveal.) Whether or not this is a reliable ac-count of how Dong Xiaowan became his concubine, what does this piece from Mao Xiang's memoir tell you about his society's attitudes towards women, marriage, and family?

Thinking Historically

If comparisons originate in our recognition of institutions and ideas that are foreign to our own, certainly the acceptance of concubines in seventeenth-century Chinese society is a sharp contrast to modern American family values. Concubines were mainly an indulgence of upper-class Chinese men, but concubinage was an institution that touched all classes of Chinese society. Poor peasants knew that they could sell their daughters into the trade, if need be. And even middle-class wives worried that a concubine might be waiting in the wings should they prove to be infertile, unable to bear a son, or otherwise displeasing to their husband or mother-in-law.

We might also compare this selection with the previous one. How does the blatant acceptance of concubinage in this selection compare to the emphasis on family stability in the Miu lineage rules? Are these documents from two different Chinas, or are they compatible? Does this selection force you to modify the contrast you drew between Ming China and modern America from the previous selection?

*mow   zhee ANG
†dong   zhow AHN

"How Dong Xiaowan Became My Concubine," in *Chinese Civilization: A Sourcebook*, 2nd ed., ed. Patricia Ebrey (New York: Free Press, 1993), 246–49.

I was rather depressed that evening, so I got a boat and went with a friend on an excursion to Tiger Hill. My plan was to send a messenger to Xiangyang the next morning and then set out for home. As our boat passed under a bridge, I saw a small building by the bank. When I asked who lived there, my friend told me that this was [the singing girl] Dong's home. I was wildly happy with memories of three years before. I insisted on the boat's stopping, wanting to see Xiaowan at once. My friend, however, restrained me, saying, "Xiaowan has been terrified by the threat of being kidnapped by a powerful man and has been seriously ill for eighteen days. Since her mother's death,[1] she is said to have locked her door and refrained from receiving any guests." I nevertheless insisted on going ashore.

Not until I had knocked two or three times did the door open. I found no light in the house and had to grope my way upstairs. There I discovered medicine all over the table and bed.

Xiaowan, moaning, asked where I had come from and I told her I was the man she once saw beside a winding balustrade, intoxicated.

"Well, Sir," she said, recalling the incident, "I remember years ago you called at my house several times. Even though she only saw you once, my mother often spoke highly of you and considered it a great pity that I never had the chance to wait on you. Three years have passed. Mother died recently, but on seeing you now, I can hear her words in my ears. Where are you coming from this time?"

With an effort, she rose to draw aside the curtains and inspected me closely. She moved the lamp and asked me to sit on her bed. After talking awhile, I said I would go, not wanting to tire her. She, however, begged me to remain, saying, "During the past eighteen days I have had no appetite for food, nor have I been able to sleep well. My soul has been restless, dreaming almost all the time. But on seeing you, I feel as if my spirit has revived and my vigor returned." She then had her servant serve wine and food at her bedside, and kept refilling my cup herself.

Several times I expressed my desire to leave, but each time she urged me to stay. . . . The following morning, I was eager to set off on the trip home, but my friend and my servant both asked me not to be ungrateful for Xiaowan's kindness as she had had only a brief chance to talk with me the previous night. Accordingly I went to say goodbye to her. I found her, fresh from her toilet, leaning against a window upstairs quite composed. On seeing my boat approaching the bank, she hurried aboard to greet me. I told her that I had to leave immediately,

---

[1]The "mother" here may well be the woman who managed her, rather than her natural mother.

but she said that she had packed up her belongings and would accompany me. I felt unable to refuse her.

We went from Hushuguan to Wuxi, and from there to Changzhou, Yixing, and Jiangyin, finally arriving at Jinjiang. All this took twenty-seven days, and twenty-seven times I asked her to go back, but she was firm in her desire to follow me. On climbing Golden Hill, she pointed to the river and swore, "My body is as constant as the direction of the Yangzi River. I am determined never to go back to Suzhou!"

On hearing her words, I turned red and reiterated my refusal, "The provincial examination is coming up soon. Because my father's recent posts have been dangerous ones, I have failed to attend to family affairs and have not been able to look after my mother on a daily basis. This is my first chance to go back and take care of things. Moreover, you have so many creditors in Suzhou and it will take a lot to redeem your singing-girl's contract in Nanjing. So please go back to Suzhou for the time being. After I have taken the examination at the end of summer, I will send word and meet you in Nanjing. At any rate, I must await the result of the examination before I even think about these matters. Insisting on it now will do neither of us any good."

She, however, still hesitated. There were dice on the table, and one of my friends said to her jokingly, "If you are ever going to get your wish [to become his concubine], they will land with the same side up." She then bowed toward the window, said a prayer, and tossed the dice. They all landed on six. All on board expressed their amazement, and I said to her, "Should Heaven really be on our side, I'm afraid we might bungle the whole thing if we proceed too hurriedly. You had better leave me temporarily, and we'll see what we can do by and by." Thus against her wishes she said goodbye, concealing her tearstained face with her hands.

I had pity for her plight but at the same time once I was on my own felt relieved of a heavy burden. Upon arrival at Taizhou, I sat for the examination. When I got home in the sixth month, my wife said to me, "Xiaowan sent her father to bring word that since her return to Suzhou, she has kept to a vegetarian diet and confined herself to her home, waiting on tiptoe for you to bring her to Nanjing as you promised. I felt awkward and gave her father ten taels[2] of silver, asking him to tell her that I am in sympathy with her and consent to her request, but she must wait till you finish the examination."

I appreciated the way my wife had handled Xiaowan's request. I then directly proceeded to Nanjing without keeping my promise to send someone to fetch her, planning to write to her after I had finished the examination. However, scarcely had I come out of the examination hall

---

[2]A tael is equivalent to about 1¼ ounce. [Ed.]

on the morning of the 15th of the eighth month when she suddenly called at my lodgings at Peach Leaf Ferry. It turned out that after waiting in vain for news from me, she had hired a boat, setting out from Suzhou and proceeding along the river with an old woman as her companion. She met with robbers on the way, and her boat had to hide among reeds and rushes. With the rudder broken, the boat could not proceed, and she had had practically nothing to eat for three days. She arrived at Sanshan Gate of Nanjing on the 8th, but not wanting to disturb my thoughts during the examination, she delayed entering the city for two days.

Though delighted to see me, she looked and sounded rather sad as she vividly described what had happened during the hundred days of our separation, including her confinement at home on vegetarian fare, her encounter with robbers on the river, and her other experiences of a voyage fraught with danger. Now she was more insistent than ever on getting her wish. The men in my literary society from Kashan, Sungjiang, Fujian, and Henan all admired her farsightedness and sincerity and encouraged her with their verses and paintings.

When the examination was over, I thought I might pass it, so hoped I would soon be able to settle my affairs and gratify her desire to become my concubine. Unexpectedly, on the 17th I was informed that my father had arrived by boat. . . . I had not seen him for two years and was overjoyed that he had returned alive from the battlefront. Without delaying to tell Xiaowan, I immediately went to meet him. . . . Before long she set out by boat in pursuit of me from the lodging house at Peach Leaf Ferry. A storm at Swallow's Ledge nearly cost her her life. At Shierhui she came on board and stayed with me again for seven days.

When the results of the examination were announced, I found my name on the list of the not quite successful candidates. I then traveled day and night to get home, while she followed weeping, unwilling to part. I was, however, well aware that I could not by myself settle her affairs in Suzhou and that her creditors would, on discovering her departure, increase their demands. Moreover, my father's recent return and my disappointment in the exams had made it all the more difficult to gratify her desire at once. On arrival at Puchao on the outskirts of my native city, I had to put on a cold face and turn ironhearted to part from her, telling her to go back to Suzhou to set her creditors at ease and thus pave the way for our future plans.

In the tenth month, while passing Jinjiang, I went to visit Mr. Zheng, the man who had been my examiner. At that time, Liu Daxing of Fujian had arrived from the capital. During a drinking party in his boat with General Chen, my friend Prefect Liu, and myself, my servant returned from seeing Xiaowan home. He reported that on arrival at Suzhou she did not change out of her autumn clothing, saying that she intended to die of cold if I did not see my way to settle her affairs promptly. On hearing this, Liu Daxing pointed to me and said, "Pijiang, you are well known as a man of honor. Could you really betray a girl like this?"

"Surely scholars are not capable of the gallant deeds of Huang Shanke and Gu Yaya," I replied.

The prefect raised his cup, and with a gesture of excitement exclaimed, "Well, if I were given a thousand taels of silver to pay my expenses, I'd start right away today!"

General Chen at once lent me several hundred taels, and Liu Daxing helped with a present of several catties[3] of ginseng. But how could it have been anticipated that the prefect, on arrival at Suzhou, failed to carry out his mission, and that when the creditors had kicked up a row and the matter had been brought to a deadlock, he fled to Wujiang? I had no chance to make further inquiries, as I returned home shortly afterwards.

Xiaowan was left in an awkward position, with little she could do. On hearing of her trouble, Qian Qianyi of Changshu went to Bantang himself and brought her to his boat. He approached her creditors, from the gentry to the townsmen, and within three days managed to clear every single debt of hers, the bills redeemed piling up a foot in height. This done, he arranged a farewell banquet on a pleasure boat and entertained her at the foot of Tiger Hill. He then hired a boat and sent someone to see her to Rugao.

On the evening of the 15th of the eleventh month when I was drinking wine with my father in our Zhuocun Hall, I was suddenly informed that Xiaowan had arrived at the jetty. After reading Qian's long interesting letter, I learned how she had gotten here. I also learned that Qian had written to a pupil of his, Zhang of the ministry of rites, asking him to redeem her singing girl's contract at once. Her minor problems at Suzhou were later settled by Mr. Zhou of the bureau of ceremonies while Mr. Li, formerly attached to that bureau, had also rendered her great assistance in Nanjing.

Ten months thereafter, her desire was gratified [and she became my concubine]. After the endless tangle of troubles and emotional pain, we had what we wanted.

---

[3]One catty is equivalent to 16 taels, 20 ounces, or a British pound. [Ed.]

23

KENNETH POMERANZ
How the Other Half Traded

The "other half" of this recent essay, written by historian Kenneth Pomeranz, refers not only to women, but to the women who were the Southeast Asian trading partners of Portuguese and then Dutch merchants in the sixteenth and seventeenth centuries. Why did these women play such an important role in European trade with Southeast Asia? How did both Europeans and Southeast Asians benefit socially and economically from these alliances?

Thinking Historically

Pomeranz enables us to make a number of comparisons about gender and family. How, for instance, was the role of women in Southeast Asia different from that of their sisters in China? How did the role and rights of women in Europe differ from those in Southeast Asia? Were gender relations more alike in Europe and Southeast Asia, or in Europe and China? How would you expect European trade with China to be different from European trade with Southeast Asia?

Even today, companies often find that keeping up the morale of employees sent overseas is difficult. But consider an earlier multinational: the Dutch East India Company (VOC) of the seventeenth and eighteenth centuries. Its outposts in India, Southeast Asia, Japan, and Taiwan were places where few Dutchwomen were willing to live; and while most men working for the company were quite willing to seek mates among indigenous women, this brought complications of its own. Given the cultural gulf separating these couples, it may be no great surprise that the private letters of these men are full of references to how hard it was to "tame" these women into the kinds of wives they expected. What may be more surprising is how hard the VOC, the Dutch Reformed Church, and other Europeans in Southeast Asia found it to break the *commercial* power of these women, many of whom were substantial traders in their own right.

Kenneth Pomeranz, "How the Other Half Traded," in Kenneth Pomeranz and Steven Topik, eds., *The World That Trade Created* (Armonk, N.Y.: M. E. Sharpe, 2006), 27–30.

Long before Europeans arrived, maritime Southeast Asia (including present-day Malaysia, Indonesia, and the Philippines) carried on a substantial long-distance trade. Many of the merchants were women — in some cases because commerce was thought too base an occupation for upper-class men, but too lucrative for elite families to abstain from completely. (Some elites carried this snobbery a step further, and held that noble women were also too lofty to barter in the marketplace or to visit the Chinese settlements where much long-distance trading was arranged; they were not, however, too noble to supervise a team of servants who carried out these businesses.) Malay proverbs of the 1500s spoke of the importance of teaching daughters how to calculate and make a profit.

More generally, these societies typically allowed women to control their own property, gave them considerable voice in the choice of husbands, and were often quite tolerant of other liaisons. The long journeys away from home that some of these women took even made it necessary to allow them, within the crude limits of available technology, to control their own fertility. (Herbal medicines, jumping from rocks to induce miscarriages, and even occasional infanticides were among the methods used.) Both the Islamic missionaries who swept through the area in the 1400s and the Christians who followed a hundred years later were appalled, and hoped to bring such women to heel.

But despite these qualms, the Portuguese, the first Europeans to establish themselves in this world, had found intermarrying with such women to be an indispensable part of creating profitable and defensible colonies. When the VOC gave up on importing Dutchwomen — having sometimes found "willing" candidates only in the orphanages or even brothels of Holland, and facing discontent among the intended husbands of these women — it turned to the daughters of these earlier Portuguese-Asian unions: they at least spoke a Western language, and were at least nominally Christian. Many had also learned from their mothers how useful a European husband could be for protecting their business interests in an increasingly multinational and often violent trading world. Councillors of the Dutch court in Batavia (present-day Jakarta), who were rarely rich themselves, but were very well placed to prevent the VOC's rules and monopoly claims from interfering with their wives' trade, were often particularly good matches for the richest of these women. Thus, arranging elite interracial marriages proved relatively easy: but making the resulting families conform to visions hatched in Amsterdam proved harder.

The VOC's principal goal, of course, was profit, and profit was best secured by monopolizing the export of all sorts of Asian goods — from pepper to porcelain — back to Europe. In theory, the Company also claimed — at least intermittently — the right to license and tax (or sink) all the ships participating in the much larger intra-Asian trade, including those of Southeast Asia's women traders. But the realities of huge oceans and numerous rivals made enforcing such a system impossible, and the VOC also faced powerful enemies within. Most Company servants soon discovered that while smuggling goods back to Holland was risky and difficult, they could earn sums by trading illegally (or semi-legally) within Asia that dwarfed their official salaries. Here their wives were a perfect vehicle for making a fortune: they were well connected in and knowledgeable about local markets, often possessed of considerable capital, and able to manage the family business continuously without being susceptible to sudden transfer by the Company.

And for some particularly unscrupulous Dutchmen there was the possibility of a kind of lucrative cultural arbitrage: after profiting from the relatively high status of Southeast Asian women, one might take advantage of their low status in Dutch law to gain sole control of the family fortune, and then perhaps even return to the Netherlands to settle down with a "proper" wife. (Though even with the law on the man's side, such a process could be very complex if the woman used her informal influence cleverly and hid her assets — in one such case the man eventually won control of most of his wife's profits, but the legal proceedings took nineteen years.)

But if men had powerful allies in the Dutch law and church, women had the climate on their side. Foreigners tended to die young in India and Southeast Asia, leaving behind wealthy widows. Such women were often eagerly sought after by the next wave of incoming European adventurers, enabling them to strike marriage bargains that safeguarded at least some of their independence; many wed and survived three or four husbands. The rare Dutchman who did live a long life in Batavia was likely to rise quite high in the VOC, become very wealthy, and marry more than once himself; but since such men (not needing a particularly well-connected or rich spouse once they'd risen this high) often chose a last wife much younger than themselves, they tended to leave behind a small circle of very wealthy widows, whose behavior often scandalized those Dutchmen who took their Calvinism seriously.

From the founding of Batavia in 1619 until the late 1800s, Dutch moralists and monopolists waged an endless battle to "tame" these women, and at least partially succeeded; later generations, for instance, seem to have conformed much more than earlier ones to European sexual mores. And as the scale of capital and international contacts needed to succeed in long-distance trade grew larger, European companies and their Chinese or Indian merchant allies — all of them male — did increasingly shrink the sphere in which these women operated.

Eventually, when late nineteenth-century innovations — the Suez Canal, telegraphs, refrigerated shipping, vaccinations, and so on — made it more and more possible to live a truly European life-style in Southeast Asia, a new generation of Dutch officials chose to bring wives with them, or to assume they would quickly return to Holland and marry there.

Even so, trade managed by Eurasian women remained a crucial part of local and regional economies: many, for instance, managed commercial real estate and money-lending operations through which they funneled profits from their husbands' activities into local development around the fringes of Southeast Asian trading cities. (Ironically, this niche may have been kept for them in part through the racism of many of their husbands, who preferred to deal with the locals as little as possible.)

As late as the turn of the twentieth century, this sphere and those who managed it refused to disappear — the Indonesian novelist Pramoedaya Toer has painted a powerful portrait of one such woman, who waged a running battle to hold on to the businesses (and children) she had handled for years against her half-mad Dutch consort and his "legal" family back in Holland. Along with most of her real-life counterparts, this fictional woman was ultimately defeated; but for three centuries, women like her had built and sustained much of the world their husbands claimed was theirs.

$$24$$

JOHN E. WILLS JR.

Sor Juana Inés de la Cruz

After the conquest of the Aztecs, the Spanish attempted to govern Mexico by converting the surviving Indians to Roman Catholicism and exploiting their labor. In addition, they encouraged fellow Spaniards to settle in the colony and imported African slaves, creating a mixed society of Europeans, Indians, and Africans. As in the rest of North America, the dividing line between slave and free was the most important social distinction. But unlike their English counterparts to the north, New Spain's colonists also distinguished between *Peninsulares*, colonists who were born in Spain, and Creoles, colonists who were born of Spanish parents in the Americas.

In the following selection a modern historian evokes the life of Sor Juana Inés de la Cruz* (1651–1695), a poet, artist, and nun who lived

---

*sohr hoo AH nah   ee NEZ   duh lah CROOZ

John E. Wills Jr., "Sor Juana Inés de la Cruz," in *1688: A Global History* (New York: W. W. Norton, 2001), 13–19.

in Mexico City in "New Spain." Sister Juana was a Creole woman and the author argues she was distinctly a product of Mexican Creole society. In what ways was she Spanish? In what ways was she Mexican? How do you think the life of a Creole woman, born and raised in the colony, would be different from that of a woman born in Spain?

Thinking Historically

The previous selection reminds us that some societies, like Southeast Asia, were less patriarchal than others. The arrival of Europeans sometimes enhanced the wealth and influence of women traders in Southeast Asia. The widows and daughters of mixed marriages often benefited from both worlds.

The daughters of Spanish settlers in the Americas had fewer opportunities for financial advancement than did the daughters of Dutch settlers in Java, and the Spanish patriarchy was as unyielding as any in Europe. Nevertheless, the culture that the Old World imported into the New provided alternatives for women that were absent in the East Indies. What were these alternatives? Were they a product of Europe, America, or the intermixture of the two?

On April 28, 1688, a long procession moved out of Mexico City, along the causeways that crossed the nearby lakes, and through the small towns and farms of the plateau, on its way toward the pass between the two volcanoes Iztaccihuatl and Popocatépetl, both more than sixteen thousand feet high, and down to the tropical port of Vera Cruz. The farmers in their villages and fields were used to a good deal of such coming and going, but this time they stopped their work to look and to call out to each other in Nahuatl, the main indigenous language, for this was no ordinary procession. Cavalry outriders and a huge coach were followed by many baggage wagons and a long line of fine coaches. The marquis of Laguna had served as viceroy of New Spain from 1680 to 1686. With their wealth, powerful connections in Madrid, and a taste for elegance and the arts, he and his wife had given the viceregal court a few years of splendor and sophistication comparable, if not to Madrid, certainly to many of the lesser courts of Europe. Now their wealthy Spanish friends were riding in their coaches as far as the Villa de Guadalupe, seeing the marquis and marchioness off on their voyage home to Spain.

> A child born of a slave shall be received,
> according to our Law, as property
> of the owner to whom fealty
> is rendered by the mother who conceived.

The harvest from a grateful land retrieved,
the finest fruit, offered obediently,
is for the lord, for its fecundity
is owing to the care it has received.
  So too, Lysis divine, these my poor lines:
as children of my soul, born of my heart,
they must in justice be to you returned;
  Let not their defects cause them to be spurned,
for of your rightful due they are a part,
as concepts of a soul to yours consigned.

These lines were written sometime later in 1688 and sent off from Mexico to the marchioness of Laguna in Spain. They make use of metaphors and classical conceits to express and conceal the feelings of the author, who had lost, with the marchioness's departure, the object of the nearest thing she had ever known to true love and, with the marquis's departure, her ultimate protection from those who found her opinions and her way of life scandalous. The trouble was not that the author was lesbian — although her feelings toward men and women were unusually complicated and unconventional, anything approaching a physical relation or even passion is most unlikely — but that she was a cloistered Hieronymite nun, who read and studied a wide range of secular books, held long intellectual conversations with many friends, wrote constantly in a variety of religious and secular styles, and betrayed in her writings sympathy for Hermetic and Neoplatonic views that were on the edge of heresy if not beyond it. Her name in religion was Sor Juana Inés de la Cruz. She is recognized today as one of the great poets in the history of the Spanish language.

Mexico in the 1680s was a society of dramatic contradictions. The elegant viceregal court and the opulent ecclesiastical hierarchy looked toward Europe for style and ideas. The vast majority of the population sought to preserve as much as possible of the language, beliefs, and ways of life that had guided them before the coming of the Spaniards; the worship of the Virgin of Guadalupe, for example, owed much to the shrine of an Aztec goddess that had been the setting of the original appearance of the Virgin to a Mexican peasant. In between the "peninsular" elite and the "Indians," the native-born "creoles" of Spanish language and culture managed huge cattle ranches and sought constantly new veins of profitable silver ore and new techniques to exploit old ones. Neither "Spanish" nor "Indian," they experienced the full force of the contradictions of Mexican society and culture.

The literary world in which Sor Juana was such an anomalous eminence thrived on these contradictions of society and culture. This was a baroque culture. The word *baroque,* originating as a Portuguese term for the peculiar beauty of a deformed, uneven pearl, suggests a range of artistic styles in which the balance and harmony of the Renaissance styles are abandoned for imbalance, free elaboration of form, playful gesture, and surprising allusion, through which the most intense of emotions and the darkest of realities may be glimpsed, their power enhanced by the glittering surface that partially conceals them. Contradiction and its partial, playful reconciliation are the stuff of the baroque style. So is the layering of illusion on illusion, meaning upon meaning. And what more baroque conceit could be imagined than the literary eminence of a cloistered nun in a rough frontier society, with a church and state of the strongest and narrowest male supremacist prejudices? Look again at the poem quoted earlier: The chaste nun refers to her poem as her child or the harvest from a grateful land. She declares her love once again to the departed marchioness.

Sor Juana was a product of Mexican creole society, born on a ranch on the shoulder of the great volcano Popocatépetl. Her mother was illiterate and very probably had not been married to her father. But some of the family branches lived in the city, with good books and advantageous connections. As soon as she discovered the books in her grandfather's library, she was consumed with a thirst for solitude and reading. Her extraordinary talents for literature and learning were recognized. When she was fifteen, in 1664, she was taken into the household of a newly arrived viceroy, as his wife's favorite and constant companion. She must have enjoyed the attention, the luxury, the admiration of her cleverness. She no doubt participated in the highly stylized exchange of "gallantries" between young men and young women. But she had no dowry. Solitude was her natural habitat. As a wife and mother, what chance would she have to read, to write, to be alone? In 1668 she took her vows in the Hieronymite convent of an order named after Saint Jerome, cloistered and meditative by rule.

This was a big decision, but less drastic than one might think. Certainly she was a believing Catholic. Her new status did not require total devotion to prayer and extinction of self. It did not imply that she was abandoning all the friendships and secular learning that meant so much to her. The nuns had a daily round of collective devotions; but many rules were not fully honored, and the regimen left her much free time for reading and writing. Each of the nuns had comfortable private quarters, with a kitchen, room for a bathtub, and sleeping space for a servant and a dependent or two; Sor Juana usually had one slave and one or two nieces or other junior dependents living in her quarters. The nuns visited back and forth in their quarters to the point that Sor Juana complained of the interruptions to her reading and writing, but outsiders spoke to the nuns only in the locutory especially provided for that purpose. From the beginning she turned the locutory into an elegant salon, as the viceroy and his lady and other fashionable people came to visit her and they passed hours in learned debate, literary improvisation, and gossip.

One of Sor Juana's most constant friends and supporters was Carlos de Sigüenza y Góngora, professor of mathematics at the University of Mexico, an eminently learned creole scholar whose position was almost as anomalous as hers. He had been educated by the Jesuits and had longed to be one of them but had been expelled from their college. He had managed to obtain his position, without a university degree, by demonstrating his superior knowledge of his subject. He had added Góngora to his name to emphasize his distant kinship, through his mother's family, with the most famous of Spain's baroque poets. But he always felt insecure among the European-born professors, churchmen, and high officials. He wrote a great deal, much of it about the history of Mexico. He was in no way Sor Juana's equal as a writer, but he probably was responsible for most of her smattering of knowledge of modern science and recent philosophy.

There was a rule of poverty among the Hieronymites, but it was generally ignored. Sor Juana received many gifts, some of them substantial enough to enable the former dowerless girl to invest money at interest. By gift and purchase she built up a library of about four thousand volumes and a small collection of scientific instruments, probably provided by Sigüenza. Her reading was broad but not very systematic, contributing to the stock of ideas and allusions she drew on constantly in her writings but giving her little sense of the intellectual tensions and transformations that were building up in Europe. She wrote constantly, in a wide variety of complex and exacting forms. Voluntarily or upon commission or request, she wrote occasional poems of all kinds for her friends and patrons. A celebration might call for a *loa*, a brief theatrical piece in praise of a dignitary. In one of hers, for example, a character "clad in sunrays" declares:

> I am a reflection
> of that blazing sun
> who, among shining rays
> numbers brilliant sons:
> when his illustrious rays
> strike a speculum,
> on it is portrayed
> the likeness of his form.

Sor Juana's standing in society reached a new height with the arrival in 1680 of the marquis and marchioness of Laguana. Even in the public festivities celebrating their arrival, she outdid herself in baroque elaborations of texts and conceits for a temporary triumphal arch erected at the cathedral. It was an allegory on Neptune, in which the deeds of the Greek god were compared to the real or imaginary deeds of the marquis. Much was made of the echoes among the marquis's title of Laguna, meaning *lake*, Neptune's reign over the oceans, and the origins of Mexico City as the Aztec city of Tenochtitlán in the middle of its great lake: an elaborate union of sycophancy to a ruler, somewhat strained classical allusion, and a creole quest for a Mexican identity. In parts of the text the author even drew in Isis as an ancestor of Neptune, and in others of her works from this time she showed a great interest in Egyptian antiquity as it was then understood, including the belief that the god Hermes Trismegistus had revealed the most ancient and purest wisdom and anticipated the Mosaic and Christian revelations. These ideas, the accompanying quasi-Platonic separation of soul and body, and her use of them to imply that a female or androgynous condition was closer to the divine wisdom than the male took her to the edge of heresy or beyond and was turned against her in later years.

Sor Juana soon established a close friendship with the marchioness of Laguna. Some of the poems she sent her are among her very finest, and they are unmistakably love poems. Some of them accompanied a portrait of the author. Several portraits in which a very handsome woman gazes boldly at us, her black-and-white habit simply setting off her own strength and elegance, have come down to us. [See Figure 4.1.]

> And if it is that you should rue
> the absence of a soul in me [the portrait],
> you can confer one, easily,
> from the many rendered you:
> and as my soul I [Sor Juana] tendered you,
> and though my being yours obeyed,
> and though you look on me amazed
> in this insentient apathy,
> you are the soul of this body,
> and are the body of this shade.

The marquis of Laguna stepped down as viceroy in 1686 but remained in Mexico until 1688. In that year Sor Juana was very busy. The marchioness was taking texts of her poems back to Spain, where they soon would be published. She added to them a play, *The Divine Narcissus*, interweaving the legend of Narcissus and the life of Jesus, which probably was performed in Madrid in 1689 or 1690. Her niece took her vows in the convent in 1688. Late in the year, after her noble friends had left, she wrote the poem quoted earlier as well as a romantic comedy, *Love Is the Greater Labyrinth*, which was performed in Mexico City early in 1689.

A large collection of her poetry was published in Madrid in 1689. The next year in Mexico she published a letter taking abstruse issue with a sermon preached decades before by the famous Portuguese Jesuit

Figure 4.1 Portrait of Sor Juana Inés de la Cruz, 1750.
This portrait of Sor Juana was done by one of Mexico's most famous
painters, Miguel Cabrera (1695–1768), the official painter of the Archbishop of Mexico. The nun sits surrounded by the emblems of her literary
life, including quill pens, inkwell, and an open volume from her enormous
library. In the original portrait, the viewer can discern a host of classical
authors lining the shelves, including Hippocrates, Virgil, and Cicero.
      Source: Schalkwijk/Art Resource, N.Y.

Antonio Vieira. Her casual way with the rules of the religious life, her
flirtings with heresy, her many writings in secular forms with intima-
tions of understanding of love inappropriate to her profession had
made her many enemies, but they could do nothing while the marquis
of Laguna and his lady were on hand to protect her. Now they closed

in. In 1694 she was forced formally to renounce all writing and humane studies and to relinquish her library and collection of scientific instruments. In 1695 she devotedly cared for her sisters in the convent during an epidemic, caught the disease, and died.

25

ANNA BIJNS

"Unyoked Is Best! Happy the Woman without a Man"

Anna Bijns* (1494–1575) was a Flemish poet who lived in Antwerp, taught in a Catholic school in that city, wrote biting criticism of Martin Luther and the Protestant Reformation, and in her many works helped shape the Dutch language. The impact of Luther, and Protestantism more generally, on the lives of women has been the subject of much debate. Luther opposed nunneries and monasticism, believing that it was the natural duty of all women to marry and bear children. At the same time, he encouraged a level of reciprocal love and respect in marriage that was less emphasized in Catholicism. The Protestant translations of the Bible from Latin also opened a pathway for individuals, including educated women, to participate in the religious life, though not as nuns. Whether or not the sentiments of this poem are more Catholic than Protestant, are they more European than Chinese? Why or why not?

Thinking Historically

No one should imagine that the ideas conveyed in this poem were typical or representative of European thought in the sixteenth century. This was obviously an extreme view that ran counter to traditional and commonly accepted ideas. Note how some phrases of the poem convey the recognition that most people will disagree with the sentiments being expressed.

*bynz

Anna Bijns, "Unyoked Is Best," trans. Kristiaan P. G. Aercke, in *Women and Writers of the Renaissance and Reformation*, ed. Katharina M. Wilson (Athens: The University of Georgia Press, 1987), 382–83.

When we are comparing documents from different cultures, we must always try to understand how representative they are of the views of the larger population. The Miu family document (selection 21) expresses the views of a single family, but lineage regulations were common in sixteenth-century China, and their ubiquity reflected an even greater consensus on the importance of the family. Anna Bijns's poem is a personal view that expresses a minority opinion. But in what sense is this a European, rather than Chinese, minority view? What sort of extreme minority views might Southeast Asian or European-American cultures produce? Do you think Anna Bijns's view might appeal to more people today than it did in the sixteenth century? If so, why?

How good to be a woman, how much better to be a man!
Maidens and wenches, remember the lesson you're about to hear.
Don't hurtle yourself into marriage far too soon.
The saying goes: "Where's your spouse? Where's your honor?"
But one who earns her board and clothes
Shouldn't scurry to suffer a man's rod.
So much for my advice, because I suspect —
Nay, see it sadly proven day by day —
'T happens all the time!
However rich in goods a girl might be,
Her marriage ring will shackle her for life.
If however she stays single
With purity and spotlessness foremost,
Then she is lord as well as lady, Fantastic, not?
Though wedlock I do not decry:
Unyoked is best! Happy the woman without a man.

Fine girls turning into loathly hags —
'Tis true! Poor sluts! Poor tramps! Cruel marriage!
Which makes me deaf to wedding bells.
Huh! First they marry the guy, luckless dears,
Thinking their love just too hot to cool.
Well, they're sorry and sad within a single year.
Wedlock's burden is far too heavy.
They know best whom it harnessed.
So often is a wife distressed, afraid.
When after troubles hither and thither he goes
In search of dice and liquor, night and day,
She'll curse herself for that initial "yes."
So, beware ere you begin.
Just listen, don't get yourself into it.
Unyoked is best! Happy the woman without a man.

A man oft comes home all drunk and pissed
Just when his wife had worked her fingers to the bone
(So many chores to keep a decent house!),
But if she wants to get in a word or two,
She gets to taste his fist — no more.
And that besotted keg she is supposed to obey?
Why, yelling and scolding is all she gets,
Such are his ways — and hapless his victim.
And if the nymphs of Venus he chooses to frequent,
What hearty welcome will await him home.
Maidens, young ladies: learn from another's doom,
Ere you, too, end up in fetters and chains,
Please don't argue with me on this,
No matter who contradicts, I stick to it:
Unyoked is best! Happy the woman without a man.

A single lady has a single income,
But likewise, isn't bothered by another's whims.
And I think: that freedom is worth a lot.
Who'll scoff at her, regardless what she does,
And though every penny she makes herself,
Just think of how much less she spends!
An independent lady is an extraordinary prize —
All right, of a man's boon she is deprived,
But she's lord and lady of her very own hearth.
To do one's business and no explaining sure is lots of fun!
Go to bed when she list,[1] rise when she list, all as she will,
And no one to comment! Grab tight your independence then.
Freedom is such a blessed thing.
To all girls: though the right Guy might come along:
Unyoked is best! Happy the woman without a man.

Regardless of the fortune a woman might bring,
Many men consider her a slave, that's all.
Don't let a honeyed tongue catch you off guard,
Refrain from gulping it all down. Let them rave,
For, I guess, decent men resemble white ravens.
Abandon the airy castles they will build for you.
Once their tongue has limed[2] a bird:
Bye bye love — and love just flies away.
To women marriage comes to mean betrayal

[1]Wants. [Ed.]
[2]Caught. [Ed.]

And the condemnation to a very awful fate.
All her own is spent, her lord impossible to bear.
It's *peine forte et dure*[3] instead of fun and games.
Oft it was the money, and not the man
Which goaded so many into their fate.
Unyoked is best! Happy the woman without a man.

[3]Long and forceful punishment; a form of torture whereby the victim was slowly crushed by heaping rocks on a board laid over his or her body. [Ed.]

26

MARY JO MAYNES
AND ANN WALTNER

Women and Marriage in Europe and China

This article is the product of a rich collaboration between historians of China and Europe who show us how a study of women and marriage is anything but peripheral to a study of these areas. Rather it can help us answer a major historical question: How do we explain the dramatic rise of Western Europe after 1500, especially in the wake of prodigious Chinese growth that continued into the sixteenth century?

The authors begin by comparing the role of religion, the state, and the family in setting marriage patterns in both China and Europe. Did Christianity allow European women more independence than Confucianism allowed women in China? In which society was the patriarchal family more powerful, and what was the relative impact of patriarchy on women in both societies? How did the age and rate at which people married in each society compare? What was the importance of Chinese concubinage and Christian ideals of chastity?

Thinking Historically

The authors' questions about marriage in Europe and China lead finally to a consideration of one of the most frequently asked comparative questions: Why did Europe industrialize before China? Do the dif-

Mary Jo Maynes and Ann Waltner, "Childhood, Youth, and the Female Life Cycle: Women's Life-Cycle Transitions in a World-Historical Perspective: Comparing Marriage in China and Europe," *Journal of Women's History*, 12, no. 4 (Winter 2001), 11–19.

ferent European and Chinese marriage patterns answer this question? What other comparative questions would we have to ask to arrive at a full answer?

Comparing Marriage Cross-Culturally

A number of years ago, we were involved in organizing a comparative historical conference on gender and kinship (our areas of specialization are Chinese and European family and women's history). Conversations that began at the conference resulted in a collection of coedited articles, but they also spurred the two of us to collaboratively teach a world history course in which family and women's history play key roles. We introduce students in that course to historical comparison by talking about marriage. In particular, we begin with a pointed comparison between the history of marriage in China and Europe based on research presented at the kinship conference.

Beginning in the late 1500s, women in northern Italy began to appeal to legal courts run by the Catholic Church when they got into disputes with their families over arranged marriages. Within the early modern Italy family system the father held a great deal of authority over his children and it was usual for the parents to determine when and whom sons and daughters married. Women and children held little power in comparison with adult men. But the Catholic Church's insistence that both parties enter into the marriage willingly gave some women an out — namely, an appeal to the Church court, claiming that the marriage their family wanted was being forced upon them without their consent. Surprisingly, these young women often won their cases against their fathers. In early modern China, by way of contrast, state, religion, and family were bound together under the veil of Confucianism. Paternal authority echoed and reinforced the political and the moral order. Religious institutions could rarely be called upon to intervene in family disputes. Therefore, young women (or young men, for that matter) had no clearly established institutional recourse in situations of unwanted marriage. So, despite the fact that paternal power was very strong in both early modern Italy and early modern China, specific institutional differences put young women at the moment of marriage in somewhat different positions.

We began with the presumption that however different the institution of "marriage" was in Italy and China, it nevertheless offered enough similarities that it made sense to speak comparatively about a category called "marriage." Parallels in the two cultures between the institution of marriage and the moment in the woman's life course that it represented make comparison useful. Nevertheless, this particular comparison also isolates some of the variable features of marriage systems that are especially significant in addressing gender relations in a world-historical context. In China, the rules of family formation and family governance were generally enforced within the bounds of each extended family group. State and religious influences were felt only indirectly through family leaders as mediators or enforcers of state and religious law. Throughout Europe, beginning in the Middle Ages, the institution of marriage was altered first by the effort of the Catholic Church to wrest some control over marriage from the family by defining it as a sacrament, and then eventually by the struggle between churches and state authorities to regulate families.

This contest among church, state, and family authorities over marriage decisions turns out to have been a particular feature of European history that had consequences for many aspects of social life. A focus on the moment of marriage presents special opportunities for understanding connections between the operation of gender relations in everyday life and in the realm of broader political developments. Marriage is a familial institution, of course, but, to varying degrees, political authorities also have a stake in it because of its implications for property transfer, reproduction, religion, and morality — in short, significant aspects of the social order. In this essay, we compare one dimension of marriage — its timing in a woman's life cycle — in two contexts, Europe and China. We argue that variations in marriage timing have world-historical implications. We examine how a woman's status and situation shifted at marriage and then suggest some implications of comparative differences in the timing and circumstances of this change of status.

The Moment of Marriage in European History

One striking peculiarity of Central and Western European history between 1600 and 1850 was the relatively late age at first marriage for men and women compared with other regions of the world. The so-called "Western European marriage pattern" was marked by relatively late marriage — that is, relative to other regions of the world where some form of marriage usually occurred around the time of puberty. In much of Europe, in contrast, men did not typically marry until their late twenties and women their mid-twenties. This practice of relatively late marriage was closely connected with the custom of delaying marriage until the couple commanded sufficient resources to raise a family. For artisans this traditionally meant having a shop and master status. For merchants it entailed saving capital to begin a business. In the case of peasant couples, this meant having a house and land and basic farming equipment. It was the responsibility of the family and the community to oversee courtship, betrothal, and marriage to assure that these conditions were met. This phenomenon was also rooted in the common practice of neolocality — the expectation that a bride and groom would set up their own household at or soon after marriage. This "delayed" marriage has attracted the attention of European historical demographers. The delay of marriage meant, quite significantly, that most European women did not begin to have children until their twenties. But this marriage pattern also has significance in other realms as well. In particular, young people of both sexes experienced a relatively long hiatus between puberty and marriage.

Unmarried European youth played a distinctive role in economic, social, cultural, and political life through such institutions as guilds, village youth groups, and universities. For the most part, historians' attention to European youth has centered on young men. Major works on the history of youth in Europe, like theories of adolescent development, tend to center on the male experience as normative. Only when gender differences in youth are recognized and the history of young women is written will the broad historical significance of the European marriage pattern become clear. Contrast between European demographic history and that of other world regions suggests a comparative pattern of particular significance for girls: Delayed marriage and childbearing meant that teenage girls were available for employment outside the familial household (either natal or marital) to a degree uncommon elsewhere. Household divisions of labor according to age and gender created constant demand for servants on larger farms; typically, unmarried youth who could be hired in from neighboring farms as servants filled this role. A period of service in a farm household, as an apprentice, or as a domestic servant in an urban household characterized male and female European youth in the lifecycle phase preceding marriage. Historians have noted but never fully explored the role young women played in European economic development, and in particular their role in the early industrial labor force.

Late marriage had gender-specific cultural ramifications as well. Whereas it was considered normal and even appropriate for teenage men to be initiated into heterosexual intercourse at brothels, in most regions of Europe, young women were expected to remain chaste until marriage. Delay of marriage heightened anxiety over unmarried women's sexuality, especially the dangers to which young women were increasingly exposed as the locus of their labor shifted from home and village to factory and city. Premarital or extramarital sexuality was uncommon, and was rigorously policed especially in the period following the religious upheavals of the Reformation in the sixteenth century. In rural areas, church and community, in addition to the family, exerted control over sexuality. Moreover, the unmarried male youth cohort of many village communities often served, in effect, as "morals police," enforcing local customs. These young men regulated courtship rituals, organized dances that young people went to, and oversaw the formation of couples. Sometimes, judging and public shaming by the youth group was the fate of couples who were mismatched by age or wealth or who violated sexual taboos. Some customs, at least symbolically, punished young men from far away who married local women, removing them from the marriage pool. Often, such a bridegroom had to pay for drinks in each village that the bridal couple passed through as they moved from the bride's parish church to their new abode — the longer the distance, the more expensive his bill.

Once married, a couple would usually begin having children immediately. Demographic evidence suggests that for most of Central and Western Europe there was virtually no practice of contraception among lower classes prior to the middle of the nineteenth century. Women had babies about every two years (more or less frequently according to region and depending on such local customs as breast-feeding length and intercourse taboos). Even though completed family sizes could be large by modern standards, the number of children most women bore was still less than if they had married in their teens. And prevailing high mortality rates further reduced the number of children who survived to adulthood.

The Moment of Marriage in Chinese History

The Chinese marriage system was traditionally characterized by early age at marriage, nearly universal marriage for women, virilocal residence (a newly married couple resided with the groom's parents), concubinage for elite men, and norms that discouraged widow remarriage. From the sixteenth through twentieth centuries, Chinese men and women married much younger on average than did their European counterparts — late teens or early twenties for women and a bit later for men. A bride typically moved to her husband's family home, which was often in a different village from her own. The moment of marriage not only meant that a girl would leave her parents but that she would also leave her network of kin and friends, all that was familiar. Families chose marriage partners, and a matchmaker negotiated the arrangements. Nothing resembling courtship existed; the bride and groom would often first meet on their wedding day.

Because a newly married Chinese couple would typically reside in an already-existing household, it was not necessary for an artisan to become established, a merchant to accumulate capital, or a peasant to own a farm before marrying. Newly married couples participated in ongoing domestic and economic enterprises that already supported the groom's family. New households were eventually established by a process of household division, which typically happened at the death of the father rather than the moment of marriage (although it could happen at other points in the family cycle as well).

Daughters were groomed from birth for marriage. They were taught skills appropriate to their social class or the social class into which their parents aspired to marry them. (In the ideal Chinese marriage, the groom was in fact supposed to be of slightly higher social status than the bride.) The feet of upper-class girls (and some who were not upper class) were bound, since Chinese men found this erotic. Bound feet also symbolically, if not actually, restricted upper-class women's movement. Thus bound feet simultaneously enhanced the sexual desirability of upper-class women and served to contain their sexuality within domestic bounds.

Virtually all Chinese girls became brides, though not all of them married as principal wives. (This contrasts with the European pattern where a substantial minority of women in most regions never married.) Upper-class men might take one or more concubines in addition to a principal wife. The relationship between a man and his concubine was recognized legally and ritually, and children born of these unions were legitimate. A wife had very secure status: divorce was almost nonexistent. A concubine's status, in contrast, was much more tenuous. She could be expelled at the whim of her "husband"; her only real protection was community sentiment. Although only a small percentage of Chinese marriages (no more than 5 percent) involved concubines, the practice remained an important structural feature of the Chinese marriage system until the twentieth century. Concubinage also provides a partial explanation of why, despite the fact that marriage was nearly universal for women, a substantial proportion of men (perhaps as high as 10 percent) never married. Also contributing to this apparent anomaly was the practice of sex-selective infanticide, a common practice that discriminated against girl babies and, ultimately, reduced the number of potential brides.

Once married, Chinese couples began to have children almost immediately, generally spacing births at longer intervals than did European couples. The reasons for this are not yet completely understood, although infanticide, extended breast-feeding, and the fairly large number of days on which sexual intercourse was forbidden all seem to have played a role in lowering Chinese family size.

Early marriage in China meant that the category of "youth," which has been so significant for European social and economic history, has no precise counterpart in Chinese history. Young Chinese women labored, to be sure, but the location of their work was domestic — either in the household of their father or husband. Female servants existed in China, but their servitude was normally of longer duration than the life-cycle servitude common in Europe. The domestic location of young women's labor in the Chinese context also had implications for the particular ways in which Chinese industries were organized, as we suggest below.

Patterns of Marriage in Europe and China

To sum up, then, there are differences of both timing of and residency before and after marriage that are particularly germane to the comparative history of young women. As demographic historians James Z. Lee and Wang Feng also have argued, "in China, females have always married universally and early . . . in contrast to female marriage in Western Europe, which occurred late or not at all." Whereas, in the nineteenth century, all but 20 percent of young Chinese women were married by age twenty, among European populations, between 60 and 80 percent of young women remained single at this age. In traditional China, only 1 or 2 percent of women remained unmarried at age thirty, whereas between 15 and 25 percent of thirty-year-old Western European women were still single. (For men, the differences though in the same direction are far less stark.) As for residence, in the Western European neolocal pattern, norms and practices in many regions resulted in a pattern whereby newly married couples moved into a separate household at marriage; but concomitant with this was their delaying marriage until they could afford a new household. In China, newly married couples generally resided in the groom's father's household. In Western Europe, the majority of postpubescent young men and many young women left home in their teenage years for a period of employment. In the early modern era, such employment was often as a servant or apprentice in either a craft or a farm household, but, over time, that employment was increasingly likely to be in a nondomestic work setting, such as a factory, store, or other urban enterprise. "Youth" was a distinctive phase in the life course of young men and increasingly of young women in Europe, although there were important gender distinctions. Such a period of postpubescent semiautonomy from parental households did not exist for Chinese youth, especially not for young women in traditional China. Young men more typically remained in their father's household and young women moved at marriage in their late teens from their own father's household to that of their husband's father.

Comparing the Moment of Marriage: Implications and Cautions

We would now like to discuss some of the world-historical implications of this important (if crude) comparison in the marriage systems of China and Western Europe. There are obviously many possible realms for investigation. For example, these patterns imply differences in young women's education, intergenerational relationships among women (especially between mothers and daughters and mothers-in-law and daughters-in-law), and household power relations. Here, we restrict our discussion to two areas of undoubted world-historical significance, namely economic development, on the one hand, and sexuality and reproduction, on the other.

The question of why the Industrial Revolution, or, alternatively, the emergence of industrial capitalism, occurred first in Europe, has been and remains salient for both European and world historians. R. Bin Wong explores this question in his innovative comparative study of economic development in Europe and China. Wong argues that there were rough parallels in the dynamics linking demographic expansion and economic growth in China and Europe until the nineteenth century. Both economies were expanding on the basis of growth of rural industrial enterprises in which peasant families supplemented agricultural work and income with part-time industrial production. What the Chinese case demonstrates, Wong argues, is that this so-called protoindustrial form of development may be viewed as an alternative route to industrialization rather than merely a precursor of factory production. Indeed, Charles Tilly has suggested that a prescient contemporary observer of the European economy in 1750 would likely have predicted such a future — that is "a countryside with a growing proletariat working in both agriculture and manufacturing."

While Wong's study is devoted to comparative examination of the economic roots and implications of varying paths to industrial development, he also connects economic and demographic growth. In particular, Wong mentions the link between marriage and economic opportunity: "in both China and Europe, rural industry supported lower age at marriage and higher proportions of ever married than would have been plausible in its absence. This does not mean that ages at marriage dropped in Europe when rural industry appeared, but the possibility was present. For China, the development of rural industry may not have lowered ages at marriage or raised proportions married as much as it allowed previous practices of relatively low ages at marriage and high proportions of women ever married to continue." What Wong does not explore is the way in which these "previous practices" that connected the low age at marriage with both virilocality and a relatively high commitment to the domestic containment of daughters and wives also had implications for patterns of economic development. In a comparative account of why Chinese industrial development relied heavily on domestic production, the fact that the young female labor force in China was to an extent far greater than that of Europe both married and "tied" to the male-headed household needs to be part of the story. This pattern of female marriage and residency held implications for entrepreneurial choice that helped to determine the different paths toward industrialization in Europe and China. World-historical comparison, taking into account aspects of gender relations and marriage and kinship systems, highlights their possible significance for economic development, a significance that has not been given proper attention by economic historians. Indeed, it is arguable that the family and marital status of the young women who played so significant a role in the workforce (especially those employed in the textile industry, which was key to early industrial development in both Europe and China) were major factors in the varying paths to development followed in China and Europe in the centuries of protoindustrial growth and industrialization.

A second set of implications concerns sexuality and reproduction. Again, we are aided by another recent study, which, in a fashion parallel to Wong's, uses Chinese historical evidence to call into question generalizations about historical development based on a European model. In their book on Chinese demographic history, Lee and Wang argue against the hegemonic Malthusian (mis)understandings according to which the family and population history to China has been seen as an example of a society's failure to curb population growth by any means other than recurrent disaster (by "positive" rather than "preventive" checks in Malthusian terms). They note the important difference in marriage systems that we have just described, but they dispute conclusions too often drawn from the Chinese historical pattern concerning overpopulation. Instead, according to Lee and Wang "persistently high nuptiality . . . did not inflate Chinese fertility, because of . . . the low level of fertility within marriage."

This second example points to another important realm for which the age at which women marry has great consequences. But the findings reported by Lee and Wang also caution scholars against leaping to comparative conclusions about one society on the basis of models established in another, even while their claims still suggest the value of comparison. We should not presume that since Chinese women were married universally and young, they therefore had more children or devoted a greater proportion of their time and energy to childbearing and child rearing than did their later married counterparts in Europe. Although the evidence is far from definitive, it nevertheless indicates that total marital fertility may have been somewhat lower in China than in Europe until the late nineteenth or early twentieth centuries. The factors in China that produced this pattern included relatively high rates of infanticide, especially of female infants, as well as different beliefs and practices about child care and sexuality. For example, babies were apparently breast-fed longer in China than in Europe (a pattern in turn related to the domestic location of women's work), which would have both increased infants' chances of survival and also lengthened the intervals between births. In the realm of sexuality, pertinent factors include both prescriptions for men against overly frequent intercourse, and coresidence with a parental generation whose vigilance included policing young couples' sexual behavior.

These two examples are meant to suggest how looking at women's life cycles comparatively both enhances our understanding of the implications of varying patterns for women's history and also suggests the very broad ramifications, indeed world-historical significance, of different ways of institutionalizing the female life cycle.

REFLECTIONS

Women's history has entered the mainstream during the last few decades. An older view, still pervasive in the academic world forty years ago, assumed women's history was adequately covered by general history, which was largely the story of the exploits of men. Political, military, and diplomatic history took precedence over historical fields seen as less resolutely masculine, such as social and cultural history.

Today, women's history not only stands independently in college and university curriculums, it has helped open doors to a wide range of new fields in social history — gender, family, childhood, sexuality, domesticity, and health, to name but a few. These new research fields have also contributed significantly to issues of general history, as the authors of the last reading show. In fact, the growth and development of new fields of research and teaching in social and cultural history have had the effect of relegating the study of presidents, wars, and treaties to the periphery of the profession. The 2006 meeting of the American Historical Association, where historians came together to talk about their work, had more sessions on women, gender, and sexuality than on politics, diplomacy, military, war, World War I, World War II, and the American Civil War, combined.

Some more traditional historians complain that this is a fad, and that sooner or later the profession will get back to the more "important" topics. But others respond that it is hard to think of anything more important than the history of half of humanity or the history of human health. This debate leads to questions about the importance of particular individuals in history. Who had a greater impact, for instance, thirtieth U.S. president Calvin Coolidge (1872–1933) or Marie Curie (1867–1934), who won the Nobel Prize for isolating radium for therapeutic purposes?

What role do individuals play on the historical canvas anyway? A president or Nobel laureate works according to social norms, available resources, supporting institutions, and the work of hundreds or thousands of others, living and dead. Forty years ago, historians put greater stress on institutions, movements, and perceived forces than they do today. In recent years, historians have looked for the "agency" of individuals and groups, perhaps in an effort to see how people can have an impact on their world. The power of slavery and the impact of imperialism have been balanced with the tales of slave revolts, the stories of successful collaborators, adapters, and resisters, and the voices of slaves and indigenous and colonized peoples. We see this in the study of women's history as well.

We began this chapter with the observation that we live in a patriarchy. Even if we are dismantling it in the twenty-first century, it was a powerful force between 1500 and 1800: a historical force, not natural, but a product of the urban revolution, perhaps, beginning about five thousand years ago. It is useful to understand its causes, describe its workings, and relate its history. But does doing so only hamper our capacity for change? Does it ignore the stories of women who have made a difference? Conversely, are women empowered, humanity enriched, by knowing how individual women were able to work within the system, secure their needs, engage, negotiate, compromise? Do the stories of a Sor Juana or the poems of an Anna Bijns inspire us? Or do they misrepresent the past and, by consequence, delude us?

Perhaps there are no easy answers to those questions, but our exercise in comparison might come in handy. The rich and varied detail of the human past should warn us against absolute declarations. We may emphasize patriarchy or emphasize women's power, but we would be foolish to deny either. In consequence, it may be most useful to ask more specific questions and to compare. Can women own property here? Is there more restriction on women's movement in this society or that? Only then can we begin to understand why here and not there, why then and not now. And only then can we use our understanding of the past to improve the present.

5

The Scientific Revolution

Europe, the Ottoman Empire, China, Japan, and the Americas, 1600–1800

HISTORICAL CONTEXT

Modern life is unthinkable apart from science. We surround ourselves with its products, from cars and computers to telephones and televisions; we are dependent on its institutions — hospitals, universities, and research laboratories; and we have internalized the methods and procedures of science in every aspect of our daily lives, from balancing checkbooks to counting calories. Even on social and humanitarian questions, the scientific method has become almost the exclusive model of knowledge in modern society.

We can trace the scientific focus of modern society to the "scientific revolution" of the seventeenth century. The seventeenth-century scientific revolution was a European phenomenon, with such notables as Nicolas Copernicus (1473–1543) in Poland, Galileo Galilei (1564–1642) in Tuscany, and Isaac Newton (1642–1727) in England. But it was also a global event, prompted initially by Europe's new knowledge of Asia, Africa, and the Americas, and ultimately spread as a universal method for understanding and manipulating the world.

What was the scientific revolution? How revolutionary was it? How similar, or different, was European science from that practiced elsewhere in the world? And how much did the European revolution affect scientific traditions elsewhere? These are some of the issues we will study in this chapter.

THINKING HISTORICALLY
Distinguishing Change from Revolution

The world is always changing; it always has been changing. Sometimes, however, the change seems so formidable, extensive, important, or quick that we use the term *revolution*. In fact, we will use the term in this and the next two chapters. In this chapter we will examine what historians call the scientific revolution. The next chapter will deal with political revolutions and the chapter following with the industrial revolution. In each of these cases there are some historians who object that the changes were not really revolutionary, that they were more gradual or limited. Thus, we ask the question, how do we distinguish between mere change and revolutionary change?

In this chapter you will be asked, how revolutionary were the changes that are often called the scientific revolution? The point, however, is not to get your vote, pro or con, but to get you to think about how you might answer such a question. Do we, for instance, compare "the before" with "the after" and then somehow divide by the time it took to get from one to the other? Do we look at what people said at the time about how things were changing? Are we gauging speed of change or extent of change? What makes things change at different speeds? What constitutes a revolution?

27

FRANKLIN LE VAN BAUMER

The Scientific Revolution in the West

In this selection, an intellectual historian of Europe summarizes the scientific revolution. Without enumerating the achievements of European science in the seventeenth century, Baumer finds evidence of the "revolutionary" nature of the transformation by referring to the popularity of scientific societies and the powerful appeal of the new scien-

Franklin Le Van Baumer, "The Scientific Revolution in the West," in *Main Currents of Western Thought*, ed. F. Le Van Baumer (New Haven: Yale University Press, 1978).

tific mentality. How does he define the scientific revolution? How does he date it? Why does he believe that it was a revolution?

Thinking Historically

What intellectual or cultural changes did the scientific revolution bring about, according to Baumer? What ideas did Europeans have about nature before the scientific revolution? Baumer suggests that we can see the scientific revolution in new intellectual institutions, educational reforms, and new careers. What were these changes? How rapid, extensive, or important were they?

In his book *The Origins of Modern Science* Professor [Herbert] Butterfield of Cambridge writes that the "scientific revolution" of the sixteenth and seventeenth centuries "outshines everything since the rise of Christianity and reduces the Renaissance and Reformation to the rank of mere episodes, mere internal displacements, within the system of medieval Christendom." "It looms so large as the real origin both of the modern world and of the modern mentality that our customary periodisation of European history has become an anachronism and an encumbrance." This view can no longer be seriously questioned. The scientific achievements of the century and a half between the publication of Copernicus's *De Revolutionibus Orbium Celestium* (1543) and Newton's *Principia* (1687) marked the opening of a new period of intellectual and cultural life in the West, which I shall call the Age of Science. What chiefly distinguished this age from its predecessor was that science — meaning by science a body of knowledge, a method, an attitude of mind, a metaphysic (to be described below) — became the directive force of Western civilization, displacing theology and antique letters. Science made the world of the spirit, of Platonic Ideas, seem unreliable and dim by comparison with the material world. In the seventeenth century it drove revealed Christianity out of the physical universe into the region of history and private morals; to an ever growing number of people in the two succeeding centuries it made religion seem outmoded even there. Science invaded the schools, imposed literary canons, altered the world-picture of the philosophers, suggested new techniques to the social theorists. It changed profoundly man's attitude toward custom and tradition, enabling him to declare his independence of the past, to look down condescendingly upon the "ancients," and to envisage a rosy future. The Age of Science made the intoxicating discovery that melioration depends, not upon "change from within" (St. Paul's birth of the new man), but upon "change from without" (scientific and social mechanics).

1

Some people will perhaps object that there was no such thing as "scientific revolution" in the sixteenth and seventeenth centuries. They will say that history does not work that way, that the new science was not "revolutionary," but the cumulative effect of centuries of trial and error among scientists. But if by "scientific revolution" is meant the occasion when science became a real intellectual and cultural force in the West, this objection must surely evaporate. The evidence is rather overwhelming that sometime between 1543 and 1687, certainly by the late seventeenth century, science captured the interest of the intellectuals and upper classes. Francis Bacon's ringing of a bell to call the wits of Europe together to advance scientific learning did not go unheeded. Note the creation of new intellectual institutions to provide a home for science — the *Academia del Cimento* at Florence (1661), the Royal Society at London (1662), the *Académie des Sciences* at Paris (1666), the Berlin Academy (1700), to mention only the most important. These scientific academies signified the advent of science as an organized activity. Note the appearance of a literature of popular science, of which Fontenelle's *Plurality of Worlds* is only one example, and of popular lectures on scientific subjects. Note the movement for educational reform sponsored by Bacon and the Czech John Amos Comenius, who denounced the traditional education for its exclusive emphasis upon "words rather than things" (literature rather than nature itself). Evidently, by the end of the seventeenth century the prejudice against "mechanical" studies as belonging to practical rather than high mental life had all but disappeared. Bacon complained in 1605 that "matters mechanical" were esteemed "a kind of dishonour unto learning to descend to inquiry or meditation upon." But the Royal Society included in its roster a number of ecclesiastics and men of fashion. The second marquis of Worcester maintained a laboratory and published a book of inventions in 1663. Not a few men appear to have been "converted" from an ecclesiastical to a scientific career, and, as Butterfield notes, to have carried the gospel into the byways, with all the zest of the early Christian missionaries.

To account historically for the scientific revolution is no easy task. The problem becomes somewhat more manageable, however, if we exclude from the discussion the specific discoveries of the scientists. Only the internal history of science can explain how Harvey, for example, discovered the circulation of the blood, or Newton the universal law of gravitation.

But certain extrascientific factors were plainly instrumental in causing so many people to be simultaneously interested in "nature," and, moreover, to think about nature in the way they did. Professor [Alfred North] Whitehead reminds us that one of these factors was medieval Christianity itself and medieval scholasticism. Medieval Christianity sponsored the Greek, as opposed to the primitive, idea of a rationally ordered universe which made the orderly investigation of nature seem possible. Scholasticism trained western intellectuals in exact thinking. The Renaissance and the Protestant Reformation also prepared the ground for the scientific revolution — not by design, but as an indirect consequence of their thinking. . . . [H]umanism and Protestantism represented a movement toward the concrete. Erasmus preferred ethics to the metaphysical debates of the philosophers and theologians. The Protestants reduced the miraculous element in institutional Christianity and emphasized labor in a worldly calling. Furthermore, by attacking scholastic theology with which Aristotle was bound up, they made it easier for scientists to think about physics and astronomy in un-Aristotelian terms. As [philosopher] E. A. Burtt has noted of Copernicus, these men lived in a mental climate in which people generally were seeking new centers of reference. Copernicus, the architect of the heliocentric theory of the universe, was a contemporary of Luther and Archbishop Cranmer, who moved the religious center from Rome to Wittenberg and Canterbury. In the sixteenth century the economic center of gravity was similarly shifting from the Mediterranean to the English Channel and the Atlantic Ocean. The revival of ancient philosophies and ancient texts at the Renaissance also sharpened the scientific appetite. The Platonic and Phythagorean revival in fifteenth-century Italy undoubtedly did a good deal to accustom scientists to think of the universe in mathematical, quantitative terms. The translation of Galen and Archimedes worked the last rich vein of ancient science, and made it abundantly clear that the ancients had frequently disagreed on fundamentals, thus necessitating independent investigation. By their enthusiasm for natural beauty, the humanists helped to remove from nature the medieval stigma of sin, and thus to make possible the confident pronouncement of the scientific movement that God's Word could be read not only in the Bible but in the great book of nature.

But no one of these factors, nor all of them together, could have produced the scientific revolution. One is instantly reminded of Bacon's statement that "by the distant voyages and travels which have become frequent in our times, many things in nature have been laid open and discovered which may let in new light upon philosophy." The expansion of Europe, and increased travel in Europe itself, not only stimulated interest in nature but opened up to the West the vision of a "Kingdom of Man" upon earth. Much of Bacon's imagery was borrowed from the geographical discoveries: He aspired to be the Columbus of a new intellectual world, to sail through the Pillars of Hercules (symbol of the old knowledge) into the Atlantic Ocean in search of new and more useful knowledge. Bacon, however, failed to detect the coincidence of the scientific revolution with commercial prosperity and the rise of the middle class. Doubtless, the Marxist Professor Hessen greatly oversimplified when he wrote that "Newton was the typical representative of the rising bourgeoisie, and in his philosophy he embodies the characteristic features of his class." The theoretical scientists had mixed motives. Along with a concern for technology, they pursued truth for its own sake, and they sought God in his great creation. All the same, it is not stretching the imagination too far to see a rough correspondence between the mechanical universe of the seventeenth-century philosophers and the bourgeois desire for rational, predictable order. Science and business were a two-way street. If science affected business, so did business affect science — by its businesslike temper and its quantitative thinking, by its interest in "matter" and the rational control of matter.

2

The scientific revolution gave birth to a new conception of knowledge, a new methodology, and a new worldview substantially different from the old Aristotelian-Christian worldview. . . .

Knowledge now meant exact knowledge: what you know for certain, and not what may possibly or even probably be. Knowledge is what can be clearly apprehended by the mind, or measured by mathematics, or demonstrated by experiment. Galileo came close to saying this when he declared that without mathematics "it is impossible to comprehend a single word of (the great book of the universe);" likewise Descartes when he wrote that "we ought never to allow ourselves to be persuaded of the truth of anything unless on the evidence of our Reason." The distinction between "primary" and "secondary qualities" in seventeenth-century metaphysics carried the same implication. To Galileo, Descartes, and Robert Boyle those mathematical qualities that inhered in objects (size, weight, position, etc.) were "primary," i.e., matters of real knowledge; whereas all the other qualities that our senses tell us are in objects (color, odor, taste, etc.) were "secondary," less real because less amenable to measurement. The inference of all this is plain: Knowledge pertains to "natural philosophy" and possibly social theory, but not to theology or the older philosophy or poetry which involve opinion, belief, faith, but not knowledge. The Royal Society actually undertook to renovate the English language, by excluding from it metaphors and pulpit eloquence which conveyed no precise meaning. The "enthusiasm" of the religious man became suspect as did the "sixth sense" of the poet who could convey pleasure but not knowledge.

The odd thing about the scientific revolution is that for all its avowed distrust of hypotheses and systems, it created its own system of nature, or worldview. "I perceive," says the "Countess" in Fontenelle's popular dialogue of 1686, "Philosophy is now become very Mechanical." "I value (this universe) the more since I know it resembles a Watch, and the whole order of Nature the more plain and easy it is, to me it appears the more admirable." Descartes and other philosophers of science in the seventeenth century constructed a mechanical universe which resembled the machines — watches, pendulum clocks, steam engines — currently being built by scientists and artisans. However, it was not the observation of actual machines but the new astronomy and physics that made it possible to picture the universe in this way. The "Copernican revolution" destroyed Aristotle's "celestial world" of planets and stars which, because they were formed of a subtle substance having no weight, behaved differently from bodies on earth and in the "sublunary world." The new laws of motion formulated by a succession of physicists from Kepler to Newton explained the movement of bodies, both celestial and terrestrial, entirely on mechanical and mathematical principles. According to the law of inertia, the "natural" motion of bodies was in a straight line out into Euclidean space. The planets were pulled into their curvilinear orbits by gravitation which could operate at tremendous distances, and which varied inversely as the square of the distance.

Thus, the universe pictured by Fontenelle's Countess was very different from that of Dante in the thirteenth, or Richard Hooker in the sixteenth century. Gone was the Aristotelian-Christian universe of purposes, forms, and final causes. Gone were the spirits and intelligences which had been required to push the skies daily around the earth. The fundamental features of the new universe were numbers (mathematical quantities) and invariable laws. It was an economical universe in which nature did nothing in vain and performed its daily tasks without waste. In such a universe the scientist could delight and the bourgeois could live happily ever after — or at least up to the time of Darwin. The fact that nature appeared to have no spiritual purpose — Descartes said that it would continue to exist regardless of whether there were any human beings to think it — was more than compensated for by its dependability. Philosophy had indeed become very mechanical. Descartes kept God to start his machine going, and Newton did what he could to save the doctrine of providence. But for all practical purposes, God had become the First Cause, "very well skilled in mechanics and geometry." And the rage for mechanical explanation soon spread beyond the confines of physics to encompass the biological and social sciences. Thus did Descartes regard animals as a piece of clockwork, Robert Boyle the human body as a "matchless engine."

Under the circumstances, one would logically expect there to have been warfare between science and religion in the seventeenth century. But such was not the case. To be sure, some theologians expressed dismay at the downfall of Aristotelianism, and the Roman Church took steps to suppress Copernicanism when Giordano Bruno interpreted it to mean an infinite universe and a plurality of worlds. But the majority of the scientists and popularizers of science were sincerely religious men — not a few were actually ecclesiastics — who either saw no conflict or else went to some lengths to resolve it. Science itself was commonly regarded as a religious enterprise. . . .

In the final analysis, however, the new thing in seventeenth-century thought was the dethronement of theology from its proud position as the sun of the intellectual universe. Bacon and Descartes and Newton lived in an age that was finding it increasingly difficult to reconcile science and religion. To save the best features of both they effected a shaky compromise. For all practical purposes they eliminated religious purpose from nature — thus allowing science to get on with its work, while leaving religion in control of private belief and morals. By their insistence that religious truth itself must pass the tests of reason and reliable evidence, John Locke and the rationalists further reduced theology's prerogatives. Bacon was prepared to believe the word of God "though our reason be shocked at it." But not Locke: "'I believe because it is impossible,' might," he says, "in a good man, pass for a sally of zeal, but would prove a very ill rule for men to choose their opinions or religion by." Good Christian though Locke might be, his teaching had the effect of playing down the supernatural aspects of religion, of equating religion with simple ethics. . . .

28

GALILEO GALILEI

Letter to the Grand Duchess Christina

One reason for thinking of European scientific developments in the seventeenth century as a revolution lies in their condemnation by established authority, particularly religious authority. Both Protestants and Catholics condemned the sun-centered model of the universe proposed by Copernicus and modified by Tycho Brahe (1546–1601) and Johannes Kepler (1571–1630). Giordano Bruno, a religious philosopher and Copernican, was burned at the stake in 1600 by the Catholic

Galileo's Letter to the Grand Duchess Christina (1615), in *The Galileo Affair: A Documentary History*, ed. and trans. Maurice A. Finocchiaro (Berkeley and Los Angeles: University of California Press, 1989), 87–90, 114–18.

Church. Galileo was investigated in 1615 and 1616 for work that gave added weight to Copernicus's theory. His use of the telescope revealed more stars than the fixed number seen by the naked eye or shown on the accepted model of the heavenly spheres of the ancient authority, Ptolemy. Galileo, by assuming that the Earth revolved around the sun (and the moon around the Earth), conceived orbits that were neater and closer to what had been observed.

This letter to the Grand Duchess Christina in 1615 shows Galileo already under siege. He had received a letter in 1613 from a supporter, Benedetto Castelli, who had been questioned by Christina (of Lorraine), the mother of the Grand Duke of Tuscany, Cosimo II de' Medici, about Galileo's views. Having left his twenty-year post at the University of Padua, Galileo was in 1613 philosopher and mathematician to the Duchy of Tuscany, and so he was in the delicate and precarious position of receiving notice of his employer's dissatisfaction with his views. This letter is his attempt to explain himself and to prevent the initiation of an inquisition. His efforts were unsuccessful. In 1633 Galileo was tried, condemned, forced to recant his views, and placed under house arrest. (The condemnation was retracted by the papacy in 1992.)

What seem to be Grand Duchess Christina's objections? How does Galileo try to answer them? How convincing would you find Galileo if you were the Grand Duchess?

Thinking Historically

What claims to new discoveries did Galileo make in this letter? In what respect did Galileo claim his work was not new? On balance, what did he perceive to be the differences between himself and his contemporaries? How is his argument "modern" or scientific? Does this letter support Baumer's interpretation of the scientific revolution?

To the Most Serene Ladyship the Grand Duchess Dowager:

As Your Most Serene Highness knows very well, a few years ago I discovered in the heavens many particulars which had been invisible until our time. Because of their novelty, and because of some consequences deriving from them which contradict certain physical propositions[1] commonly accepted in philosophical schools, they roused against

---

[1]In *The Starry Messenger* (Venice, 1610) Galileo had described his discovery, through telescopic observation, of lunar mountains, four satellites of Jupiter (which he named "Medicean planets"), the stellar composition of the Milky Way and of nebulas, and the existence of thousands of previously invisible fixed stars. Within a few years, Galileo added to these his observations of sunspots, the phases of Venus, and Saturn's rings.

me no small number of such professors, as if I had placed these things in heaven with my hands in order to confound nature and the sciences. These people seemed to forget that a multitude of truths contribute to inquiry and to the growth and strength of disciplines rather than to their diminution or destruction, and at the same time they showed greater affection for their own opinions than for the true ones; thus they proceeded to deny and to try to nullify those novelties, about which the senses themselves could have rendered them certain, if they had wanted to look at those novelties carefully. To this end they produced various matters, and they published some writings full of useless discussions and sprinkled with quotations from the Holy Scripture, taken from passages which they do not properly understand and which they inappropriately adduce.[2] . . .

These people are aware that in my astronomical and philosophical studies, on the question of the constitution of the world's parts, I hold that the sun is located at the center of the revolution of the heavenly orbs and does not change place, and that the earth rotates on itself and moves around it. Moreover, they hear how I confirm this view not only by refuting Ptolemy's and Aristotle's arguments, but also by producing many for the other side, especially some pertaining to physical effects whose causes perhaps cannot be determined in any other way, and other astronomical ones dependent on many features of the new celestial discoveries; these discoveries clearly confute the Ptolemaic system, and they agree admirably with this other position and confirm it. Now, these people are perhaps confounded by the known truth of the other

---

[2]Galileo has been notified that Cardinal Bellarmine finds the Copernican theory heretical because the sun must go around the Earth according to Psalm 19:

The heavens declare the glory of God;
. . . .
In them hath he set a tabernacle for the sun,
Which is as a bridegroom coming out of his chamber,
And rejoiceth as a strong man to run a race.
His going forth is from the end of the heaven,
And his circuit unto the ends of it:
And there is nothing hid from the heat thereof. (19:1, 4–6 King James Version)

The Grand Duchess mentioned to Castelli the passage in Joshua 10:12–13 (KJV):

Then spake Joshua to the Lord in the day when the Lord delivered the Amorites before the children of Israel, and he said in the sight of Israel, Sun, stand thou still upon Gibeon; and thou, Moon, in the valley of Ajalon. And the sun stood still, and the moon stayed, until the people had avenged themselves upon their enemies. Is not this written in the book of Jasher? So the sun stood still in the midst of heaven, and hastened not to go down about a whole day.

Thus, the Bible seemed to indicate that the sun revolved around the Earth. [Ed.]

propositions different from the ordinary which I hold, and so they may lack confidence to defend themselves as long as they remain in the philosophical field. Therefore, since they persist in their original self-appointed task of beating down me and my findings by every imaginable means, they have decided to try to shield the fallacies of their arguments with the cloak of simulated religiousness and with the authority of Holy Scripture, unintelligently using the latter for the confutation of arguments they neither understand nor have heard.

At first, they tried on their own to spread among common people the idea that such propositions are against Holy Scripture, and consequently damnable and heretical. Then they realized how by and large human nature is more inclined to join those ventures which result in the oppression of other people (even if unjustly) than those which result in their just improvement, and so it was not difficult for them to find someone who with unusual confidence did preach even from the pulpit that it is damnable and heretical; and this was done with little compassion and with little consideration of the injury not only to this doctrine and its followers, but also to mathematics and all mathematicians. Thus, having acquired more confidence, and with the vain hope that the seed which first took root in their insincere minds would grow into a tree and rise toward the sky, they are spreading among the people the rumor that it will shortly be declared heretical by the supreme authority. They also know that such a declaration not only would uproot these two conclusions, but also would render damnable all the other astronomical and physical observations and propositions which correspond and are necessarily connected with them; hence, they alleviate their task as much as they can by making it look, at least among common people, as if this opinion were new and especially mine, pretending not to know that Nicolaus Copernicus was its author or rather its reformer and confirmer. Now, Copernicus was not only a Catholic but also a clergyman and a canon, and he was so highly regarded that he was called to Rome from the remotest parts of Germany[3] when under Leo X the Lateran Council was discussing the reform of the ecclesiastical calendar; at that time this reform remained unfinished only because there was still no exact knowledge of the precise length of the year and the lunar month. Thus he was charged by the Bishop of Fossombrone,[4] who was then supervising this undertaking, to try by repeated studies and efforts to acquire more understanding and certainty about those celestial motions; and so he undertook this study, and, by truly Herculean labor and by his admirable mind, he made so much progress in this science and acquired such an exact knowledge of the periods of celestial

---

[3]Actually Poland.
[4]Paul of Middelburg (1445–1533).

motions that he earned the title of supreme astronomer; then in accordance with his doctrine not only was the calendar regularized,[5] but tables of all planetary motions were constructed. Having expounded this doctrine in six parts, he published it at the request of the Cardinal of Capua[6] and the Bishop of Kulm;[7] and since he had undertaken this task and these labors on orders from the Supreme Pontiff, he dedicated his book *On Heavenly Revolutions* to the successor of the latter, Paul III. Once printed this book was accepted by the Holy Church, and it was read and studied all over the world without anyone ever having had the least scruple about its doctrine.[8] Finally, now that one is discovering how well founded upon clear observations and necessary demonstrations this doctrine is, some persons come along who, without having even seen the book, give its author the reward of so much work by trying to have him declared a heretic; this they do only in order to satisfy their special animosity, groundlessly conceived against someone else who has no greater connection with Copernicus than the endorsement of his doctrine.

Now, in matters of religion and reputation I have the greatest regard for how common people judge and view me; so, because of the false aspersions my enemies so unjustly try to cast upon me, I have thought it necessary to justify myself by discussing the details of what they produce to detest and abolish this opinion, in short, to declare it not just false but heretical. They always shield themselves with a simulated religious zeal, and they also try to involve Holy Scripture and to make it somehow subservient to their insincere objectives; against the intention of Scripture and the Holy Fathers (if I am not mistaken), they want to extend, not to say abuse, its authority, so that even for purely physical conclusions which are not matters of faith one must totally abandon the senses and demonstrative arguments in favor of any scriptural passage whose apparent words may contain a different indication. . . .

---

[5]Though the Copernican system did play a role in the reform of the calendar, the new Gregorian calendar was constructed on the basis of non-Copernican ideas.

[6]Cardinal Nicolaus von Schoenberg (1472–1537), archbishop of Capua.

[7]Tiedemann Giese (1480–1550), Polish friend of Copernicus.

[8]Of course, Galileo had no way of knowing that one Giovanni Maria Tolosani had had quite a few scruples about it.

29

NATALIE ZEMON DAVIS

Metamorphoses: Maria Sibylla Merian

Davis, a modern historian, writes here of a woman scientist and artist, Maria Sibylla Merian* (1647–1717), whose work graphically illustrates the new approaches to nature in the seventeenth century. What did Merian accomplish? What do her accomplishments suggest about the history of science?

Thinking Historically

What aspects of Merian's work were radically new or revolutionary? What elements were continuations of traditional ideas? How might the idea of metamorphoses apply to her work and the scientific revolution?

In June 1699, . . . Maria Sibylla Merian and her daughter Dorothea were boarding a boat in Amsterdam, bound for America. Their destination was Suriname, where they intended to study and paint the insects, butterflies, and plants of that tropical land.

At age fifty-two, Maria Sibylla Merian was a person of some reputation. As early as 1675, when she was a young mother living with her husband in Nuremberg, the learned painter Joachim Sandrart had included her in his *German Academy*, as he called his history of German art. Not only was she skilled in watercolor and oils, in painting textiles and engraving copperplates; not only could she render flowers, plants, and insects with perfect naturalness; but she also was a knowing observer of the habits of caterpillars, flies, spiders, and other such creatures. A virtuous woman and a fine housekeeper (despite all the insects), Merian, said Sandrart, could be likened to the goddess Minerva. A few years later, when she published the two volumes of her *Wonderful Transformation and Singular Plant-Food of Caterpillars*, a Nuremberg luminary, Christopher Arnold, sang in verse of all the men who were being equaled by this ingenious woman. Her work was *"verwunderns"* — "amazing."

*ma REE ah   sih BIHL ah   meh ree AHN

Natalie Zemon Davis, *Women on the Margins: Three Seventeenth-Century Lives* (Cambridge: Harvard University Press, 1995), 140–41, 147–48, 149–50, 154–56, plate 23.

Then, in 1692, another kind of singularity was noted about Maria Sibylla Merian, for a different set of readers. Petrus Dittelbach, a disaffected member of the Labadists (a radical Protestant community in the Dutch province of Friesland) published an exposé of the conduct of his former coreligionists. Among them was "a woman of Frankfurt am Main" who had left her husband, the painter Johann Andreas Graff, in Germany to find peace among the Labadists of Wieuwerd. When Graff came to get her back, he was informed by the leading Brothers that a believer like Maria Sibylla was freed from marital obligations toward an unbeliever like him. Refused entry into the community, the husband stayed around for a time doing construction work outside its walls, and then left. Dittelbach had heard that he was going to break his matrimonial tie, and indeed, about the time *The Decline and Fall of the Labadists* appeared in print, Graff was asking the Nuremberg town council for a divorce from Maria Sibylla so that he could marry someone else.

These accounts suggest the turnings in the life of the artist-naturalist Maria Sibylla Merian. And there were more changes to come. She sailed back from America laden with specimens, published her great work *Metamorphosis of the Insects of Suriname*, amplified her *European Insects*, and was an important figure in the circle of Amsterdam botanists, scientists, and collectors till her death in 1717. . . .

. . . Her *Raupen* of 1679, or (to give the title in English) the *Wonderful Transformation and Singular Flower-Food of Caterpillars . . . Painted from Life and Engraved in Copper*, [was] followed by a second volume in 1683. In each of the hundred copperplates (fifty per volume, available in black and white or handcolored, depending on the buyer's wish and purse), one or more species of insect were depicted from life, in their various stages: caterpillar or larva; pupa with or without cocoon; and moth, butterfly, or fly, in flight or at rest (sometimes in both states). Many of the plates included the egg stage as well. Each picture was organized around a single plant, represented most often in the flowering stage and sometimes in the fruit stage; the plant was selected to show the leaves upon which the caterpillar fed and the places on the leaves or stem (or on the ground nearby) where the female laid its eggs. Each plant was identified by its German and Latin names, and a page or two of German text facing the picture gave Maria Sibylla's observations on how her insect specimen had looked and behaved at each stage, often with exact dates, and her reactions to its appearance. She did not give names to individual species of moths and butterflies — in fact, her contemporaries had names for only a small number of them — but her descriptions yielded individual life histories.

Here is what she said of an insect shown in its stages from egg to moth on a cherry plant (pictured in the illustrations in this volume):

Many years ago when I first saw this large moth, so prettily marked by nature, I could not marvel enough over its beautiful gradation of color and varying hue, and I made use of it often in my painting. Later, as through God's grace I discovered the metamorphosis of caterpillars, a long time went by until this beautiful moth appeared. When I caught sight of it, I was enveloped in such great joy and so gratified in my wishes that I can hardly describe it. Then for several years in a row I got hold of its caterpillars and maintained them until July on the leaves of sweet cherries, apples, pears, and plums. They have a beautiful green color, like the young grass of spring, and a lovely straight black stripe the length of the back, and across each segment also a black stripe out of which four little white round beads glisten like pearls. Among them is a yellow-gold oval spot and under them a white pearl. Underneath the first three segments they have three red claws on each side, then two empty segments, after which there are four little green feet of the same color as the caterpillars, and at the end again a foot on both sides. Sprouting out of each pearl are long black hairs, together with other, smaller ones, so stiff that one could almost be pricked by them. Strange to note, when they have no food, this variety of caterpillars devour each other, so great is their hunger; but so soon as they obtain [food], they leave off [eating each other].

When such a caterpillar attains its full size, as you can see [in my picture] on the green leaf and stem, then it makes a tough and lustrous cocoon, bright as silver and oval round, wherein it first sheds and expels its entire skin and changes itself into a liver-colored date stone [*Dattelkern*, her usual word for pupa], which stays together with the cast-off skin over the caterpillar. It remains thus motionless until the middle of August, when finally the moth of such laudable beauty comes out and takes flight. It is white and has gray spotted patches, two yellow eyes, and two brown feelers (Hörner). On each of the four wings are a few round circles in and about each other, which are black and white as well as yellow. The ends of the wings are brown, but near the tips (by which I mean only the ends of the moth's two outer wings) are two beautiful rose-colored spots. By day the moth is quiet, but at night very restless.

Her concern with beauty linked her to the still-life tradition in which she had been formed, and she herself acknowledged in her 1679 preface that her juxtaposition of plants and insects owed something to the artist's concern for adornment. She was also building on earlier efforts to achieve "naturalistic" or "mimetic" representations of flora and fauna. Detailed and lifelike pictures of insects and plants can be found in the margins of Netherlandish prayerbooks as early as the late fifteenth century, well before they surfaced in Dutch still-lifes in watercolor and oil. To give an example of the quest for precision close to home, Georg Flegel, Jacob Marrel's first teacher in Frankfurt, did small, careful studies of insects (one of them followed a silkworm from egg to moth); and flies, dragonflies, beetles, and butterflies appear among the foods, fruits, sugars, birds, and wines of Flegel's larger oil paintings.

But Maria Sibylla Merian had something else in mind when she did her insect studies from life. The moths and caterpillars of her *Raupen* did not just add to the "lively" (*"lebendig"*) quality of flower pictures, as in the bouquets and wreaths painted by her stepfather Marrel and his student Abraham Mignon. The insects were there for themselves. When necessary, Merian sacrificed verisimilitude (the way things might look to an observer) for a decorative portrayal of the stripes and spikes and legs the caterpillar actually had (what a nature lover must know about an insect).

Above all, her insects and plants were telling a life story. Time moved in her pictures not to suggest the general transience of things or the year's round of the most precious blossoms, but to evoke a particular and interconnected process of change. Her insects were not placed to convey metaphorical messages, as was the practice of many still-life painters and specifically of her step-father's Utrecht teacher, Jan Davidsz de Heem (the butterfly as the symbol of the resurrected soul, the fly as the symbol of sinfulness, and so on). The *Ignis* of Joris Hoefnagel, a remarkable collection of insect watercolors by an artist-naturalist of the late sixteenth century, was designed like an emblem book, each picture preceded by a biblical quote or adage and followed by a poem. Merian's work was infused with religious spirit, as we shall see, but, except for a nod at the goodness of the bee, there were no allegorical comments in her texts.

If Maria Sibylla recentered flower painting around the life cycle of moths and butterflies and the plant hosts of their caterpillars, how different were her volumes of 1679 and 1683 from the more narrowly scientific insect books of her day? The 1660s were important years for the history of entomology: sustained observation and improved magnification allowed much new understanding of the anatomy and molting of insects and laid to rest among naturalists the belief in abiogenesis (that is, spontaneous generation of certain insects from decaying matter). New systems of classification were tried out, quite different from those used in Renaissance encyclopedias such as the one the Merian brothers had illustrated and published in 1653. There Jan Jonston had followed Thomas Mouffet (and Aristotle) in making the possession of wings a major criterion for classification: wingless caterpillars were treated along with worms in chapters separate from butterflies and moths, and metamorphosis was accordingly slighted. . . .

Merian's goal was simply ill-served by boundary classifications. Her subject was a set of events — "you'll find in this volume more than a hundred transformations [*Verwandlungen*]," she said in 1683 — and to represent them properly meant crossing the line between orders and putting the plant and animal kingdoms in the same picture. Yet even while lacking the logic of classification, her sequence was not "tumultuous." Emerging from the sensibility of two artists, Merian and her publisher-husband Graff, the books moved the reader's eye through the transformations by a visually striking and pleasurable path. The "method" of the *Raupen* — highly particular pictures and accounts strung together by an aesthetic link — had scientific importance quite apart from the new species contained on its pages. It made the little-studied process of metamorphosis easy to visualize and remember, and insisted on nature's connections, a long-term contribution. It also fractured older classification systems by its particularism and surprising mixtures, and so cleared the ground for those like Swammerdam who were proposing a replacement.

Publishing the Raupen was "remarkable" for a woman, as Christopher Arnold told readers in his opening poem of 1679 — "remarkable that women also venture to write for you / with care / what has given flocks of scholars so much to do." Merian herself drew on her female status only once, perhaps disingenuously: in the midst of her description of the insects on the goose-foot plant, she imagined her readers asking whether the thousands of exceptionally large caterpillars during that year of 1679 would not lead to much damage. "Whereupon, following my womanly simplicity [*meiner Weiblichen Einfalt*] I give this answer: the damage is already evident in empty fruit trees and defective plants."

But can we go deeper than Arnold's "beyond-her-sex" topos and Maria Sibylla's modesty topos? Can we ask whether her experience or cultural habits as a seventeenth-century woman helped generate her ecological vision of nature and the crossing of boundaries in her particular narratives?

For the seventeenth century, Maria Sibylla Merian is a sample of one. Other women still-life painters of her day, such as Margaretha de Heer from Friesland, included insects in their pictures, but did not go so far as to breed and study them (Merian's daughters would do so under her influence, but only much later). Other women of her day collected butterflies, moths, and caterpillars, but did not write about or represent them. John Ray's four daughters all brought him specimens, but it was only he who wrote down the observations, naming each caterpillar after the daughter who had collected it. Moreover, Ray had been attentive to the habitat of insects in his early observations, even while making classification his most important goal, and continued to include metamorphoses in his descriptions of individual insects when he was aware of them.

Still Merian was a pioneer, crossing boundaries of education and gender to acquire learning on insects and nurturing daughters as she observed, painted, and wrote. Her focus on breeding, habitat, and metamorphosis fits nicely with the domestic practice of a seventeenth-century mother and housewife. We have here not a female mind uneasy with analysis or timelessly connected to the organic (images that have been thoroughly challenged in recent scholarship), but a woman perched for scientific enterprise on a creative margin — for her a buzzing ecosystem — between domestic workshop and learned academy.

More explicitly important to Maria Sibylla Merian than her gender was the legitimation, nay, the sanctification of her entomological task by religion: "These wondrous transformations," she wrote in her 1679 preface to the reader, "have happened so many times that one is full of praise for God's mysterious power and his wonderful attention to such insignificant little creatures and unworthy flying things . . . Thus I am moved to present God's miracles such as these to the world in a little book. But do not praise and honor me for it; praise God alone, glorifying Him as the creator of even the smallest and most insignificant of these worms.". . .

Maria Sibylla had not yet undergone her conversion experience when she began to publish the *Raupen*, but her stress on God's creativity in nature and her "enthusiasm" in talking about insects and their beauty surely prepared her ears for the prophetic and lyrical cadences that soon were to fill her world. As Jean de Labadie had said some years before: "Everything we hear or see announces God or figures him. The song of a bird, the bleating of a lamb, the voice of a man. The sight of heaven and its stars, the air and its birds, the sea and its fish, the land and its plants and animals . . . Everything tells of God, everything represents him, but few ears and eyes try to hear or see him." Maria Sibylla was one of those trying to see.

30

LADY MARY WORTLEY MONTAGUE

Letter on Turkish Smallpox Inoculation

Lady Mary Wortley Montague, an English aristocrat, came down with smallpox in 1715. She survived, but was badly scarred by the rash that accompanied the often-fatal disease. Her younger brother died from smallpox, one of the tens of thousands who succumbed in epidemics across Europe and around the world in the eighteenth and nineteenth centuries. Two years after her recovery Montague traveled to Istanbul with her husband, who was the British ambassador to the Ottoman Empire. There, she witnessed a new approach to warding off smallpox infections, as she described in the following letter to a friend in England. What process does Montague describe in her letter? What was her response to the events she witnessed in Turkey?

Thinking Historically

This letter provides a clear example of how scientific observation can change the material world in which we live. After observing the Turkish smallpox inoculation Montague had her son and daughter inoculated. In fact, she became an advocate for smallpox inoculation in England and played an important role in persuading the English medical profession to support the innovative procedure. Montague paved the way for a safer vaccine, developed by Edward Jenner in 1796, that would eventually eradicate the disease from the planet.

Despite her admirable efforts, it was difficult to convince Europeans to embrace smallpox inoculation, which had been practiced in Asia for centuries. Even though the effectiveness of this technology came to be recognized in England during Montague's lifetime, the French and other Europeans, according to Voltaire, thought that the English were "fools and madmen" for experimenting with inoculation. What does this suggest about the nature of scientific discovery? Besides lack of knowledge, what other obstacles need to be overcome?

Letters of Lady Mary Wortley Montague, written during her travels in Europe, Asia, and Africa, to which are added poems by the same author (Bordeaux, J. Pinard, 1805). The UCLA Louis M. Darling Biomedical Library, History and Special Collections Division.

To Mrs. S. C., Adrianople, April 1, O.S.

A Propos of distempers, I am going to tell you a thing, that will make you wish yourself here. The small pox, so fatal, and so general amongst us, is here entirely harmless, by the invention of ingrafting, which is the term they give it. There is a set of old women, who make it their business to perform the operation, every autumn, in the month of september, when the great heat is abated. People send to one another to know if any of their family has a mind to have the small-pox; they make parties for this purpose, and when they are met (commonly fifteen or sixteen together) the old woman comes with a nut-shell full of the matter of the best sort of small pox, and asks what vein you please to have opened. She immediately rips open than you offer to her, with a large needle (which gives you no more pain than a common scratch), and puts into the vein as much matter as can lie upon the head of her needle, and after that, binds up the little wound with a hollow bit of shell, and in this manner opens four or five veins. The Grecians have commonly the superstition of opening one in the middle of the forehead, one in each arm, and one in the breast, to mark the sign of the cross; but this has a very ill effect, all these wounds leaving little scars, and is not done by those that are not superstitious, who choose to have them in the legs, or that part of the arm that is concealed. The children or young patients play together all the rest of the day, and are in perfect health to the eighth.

Then the fever begins to seize them, and they keep their beds two days, very seldom three. They have very rarely above twenty or thirty in their faces, which never mark, and in eight days time they are as well as before their illness. Where they are wounded, there remains running sores during the distemper, which I don't doubt is a great relief to it. Every year thousands undergo this operation, and the French ambassador says pleasantly that they take the small-pox here by way of diversion, as they take the waters in other countries. There is no example of any one that has died in it, and you may believe I am well satisfied of the safety of this experiment, since I intend to try it on my dear little son. I am patriot enough to take pains to bring this useful invention into fashion in England, and I should not fail to write to some of our doctors very particularly about it, if I knew any one of them that I thought had virtue enough to destroy such a considerable branch of their revenue, for the good of mankind. But that distemper is too beneficial to them, not to expose to all their resentment the hardy wight[1] that should undertake to put an end to it. Perhaps if I live to return, I may, however have the courage to war with them. Upon this occasion, admire the heroism in the heart of

Your friend, etc. etc.

[1]Creature.

31

LYNDA NORENE SHAFFER
China, Technology, and Change

In this essay an important contemporary world historian asks us to compare the revolutionary consequences of scientific and technological changes that occurred in China and Europe before the seventeenth century. What is Shaffer's argument? In what ways was the European scientific revolution different from the changes in China she describes here?

Thinking Historically

What exactly was the impact of printing, the compass, and gunpowder in Europe? What was the "before" and "after" for each of these innovations? What, according to Shaffer, was the situation in China before and after each of these innovations? Were these innovations as revolutionary in China as they were in Europe?

Francis Bacon (1561–1626), an early advocate of the empirical method, upon which the scientific revolution was based, attributed Western Europe's early modern take-off to three things in particular: printing, the compass, and gunpowder. Bacon had no idea where these things had come from, but historians now know that all three were invented in China. Since, unlike Europe, China did not take off onto a path leading from the scientific to the Industrial Revolution, some historians are now asking why these inventions were so revolutionary in Western Europe and, apparently, so unrevolutionary in China.

In fact, the question has been posed by none other than Joseph Needham, the foremost English-language scholar of Chinese science and technology. It is only because of Needham's work that the Western academic community has become aware that until Europe's take-off, China was the unrivaled world leader in technological development. That is why it is so disturbing that Needham himself has posed this apparent puzzle. The English-speaking academic world relies upon him and repeats him; soon this question and the vision of China that it implies will become dogma. Traditional China will take on supersociety

Lynda Norene Shaffer, "China, Technology and Change," *World History Bulletin*, 4, no. 1 (Fall/Winter, 1986–1987), 1–6.

qualities — able to contain the power of printing, to rein in the potential of the compass, even to muffle the blast of gunpowder.

The impact of these inventions on Western Europe is well known. Printing not only eliminated much of the opportunity for human copying errors, it also encouraged the production of more copies of old books and an increasing number of new books. As written material became both cheaper and more easily available, intellectual activity increased. Printing would eventually be held responsible, at least in part, for the spread of classical humanism and other ideas from the Renaissance. It is also said to have stimulated the Protestant Reformation, which urged a return to the Bible as the primary religious authority.

The introduction of gunpowder in Europe made castles and other medieval fortifications obsolete (since it could be used to blow holes in their walls) and thus helped to liberate Western Europe from feudal aristocratic power. As an aid to navigation the compass facilitated the Portuguese- and Spanish-sponsored voyages that led to Atlantic Europe's sole possession of the Western Hemisphere, as well as the Portuguese circumnavigation of Africa, which opened up the first all-sea route from Western Europe to the long-established ports of East Africa and Asia.

Needham's question can thus be understood to mean, Why didn't China use gunpowder to destroy feudal walls? Why didn't China use the compass to cross the Pacific and discover America, or to find an all-sea route to Western Europe? Why didn't China undergo a Renaissance or Reformation? The implication is that even though China possessed these technologies, it did not change much. Essentially Needham's question is asking, What was wrong with China?

Actually, there was nothing wrong with China. China was changed fundamentally by these inventions. But in order to see the changes, one must abandon the search for peculiarly European events in Chinese history, and look instead at China itself before and after these breakthroughs.

To begin, one should note that China possessed all three of these technologies by the latter part of the Tang dynasty (618–906) — between four and six hundred years before they appeared in Europe. And it was during just that time, from about 850, when the Tang dynasty began to falter, until 960, when the Song dynasty (960–1279) was established, that China underwent fundamental changes in all spheres. In fact, historians are now beginning to use the term *revolution* when referring to technological and commercial changes that culminated in the Song dynasty, in the same way that they refer to the changes in eighteenth- and nineteenth-century England as the Industrial Revolution. And the word might well be applied to other sorts of changes in China during this period.

For example, the Tang dynasty elite was aristocratic, but that of the Song was not. No one has ever considered whether the invention of

gunpowder contributed to the demise of China's aristocrats, which occurred between 750 and 960, shortly after its invention. Gunpowder
may, indeed, have been a factor although it is unlikely that its importance lay in blowing up feudal walls. Tang China enjoyed such internal
peace that its aristocratic lineages did not engage in castle-building of
the sort typical in Europe. Thus, China did not have many feudal fortifications to blow up.

The only wall of significance in this respect was the Great Wall,
which was designed to keep steppe nomads from invading China. In
fact, gunpowder may have played a role in blowing holes in this wall,
for the Chinese could not monopolize the terrible new weapon, and
their nomadic enemies to the north soon learned to use it against them.
The Song dynasty ultimately fell to the Mongols, the most formidable
force ever to emerge from the Eurasian steppe. Gunpowder may have
had a profound effect on China — exposing a united empire to foreign
invasion and terrible devastation — but an effect quite opposite to the
one it had on Western Europe.

On the other hand, the impact of printing on China was in some
ways very similar to its later impact on Europe. For example, printing
contributed to a rebirth of classical (that is, preceding the third century
A.D.) Confucian learning, helping to revive a fundamentally humanistic
outlook that had been pushed aside for several centuries.

After the fall of the Han dynasty (206 B.C. – A.D. 220), Confucianism had lost much of its credibility as a world view, and it eventually
lost its central place in the scholarly world. It was replaced by Buddhism, which had come from India. Buddhists believed that much
human pain and confusion resulted from the pursuit of illusory pleasures and dubious ambitions: Enlightenment and, ultimately, salvation
would come from a progressive disengagement from the real world,
which they also believed to be illusory. This point of view dominated
Chinese intellectual life until the ninth century. Thus the academic and
intellectual comeback of classical Confucianism was in essence a return
to a more optimistic literature that affirmed the world as humans had
made it.

The resurgence of Confucianism within the scholarly community
was due to many factors, but printing was certainly one of the most important. Although it was invented by Buddhist monks in China, and at
first benefited Buddhism, by the middle of the tenth century, printers
were turning out innumerable copies of the classical Confucian corpus.
This return of scholars to classical learning was part of a more general
movement that shared not only its humanistic features with the later
Western European Renaissance, but certain artistic trends as well.

Furthermore, the Protestant Reformation in Western Europe was in
some ways reminiscent of the emergence and eventual triumph of Neo-
Confucian philosophy. Although the roots of Neo-Confucianism can be

found in the ninth century, the man who created what would become its most orthodox synthesis was Zhu Xi (Chu Hsi, 1130–1200). Neo-Confucianism was significantly different from classical Confucianism, for it had undergone an intellectual (and political) confrontation with Buddhism and had emerged profoundly changed. It is of the utmost importance to understand that not only was Neo-Confucianism new, it was also heresy, even during Zhu Xi's lifetime. It did not triumph until the thirteenth century, and it was not until 1313 (when Mongol conquerors ruled China) that Zhu Xi's commentaries on the classics became the single authoritative text against which all academic opinion was judged.

In the same way that Protestantism emerged out of a confrontation with the Roman Catholic establishment and asserted the individual Christian's autonomy, Neo-Confucianism emerged as a critique of Buddhist ideas that had taken hold in China, and it asserted an individual moral capacity totally unrelated to the ascetic practices and prayers of the Buddhist priesthood. In the twelfth century Neo-Confucianists lifted the work of Mencius (Meng Zi, 370–290 B.C.) out of obscurity and assigned it a place in the corpus second only to that of the *Analects of Confucius*. Many facets of Mencius appealed to the Neo-Confucianists, but one of the most important was his argument that humans by nature are fundamentally good. Within the context of the Song dynasty, this was an assertion that morality could be pursued through an engagement in human affairs, and that the Buddhist monks' withdrawal from life's mainstream did not bestow upon them any special virtue.

The importance of these philosophical developments notwithstanding, printing probably had its greatest impact on the Chinese political system. The origin of the civil service examination system in China can be traced back to the Han dynasty, but in the Song dynasty government-administered examinations became the most important route to political power in China. For almost a thousand years (except the early period of Mongol rule), China was governed by men who had come to power simply because they had done exceedingly well in examinations on the Neo-Confucian canon. At any one time thousands of students were studying for the exams, and thousands of inexpensive books were required. Without printing such a system would not have been possible.

The development of this alternative to aristocratic rule was one of the most radical changes in world history. Since the examinations were ultimately open to 98 percent of all males (actors were one of the few groups excluded), it was the most democratic system in the world prior to the development of representative democracy and popular suffrage in Western Europe in the eighteenth and nineteenth centuries. (There were some small-scale systems, such as the classical Greek city-states, which might be considered more democratic, but nothing comparable in size to Song China or even the modern nation-states of Europe.)

Finally we come to the compass. Suffice it to say that during the Song dynasty, China developed the world's largest and most technologically sophisticated merchant marine and navy. By the fifteenth century its ships were sailing from the north Pacific to the east coast of Africa. They could have made the arduous journey around the tip of Africa and on into Portuguese ports; however, they had no reason to do so. Although the Western European economy was prospering, it offered nothing that China could not acquire much closer to home at much less cost. In particular, wool, Western Europe's most important export, could easily be obtained along China's northern frontier.

Certainly, the Portuguese and the Spanish did not make their unprecedented voyages out of idle curiosity. They were trying to go to the Spice Islands, in what is now Indonesia, in order to acquire the most valuable commercial items of the time. In the fifteenth century these islands were the world's sole suppliers of the fine spices, such as cloves, nutmeg, and mace, as well as a source for the more generally available pepper. It was this spice market that lured Columbus westward from Spain and drew Vasco Da Gama around Africa and across the Indian Ocean.

After the invention of the compass, China also wanted to go to the Spice Islands and, in fact, did go, regularly — but Chinese ships did not have to go around the world to get there. The Atlantic nations of Western Europe, on the other hand, had to buy spices from Venice (which controlled the Mediterranean trade routes) or from other Italian city-states; or they had to find a new way to the Spice Islands. It was necessity that mothered those revolutionary routes that ultimately changed the world.

Gunpowder, printing, the compass — clearly these three inventions changed China as much as they changed Europe. And it should come as no surprise that changes wrought in China between the eighth and tenth centuries were different from changes wrought in Western Europe between the thirteenth and fifteenth centuries. It would, of course, be unfair and ahistorical to imply that something was wrong with Western Europe because the technologies appeared there later. It is equally unfair to ask why the Chinese did not accidentally bump into the Western Hemisphere while sailing east across the Pacific to find the wool markets of Spain.

SUGITA GEMPAKU

A Dutch Anatomy Lesson in Japan

Sugita Gempaku* (1733–1817) was a Japanese physician who, as he tells us here in his memoir, suddenly discovered the value of Western medical science when he chanced to witness a dissection shortly after he obtained a Dutch anatomy book.

What was it that Sugita Gempaku learned on that day in 1771? What were the differences between the treatments of anatomy in the Chinese *Book of Medicine* and the Dutch medical book? What accounts for these differences?

Thinking Historically

How might the Dutch book have changed the way the author practiced medicine? How did it change his knowledge of the human body? How did it change the relevance of his knowledge of the human body to the medicine he practiced? How revolutionary was the new knowledge for Sugita Gempaku?

Whenever I met Hiraga Gennai (1729–1779), we talked to each other on this matter: "As we have learned, the Dutch method of scholarly investigation through field work and surveys is truly amazing. If we can directly understand books written by them, we will benefit greatly. However, it is pitiful that there has been no one who has set his mind on working in this field. Can we somehow blaze this trail? It is impossible to do it in Edo. Perhaps it is best if we ask translators in Nagasaki to make some translations. If one book can be completely translated, there will be an immeasurable benefit to the country." Every time we spoke in this manner, we deplored the impossibility of imple-

*SOO gee tah   gehm PAH koo

Sugita Gempaku, *Ranto Kotohajime* (The Beginning of Dutch Studies in the East), in David J. Lu, ed., *Japan: A Documentary History*, vol. I (Armonk, N.Y.: M. E. Sharpe, 2005), 264–66. Iwanami Shoten, *Nihon Koten Bunka Taikei* (Major Compilation of Japanese Classics), vol. 95 (Tokyo: Iwanami Shoten, 1969), 487–93.

menting our desires. However, we did not vainly lament the matter for long.

Somehow, miraculously I obtained a book on anatomy written in that country. It may well be that Dutch studies in this country began when I thought of comparing the illustrations in the book with real things. It was a strange and even miraculous happening that I was able to obtain that book in that particular spring of 1771. Then at the night of the third day of the third month, I received a letter from a man by the name of Tokuno Bambei, who was in the service of the then Town Commissioner, Magaribuchi Kai-no-kami. Tokuno stated in his letter that "A post-mortem examination of the body of a condemned criminal by a resident physician will be held tomorrow at Senjukotsukahara. You are welcome to witness it if you so desire." At one time my colleague by the name of Kosugi Genteki had an occasion to witness a post-mortem dissection of a body when he studied under Dr. Yamawaki Tōyō of Kyoto. After seeing the dissection firsthand, Kosugi remarked that what was said by the people of old was false and simply could not be trusted. "The people of old spoke of nine internal organs, and nowadays, people divide them into five viscera and six internal organs. That [perpetuates] inaccuracy," Kosugi once said. Around that time (1759) Dr. Tōyō published a book entitled *Zōshi* (*On Internal Organs*). Having read that book, I had hoped that some day I could witness a dissection. When I also acquired a Dutch book on anatomy, I wanted above all to compare the two to find out which one accurately described the truth. I rejoiced at this unusually fortunate circumstance, and my mind could not entertain any other thought. However, a thought occurred to me that I should not monopolize this good fortune, and decided to share it with those of my colleagues who were diligent in the pursuit of their medicine. . . . Among those I invited was one [Maeno] Ryōtaku (1723–1803). . . .

The next day, when we arrived at the location . . . Ryōtaku reached under his kimono to produce a Dutch book and showed it to us. "This is a Dutch book of anatomy called *Tabulae Anatomicae*. I bought this a few years ago when I went to Nagasaki, and kept it." As I examined it, it was the same book I had and was of the same edition. We held each other's hands and exclaimed: "What a coincidence!" Ryōtaku continued by saying: "When I went to Nagasaki, I learned and heard," and opened his book. "These are called *long* in Dutch, they are lungs," he taught us. "This is *hart*, or the heart. When it says *maag* it is the stomach, and when it says *milt* it is the spleen." However, they did not look like the heart given in the Chinese medical books, and none of us were sure until we could actually see the dissection.

Thereafter we went together to the place which was especially set for us to observe the dissection in Kotsukahara. . . . The regular man who performed the chore of dissection was ill, and his grandfather, who was ninety years of age, came in his place. He was a healthy old man. He had experienced many dissections since his youth, and boasted that he dissected a number of bodies. Those dissections were performed in those days by men of the *eta*[1] class. . . . That day, the old butcher pointed to this and that organ. After the heart, liver, gall bladder, and stomach were identified, he pointed to other parts for which there were no names. "I don't know their names. But I have dissected quite a few bodies from my youthful days. Inside of everyone's abdomen there were these parts and those parts." Later, after consulting the anatomy chart, it became clear to me that I saw an arterial tube, a vein, and the suprarenal gland. The old butcher again said, "Every time I had a dissection, I pointed out to those physicians many of these parts, but not a single one of them questioned 'what was this?' or 'what was that?'" We compared the body as dissected against the charts both Ryōtaku and I had, and could not find a single variance from the charts. The Chinese *Book of Medicine* (*Yi Jing*) says that the lungs are like the eight petals of the lotus flower, with three petals hanging in front, three in back, and two petals forming like two ears and that the liver has three petals to the left and four petals to the right. There were no such divisions, and the positions and shapes of intestines and gastric organs were all different from those taught by the old theories. The official physicians, Dr. Okada Yōsen and Dr. Fujimoto Rissen, have witnessed dissection seven or eight times. Whenever they witnessed the dissection, they found that the old theories contradicted reality. Each time they were perplexed and could not resolve their doubts. Every time they wrote down what they thought was strange. They wrote in their books. "The more we think of it, there must be fundamental differences in the bodies of Chinese and of the eastern barbarians [i.e., Japanese]." I could see why they wrote this way.

That day, after the dissection was over, we decided that we also should examine the shape of the skeletons left exposed on the execution ground. We collected the bones, and examined a number of them. Again, we were struck by the fact that they all differed from the old theories while conforming to the Dutch charts.

The three of us, Ryōtaku, [Nakagawa] Junan (1739–1786), and I went home together. On the way home we spoke to each other and felt the same way. "How marvelous was our actual experience today. It is a shame that we were ignorant of these things until now. As physicians who serve their masters through medicine, we performed our duties in complete ignorance of the true form of the human body. How disgraceful it is. Somehow, through this experience, let us investigate further the truth about the human body. If we practice medicine with this knowledge behind us, we can make contributions for people under heaven

---

[1]The eta were an untouchable caste in Japan, defined by their restriction to certain occupations associated with death — tanning or working with hides, cremating the dead, butchering meat, and, thus, doing autopsies. They could not be physicians. [Ed.]

and on this earth." Ryōtaku spoke to us. "Indeed, I agree with you wholeheartedly." Then I spoke to my two companions. "Somehow if we can translate anew this book called *Tabulae Anatomicae*, we can get a clear notion of the human body inside out. It will have great benefit in the treatment of our patients. Let us do our best to read it and understand it without the help of translators." Ryōtaku responded: "I have been wanting to read Dutch books for some time, but there has been no friend who would share my ambitions. I have spent days lamenting it. If both of you wish, I have been in Nagasaki before and have retained some Dutch. Let us use it as a beginning to tackle the book together." After hearing it, I answered, "This is simply wonderful. If we are to join our efforts, I shall also resolve to do my very best." . . .

The next day, we assembled at the house of Ryōtaku and recalled the happenings of the previous day. When we faced that *Tabulae Anatomicae*, we felt as if we were setting sail on a great ocean in a ship without oars or a rudder. With the magnitude of the work before us, we were dumbfounded by our own ignorance. However, Ryōtaku had been thinking of this for some time, and he had been in Nagasaki. He knew some Dutch through studying and hearing, and knew some sentence patterns and words. He was also ten years older than I, and we decided to make him head of our group and our teacher. At that time I did not know the twenty-five letters of the Dutch alphabet. I decided to study the language with firm determination, but I had to acquaint myself with letters and words gradually.

33

BENJAMIN FRANKLIN

Letter on a Balloon Experiment in 1783

Benjamin Franklin (1706–1790) was the preeminent statesman, diplomat, and spokesman for the British colonies that became the United States during his long lifetime. Trained as a candle maker and printer, he became a journalist, publisher, merchant, homespun philosopher, and inveterate inventor. He invented the lightning rod, the Franklin stove, bifocals, and the medical catheter, among other things. His

---

Nathan G. Goodman, ed., *The Ingenious Dr. Franklin, Selected Scientific Letters of Benjamin Franklin* (Philadelphia: University of Pennsylvania Press, 1931), 99–102.

inventions sprang from a gift of immense curiosity and an exhaustive reading in the science of his day.

Franklin, sometimes called "the first American," represented the fledging Republic in France during the Revolution, ensuring French participation against the British. In 1783 he signed the second Treaty of Paris, by which the British recognized the independence of the United States. Franklin was the only founding father to sign the Declaration of Independence (1776), the Treaty of Paris (1783), and the Constitution of the United States (1789). Throughout his life Franklin furthered his interest in scientific experiment and invention. In December of 1783, he wrote to a friend about a recent invention that fascinated him: an early experiment in air travel in a balloon. What did Franklin see and what did it mean to him?

Thinking Historically

What evidence do you see in this letter that the scientific revolution was a genuinely revolutionary change? What was revolutionary about it? What evidence do you see that the people of the time thought they were living in a revolutionary age? How would you compare their attitudes with those of people today toward modern technological innovations?

TO
Sir Joseph Banks

Passy, Dec. 1, 1783.

Dear Sir: —
In mine of yesterday I promised to give you an account of Messrs. Charles & Robert's experiment, which was to have been made this day, and at which I intended to be present. Being a little indisposed, and the air cool, and the ground damp, I declined going into the garden of the Tuileries, where the balloon was placed, not knowing how long I might be obliged to wait there before it was ready to depart, and chose to stay in my carriage near the statue of Louis XV, from whence I could well see it rise, and have an extensive view of the region of air through which, as the wind sat, it was likely to pass. The morning was foggy, but about one o'clock the air became tolerably clear, to the great satisfaction of the spectators, who were infinite, notice having been given of the intended experiment several days before in the papers, so that all Paris was out, either about the Tuileries, on the quays and bridges, in the fields, the streets, at the windows, or on the tops of houses, besides the inhabitants of all the towns and villages of the environs. Never before was a philosophical experiment so magnificently attended. Some

guns were fired to give notice that the departure of the balloon was near, and a small one was discharged, which went to an amazing height, there being but little wind to make it deviate from its perpendicular course, and at length the sight of it was lost. Means were used, I am told, to prevent the great balloon's rising so high as might endanger its bursting. Several bags of sand were taken on board before the cord that held it down was cut, and the whole weight being then too much to be lifted, such a quantity was discharged as to permit its rising slowly. Thus it would sooner arrive at that region where it would be in equilibrio with the surrounding air, and by discharging more sand afterwards, it might go higher if desired. Between one and two o'clock, all eyes were gratified with seeing it rise majestically from among the trees, and ascend gradually above the buildings, a most beautiful spectacle. When it was about two hundred feet high, the brave adventurers held out and waved a little white pennant, on both sides [of] their car, to salute the spectators, who returned loud claps of applause. The wind was very little, so that the object though moving to the northward, continued long in view; and it was a great while before the admiring people began to disperse. The persons embarked were Mr. Charles, professor of experimental philosophy, and a zealous promoter of that science; and one of the Messieurs Robert, the very ingenious constructors of the machine. When it arrived at its height, which I suppose might be three or four hundred toises, it appeared to have only horizontal motion. I had a pocket-glass, with which I followed it, till I lost sight first of the men, then of the car, and when I last saw the balloon, it appeared no bigger than a walnut. I write this at seven in the evening. What became of them is not yet known here. I hope they descended by daylight, so as to see and avoid falling among trees or on houses, and that the experiment was completed without any mischievous accident, which the novelty of it and the want of experience might well occasion. I am the more anxious for the event, because I am not well informed of the means provided for letting themselves down, and the loss of these very ingenious men would not only be a discouragement to the progress of the art, but be a sensible loss to science and society.

I shall inclose one of the tickets of admission, on which the globe was represented, as originally intended, but is altered by the pen to show its real state when it went off. When the tickets were engraved the car was to have been hung to the neck of the globe, as represented by a little drawing I have made in the corner.

I suppose it may have been an apprehension of danger in straining too much the balloon or tearing the silk, that induced the constructors to throw a net over it, fixed to a hoop which went round its middle, and to hang the car to that hoop.

Tuesday morning, December 2d. — I am relieved from my anxiety by hearing that the adventurers descended well near L'Isle Adam before sunset. This place is near seven leagues from Paris. Had the wind blown fresh they might have gone much farther.

If I receive any further particulars of importance, I shall communicate them hereafter.

With great esteem, I am, dear sir, your most obedient and most humble servant,

FRANKLIN

P.S. *Tuesday evening.* — Since writing the above I have received the printed paper and the manuscript containing some particulars of the experiment, which I enclose. I hear further that the travellers had perfect command of their carriage, descending as they pleased by letting some of the inflammable air escape, and rising again by discharging some sand; that they descended over a field so low as to talk with the labourers in passing, and mounted again to pass a hill. The little balloon falling at Vincennes shows that mounting higher it met with a current of air in a contrary direction, an observation that may be of use to future aerial voyagers.

REFLECTIONS

Was there a scientific revolution in the seventeenth and eighteenth century? By most measures we would have to say "yes." There were new polished-glass instruments with which to observe and measure; books, theories, diagrams, debates, and discoveries emerged at a dizzying pace. Age-old authorities — Aristotle, Ptolemy, even the Bible — were called into question. The wisdom of the ages was interrogated for evidence and forced to submit to tests by experiment. But these changes would not have constituted a revolution if they occurred in a vacuum.

Maria Sibylla Merian's metaphor is perhaps most appropriate. There was a metamorphosis — a change from one way of looking at the world to another. We might even say it was a change from a medieval manner of wearing the world like a robe to a modern view of the world as a stage, as a reality seen through a window, something separate that could be touched, weighed, measured, even bought and sold.

However we choose to characterize the changes in scientific thinking during this period, it is important to emphasize the revolutionary impact of the European scientific revolution of the seventeenth century without slighting the scientific and technological achievements of other civilizations. Many of the scientific developments in Europe sprang from foreign innovations, and in some fields Europe was not as advanced as other societies. Yet the scientific revolution's unique combination of observation and generalization, experimentation and mathematics, induction and deduction established a body of knowledge and a method for research that proved lasting and irreversible.

Why was it that China, so scientifically and technologically adept during the Sung dynasty, pictured hearts and lungs as flower petals in the late-Ming and early-Ch'ing seventeenth century? Was it that Chinese science lost momentum or changed direction? Or does such a question, as Lynda Shaffer warns, judge China unfairly by Western standards? Do the petal hearts reflect a different set of interests rather than a failure of Chinese science?

Chinese scientists excelled in acupuncture, massage, and herbal medicine, while European scientists excelled in surgery. It turned out that the inner workings of the human body were better revealed in surgical dissection than in muscle manipulation or in oral remedies. And, as Sugita Gempaku reminds us, the Europeans not only cut and removed, they also named what they found and tried to understand how it worked. Perhaps the major difference between science in Europe and that in India, China, and Japan in the seventeenth century was one of perspective: Europeans were beginning to imagine the human body as a machine and asking how it worked. In some respects, the metaphor of man as a machine proved more fruitful than organic metaphors of humans as plants or animals.

Asking probing questions and testing the answers also changed our understanding of the heavens. If mathematical calculations indicated that a star would appear at a particular spot in the heavens and it did not, Galileo might just as soon have questioned the observation as the math. From the seventeenth century on, scientists would check one or the other on the assumption that observation and mathematics could be brought together to understand the same event, that they would have to be in agreement, and that such agreement could lead to laws that could then be tested and proved or disproved.

It is this method of inquiry, not the discoveries, that was new. For the scientific method that emerged during this period constituted a systematic means of inquiry based on agreed-upon rules of hypothesis, experimentation, theory testing, law, and dissemination. This scientific inquiry was a social process in two important ways: First, any scientific discovery had to be reproducible and recognized by other scientists to gain credence. Second, a community of scientists was needed to question, dismiss, or validate the work of its members.

Finally, we return to Baumer's emphasis on the societies of seventeenth-century science. The numerous organizations in Europe are testaments not only to a growing interest in science but to a continuing public conversation. Science in Europe thus became a matter of public concern, a popular endeavor. Compare the masses of Parisians Ben Franklin described who turned out to view the balloon experiment with the few physicians gathered around Sugita Gempaku who could learn from the expertise of outcast butchers.

Ultimately, then, the difference between European science and that of India or China in the seventeenth century may have had more to do with society than with culture. The development of modern scientific methods relied on the numerous debates and discussions of a self-conscious class of gentlemen scientists in a Europe where news traveled quickly and ideas could be translated and tested with confidence across numerous borders. To what extent does science everywhere today demonstrate the hallmarks of the seventeenth-century scientific revolution?

6

Enlightenment and Revolution

Europe and the Americas, 1650–1850

HISTORICAL CONTEXT

The modern world puts its faith in science, reason, and democracy. The seventeenth-century scientific revolution established reason as the key to understanding nature, and its application-directed thought, organized society, and measured governments during the eighteenth-century Enlightenment. Most — though, as we shall see, not all — people believed that reason would eventually lead to freedom. Freedom of thought, religion, and association, and political liberties and representative governments were hailed as hallmarks of the Age of Enlightenment.

For some, enlightened society meant a more controlled rather than a more democratic society. Philosophers like Immanuel Kant and Jean-Jacques Rousseau wanted people to become free but thought most people were incapable of achieving such a state. Rulers who were called "enlightened despots" believed that the application of reason to society would make people happier, not necessarily freer.

Ultimately, however, the Enlightenment's faith in reason led to calls for political revolution as well as for schemes of order. In England in the seventeenth century, in America and France at the end of the eighteenth century, and in Latin America shortly thereafter, revolutionary governments were created according to rational principles of liberty and equality that dispatched monarchs and enshrined the rule of the people. In this chapter we will concentrate on the heritage of the Enlightenment, examining competing tendencies toward order and revolution, stability and liberty, equality and freedom. We will also compare the American and the French Revolutions, and these with the later revolutions in Latin America. Finally, in reflection, we will briefly compare these distinctly European and American developments with processes in other parts of the world.

193

THINKING HISTORICALLY
Close Reading and
Interpretation of Texts

At the core of the Enlightenment was a trust in reasoned discussion, a belief that people could understand each other, even if they were not in agreement. Such understanding demanded clear and concise communication in a world where the masses were often swayed by fiery sermons and flamboyant rhetoric. But the Enlightenment also put its faith in the written word and a literate public. Ideas were debated face to face in the salons and coffeehouses of Europe and in the meeting halls of America, but it was through letters, diaries, the new world of newspapers, and the burgeoning spread of printed books that the people of the Enlightenment learned what they and their neighbors thought.

It is appropriate then for us to read the selections in this chapter — all primary sources — in the spirit in which they were written. We will pay special attention to the words and language that the authors use and will attempt to understand exactly what they meant, even why they chose the words they did. Such explication is a twofold process; we must understand the words first and foremost; then we must strive to understand the words in their proper context, as they were intended by the author. To achieve our first goal, we will paraphrase, a difficult task because the eighteenth-century writing style differs greatly from our own: Sentences are longer and arguments are often complex. Vocabularies were broad during this period, and we may encounter words that are used in ways unknown to us. As to our latter goal, we must try to make the vocabulary and perspective of the authors our own. Grappling with what makes the least sense to us and trying to understand why it was said is the challenge.

34

DAVID HUME

On Miracles

The European Enlightenment of the eighteenth century was the expression of a new class of intellectuals, independent of the clergy but allied with the rising middle class. Their favorite words were *reason, nature,* and *progress.* They applied the systematic doubt of René Descartes (1596–1650) and the reasoning method of the scientific revolution to human affairs, including religion and politics. With caustic wit and good humor, they asked new questions and popularized new points of view that would eventually revolutionize Western politics and culture. While the French *philosophes* and Voltaire (1694–1778) may be the best known, the Scottish philosopher David Hume (1711–1776) may have been the most brilliant. What does Hume argue in this selection? Does he prove his point to your satisfaction? How does he use reason and nature to make his case? Is reason incompatible with religion?

Thinking Historically

The first step in understanding what Hume means in this essay must come from a careful reading — a sentence-by-sentence exploration. Try to paraphrase each sentence, putting it into your own words. For example, you might paraphrase the first sentence like this: "I've found a way to disprove superstition; this method should be useful as long as superstition exists, which may be forever." Notice the content of such words as *just* and *check.* What does Hume mean by these words and by *prodigies?*

The second sentence is a concise definition of the scientific method. How would you paraphrase it? The second and third sentences summarize the method Hume has discovered to counter superstition. What is the meaning of the third sentence?

In the rest of the essay, Hume offers four proofs, or reasons, why miracles do not exist. How would you paraphrase each of these? Do you find these more or less convincing than his more general opening and closing arguments? What does Hume mean by *miracles?*

The Philosophical Works of David Hume (Edinburgh: A. Black and W. Tait, 1826).

I flatter myself that I have discovered an argument . . . , which, if just, will, with the wise and learned, be an everlasting check to all kinds of superstitious delusion, and consequently will be useful as long as the world endures; for so long, I presume, will the accounts of miracles and prodigies be found in all history, sacred and profane. . . .

A wise man proportions his belief to the evidence. . . .

A miracle is a violation of the laws of nature; and as a firm and unalterable experience has established these laws, the proof against a miracle, from the very nature of the fact, is as entire as any argument from experience can possibly be imagined. . . . Nothing is esteemed a miracle, if it ever happens in the common course of nature. It is no miracle that a man, seemingly in good health, should die on a sudden; because such a kind of death, though more unusual than any other, has yet been frequently observed to happen. But it is a miracle that a dead man should come to life; because that has never been observed in any age or country. There must, therefore, be an uniform experience against every miraculous event, otherwise the event would not merit that appellation. And as an uniform experience amounts to a proof, there is here a direct and full *proof*, from the nature of the fact, against the existence of any miracle. . . .

(Further) there is not to be found, in all history, any miracle attested by a sufficient number of men, of such unquestioned good sense, education, and learning, as to secure us against all delusion in themselves; of such undoubted integrity, as to place them beyond all suspicion of any design to deceive others; of such credit and reputation in the eyes of mankind, as to have a great deal to lose in case of their being detected in any falsehood. . . .

Secondly, We may observe in human nature a principle which, if strictly examined, will be found to diminish extremely the assurance, which we might, from human testimony, have in any kind of prodigy. . . . The passion of *surprise* and *wonder*, arising from miracles, being an agreeable emotion, gives a sensible tendency towards the belief of those events from which it is derived. . . .

With what greediness are the miraculous accounts of travellers received, their descriptions of sea and land monsters, their relations of wonderful adventures, strange men, and uncouth manners? But if the spirit of religion join itself to the love of wonder, there is an end of common sense; and human testimony, in these circumstances, loses all pretensions to authority. A religionist may be an enthusiast, and imagine he sees what has no reality: He may know his narrative to be false, and yet persevere in it, with the best intentions in the world, for the sake of promoting so holy a cause: Or even where this delusion has not place, vanity, excited by so strong a temptation, operates on him more powerfully than on the rest of mankind in any other circumstances; and self-interest with equal force. . . .

The many instances of forged miracles and prophecies and supernatural events, which, in all ages, have either been detected by contrary evidence, or which detect themselves by their absurdity, prove sufficiently the strong propensity of mankind to the extraordinary and marvellous, and ought reasonably to beget a suspicion against all relations of this kind.[1] . . .

Thirdly, It forms a strong presumption against all supernatural and miraculous relations, that they are observed chiefly to abound among ignorant and barbarous nations; or if a civilized people has ever given admission to any of them, that people will be found to have received them from ignorant and barbarous ancestors, who transmitted them with that inviolable sanction and authority which always attend received opinions. . . .

I may add, as a *fourth* reason, which diminishes the authority of prodigies, that there is no testimony for any, even those which have not been expressly detected, that is not opposed by any infinite number of witnesses; so that not only the miracle destroys the credit of testimony, but the testimony destroys itself. To make this the better understood, let us consider, that in matters of religion, whatever is different is contrary; and that it is impossible the religions of ancient Rome, of Turkey, of Siam, and of China, should all of them be established on any solid foundation. Every miracle, therefore, pretended to have been wrought in any of these religions (and all of them abound in miracles), as its direct scope is to establish the particular system to which it is attributed; so has it the same force, though more indirectly, to overthrow every other system. In destroying a rival system, it likewise destroys the credit of those miracles on which that system was established, so that all the prodigies of different religions are to be regarded as contrary facts, and the evidences of these prodigies, whether weak or strong, as opposite to each other. . . .

Upon the whole, then, it appears, that no testimony for any kind of miracle has ever amounted to a probability, much less to a proof; and that, even supposing it amounted to proof, it would be opposed by another proof, derived from the very nature of the fact which it would endeavour to establish. It is experience only which gives authority to human testimony; and it is the same experience which assures us of the laws of nature. When, therefore, these two kinds of experience are contrary, we have nothing to do but to subtract the one from the other, and embrace an opinion either on one side or the other, with that assurance which arises from the remainder. But according to the principle here explained, this subtraction with regard to all popular religions amounts to an entire annihilation; and therefore we may establish it as a maxim, that no human testimony can have such force as to prove a miracle, and make it a just foundation for any such system of religion.

[1]Accounts of miracles. [Ed.]

35

DENIS DIDEROT

Supplement to the Voyage of Bougainville

French *philosophe* Denis Diderot* (1713–1784) personified the Enlightenment with his literary wit, faith in reason, passion for universal knowledge, and constant challenge to custom, convention, and censorship. He wrote his great *Encyclopedia* of seventeen volumes, a compendium of the wisdom of the eighteenth century, amidst a life of philosophical treatises, provocative popular essays, numerous marriages and affairs, and periods of imprisonment for his writings.

His *Supplement to the Voyage of Bougainville*† (1772) is a literary invention presented as if it were a recently discovered addition to the famous 1768 account of the voyage to Tahiti by the French explorer, Louis-Antoine de Bougainville. Bougainville's very popular *Voyage around the World* spread the idea of the South Sea Islanders as "noble savages," untarnished by civilization, free to lead a life in tune with nature. Such accounts became a literary model for European self-criticism.

In this passage, Diderot uses the departure of the French from Tahiti as an opportunity for an old Tahitian to wish them good riddance. What criticisms does Diderot's old Tahitian make of the French and their civilization?

Thinking Historically

The idea of presenting one's philosophical ideas in a "long-lost" book or in the voice of "the native" was an old technique in the eighteenth century, possibly initiated as early as 1516 in Thomas More's classic work in which a traveller describes an ideal world called *Utopia*. For both Diderot and More, the use of the foreigner's voice provided the author with a bit of distance for protection from the censor, or worse, the police and jailer. Under the guise of "only reporting what others said," the author could try out new and sometimes radical ideas. It is likely, however, that the speech Diderot put in the mouth of the old Tahitian in this section represented Diderot's own ideas about French civilization.

*dee duh ROH
†boo gan VEEL

Denis Diderot, *Supplement to the Voyage of Bougainville*, Part II, "The Old Man's Farewell" (Essex, U.K.: Project Gutenberg, University of Essex, 2006), http://courses.essex.ac.uk/cs/cs101/txframe.htm.

Bear in mind that Diderot is writing on the eve of the French Revolution, which broke out in 1789. While no one foresaw the future in 1772, the strains of the old regime were evident to many philosophers of the Enlightenment like Diderot: an indifferent monarchy; a depleted treasury to be worsened by aid to the American Revolution; a creakingly inequitable Parliament where the nobility and clergy each had as much representation as everyone else. What evidence do you see of Diderot's concern about these issues? In addition, thinkers like Voltaire and Diderot were critical of French colonialism and slavery. What evidence do you see of this critique in this document? What other criticisms does Diderot make of French civilization?

Part II, "The Old Man's Farewell"

He was the father of a large family. On the arrival of the Europeans, he cast looks of disdain at them, showing neither astonishment, fright, nor curiosity. [The presence of this old man and his attitude to the Europeans are mentioned by Bougainville.] They came up to him: he turned his back on them and retired into his cabin. His silence and his anxiety revealed his thoughts too well. He groaned within himself over the happy days of his country, now for ever eclipsed. On the departure of Bougainville, as the inhabitants rushed in a crowd on to the beach, attached themselves to his clothing, hugged his comrades in their arms and wept, this old man advanced, severe in mien, and said: "Weep, luckless Tahitiens weep, but for the arrival not for the departure of these ambitious and wicked men. One day you will know them better. One day they will return, holding in one hand the morsel of wood you see attached to this man's belt, in the other, the iron which hangs from that man's side: they will return to throw you into chains, to cut your throats, or to subject you to their extravagance and vices: one day you will serve under them, as corrupted, as vile, as luckless as they. One consolation I have. My life is drawing to its close. And the calamity I announce to you, *I* shall not see. O Tahitiens, my friends, there is one method which might save you from your tragic future. But I would rather die than advise it. Let them withdraw and live."

Then addressing Bougainville, he added:

"And thou, chief of the brigands who obey thee, quickly push off thy vessel from our shore. We are innocent; we are happy: and thou canst not but spoil our happiness. We follow the pure instinct of nature: thou hast sought to efface its character from our souls. Here all things belong to all men. Thou hast preached some strange distinction between thine and mine. Our daughters and our wives were held in common by us all: thou hast shared this privilege with us, and thou hast come and inflamed them with frenzies unknown before. They have lost their reason in thy arms. Thou hast become ferocious in theirs. They have come to hate each other. You have slaughtered each other for them: they have come back stained with your blood. We are free: and see thou hast planted in our earth the title of our future slavery. Thou art neither god nor demon. Who art thou then to make slaves? Orou! thou who understandest the language of these men, tell us all as thou hast told me, what they have written on this metal blade! *This country is ours.* This country is thine! And why? Because thou hast set foot there? If a Tahitien disembarked one day upon your shores, and graved upon one of your stones or on the bark of one of your trees: *This country belongs to the inhabitants of Tahiti,* what wouldst thou think of such a proceeding? Thou art the stronger! But what of that? When someone took from you one of those rubbishy trifles with which your hut is filled, thou didst cry out and take thy revenge. Yet at that moment thou wast projecting in the depth of thy heart the theft of a whole country. Thou art not a slave. Thou wouldst suffer death rather than become one, yet us thou wouldst enslave. Thinkest thou then that the Tahitien cannot defend his liberty and die? He, whom thou wishest to seize like an animal, the Tahitien, is thy brother. You are both children of nature. What right hast thou over him that he has not over thee? Thou art come. Did we fall upon thee? Did we pillage thy ship? Did we seize thee and expose thee to the arrows of our enemies? Did we yoke thee to our animals toiling in the fields? No. We have respected our image in thee. Leave us our customs. They are wiser and more honourable than thine. We have no wish to barter what thou callest our ignorance against thy useless knowledge. We possess all that is necessary and good for us. Do we deserve contempt because we have not known how to fabricate for ourselves wants in superfluity? When we are hungry we have enough to eat; when we are cold the means to clothe ourselves. Thou hast entered our cabins. What, in thy opinion, is lacking? Pursue as long as thou wilt what thou callest the commodities of life. But permit sensible beings to stop, when by continuing their painful labour they will gain but imaginary good. If thou persuadest us to cross the narrow limit of necessity, when shall we stop working? What time will be left over for enjoying ourselves? We have reduced to the smallest possible the sum of our annual and daily toil, because to us nothing seems better than repose. Go back to thine own country to trouble and torment thyself as much as thou wilt. Trouble us neither with thy artificial needs, nor thy imaginary virtues. Look at these men: how straight, healthy, and robust they are! Look at these women. How straight, healthy, fresh, and fair they are. Take this bow. It is mine. Call to help thee, one, two, three, four of thy comrades and try to bend it. I bend it myself alone. I plough the earth. I climb the mountain. I pierce the forest. I cover a league of the plain in less than an hour. Thy young companions can scarcely follow me, and I am ninety years old and more. Woe to this island! Woe to all Tahitiens present and to come for the day of this thy visit! We only know one illness that to which man, animal, and plant have been condemned, old age: and thou hast brought to us another. Thou hast infected our blood. Perhaps we shall have to exterminate with our own hands, our daughters, our wives, our children: the men who have approached thy women: the women who have approached thy men. Our fields will be damp with the impure blood which has passed from thy veins into ours: else our children will be condemned to nourish and perpetuate the ill thou hast given to their fathers and mothers and to transmit it for ever to their descendants. Wretch! thou wilt be guilty of the ravages that follow thy fatal embraces or of the murders we shall commit to check the poison! Thou speakest of crimes! Knowest thou a greater than thine own? What with thee is the punishment for the man who kills his neighbour? Death by iron. And what for the coward who poisons him? Death by fire. Compare thy crime to this latter one, and tell us, poisoner of nations, the punishment thou deservest. A moment ago the young Tahitien maiden abandoned herself with transport to the embraces of the Tahitien boy: she waited with impatience till her mother (authorized by her reaching the nubile age), raised her veil and bared her throat. She was proud to excite the desires or to fix the amorous gaze of the stranger, her parents or her brother. She accepted fearlessly and shamelessly, in our presence, midst a circle of innocent Tahitiens, to the sound of flutes, between the dances, the caresses of him her young heart and the secret voice of her senses had chosen. The idea of crime and the danger of disease have come with thee amongst us. Our pleasures, formerly so sweet, are accompanied by remorse and terror. That man in black, next you, who listens to me, has spoken to our boys. I know not what he has said to our girls. But our boys hesitate: our girls blush. Plunge if thou wilt into the dark forest with the perverse partner of thy pleasures, but allow the good and simple Tahitiens to reproduce without shame, in the face of heaven and the open day. What sentiment more honourable and greater couldst thou find to replace the one we have breathed into them and which animates their lives? They think the moment has come to enrich the nation and the family with a new citizen and they glory in it. They eat to live and grow. They grow to multiply, they find there neither vice nor shame. Listen to the succession of thy crimes. Scarcely hadst thou appeared among them, but they turn thieves. Scarcely hadst thou descended on our soil, but it smoked blood. That Tahitien who ran to meet thee, who greeted thee, who received thee crying *Taio, friend, friend*: you killed him. And why, did you kill him? Because he had been seduced by the glitter of thy little serpents' eggs. He gave thee his fruits: he offered thee his wife and daughter: he yielded thee his cabin. And thou hast killed him for a handful of these grains, which he took from thee without asking. And this people? At the sound of thy deadly firearms, terror seized them and they fled into the mountain. But understand they would have speedily come down again. Without me you may be sure you would all have perished in an instant. Why have I calmed, why have I restrained them? Why do I restrain them even now? I do not know. For thou deservest no sentiment of pity. Thou hast a ferocious soul which never felt it. Thou didst walk, thou and thine, in our island: thou hast been respected: thou hast enjoyed everything: thou hast found in thy way neither barrier nor refusal: thou wast invited in: thou sattest down: there was laid out before thee the abundance of the country. Didst thou wish for our young girls? Save for these, who have not yet the privilege of showing face and throat, their mothers presented thee them all quite naked. Thine the tender victim of hostly duty. For her and for thee the ground hast been scattered with leaves and flowers: the musicians have tuned their instruments: nothing has troubled the sweetness nor hindered the liberty of her caresses or thine. The hymn was chanted, the hymn which exhorted thee to be a man and our child to be a woman, a woman yielding and voluptuous. There was dancing round your bed, and it is on leaving the arms of this woman, after feeling on her breast the sweetest rapture, that thou hast killed her brother, her friend, her father perhaps. Thou hast done worse still. Look this way. See this enclosure stiff with arms: these arms which had only menaced our enemies, they are turned against our own children: see the wretched companions of our pleasures: see their sadness. See the grief of their fathers: the despair of their mothers. In that place they have been condemned to perish by our hands or by the ills that thou hast done them. Withdraw unless thy cruel eyes take pleasure in spectacles of death: withdraw, go, and may the guilty seas which have spared thee in thy voyage gain their own absolution and avenge us by swallowing thee up before thy return. And you, Tahitiens, return to your cabins every one of you and let these unworthy strangers hear on their departure but the moaning wave, and see but the foam whose fury whitens a deserted beach."

He had scarcely finished, but the crowd of inhabitants had disappeared. A vast silence reigned over all the island. Nothing was heard but the shrill whistle of the winds and the dull noise of the water along all the coast. One might have thought that air and water, responsive to the old man's voice, were happy to obey him.

36

The American Declaration of Independence

If anyone had taken a poll of Americans in the thirteen colonies as late as 1775, independence would not have won a majority vote anywhere. Massachusetts might have come close, perhaps, but nowhere in the land was there a definitive urge to separate from the British Empire. Still, three thousand miles was a long way for news, views, appointees, and petitions to travel and tensions between the colonies and Britain had been growing.

Of course, each side looked at the cost of colonial administration differently. The British believed that they had carried a large part of the costs of migration, administration of trade, and control of the sea, while the colonists resented the humiliation resulting from their lack of political representation and the often inept royal officials and punitive legislation imposed on them from afar by the Parliament and the king.

By the spring of 1775, events were rapidly pushing the colonies toward independence. In April, British troops engaged colonial forces at Lexington and Concord, instigating a land war that was to last until 1781. In the midst of other urgent business, most notably raising an army, the Continental Congress asked a committee that included Thomas Jefferson, Benjamin Franklin, and John Adams to compose a statement outlining these and other reasons for separation from Britain. Jefferson wrote the first draft, the bulk of which became the final version accepted by the Continental Congress on July 4, 1776.

The Declaration of Independence was preeminently a document of the Enlightenment. Its principal author, Thomas Jefferson, exemplified the Enlightenment intellectual. Conversant in European literature, law, and political thought, he made significant contributions to eighteenth-century knowledge in natural science and architecture. Benjamin Franklin and other delegates to the Congress in Philadelphia were similarly accomplished.

It is no wonder, then, that the Declaration and the establishment of an independent United States of America should strike the world as the realization of the Enlightenment's basic tenets. That a wholly new country could be created by people with intelligence and foresight, according to principles of reason, and to realize human liberty was heady stuff.

A Documentary History of the United States, ed. Richard D. Heffner (New York: Penguin Books, 1991), 15–18.

What were the goals of the authors of this document? In what ways was the Declaration a call for democracy? In what ways was it not?

Thinking Historically

Before interpreting any document, we must read it carefully and put it into context — that is, determine the what, where, and why. Some of this information may be available in the text itself. For instance, whom is the Declaration addressed to? What is the reason given for writing it?

We interpret or extract meaning from documents by asking questions that emerge from the reading. These questions may arise from passages we do not understand, from lack of clarity in the text, or from an incongruence between the text and our expectations. It may surprise some readers, for example, that the Declaration criticizes the king so sharply. To question this might lead us to explore the need for American colonists to defend their actions in terms of British legal tradition. For years, the American colonists blamed the king's ministers for their difficulties; in July 1776 they blamed the king — a traditional sign of revolutionary intent in England, which meant efforts toward independence were imminent.

Consider also the disparity between the lofty sentiments of liberty and independence and the existence of slavery in the Americas. How is it possible that Jefferson and some of the signers of the Declaration could own slaves while declaring it "self-evident that all men are created equal"? To whom did this statement apply?

In Congress, July 4, 1776, the Unanimous Declaration of the Thirteen United States of America

When in the course of human events, it becomes necessary for one people to dissolve the political bands which have connected them with another, and to assume among the powers of the earth, the separate and equal station to which the Laws of Nature and of Nature's God entitle them, a decent respect to the opinions of mankind requires that they should declare the causes which impel them to the separation.

We hold these truths to be self-evident, that all men are created equal, that they are endowed by their Creator with certain unalienable rights, that among these are life, liberty, and the pursuit of happiness. That to secure these rights, governments are instituted among men, deriving their just powers from the consent of the governed. That whenever any form of government becomes destructive of these ends, it is the right of the people to alter or to abolish it, and to institute new government, laying its foundation on such principles and organizing its powers in such form, as to them shall seem most likely to effect their safety and happiness. Prudence, indeed, will dictate that governments long established should not be changed for light and transient causes; and accordingly all experience hath shown, that mankind are more disposed to suffer, while evils are sufferable, than to right themselves by abolishing the forms to which they are accustomed. But when a long train of abuses and usurpations, pursuing invariably the same object evinces a design to reduce them under absolute despotism, it is their right, it is their duty, to throw off such government, and to provide new guards for their future security. Such has been the patient sufferance of these Colonies; and such is now the necessity which constrains them to alter their former systems of government. The history of the present King of Great Britain is a history of repeated injuries and usurpations, all having in direct object the establishment of an absolute tyranny over these States. To prove this, let facts be submitted to a candid world.

He has refused his assent to laws, the most wholesome and necessary for the public good.

He has forbidden his Governors to pass laws of immediate and pressing importance, unless suspended in their operation till his assent should be obtained; and when so suspended, he has utterly neglected to attend to them.

He has refused to pass other laws for the accommodation of large districts of people, unless those people would relinquish the right of representation in the Legislature, a right inestimable to them and formidable to tyrants only.

He has called together legislative bodies at places unusual, uncomfortable, and distant from the depository of their public records, for the sole purpose of fatiguing them into compliance with his measures.

He has dissolved representative houses repeatedly, for opposing with manly firmness his invasions on the rights of the people.

He has refused for a long time, after such dissolutions, to cause others to be elected; whereby the legislative powers, incapable of annihilation, have returned to the people at large for their exercise; the State remaining in the meantime exposed to all the dangers of invasion from without and convulsions within.

He has endeavoured to prevent the population of these states; for that purpose obstructing the laws of naturalization of foreigners; refusing to pass others to encourage their migration hither, and raising the conditions of new appropriations of lands.

He has obstructed the administration of justice, by refusing his assent to laws for establishing judiciary powers.

He has made judges dependent on his will alone, for the tenure of their offices, and the amount and payment of their salaries.

He has erected a multitude of new offices, and sent hither swarms of officers to harass our people, and eat out their substance.

He has kept among us, in times of peace, standing armies without the consent of our legislatures.

He has affected to render the military independent of and superior to the civil power.

He has combined with others to subject us to a jurisdiction foreign to our constitution, and unacknowledged by our laws; giving his assent to their acts of pretended legislation:

For quartering large bodies of armed troops among us:

For protecting them, by a mock trial, from punishment for any murders which they should commit on the inhabitants of these States:

For cutting off our trade with all parts of the world:

For imposing taxes on us without our consent:

For depriving us in many cases, of the benefits of trial by jury:

For transporting us beyond seas to be tried for pretended offences:

For abolishing the free system of English laws in a neighbouring Province, establishing therein an arbitrary government, and enlarging its boundaries so as to render it at once an example and fit instrument for introducing the same absolute rule into these Colonies:

For taking away our Charters, abolishing our most valuable laws, and altering fundamentally the forms of our governments:

For suspending our own Legislatures, and declaring themselves invested with power to legislate for us in all cases whatsoever.

He has abdicated government here, by declaring us out of his protection and waging war against us.

He has plundered our seas, ravaged our coasts, burnt our towns, and destroyed the lives of our people.

He is at this time transporting large armies of foreign mercenaries to complete the works of death, desolation, and tyranny, already begun with circumstances of cruelty and perfidy scarcely paralleled in the most barbarous ages, and totally unworthy the head of a civilized nation.

He has constrained our fellow citizens taken captive on the high seas to bear arms against their country, to become the executioners of their friends and brethren, or to fall themselves by their hands.

He has excited domestic insurrections amongst us, and has endeavoured to bring on the inhabitants of our frontiers, the merciless Indian savages, whose known rule of warfare, is an undistinguished destruction of all ages, sexes, and conditions.

In every state of these oppressions we have petitioned for redress in the most humble terms: our repeated petitions have been answered only by repeated injury. A prince whose character is thus marked by every act which may define a tyrant is unfit to be the ruler of a free people.

Nor have we been wanting in attention to our British brethren. We have warned them from time to time of attempts by their legislature to extend an unwarrantable jurisdiction over us. We have reminded them of the circumstances of our emigration and settlement here. We have appealed to their native justice and magnanimity, and we have conjured them by the ties of our common kindred to disavow these usurpations, which would inevitably interrupt our connections and correspondence. They too have been deaf to the voice of justice and of consanguinity. We must, therefore, acquiesce in the necessity, which denounces our separation, and hold them, as we hold the rest of mankind, enemies in war, in peace friends.

We, therefore, the Representatives of the United States of America, in General Congress assembled, appealing to the Supreme Judge of the world for the rectitude of our intentions, do, in the name, and by authority of the good people of these Colonies, solemnly publish and declare, That these United Colonies are, and of right ought to be Free and Independent States; that they are absolved from all allegiance to the British Crown, and that all political connection between them and the State of Great Britain, is and ought to be totally dissolved; and that as Free and Independent States, they have full power to levy war, conclude peace, contract alliances, establish commerce, and to do all other acts and things which Independent States may of right do. And for the support of this declaration, with a firm reliance on the protection of Divine Province, we mutually pledge to each other our lives, our fortunes, and our sacred honor.

37

The French Declaration of the Rights of Man and Citizen

The founding of the Republic of the United States of America provided a model for other peoples chafing under oppressive rule to emulate. Not surprisingly then, when the French movement to end political injustices turned to revolution in 1789 and the revolutionaries convened at the National Assembly, the Marquis de Lafayette (1757–1834), hero of the American Revolution, proposed a Declaration of the Rights of Man and Citizen. Lafayette had the American Declaration in

A Documentary History of the French Revolution, ed. John Hall Stewart (London: Macmillan, 1979).

mind, and he had the assistance of Thomas Jefferson, present in Paris as the first United States ambassador to France.

While the resulting document appealed to the French revolutionaries, the French were not able to start afresh as the Americans had done. In 1789 Louis XVI was still king of France: He could not be made to leave by a turn of phrase. Nor were men created equal in France in 1789. Those born into the nobility led lives different from those born into the Third Estate (the 99 percent of the population who were not nobility or clergy), and they had different legal rights as well. This disparity was precisely what the revolutionaries and the Declaration sought to change. Inevitably, though, such change would prove to be a more violent and revolutionary proposition than it had been in the American colonies.

In what ways did the Declaration of the Rights of Man and Citizen resemble the American Declaration of Independence? In what ways was it different? Which was more democratic?

Thinking Historically

The French Declaration is full of abstract, universal principles. But notice how such abstractions can claim our consent by their rationality without informing us as to how they will be implemented. What is meant by the first right, for instance? What does it mean to say that men are "born free"? Why is it necessary to distinguish between "born" and "remain"? What is meant by the phrase "general usefulness"? Do statements like these increase people's liberties, or are they intentionally vague so they can be interpreted at will?

The slogan of the French Revolution was "Liberty, Equality, Fraternity." Which of the rights in the French Declaration emphasize liberty, which equality? Can these two goals be opposed to each other? Explain how.

The representatives of the French people, organized in National Assembly, considering that ignorance, forgetfulness, or contempt of the rights of man are the sole causes of public misfortunes and of the corruption of governments, have resolved to set forth in a solemn declaration the natural, inalienable, and sacred rights of man, in order that such declaration, continually before all members of the social body, may be a perpetual reminder of their rights and duties; in order that the acts of the legislative power and those of the executive power may constantly be compared with the aim of every political institution and may accordingly be more respected; in order that the demands of the citizens, founded henceforth upon simple and incontestable principles, may always be directed towards the maintenance of the Constitution and the welfare of all.

Accordingly, the National Assembly recognizes and proclaims, in the presence and under the auspices of the Supreme Being, the following rights of man and citizen.

1. Men are born and remain free and equal in rights; social distinctions may be based only upon general usefulness.

2. The aim of every political association is the preservation of the natural and inalienable rights of man; these rights are liberty, property, security, and resistance to oppression.

3. The source of all sovereignty resides essentially in the nation; no group, no individual may exercise authority not emanating expressly therefrom.

4. Liberty consists of the power to do whatever is not injurious to others; thus the enjoyment of the natural rights of every man has for its limits only those that assure other members of society the enjoyment of those same rights; such limits may be determined only by law.

5. The law has the right to forbid only actions which are injurious to society. Whatever is not forbidden by law may not be prevented, and no one may be constrained to do what it does not prescribe.

6. Law is the expression of the general will; all citizens have the right to concur personally, or through their representatives, in its formation; it must be the same for all, whether it protects or punishes. All citizens, being equal before it, are equally admissible to all public offices, positions, and employments, according to their capacity, and without other distinction than that of virtues and talents.

7. No man may be accused, arrested, or detained except in the cases determined by law, and according to the forms prescribed thereby. Whoever solicit, expedite, or execute arbitrary orders, or have them executed, must be punished; but every citizen summoned or apprehended in pursuance of the law must obey immediately; he renders himself culpable by resistance.

8. The law is to establish only penalties that are absolutely and obviously necessary; and no one may be punished except by virtue of a law established and promulgated prior to the offence and legally applied.

9. Since every man is presumed innocent until declared guilty, if arrest be deemed indispensable, all unnecessary severity for securing the person of the accused must be severely repressed by law.

10. No one is to be disquieted because of his opinions, even religious, provided their manifestation does not disturb the public order established by law.

11. Free communication of ideas and opinions is one of the most precious of the rights of man. Consequently, every citizen may speak,

write, and print freely, subject to responsibility for the abuse of such liberty in the cases determined by law.

12. The guarantee of the rights of man and citizen necessitates a public force; therefore, is instituted for the advantage of all and not for the particular benefit of those to whom it is entrusted.

13. For the maintenance of the public force and for the expenses of administration a common tax is indispensable; it must be assessed equally on all citizens in proportion to their means.

14. Citizens have the right to ascertain, by themselves or through their representatives, the necessity of the public tax, to consent to it freely, to supervise its use, and to determine its quota, assessment, payment, and duration.

15. Society has the right to require of every public agent an accounting of his administration.

16. Every society in which the guarantee of rights is not assured or the separation of powers not determined has no constitution at all.

17. Since property is a sacred and inviolate right, no one may be deprived thereof unless a legally established public necessity obviously requires it, and upon condition of a just and previous indemnity.

$$\boxed{38}$$

MARY WOLLSTONECRAFT

A Vindication of the Rights of Woman

Mary Wollstonecraft (1759–1797) lived a short but influential life as a writer in England and France in the midst of the French Revolution. She wrote *A Vindication of the Rights of Woman* (1792) in response to the radical changes that were occurring in France. She also lent support to Thomas Paine's radical *Rights of Man* (1791) which challenged conservative Edmund Burke's critical *Reflections on the Revolution in France* (1790).

The American and French revolutions enshrined many of the ideas and much of the language of the eighteenth-century Enlightenment. The very success of these revolutions demonstrated the power of En-

---

Mary Wollstonecraft, *A Vindication of the Rights of Woman* (Boston: Peter Edes, 1792). Spelling Americanized.

lightenment ideas about freedom and equality and, thus, inspired other marginalized groups to wonder about their own rights. If all men were created equal, then what about slaves? If kings and their governments could be overthrown and replaced by the rule of "the people," why, then, did women have no power politically — they were people too, weren't they? Mary Wollstonecraft, sometimes called the first feminist, was one of those who wondered about this, and who took Enlightenment reasoning a step further.

The male thinkers of the Enlightenment had been content to declare the "rights of man" as sufficient protection for women, assuming that "man" stood for mankind. Wollstonecraft forced them to confront that when they declared that "all men" are created equal, they did not mean to include women. In fact, they believed that women did not have the same rational faculties as men, and that women were principally meant to attend to their appearance and the service of the naturally dominant sex. Wollstonecraft pointed out that women were trained by society to accept these insults as part of the "natural" state of things.

Modern feminists sometimes distinguish between two types of demands: political/legal and cultural. Generally political and legal demands are easier to identify and label — like the right to vote or the right to own property — and the only requirement for these rights to become available to women is that legislation be enacted. Cultural demands are often more subtle and complicated and require changes in the way people think. Which of Wollstonecraft's demands are political or legal? Which are cultural? Which of her demands have been realized since 1792? Which have not?

Thinking Historically

When Jefferson wrote that "all men are created equal," he was writing in the language of eighteenth-century enlightened universalism. But he did not imagine that any of his contemporaries would think the document included women or African slaves. Notice how Mary Wollstonecraft speaks of man in general in most of the first chapter and then turns to "men" in most of the rest of the selection. Why do you think she changes her focus from mankind to men?

In addition to the enormous differences between eighteenth-century and modern vocabulary and writing styles, both the questions and the answers of the eighteenth century were different from our own. Most people today would answer eighteenth-century questions very differently from the way they were answered then. If asked, few people today, for instance, would say that men alone should be educated. The idea that both men and women should be educated is an example of an idea that was new in 1792, but is now almost universally accepted. What other ideas does Wollstonecraft express that have since become fairly universal?

In addition, we no longer ask some of the questions that were asked in the eighteenth century. What examples do you see here of questions that are generally no longer asked? What other kinds of questions have we stopped asking? Why?

Chap. I. The Rights and Involved Duties of Mankind Considered

In the present state of society it appears necessary to go back to first principles in search of the most simple truths, and to dispute with some prevailing prejudice every inch of ground. To clear my way, I must be allowed to ask some plain questions, and the answers will probably appear as unequivocal as the axioms on which reasoning is built; though, when entangled with various motives of action, they are formally contradicted, either by the words or conduct of men.

In what does man's pre-eminence over the brute creation consist? The answer is as clear as that a half is less than the whole; in Reason.

What acquirement exalts one being above another? Virtue, we spontaneously reply.

For what purpose were the passions implanted? That man by struggling with them might attain a degree of knowledge denied to the brutes, whispers Experience.

Consequently the perfection of our nature and capability of happiness must be estimated by the degree of reason, virtue, and knowledge that distinguish the individual, and direct the laws which bind society: and that from the exercise of reason, knowledge and virtue naturally flow is equally undeniable, if mankind be viewed collectively.

The rights and duties of man thus simplified, it seems almost impertinent to attempt to illustrate truths that appear so incontrovertible; yet such deeply rooted prejudices have clouded reason, and such spurious qualities have assumed the name of virtues, that it is necessary to pursue the course of reason as it has been perplexed and involved in error, by various adventitious circumstances, comparing the simple axiom with casual deviations.

Men, in general, seem to employ their reason to justify prejudices, which they have imbibed, they cannot trace how, rather than to root them out. The mind must be strong that resolutely forms its own principles; for a kind of intellectual cowardice prevails which makes many men shrink from the task, or only do it by halves. Yet the imperfect conclusions thus drawn, are frequently very plausible, because they are built on partial experience, on just, though narrow, views. . . .

Chap. II. The Prevailing Opinion
of a Sexual Character Discussed

To account for, and excuse the tyranny of man, many ingenious arguments have been brought forward to prove, that the two sexes, in the acquirement of virtue, ought to aim at attaining a very different character: or, to speak explicitly, women are not allowed to have sufficient strength of mind to acquire what really deserves the name of virtue. Yet it should seem, allowing them to have souls, that there is but one way appointed by Providence to lead *mankind* to either virtue or happiness.

If then women are not a swarm of ephemeron triflers, why should they be kept in ignorance under the specious name of innocence? Men complain, and with reason, of the follies and caprices of our sex, when they do not keenly satirize our headstrong passions and groveling vices. Behold, I should answer, the natural effect of ignorance! The mind will ever be unstable that has only prejudices to rest on, and the current will run with destructive fury when there are no barriers to break its force. Women are told from their infancy, and taught by the example of their mothers, that a little knowledge of human weakness, justly termed cunning, softness of temper, *outward* obedience, and a scrupulous attention to a puerile kind of propriety, will obtain for them the protection of man; and should they be beautiful, every thing else is needless, for, at least, twenty years of their lives. . . .

How grossly do they insult us who thus advise us only to render ourselves gentle, domestic brutes! For instance, the winning softness so warmly, and frequently, recommended, that governs by obeying. What childish expressions, and how insignificant is the being — can it be an immortal one? who will condescend to govern by such sinister methods! "Certainly," says Lord Bacon,[1] "man is of kin to the beasts by his body; and if he be not of kin to God by his spirit, he is a base and ignoble creature!" Men, indeed, appear to me to act in a very unphilosophical manner when they try to secure the good conduct of women by attempting to keep them always in a state of childhood. . . .

Chap. IV. Observations on the State of Degradation
to Which Woman Is Reduced by Various Causes

. . . The power of generalizing ideas, of drawing comprehensive conclusions from individual observations, is the only acquirement, for an immortal being, that really deserves the name of knowledge. Merely to observe, without endeavoring to account for any thing, may (in a very

---

[1] Francis Bacon (1561–1626), English philosopher, writer, and statesman. [Ed.]

incomplete manner) serve as the common sense of life; but where is the store laid up that is to clothe the soul when it leaves the body?

This power has not only been denied to women; but writers have insisted that it is inconsistent, with a few exceptions, with their sexual character. Let men prove this, and I shall grant that woman only exists for man. I must, however, previously remark, that the power of generalizing ideas, to any great extent, is not very common amongst men or women. But this exercise is the true cultivation of the understanding; and every thing conspires to render the cultivation of the understanding more difficult in the female than the male world.

I am naturally led by this assertion to the main subject of the present chapter, and shall now attempt to point out some of the causes that degrade the sex, and prevent women from generalizing their observations. . . .

Ah! why do women, I write with affectionate solicitude, condescend to receive a degree of attention and respect from strangers, different from that reciprocation of civility which the dictates of humanity and the politeness of civilization authorize between man and man? And, why do they not discover, when "in the noon of beauty's power," that they are treated like queens only to be deluded by hollow respect, till they are led to resign, or not assume, their natural prerogatives? Confined then in cages like the feathered race, they have nothing to do but to plume themselves, and stalk with mock majesty from perch to perch. It is true they are provided with food and raiment, for which they neither toil nor spin; but health, liberty, and virtue, are given in exchange. But, where, amongst mankind has been found sufficient strength of mind to enable a being to resign these adventitious prerogatives; one who, rising with the calm dignity of reason above opinion, dared to be proud of the privileges inherent in man? And it is vain to expect it whilst hereditary power chokes the affections and nips reason in the bud. . . .

"I have endeavoured," says Lord Chesterfield,[2] "to gain the hearts of twenty women, whose persons I would not have given a fig for." . . .

I lament that women are systematically degraded by receiving the trivial attentions, which men think it manly to pay to the sex, when, in fact, they are insultingly supporting their own superiority. It is not condescension to bow to an inferior. So ludicrous, in fact, do these ceremonies appear to me, that I scarcely am able to govern my muscles, when I see a man start with eager, and serious solicitude to lift a handkerchief, or shut a door, when the *lady* could have done it herself, had she only moved a pace or two. . . .

---

[2] Philip Dormer Stanhope, fourth earl of Chesterfield (1694–1773), English statesman, diplomat, and wit. [Ed.]

Mankind, including every description, wish to be loved and re-spected for *something*; and the common herd will always take the near-est road to the completion of their wishes. The respect paid to wealth and beauty is the most certain, and unequivocal; and, of course, will al-ways attract the vulgar eye of common minds. Abilities and virtues are absolutely necessary to raise men from the middle rank of life into no-tice; and the natural consequence is notorious; the middle rank con-tains most virtue and abilities. Men have thus, in one station, at least, an opportunity of exerting themselves with dignity, and of rising by the exertions which really improve a rational creature; but the whole fe-male sex are, till their character is formed, in the same condition as the rich: for they are born, I now speak of a state of civilization, with cer-tain sexual privileges, and whilst they are gratuitously granted them, few will ever think of works of supererogation,[3] to obtain the esteem of a small number of superior people. . . .

Women, commonly called Ladies, are not to be contradicted in company, are not allowed to exert any manual strength; and from them the negative virtues only are expected, when any virtues are ex-pected, patience, docility, good-humor, and flexibility; virtues incom-patible with any vigorous exertion of intellect. Besides, by living more with each other, and being seldom absolutely alone, they are more under the influence of sentiments than passions. Solitude and reflec-tion are necessary to give to wishes the force of passions, and to en-able the imagination to enlarge the object, and make it the most desir-able. The same may be said of the rich; they do not sufficiently deal in general ideas, collected by impassioned thinking, or calm investiga-tion, to acquire that strength of character on which great resolves are built.

Chap. XII. On National Education

The good effects resulting from attention to private education will ever be very confined, and the parent who really puts his own hand to the plow, will always, in some degree, be disappointed, till education be-comes a grand national concern. A man cannot retire into a desert with his child, and if he did he could not bring himself back to childhood, and become the proper friend and play-fellow of an infant or youth. And when children are confined to the society of men and women, they very soon acquire that kind of premature manhood which stops the growth of every vigorous power of mind or body. In order to open their faculties they should be excited to think for themselves; and this

[3]More than is necessary. [Ed.]

can only be done by mixing a number of children together, and making them jointly pursue the same objects.

Let an enlightened nation then try what effect reason would have to bring them back to nature, and their duty; and allowing them to share the advantages of education and government with man, see whether they will become better, as they grow wiser and become free. They cannot be injured by the experiment; for it is not in the power of man to render them more insignificant than they are at present.

To render this practicable, day schools, for particular ages, should be established by government, in which boys and girls might be educated together. The school for the younger children, from five to nine years of age, ought to be absolutely free and open to all classes. . . .

After the age of nine, girls and boys, intended for domestic employments, or mechanical trades, ought to be removed to other schools, and receive instruction, in some measure appropriated to the destination of each individual, the two sexes being still together in the morning; but in the afternoon, the girls should attend a school, where plain-work, mantua-making, millinery, etc. would be their employment.

The young people of superior abilities, or fortune, might now be taught, in another school, the dead and living languages, the elements of science, and continue the study of history and politics, on a more extensive scale, which would not exclude polite literature.

Girls and boys still together? I hear some readers ask: yes. And I should not fear any other consequence than that some early attachment might take place; which, whilst it had the best effect on the moral character of the young people, might not perfectly agree with the views of the parents, for it will be a long time, I fear, before the world is so far enlightened that parents, only anxious to render their children virtuous, will let them choose companions for life themselves. . . .

In short, in whatever light I view the subject, reason and experience convince me that the only method of leading women to fulfill their peculiar duties, is to free them from all restraint by allowing them to participate in the inherent rights of mankind.

Make them free, and they will quickly become wise and virtuous, as men become more so; for the improvement must be mutual, or the injustice which one half of the human race are obliged to submit to, retorting on their oppressors, the virtue of man will be worm-eaten by the insect whom he keeps under his feet.

Let men take their choice, man and woman were made for each other, though not to become one being; and if they will not improve women, they will deprave them!

39

TOUSSAINT L'OUVERTURE
Letter to the Directory

When the French revolutionaries proclaimed the Declaration of the Rights of Man and Citizen in 1789, the French colony of Saint-Domingue[1] (now Haiti) contained a half million African slaves, most of whom worked on the sugar plantations that made France one of the richest countries in the world. Thus, the French were confronted with the difficult problem of reconciling their enlightened principles with the extremely profitable, but fundamentally unequal, institution of slavery.

French revolutionaries remained locked in debate about this issue when in 1791, the slaves of Saint-Domingue organized a revolt that culminated in establishing Haiti's national independence twelve years later. François Dominique Toussaint L'Ouverture,* a self-educated Haitian slave, led the revolt and the subsequent battles against the French planter class and French armies, as well as the Spanish forces of neighboring Santo Domingo, now the other half of the island known as the Dominican Republic and the antirevolutionary forces of Britain, all of whom vied for control of the island at the end of the eighteenth century.

At first Toussaint enjoyed the support of the revolutionary government in Paris; in the decree of 16 Pluviôse (1794) the National Convention abolished slavery in the colonies. But after 1795, the revolution turned on itself and Toussaint feared the new conservative government, called the Directory, might send troops to restore slavery on the island.

In 1797 he wrote the Directory the letter that follows. Notice how Toussaint negotiated a difficult situation. How did he try to reassure the government of his allegiance to France? At the same time, how did

---

[1]san doh MANG   Santo Domingo was the Spanish name for the eastern half of Hispaniola (now the Dominican Republic). Saint-Domingue was the French name for the western half of the island, now Haiti. San Domingo, which is used in the text, is a nineteenth-century abbreviation for Saint-Domingue. To further complicate matters, both the Spanish and French sometimes used their term for the whole island of Hispaniola. Spain controlled the entire island until 1697 when the Spanish recognized French control of the west. [Ed.]
  *too SAN   loo vehr TUR

Toussaint L'Ouverture, "Letter to the Directory, November 5, 1797," in *The Black Jacobins*, ed. C. L. R. James (New York: Vintage Books, 1989), 195–97.

he attempt to convince the Directory that a return to slavery was unthinkable?

Thinking Historically

Notice how the author is torn between the ideals of the French Revolution and the interests of the people of Saint-Domingue. Where did Toussaint's true loyalty lie? At the time he wrote this letter events had not yet forced him to declare the independence of Saint-Domingue (Haiti); this would not happen until January 1, 1804. But, according to the letter, how and why did Toussaint regard the principles of the French Revolution as more important than his loyalty to France?

. . . The impolitic and incendiary discourse of Vaublanc has not affected the blacks nearly so much as their certainty of the projects which the proprietors of San Domingo are planning: insidious declarations should not have any effect in the eyes of wise legislators who have decreed liberty for the nations. But the attempts on that liberty which the colonists propose are all the more to be feared because it is with the veil of patriotism that they cover their detestable plans. We know that they seek to impose some of them on you by illusory and specious promises, in order to see renewed in this colony its former scenes of horror. Already perfidious emissaries have stepped in among us to ferment the destructive leaven prepared by the hands of liberticides. But they will not succeed. I swear it by all that liberty holds most sacred. My attachment to France, my knowledge of the blacks, make it my duty not to leave you ignorant either of the crimes which they meditate or the oath that we renew, to bury ourselves under the ruins of a country revived by liberty rather than suffer the return of slavery.

It is for you, Citizens Directors, to turn from over our heads the storm which the eternal enemies of our liberty are preparing in the shades of silence. It is for you to enlighten the legislature, it is for you to prevent the enemies of the present system from spreading themselves on our unfortunate shores to sully it with new crimes. Do not allow our brothers, our friends, to be sacrificed to men who wish to reign over the ruins of the human species. But no, your wisdom will enable you to avoid the dangerous snares which our common enemies hold out for you. . . .

I send you with this letter a declaration which will acquaint you with the unity that exists between the proprietors of San Domingo who are in France, those in the United States, and those who serve under the English banner. You will see there a resolution, unequivocal and carefully constructed, for the restoration of slavery; you will see there that their determination to succeed has led them to envelop themselves in the mantle of liberty in order to strike it more deadly blows. You will see that they are counting heavily on my complacency in lending myself to their perfidious views by my fear for my children. It is not astonishing that these men who sacrifice their country to their interests are unable to conceive how many sacrifices a true love of country can support in a better father than they, since I unhesitatingly base the happiness of my children on that of my country, which they and they alone wish to destroy.

I shall never hesitate between the safety of San Domingo and my personal happiness; but I have nothing to fear. It is to the solicitude of the French Government that I have confided my children. . . . I would tremble with horror if it was into the hands of the colonists that I had sent them as hostages; but even if it were so, let them know that in punishing them for the fidelity of their father, they would only add one degree more to their barbarism, without any hope of ever making me fail in my duty. . . . Blind as they are! They cannot see how this odious conduct on their part can become the signal of new disasters and irreparable misfortunes, and that far from making them regain what in their eyes liberty for all has made them lose, they expose themselves to a total ruin and the colony to its inevitable destruction. Do they think that men who have been able to enjoy the blessing of liberty will calmly see it snatched away? They supported their chains only so long as they did not know any condition of life more happy than that of slavery. But to-day when they have left it, if they had a thousand lives they would sacrifice them all rather than be forced into slavery again. But no, the same hand which has broken our chains will not enslave us anew. France will not revoke her principles, she will not withdraw from us the greatest of her benefits. She will protect us against all our enemies; she will not permit her sublime morality to be perverted, those principles which do her most honour to be destroyed, her most beautiful achievement to be degraded, and her Decree of 16 Pluviôse which so honours humanity to be revoked. *But if, to re-establish slavery in San Domingo, this was done, then I declare to you it would be to attempt the impossible: we have known how to face dangers to obtain our liberty, we shall know how to brave death to maintain it.*

This, Citizens Directors, is the morale of the people of San Domingo, those are the principles that they transmit to you by me.

My own you know. It is sufficient to renew, my hand in yours, the oath that I have made, to cease to live before gratitude dies in my heart, before I cease to be faithful to France and to my duty, before the god of liberty is profaned and sullied by the liberticides, before they can snatch from my hands that sword, those arms, which France confided to me for the defence of its rights and those of humanity, for the triumph of liberty and equality.

40

SIMÓN BOLÍVAR

A Constitution for Venezuela

As we have seen, the Enlightenment principles of reason, human rights, and equality ignited revolutions on both sides of the Atlantic. In Europe, these revolutions overturned kings and tyrannies, marshaling national citizen armies and creating parliamentary democracies. In the American colonies, the revolutions took shape as anticolonial struggles for independence. Sometimes the effort to create both an independent nation *and* a democracy proved overwhelming.

Simón Bolívar* (1783–1830), called "the Liberator," successfully led the Latin American revolution for independence from Spain between 1810 and 1824. (See Map 6.1.) In 1819, he became president of Venezuela and of what is today Colombia, Ecuador, and Panama, and he gave the speech on the Constitution of Venezuela that follows.

What does Bolívar see as the difference between the independence of Spanish-American colonies and that of the American colonies? What does he mean when he says that Latin Americans have been denied "domestic tyranny"? Would you call Bolívar a "democrat"? Is he more or less democratic than the French or North American revolutionaries? What kind of society do you think would result from the constitution he envisions?

Thinking Historically

How does Bolívar characterize the revolutionary population of South America? How does he think this population differs from the North American revolutionaries? What do you think accounts for this difference?

In what ways did the revolutionaries of South America, North America, and France see their problems and needs differently? How did Bolívar propose to solve what he perceived to be the unique problems of South America? What do you think of his solution?

*see MOHN   boh LEE vahr

Selected Writings of Bolívar, comp. Vincent Lecuna, ed. Harold A. Bierck Jr., 2 vols. (New York: Colonial Press, 1951), 175–91.

Map 6.1 Latin American Independence, 1804–1830

Let us review the past to discover the base upon which the Republic of Venezuela is founded.

America, in separating from the Spanish monarchy, found herself in a situation similar to that of the Roman Empire when its enormous framework fell to pieces in the midst of the ancient world. Each Roman division then formed an independent nation in keeping with its location or interests; but this situation differed from America's in that those members proceeded to reestablish their former associations. We, on the contrary, do not even retain the vestiges of our original being. We are not Europeans; we are not Indians; we are but a mixed species of aborigines and Spaniards. Americans by birth and Europeans by law, we find ourselves engaged in a dual conflict: We are disputing with the natives for titles of ownership, and at the same time we are struggling to maintain ourselves in the country that gave us birth against the opposition of the invaders. Thus our position is most extraordinary and complicated. But there is more. As our role has always been strictly passive and political existence nil, we find that our quest for liberty is now even more difficult of accomplishment; for we, having been placed in a state lower than slavery, had been robbed not only of our freedom but also of the right to exercise an active domestic tyranny. Permit me to explain this paradox.

In absolute systems, the central power is unlimited. The will of the despot is the supreme law, arbitrarily enforced by subordinates who take part in the organized oppression in proportion to the authority that they wield. They are charged with civil, political, military, and religious functions; but, in the final analysis, the satraps of Persia are Persian, the pashas of the Grand Turk are Turks, and the sultans of Tartary are Tartars. China does not seek her mandarins in the homeland of Genghis Khan, her conqueror. America, on the contrary, received everything from Spain, who, in effect, deprived her of the experience that she would have gained from the exercise of an active tyranny by not allowing her to take part in her own domestic affairs and administration. This exclusion made it impossible for us to acquaint ourselves with the management of public affairs; nor did we enjoy that personal consideration, of such great value in major revolutions, that the brilliance of power inspires in the eyes of the multitude. In brief, Gentlemen, we were deliberately kept in ignorance and cut off from the world in all matters relating to the science of government.

Subject to the three-fold yoke of ignorance, tyranny, and vice, the American people have been unable to acquire knowledge, power, or [civic] virtue. The lessons we received and the models we studied, as pupils of such pernicious teachers, were most destructive. We have been ruled more by deceit than by force, and we have been degraded more by vice than by superstition. Slavery is the daughter of darkness: An ignorant people is a blind instrument of its own destruction. Ambition and intrigue abuse the credulity and experience of men lacking all political, economic, and civic knowledge; they adopt pure illusion as reality; they take license for liberty, treachery for patriotism, and vengeance for justice. This situation is similar to that of the robust blind man who, beguiled by his strength, strides forward with all the assurance of one who can see, but, upon hitting every variety of obstacle, finds himself unable to retrace his steps.

If a people, perverted by their training, succeed in achieving their liberty, they will soon lose it, for it would be of no avail to endeavor to explain to them that happiness consists in the practice of virtue; that the rule of law is more powerful than the rule of tyrants, because, as the laws are more inflexible, every one should submit to their beneficent austerity; that proper morals, and not force, are the bases of law; and that to practice justice is to practice liberty. Therefore, Legislators, your work is so much the more arduous, inasmuch as you have to reeducate men who have been corrupted by erroneous illusions and false incentives. Liberty, says Rousseau, is a succulent morsel, but one difficult to digest. Our weak fellow-citizens will have to strengthen their spirit greatly before they can digest the wholesome nutriment of freedom. Their limbs benumbed by chains, their sight dimmed by the darkness of dungeons, and their strength sapped by the pestilence of servitude, are they capable of marching toward the august temple of Liberty without faltering? Can they come near enough to bask in its brilliant rays and to breathe freely the pure air which reigns therein? . . .

The more I admire the excellence of the federal Constitution of Venezuela, the more I am convinced of the impossibility of its application to our state. And to my way of thinking, it is a marvel that its prototype in North America endures so successfully and has not been overthrown at the first sign of adversity or danger. Although the people of North America are a singular model of political virtue and moral rectitude; although the nation was cradled in liberty, reared on freedom, and maintained by liberty alone; and — I must reveal everything — although those people, so lacking in many respects, are unique in the history of mankind, it is a marvel, I repeat, that so weak and complicated a government as the federal system has managed to govern them in the difficult and trying circumstances of their past. But, regardless of the effectiveness of this form of government with respect to North America, I must say that it has never for a moment entered my mind to compare the position and character of two states as dissimilar as the English-American and the Spanish-American. Would it not be most difficult to apply to Spain the English system of political, civil, and religious liberty? Hence, it would be even more difficult to adapt to Venezuela the laws of North America. Does not *L'Esprit des Lois* state that laws should be suited to the people for whom they are made; that it would be a major coincidence if those of one nation could be adapted to another; that laws must take into account the physical conditions of the country, climate, character of the land, location, size, and mode of living of the people; that they should be in keeping with the degree of liberty that the Constitution can sanction respecting the religion of the inhabitants, their inclinations, resources, number, commerce, habits, and customs? This is the code we must consult, not the code of Washington! . . .

Venezuela had, has, and should have a republican government. Its principles should be the sovereignty of the people, division of powers, civil liberty, proscription of slavery, and the abolition of monarchy and privileges. We need equality to recast, so to speak, into a unified nation, the classes of men, political opinions, and public customs.

Among the ancient and modern nations, Rome and Great Britain are the most outstanding. Both were born to govern and to be free and both were built not on ostentatious forms of freedom, but upon solid institutions. Thus I recommend to you, Representatives, the study of the British Constitution, for that body of laws appears destined to bring about the greatest possible good for the peoples that adopt it; but, however perfect it may be, I am by no means proposing that you imitate it slavishly. When I speak of the British government, I only refer to its republican features; and, indeed, can a political system be labelled a monarchy when it recognizes popular sovereignty, division and balance of powers, civil liberty, freedom of conscience and of press, and all that is politically sublime? Can there be more liberty in any other type of republic? Can more be asked of any society? I commend this Constitution to you as that most worthy of serving as model for those who aspire to the enjoyment of the rights of man and who seek all the political happiness which is compatible with the frailty of human nature.

Nothing in our fundamental laws would have to be altered were we to adopt a legislative power similar to that held by the British Parliament. Like the North Americans, we have divided national representation into two chambers; that of Representatives and the Senate. The first is very wisely constituted. It enjoys all its proper functions, and it requires no essential revision, because the Constitution, in creating it, gave it the form and powers which the people deemed necessary in order that they might be legally and properly represented. If the Senate were hereditary rather than elective, it would, in my opinion, be the basis, the tie, the very soul of our republic. In political storms this body would arrest the thunderbolts of the government and would repel any violent popular reaction. Devoted to the government because of a natural interest in its own preservation, a hereditary senate would always oppose any attempt on the part of the people to infringe upon the jurisdiction and authority of their magistrates. It must be confessed that most men are unaware of their best interests, and that they constantly endeavor to assail them in the hands of their custodians — the individual clashes with the mass, and the mass with authority. It is necessary, therefore, that in all governments there be a neutral body to protect the injured and disarm the offender. To be neutral, this body must not owe its origin to appointment by the government or to election by the people, if it is to enjoy a full measure of independence which neither fears nor expects anything from these two sources of authority. The hereditary senate, as a part of the people, shares its interests, its sentiments, and its spirit. For this reason it should not be presumed that a hereditary senate would ignore the interests of the people or forget its legislative duties. The senators in Rome and in the House of Lords in London have been the strongest pillars upon which the edifice of political and civil liberty has rested.

At the outset, these senators should be elected by Congress. The successors to this Senate must command the initial attention of the government, which should educate them in a *colegio* designed especially to train these guardians and future legislators of the nation. They ought to learn the arts, sciences, and letters that enrich the mind of a public figure. From childhood they should understand the career for which they have been destined by Providence, and from earliest youth they should prepare their minds for the dignity that awaits them.

The creation of a hereditary senate would in no way be a violation of political equality. I do not solicit the establishment of a nobility, for as a celebrated republican has said, that would simultaneously destroy equality and liberty. What I propose is an office for which the candidates must prepare themselves, an office that demands great knowledge and the ability to acquire such knowledge. All should not be left to chance and the outcome of elections. The people are more easily deceived than is Nature perfected by art; and, although these senators, it is true, would not be bred in an environment that is all virtue, it is equally true that they would be raised in an atmosphere of enlightened education. Furthermore, the liberators of Venezuela are entitled to occupy forever a high rank in the Republic that they have brought into existence. I believe that posterity would view with regret the effacement of the illustrious names of its first benefactors. I say, moreover, that it is a matter of public interest and national honor, of gratitude on Venezuela's part, to honor gloriously, until the end of time, a race of virtuous, prudent, and persevering men who, overcoming every obstacle, have founded the Republic at the price of the most heroic sacrifices. And if the people of Venezuela do not applaud the elevation of their benefactors, then they are unworthy to be free, and they will never be free.

A hereditary senate, I repeat, will be the fundamental basis of the legislative power, and therefore the foundation of the entire government. It will also serve as a counterweight to both government and people; and as a neutral power it will weaken the mutual attacks of these two eternally rival powers. In all conflicts the calm reasoning of a third party will serve as the means of reconciliation. Thus the Venezuelan senate will give strength to this delicate political structure, so sensitive to violent repercussions; it will be the mediator that will lull the storms and it will maintain harmony between the head and the other parts of the political body.

REFLECTIONS

The Enlightenment and its political legacies — secular order and revolutionary republicanism — were European in origin but global in impact. In this chapter, we have touched on just a few of the crosscurrents of what some historians call an "Atlantic Revolution." A tide of revolutionary fervor swept through France, the United States, and Latin

America, found sympathy in Russia in 1825, and echoed in the Muslim heartland, resulting in secular, modernizing regimes in Turkey and Egypt in the next century.

The appeal of the Enlightenment, of rationally ordered society, and of democratic government continues. Elements of this eighteenth-century revolution — the rule of law; regular, popular elections of representatives; the separation of church and state, of government and politics, and of civil and military authority — are widely recognized ideals and emerging global realities. Like science, the principles of the Enlightenment are universal in their claims and often seem universal in their appeal. Nothing is simpler, more rational, or easier to follow than a call to reason, law, liberty, justice, or equality. And yet every society has evolved its own guidelines under different circumstances, often with lasting results. France had its king and still has a relatively centralized state. The United States began with slavery and still suffers from racism. South American states became free of Europe only to dominate Native Americans, and they continue to do so. One democratic society has a king, another a House of Lords, another a national church. Are these different adaptations of the Enlightenment ideal? Or are these examples of incomplete revolution, cases of special interests allowing their governments to fall short of principle?

The debate continues today as more societies seek to realize responsive, representative government and the rule of law while oftentimes respecting conflicting traditions. Muslim countries and Israel struggle with the competing demands of secular law and religion, citizenship and communalism. Former communist countries adopt market economies and struggle with traditions of collective support and the appeal of individual liberty.

Perhaps these are conflicts within the Enlightenment tradition itself. How is it possible to have both liberty and equality? How can we claim inalienable rights on the basis of a secular, scientific creed? How does a faith in human reason lead to revolution? And how can ideas of order or justice avoid the consequences of history and human nature?

The great revolutionary declarations of the Enlightenment embarrass the modern skeptic with their naïve faith in natural laws, their universal prescriptions to cure all ills, and their hypocritical avoidance of slaves, women, and the colonized. The selections by Diderot, Toussaint, and Wollstonecraft, however, remind us that Enlightenment universalism was based not only on cool reason and calculation and the blind arrogance of the powerful. At least some of the great Enlightenment thinkers based their global prescription on the *felt* needs, even the sufferings, of others. For Diderot, Toussaint, and perhaps especially, Wollstonecraft, the recognition of human commonality began with a capacity for empathy that the Enlightenment may have bequeathed to the modern world.

Volume One Acknowledgments

John Aberth. "Ahmad al-Maqrizi, the Plague in Cairo." From *The Black Death: The Great Mortality of 1348–1350* by John Aberth. Copyright © 2005 by Bedford/St. Martin's. Reproduced by permission of Bedford/St. Martin's.

S. A. M. Adshead. "China and Rome Compared." Excerpts from *China in World History.* Copyright © 2000. Reprinted by permission of Palgrave Macmillan.

Natalie Angier. "Furs for Evening, But Cloth Was the Stone Age Standby." From *The New York Times*, December 14, 1999. Copyright © 1999 by The New York Times. Reprinted with permission.

Anonymous. Excerpt from "Chandogya Upanishad." In *The Upanishads: Breath of the Eternal*, translated by Juan Mascaro. Copyright © by Juan Mascaro. Reprinted with permission of Penguin Books, Ltd.

Anonymous. Excerpt from *The Bhagavad-Gita: Caste and Self* translated by Barbara Stoler Miller. Copyright © 1986 by Barbara Stoler Miller. Used by permission of Bantam Books, a division of Random House, Inc.

Anonymous. Excerpt from *The Epic of Gilgamesh*, translated by N. K. Sanders. Copyright © 1972 by N. K. Sanders. Reprinted with the permission of Penguin Books, Ltd.

Anonymous. "The Rig-Veda: Sacrifice as Creation." Excerpt from *Sources of Indian Tradition*, Second Edition, by Ainslie T. Embree. Copyright © 1988 by Columbia University Press. Reprinted with the permission of the publisher.

Anonymous. "Svetasvatara Upanished." From *The Upanishads: Breath of the Eternal*, translated by Swami Prabhavananda and Frederick Manchester. Copyright © 1948, 1957 by The Vedanta Society of Southern California. Reprinted with permission.

Anonymous. "The Upanishads: Karma and Reincarnation." Excerpt from *The Hindu Tradition: Readings in Oriental Thought*, edited by Ainslie T. Embree. Copyright © 1966 by Random House, Inc. Used by permission of Random House, Inc.

Aristophanes. Excerpt from *Lysistrata*, edited by William Arrowsmith, translated by Douglass Parker. Copyright © 1964 by William Arrowsmith. Used by permission of Dutton Signet, a division of Penguin Group (USA) Inc.

Aristotle. "The Athenian Constitution." From *Aristotle, Politics and the Athenian Constitution*, translated by John Warrington. Copyright © 1959 by John Warrington. Reprinted with the permission of David Campbell Publishers, Ltd.

Ban Zhao. "Lessons for Women." From *Pan Chao: Foremost Woman Scholar of China, First Century A.D.: Background, Ancestry, Life and Writings of the Most Celebrated Chinese Woman of Letters,* translated by Nancy Lee Swann. Copyright © The East Asian Library and the Gest Collection, Princeton University. Reprinted by permission of Princeton University.

William Theodore De Bary. Excerpts from "The Buddha's First Sermon," "Buddhism and Caste," and "Buddhism in China" (Hung-ming chi, in Taisho daizokyo, LII, 1-7). From *The Buddhist Tradition in India, China and Japan* by William Theodore De Bary. Copyright © 1969 by William Theodore De Bary. Used by permission of Random House, Inc.

Jerry H. Bentley. "The Spread of World Religions." From *Old World Encounters: Cross-Cultural Contacts and Exchanges in Pre-Modern Times.* Copyright 1992 by Oxford University Press, Inc. Used by permission of Oxford University Press, Inc.

Goitein, *Journal of Jewish Studies*, volume 3, #4. Copyright © 1952 by S. G. Goitein. Reprinted by permission of the *Journal of Jewish Studies*. "Cairo: An Islamic City in Light of the Geniza." Translated and edited by Ira M. Lapidus. From *Middle Eastern Cities*. Copyright © 1969 by the Regents of the University of California Press. Reprinted by permission of the publisher.

Gregory Guzman. "Were the Barbarians a Negative or Positive Factor in Ancient and Medieval History?" From *The Historian*, August 1988. Reprinted with the permission of the author.

Gabriel de' Mussis. "Origins of the Black Death." From *The Black Death* by Rosemary Horrox. Copyright © 1994 Manchester University Press, Manchester, UK. Reprinted by permission.

Sarah Shaver Hughes and Brady Hughes. Excerpt from "Women in Ancient Civilizations." As published in *Women's History in Global Perspective*, vol. 2, pp. 26–30 and 36–40. Copyright © 1998 by Sarah Shaver Hughes and Brady Hughes. Reprinted with permission of the American Historical Association and the authors.

G. W. B. Huntingford. Excerpt from *The Glorious Victories of 'Āmda Ṣeyon: King of Ethiopia*. Translated by G. W. B. Huntingford. Copyright © 1965. Published by Oxford University Press. Reprinted by permission.

Ibn al-Athir. "The Conquest of Jerusalem." Excerpt from *Arab Historians of the Crusades: Selected and Translated from the Arabic Sources*, edited and translated by E. J. Costello. Islamic World Series, 1969. Copyright © 1969 Routledge & Kegan Paul, Ltd. Reprinted by permission of Copyright Clearance Center, via the format Textbook.

John of Plano Carpini. Excerpt from *History of the Mongols*; Guyuk Khan, "Letter to Pope Innocent IV," excerpts from "Narrative of Brother Benedict the Pole," and excerpt from *The Journey of William of Rubrick* from *Mission to Asia: Narratives and Letters of the Franciscan Missionaries to Mongolia and China in the Thirteenth and Fourteenth Centuries*, translated by a nun of Stanbrook Abbey, edited by Christopher Dawson. Copyright © 1955. Reprinted with permission of The Continuum International Publishing Group.

Kalidasa. Excerpt from *Shakuntala*. Translated by Barbara Stoler Miller. From *Theatre of Memory: The Plays of Kalidasa*, edited by Barbara Stoler Miller. Copyright © 1984 Columbia University Press. Reprinted with permission.

Gerda Lerner. "The Urban Revolution: Origins of Patriarchy." From *The Creation of Patriarchy*. Copyright © 1986, 1987 by Gerda Lerner. Used by permission of Oxford University Press, Inc.

Bernard Lewis. "Peace Terms with Jerusalem," from "Al Tabari, Tarik al-Rusulcwa'l muluk" (Leiden: Brill), published in *Islam from the Prophet Muhammad to the Conquest of Constantinople*, edited and translated by Bernard Lewis. Vol. I: Politics and War. Excerpt from Vol II: Religion and Society. Published by Harper & Row, 1974.

Miriam Lichtheim. "Advice to the Young Egyptian: Be a Scribe." From *Ancient Egyptian Literature: A Book of Readings, Volume 2; The New Kingdom* by Miriam Lichtheim. Copyright © 1976 by the University of California Press Books. Reproduced with permission of University of California Press Books in the format Textbook via Copyright Clearance Center.

Liu Tsung-yuan. "Camel Kuo the Gardner" from *An Anthology of Chinese Literature: From Early Times to the Fourteenth Century*, edited by Cyril Birch.

Copyright © 1965 by Grove Press, Inc. Used by permission of Grove/Atlantic, Inc.

Livy. Excerpt from *Women's Life in Greece and Rome,* Second Edition. Mary R. Lefkowitz and Maureen B. Fant, eds. Copyright © 1992. Reprinted with the permission of The Johns Hopkins University Press.

G. E. R. Lloyd. "Chinese and Greco-Roman Innovation." Excerpts from *The Ambitions of Curiosity* by G. E. R. Lloyd. Copyright © 2002 by G. E. R. Lloyd. Reprinted with the permission of Cambridge University Press.

Magnus Magnusson and Hermann Palsson. "Eiric's Saga." From *The Vinland Sagas: The Norse Discover America,* translated with an introduction by Magnus Magnusson and Hermann Palsson (Penguin Classics, 1965). Copyright © Magnus Magnusson and Hermann Palsson, 1965. Reprinted by permission of Penguin Books Ltd.

Marco Polo. Excerpt from *Marco Polo: The Travels,* translated by Ronald Latham. Copyright © 1958 by Ronald Latham. Reprinted with the permission of Penguin Books, Ltd.

William H. McNeill. "Greek and Indian Civilization." From *A World History,* Second Edition. Copyright © 1971 by Oxford University Press. Reprinted by permission of the author. "Consequences of the Black Death in Europe." From *Plagues and Peoples* by William H. McNeill. Copyright © 1976 by William H. McNeill. Used by permission of Doubleday, a division of Random House, Inc.

Mirabai. Excerpt from Bhakti poems, from *Sources of Indian Tradition,* Volume I: From the Beginning to 1800, 2nd edition. Edited by Ainslee Embree. Copyright © 1988 Columbia University Press. Reprinted with permission.

Ichisada Miyazaki. "The Chinese Civil Service Exam System." From *China's Examination Hell,* translated by Conrad Schirokauer. Copyright 1976. Reprinted by permission of the publishers, Weatherhill, Inc.

R. K. Narayan. Excerpt from *The Ramayana* by R. K. Narayan. Copyright © R. K. Narayan 1972. Used by permission of the Wallace Literary Agency, Inc.

Pliny. "Pliny Consults the Emperor Trajan." [Letters 10: 96-97] From *Pliny Secundus: Letters and Panegyricus,* Volume II, Loeb Classical Library, Volume 59, translated by Betty Radice. Copyright © 1969 by the President and Fellows of Harvard College. The Loeb Classical Library ® is a registered trademark of the President and Fellows of Harvard College. Reprinted by permission of the publishers and the Trustees of the Loeb Classical Library.

Roxanne Prazniak. "Ban Zhao and the End of Chinese Feudalism." From *Dialogues Across Civilizations* by Roxanne Prazniak. Copyright © 1996 Westview Press. Reprinted by permission of Copyright Clearance Center.

Kevin Reilly. "Cities and Civilizations," and "Love in Medieval Europe, India, and Japan." From *The West and the World: A History of Civilization,* Second Edition. Copyright © 1989 by Kevin Reilly. Reprinted by the permission of Pearson Education Inc.

Lynda Shaffer. "Southernization." From *Journal of World History* 5, no. 1, Spring 1994. Copyright © 1994 by the University of Hawaii Press. Reprinted with the permission of the publishers. All rights reserved.

Murasaki Shikibu. Excerpts from *The Tale of Genji,* Volume 1, by Lady Murasaki. Translated by Arthur Waley. Originally published by Houghton Mifflin Company. Copyright © by permission of The Arthur Waley Estate. All rights reserved.

Marjorie Shostak. "Memories of a !Kung Girlhood." From *Nisa: The Life and Words of a !Kung Woman.* Copyright © 1981 by Marjorie Shostak. Reprinted with the permission of Harvard University Press.

J. W. Thomas. Excerpt from *Ulrich von Liechtenstein's The Service of Ladies,* translated by J.W. Thomas. Copyright © 1969. Published by arrangement with North Carolina Press (1969). Reprinted with permission.

Burton Watson. Excerpt from *The Lotus Sutra,* translated by Burton Watson. Copyright © 1993 by Burton Watson. Reprinted by permission of Columbia University Press.

Lynn White Jr. The Historical Roots of Our Ecological Crisis." From *Science* 155: 1203-07 (1967). Copyright © 1967 AAAS. Reprinted by permission.

Volume Two Acknowledgments

Chinua Achebe. "An Image of Africa: Racism in Conrad's *Heart of Darkness.*" First published in *Massachusetts Review* 18 (1977): 782–94. Copyright © by Chinua Achebe. Reprinted by permission of David Higham Associates, Limited.

"Aztec Account of the Conquest." From *The Broken Spears: The Atzec Account of the Conquest of Mexico,* by Miguel Leon-Portilla. Copyright © 1962, 1990 by Miguel Leon-Portilla. Expanded and Updated Edition © 1992 by Miguel Leon-Portilla. Reprinted by permission of Beacon Press, Boston.

Benjamin Barber. Excerpt from *Jihad vs. McWorld: How Globalism and Tribalism Are Reshaping the World.* Copyright © 1995 by Benjamin R. Barber. Used by permission of Times Books, a division of Random House, Inc.

Franklin Le Van Baumer. "The Scientific Revolution in the West." From *Main Currents of Western Thought,* edited by Franklin Le Van Baumer. Copyright © 1978 by Franklin Le Van Baumer. Reprinted by permission of Yale University Press.

Anna Bijns. "Unyoked Is Best! Happy Is the Woman without a Man." From *Women Writers of the Renaissance and Reformation,* edited by Katharina M. Wilson. Copyright 1987 by The University of Georgia Press. Reprinted by permission of The University of Georgia Press.

David Cannadine. Excerpt from *Ornamentalism: How the British Saw Their Empire.* Copyright © 2005. Reprinted by permission of Oxford University Press.

Iris Chang. Excerpt from *The Rape of Nanking: The Forgotten Holocaust of World War II.* Copyright © 1997 by Iris Chang. Reprinted with the permission of Basic Books, a member of Perseus Books, LLC.

John H. Coatsworth. "Economic Trajectories in Nineteenth-Century Latin America." From *Latin America and the World Economy since 1800,* edited by John H. Coatsworth and Alan M. Taylor. Copyright © 1998 by Harvard University Press. Reprinted by permission.

Natalie Zemon Davis. Excerpted text from *Women on the Margins: Three Seventeenth-Century Lives* by Natalie Zemon Davis. The Belknap Press of Harvard University Press. Copyright © 1995 by the President and Fellows of Harvard College. Reprinted by permission of the publisher.

Carolina Maria de Jesus. Excerpts from *Child of the Dark: The Diary of Carolina Maria de Jesus* by Carolina Maria de Jesus, translated by David St. Clair. Translation copyright © 1962 by E. P. Dutton & Co., Inc., New York and Souvenir Press Ltd., London. Used by permission of Dutton, a division of Penguin Group (USA) Inc.

Bernal Díaz. Excerpt from *The Conquest of New Spain* by Bernal Díaz. Translated by J. M. Cohen (Penguin Classics, 1963). Copyright © J. M. Cohen, 1963. Reprinted by permission of Penguin Group, UK.

Diane Dixon. "Michelle, Top Woman in a Macho World." From *The Observer,* Sunday, April 2, 2006. Copyright © Guardian Newspapers Limited, 2006. Reprinted with permission.

Bartolomeo de Las Casas. Excerpt from *Bartolomeo de Las Casas: A Selection of His Writings* by Bartolomeo de Las Casas, translated by George Sanderlin. Copyright © 1971 by Alfred A. Knopf, a division of Random House, Inc. Used by permission of Alfred A. Knopf, a division of Random House, Inc.

Assia Djebar. "Growing Up in Algeria." From *Fantasia: An Algerian Cavalcade,* translated by Dorothy S. Blair. Copyright © 1993 Dorothy S. Blair. Reprinted by permission of Heinemann (Portsmouth, NH).

Abba Eban. "The Refugee Problem." From *The Arab-Israeli Reader* by Walter Laqueur and Barry Rubin. Copyright © 1969, 1970 by B. L. Mazel, Inc. Copyright © 1976 by Walter Laqueur. Copyright © 1984, 1995, 2000 by Walter Laqueur and Barry Rubin. Used by permission of Viking Penguin, a division of Penguin Group (USA) Inc.

Patricia Buckley Ebrey. "Family Instructions for the Miu Lineage," and "How Dong Xiaowan Became My Concubine." From *Chinese Civilization: A Sourcebook*, Second Edition by Patricia Buckley Ebrey, ed. Copyright © 1993 by Patricia Buckley Ebrey. Reprinted with the permission of The Free Press, a division of Simon & Schuster Adult Publishing Group. All rights reserved.

Ainslee T. Embree. "Bada'uni, Akbar and Religion." From *Sources of Indian Tradition* by Ainslee T. Embree. Copyright © 1988 by Ainslee T. Embree. Reprinted by permission of Columbia University Press.

Olaudah Equiano. "Enslaved Captive." From *Africa Remembered: Narratives by West Africans from the Era of the Slave Trade.* by Phillip D. Curtin, ed. Waveland Press, Inc., 1967 (reissued 1997). All rights reserved.

Joachim C. Fest. "The Rise of Hitler." From *Hitler,* English translation by Clara and Richard Winston. Copyright © 1973 by Verlag Ullstein. English translation © 1974 by Harcourt, Inc. Adapted by permission of Harcourt, Inc.

Betty Friedan. Excerpts from "The Problem That Has No Name." From *The Feminine Mystique.* Copyright © 1983, 1974, 1973, 1963 by Betty Friedan. Used by permission of W. W. Norton & Company, Inc.

David Fromkin. "On the Balfour Declaration." From *A Peace to End All Peace* by David Fromkin. Copyright © 1989 by David Fromkin. Used by permission of HarperCollins Publishers.

Galileo Galilei. "Letter to the Grand Duchess Christina." From *The Galileo Affair: A Documentary History*, edited and translated by Maurice A. Finocchiaro. Copyright © 1989 by University of California Press Books. Reproduced with permission of University of California Press Books in the format Textbook via Copyright Clearance Center.

Mohandas K. Gandhi. Excerpt from *Hind Swaraj or Indian Home Rule.* Reprinted by permission of the Navajivan Trust.

Glenn Garvin and Edward Hegstrom. "Report: Maya Indians Suffered Genocide." Copyright © 1999 by the *Miami Herald.* Reproduced with permission of Miami Herald in the format Textbook via Copyright Clearance Center.

Sugita Gempaku. "A Dutch Anatomy Lesson in Japan." From *Sources of Japanese History*, Volume 1, edited by David John Lu (McGraw-Hill, 1974). Reprinted by permission of David Lu.

Sherif Hetata. "Dollarization, Fragmentation, and God." Excerpts from *The Cultures of Globalization* edited by Fredric Jameson and Masao Miyoshi. Copyright © 1998 Duke University Press. Used by permission of the publisher. All rights reserved.

Heinrich Himmler. "Secret Speech at Posen." From *A Holocaust Reader* edited by Lucy S. Dawidowicz. Copyright © 1976 by Lucy S. Dawidowicz. Reprinted by permission of Behrman House.

Joseph Kahn. "Letter from Asia: China Has an Ancient Mariner to Tell You About." From *The New York Times*, July 20, 2005. Copyright © 2005 by The New York Times Company. Reprinted by permission.

Jawaharlal Nehru. "Gandhi." From *Toward Freedom: The Autobiography of Jawaharlal Nehru*. Reprinted by permission of the Jawaharlal Nehru Memorial Fund.

George Orwell. Excerpt from *Burmese Days* by George Orwell. Copyright © by George Orwell and renewed 1962 by Sonia Pitt-Rivers. Reprinted by permission of Harcourt, Inc. and Bill Hamilton as the Literary Executor of the Estate of the Late Sonia Brownell Orwell and Seeker & Warburg, Ltd.

Jurgen Osterhammel. Excerpt from *Colonialism*, translated by Shelly Frisch. Copyright © 1997 by Shelly L. Frisch. Reprinted with the permission of Markus Weiner Publishers.

Arnold Pacey. "Asia and the Industrial Revolution." From *Technology in World Civilizations: A Thousand Year History*. Copyright 1990. Reprinted by permission of MIT Press, Cambridge, Mass.

Kenneth Pomeranz. "How the Other Side Traded." From *The World That Trade Created: Society, Culture, and the World Economy, 1400 to the Present*, 2nd edition by Kenneth Pomeranz and Steven Topik. Copyright © 2006 by M. E. Sharpe, Inc. Reprinted with permission.

Donald Quataert. Excerpts from *The Ottoman Empire, 1700–1922*. Copyright © 2000 by Donald Quataert. Reprinted with the permission of Cambridge University Press.

Erich Maria Remarque. Excerpt from *All Quiet on the Western Front* by Erich Maria Remarque. "Im Western Nichts Neues." Copyright 1928 by Ullstein A. G.; Copyright renewed © 1956 by Erich Maria Remarque. "All Quiet on The Western Front." Copyright 1929, 1930 by Little, Brown and Company. Copyright renewed © 1957, 1958 by Erich Maria Remarque. All rights reserved. Reprinted by permission of Pryor Cashman Sherman and Flynn LLP.

Andrew C. Revkin. "Climate Data Hint at Irreversible Rise in Seas." From *The New York Times*, March 24, 2006. Copyright © 2006 by The New York Times Company. Reprinted with permission.

Matteo Ricci. "Jesuit Missionaries in Ming China." From *China in the Sixteenth Century* by Matteo Ricci, translated by Louis J. Gallagher. Copyright © 1942, 1953 and renewed 1970 by Louis J. Gallagher, S.J. Used by permission of Random House, Inc.

John Roach. "By 2050 Warming to Doom Million Species, Study Says." From *National Geographic News*, July 12, 2004. Copyright © 2004 by National Geographic Society. Reprinted with permission.

Larry Rohter. "With Big Boost from Sugar Cane, Brazil Is Satisfying Its Fuel Needs." From *The New York Times*, April 10, 2006. Copyright © 2006 by The New York Times Company. Reprinted with permission.

Kirkpatrick Sale. Excerpt from *The Conquest of Paradise*. Copyright © 1990 Kirkpatrick Sale. Used by permission of Alfred A. Knopf, a division of Random House, Inc.

Lynda Norene Shaffer. "China, Technology and Change." From *World History Bulletin* 4, no. 1 (Fall/Winter, 1986–87): 1–6. Copyright © 1987. Reprinted with permission.

Ari Shavit. "An Interview with Benny Morris." From *Ha'aretz*, January 9, 2004. Copyright © 2004 by Ari Shavit. Reprinted with permission of Ha'aretz Syndication Service.

Jonathan Spence. "The Late Ming Empire." From *The Search for Modern China*. Copyright © 1990 by Jonathan Spence. Used by permission of W. W. Norton & Company, Inc. Includes Tang Xianzu, excerpts from *The Peony Pavilion*, translated by Cyril Birch. Copyright © 1980 by Indiana University Press. Reprinted with the permission of the publishers.

Luther Standing Bear. Excerpt from *Land of the Spotted Eagle* by Luther Standing Bear. Copyright © 1933 by Luther Standing Bear. Renewal Copyright 1960 by May Jones. Reprinted by permission of the University of Nebraska Press.

Peter N. Stearns. "The Industrial Revolution Outside the West." From *Industrial Revolution in World History* by Peter N. Stearns. Copyright © 1998 by Westview Press. Reprinted by permission of Westview Press, a member of Perseus Books, LLC.

Jean-François Steiner. Excerpt from *Treblinka*. English translation copyright © 1967 by Simon & Schuster, Inc. Reprinted with the permission of Simon & Schuster Adult Publishing Group.

Theodore von Laue. Excerpt from *The World Revolution of Westernization: The Twentieth Century in Global Perspective*. Copyright 1987 by Oxford University Press, Inc. Used by permission of Oxford University Press, Inc.

John E. Wills Jr. "Sor Juana Inés de la Cruz." From *1688: A Global History*. Copyright © 2001 John E. Wills Jr. Used by permission of W. W. Norton & Company, Inc.

Iwasaki Yataro. "Letter to Employees of the Mitsubishi Company." From *Sources of Japanese History*, Volume II, by David Lu, ed. Copyright © 1974 (McGraw-Hill). Reprinted by permission of David Lu.

Fukuzawa Yukichi. "Datsu-a Ron (On Saying Good-bye to Asia)." From *Japan: A Documentary History*, Vol II: *The Late Tokugawa Period to the Present* by David J. Lu, ed. Translation copyright © 1997 by David J. Lu. Reprinted by permission of M. E. Sharpe, Inc.

Zheng He. "Inscription to the Goddess." From *China and Africa in the Middle Ages*, ed. Teobaldo Filesi, translated and inscribed by David Morrison. Copyright © 1972 by David Morrison. Reprinted with permission of the publisher.